RAISE THE CLANS

THE WARGAMER'S GUIDE TO
THE JACOBITE REBELLIONS

To Steve

Best wishes

MARTIN HACKETT

AMBERLEY

First published 2014

Amberley Publishing
The Hill, Stroud
Gloucestershire, GL5 4EP

www.amberley-books.com

British Library Cataloguing in Publication Data.
A catalogue record for this book is available from the British Library.

ISBN 978 1 4456 0379 7 (print)
ISBN 978 1 4456 2145 6 (ebook)

Typeset in 10pt on 12pt Minion Pro.
Typesetting and Origination by Amberley Publishing.
Printed in the UK.

CONTENTS

Preface

My first recollection of knowing anything about the Jacobite rebellions was my father repeatedly singing snatches of the Skye Boat Song: 'Speed, bonnie boat, like a bird on the wing, onward the sailors cry/ Carry the lad that's born to be King, over the sea to Skye.'

I can still remember asking my father who the song was about; I was standing in the kitchen, holding tightly to a wooden plinth as instructed, and I would be perhaps seven or eight years old.

My father replied, 'Come on, you know this.' I thought for a moment and then said, 'Jesus', though on uttering Christ's name I was not really sure that I was correct. My dad laughed aloud and managed to look exasperated at the same time. 'No!' he jovially replied, 'not Jesus, think again.'

'Ohhhhh, I know, it's Bonnie Prince Charlie.' 'Yes son, Bonnie Prince Charlie.' And with that he went back to work with his drill and screwdriver on the kitchen units we were fitting, and I was dutifully holding, while the strains of 'over the sea to Skye' began again and my father told me potted bits of what he knew of the Stuart prince and his quest for the throne.

From that early encounter my interest in the Stuart era developed, as did my liking for military history in general. By my mid-teens, the English Civil War had become my specialist subject. Armies of model figures representing the Royalists and Parliamentarians followed, and then, as new figures appeared for the Jacobite Rebellions, I was able to collect and start to recreate in miniature those battles along with my long-standing friend Jonathan Worton. Jon is one of the finest figure painters and scratch build modellers to ever grace a wargames table and together we have won many best demonstration game awards across the UK at some of the numerous wargame conventions. From the need to recreate these historical battles on the tabletop in miniature comes the set of rules that you will find in the penultimate chapter of the book. As with all of my wargame rule systems, it is designed to be both swift to play while at the same time accurately recreating what happened in reality.

Warfare is simultaneous; one side does not shoot and then let the other side have a go. Therefore the rules have to be rigid enough to give accurate casualty figures and morale results while at the same time giving the commanders an air of uncertainty as to whether their miniature men will perform the way that they want them to. So, within the rules there is that little element of chance that creeps into everyday life and which was certainly present in every battle that has ever been fought throughout humankind's history.

My aim, therefore, with this book is threefold; firstly, to put into one work the information necessary for someone to understand in detail the military campaigns for all of those Jacobite rebellions which commenced from Scotland; secondly, to arm the reader with knowledge as to where these battle sites can be found, along with other historical locations connected with the Stuart uprisings, so that they can be visited by both the more general historian as well as the keen wargamer; finally, to provide the wargaming enthusiast with a set of rules that allows the complex battles of this period to be accurately recreated in miniature in whatever scale the gamer prefers. Therein lies the greatest challenge to any writer of wargame rules, but especially so with the Jacobite rebellions. Over a fifty-seven-year period, the Jacobites gained some considerable victories. Even in the last great uprising – the '45 as it is commonly known – the Jacobites only lost one major battle; sadly for the Stuart cause it was the last battle, Culloden. So in order to create a comprehensive wargame system, which is a fair reflection of what happened given the number of Jacobite successes, I have included rules for both the weather and the terrain. This is because it was when these two factors combined (a common occurrence) that the Jacobite force gained a sufficient advantage over their Government opponents. That advantage was rightly exploited, laying the foundations of Jacobite success. Those natural elements on a local scale always seemed to favour the Stuarts, but ironically it was the weather on a national scale that would prevent the very Continental support that each Jacobite rising would need if it was to stand a realistic chance of success. There was one other fundamental element that had more impact on whether a Jacobite rising would be successful or not and that was the ability of the Stuart claimant, on his arrival in Scotland, to 'raise the clans' to his standard.

General Touring Information

In every case the author has personally visited and photographed each battle site listed within this book, many of them within the last six months, so that the information read and the photographs you see should be as accurate and as up to date as possible and all those photographs without a specific credit were taken by the author. The majority of the photographs were taken during the winter months, so when touring be prepared for some fields to look different if they are rich with abundant crops where once bare soil lay. Similarly, the natural spring and summer growth of hedges and trees may now obscure some landmarks that were clearly visible before. Also, the land use, infrastructure, road systems and rights of way can all change, sometimes at very short notice. If you encounter difficulties in following any tour then we would very much like to hear about it so that we can incorporate changes in future editions; your comments should be sent to the publisher at the address provided at the front of this book. To derive maximum value and enjoyment from your exploration of these battle sites, we would suggest that you equip yourself with the following items:

Appropriate Maps. A general road map to navigate to the appropriate location and if more detail is required, then either the Landranger or Explorer series of maps from the Ordnance Survey, which are available from all good book sellers in most high streets of the UK, would be ideal.

Lightweight waterproof clothing and robust footwear are essential, especially if you leave the footpaths of built-up areas.

A compass is always a useful tool, and it allows the reader to verify the locations of troops and their movements upon the battlefield.

A camera and spare films. The author always carries cheap disposable cameras as emergency cover for his more expensive equipment and they have saved the day on more than one occasion.

A notebook to record details of any photographs taken and any changes that may have occurred.

Food, drink and fuel. Although in Britain you are in theory never far from a retail outlet, there are roads in Wales and Scotland where, even in the twenty-first century, passing another car can be a rarity (especially in winter), and finding somewhere to top up your fuel tank can be a challenge. It is, therefore, sensible to always ensure that the fuel tank is full and take spare drinking water with you and some light refreshments, particularly if you are planning to do some full-length walks or circular tours.

Binoculars. An excellent aid, especially when verifying the location and interpreting how much each army could have seen of the other when they were deploying for battle.

The author has visited all of the sites by car as few of them are accessible by rail. Within each chapter are details on other attractions to see in the area, but this is not a definitive list; as the reader will appreciate, whole brochures are available on some towns and cities and it would be impossible to include every attraction, or indeed cater for every taste. The author would advise anyone planning to visit any of these sites to contact the local tourist office as they can provide news of any special events and are generally happy to post out information, including maps and places with accommodation. The author has contacted or visited over twenty tourist offices in the last year and has received excellent service from all of them. For those disabled visitors wishing to visit a battle site, please take note of the routes and location points detailed, and while it may not be possible to explore a complete site due to the nature of the terrain, many of the salient points that can be reached by road are visible without leaving a vehicle.

Some Dos and Don'ts

Touring a battlefield can be an interesting, rewarding and sometimes emotional experience, especially if you have studied the battle beforehand, or are related to people that were involved in it. However, it is clear from my tours that although there are some locals familiar with the battle having been fought within their vicinity, there will also be people who are totally unaware that there was any kind of military action in their area, so be patient if you are quizzed and simply explain the reason for your interest in their domain. Many sites have clearly marked routes that are along public rights of way; for example, a long-distance footpath may cross a battle site. Therefore, when walking, please keep to these designated rights of way, but if you do stray and you are asked to leave the land you are on, please do so immediately by the quickest and safest way possible. It is especially important in Scotland to keep to the designated paths, as there are bogs and ditches that lie unseen, covered by layers of moss and heather, which can cause injury if one is unlucky enough to step down into one. Always be aware, especially in rural areas, of not blocking gates or drives to farms when choosing a place to park. If you take a dog with you, and Rosie accompanied the author on all of his walks without any problem, remember that there are times when the dog must be on the lead both in the town and the country; this is both for the dog's safety, and that of wildlife and farm animals. If there is no clear parking place, then choose an open stretch of road where vehicles coming from both directions can clearly see your position. If you have to use a gate to continue your walk then please ensure that the gate is closed behind you before you move on. Do not feed animals that you find on the walks; it is dangerous to the animal and potentially dangerous to the person providing the food, as these are wild animals, not domesticated pets. The owner of one estate upon which a Jacobite battle site encroaches was fortunate enough to see and stop a woman feeding crisps to one of her Highland cows; the woman was pleased that the cow appreciated the crisps sufficiently to nuzzle the 24-inch pointed horns up the side of her head and face, unaware that a sudden move could have led to her being gored or blinded.

Many country estates have shoots or equestrian events and, although the author is unaware of any battle sites in this book being near such an estate, as stated above, things change. Therefore if you hear gunshots, or there are signs indicating that there is a shoot or a cross-country event in progress, make sure that you are on the correct route, and, if unsure, try and verify with the local farmer or landowner where the event is taking place and what walks will be affected. A word of caution in relation to battlefields in general, but particularly to those found in the more remote parts of Wales and Scotland: take care and wear appropriate clothing and footwear when exploring these sites. Some of these battles were fought over very rough terrain, with bogs, streams, waterfalls, water-cut ravines and hidden drops in what looks like a flat moor or hillside. If travelling alone, it is worth advising someone where you are going to and when you are likely to be back. Mobile phone signals are not strong in all places and should the walker incur an injury or a sudden illness, at least there will be someone with knowledge of where you were intending to be on that day.

Finally, if, as one sometimes reads in the press, someone finds an artefact, leave it where it is and mark its location with a stone or stick and then photograph a landmark in relation to the object so that it can be found, or use GPS if possible. Then contact the landowner and the local police, who will be able to put you in touch with the relevant archaeological department. If it is likely that the artefact could be damaged or taken by someone else by leaving it, mark the position in some way and record the location as above before removing the object. The discovery should then be reported to the local landowner or the local police, who will take all the necessary details. As regards stone structures such as castles, walls and buildings, or memorials or cairns that have been placed there to remember the dead, then these should not be damaged, or marked in any way, and nothing should be removed from the site. If you wish, flowers may be placed at the site as your own mark of remembrance.

The Jacobite Battle Sites

The majority of the historical places and battle sites covered in this book are largely unchanged, with the exception of Prestonpans, which has been almost covered in housing and industrial developments, and Falkirk, where the northern side of the battlefield has again been urbanised. However, within the built-up areas of Preston and Dunkeld, many of the original shapes of the streets or the locations of where the streets were are still visible and well worth the exploration. Some sites have a good local information board and the battle site at Killiecrankie has a good visitor centre. Both Glencoe and Culloden, which are in the care of the Scottish National Trust, have state-of-the-art centres with cafeterias, shops and a wealth of information. For visitors who struggle with mobility, many of the sites can be seen safely from roadside pull-ins, which are found in abundance along the majority of the Scottish roads. Even at places like Glenshiel and Sheriffmuir, which are fairly isolated, the roads pass close enough to the key locations that anyone can take it all in.

Introduction

When one walks upon a battlefield for the first time one feels a range of emotions: sadness, sometimes an air of foreboding, and a sort of oppressiveness that seems to push down upon you. Conversely, there is sometimes an air of lightness and euphoria. This is a good time to question whether you are actually standing where people were slain and to revisit your notes and references. The battle sites in Scotland are particularly atmospheric; maybe it is the narrowness of the glens and the height of the overpowering mountains that rise steeply on either side of you, sometimes to many thousands of feet. The author has visited Culloden many times, from the late 1970s until this very year. There is always an air of foreboding on Drummossie Moor – Culloden Moor's more rightful name. It is as if the landscape reflects the pain of the event it witnessed. Is this atmosphere created by the knowledge of the slaughter that occurred there following the battle, or does a deathly, magnetic imprint linger upon the land?

For almost forty years now, the author has walked and studied military sites, castles, hillforts, bays and battlefields. Around half of those places, the author has visited alone, which has not been through choice but through circumstances. It is comforting to have someone with you, not only because you can discuss the evidence as to where a battle might have been fought, but because you can share your feelings and see if those people with you are similarly affected. The ability to refer to and to debate what is documented on a battle while standing on the actual location allows a stimulated discussion to develop as to where the battle would have been fought. This can lead to a fundamental matter such as whether it was fought east–west or north–south; such simple contrasts can make a huge difference to the interpretation of a battle. For any of you that may have read any of the author's previous works, you will know that the battlefield interpretation springs from what knowledge we have of where the armies ended up *after* the battle. Then, while standing upon the different parts of the battlefield, one can work out from the topography how the armies were most likely to have been deployed. From that, one can work out how the battle would have unfolded to eventually reach the point where the troops left the field, thus completing the circle of interpretation. At each critical point within the battle, the movements of the troops are reassessed to make sure they are logical in the context of that particular moment. This may read as rather a lot of guesswork, and to a certain extent it is, but it is based upon the logical interpretation of known military dispositions and tactics, rather than simply obscure speculation, and this can *only* be done when on site. The choice

Sometimes a battlefield walk can be in the most stunning of places, such as here on Majorca.

of where to fight is dependent upon the type of troops that are fighting, so, armed with knowledge of the composition of an army of a given period, one can surmise as to the terrain that a general would have picked for his troops. No matter whether one is examining a battle from the Ancient period, the Dark Ages, or from the Jacobite wars (a time when the horse and the musket had combined to become the twin masters of the battlefield), there are certain elements which are fundamental (although the mechanisation of war altered these common elements). One must understand that for the most part (and there are of course exceptions which prove the rule), the military commanders of those times knew the capabilities of their troops, the type of terrain that their men would perform best upon, and therefore where not to deploy so as to put their army at risk of defeat. This practical knowledge can be brought into play when examining potential battle sites, always making allowances in case the terrain may have been altered by mining, quarrying, erosion or construction. Generals would always look to find terrain where the infantry – for, almost without exception, it was the infantry that made up the majority of the troops within an army – could deploy with room to fight, but with their flanks and rear protected. Cavalry does not deploy on the steep sides of hills or behind deep rivers that they cannot ford at need; this is because horsemen need open and fairly flat, rolling terrain, so as to be able to move smoothly and charge at need into their enemy. Cavalry are used to support the infantry and to exploit a weakness in the enemy's lines so as to turn an enemy flank, or to get behind the enemy's lines to attack from the rear. Light infantry need rough and broken terrain to try and get close enough to harass the enemy without getting into a direct fire-fight or melee, and often look to snipe at their opponents and then withdraw.

When examining the battles from the Jacobite risings, one has to allow for the differences between the two armies and how their choice of ground could be in sharp contrast one to another. There was such a difference in fighting between the old style of the Highlanders when compared to and pitted against the modern Government army. The Government army fought with neat ranks and columns, moved with parade ground symmetry and formed neat lines with its infantry and cavalry, both of which were in turn supported by artillery pieces in battle, which were designed to keep pace with the army while on the move. Although some units within the Jacobite armies required similar terrain to that of the Government troops opposing them, the terrain of choice for the Highlanders was in sharp contrast to the professional armies. They chose rough, broken terrain, steep hills, rocky outcrops, misty marshes and patches of woodland, all of which would be uncomfortable for the parade ground troops of the Government armies if they were caught unawares. It is no surprise that as the British Empire expanded, its army diversified as it changed to deal with new enemies, fought in scrub or wilderness. Certain regiments became ever more specialist in their style of fighting and some of the finest troops in the British Army were formed from the ranks of Scottish clansmen to operate in such difficult terrain.

We will examine the opposing armies that fought in those uprisings and identify the weapons and the tactics that they employed. The military campaigns will be followed, revealing a clear picture of the moves, feints and countermoves, so that the reader will understand how time and again fortune favoured one side and then another as they vied to gain the upper hand. The pitched battles that were fought within those campaigns will also be narrated in detail, allowing both the historian and the wargamer to understand the reasons why one force triumphed over another, and to consider what ultimately led to the demise of the Jacobite claim. The final chapter contains a complete set of wargame rules to allow the armchair general to recreate in miniature these important milestones in British history. The final sections are appendices, which list details of relevant visitor centres where people can learn more about the Jacobite rebellions, quick reference tables to speed up the mechanics of the wargame rules, and a section which provides details of suppliers of miniature figures and gaming accessories.

On some battlefields there are monuments erected by local people or by national societies; on others there is nothing save the vegetation that feeds the livestock who, generation after generation, have grazed the ground unknowing of the men that fought and fell there before them. Do they matter, these battlefields that were fought over by people that perished between ten and thirteen generations ago? The answer is yes, they do matter, because today, even after more than 250 years have elapsed since the last of the Jacobite Rebellions, descendants of those who died still lay wreaths on the battle sites in memory of their ancestors. Yet in some cases, within twenty-four hours of those wreaths being laid, they are uplifted from their cairn, torn asunder and the flowers scattered across the battlefield to rot just like the dead would have lain centuries before. Clearly, feelings still run high and this kind of wanton, cowardly desecration merely symbolises the lack of understanding and unforgiving bigotry that runs through mankind. If mankind does not understand the past, then there can be no hope going forward. People should endeavour to understand why these battles were fought, and commemorate all those who lost their lives, regardless of which side they fought on.

The Jacobite Cause

Introduction

The rich and fertile lands of the British Isles have experienced more than two millenniums of warfare. The earliest disputes would have been tribal, localised feuding over a well-stocked fish lake or a particularly fertile valley. These disputes would have been very much in the style of the micro-wars fought between the Scottish clans: they would be local skirmishes over land and cattle, or occasionally long-standing feuds between different clans or sometimes even branches of the same clan. Following centuries of invasion by waves of Germanic and Danish peoples, the indigenous Celts (themselves originally invaders from the Alpine areas of Europe) were marginalised to the edges of Britain and the Anglo-Saxons finally reigned supreme. For century after century these invaders-turned-settlers fought for mastery until first an Anglo-Saxon and then a Norman hierarchy prevailed; Angleland, or England, had been born. Yet for almost a thousand years afterwards, until 1746, there would be further warfare: periods of civil warfare where men fought for factions determined to seize power. Whatever the pretence was, it all came down to one thing: all of these men, though occasionally a woman was involved in the plotting, were vying to see who would sit on the throne of England and rule the realm.

From the early feuding between the Celtic tribes of Iron Age Britain to the troubles in Northern Ireland in the twentieth and the twenty-first centuries, there has not been a century without some form of conflict on British soil. These many wars repeatedly saw regular paid armies, private regiments, paid mercenaries, volunteers, and even regiments from armies from countries across mainland Europe, shed their blood on British soil in the name of one cause or another. Sometimes, these armies fought in the name of, or hid under the broad cloak of, 'religion'. The Jacobite Wars span a period of almost sixty years, from 1689 to 1746, and they contain in that one short period many of these different elements: men sent from Spain and France fought alongside Irish mercenaries in mostly small armies, which were rallied in varying degrees of competence, to aid the cause of James Edward Stuart and Charles Edward Stuart, the Old and Young Pretenders respectively, in their quest to regain the British throne.

We cannot call the armies that repelled these rebellions in Britain either English or British. The troops that marched and died were fighting for the British Government and we shall hereafter refer to those forces as those of the 'Government'. But these troops were not simply Government troops; they were an amalgamation of men drafted from the

Continent to supplement home forces assembled from England, Wales, Scotland, Ireland, the Netherlands and Germany. This was very much a 'civil' war, where brother fought against brother, father against son, and even wife against husband. At the core of the final rising in 1746, when the Duke of Cumberland led the Government forces in the Culloden campaign, he would eventually face his own cousin, Charles Edward Stuart, across that mile of rugged, desolate, moor. At their heart, these rebellions were in essence a family feud for the throne.

Map A
Key settlements of the Jacobite Rebellions

Main areas of Jacobite support but which never all rose together

Background

To understand the Jacobite rebellions, we need to go back several generations and briefly examine how the Stuart monarchy came to polarise opinion in the late seventeenth and early eighteenth centuries. There were those who trembled at the thought of a Stuart restoration, while in sharp contrast there were those who were prepared to risk their necks to champion the Stuart cause. This diversity would lead not only to a whole series of rebellions and wholesale wars, but finally to legislation. This legislation took the form of anti-Catholic laws, which survive on the statute book, directly affecting the British monarchy until this day. The Act of Settlement of 1701 disqualified a Catholic monarch, or anyone married to a Catholic, from succeeding to the throne of England and Wales and it was only in 2013 that a slight amendment was made. It should be emphasised that until 1707, when the two Acts of Union were passed, England and Scotland remained autonomous, even though they had shared a common monarch since 1603. The 2013 amendment to the Act of Settlement permits a monarch to inherit even if married to a Catholic, as long as the monarch themselves is still a Protestant.

We may not think that we are condoning and perpetuating this anti-Catholic sentiment, yet each year, on or around 5 November, the British celebrate 'Guy Fawkes Night', when firework displays can be seen the length and breadth of Britain, often centred on an enormous bonfire. Atop that bonfire sits an effigy: the representation of Guy Fawkes. This traditional autumn celebration recalls Fawkes' involvement in an attempt to assassinate James I and Parliament in 1605. However, it has to a large extent lost its traditional sectarian connotations; indeed, the only place in England where the festival still retains the custom of the burning of an effigy of the Pope is the town of Lewes in East Sussex, where the festival is the town's main event of the year and where friendly competition survives as people compete to prepare the best float. However, the roots of unrest were sown shortly before 1605, in 1603, when Elizabeth I died without an heir, leaving England without a monarch. Thus England in 1603 found herself in the very position which Henry VIII had feared and tried so hard and with increasing desperation to avoid during his lifetime. With Elizabeth's death, the Tudor Royal House came to its quiet end. This left James VI of Scotland as the only legitimate heir, and by being offered and accepting the English crown he thereby united the thrones of England and Scotland under one monarch for the very first time, becoming James VI of Scotland and James I – and the first Stuart king – of England (hereafter referred to as James I).

Following her father's foundation of the Church of England, Elizabeth I sought to maintain that separation throughout her lifetime. Elizabeth survived even in spite of Pope Pius V's attempt to depose her with the papal bull *Regnans in Excelsis* of 1570, in which Elizabeth was declared a heretic. The Pope was therefore seeking to remove the duty of allegiance which Elizabeth's subjects owed to her, but it only served to weaken the position of Elizabeth's Catholic subjects as they tried to juggle their loyalty to the crown and loyalty to their faith. Trying to maintain both allegiances at one time was not easy and as a result we see certain members of the aristocracy forced to construct private chapels and hidden 'priest holes' in their own houses for their private worship of the Catholic faith. Outwardly they are maintaining their loyalty to Elizabeth; inwardly they are at peace with their faith. Following the papal bull, the Spanish Armada in 1588 was the only main military threat to Protestant England, but this lavish, and in the end vain, attempt to force Catholicism upon England only served to further unite the majority of the country against their 'Popish' enemies. Thereafter, politically astute councillors could play upon the people's fears and they ensured that the threat of the 'demonic' Catholic religion (as they saw it) was maintained. This was not only served to preserve England's independence from Rome, it also provided Elizabeth's fleet of experienced and talented sailors with a reason to attack and pillage French and Spanish Catholic possessions overseas. Many of these small wars, which are labelled as 'religious', were simply open acts of an aggressive foreign policy carried out with the monarch's blessing as they looked to expand their frontiers, trade and wealth through simple acquisition. Despite the wealth gained by these sea-dogs, Elizabeth I was creating an ever-increasing debt.

With the accession of James I there was some concern among the Protestant nobility that the new king would be too lenient with the Catholics and there were similar concerns as regarded his passive foreign policy. One of the first things James I did was to look to bring the ongoing war with Catholic Spain to an end and to give some of his Scottish and Catholic aristocracy favourable court positions, causing disquiet among Elizabeth's staunchest supporters. However, the English Parliament was shaken in 1605 by the exposure of the Gunpowder Plot, which, it has been calculated, would have caused the death of everyone within the House of Parliament, should Guy Fawkes have succeeded in lighting the fuse at the time of the opening of Parliament. Following the eventual cornering of the conspirators in the Midlands and their subsequent trials and executions, James hardened his policy and although he did not inflict any further direct brutality upon the Catholics, he passed the Popish Recusants Act of 1605, which forbade Roman Catholics from practising the professions of either law or medicine and even from acting as a guardian or trustee. More importantly, fearing another assassination attempt (there had been several attempts upon Elizabeth in her reign), it allowed local magistrates to search the houses of known Catholics for stores of arms. The Act also provided a new oath of allegiance, which denied the Pope of any power to depose a British monarch. Finally, any Catholic who did not receive the sacrament at least once a year in his own Church of England parish church was to be fined £60 or to forfeit two-thirds of his land. The Recusancy Acts had originally been brought in under Elizabeth I to restrict Catholic freedoms and James applied these as a warning, it seems, to other plotters that a heavy hand would fall on those who sought to bring him down. In 1605, more than 5,000 people were convicted of recusancy, of whom over 100 were landowners.

How much the gunpowder plot was the clever plan of disgruntled Catholics, and how much of it was a clever piece of Government propaganda designed to control the largely Protestant public through fear of a return to a Catholic state, we will probably never know. Certainly it suited Parliament to have the people fearful of the Catholics; it meant they fought better when pitted against armies or navies from France and Spain and it meant the King was wary of too much Catholic freedom. Although James brought in or practised these harsh laws, they were not so strictly enforced, especially as time passed from the 1605 plot. James, therefore, throughout his reign, trod a successful tightrope, which had on one side his commitment to the Protestant throne and on the other his commitment to his Scottish and Catholic favourites. In addition, he succeeded in his desire to keep peace within his realm and with his Catholic neighbours, France and Spain. However, those Stuarts that succeeded him were not able to maintain the balance. Importantly, however, James's reign laid one very important foundation: he may have been the first Stuart king of England, but there had been a Stuart monarch for the Scottish people since 1371 and if an English parliament threatened a Stuart king of both kingdoms, then trouble would ensue and this is exactly what occurred for the next 121 years.

If religion was one cause of unease towards the Stuarts then debt was another and this became the Achilles heel for Charles I. James I and VI had inherited a debt of £400,000 from Elizabeth, and James tried to bring down this financial millstone by not getting embroiled in the hugely destructive Thirty Years War. This pan-European war started in 1618 as a small religious dispute between Protestant and Catholic states which were part of the Holy Roman Empire. However, it quickly grew to encompass the major powers of Western Europe, with Sweden, the Holy Roman Empire, France and Spain all involved. Shortly after James's death, and as a result of wars being fought with France between 1627 and 1629 and Spain between 1625–1630, the debt under Charles I quickly grew to £1 million. The money wasted by England in 1627/8 when she first attacked and then aided the Protestant Huguenots against France was far out of proportion to any benefit gained against the French. The finances of the Kingdom, when income from taxation and custom duties was balanced against expenditure, would just about nett out. Once at war the expenditure far outweighed the income and in fact the trend has been the same ever since. It is perhaps poignant to note at this point that Britain's national debt rose exponentially after its three great wars; over the Napoleonic Wars between 1792 and 1815 it rose to £850 million; after the First World War (1914 to 1918) it had reached £7.4 billion; and after the Second World War (1939 to 1945) it had reached a staggering £24.7 billion and the British borrowing that was undertaken to fund a war in order to save humanity was only finally paid off in December 2006!

It was Charles I's efforts to deal with the debt by oppressive taxation and without recourse to Parliament which shut the lid on a barrel of unstable gunpowder with the fuse well alight. His cause was made worse by attempting to bring uniformity within the Church in both of his kingdoms. His father James had succeeded in bringing bishops back into the Scottish Kirk system; Charles tried to go one better and impose a Book of Common Prayer, to be used in the Kirk in 1637. This sparked rioting in Scotland and led to a formalised opposition in the National Covenant. The matter was made worse when in successive years Scottish armies marched on England. The first incursion, known as the First Bishops' War of 1639, was settled without bloodshed but increased the burden of debt. The second invasion, and therefore the Second Bishops' War, of 1640 led to an English defeat at the Battle of Newburn and a humiliating settlement with the Scots. Charles negotiated and agreed to all of the demands of the Scottish Parliament. Further in debt, he now had to recall his English Parliament; faced with the Grand Remonstrance, a list of grievances against the King (and those ministers who ill advised him), Charles attempted to take control of Parliament by force; failing to arrest those members who he believed were plotting against him, he left London and began a tour of England,l proclaiming that he would uphold the Protestant faith and defend his people.

Thus began nine years of civil war in which many tens of thousands of soldiers and civilians alike died, as disease marched with the armies to their deaths. The Civil War was realy three separate wars: 1642 to 1646; 1648 and 1649 to 1651. One man rose to the fore as the civil wars unfolded, he was a Parliamentarian master of horse, a cavalry commander and his name was Oliver Cromwell. His religious zeal and dictatorial attitude were to leave stains on these isles which have not been washed away even unto today. As regards the Civil War, ultimately Parliament was successful but after it failed to agree a personal settlement with the King, Cromwell decided that the only thing that could be trusted was himself and his own army, for Cromwell was now the master of the most powerful force in England. Cromwell mistrusted most of his own Parliament and certainly he mistrusted the King, and with them both, in Cromwell's eyes, incapable of being honest enough to work together for the common good, he decided to rule without them. Although not present at Pride's Purge, it is most likely that Cromwell was behind the use of force when General Pride (a subordinate but well known general who had served Cromwell at the overwhelming victory of Preston in 1648) took over Parliament by force in December 1648. Cromwell returned soon after Pride had taken control and ensured, by the use of the army, that only those who would find Charles guilty would sit on his trial. Cromwell now provided a trial which had no legal authority and the commissioners (judges) found the King guilty of treason against his own people, for which he was executed on 30 January 1649.

Cromwell, however, had not only killed the King of England but the King of Scotland as well. Although the Scots had helped Parliament in the first civil war, it was on the understanding that first they would be handsomely paid for their help and secondly that England would undertake the Scottish Kirk system of presbyteries after the war was concluded; whatever the understanding, Parliament reneged on their agreement. This insult, followed by the execution of a Stuart King, now led the Scots to rise in open revolt. Cromwell went north and beat the Scots at the Battle of Dunbar in September 1650, not far from Edinburgh. Undaunted, the Scots rose again in 1651 and marched south; eventually, in a great battle fought in and around Worcester in September 1651, the combined Scottish-Royalists were defeated and after a long and weary road Charles II escaped to exile in France. The first of the many Stuart exiles had begun.

However, Parliament found that it could not function without a figurehead, without a monarch, and turned to Oliver Cromwell to become King, an offer he wisely declined. However, Cromwell saw himself as the man to rule England through her troubled times and took the title of Lord Protector, ruling at times through the army and his appointed Major-Generals, who were each responsible for different areas of the country to manage. Cromwell's legacy was a strong and efficient army but he also left a trail of atrocities. It seems that Cromwell believed he had an almost divine right to rule dictatorially if necessary, yet he had overthrown and executed Charles I for the very same thing. Even among his own he was ruthless. A Levellers' rising broke out in 1648 to 1649 among men who had fought for freedom from tyranny and who now wanted equality for all. The rebellion was swiftly put down and the leaders executed. Ireland had openly risen in revolt against English control during the reign of Charles I and in consequence, once the King was dead and England relatively quiet, Cromwell turned his attention to those Royalists and rebels in Ireland. The suppression and subsequent massacres of Cromwell's campaigns between 1649 and 1653 are still resonate there to this day: at Drogheda, around 700 innocent men, women, children, prisoners and even Catholic priests were killed in addition to the 2,700 soldiers that had resisted the siege. At the end of the campaign, Catholic lands were distributed among the English already settled in Ireland, and to the Parliamentary soldiers who had fought for Oliver Cromwell. In ruling in this manner Cromwell instilled in Parliament a mistrust of the army and in later decades this fear returned so that after each war that Britain was involved in, the army was greatly reduced. This left the country with a very small standing army and left Britain open to the threat of both rebellion and invasion.

Just who Oliver Cromwell envisaged succeeding him is open to much debate; but upon his death in September 1658 the tile of Lord Protector passed without any legal precedent to his third son, Richard Cromwell. Richard inherited a debt that now stood at £2 million and he inherited not only the stewardship of the crown but also the army. This was a major weakness as he had no military experience, having not taken up arms in the Civil War and this meant he did not have the confidence of the army. From the first, Richard was found seriously wanting and with neither the respect of the army nor Parliament, he was a mere figurehead until the two rival powers clashed in 1659. Richard resigned his office of Lord Protector in May 1659 and England was once more without a head of its people or its Church. A series of minor rebellions and armies gathered and marched but it seems that neither Parliament nor the army wanted to return to an all-out war. Parliament limited the power of the army to influence parliamentary affairs and eventually, after Parliament had met and negotiations were completed to the satisfaction of all, Charles II returned to London upon 29 May 1660, his birthday, to ascend the throne eleven years after his father's death.

This restoration of the monarchy in 1660 brought with it a commitment from Charles II to uphold the Church of England and he did so by passing the Act of Uniformity in 1662, which set out common standards for prayer and Church services and restored much that Cromwell's puritanical stewardship had banished. Theatres reopened and bawdy plays mirrored the mood of the majority of people , who rejoiced in a return to freedoms of expression which had been buried under the Protectorate. Charles was even able to reinstate the Episcopacy in Scotland. Despite his popularity, the dread of a Catholic resurgence was ever in people's minds and even events such as the Great Plague in 1665 and the Great Fire of London in 1666 were attributed to Catholic plots, and there are reports of people fleeing their homes in London and in other provincial towns for fear that they would 'have their throats cut' by rising Papists.

The Stuart lines of succession. Top left to right: James II; James Francis Stuart (Old Pretender); Charles Edward Stuart (Young Pretender); Charles Edward Stuart in old age; James Fitz James. Bottom left to right: Mary II; William III; Anne; George I; George II. (Jackdaw Publications London No. 15)

Such was the hysteria against Catholics that where the Great Fire of London was thought to have started in Pudding Lane, an inscription ascribing the fire to 'Popish frenzy' was engraved upon the monument. The building was the King's own bakers and this inflammatory inscription was only removed in 1831. Anti-Catholic feeling was also fuelled by doubts over the religious allegiance of the King and his international alliances. In May 1662 Charles II married a Catholic, Catherine of Braganza, who was a princess of Portugal, and later formed an alliance with France against the Protestant Netherlands. France was now the foremost Catholic nation, having superseded a declining Spain by destroying the Spanish army at Rocroi in 1643. Charles did not help himself by quelling fears of his hidden Catholicism. In 1670 Charles II entered into the secret Treaty of Dover, an alliance with his first cousin King Louis XIV of France. In this treaty Louis agreed to aid Charles in the Third Anglo-Dutch War, and also to pay Charles a pension. Charles for his part secretly promised to convert to Catholicism at an unspecified future date, a promise he was to keep upon his deathbed. In 1672 Charles attempted to introduce religious freedom for Catholics, and also Protestant dissenters, with a Royal Declaration of Indulgence; however, the English Parliament were unhappy with the bill and forced Charles to withdraw it. Further chaos reigned towards the end of Charles II's reign when, from 1679 to 1682, a man named Titus Oates succeeded, through devious letters and manuscripts, in convincing the hierarchy of Church and State that there was a 'Popish Plot' to assassinate the King and his brother. The crisis saw some extraordinary developments. Catholics were forbidden within a radius of twenty miles of London, and despite hard cross-examinations Oates was so convincing that chaos and affray ensued and innocent people were tried and executed as conspirators. Seizing upon the anti-Catholic tide, Shaftesbury publicly demanded that the King's brother, James, should be excluded from the royal succession, so that at the end of 1678 Parliament passed a bill, a second Test Act, which excluded Catholics from membership of both Houses of Parliament, a law that was not repealed until 1829.

Furthermore, this crisis gave rise to the foundation of our modern political system as the pro-exclusion Whig and the anti-exclusion Tory parties developed. These two parties steadily became established and would vie for power until the mid-nineteenth century when the Whig party slowly broke into different factions, leading to the formation of the Liberal and Unionist parties. The Whigs fundamentally stood for the power of Parliament over the monarchy and for the established Church of England, but also for trade and industrial and agricultural development. The Tories were more traditional, supporters of an absolute monarchy, and generally they were supports of Roman Catholic faith. Charles II naturally sided with the Tories following the discovery of the Rye House Plot in 1683, which threatened to murder Charles and James. The resultant investigation and recriminations resulted in some Whig leaders being killed and others forced into exile. Charles, like his father, had now had enough of Parliaments and dissolved the English Parliament in 1681, choosing to rule alone until his death on 6 February 1685, when it would seem his own true faith was finally acknowledged. Whatever blood had been shed in these sporadic anti-Catholic purges during Charles II's reign would be as nothing compared to what would transpire thereafter. Despite fathering at least eight illegitimate children, Charles's wife, Catherine, bore him no live children. As his illegitimate children were excluded from the succession, he was succeeded by his brother James, whose suitability had already been challenged by Anthony Ashley Cooper, the First Earl of Shaftesbury, at the height of the Titus Oates scandal. Perhaps Shaftesbury saw what was coming: it is quite incredible but once more the failure of a monarch to produce a legitimate heir would lead to a major crisis in the realm of both kingdoms and this crisis would continue for over sixty years.

Whereas Charles II had been circumspect where his faith was concerned, James II was not so covert. James, as Duke of York and heir apparent, renounced his office of Lord High Admiral rather than swear an Oath under the new Test Act of 1673, thereby clearly showing his hidden Catholic faith. Following the death of his devoted first wife Anne Hyde in 1671, he remarried in 1673 to Maria d'Este, a Catholic princess from the Italian state of Modena, further strengthening his Catholic ties; with Mary of Modena, as she is known, being a personal favourite of Louis XIV, the French King was now the unrivalled champion of the Catholic World. Soon after becoming king, James faced two rebellions, both of which had begun in Holland. The major rebellion was in southern England and was led by his nephew the Duke of Monmouth, one of Charles II's illegitimate children. The second smaller rebellion rose in Scotland and was led by Archibald Campbell, the Earl of Argyll. Argyll sailed to Scotland and, on arriving there, raised recruits mainly from among his own clan, the Campbells. But around 300 men was all Argyll could muster and he was quickly defeated and captured at Inchinnan on 18 June 1685, the northern rebellion posing little threat to James's position. In contrast, Monmouth's rebellion was more dangerous and began when Monmouth proclaimed himself King at Lyme Regis on 11 June 1685. Monmouth's recruiting raised a mostly peasant army, which at its peak rose to around 5,000 men, and for a while he posed a serious threat to the west of England. The King's army, which was led by the Earl of Feversham and John Churchill, finally overpowered the rebels at the Battle of Sedgemoor on 6 July 1685, when the rebels tried a night attack near the village of Westonzoyland on the Somerset Levels. Monmouth himself was captured and executed at the Tower of London on 15 July and the trials that followed, most notably under Judge George Jeffreys, condemned many of the rebels to transportation and indentured servitude in the West Indies. The trials became known as the Bloody Assizes as 333 rebels were executed and 814 transported, so that local gentry in Somerset feared there would be insufficient men to work the land such was the depopulation of male labour. Ironically, it was these failed rebellions that led James to take measures which in turn alienated his people and led to a rebellion to remove him from the throne.

Both rebellions were defeated easily enough, but they massively hardened James's resolve against any as he saw as his enemies. In order to strengthen his own position, James sought safety in an enlarged standing army under his control and to the people this instantly brought back the old fears of authoritarian rule. Their memories were long and it was only one generation since Oliver Cromwell's army had ruled the land. In addition, people feared the billeting of soldiers near their towns and villages and the trouble and disease that might come with an army. Of more concern to Parliament was the growing number of regimental commands being given to James's Catholic friends, and without the need to take the same oath which James himself had refused to take just twelve years earlier under the Test Act. Parliament, which had supported James, now refused to agree to James's requests and they were even more alarmed when the King's Secretary of State, the Earl of Sunderland, began replacing senior office-holders at court with James's Catholic favourites. James was keeping all his friends close and looking to build a wall of both political and military strength that he believed would see him through any future crisis. However, within Parliament James had begun to lose the confidence of many of his former Anglican supporters and any lingering support vanished when once more religious matters came to a head.

In 1687 James issued the Declaration of Indulgence, in which he used his dispensing power to negate the effect of laws punishing Catholics and Protestant Dissenters, even going on a speaking tour to explain his reason for the act to people in the west of the country. At the same time James provided partial toleration in Scotland, using his same dispensing power to grant full relief to Catholics and partial relief to Presbyterians. In 1688, James ordered this declaration be read from the pulpits of every Anglican church and he also began to interfere with the traditional way in which the Anglican Church managed education; he tried to force the colleges of Oxford and Cambridge to accept Catholics in positions of authority, including the office of president at Magdalen College. People are open to change when they can see a good reason for it, and if change is introduced slowly and with forethought. In the years 1687 to 1688 we see an ever increasing number of changes being pushed through by James, all designed to enhance the position of Catholics in society, believing that he now had enough friends in the right places to support him should any insurgency arise. All that James succeeded in doing was alienating the key bodies of men that he needed to stay in power: the Church and Parliament. Matters came to a head when seven bishops, including the Archbishop of Canterbury, submitted a petition requesting the reconsideration of the King's religious policies as they objected to having to preach from the pulpit the aforementioned declaration. The seven clergy were arrested and tried for seditious libel, while a short time later Queen Mary gave birth on 10 June to a son and heir, James Francis Edward Stuart. Clearly King James now had a Catholic son and heir and the possibility of a Catholic Stuart dynasty was in place. This son precluded James's Protestant daughters from his first marriage and the toleration which Parliament had shown to James was finally removed. Certain Protestant nobles had already made overtures to William of Orange when they first knew that the Queen, Mary of Modena, was pregnant; the subsequent birth of a healthy son reinforced their conviction that a Protestant champion was needed. At the end of June 1688 a group of seven nobles invited the Prince of Orange to come to England with an army as they now fully believed that William and his wife Mary, the daughter of James II and VII and a lady who had kept faith with her Protestant religion, would be accepted. Mary was next in line to her father and so the legitimacy could not be contested if James could be removed from office. James continued to press on with plans to make his own position more secure and was on the verge of calling a general election when it became clear that William would accept the offer before him and invade. Louis XIV, on seeing the situation unfold before him, offered James the support of French troops, but James declined, believing his own force of 20,000 men was sufficient to deal with the invasion. William landed, ironically, on the infamous date of 5 November 1688 and he had 15,000 men with him. William adopted a policy of no intervention in local affairs; he forbad his men to take anything from the local population and maintained his advance through his own supply lines. William's plan of a slow, steady but relentless march towards London eventually told as James now began to try and undo those policies that he had begun to implement, but it was too late. James's army began to desert; his followers, who had been dismissed as 'evil' counsellors, were gone. He was effectively alone, save for a few loyal friends. James had already sent his wife and his young son and heir to the throne abroad to France; it was now James's turn to flee.

James II's flight from London was nothing short of farcical and it began in disguise on 11 December from Whitehall. James II had only got as far as Faversham before he was seized and brought back to London. After a few days James II was taken and imprisoned in Rochester, but was 'allowed' to escape on 23 December, fleeing swiftly to France where he was re-united with his wife and young son and heir. William deemed that it was safer to let James flee quietly abroad than risk turning him into a martyr at home, which might inflame the fickle population. James II's reign was over. This shows just how cruel 'the twists of fate' are in the history of the Stuarts. England in 1688 wanted a Protestant king and only three years earlier the Duke of Monmouth had claimed the throne on those very grounds as he stood for a Protestant monarchy and challenged the legitimacy of James to rule because of his clear Catholicism. The second thing in Monmouth's favour was that he was the eldest son of Charles II and a direct if illegitimate claimant. How different would the history of the three kingdoms have been if Monmouth had succeeded in his rebellion and continued the Stuart dynasty as a Protestant one, without the need for recourse to Hanoverian relatives, instigating the series of rebellions that followed? Hindsight is a wonderful thing.

This book was completed in spring 2014, at a poignant time as the ongoing debate on Scottish independence closes in on the Autumn referendum. The Scottish National Party (the SNP), led by Alex Salmond, are campaigning for the full devolution of Scotland; well, 'full' in the sense that they want to govern their own affairs, yet they still want to keep key elements of the British Union that will support them. So they want to keep the Pound as their currency and also be part of the European Union (EU) while being a separate country in almost everything else. Neither of these two fundamental cornerstones are easy to maintain if the SNP achieve their goal of Scottish independence, and these facts have been made clear by both the British and European parliaments. The SNP believe that economically they will be in a stronger financial situation given the United Kingdom's debt position if they can be removed from it. But Scotland has helped to build that debt; its Members of Parliament have sat in positions of power at Westminster and made collective decisions on the British economy. One cannot just pick the cherries from the tin of fruit salad, one has at some point to eat the other lesser sweet fruit as well; and devolution from the United Kingdom would raise serious issues with regards to defence and the apportion of the ongoing national debt. There are people working in Scotland who rely on English companies and English contracts, there are people in England who rely on Scottish companies and contracts. The Better Together campaign which has the support of the three main United Kingdom political parties, Labour, Conservative and Liberal Democrats, all of whom firmly believe that the devolved policy-making powers which the Scottish Parliament already has is power enough and that further disintegration will be to the detriment of all the peoples of the United Kingdom. The year 2014 measures exactly 325 years since the Scottish people found themselves for the first time in exactly the same situation as the voters this year: who to support. Some Scottish people relied on English trade and there were Scottish regiments in the Government army, as there are today. For the vast majority of people, the politics and the complexities of national affairs were secondary to two things: their religion (which was far more important in the last part of the seventeenth and the early part of the eighteenth centuries than it is today) and their ability to feed and clothe themselves. And it is the latter and how someone would be affected personally that really matters: both 300 years ago and today, it mostly comes down to the money which someone has. Which of the two monarchs would ensure that an individual would be better off financially if they followed them? We are fortunate that we have a rare insight into the plight of the clans living in the Western Highlands which shows why so many Highlanders were willing to follow the Stuart banner, march long distances and die for a cause which offered them a chance of something better. A clansman who was waiting in prison to be executed is reported to have said: 'My lord, for the two kings [i.e. James Stuart and George of Hanover] and their right, I care not a farthing. But I was starving. And, by God, if Mohammed had set up a standard in the Highlands I would have been a good Muslim for bread and stuck close to the Jacobite party, for I must eat.' This remark was not made and is in no way meant to be insulting in any way to the Prophet Mohammed; what the clansman was saying was that if someone had come from as East as anyone could go in the known World at that time and they had offered him money enough to eat with, then he would have followed their banner. This poverty was the plight of many of the clans living in the western fringes of Scotland. The rugged Highland region was generally poor of pasture, low on any kind of industry and far removed from any centres of commerce, even speaking the Gaelic language as a first tongue. The old clan ways were adhered to with a strict code of allegiance from the family. It was the clan chiefs of the Highlands and the gentry of the Lowlands who had to ask themselves the same kind of searching economic question which the Scottish people will vote on later this year. For the people 300 years ago, the question was whether they would be better off under a traditional Scottish descended Catholic Stuart monarch, or under a Parliament led from Westminster under a Protestant Dutch or even a Protestant German King?

3

The Armies of
the Jacobite Rebellions

As we touched upon in the introduction, the armies that repeatedly faced each other during this series of rebellions were for the most part very different in their composition. The Government armies were formed for the most part soldiers who were trained, dressed in a uniform manner and paid a wage for their pains. The Jacobites were individual fighting men with an inbred fighting spirit and an iron resolve which was honed in their inter-clan wars and local disputes which turned into conflict, normally over the theft of one or the other's cattle. The general fighting men of both sides were very poor (even men of the clan chiefs lived on what we call today the poverty line) and very, very few of these men ever made it out of the ranks through ability. Leading the armies for both sides were wealthy men, society men who had gone into soldiering because that is what the sons of rich people did if they were not going to manage their father's estate; the Duke of Cumberland, who led the final campaign for the Hanoverians, was as high in society as one could get, being a Prince of the realm. The leaders of the Jacobites were also for the most part high up in the peerage, lords, dukes and earls who believed in the old established order and the Catholic Church. Finally, there were the mercenaries; although mighty invasions were planned, only small numbers of regular troops sent by France and Spain fought for the Jacobite cause, but they were regular soldiers, trained in discipline and control, and were a contrast to the rest of the Jacobite armies.

If the clans could be roused, then at any time the Stuarts could call on an army of between 5,000 and 10,000 men. However, it has been estimated that if all the male population of the clans had turned out in one rising, an army of 25,000 or maybe 30,000 could have been formed, though the majority would have been very poorly armed. For any rising to work, a Stuart pretender to the throne needed the clans together with outside Catholic support. Time and again such support was proffered and time and again for a variety of reasons it failed to materialise. In sharp contrast the British Government, after every European war, successful or not, sought to reduce its army to the bare minimum, only to have to recruit and train an army the next time there was an international crisis. This fear of a standing army went back to the days immediately after the end of the third phase of the English Civil War in 1651, when having already executed Charles I in 1649, Cromwell went on to rule eventually through the use of force when he found 'his' Parliament as intransigent as the one Charles had railed against. Politicians' memories were long and they feared that any large standing army would be vulnerable to subversion against its own people, and especially its Parliament, if unpopular decisions were taken. Thus it was that after both William III and the Duke of Marlborough had built and trained a disciplined force, it was largely disbanded after the respective peace treaties were signed. So if a rebellion occurred on home soil during a time of peace in Europe then Britain's standing army was small; if a rebellion broke out during a European conflict then the army was often abroad and invalided and militia forces were left to garrison and defend the country. In 1744, of the 10,000 troops stationed for the defence of Britain, some 7,000 were deployed to defend London and the south-east corner of England. These latter points were not lost on the spies from France and Spain. There were also Highland clans that fought with the Government with distinction and loyalty. As a general rule the clans that supported the Jacobite cause tended to be of a Roman Catholic or Scottish Episcopalian persuasion, while those clans which tended to be Presbyterian sided with the British Government.

Infantry

In warfare, as well as in politics, the late seventeenth century was a period of transition. A generation before, when the English Civil War had broken out, an army was made up of different types of combatant. A regiment of troops in the English Civil Wars was formed of two types of infantrymen, or foot: these were the musketeer and the pikeman. The role of the pikeman was to protect the slow-firing musketeers from marauding cavalry, giving the musketeers time to reload and fire their cumbersome matchlock muskets. Once each side had softened the other up with a volley or two of musketry the regiment would advance, with the pikemen going forward to deliver the final charge, trying to frighten or push the enemy off the field of battle. At the outset of the English Civil War the ratio of pike to musket was supposed to be 1:2. In reality, and certainly in the Royalist armies, it was at least 3:1 in favour of the pike. By the end of the war it had completely changed, with nearly all the Royalist foot regiments consisting of men who were solely armed with muskets, preferring to fire and then charge using their musket butts as the offensive weapon. The New Model Army in 1645 was reformed under Thomas Fairfax along traditional lines, with one pikeman to every two musketeers and so for a while the two weapons were still used together.

However, by 1670 a new invention began to creep into all of the western European armies. According to the most accurate estimate, at some time in the 1660s a small sharp blade attachment appeared, called a bayonet appeared; the word had been around for some time and meaning a blade hung on the belt when out hunting. It was now re-made in a simple version to fit into a musket and allocated to the French infantry regiments. The idea was that the musketeer could insert the bayonet into the muzzle of his own musket after shooting off a final volley and turn his firearm into a short pike, an attacking melee weapon of his own. Acting as a unit once a series of musket volleys had been shot, the order to 'fix bayonets' would be given and the musketeers could advance as one to deliver a charge of their own. This early design of bayonet was referred to as a 'plug' bayonet because it fitted into the mouth of the musket barrel and at once the drawback can be seen: it prevented the musket from being fired, which meant if you were not quick enough with your last volley and fitting your bayonet it was possible for a charging enemy to hit you before you were ready with disastrous results, Killiecrankie being a prime example. The other drawback was that if the bayonet was not fully fitted into the socket then it could accidently slip out during combat, leaving the musketeer to revert to the age-old practice of clubbing the musket at his adversary. The most important development came later in the 1680s, when the ring or socket bayonet was invented. This bayonet slipped over the mouth of the musket barrel, and slid down the outside of the barrel before being twisted and locked into a small but strong fixing which held the bayonet in place until the musketeer wanted to remove it. This innovation meant two things: firstly that the bayonet was solidly fixed to the musket and would not dislodge during hand-to-hand combat thus giving the musketeer greater confidence in its fighting ability; secondly, because the barrel was not blocked the musketeer could carry on firing until the last possible moment before either engaging in charging or counter-charging the enemy. This design of socket bayonet would remain basically unchanged for the next 250 years and would be used across the world, notably by the massed armies of the Napoleonic Wars, where the red-coated British infantry would become synonymous with great firepower and a thin red line of steel. At the start of the Stuart uprisings, then, the Government units still had a few pikemen at a ratio of around ten muskets to each pike, the majority of muskets being matchlocks. After 1700 the Government foot would all be armed with flintlock muskets, save for the officers, who carried spontoons, a type of short halberd which they used for dressing the ranks into neat lines. The British infantry unit traditionally formed up in three lines and would fire either in lines by volley or in small groups called platoons, which meant the volley was smaller than the whole line firing but kept up a constant fire upon the enemy.

The Jacobite style of fighting went back over 1,000 years to the times of individual prowess and fighting ability, the same spirit with which the ancient Celts had fought the Romans. Yes, they had adapted to new weapons, firstly the bow and then the pistol and the musket, but the Highlanders never had the volume of muskets necessary to equip a whole army, and after they had fired their first volley, often from the hip while on the run, they would discard the musket, ready to charge home. As was repeatedly seen during the great risings, when they were asked to win a battle by means of a fire-fight, they lost. For the most part they were not drilled, though Lord Murray in the '45 Rebellion did try to instil some practical manoeuvres and certainly the Jacobite retreat from Culloden was well executed. In contrast to the regularity of equipment carried by their opponents, the Jacobites carried a variety of weapons: whatever they had when they left home supplemented by anything they were given or plundered during the campaign. Repeatedly in letters to the French Kings whenever an invasion was mentioned, the repeated requests from the clans came for arms, munitions and money. The Jacobites carried muskets, pistols, dirks (short knives), and sometimes a 'Lochaber axe', a long polearm which held on to favour with the Jacobites in the absence of any other weapon. Some men still carried small shields called targes, which were made

Cannon balls, grape shot, musket and pistol balls, 12 inch ruler for scale. (Author's collection)

from wood, covered in leather and often studded in a geometric pattern; some targes had a device for screwing a small blade into the outside centre so that the shield was an offensive as well as a defensive weapon when crashing into melee. On page 20 of his book *Memoirs of the Lord Viscount Dundee, The Highland Clans* (published by F. E. Robinson & Company in 1903), Henry Jenner gives a clear picture of how the Highlanders reacted once given the order for the advance: they discarded their 'plads, haversacks, and all other utensils, and marched resolutely and deliberately in their shirts and doublets, with their fusils (muskets), swords, targets, and pistols ready...' The Highland charge was by all accounts a fearsome sight to behold; it began as Henry Jenner describes, with the discarding of all surplus kit, which was simply left where it fell. The Charge would then gain momentum until the Highlanders were within perhaps fifteen seconds of hitting the enemy, at which point they would fire their muskets to cause as much confusion as possible before the charge made contact and also to draw their opponents' volley at long and less effective range. Once fired, the muskets were dropped to the ground and the pistols were then drawn to fire in to the face of the enemy before these firearms were also thrown aside. Finally, at the last second, either the claymore or the broadsword would be drawn and brought crashing down onto the head, or across the face, of the man before them; it took brave men to withstand such an assault. It is significant that Cumberland reported that when his troops scoured the battlefield they recovered 2,320 firelocks but only 190 broadswords, clearly illustrating the improvement in the quantity of muskets carried at the end of the campaign compared to the start, when many Jacobites had only scythes or pitchforks.

Cavalry

The many different types of military horsemen during the Renaissance period is so vast that it commands a book in its own right; fortunately, by the late seventeenth century this variety had given way to two distinct types, the heavy cavalry and the dragoons. The dragoons were the lighter side of the mounted arm and were armed with carbines and bayonet as well as with pistols and a sword and their original aim was to act as mounted infantry, performing a variety of tasks. They could take up an advance position, often occupying woods or lanes, from which they could harass an enemy flank, Naseby in 1645 being a good example of their effectiveness. Alternatively, they could become involved in fighting in built-up areas or in difficult terrain such as their uphill advance on foot to the Royalists' ridge at Stow-on the-Wold in 1646. Finally, as they were light horsemen they could perform two campaign roles, one being to scout out the enemy before a battle and the other to harass and chase the enemy once they had broken away from the battle in rout. The dragoon was therefore the most versatile role in the army. The heavy cavalry still wore either a cuirass for chest protection or a thick buff leather coat for more complete coverage and charged home with the sword, sometimes shooting pistols if time allowed, so these charges were reminiscent of both Prince Rupert and Cromwell's tactics during the English Civil War. This practice of separating the two types of cavalry continued on the Continent but during the War of the Spanish Succession (1700–1713) the British Government realised that the dragoons were much cheaper to maintain and much more flexible in their ability that the more expensive heavy cavalry units and when the '15 Rebellion broke out the need for fresh regiments led to the creation of thirteen new dragoon regiments. These British dragoons undertook all the roles of the mounted troops, charging home when required and dismounting and fighting as infantry at need, and became invaluable to the Government force.

Again, in sharp contrast to the British mounted arm, it was all the Jacobites could do to raise any horsemen at all, especially in the first few risings, where their mounted men came from the gentry and wealthier clans, who could afford horses. In the '45 rising they did have a company of the loyal French-Irish Fitzjames's Horse, at its strongest only around 130 men and not all of those with horses, and a unit of Baggot's Hussars as well as number of mounted clansmen. Almost invariably the newly raised and very small troops of cavalry had to give up their horses to these two more regular troops of horsemen as there was a permanent shortage of horses within the Jacobite army. These two troops of horse were equipped in the same manner as the British dragoons and, although small, behaved well when called to action.

Artillery

The common smooth-bore cannon was the mainstay of all artillery units at this time and capable, depending on its calibre, of sending a solid lump of iron (a cannon-ball) between a half and a mile and half. The destruction caused by a cannon ball was through the violence of its actual passage in smashing into and careering through the enemy ranks. At close quarters the large cannon ball was replaced by sacks of musket balls which resembled bunches of grapes. This 'grape' shot was devastating at close range as a gun could shoot out hundreds of musket balls in one blast and did considerable damage to the Jacobite charge at Culloden. The variety of calibre, construction material and type of carriage throughout the sixteenth and early seventeenth centuries was as wide as the types of horsemen. Across Europe cannons were made by individual experts, masters of their craft ,but this was regulated in England by the Royal Ordnance, which began in 1414 and existed under various names until 1855; its headquarters were in the Tower of London. It regulated the types of cannon by the weight of shot fired: 3lb, 4lb, and so forth. Cannons were cast in iron or bronze (often called brass) and their quality was very inconsistent, so that cannons could split open when being fired. The British artillery train was poor and consisted mostly of cannons used for the defence of forts and castles. In 1716, in a positive move for this military craft, the Royal Regiment of Artillery was formed so that by the '45 campaign Cumberland was able to deploy an efficient artillery arm on the battlefield and so combine his three arms in a coordinated and tactical battle plan. This included the other type of artillery in battlefield use, the mortar. The heavy mortar had been around for centuries as an early form of howitzer which, instead of shooting a solid cannonball, fired a hollow metal ball or shell which exploded once the fuse which stuck through a hole in the top had burned into the heart of the missile, scattering shrapnel through 360 degrees. Originally designed for use in large scale sieges, the Coehorn had been invented in the Netherlands by Menno van Coehoorn in 1674 and naturally William of Orange, with his experiences in the Dutch army, added these light and versatile weapons to his artillery train. These small devoices made a significant contribution in several of the Jacobite battles.

A captured coehorn mortar abandoned by the Jacobites at Kedleston Hall. (Courtesy of the National Trust)

The Jacobite artillery train was always weak and relied on what they could remove from the capture of an enemy garrison or town armoury or plunder after a victorious battle and the majority of all their canon were light guns, probably either 3lb or less, so that they could be moved at the same speed as the Highlanders marched. There was no place for a massive siege train, even though the Jacobites did attempt several sieges. Only during the latter half of the '45 Rebellion, when some trained French artillerymen joined Prince Charles's army, did the rebels have an effective artillery unit. The chassis of the cannon, being made of wood, was susceptible to poor weather, causing the wood to weaken or twist, rendering the cannon unreliable and difficult to move. Since they were first invented, cannons had been painted; many were given their own pet name, showing the affinity between the guns' captain and his livelihood. In war it was essential across a massive battlefield for the officers to see whose cannons were where and so the cannons were painted in standard colours by army to make this recognition easier. The British guns were red until 1756, when they changed to grey, while the French were a bright lime/grass green, while any cannons bought over to England by William III may have been orange or blue. The Jacobites, as they used captured guns, would most likely have had a mixture of these and perhaps other colours depending on the age of the artillery piece.

Women

Throughout the book the author will refer to fighting men, as these were the overwhelming majority of combatants; however not every soldier was a man. There is evidence in many of the eighteenth-century wars that some women delicately disguised themselves as men so as to march with a loved one or to seek a loved one that they had lost; by cutting their hair short, pretending to shave and binding the breasts flat, if a woman could march, fight and shoot a musket then might she remain undetected? There is even a suggestion that women were on board ships in the navy, not excluded as all our childhood history taught us. Fanciful, perhaps, until one reads of Christian Davies, who served as an infantryman from 1697 until 1701 and then for a further five years as a dragoon in the Royal Scots Greys from 1701 until discovered in 1706 while still searching after all those years for her husband. While in the Scots Greys she was wounded at the Battle of Schellenberg but was not willing to be invalided and, with a musket ball in her upper thigh, she fought at the Battle of Blenheim. Even after discovery she still kept a role within the army and eventually lived as a Chelsea Pensioner until she died and was buried there.

The Government Army Dress

Nearly all of the units that fought in all of the Jacobite rebellions were red-coated soldiers and the vast majority of those were regiments of foot. In the early risings at the end of the seventeenth century the coats were still the long, flat-style coat without turnbacks but with coloured cuffs to identify the unit and the same simple, black, broadbrimmed hat that had been worn for much of the century was still in vogue; the rest was as follows. The headgear of the uniform by the eighteenth century still consisted of a broadbrimmed hat which could be turned up into the famous tricorn, or if they were one of the elite companies of the regiment they wore the mitre cap as a sign that they were the Grenadiers, the strongest and most experienced men of the unit. The rest of the uniform was consistent throughout the risings and consisted of: a shirt (white), a neckcloth (white), a waistcoat, a knee-length coat, breeches, stockings and shoes; boots were only for mounted men. In the seventeenth century breeches could be any colour but by the eighteenth these were all red, except for Royal regiments, which were blue. The warm woollen coat would have a facing colour chosen by the colonel of the regiment, yellow, cream, blue, white and green were all popular, and in different shades of those bold colours. Although these were partly used to distinguish one unit from another, eventually it was the pattern of the coloured stitching of the lace or tapes around the coat which set aside one unit from another. One stipulation of the army was that all of the horses for a dragoon regiment should be black, while the Scots Greys were to have, as their name suggests, horses which were of a grey colour. There were two unusual units that fought in the Culloden campaign, the first being the Georgia Rangers, who were destined for North America, having sailed from London, but were relieved of their orders by Cumberland at Hull and went on to fight in the autumn 1745 campaign. These rangers were equipped and dressed to fight in the wilderness in North America so they wore green uniforms and wore leather caps rather than the usual tricorn. The second unit was the small personal unit of bodyguards for the Duke of Cumberland. He had sixteen Austro-Hungarian/German Hussar troopers from Hanover who wore a green dolmen and pelisse and a crimson waistcoat and breeches which had scarlet trim; a brown fur kolpak hat was worn and dragoon or Hessian style riding boots.

The Highland clans and the early independent companies that fought for the Government wore a hybrid of the two uniforms. They wore a short red jacket but wore their plaid to set them aside as a Scottish regiment and wore a bonnet with a red cross upon it. The Dutch units that fought for the Government in the 1719 rebellion wore blue or grey long coats, again with coloured cuffs of orange, white and red to identify the unit. For all the Government's desire for its army to perform well, its men often endured considerable hardship on campaign: in the '45 Rebellion Ligonier had to repeatedly ask for extra shoes for the infantry, because their own were so worn, and with the winter being so harsh he requested extra blankets too, which had never before been supplied to the infantry, this being in fact the first time in British Army history that such a request had been considered. In *The Bloody Eleventh, A history of the Devonshire Regiment* by R.E.R. Robinson, 1988, a quote from Ligonier shows two important elements of the '45 campaign: firstly, how hard it was for the 'poor bloody infantry' when marching and countermarching to intercept the enemy; and secondly why, when Cumberland was duped into heading for Wales (only to find that the Jacobites had reached Derby), he

A grenadier from Pulteney's 13th Foot gives fire. (Courtesy of the Lace Wars)

knew that if the Jacobites kept on to Derby then, with his men exhausted, they would not be able to catch the prince and his army: Cumberland … because they (the infantry) 'had scarcely halted six hours these ten days, had been without victuals for twenty-four hours, and had been exposed to the coldest nights I ever felt without shelter, for the country produced not straw for two battalions . . . '

The Jacobite Army Dress

The mainstay of all the Jacobite army were its Highland clansmen but although some clans may have had a regular cloth colour or family weave, the tartans that the clans proudly display today do not necessarily go back to the Jacobite period. These men were used to living and working in a harsh climate and capable of surviving and fighting on slim rations. Many of the clans were poor and the promise of pay in gold and honour for the clan for ever under a restored Stuart monarchy was more than tempting when all that lay ahead for many of them was simple: a stagnation, a rotation of the farming year which provided just enough to get through to the next year. The Highland clan system was feudal, with homage paid to the clan chief (or laird), and if he called out the clan to war, to war it went. Similarly, if the chief stayed at home the clan stayed at home and did not get involved even if the majority of clansmen had sympathy with the Stuart cause. The style of clothing and the type of weaponry that the Highlanders would have carried in the first rising and in the last would have been the same: nothing had changed in those sixty years to alter the attire and the weaponry would have been whatever was to hand. The Jacobite clothing was a long shirt, around which was wrapped the plaid, which was at least two yards by four yards long, but in many caseswas six yards long. The plaid was wrapped around the waist first and then up and over the shoulder to cover the upper body, the whole being kept together at the waist with a belt and sometimes at the shoulder with a broach. A cross belt might be worn to carry a small bag for personal belongings, shot and powder, while the dirk, the small knives they carried, would be stored in their long socks. A sword could also be pushed through the man waist belt, as would any pistols. Many of the men at the start of the '45 Rebellion were very poor in both clothing and weaponry and when the army marched into Edinburgh many were in just shirts or simple plaid and with little else with them. The fact that so little changed over the time period means that the gamer can pretty much use any Highlander unit as any other, and the same army can be used in any of the risings. The regular French and Irish troops that fought for the Stuarts wore very similar uniforms to the British, with blue coats with red facings and red coats with black facings respectively. The Spanish troops that fought against the Dutch in the 1719 rising wore white coats and breeches with possibly red, yellow or blue waistcoats and cuffs with red stockings and shoes.

Standards

Every Government regiment and every Highland clan would have carried a standard, the rallying point for the men to stand by their comrades. The Government regiments carried a flag, the base colour of which was the same as the facing colour of the regiment, with the individual motif of the current or previous colonel. Many of the clans carried the blue saltire known across the world as a symbol for Scotland, but in addition many individual clans had their own traditional flags as well. Many of the different flags that were carried, together with the exact coat colours and facings of the regular regiments involved in the Jacobite campaigns, can be found on a suitable internet search engine and the author would recommend the enthusiast to seek out the units he wishes to recreate from that source or to refer to the bibliography for further reading. To aid the gamer, many of the flags are available to purchase in colour and in the right scale for the army being collected through one of the many companies that now makes ready-to-use flags for wargamers.

Spies

Many people, when first thinking of spies, would come up with the name James Bond, the archetypal British agent who has been with us for over sixty years. Spies have been around ever since there were armies, maybe not by that name, but certainly in the way they behave. From the earliest days of spying everyone had their price, be it money,

The basic camp of a regular regiment.

power or sexual favours, but money was the main driver for people to betray their own side. Religious or political conscience or potential political gain influenced many to look for friends abroad and so betray their own country, and finally there were the Government spies, paid professionals with the wit, guile and charm to be accepted at the heart of the enemy's circle and even succeeding in influencing their unknowing 'friends'. In this period from 1680 to 1750 it is these latter two types of spy that dominate, the Government employing people on the Continent to try and determine the French, Spanish and even Swedish plots against Britain while at the same time planting their own spies among the Jacobite ranks. The news that was bought to the Jacobite command at Derby that there was a new army of 9,000 men blocking their route to London was a lie planted by Dudley Bradstreet, who was a planted Government spy.

Size of the Army

The question of the available troops for both sides at the start of a battle is an almost ubiquitous one when looking at any battle, from any era of history: it is virtually impossible to know exactly how many men took part. One of the problems with sources for the eighteenth century is that they often list an army by brigade or regiment rather than the actual number of men and in some cases the name of the regiment changes because for the British Army it was the name of the colonel which named the regiment. Only after 1748 were the regiments awarded a regimental number to be permanently associated with. As has been shown throughout history the numbers within a unit titled as a regiment is never consistent, as such units were rarely at full strength. Wherever possible, the author has listed what are the most likely numbers of men involved in a given battle. However, with the extent of modern battlefield archaeology and archive research continuing to throw up new information, the author accepts that some of the numbers may be questioned. For the gamer wishing to recreate the battles of the campaigns that follow, then the players will simply apportion the size of the battle to the number of models that they have available.

Battles or Skirmishes?

The armies that fought in these rebellions were not huge in terms of the numbers of men involved when compared to the 50,000-strong armies marching and fighting in mainland Europe. For the most part neither side mustered more than 10,000 men a time. Although in total Cumberland had 30,000 men at his disposal, they were split into three armies and were strategically placed to hem the Prince and his army in the North, keeping the pretender well away from the seat of power in London. So the battles we will examine in this book were small by European standards but reflective in size of many of the hundreds of battles that have been fought across the British Isles. In the Dark Ages any encounter with more than a thousand men a side would be considered a good sized battle; in the English Civil war 5,000 men a side was a large battle; whereas in the Napoleonic wars only a battle with 50,000 men a side would be considered as large: it is all relative to the men available and the land mass available. Britain by comparison with many of the countries in Europe with which it has vied for centuries in the past is a country with a small overall landmass and did not have the populations that some of the countries had, and consequently the armies were proportionally smaller.

Settlements

The majority of built-up areas in eighteenth-century Scotland were much smaller than their English counterparts. The largest centres were the ports, where trade stimulated economic growth and prosperity, and by the addition of associated trades the port would expand, thereby stimulating more growth and expansion and so the growth continued. Edinburgh was dominated by the castle, but as we will see later the city could be taken and used by the Jacobites even though the castle remained in Government hands. Today the city is enormous and areas like Coltbridge which were on the edge of the city are now closer to the centre than the outskirts.

Battlesites

If the towns and villages have changed dramatically then it is refreshing that the majority of the battlesites have not changed too drastically, and would be recognised if the soldiers were to return to re-fight the battle today. Some have been split by roads or rail, both at Killiecrankie for example, while some have almost been lost completely under the weight of urban expansion, as at Prestonpans. Unfortunately, others such as Sheriffmuir and Glenshiel have been affected by agricultural change, mostly forestry plantations, though the underlying shape of the land has not be altered. Many of these sites now have information boards to accompany the earlier cairns which mark the approximate site of the battle, because for the majority of sites it is very difficult to know exactly where the battle was fought. Modern battlefield archaeology is allowing us, through its increasing accuracy, to hone in on where the most vigorous fights of a battle took place, but that only tells part of the story. A large quantity of military scrap, either broken or intact, can be found on a battlesite as long as the soil is not so acidic as to corrode the items away; things such as buttons, bits of weaponry, buckles and bits of leather straps may tell where a violent melee was fought. Meanwhile, hundreds of musket balls and some cannon balls will tell where the shot from an army was falling but not from which direction it necessarily came, and this where the written accounts have to be correlated with the archaeological evidence. At Culloden an enormous effort has been made to put the moor back to as close as to how it would have looked at the time of the battle as possible. Flags mark the front lines of the armies and information plaques identify the location, name and number of men for individual units, with detailed markers as one walks across the terrain. Culloden is one of those few exceptions where a huge amount of interpretation has been done for the visitor. At the majority of battlesites it is the imagination of the reader, illuminated by the writings of an author, that have to create the pictures of how a battle unfolded; the author hopes that in the chapters that follow, he has been able to bring these Jacobite campaigns to life for you.

4

The Inglorious Rebellions
1688–1697

The arrival of William and Mary in 1688 is known as the Glorious Rebellion because it was claimed that the revolution was achieved without bloodshed. It is true that there was no major battle in the initial campaign, as James's army capitulated in a series of desertions and retreats, but it was certainly not bloodless, as the encounters at Wincanton in Somerset and at Reading in Berkshire confirm. The revolution has been labelled as the 'Sensible' revolution as it gave all three parties what they wanted: Britain got a Protestant monarch without another destructive civil war, William got a Protestant Britain which provided him a superb navy with which to fend off France from his native Netherlands and James was able to escape with his life to Catholic France. The initial rebellion may have been mostly bloodless but the consequences created a situation which would lead to bloodletting for the next fifty-eight years as James and his heirs unceasingly planned to regain the lost throne.

On 13 February William and Mary were proclaimed joint sovereigns of England and Ireland following a lengthy series of debates and arguments in Parliament, where the questions of succession had to be agreed before William and Mary could jointly rule. Following similar debates in the Scottish Parliament, the throne was eventually declared vacant on 4 April when James's supporters left the chamber and debate, and so finally on 11 May 1689 William and Mary were able to accept the offer of the Scottish crown and became joint sovereigns there too. The political calm before the military storm was over.

Once in France James was soon closeted with his ally and friend King Louis XIV, who showed great sympathy for James's plight. Louis had continued his expansion plans for the French territories by invading the Palatinate in 1688, seizing the initiative because his opponents in Austria were occupied with a Turkish threat and in the Netherlands William was preparing to invade England to evict James. With Louis now at war with three countries, as William had brought England into the war as expected to support the Netherlands, Louis knew that by supporting James he would drain resources from Williams's continental armies. Louis put plans into motion at once and assisted James with money, ships and troops for his expedition to Ireland. In supporting James in his attempt to regain his throne, Louis XIV was hitting the English from the rear, causing them to move ships and troops away from other parts of the world, so allowing the French more leeway in their movements to expand their empire; Louis saw the time and money he gave to James as a sound investment.

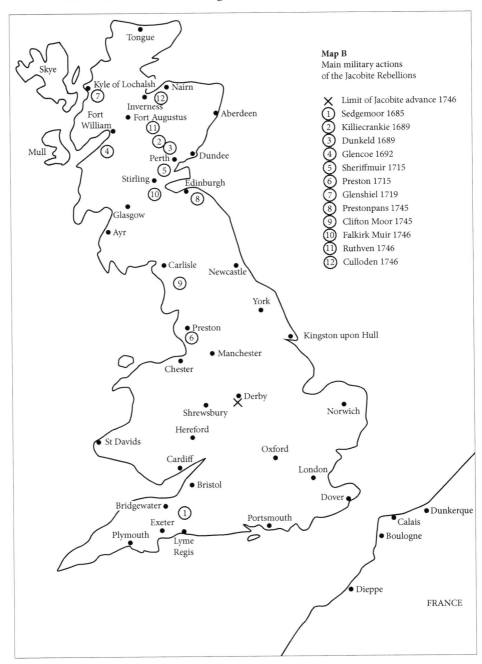

Tongue

Skye

Kyle of Lochalsh ● Nairn
⑦
Inverness ⑫
Fort
William ● Fort Augustus ● Aberdeen
⑪
Mull ② ③
④ Perth ● ● Dundee
⑤
Stirling ● Edinburgh
⑩ ⑧

● Glasgow

● Ayr

● Carlisle
⑨ Newcastle ●

● York

● Preston
⑥ Kingston upon Hull ●
● Manchester
Chester ●

● Derby
✗
Shrewsbury ● Norwich ●
Hereford ●
● St Davids
Cardiff ● Oxford ●
● London
● Bristol
Dover ●
Bridgewater ●
① ● Dunkerque
Exeter Portsmouth ● ● Calais
Plymouth ● Lyme ● Boulogne
Regis

● Dieppe

FRANCE

Map B
Main military actions
of the Jacobite Rebellions

✗   Limit of Jacobite advance 1746
①   Sedgemoor 1685
②   Killiecrankie 1689
③   Dunkeld 1689
④   Glencoe 1692
⑤   Sheriffmuir 1715
⑥   Preston 1715
⑦   Glenshiel 1719
⑧   Prestonpans 1745
⑨   Clifton Moor 1745
⑩   Falkirk Muir 1746
⑪   Ruthven 1746
⑫   Culloden 1746

In February 1689 James landed in Ireland to begin his campaign against the Protestants there, while on 16 April 1689 Viscount Dundee, known as Bonnie Dundee, raised James's standard upon Law Hill in Dundee. There were just fifty men with him, though letters were on the way from Ireland stating that James would be sending Irish troops to support the rising in Scotland. The plan was to give William a war to fight on two home fronts, as well as on the Continent, stretching his resources to the maximum. The recruitment of followers to Dundee's cause proved very difficult, for William of Orange had not been idle. Hearing of Dundee's arrival in Scotland, he ordered the Scottish Parliament to send Major-General Hugh Mackay of Scourie to intercept and destroy Dundee's rebellion. The news that Mackay was marching against Dundee galvanised some of the Western clans into action. Support now came from the Highlands, and eventually 300 Irish troops did arrive at Kintyre under the command of the aptly named Colonel Cannon. The geographical structure of the Highlands, with many high mountains split by narrow river valleys and sea-lochs, limited the routes by which armies could travel efficiently. Accordingly, intelligence on what the enemy's movements were, or plans might be, was crucial. Armed with that knowledge, someone with a sound understanding of the terrain had a great strategic advantage over his opponent. Making his way from the Highlands with the nucleus of a fighting force, Dundee made for Blair Castle, Blair Atholl, as it is better known, and the home of the Atholl family since 1269. This was a vital strongpoint as it guards the main route north through the central Highlands of Scotland from Perth, via Pitlochry and Kingussie, to Inverness. At Blair Atholl the Marquis of Atholl was playing the time honoured game of 'wait and see who wins' before he committed himself to one side or the other, but there was nothing he could do to prevent Dundee's men from securing the castle as their base. Through intelligence Dundee knew that Mackay, who had been fruitlessly pursuing him for some three months, was now at Perth with an army of regular troops. The majority of Dundee's army were Highlanders and they were eager to march at once to tackle Mackay's force as soon as possible; they fretted and became frustrated at their inability to close with the enemy who was now just two days away. Dundee also knew that from Perth, Mackay would make for Blair Atholl; it was the next obvious move, being an important stronghold on the main road north, so Mackay had to come through the pass of Killiecrankie. The skill of Dundee as a general is clearly shown as he managed to keep the clan leaders content with the assurance that they would get their chance at Mackay's men when the time was right and they were sure of victory. Dundee managed to convince them that the most suitable terrain for such an attack was the sloping ground to the north-east of Killiecrankie and that Mackay would have to be given uninterrupted passage to draw his army out into the open from the narrow confines of the river valley. Having met his clans, Dundee realised that any kind of defensive, drawing, feint or other subtle manoeuvre was out of the question: once released, the wave of the Highland charge would either envelope the enemy or break upon it – there was no middle way. Having laid his plans Dundee sent the majority of his force north-east from Blair Atholl in a circulatory clockwise march that would bring them onto the lower slopes of Creag Eallaich. This mountain, sitting many hundreds of feet above the road and river, would give the army a perfect view over anything moving through the valley below. Dundee had very few cavalry in his army but he sent them on a separate march away from the rest of his army in order to draw Mackay's attention away from the mountains to his right as he emerged from the pass of Killiecrankie. Accordingly, the first sighting Mackay's scouts had of the Jacobite forces was a small unit of cavalry coming towards them from the direction of Strathgarry and Blair Atholl. Mackay was probably convinced that these horsemen were Dundee's own skirmish patrols, out looking for the Government army; he took the bait and followed the retreating horsemen into the valley which widened before him.

Too late, Mackay realised his predicament when he saw the Clans marching up onto the high ground to his right. Retreat for Mackay's men was impossible because the Jacobites would soon be no more than a musket shot away, so if the Williamites tried to turn and run then a Highland charge would catch them deploying and they would be crushed. Mackay had no choice but to deploy on the ground that Dundee had chosen for him; he therefore sent his men up the first slope of the hill, to the right of the narrow road that had been their path for the fifteen miles from Dunkeld, and they began to deploy in the face of the Highlanders above.

Mackay knew that his position was precarious. The enemy were some 400 feet above him on sloping ground and to his rear was the treacherous bank of the river Garry, with no escape route should his army be worsted. Yet Mackay did have some advantages; his army was twice the size of Dundee's, and his men were regulars trained in disciplined firing, which meant that they should easily be able to fire two or three volleys per minute.

Killiecrankie, looking down towards Urrard House and Mackay's left wing.

As Mackay's men deployed he encouraged them with these facts and assured them that if they stood firm then their volleys would win the day. Mackay knew that the terrain was such that once deployed there would be no room to manoeuvre and so he decided to risk having no reserve so as to be able to bring all his available firepower to bear on the enemy. To achieve this Mackay dispensed with a second line of foot troops and instead he placed his two units of cavalry to act as a reserve behind the centre of his infantry. He also placed a few infantry in Urrard House, presumably because this would be a rallying point if his troops buckled from the Highlanders assault. Mackay also feared being outflanked, especially towards the narrow Killiecrankie pass through which his army had just marched; if his army was defeated and they were cut off from that passage out of the Highlands, Mackay knew that none of them would escape. To ensure therefore that he could not be outflanked, Mackay extended his line, which meant that once his army was deployed it was only three ranks deep, a very thin red line. Mackay's army numbered around 4,600 foot and perhaps 400 horse and consisted of newly raised or inexperienced lowland Scots and three experienced Scottish Dutch regiments.

1. Lauder's fusiliers 200 men
2. Balfour's regiment 660 men
3. Ramsay's regiment 660 men
4. Kenmure's regiment 770 men
5. Leven's regiment 870 men
6. Mackay's regiment 550 men
7. Hasting's regiment 850 men
8. Weem's Highland company 200 men

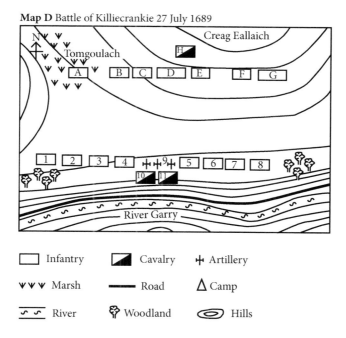

Map D Battle of Killiecrankie 27 July 1689

☐ Infantry	◣ Cavalry	✛ Artillery
⌄⌄⌄ Marsh	▬▬ Road	△ Camp
∿∿ River	🌳 Woodland	◎ Hills

Dundee knew that to stand a chance of victory his men had to break the Government troops with their first charge. The majority of Highlanders did not have any firearms and there was no way that they could enter into a fire fight with the Williamite army, so a long drawn out encounter, despite the advantage of ground which the Jacobites held, was out of the question. The majority of their weapons were for hand-to-hand combat; knives and the long-handled Lochaber axes seem to have been the predominant weapons, with many Highlanders not having their infamous broadsword or targe. Having seen the deployment below him, Dundee arranged his troops in columns by clan.

So instead of charging downhill in a drawn out line, giving all of Mackay's infantry a target straight ahead of them, seven densely packed columns would charge, aiming to hit certain Government regiments ahead of them but risking flanking fire from those Government regiments not engaged with the enemy. This was a risky strategy but Dundee gambled that the flanking regiments would not have time to manoeuvre into position before the Highland charge was past them and their would be fire useless unless they risked firing into a melee which involved more of their own troops than their enemies. Dundee only had a little over 2,000 men. As Mackay looked up the hill of Creag Eallaich above him, he would have seen eight Jacobite units deployed from left to right as follows:

A. Sir John MacLean 200 men

B. Purcell's Irish regiment under Colonel Cannon 400 men

C. Clanranald Macdonalds 480 men

D. Glengarry Macdonells 300 men

E. Cameron's of Locheil 500 men

F. Sir Alex Maclean and other smaller clans 200 men

G. Macdonalds of Sleat 300 men.

H. Bonnie Dundee and the Earl of Dunfermline's Horse 50 men

Looking down from the hill where the Jacobites sat goading Mackay at Killiecrankie 1689.

This meant that when the charge came Dundee would be throwing 1,400 men on his right against the 2,290 men on Mackay's left, while the 2,470 men on Mackay's right would be receiving an attack from Dundee's left flank and the remaining 540 men.

It seems that all the deployment was completed by early afternoon, and then the psychological warfare began. Dundee was determined that his small army would not strike until the time was right. It was high summer; the sun was behind Mackay's men and into the faces of the Jacobites and Dundee was prepared to wait for it to dip behind the mountains across the valley to the west so that his men would have a clear view when they charged. Dundee also knew that the Government troops had been marching for some weeks in pursuit of his Jacobite force. Now they had arrived in the morning after another long march from Perth, then they had deployed and now they were standing at the ready, waiting for the Jacobite advance to begin. Therefore the longer they were kept on their feet, the more fatigued they would become and the less attentive, hotter and more restless they would be while stood at attention with full kit. If Dundee could restrain the Clans for the rest of the sunny afternoon then the regulars would be at their weakest by early evening. To increase the pressure on their intended victims, the Highlanders started their howls, intimidating, eerie calls that made the blood run cold to hear them. For hours the Highlanders sat and waited; they bayed at the Williamite men below them, ignoring the musket and intermittent cannon shots that Mackay sent into their ranks to try and intimidate them into charging. Dundee and the Highlanders held their nerve, prepared to wait for the right time, and this control of the Clans clearly demonstrates Dundee's tremendous leadership.

About eight o'clock in the evening, Dundee gave the order to advance. With each Clan having a nominated Government regiment to assault, the 2,000 men began their charge. Although accustomed to such terrain, it cannot have been easy for the Highlanders to move rapidly over the sloping rough ground, especially as their momentum gathered with the advance. Mackay had seen the ground before his men as a killing field and at approximately 80 yards his men let forth a tremendous volley. Mackay had been proved right for as many as 700 Highlanders fell to the floor, if not killed outright then certainly out of the battle, so literally in a flash one third of the Jacobite force was downed, but the remainder poured on through what was now a mist of smoke punctuated by the cries of screaming men. Despite the galling losses the Highlanders screamed as they charged in, and it was more than Mackay's men could bear. The Jacobites fired their running volley at about 50 yards from the Government line before drawing their swords and crashing, pistols firing, blades swirling, into the red-coated troops.

The Government troops on the left had failed to reload and fire a second volley into the closing Jacobites; and then they struggled to fix their plug bayonets into position and so they had to fend off their opponents with their musket-butts. The Government troops on the left of Urrard House all broke into rout; Mackay, seeing that his right regiments were still intact, called for his cavalry to advance with him and assault the Jacobite units so as to try and stabilise the situation. As Mackay rode forward he turned and looked behind him and shuddered to find that only one sergeant had followed him, as the rest of his horsemen had turned and fled as Mackay's disintegrating left wing infantrymen ran through them. Mackay, by a miracle, passed unscathed through the Highlanders' ranks and ended higher up the hill, alone on the heather, looking down on his army's destruction. At this crucial moment in the battle Dundee himself had led his own cavalry units down the hill, and he saw Dunfermline to go on and capture the Government cannon, but then at the crucial moment of the battle another steady volley of musket fire from Mackay's own regiment hit the Jacobite horse, including the General himself, and Dundee fell, mortally wounded, to the ground.

Their end was swift, with the battle effectively over in fewer than 20 minutes. Mackay eventually arrived back at Stirling with fewer than 500 men; it is estimated that at least 2,000 died on the field, and at least another 500 were killed in the rout that followed; the remaining 2,000 scattered to who knows what end. Some indication of the brutality of those few minutes of hand-to-hand fighting comes from a quote from an eyewitness of the battle, Sir Ewen Cameron of Lochiel, who says in the work, *Memoirs of Sir Ewen Cameron of Lochiell, Chief of the Clan Cameron* by John Drummond (Edinburgh: The Abbotsford Club, 1842):

> When day returned, the Highlanders went and took a view of the field of battle, where the dreadful efforts of their fury appeared in many horrible figures. The enemy lay in heaps almost in the order they were posted; but so disfigured with wounds, and so hashed and mangled, that even the victors could not look upon the amazing proofs of their own ability and strength without surprise and horror. Many had their heads divided into two halves by one blow, others had their sculls cutt-off above the eares by a back-strock...

The fields where the Government troops routed at Killiecrankie in 1689.

So why was the battle so decisive? As explained in the chapter on soldiering, at the time of Killiecrankie warfare was going through a transmission and this Government army was caught in that cross-over between the old pike and slow firing musket way of fighting and the new, quicker way of firing a musket and then defending yourself with the bayonet. The speed of the traditional but now archaic Jacobite charge coupled with the slowness of the redcoats to re-load meant that the Government volleys did not bring down enough men, though this may have been because some of MacKay's units on the left flank failed to advance and they may have even ran without firing a shot. Whereas in the later risings the Government volleys could be devastating, at Killiecrankie they were not sufficient to stop the Highland charge. Once caught up in a melee, the Government units were not trained sufficiently to work together as a disciplined, cohesive body capable of standing and defending each other and their associated units. Once a unit in a single line of troops has crumpled then it exposes the flanks of the units either side, and so puts them at greater risk and then the breakthrough dominoes along the line. The right wing crumpling under the onslaught while the left wing collapsed without a fight left the guns and the Horse exposed. It is understood that the Horse did release a volley with their carbines before turning and fleeing themselves. At Killiecrankie all the elements of battle conspired against the Government army, but surely that should reflect on Dundee's knowledge and his ability to exploit the weaknesses of his opponent? Mackay's decision to go for all out firepower and not to have a second line or at least a reserve of foot may have succeeded if all of his units had got off two volleys before the Jacobites hit his men: to only get off perhaps half or two-thirds of one volley across the whole line meant that with no time to fit bayonets the Williamite infantry were lambs doomed to the slaughter.

The cairn to the fallen of Killiecrankie in the grounds, Urrard House. (Courtesy of Urrard House)

The battle was a massive victory for the Jacobites but it had come at a very high price. Dundee, their master strategist and tactician, was lost and at least a third of the Highlanders had perished alongside him. After Killiecrankie, Colonel Cannon, leader of the small Irish regiment, took command of the Jacobite forces. First, the Highlanders returned to Blair Atholl with Bonnie Dundee's body for burial. In contrast to their fortunes, the victory galvanised more clans into believing that victory could be achieved and they descended on Blair Atholl, where the Jacobite ranks swelled to around 5,000, now joined by the Atholl brigade themselves. The other key element gained from the victory was the capture of most of the Government baggage train, which ran to around 1,200 pack horses in addition to the equipment which could be collected from the dead upon the field. The muskets may have been coming close to obsolete but they were better than what the Highlanders currently had and the additional clothing, footwear and food was always welcome to an army on the march. It is worth noting that the Scots Greys had been formed in 1681 with the brief that they were responsible for keeping civil order in Scotland, and this involved the regiment in expeditions against various rebellious clans who showed any protests towards the monarchy. In 1688, the regiment was quartered in London at the start of the Glorious Revolution but took the side of William and Mary after James's departure, and the men were kept together and taken into the new king's army. Then it was ordered back to Scotland to continue its policing duties. For their service against the Jacobites at the Battle of Killiecrankie the regiment's title as a Royal Regiment was confirmed and they were ranked as the 4th Dragoons from thereon.

Cannon, however, did not possess the energy or the sense of purpose which Dundee had had and it was without any cohesive plan that Cannon marched north to muster more recruits, unless it was to draw Mackay's force more into hostile territory. Thus began a series of long marches and counter-marches, first north-east towards Aberdeen and then back south-west again. Despite Mackay's major setback at Killiecrankie his response was most creditable and the fact that the Jacobites did not follow up their victory meant that he had time to regroup ready to continue blocking the Jacobites' route south. Given that he knew his infantry arm was shattered, he left his remaining infantry units to recover and sent all of his available cavalry out on patrols, and his cavalry succeeded in creating enough local concern to stop the rising spreading further and forced Cannon to keep on the move. Wherever the Jacobites marched, they were shadowed and their attempted destination thwarted by Mackay, who used his 1,200 dragoons to patrol potential Jacobite routes and occupy key settlements. If Mackay's spies were keeping him informed then the Jacobite spy ring was also working well and Cannon learned that the road south to Stirling was only guarded by a single unit at Dunkeld. The Highlanders now began another march, but this time they were heading in the right direction for a rebellion – south! Their march took them past the site of their recent victory at Killiecrankie and so on towards Perth. Cannon was wily enough to not march blindly into Dunkeld and reconnoitred the town before choosing to attack from the north and west, having first sent the baggage and stores back to the safe haven of Blair Atholl. Cannon had several thousand men with him, his army almost twice that which

Dundee had at Killiecrankie. As well as the survivors from the battle, there were units of men from the Appin Stewarts, the MacGregors, the MacDonalds from Glencoe and above all a significant number of the Atholl men now that the victory of Killiecrankie and had convinced the Marquis of Atholl to support the cause.

Hills surround Dunkeld on three sides, west, north and east; only the southern side of the town is an open valley but that is dominated by the fast flowing River Tay. Cannon's men, as the dawn light rose, made their way to the surrounding hills, from where they could see the settlement below them. They arrived at Dunkeld to find that it was being defended by the Earl of Angus's regiment, the Cameronians (arch enemies of the Atholl men), led by Colonel Cleland who, as they watched, was busy organising his men, who were in the act of fortifying the town against the approaching Jacobites.

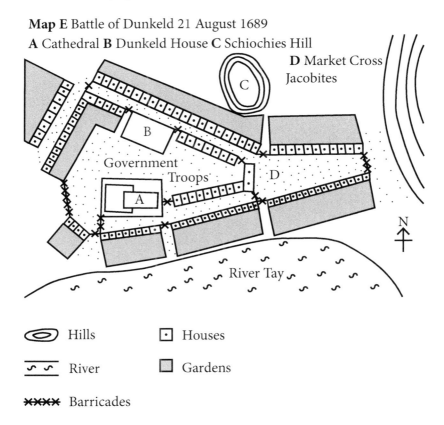

Map E Battle of Dunkeld 21 August 1689
A Cathedral **B** Dunkeld House **C** Schiochies Hill
D Market Cross
Jacobites
Government Troops
River Tay
N

Hills   Houses

River   Gardens

Barricades

The estimates vary as to the number of men Cleland had available; anything from 600 to 1,000 is possible but realistically it was probably no more than 500 to 600 who were preparing to defend the town. Their sudden predicament was not helped by their lack of any artillery and by the fact that they did not have much ammunition. So while some of Cleland's men prepared barricades, others were stripping lead from the roof of Dunkeld House to cast musket balls for their shot. It was not unknown for men to cast their own shot from small ingots or bars of lead, particularly before and during sieges, when a lot more ammunition would be required, and rows of precast shot together with the wooden moulds have been found on English Civil war siege sites.

Schiochies Hill at Dunkeld, now renamed Stanley Hill.

Early on the morning of 21 August, around seven, the Jacobite advance began with an assault led by the MacLeans on Schiochies Hill to the north of the town, where a Captain Hay was defending that key outpost for Cleland. The overwhelming firepower and the ferocity of the charge of around a hundred men led by Sir Alexander MacLean quickly drove Hay's company back into the protection of their triangular strong-point. Although an initial victory, Sir Alexander MacLean broke a leg in the charge and was out of action, robbing Cannon of a brave and organised clan commander. This success was followed by a general assault on those three sides of the town that were away from the river. The Jacobites probed and tested the Williamite defences and the defenders were slowly pushed back deeper and deeper into a progressively smaller and smaller area of the town. A firefight then ensued which lasted for at least three hours until, after a total of almost four hours of sporadic assaults, the Jacobites had succeeded in killing both Colonel Cleland and his second in command, a major, which then left the next senior officer, a Captain Munro, in possession of what was left of the regiment. At around 11.00 Munro, seeing that many of the houses within Dunkeld were now alight, and that his defences were weakened by his ongoing losses at the barricades, decided to pull his remaining men back into safety of Dunkeld House, which was now the last

The main square in Dunkeld.

The River Tay at Dunkeld running past the cathedral.

remaining intact building in the centre of the defensive perimeter and presumably was more solid that the other town houses, having a lead and tiled roof, whereas many of the other houses seem to have had roofs made of thatch given the ease, which the fires seem to have spread. Those fires which had started spasmodically had now spread to much of the town, having been either started deliberately or simply caught fire from all of the hot match and hot shot being fired from all directions, both from within and from outside the town. These fires eventually merged to engulf the whole town, destroying all but three of the houses. The phoenix town that grew up from these ashes was situated more to the east than the original settlement but the ruins of the cathedral and the renamed Stanley Hill allow the visitor to appreciate the layout of the original battle.

Whether by some pre-arranged signal or not, just as Munro was retreating into Dunkeld House for a final stand, the Jacobites suddenly ceased their attack. It is unsure as to why the assault filtered out and in fact Mackey and the Cameronians surely feared that some final main assault was about to be unleashed, but it seems that the Jacobites just gave up and began to retreat out of the town. There are several reasons why the battle simply ground to a halt in the late morning, and the most likely one is that their ammunition had simply run out after three to four hours of intermittent musket shooting. The Jacobites would have fired off many thousands of musket-balls at their enemy and it is likely that this running low of ammunition coincided with a number of accumulated losses, at which point the clan leaders decided that enough was enough. This is hardly surprising given that the Jacobite tactics were not suited to direct assaults: neither sieges nor street fighting were something that the clans were used to. A Jacobite battle was often over in a few minutes, and certainly never lasted for a whole morning. They had done well to fight for so long as even their muskets were not suited to street fighting, as most were either antiquated firearms from previous wars or matchlocks which had been so recently captured after the victory at Killiecrankie. Matchlocks were effective if used by trained men in disciplined regiments, where the volume of shot would be destructive. Fighting among houses in skirmishing lines while trying to shoot a musket by plunging in a lighted fuse into an open pan is difficult enough when in organised ranks, but when engaging an enemy that is almost hidden from your view and you have to expose yourself to shoot it is far from ideal. The Cameronians would have been armed with flintlocks, far safer and easier to discharge in a confined space than the old fashion matchlock. From Cannon's point of view, he had no artillery with which to inflict long range damage on the well dug-in defenders but outnumbering the Williamite troops at around six or even eight to one, he must have felt confident of a victory.

The Jacobites did succeed in destroying most of the town but the Government force had held on. Casualties, as ever, are difficult to determine; Cannon claimed 200 of the enemy dead and only some twenty men from the Jacobite army. An 'exact narrative' quoted in Cassell's battlefield survey lists just seventeen killed, including officers, and thirty-three other ranks wounded among the Camerons, with around 300 of the Jacobites slain. This on the other hand seems too low a number for the defenders, given that they were driven back from all of the initial barricades. Certainly the marauding

Jacobites in the open, approaching barricades, would be a much better target for a firelock musketeer than a man behind a barricade would be when being targeted by an inexperienced clansman with a matchlock. Overall, then, one would think that from the conflicting numbers reported that around a hundred of the Camerons and as many as three to four hundred of the Jacobites were either killed or wounded, certainly rendered hors de combat. With the Jacobite casualties at around ten per cent from this style of fighting, you can imagine their clan elders calling for a withdrawal. Having been worsted, but with Cannon claiming a victory, for which James later rewarded him, the Highlanders returned along the valley north to Blair Atholl, before slowly drifting back to their own homes in the mountains for the autumn and winter, while Cannon and his remaining Irish troops under Purcell eventually wintered and almost starved to death on the island of Mull. Despite being outside the normal campaigning season, Cannon tried to rally the clans to meet and plan a strategy for 1690 but few were forthcoming as first harvesting and then raiding and petty clan disputes came more to the fore than any planned uprising to support James and his cause.

At Dunkeld there is a possible connection to another famous Scottish King, Macbeth. Birnam Wood, so important in the prophecy of Macbeth's downfall, was once a mighty forest and it still exists today. Alongside the river, which was once surrounded by the forest, grows one of the ancient oaks that once filled the forest. This mighty tree is worth the half a mile walk along the banks of the River Tay from the centre of Dunkeld, as the photograph shows.

All of this lethargy in the Highlands meant that Mackay's strategy of containment worked well and with the bare minimum of men, he was able to provide a sufficient presence to deter the clans from rising in any number. This was just as well, for as this micro-war in Scotland moved into 1690 William III was planning a major campaign in Ireland to crush James's rebellion, which was very slowly gaining momentum and greatly overshadowed the Scottish rising. Indeed, William planned to recall all of Mackay's horse, all of the non-Scottish regiments and even some of his loyal Scottish units to support his Irish expedition. Had the Jacobites got news of this reduction in the Government forces then they could have acted to threaten the border and prevent troops from being sent to thwart James in Ireland, but they did not and instead the only crumbs of comfort they got was that James was sending both infantry and horsemen, money and supplies to equip and feed a strong army. But the clans had heard this the previous year and over the next fifty years it would become a hoary old chestnut to the clan leaders' ears; it was a promise that they would hear every time from the first rising to the last but due to a range of circumstances, they would never see any of those promises fulfilled.

By way of meeting his promise James sent Major General Thomas Buchan with a few reinforcements and some much needed money to pay those professional soldiers still willing to fight for the cause. Buchan was an Aberdeen man and it was hoped that his arrival would regenerate the rising in both the Highlands and around his homeland. In April 1690 Buchan called for the Highland clans to rise and march east with him to begin a fresh rising. His force was small; at best he had 1,500 men, though it is likely to

The ruined cathedral at Dunkeld defended by the Cameronians.

The streets of Dunkeld are still narrow.

An aside from the Jacobites – the oldest oak tree from Birnam wood.

have been less than a thousand including his own regiment. Few Highlanders had joined Buchan, just the Macleans of note, but Buchan did have Cannon with the remainder of the Irish troops from Purcell's regiment. They marched towards Aberdeen, taking a route along the Spey Valley which was into the Laird of Grant's territory, and with Grant a committed Williamite it was a significant gamble, though one which Buchan believed was right to take as he believed that Grant's clan was loyal to the Stuarts. Their route brought them on the evening of 30 April to the village of Cromdale, where the ruined Lethendry castle sat upon flat ground alongside the Spey and where, within a short distance, the river was crossable at three different places. The river is wide and fast flowing and the control of such crossings is vital to an army. The site was also not far from the Government garrison at Ballachastell and not all of the clans were content with the position in which Buchan had chosen to camp. The Jacobites knew that Sir Thomas Livingstone, the garrison commander at Inverness, was pursuing them with a force of dragoons and MacDonald of Keppoch chose to quarter his men on the higher ground at Dalchapple, which was away from the main camp, rather than risk being caught in the valley.

Livingstone's force consisted of around 400 horse and 800 foot and they had been closing in on Buchan's men for some days; having received intelligence from Ballachastell that the Jacobites had arrived, Livingstone urged his men on to continue their pursuit into the evening. The Government force kept on long after dark and eventually arrived

The River Spey at Cromdale, where the Jacobites failed to defend the crossings.

around two a.m. on 1 May. Their route brought them to the hills above Cromdale, from where they could overlook their quarries' positions, where the evening fires betrayed the Jacobite encampment. Livingstone apparently consulted his men as to their willingness to continue the action forthwith. In spite of the long march, the Government troops were eager to take just a brief rest and then attack. Despite the low-lying land Buchan had laid out his defences well; his camp was in the centre with pickets around the perimeter and, most importantly, three platoons of forty-five men each to guard the three river crossings. These points on the Spey were the weak points in Buchan's defences and should perhaps have been barricaded at the water's edge rather than just manned. Having let his men rest, Livingstone ordered his 400 cavalry to attack; the flat nature of the flood-plain fields beside the river was perfect for the cavalry should they succeed in getting across the river. The three dragoon units were organised as follows. There were around 200 of the Scots Greys and two units of mounted militia, each of which had around 100 men under the command of Gordon Edinglassie and the Master of Forbes respectively.

By distracting the Jacobites who were guarding the fords by attacking the crossing by the kirk with a minor force, Livingstone drew off the remaining two platoons of pickets from the other two fords. It was an old-fashioned ruse but it worked and with the two fords now unguarded, the Government horse were able to ride straight through the river unopposed and into the main camp, where they attacked the startled Jacobites as they awoke. The nature of the location meant that the valley was prone to mist and fog and this natural phenomena began to collect as the Government attack began, an event that

The Cromdale Burn; the dragoons attacked to the right of this small river.

was repeated when the author visited the site. This clearly saved some of the Jacobites as they fled in their shirts into the shrouded hills to escape. The battle was an easy victory for the Williamite men; the initial assault killed hundreds of Jacobites, most of whom would have barely been aware of what was happening as they awoke from sleep before they were struck down.

In total around 400 were killed, though as they rallied to defend themselves they did inflict as many as 100 casualties on the Government forces. Cannon and Buchan both escaped, but the next day pockets of fleeing Jacobites were surrounded and captured in a series of small skirmishes, including around 100 (who may have been the Macdonalds of Keppoch) on Granish Moor. Despite other small skirmishes and attempted gatherings, the war in Scotland and so the Scottish threat to William was over. For his success with his holding strategy Mackay was allowed to keep his small army and in June 1690, with some 6,000 men, he began to impose himself upon the Highland region. The Government fort at Inverlochy on Loch Linnhe was revamped and enlarged and re-named Fort William as the new King looked to stamp his authority on to a region hitherto dominated by the clans.

Ireland

The situation in Scotland could not have been in sharper contrast to that in Ireland. James's support in Ireland was almost universal and far greater than in Scotland. Upon his arrival in 1689 he was greeted as a saviour because James's 1687 Declaration of Indulgence, which had caused consternation in England, would allow Catholics to practice their religion without question. Once safely delivered James strengthened his support by promising the Irish Parliament that eventually they would have the right to self-determination, freed from the yoke of a future English Government. For both the Irish people and gentry their support was given willingly to James as they looked to secure the return of their own lands, which had been confiscated and redistributed by Oliver Cromwell. All Irish Catholics wanted the removal of Cromwell's laws, which had forbidden Catholics to sit in their own parliament and to practice their own religion. So the 1689 rising behind James was really a rekindling of the religious rebellions from fifty years earlier, which Cromwell had eventually supressed in brutal fashion. Men flocked to the Stuart cause and James was able to lead an army which had been raised and led by Richard Talbot, the First Earl of Tyrconnel. By early 1690, the Catholic forces controlled all of Ireland, save for the province of Ulster. Holding out in Ulster against James's ever encroaching army was the Duke of Schomberg, a Huguenot from France whose lands had been confiscated by Louis XIV. William appointed this loyal Protestant to the position of Master-General of the Ordnance, with authority to lead the expeditionary force against the growing might of James's forces in Ireland. In August 1689 Schomberg landed in Ireland with around 20,000 men and quickly captured Carrickfergus before marching unopposed through what was now a clearly devastated country. Seizing up the military situation very quickly, Schomberg realised that his raw troops, regiments in some cases which had only just been trained, were no match for the much larger force of fanatical Catholics led by James. He therefore decided to entrench the Government force in the town of Dundalk and await William's main force next spring. Schomberg's force was to suffer heavy losses during the winter cessation in hostilities as diseases ravished his army. The only positive for Schomberg during those harsh months was the success which small groups of irregular cavalry were having in harrying and frustrating James's probing advances. These Protestants, who called themselves the Inniskillingers, but were known to the majority as Scots-Irish, were smaller groups of light cavalry who undertook defensive patrols.

William landed in Ireland at Carrickfergus in Ulster on 14 June 1690 and, having laid his plans, marched south to take Dublin with his and Schomberg's forces now united. James chose to place his line of defence on the River Boyne, around 30 miles north from Dublin, where he rightly saw the river as a formidable obstacle which could be held by determined men. William's army reached the banks of Boyne on 29 June but the King was lucky to escape with his life while he was surveying James's position on the other side of the river.

William's army was around 36,000 strong, composed of troops from many countries including France, the Netherlands, Denmark as well as England, Scotland and Wales; most of the men were trained and some of the Dutch and Danish troops were highly trained and armed with the latest flintlock muskets. James had fewer men, not more than 25,000, and of these only 6,000 were regular troops from France. There were some good quality cavalry which had been raised from among the Irish gentry but the rest of his army was predominantly poorly armed peasants who had been given rudimentary training and who were armed with improvised weapons such as scythes, a small minority having any proper weapons such as pikes or muskets; even the regular infantry were equipped with the inferior matchlock musket. The political and religious complexity of these Jacobite wars and the men that fought in them can clearly be seen when the Boyne campaign is further analysed. Not only were the troops that fought in William's army from an alliance of countries concerned about the power that a combined Catholic Britain and France would have over the rest of Europe but also William's elite troops were his blue guards, who just happened to be formed from Dutch Catholics. Even though Louis XIV was championing Catholicism, Pope Alexander VIII supported William and his army against James because the Vatican feared the rising power of France, which had been unchecked thus far.

William fought and beat James at the Battle of the Boyne on 1 July 1690, though it was a hard fought battle and the outcome was still in the balance when James gave the order to retreat. It was that order which probably cost the Catholics both the battle and the war. For James it was London, when he was still the King, all over again; then William had approached from the west and James had lost his nerve and fled; this time William has come from the north but the outcome was the same – James did not have the stomach to be a King. His inability to stand and face danger outraged his loyal followers, and they coined the nickname in Gaelic of 'Seamus a'chaca' or James the Shit; he would not be the first Stuart to incur the wrath of his subjects.

For William, the retreat of his enemy secured his victory but there were losses too; although not many of his men had been killed outright thousands were wounded and among the dead was Schomberg, who was killed in the battle along with many other officers. However, when one considers the overall numbers of men involved then the total casualties were light by the standards of comparative battles of the day; some 2,000 men killed from such a major engagement is only 4 per cent of the combatants. Indeed, James's army was still in good order with some of his regiments uncommitted and his cavalry screened his retreating infantry well, giving it time to escape. While William steadily pursued the Catholic army retreating before him, James fled to Dublin and then swiftly back to France to resume his exile. James had tossed aside his largest army and with it his greatest personal chance to regain his throne. It was not clear that the battle was going to be lost, but by throwing in the towel James condemned his army to defeat; he had let himself down, and worse he had let down all those thousands of supporters who were relying upon him.

Williams's victory in Ireland was not complete with James's departure; the war for the throne was far from over and although some of the peasantry deserted in droves, there were still the regular regiments to be dealt with. News then came to William that on 30 June 1690, at the Battle of Beachy Head, a French fleet had delivered a crushing defeat on the combined Anglo-Dutch fleets. The French of sixty-eight ships had defeated the allies' smaller fleet of fifty-six ships, sinking about nine ships and capturing one; there were heavy crew losses on both sides during the engagement. Despite the defeat, the allies had prevented the French from destroying the entire fleet and the channel was not clear for the French to invade, which was England's greatest fear as a war on potentially three fronts would have pushed William's resources to the limit.

So even as James was sailing back to France and William was closing in on Dublin, he received a clear indication that there was still much for William to do before his shores would be secure. A year later another massive battle was fought at Aughrim on 12 July 1691, when after a titanic struggle the 17,400 Williamite men led by Godard van Reede, Baron de Ginkel and General Mackay defeated the 20,000 Catholics under Charles Chalmont, Marquis de St Ruth. Aughrim was a galling battle, with around 10 per cent of the Government troops killed and around 40 per cent of the Irish force. With this crushing defeat the remaining core of the Catholic army fled Dublin and made for Limerick to form another defensive position behind the River Shannon. This proved to be a successful strategy and eventually, after losing 3,000 of his finest men in assaults and over 2,000 men to disease, William decided that there was no military solution to the enforced stalemate and he agreed a settlement, which became ratified as the Treaty of Limerick on 3 October 1691. As part of the treaty 14,000 men of James's Irish Brigade chose to leave and go to France, with their families where applicable, and they would continue to serve James as men of the Irish Brigade, regiments that would be loyal to France and the Stuarts, fighting with distinction under French command. A further 1,000 men chose to join William's army and the remaining 2,000 were allowed to return to their homes.

Scotland

Having shown leniency in Ireland, William was chastised back home and although the Treaty of Limerick stood, soon harsher controls were once more introduced against Catholics under the Penal Laws, which again reduced Irish land holding, forbade them from owning weapons or from joining the legal profession. Meanwhile, in Scotland things were still far quieter than they were in Ireland. William did not want to have around 6,000 troops stationed north of the border just to keep the Highland clans from rising and causing trouble upon his flank at home; William wanted all of his money and troops focused on defeating Louis XIV and restabilising the whole of Western Europe. Mackay left Colonel Hill in charge of Fort William on 1 July 1691 and he withdrew some of his 6,000 men south, and with things so calm William felt that it was also time to show clemency to the clans that had risen against him in Scotland. A few weeks later, on 17 August, William issued a proclamation which offered a pardon to all those clans who would take an oath of allegiance to him by 1 January 1692. The clan chiefs had previously sworn an oath to James and such was their loyalty to him that they felt that they could not now bow to William, unless James had first sanctioned such a move. Communication in the late seventeenth century was slow, so that there followed months of inactivity until James's permission finally came through in late December. This left the clan leaders precious little time to meet William's deadline and make their way to the appropriate officers to swear their oaths. Alistair MacDonald of Glencoe, who was the aged chief of the Clan Iain Abrach, failed to meet the appointed deadline and played right into the hands of William's Secretary of State, Sir John Dalrymple, who was also Master of Stair. Dalrymple was hardly the diplomat for fine negotiations; he hated the Jacobites and he hated the Highlanders and he believed that the way to police the two disruptive

Wade's military road crosses one of his bridges at the head of Glencoe.

elements, who were often akin, was to make an example of a clan, a clan that had stepped out of line. Alistair MacDonald reached Colonel Hill before the deadline, but, whether by accident or design, Hill could not administer the oath, and MacDonald was forced to travel further to Inverary (through thick snow) only to find when he arrived that Sir Colin Campbell was not at home when he arrived and the oath could not be sworn; the Macdonalds of Glencoe had stepped out of line. The certificate was issued on 6 January but Colin Campbell warned MacDonald that the paper was technically invalid as he had, after all, had five months to swear his oath, and the other clans had all done so in time.

Prepared for such a moment as this, Dalrymple had even picked the infantry regiment he felt could administer such a lesson, the Earl of Argyll's. This regiment was partly officered by some Campbell gentry, including Robert Campbell of Glenlyon. Robert Campbell had, at the age of fifty-nine, been forced back into the army to rebuild his finances, partly from having lost too much at cards while trying to live the high life and partly from having had his lands repeatedly ravaged by the MacDonnells of Keppoch and the Macdonalds of Glencoe. Dalrymple was convinced that a loyal clan regiment of around 800 men committed to carrying out their orders without question and which had grounds for revenge would strike such fear into the hearts of the clans that they would not dare step out of line again, whatever the cause. In January 1692 Dalrymple wrote to Sir Thomas Livingstone, the aforementioned victor of Cromdale, who was now the Commander-in-Chief Scotland, ordering him to strike ruthlessly at any oath-refusing rebels and not to trouble with prisoners. Further orders were issued which included an authorisation from King William himself dated 16 January which left no doubt that the people in the Glencoe valley were to be wiped out. Orders came down the military chain of command, from Livingstone to Hill and from Hill to Robert Campbell, who was instructed to be both secret and sudden.

Map F Massacre of Glencoe 13 February 1692

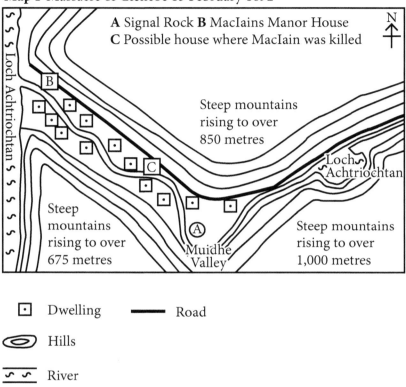

⊡	Dwelling	▬▬	Road
◎	Hills		
ᔕ ᔕ	River		

Slaughter under Trust

On 1 February 1692 the Argyll regiment left Fort William for the march to Glencoe. He had perhaps 800 men with him, but only a couple of companies, 120 men, were to be billeted upon Alistair MacDonald's family. There is uncertainty as to the number of soldiers deployed, whether it was 120 as planned or just sixty, which is what the muster roll of 1691 states. The rest of the regiment were to bide their time within striking distance and at the appointed time seal off each end of the valley so that none of the clan could escape. This was to be ethnic cleansing on a family scale with around 500 men, women and children concentrated in the valley for the winter, more scattered dwellings in the higher hills and mountains reserved for summer occupation. There was no large and lordly hall in the valley to receive a sudden large party of men, and so when Robert Campbell arrived seeking shelter and nourishment, he knew that his men

The steep, inhospitable sides of the Glencoe valley.

would be billeted in a string of houses across the valley. There could have been no easier setting for the Argyll men to carry out their orders; they would be able to unleash a series of simultaneous but isolated attacks, each one small and confined and much easier than if Argyll's were having to take on a clan chief and all his men inside a clan castle. Campbell was met by members of the clan and showed them papers that he was to be billeted upon demand if necessary and also that he was authorised to collect arrears of the cess and hearth tax, which was a new tax which had been imposed in 1690. The three senior officers of the Argylls even gave their paroles of honour as testament that they were there with no hostile intentions. Satisfied with the papers and in spite of the past differences between the two groups of men, the Argylls were told that they were welcome and the men settled down to living with the MacDonalds. These rank and file would have been billeted three maybe four to a house, scattered across all the settlement so that each group could take their part when the order came to attack. The time seems to have passed off convivially, with sports in the day, song, dance and merriment in the evenings provided by the hosts and appreciated by the guests; despite the hardship which the clan was already feeling with the winter storms, they managed to find food enough for all.

There is no certainty today as to where the houses, small hall or basic cottages of the clan would have been. Very few traces remain from any of the dwellings there at this time and there is conjecture about where exactly Alistair MacDonald and his wife lived while among their clan and away from their main house at the mouth of the river, well down the valley. It is unlikely that as the clan shepherd he would have strayed far from his flock with such unwelcome visitors under their roofs. The valley is mentioned as having been densely populated in some parts, and so for interpretation the author has positioned dwellings upon the most likely areas of flat land adjacent to the river, which would have provided the water supply for the families. Robert Campbell was reputed to have been playing cards in the early evening with the two sons of Alistair MacDonald when he received from a runner a letter instructing him to 'fall upon the rebells the MacDonalds of Glenco and put all to the sword under seventy' signed by Robert Duncanson, his commanding officer, on 12 February 1692. Making his excuses to his hosts that his men were needed for an urgent matter, he left the house having first accepted an offer to dine with Alistair and his family the next evening. Despite the scattered nature of his men, Campbell somehow managed to gather his senior men together, presumably by some prearranged signal, and to issue them with the orders he had so lately received. Although the men took their orders readily and dispersed to prepare for their attack at the prearranged hour, not all of the men could now stomach the orders and some slipped away from the valley. An officer named Robert Stewart fled and two privates who were MacEacherns and therefore related to the MacDonalds appear to have also fled, but only after giving some kind of warning to some of the MacDonalds. How much the ordinary men knew of this planned assault cannot be certain, but there are reports that some of the soldiers hinted to their hosts that things were going to happen that night, one soldier even telling a great stone that it would not lie there so 'peaceful' if it knew what was 'to happen tonight', the soldier apparently making sure a child was in ear-shot of his prophetic words. Campbell laid his plans carefully and now doubled the guards within the immediate vicinity of the settlement. For the rest of the valley he was already assured that patrols of his men and a force led by Hamilton, which would come over the mountains to the north and descend the staircase at the head of the valley, which would seal off the glen from all other access points. This would ensure that there were no unguarded escape routes, not only at the top and bottom but also where the valley sides opened out in to small passes on either side of the glen. His plans laid, all Campbell had to do now was to sit and wait for the appointed time to tick round and he could launch his attack; the time was set for five the following morning.

By ten on the evening of 12 February all the houses were at rest, though an uneasy dread must have filled the air. The night was a raw one, with a freezing wind blowing from the north which quickly brought snow, which became a full blown blizzard. It seems few of the MacDonalds were asleep; the rumours must have reached some of their ears and played upon their minds. Certainly the two sons of Alistair were uneasy and they questioned the soldiers, including Campbell, and their intentions directly before approaching their own father with their concerns, but both elderly men assured the sons that there was nothing amiss. The rank and file too were restless, knowing that they had seven hours to wait before the allotted time of the assault. The sons of Alistair were taking no chances and it seems that they were prepared for some type of attack. At some time

Looking from the lower glen up towards Signal Rock and the head of Glencoe.

on the fateful early morning, at the big sweeping bend of the valley upon a jutting rocky outcrop, a burning brand was waved to signal to the troops that the deed must begin.

Watchful eyes saw bands of soldiers' bayonets at the ready, moving just before five towards the houses; cries of alarm followed and, foolishly for the plan, some of the soldiers fired their muskets. The whole valley was now awake and all secrecy lost. In the ensuing chaos, many of the families managed to escape into the wilds of the early morning storm, the atrocious weather both an aid to them fleeing but also a killer, with the deadly cold causing hyperthermia. Campbell had specific instructions to ensure that Alistair MacDonald (the old fox as he was referred to) and his sons were killed. MacDonald himself was shot in his bedroom, in the back and head; his wife was attacked for trying to help her husband and stripped naked, with even her rings ripped from her fingers, before she escaped into the white landscape, managing to stumble into another group of refugees, but she would die of the cold and her injuries within twenty-four hours. The two sons escaped with their families as the houses of the clan were set alight by the marauding soldiers below them in the valley but others were not so lucky; some were killed in their houses, others taken out and executed, even children begging for mercy were shot or stabbed without compassion. There were miraculous escapes, including a MacDonald who was taken outside from a house at Achnanon to be executed; feigning injury, he was led to a wall as the soldiers prepared their muskets, and seizing his plaids and rushing the small line, he managed to throw the plaid in their faces and disappear behind them into the dawn, the men firing wildly after him into the darkness, but no bullet found its target. With the deed in action Major Duncanson and Captain Drummond arrived to see that Campbell had carried out his orders to the letter. Neither man was satisfied with Campbell's work and criticised the lack of bodies from the ambush. Campbell had had enough but had to continue his orders with Duncanson on hand to comment on the pitiful body count as the results of his men's work became clearer in the light of day.

Thirty-eight of the clan had been murdered and some 900 cattle, 200 horses and a large number of sheep and goats were confiscated. Significantly from a potential total of 500, at least 400, maybe more, had escaped the butchery, though it is thought that a further forty perished in what remained of the biting winter storm. How many starved afterwards because their livelihoods and animals were taken away will never be fully known, but the clan recovered manfully within a short space of time, as will be seen in the following chapters.

An enquiry was to follow in 1695, and within a month it had delivered a full report; the matters of culpability, with regards to the King himself and the senior officials involved, was left to the King's conscience but no action was taken against any of them. Hamilton was found guilty of murder and many found guilty of 'murder under trust', and although the men named were called to trial none were ever brought forward. William deemed that he needed the men more in his ranks abroad in Flanders than British justice needed them in Court.

This, then, was a massacre of Scottish Highlanders by a Scottish regiment with Scottish Lowlander officers under the orders of a Dutch King on the throne of three Kingdoms which he looked to rule both fairly and justly. The purpose behind such a barbaric act was to quell the seeds of rebellion before they ever started again and by putting such fear into the clans that they would think long and hard before committing to follow a Stuart again. This massacre, following on so swiftly after the peace settlement in Ireland, certainly had the effect of quietening the Highlands. It was winter and certainly not a season for any campaigning, so as ever the clans watched and waited for further news of James. There was still talk of a French invasion following their earlier naval victory at Beachy Head and this time it was for real. Louis XIV knew that if he was to defeat the Netherlands then he needed to prevent William III having at his disposal the entire British Army. With the rebellions in both Scotland and Ireland having failed, Louis believed that it was time to try a direct assault on the English coast, his infantry forces now increased by the regiments returned from Limerick, his 'wild geese'. In preparation Louis once more gave support and James assembled a re-organised force of around 16,000 men, mainly from his failed campaign in Ireland. His infantry were assembled at Saint-Vaast-la-Hougue while the cavalry and guns were ready to be loaded into transports at Le Havre. What was to follow was one of the largest naval battles ever fought under sail. The French fleet, when finally assembled under Tourville, numbered forty-four ships of the line and around forty other large vessels, including some large transports and cannon bearing galleys. The Anglo-Dutch fleet outnumbered the French, able to command eighty-two ships of the line as well as thirty-eight other large vessels. A series of battles were fought between Barfleur and La Hogue. The first encounter took place off Barfleur but it was an indecisive encounter and although considerable superficial damage was done to both fleets, with several thousand sailors killed on each side, no ships were sunk. Further along the Channel, an action at Cherbourg was more decisive as three French ships went down with no losses sustained by the allied fleet. Finally, off Saint-Vaast-la-Hougue a further twelve French ships were sunk and once again the Anglo-Dutch fleets escaped with losses but with all ships afloat. The allies were avenged for their defeat off Beachy Head two years earlier and James's army was once more stranded upon the French coast and Louis XIV's threat of invasion of England was lifted. Incredibly, although James's plans were in ruins, he was heard to exclaim that only his 'Jack-tars' could have delivered such a victory. William III was now secure at home, his combined navies were masters of the western European seaways and catastrophic harvest failures in mainland Europe in 1692, 3 and 4 led to a gradual decrease in France's influence as she struggled economically to support the enormous armies totalling 400,000 men which Louis could put into the field. The war which had been raging since 1688 now slackened in intensity and finally in 1697 the Treaty of Ryswick brought to a close a period of European warfare variously known as The Nine Years' War, The War of the Grand Alliance or The War of the League of Augsburg. William's involvement was fundamental as his home nation of the Netherlands was under threat from the expansionism of Louis and France but the harsh realities of the cost of war had come home to Louis and peace allowed Europe to catch its breath. William, content that he had achieved all of his aims, could also turn more attention to matters back home.

The memorial to the MacDonalds in Glencoe.

Conclusions

The dividing line between success and failure is often minute. In the immediate aftermath of William's arrival, with active rebellions in both Scotland and Ireland and with William already fighting a war on the Continent, was the moment when Louis XIV should have committed to a French invasion of England. The piecemeal way in which the rebellions and invasions unfolded, Scotland 1689, Ireland 1690 to 91 and then the failed French invasion of 1692, allowed William to deal with each one in turn, without being overstretched. If any rising was going to succeed in putting a Stuart heir back on the throne of England, it had to be done at a time when England was weak, when the idea was fresh and when the maximum amount of support could be gained from France and Spain; the first few years of William's reign was the perfect time to strike.

On a more local level, had the enigmatic Dundee not been killed then it is most likely that he would have been able to raise more than the 5,000 Highlanders that assembled at Blair castle after Killiecrankie, and that his guile would not have seen his army embarrassed by a regiment in Dunkeld. Any rebellion relies on the strength, belief and charisma of its leadership. In Dundee the Jacobites had a natural, intelligent, charismatic commander who gained the trust, respect and so the unquestioning support of his men. Cannon, although by rank the next in line to command, was simply not the same calibre of man as Dundee and lacked the military intelligence and the political diplomacy to unite the clan leaders, who could be truculent on occasion. Despite the ineptitude which crept into the rebellion in Scotland after Dundee's death, the Jacobites had been more frustrated than defeated and if only James or Louis could have given the Scottish rising anywhere near as much support as the Irish rising enjoyed in 1690, then the threat to William's place upon the throne would have been that much greater. It was going to be over in Scotland once Buchan made the fatal mistake in his first campaign of allowing himself to be cornered and defeated and any support that he might have gained with a victory was wiped out within a few weeks, and successive failures in so short a time closely followed by the massacre at Glencoe clearly made the clans think on any further actions.

James II seems to have suffered from a great weakness of resolve coupled with that inherited Stuart stubbornness. Having alienated his country through ignoring his advisors and trying to enforce Catholicism on a Protestant nation, he then fled the country to save his own skin, fearing perhaps the same retribution that had been meted out to his father Charles I. James II was fine when plotting his strategy from the safety of France and while things were moving in his direction, but the moment there was any reverse, especially if he was on home soil, his nerve seems to have failed him. James seems to have failed to understand that the world had changed; a monarch could no longer rule, as Charles had tried, with a divine right. Louis XIV's old style of leadership, which James tried so hard to copy, was outdated and would, albeit almost a century later, lead to the French Revolution. Britain had already had her revolution between 1642 to 1651 and would not need another one to allow her Government and people to ultimately work together to forge a country. Britain was becoming a modern country and would become an economic power through her expanding empire and through industrial innovation, part of which was initially fuelled by the refugee Huguenots expelled from Louis's France. France in contrast lurched and struggled with the inequality between her rich minority and the poor majority as her desire for empire was repeatedly challenged by the expanding British one. There was no way that the majority of British people wanted to risk a return to a despotic leader and the Government took steps in 1701 to ensure that such an eventuality would not occur by passing the Act of Settlement.

It is worth considering, however, that had the Stuarts set their goal a little lower, perhaps king of a separate Ireland or Scotland, then this may have been achievable, for in those countries, especially in Ireland, James had far greater support than in England. Certainly if William had been forced to fight a war on three fronts then he may have been forced to give up Scotland or more likely Ireland rather than his Dutch homeland; any properly co-ordinated attacks could have forced William into a difficult compromise. Such co-ordination was never mastered for the Stuart cause and the elements which dogged the first rising would come back to haunt all of the others.

5

The Old Pretender 1698–1720

Succession and Union

The quiet final three years at the end of the seventeenth century continued into the start of the early eighteenth as the western European powers recovered after their epic struggle of the War of the League of Augsburg. For the British Government the failure of William and Mary, as well as now Mary's sister Anne, to produce any surviving children still left the way open for a resurgent Stuart to claim the throne and they feared further rebellions. The Act of Settlement, which had been drafted in 1700, finally received Royal Ascent in 1701 and gave the full succession of the English and Irish crowns and thrones to the Electress Sophia of Hanover, who was the most junior of the Stuarts, being a granddaughter of James VI and I, but her line were committed Protestants. By this Act the Government finally had a constitutional solution to offset a Stuart claimant of Catholic persuasion, whatsoever befell William or Anne from thereon in.

While the Act of Settlement was awaiting its royal signature, the thing which Europe had feared for some time came to pass: Charles II of Spain died on 1 November 1700, throwing open the question of who would rule the crumbling Spanish Empire. Spain was no longer a great power but she still commanded a massive empire, then the largest in the world, and in Europe she still held lands in much of Italy, half of the Netherlands and numerous islands in the Mediterranean. Louis XIV declared that Philip of Anjou, now Philip V of Spain, should be king and succeed to the throne of France after his own death. Louis envisaged a united France and Spain and their combined wealth and substantial empires terrified the smaller European countries, who feared that Louis XIV would dominate the whole of Western Europe. This fear allowed William to once again build an alliance of all those countries opposed to Louis's plan, together with the Austrian Empire in central Europe. Thus, in July 1701, armed conflict began in Europe in the form of the War of the Spanish Succession when Austrian forces under Prince Eugene of Savoy invaded the Duchy of Milan, a Spanish territory; Britain and France were at war again!

Shortly after, on 16 September 1701, James II died still in exile at Saint-Germain-en-Laye. Louis at once recognised his son James Edward Stuart as James III and VIII; with the full ceremony befitting a King, it was proclaimed with trumpets around the vicinity of the town. The title was recognised by both the Pope and the King of Spain and James became known as the 'Old Pretender'. And just six months later, on 8 March 1702, William was also dead: he died from pneumonia following complications with a broken collarbone, obtained during a fall while out riding, his horse having apparently stumbled over a mole hill. This simple accident led to the Jacobites creating a toast to 'the little gentleman in the black velvet waistcoat'. William's death, however, found Britain in a much stronger political position than she had been in when William accepted the throne, the Bill of Rights and the Act of Settlement giving Britain a solid foundation for her future, and William's dying wish was that the two countries of England and Scotland be joined. William was succeeded by Queen Anne and the focus at the beginning of her reign was the continued success of Britain's army in Europe, where John Churchill, who had fought at Sedgemoor back in 1685, succeeded with his ally Prince Eugene in soundly defeated the French at Blenheim on 13 August 1704, to be followed by a further victory at Ramillies on 23 May 1706.

The success abroad was complemented by even more dramatic events at home, where after protracted negotiations plans came together to formalise the Union of England and Scotland into one monarchy under one Parliament. Such a move would see the monarch as the official ruler of all three kingdoms and for the first time wearing one crown and with a combined Parliament. Accordingly, a group of commissioners was established in both countries to examine the issues which would need to be resolved prior to any agreement being signed. In the early 1700s Scotland was going through a financial crisis brought about by a succession of bad harvests and by people investing in the Darien Scheme. This latter enterprise was a project in the 1690s to establish a Scottish trading colony on the Isthmus of Panama in the central Americas. The whole project was a fiasco; there was a complete lack of leadership and basic organisation; there was improper provisioning and no basic planning, and the expected demand for goods never materialised. Eventually, after a siege by the Spanish against an outpost devastated by disease and a shortage of food, the colony was abandoned in April 1700. Unfortunately for Scotland, it is estimated that the Darien Company was financially backed by a quarter of the total money circulating in Scotland at the turn of the century. This left many people on the verge of bankruptcy and if lessons had been learnt from this then maybe the South Sea Bubble that followed just a generation later would not have been so damaging. The financial hardship of Scotland did two things; it led some people to believe that they would be better off under the Union, while for others a Stuart King seemed more palatable. Many commissioners had invested heavily and so lost heavily in the failed Darien Scheme and saw possible compensation from the money which England was willing to offer to Scotland for what Scotland had lost in the past and might lose in the future. The sum granted to Scotland was £398,085 and 10s to offset future liability towards the English national debt. However, this was not the only money being swilled in a northerly direction as large sums were paid to the Earl of Glasgow and the second Duke of Queensberry, James Douglas, who was the Queen's Commissioner in the Scottish Parliament and Keeper of the Privy Seal of Scotland from 1705 to 1709. The money was apparently compensation for various losses incurred but Robbie Burns summed it up as follows: 'We're bought and sold for English Gold, Such a Parcel of Rogues in a Nation.' Money was also used to hire spies, one of whom was the author Daniel Defoe, and he reported that there were violent demonstrations against the Union and that for every Scot in favour there were ninety-nine against. The Act of Union was in fact two separate acts, the Union with Scotland Act 1706 passed by the Parliament of England and the Union with England Act passed in 1707 by the Parliament of Scotland. They put into effect the terms of the Treaty of Union that had been agreed on 22 July 1706, based upon the negotiations between the two sets of commissioners representing the parliaments of each country. The Acts joined the Kingdom of England and the Kingdom of Scotland together.

In summary the salient points of the combined Acts were as follows. As regards sharing Government, they allowed Scotland to send representative peers from the Peerage of Scotland to sit in the House of Lords. It also guaranteed that the Church of Scotland would remain the established Church in Scotland, and that Scottish law would remain separate to the law of England and Wales (which it still does to this day) and coupled with that, the Court of Session would also remain within Scotland. Other provisions included the reinstatement of the Act of Settlement 1701, which was particularly aimed at the Stuarts, as was the continuing ban on Roman Catholics from taking the throne. Finally, it also created an excise and customs union as well as a monetary one. The two countries were finally combined as one on 1 May 1707. In Scotland it was the Duke of Queensberry who was largely responsible for the successful passage of the Union act by the Scottish Parliament so that eventually the two separate Bills were approved.

It was the lure of English gold that had won the day with the decision makers, but not with the common people. Such was the reaction in Scotland as protests erupted across the major towns and cities that the parliament had to impose martial law. In his television programme *The History of Britain* Simon Schama eloquently sums up the situation which surrounded the idea of a union between the two countries: 'What began as a hostile merger would end in a full partnership in the most powerful going concern in the world ... it was one of the most astonishing transformations in European history'.

The Grand Invasion of 1708

How much faith Louis really had in the ability of the Stuarts to regain the throne and how much he simply used them as a shield to draw off British troops from mainland Europe will probably never be known. Certainly, time and again, and especially when things were going against him, Louis seemed capable of finding the resources to fund an expedition to support the Jacobite cause. In February 1708, with the War of the Spanish Succession going increasingly against the French in the Low Countries, Louis assembled a force of 6,000 men consisting of six French regiments and three regiments from the Irish corps. A fleet of fifteen transport ships and five men of war were ready to carry the invasion force to Scotland. Much of the evidence which had been provided to Louis for him to take the decision to invade at this time came from a Colonel Hooke, who was the official French agent in Scotland. Hooke had been with Monmouth at Sedgemoor before being later pardoned by James; Hooke then converted to Catholicism and later fought alongside James at the Boyne. Hooke reported that the Act of Union, though popular with the Scottish Whig minority, was unpopular with the vast majority of the Scottish people. Hooke put before Louis a verbal list of clans that had promised to rise if a French army invaded Scotland, where they promised as many as 25,000 men would flock to the Stuart banner. Hooke also brought a list of demands which the clans had said must be met if the rebellion was to have a chance of succeeding: the clans would provide the men, but the supplies of weapons would have to come from France. Scotland, like much of Europe, had been blighted by a series of poor harvests, and many had lost money in the grandiose financial adventure of the Darien scheme. They requested 8,000 men at arms, weapons for the entire Scottish army, artillery, ammunition and grenades as well as 100,000 pistoles (a small gold coin and the equivalent of around £20 million today) and finally the officers to train the Scottish army. How much of these requests Louis was able to meet is not certain but 6,000 troops was 75 per cent of the amount requested and one must assume that having committed regiments of his own army as well as the Irish corps, he would have contributed some additional weapons and ammunition as well.

Map C
Naval engagements of
the Jacobite rebellions

(A) Firth of Forth 1708
(B) Off Cornwall 1745
(C) Tongue 1746
(D) Loch nan Uamh 1746

On 8 March, having waited for a series of channel storms to abate, the French fleet finally set sail for Scotland, unsure even as to which port it was making for until they were under way. The expedition was commanded by a brave rear-admiral, Claude Forbin, Count de Forbin-Gardanne. He was experienced in war both on land and sea and was respected for his record of success in both arms of military service. Despite his own impetuosity of character, Forbin was not convinced that James's expedition was going to be a success; he had grave doubts about both the size of the force he was carrying and how many Jacobites would rise to meet his illustrious charge when safely delivered. Edinburgh was said to be jubilant at the thought of the King returning and plans were in place for signals to be exchanged between the ships and the shore so that those ashore could be ready to assist James and his army upon arrival. On land, Edinburgh was poorly prepared. Lord Leven the English commander at Edinburgh stated that he had few men and that he had no clothing and no provisions, so effectively he had nothing with which to prevent a Jacobite army from capturing the city. The newly promoted Admiral Byng, however, was forewarned of the plot and with a fleet of thirty-eight ships he was awaiting the French invasion fleet, and when they appeared he calmly closed in behind the French ships now trapped in the Firth of Forth. Seeing that it was impossible to land safely either James or any of his supplies, the French Admiral Forbin ordered his ships to bear down on the awaiting English, who were blocking his route to the open sea. Forbin's fleet gave Byng the impression that they were going to attack and so Byng reduced his sail in preparation for battle, but instead the French ships piled on all their available sail and sped past the surprised English fleet and headed east with the wind behind them and the English in pursuit. The English succeeded in capturing one ship and with the wind blocking any attempt to sail towards the coast, Forbin concluded that the only thing he could so was to return to Dunkirk with the army and his ships intact. Byng was content to sit off the coast, his job for the moment was done.

Once back in France, there was much debate and questioning of loyalties and plots, mirrored in Britain as Queen Anne questioned the loyalty of some Scottish lords; some castles in Scotland were appropriated and men were billeted at Blair Atholl. Britain had been saved, but partly by luck. The French invasion which would have been the spark to light the fuse of a massive Scottish rebellion had been thwarted this time by a combination of the weather and some accurate British intelligence. The most significant consequence of the attempted invasion was that when the first general election was held after the Union in 1708, the Whigs won a majority for the first time, allowing them to strengthen their hold on positions in authority within local government, in the Church of England and even in the armed forces.

The War of the Spanish Succession continued until the Peace of Utrecht in 1713, a collaboration of different treaties which between them settled the conflicts between the respective countries which had been involved in the war. Britain's armies had fought and triumphed and this was reflected in the terms of the peace, under which Spain ceded Gibraltar and Minorca to Britain while France ceded territories in North America, namely its claims to Newfoundland, the Hudson's Bay Company and Nova Scotia; Britain's empire had expanded at the cost of its near neighbours.

The Firth of Forth from Musselburgh, where the French fleet were driven off in 1708.

Upon the cessation of hostilities, the first thing that the Government chose to do was to stand down much of the army; as explained in Chapter Three, either for fear of a coup d'état or because of the cost of maintaining an army, often both, successive parliaments ever since the Restoration in 1660 had looked to limit the size of the army. This is exactly what happened straight after the War of the Spanish Succession concluded and the reliable and experienced army which Marlborough had so painstakingly trained and moulded was slowly taken apart. Of course, this was just what any foreign power and particularly a Stuart claimant wanted to see; a reduction in the armed forces was welcome news to all Catholics, both at home and abroad. Having lived to see the triumphs of the Peace of Utrecht, Queen Anne died on 1 August 1714 and her nominated successor Sophia had died just a few weeks before, on 8 June. This brought to the throne James VI and I's great-grandson, George the Elector of Hanover, who on becoming King George I started the Hanoverian dynasty. The distance meant that it was some time before the new monarch could be summoned and he eventually arrived at Greenwich on 18 September and he was crowned in Westminster Abbey on 20 October 1714.

The Great Rising – The 15

From the moment of Anne's death there were rumours of plots being hatched on both sides of the Channel to being the Stuarts back to the now British throne. General Election victories in 1710 and 1713 had given the Tories large majorities and their success at bringing the War of the Spanish Succession to an end furthered their power with widespread public support. But immediately after his succession George I had reversed the fortunes of the Tories by appointing Whig members to his cabinet as they had supported and aided his succession. So although the succession of George I had at first passed off largely without incident, but under the calm surface there were many rumblings of discontent, and not least from some of those now out of favour Tories. From March 1715 the Stuart movement intensified and in sharp contrast to the previous risings, there was now widespread support in England and Wales as well as Scotland for a rebellion against the new German king.

The first signs of any sentiments moving towards James were simple, subtle toasts to James, but small riots in provincial towns and protests by regiments of the army over the state of their uniforms and conditions did not help to lay to rest the clamour that something was amiss. The general ground-swell of support for James grew. For the first time since the succession: those discontented with the thought of a German monarch had someone to sympathise with them. On 10 June, which was James's birthday, the first signs of rebellion were visible as open demonstrations took place in the north and west of Britain; there were riots in Leeds, an arson attack in Manchester, and in Somerset and Gloucestershire open drinking and 'tumultuous' singing of Jacobite songs, a Whig who complained being badly beaten for his pains. Action was taken in London, with a defensive camp being established in Hyde Park which was furnished with artillery moved there from the Tower of London and aside from London and the surrounding counties the odour of rebellion grew ever more pungent. A rebellion in Cornwall in August 1715 was nipped in the bud as the instigators, James Butler, Second Duke of Ormonde, and Henry St John, the First Viscount Bolingbroke (who were both men of some standing in the High Tories) had intrusted their scheme to capture the cities of Exeter, Plymouth and then Bristol to a Colonel Maclean. It turned out that Maclean was a Whig spy, who supplied the names of the Jacobite leaders in the South West to Hugh Boscawen of Tregothnan, who was the Government representative in Cornwall, and he called out the militia, which quickly put an end to any attempt at a rising. With both Bolingbroke, and later Ormonde, fleeing abroad as Parliament began to suspect the two men of plotting against the Crown, in their absence they were stripped of titles and their offices were extinguished and it was left to those less well known Jacobite supporters to take the rap. Many were arrested, some were convicted and one died in prison, but others were acquitted, with a celebration party being held upon their return home. The important thing for George I was that this far flung rebellion at the edge of his kingdom had failed to even get started but in prudence, across Wales and in London, all prominent Jacobite sympathisers were being kept under surveillance.

However, in the north of England and especially in Scotland, the rebellion took hold with some speed. In Scotland the defence of the new Hanoverian Britain depended on John Campbell, the second Duke of Argyll, who had succeeded to the title from his father in 1705. Campbell had supported the Act of Union and for this and for his military career he was created Baron Chatham and Earl of Greenwich, and as a skilled politician he worked with the Duke of Somerset and helped to secure the Hanoverian succession. Campbell also fought with distinction in the War of the Spanish Succession, under the Duke of Marlborough, and he was an experienced commander but following the Peace of Utrecht Britain quickly reduced her standing army, leaving precious few men to defend the realm. Argyll's spies kept him well informed of the Jacobites' movements, which allowed him to keep the routes south under surveillance. The Jacobite plans for a rising to coincide with a French invasion had long been laid between James and the Earl of Mar, who had been corresponding for some time on what they planned to be a major rebellion. With the plots laid in August 1715, James called on Mar to raise the clans again and leaving London, he brought the clans together and raised the old Scottish standard at Braemar on 6 September. In contrast to the earlier risings, Mar's proclamation brought in an alliance of not only the Highland clans but also some of the Lowlanders too. They quickly captured Inverness and then moved swiftly south to capture Perth on 14 September. Mar's army was now around 1,000 horse and 5,000 foot, with the promise of some 2,500 Highlanders on the march from the western side of Scotland and a further 3,500 from the far north. There were also promises that James was on the way from France with troops for two separate landings, one in Cornwall, the other in Scotland; everything was moving the Jacobites' way. Mar gathered his forces at Perth and his strength grew daily; they even succeeded in capturing weapons intended for the Government troops in the northern Highlands, thus robbing Lord Sutherland, the Hanoverian leader there, of much needed supplies. The only minor setback for Mar, but a boon for the English rebels, was that Brigadier William Mackintosh of Borlum, who had captured Inverness for the Jacobites and who was a proven soldier, became separated from the rest of the Scottish forces. Mackintosh, with around 2,000 men, arrived on 9 October and instead of linking up with Mar or outflanking Argyll chose instead to cross the Firth of Forth in local fishing boats from Burntisland and attempt an attack on Edinburgh. Thwarted there, Mackintosh led his men south on the long march towards England. There is conjecture as to whether Mar intended Mackintosh to attempt the attack on Edinburgh and then move south whether the capital was captured or not. Mackintosh's men would have been a boost to Mar's forces, which had to force Argyll to fight so that he could be beaten and open the way to the south for Mar's army. On 14 October Argyll, learning of Mackintosh's recent threat, retired his forces to Edinburgh to regroup and to organise his force following the arrival of reinforcements. On 16 October Mar moved his force from Perth to Dunblane while Argyll now left Edinburgh and returned to Stirling, so Mar retreated to Perth.

This game of cat and mouse is difficult to fathom: Mar had a much larger army than Argyll and delay, while it allowed more Jacobites to arrive, also gave time for more Government reinforcements to be sent; furthermore, the Jacobite army was always prone to desertions during periods of inactivity, not from a fear of any fighting that lay ahead but from a 'I have better things to do at home' feeling. The only reason which may have been seriously delaying Mar was the absence of his King, together with the troops, money and weapons promised by the French, but James was delayed in France by an event which was to have a serious impact on the whole Stuart strategy. On 1 September Louis XIV died; Louis, having reigned so long, was succeeded by his great-grandson Louis XV, yet Louis was only five years old and too young to inherit and the Regent, the Duke of Orleans, was the power behind the throne until Louis could take the reins of monarchy when he came of age at thirteen in 1723. The Duke of Orleans was a shrewd statesman and after a succession of expensive wars, which together with failed harvests had left the French state under crippling economic pressures, he wanted to build a better relationship with her near neighbour Britain. Orleans now prevaricated upon the aid of men, arms, money and ships which Louis had promised for the next Jacobite rising. Having come off considerably worse than the British in the War of the Spanish Succession, Orleans was not going to provoke another war with Britain if he could avoid it. This left James with no clear answer as to when the promised expedition would begin and his frustration grew as time continued to slip away from the instructions he had given to Mar. Unbeknown to James, his rebellion was well under way and support was growing but not in an organised way; there was no clear, co-ordinated plan and two separate campaigns were under way, neither one with a clear objective.

The Campaign in England

So while James kicked his heels in France, in the north-east of England there were poor agricultural yields, and a crisis in the coal-mining industry loomed as the surface yields declined and deeper mines were needed to prevent flooding. Catholic clergy and Tory gentry were both suffering financially following the death of Anne. United by common complaint and led by their local Member of Parliament for Northumberland, Thomas Forster, a group of around 300 horsemen proclaimed James their king at Warkworth, on 9 October. United, they marched on Newcastle, intent on capturing and rousing the city, which quietly refused to surrender to them. Frustrated at this first setback but not undaunted, the horsemen, which included the Earl of Derwentwater, one of the illegitimate children of Charles II, headed north across the Cheviots and met up with Mackintosh, still heading south at Kelso. There followed several days of debate as to which route to take next. Mackintosh wanted this small army to inspire the rest of the Lowlands, the Dumfries and Glasgow areas, to join the rising. The English were determined to march through Lancashire and on towards Liverpool, where they expected that thousands of recruits would flock to their sides. News that General Carpenter was advancing from Newcastle

The modern Ribble Bridge at Preston.

with 1,000 troops convinced the Jacobites that their route should be towards England and so they moved south-west, so that while Carpenter headed north and reached Jedburgh on 30 October, Mackintosh's men crossed into England. Carpenter, receiving fresh intelligence of the Jacobites' proposed route south, retraced his steps to Newcastle before swinging south-west to come across the Pennines and down to Preston. Carpenter knew that in Cheshire, away to the south, General Wills was preparing for the approaching Jacobite army.

The Jacobites' advance was steady and they reached Preston on 9 November, and Forster was keen for them to press on the next day towards Liverpool. The only opposition to their long march was some Westmorland militia, but they dispersed back to their homes as the rebels marched on. The rebels were able to collect the weapons abandoned by the retreating militia; some had muskets, others simple pitchforks, but all that was abandoned was cheerfully gathered by the Jacobites, who took them all to supplement their own armaments. Their army did not grow as they marched south and although a few men did join their ranks, they also lost men, who would slip away quietly in the night to begin the long walk home. However, Forster's mounted patrols found that the countryside south of Preston was already in Government hands. This meant that the bridges that they needed to cross to continue a push south to either Manchester or Liverpool (both cities were hordes of Jacobite sympathisers were expected to join them) were already guarded and the Jacobites could go no further south without a fight or face the threat of retreat north – a retreat which would be harassed by dragoons all the way. Forster, seeing that his force was now vulnerable to the encroaching Government counter-campaign, became most 'dispirited' and instead of making plans or reading despatches, he retired to his bed. The remaining senior commanders then held a council of war and decided to stay and fight. In preparation they barricaded the centre of Preston, forming a defensive network of barriers, some laid behind one another, providing strong fall-back positions so that they could resist repeated attacks. They initially posted a force of 100 men under Farquharson on the

Fishergate in the centre of Preston.

Ribble Bridge, but Forster, seeming refreshed after his night's rest, withdrew the men into the central ring of defences. After such careful planning, it seems incredible that anyone within the Jacobite army, including Forster, could neglect to place any barricade at the main bridge into the town, particularly as they took such pains to defend the Fishergate, which led to the main southern crossing – the ford at Penwortham.

By not barricading the southern bridge, the way was open for the Government troops to get over the River Ribble and thereby gain a foothold on the southern side of the town unopposed. The only good news for Forster was that he had more recruits as some poorly armed Lancashire men had come to join the Jacobites; but they were so poorly armed with a miscellany of weapons that Mackintosh commented that if he had 'ten thousand of them, I'd fight them all with a thousand of his (Wills') dragoons'. Clearly, the Jacobites, by retrieving discarded hand-held polearms, were not well equipped, but they did take six small naval cannon from their scouring of Lancaster which would have been useful to shoot from a barricade down the narrow lanes of a seventeenth-century town. Such artillery pieces would have been formidable if entrenched around the aforementioned Ribble Bridge. How many men of James's English rebellion made it to Preston is questionable – they certainly had more men than were seeking to thwart them. They should have had at least 2,300 men made up of the combined forces of Mackintosh and Forster, and, given that they had received support from small groups of recruits joining them on the journey south, as well as a fresh influx while at Preston, their total force must have been around 3,000 men, even allowing for the ubiquitous desertion which occurred en route as men left to begin the already long journey home.

The strategy of the of the opposing commanders shows a marked contrast: while Forster's strategy was epitomised by the lack of a coherent plan throughout the campaign and at key moments lapses into apathy, General Wills' approach was calm and proficient. Forster's plan seems to have been to march his army south, gathering recruits as he

Map H Battle of Preston 13/14 November 1715

A Mitre Inn
B Sir Henry Houghtons House
C Parish Church
D Tithebarn Street Barricade

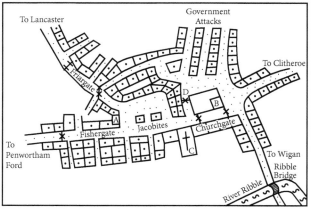

Bridge   Houses

River   Barricades

went, providing the impetus to continue south; a self-perpetuating march, presumably towards London. There was no coordinated plan to wait for James to arrive or to meet up with any secondary invasion marching from the Highlands. Whereas Wills, with intelligence on the numbers marching towards him, first secured his defences and then forced Forster to make the decision as to whether to stand and fight or to retreat.

Wills had marched north from Cheshire on 10 November and had secured all of the key river crossings as he came north, thereby ensuring that his supply routes were guarded and that there was nowhere that the Jacobites could attempt to cross into Liverpool or Wales without combat. Wills had four regiments of dragoons and one unit of foot soldiers and stopped to collect another regiment of dragoons at Wigan. Presumably he would have left companies of foot soldiers to guard the bridges, and one imagines that they would all have been barricaded to aid their defence. Having reached the outskirts of Preston, Wills surrounded the whole town, instructing his dragoons to take up a position on each of the main roads leading into the town's centre. Wills' encircling force at Preston was somewhat smaller than the Jacobite force, numbering around 1,600 men, and Wills took the unusual decision to split up his units and recombine them in mixed units so that colleagues from a single unit of dragoons were approaching the enemy from opposite sides of the town. Presumably this was for morale purposes; had a single unit been defeated in an assault, it may have caused the whole unit to bolt from the town, but by combining mixed squadrons together, Wills was trying to prevent part of a unit from looking bad in the eyes of another. Thus Pitt's, Wynn's, Stanhope's, Munden's, Honeywood's and Dormer's dragoons were brigaded for the attack. Brigadiers Dormer and Munden's forces attacked from the north down the Lancaster road., each brigadier with 200 men. Local volunteers and militia – around 400 men – were left to guard the fords and the Ribble Bridge, but they were kept well away from the main combat area. Finally, from the east would come the main assault: Brigadier Honeywood would lead 400 of Preston's men, the Cameronians, 200 brigaded dragoons, and a reserve of 200 of his dragoons.

The battle began just after lunchtime on Saturday 12 November, when Honeywood's assault was launched against the most easterly barrier on Church Street. However, the Jacobites were well entrenched, shooting from every conceivable place, cellars, windows, rooftops and doorways, as well as the barricades, The Highlanders poured musket fire into the attacking redcoats, supported by two of the six ship's cannons. The first shot was so bad as to be reputed to have hit a chimney, which suggests that their trajectory was not set for street fighting. However, further rounds seem to have hit home as after some initial advances the Government troop withdrew, having suffered considerable losses – at least 120 men were killed and perhaps as many as 150. The first assault having failed, Wills then sent in his dragoons from the north, who made some progress before being outgunned in a similarly galling fashion to Honeywood's forces and were driven off with losses of around 100 men. The eastern attack having failed, the Jacobites withdrew to their second positions, thus strengthening their centre. The Government troops, seeing this retreat, advanced and succeeded in setting on fire some of the houses close to the barricades. The wind blew the smoke and the flames south, so it did no damage to the Jacobite positions, but it did allow some of the Cameronians, under cover of the smoke, to get into position to shoot at the defending rebels. As the late autumn night drew in, one humorous but widely reported incident took place, showing that even in the midst of gruesome battle, humanity sometimes steals the show. As darkness fell, an order went out that all the Government troops who had secured houses around the town should light candles in the windows to show where they were. The Jacobites, from their central position within the town, could see all of these lights appearing and cheerfully shot at their Government opponents, who were exposing their positions. In a bizarre turn of events – and the fore-runner of a subsequent catch-phrase from the BBC Television series *Dad's Army* – runners were sent out by the Government command, shouting to their comrades to 'Put that light out'. The terrified townsfolk of Preston, fearing for their own safety, proceeded to place lighted candles in all their windows so that the whole town was alighted by their actions. On seeing this, the spasmodic shooting stopped, and reports stated that both sides were 'amused' by the action. Despite the poor light for open shooting, both sides periodically exchanged shots during the night, though no casualties were reported.

The first day had been a resounding success for the Jacobites; they had driven off repeated attacks and caused ten times the casualties they had suffered, but it seems that something was wrong. The militia and local volunteers guarding the southern side of the town that ran alongside the River Ribble must have vacated their posts or become complacent and grouped around the Ribble Bridge, because in the night hundreds of the rebels deserted James's cause. Finding Penwortham Ford unguarded, around 1,300 men vanished into the Lancashire night. Did they steal ships and head north, sensing that this unguarded port might be their last chance to escape north with anything they had gained so far? It seems that a lot of those who slunk away were the newest recruits – locals for whom the musket exchanges had been just too close for comfort. The morning was to bring more bad news for Forster: General Carpenter had arrived overnight, not only with his own force of 1,000 cavalry, but commanding a further 1,500 men under the Earl of Carlisle and Lord Lumley, who had clearly rallied their own local militia.

The early Sunday morning was noisily shattered when just before dawn, Honeywood launched a fresh assault on the church barricade, yet the attack was again repulsed and Wills withdrew his men to consider his next move; however, that decision was taken away from him by the arrival of the more senior officer, General Carpenter. On reconnoitring the enemy's positions and realising that Wills had not blocked all of the escape routes the previous evening, Carpenter was furious and instantly closed the hole through which so many rebels had bolted the night before with a unit of dragoons. It seems incredible that the thorough Wills had now caught the same apathy which had blighted Forster; perhaps he wanted some of the rebels to escape to allow him more chance of taking the town. What is strange is why any of the Jacobites chose to flee, given the way they had seen off the regular troops the first day. Perhaps they feared that their ammunition was running low and that in a fire fight and with no way of escape, they would eventually be defeated. Certainly Forster believed that their cause was lost. The Scots wanted to risk an all-out

The River Ribble at Penwortham, which was fordable at low tide.

assault to try and break out and take as many of the Government troops with them as they could, but Forster resisted and looked to sue for terms with Carpenter.

With both the town completely sealed off from outside and now outnumbering his enemy, Carpenter was in a strong position. Throughout Sunday 13 November there were some protracted negotiations, during which an innocent drummer boy was killed, but Carpenter was prepared to wait as the Jacobites thrashed out their now hopeless position among themselves to see if there were any possible solutions to their predicament. The terms offered to Forster were simply that the rebels were 'prisoners of discretion', which in base terms meant that they had no rights at all. Such was the fury with which the Scots met this news that a Highland officer named Murray went to shoot Forster, but the shot was knocked wide by a man named Patten. Eventually the Jacobites agreed to surrender on 14 November at 7 a.m. and the rank and file laid down their arms in the market place before being marched off to the church, where they were imprisoned and fed on bread and water for a month. The officers gave up their swords at the entrance to the church, the senior officers being allowed to surrender their weapons in private and to remain imprisoned in the various inns within the town. Some were eventually transferred to Lancaster Castle, and others to Liverpool, where they were tried, but by then some had already died in captivity. While trying to decide their own fate, Mar had fought the Government army at Sheriffmuir, but that news was still to reach the Jacobites holed up in Preston.

How appalling the Jacobite desertions during the night between the two battles must have been, as the roll call of the surrendered Jacobite forces testifies: Baynes lists in his account of the battle a telling summary of the final losses. The Government lost 145 killed (3 officers) and 131 wounded. The Jacobites lost just seventeen killed and twenty-five wounded, but 1,485 surrendered, of whom 463 were English. This means that just over 1,500 men were present and that almost half had deserted in a single night

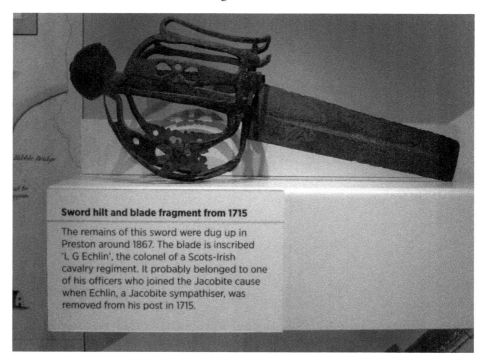

Jacobite Sword Hilt. (Courtesy of Preston Museum)

Moor Park, Preston, where the Jacobite prisoners were gathered after the battle.

– on such fickle shoulders was James's cause resting. For the treatment of the Jacobites after the battle, they may as well have died in the glory of a final charge. For those that surrendered, hanging, a firing squad, death in prison, or transportation to the colonies were the most common sentences that awaited them. A few would survive all of these terrors and return to England to try and extract revenge thirty years later. The battles at Preston and Dunkeld clearly illustrate that the leadership of the Jacobites was not capable of fighting on terms other than their own, historical way – the manic, all for glory, charge. Outnumbering the enemy at Dunkeld, they could not break into the defences, and when outnumbering the enemy from within defences at Preston, they could not break out! The defenders inflicted far greater casualties than they suffered, and with Penwortham Ford unguarded the whole Jacobite army could have slipped away in the night in a proper withdrawal. It is not hard to see why the majority of the Jacobites did not want to surrender and would have preferred a 'death or glory' charge for freedom when the alternative was surrender on zero terms followed by brutal punishment.

The Campaign in Scotland

On 4 and 5 November, Mar was reinforced by 2,500 men of the western clans and a further 2,000 from the north of Scotland under Lord Seaforth, bringing his army up to around 10,000 men. Feeling confident of victory without the need for French reinforcements, Mar once more advanced towards Stirling in order to cross the River Forth and to continue south towards Edinburgh. Argyll's scouts were aware of the rebels' movements and Argyll moved from Edinburgh towards Stirling to intercept the Jacobites' advance. Argyll drew up his men on the high ground east of Dunblane, while Mar's army was deployed further north near Kinbuck, close to the Allan Water in a defensive position, with the river protecting the army's right flank and rear. This was a sound deployment given that Argyll's men were close and strong in horse, which was always a Jacobite weakness. Argyll, then, had won the race to block the Jacobite advance and he had the possession of the high ground on the edge of Sheriffmuir – a commanding position but not a strong one. Some historians question whether Mar even knew where Argyll and his army were, but it is unlikely, with such a large force and plenty of light horsemen at his disposal, that Mar's scouts had not located the smaller Government army. If Mar had not known where the enemy army was, then why did his army take their time the next morning and then march straight for Argyll's position? Surely this was because Mar wanted to fully appreciate where his opponent was and what strength he had brought to the field? Whatever the reason was, on the late morning of 13 November, Mar formed his army up into two columns, one led by himself and the other by Hamilton, and marched up the northern side of Sheriffmuir, the cavalry at the head of the columns and presumably, although small in number, screening the main strength of the Jacobite infantry that followed. The gently sloping plateau of this moor is not the easiest ground to cross in modern boots and walking gear, so for an army to manoeuvre upon it would be even more difficult. The mass of long grasses, tangled clumps

The desolation of Sheriffmuir almost unchanged since 1715.

of heather and small bushes, deep sphagnum moss, isolated pools and small clumps of trees made walking in a straight line difficult. A regiment of men could lie down and they would simply disappear from sight, so that, coupled with the slope that falls around the edges of the moor, makes the visibility and action of command very difficult.

Seeing that the Jacobites were advancing towards the higher ground to the east of his current position, Argyll moved forward to counter the rebels' plan, spreading his own line thinly to accommodate the greater number of men that Mar was able to field against him. This seems to bring into question the skill of Argyll's scouting troops. This is because if Argyll had known that Mar's men were approaching from the north then surely he would have deployed at the first opportunity on the higher ground, preventing Mar from gaining the upper hand. It seems more likely from Argyll's initial actions that he expected Mar to come from the east and had set his men up to defend their escape route west and then south rather than risk having his flank turned and his army pinned by half of Mar's force while the other half by-passed Argyll's men and led the invasion south. This was something that Argyll could not allow to happen – at all costs he could not let the Jacobites pass him and advance south and he had to stop them while he had a chance, even though he was considerably outnumbered.

Quoted numbers for armies are always open to interpretation: often the number of fighting men in an army was reduced below its paper strength, through the posting of small units to guard lines of communication, bridges and fords and of course their camp. At Sheriffmuir, Argyll is stated to have had 3,160 troops to Mar's 8,797, but as many as 1,340 men appear to have been left, not only to guard key positions and cover any retreat, but also to act as a fresh reserve for any subsequent military action. Yet even allowing for those men that Mar had left at Perth as reserves, his advantage of almost 2:1 should have been sufficient for his army to carry the day with ease.

Argyll's army was made up as follows, with 960 cavalry and 2,200 foot soldiers, the foot soldiers being brigaded under Major-General Wightman. Other commanders present were lieutenant generals Evans and Whetham.

1. Carpenter's dragoons, 180 men
2. Kerr's dragoons, 180 men
3. Stair's dragoons, 180 men
4. General Wightman's foot soldiers, 1630 men
5. Earl of Portmore's dragoons – Scots Greys, 180 men

Map G Battle of Sheriffmuir 13 November 1715

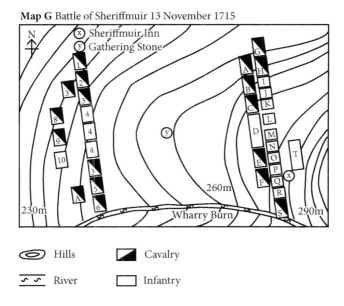

6. Evans' dragoons, 180 men
7. Volunteer Gentlemen, 60 men
8. Dragoon reserve I – made up of a squadron take from front dragoon units
9. Dragoon reserve II – made up of a squadron take from front dragoon units
10. Foot reserve – 570 men from Egerton's and Orrery's (Scots fusiliers)

Although the Earl of Mar's army was considerably larger than Argyll's with 7,457 on the field, he was slightly weaker in his total number of cavalry with 807, but he was far superior in foot soldiers with 6,650. Mar led his column onto the right side of the moor and placed himself on the extreme right of the front line; for the size of his force, he had few senior officers to assist him. General Hamilton took command of the second column when marching onto the battlefield and so the left of the Jacobite army. Other listed senior officers were the Adjutant-General, a Colonel William Clepham, and the Quartermaster-General, who was Peter Smith.

A & B. Huntly's cavalry, 250 men

C. Stirling cavalry, 77 men

D. General Gordon's Highlanders, 2,970 men

E. Perthshire cavalry, 70 men

F. Fife cavalry, 90 men

G & H. Earl Marischal's cavalry, 180 men

I, J & K. Seaforth's Highlanders, 700 men

L & M. Huntly's battalions, 800 men

N. Panmure, 420 men

O. Tullibardine, 400 men

P. Drummond, 500 men

Q. Strathallan, 300 men

R. Robertson, 200 men

S. Angus cavalry, 100 men

T. Reserves, 400 men

It is not totally certain whether either side had any artillery and if they did, whether they succeeded in deploying them in time to be used, given the speed with which the battle commenced. The weather had been particularly cold and much of the moor was frozen hard and so much easier to cross than when in a state of sodden moss or peat. The battle began around noon in response to the movements being made by their opponents deploying, rather than from any strategic planning, as each side sought to capitalise on what it deemed to be mistakes made by the other as they deployed. The fact that the Government army moved to the right at the same time as the two Jacobite columns separated when they came up onto the moor caused disruption to both armies, for neither was properly prepared when the battle actually began. Mar, seeing Argyll's left wing being stretched as his right wing expanded to meet Hamilton's higher deployment, gave the order to charge. Meanwhile, Argyll, seeing Mar's left wing unformed as Hamilton hurried onto the top of the moor, also gave the order to charge. Mar's right wing charge was led by the Captain of Clanranald, who within seconds of the order being given was shot and killed. The clan chief being slain caused the Highlanders to halt. Seeing the hesitation, Glengarry rushed forward and cried 'Revenge! Revenge! Today for revenge and tomorrow for mourning' – these Highlanders were MacDonalds who had been the intended victims of the Glencoe massacre under the earlier Duke of Argyll's banner, and this charge was a chance for their payback. While Argyll's left flank was crumbling under the Highland charge, his own right flank was pushing back Mar's left wing as his dragoons charged and pushed back the disordered units that Hamilton was trying to deploy. Therefore, simultaneously both charges were successful, with the two left wings of both armies collapsing, and Argyll's in total rout. Mar's Highlanders chased Argyll's foot soldiers and dragoons back down the hill towards the Wharry Burn and the direction of Dunblane.

Mar's left wing, however, behaved much better than the Government troops who had fled so easily, and against the repeated charges of Argyll's dragoons they fought a

The Wharry Burn at Sheriffmuir.

series of fighting withdrawals, during which the dragoons are reputed to have charged no less than a dozen times. This series of assaults would last for a staggering three hours before eventually the Highlanders were forced back to their camp near the Allan Water. The uneven nature of the Sheriffmuir terrain meant that neither Argyll nor Mar could actually see what was happening to the different parts of their armies. Mar did not know his left had been pushed back and Argyll did not know that his left wing had completely disintegrated. These undulations and hidden dips may also account for some of the accusations which were levelled at certain units and sub-commanders after the battle, as although neither side lost the battle, certainly the Jacobites could have gone on to win it if Mar and Hamilton had fully appreciated what was happening across the whole battlefield. Such accusations always look to find out traitors and cowards, and Drummond, an aide-de-camp for Hamilton, and the Marquess of Huntley were both accused of these 'crimes' immediately after the battle. Drummond is certainly suspect, as he seems to have told Hamilton that Mar's right had given way when of course it had triumphed, causing Hamilton to fight his impressive defensive retreat when in fact he could have afforded to push on and drive the dragoons back, using his cavalry to assault the enemy rather than defend his infantry. Huntley's cowardice is not justified given that although outnumbered, his small unit of cavalry repeatedly aided Hamilton's retreat.

By around 2 p.m. Mar was able to rally his men from their slaughter of the fleeing Hanoverian troops and supporters and they formed up in good order in the position where the Scots Greys had started the battle some two hours earlier. Mar had around 4,000 men and let them rest as he assessed the battlefield, quiet save for the cries of the wounded, and what to do next. Argyll eventually got news that his left wing had been destroyed and it came as something of a wake-up call when he must have realised how lax he had been to get involved personally in a fight which only involved half of the force he was responsible for. Argyll quickly rallied his men from their pursuit in the valley, something which was no mean feat in itself given the erratic behaviour of British cavalry in general, and his force of just over 1,000 men was back on the edge of Sheriffmuir by 3 p.m. Argyll deployed his force, which was roughly equal in foot soldiers and cavalry, in the traditional manner, with two brigades of foot soldiers in the centre and his cavalry shared equally on each wing. He is reported to have also had two cannon, which he placed in front of his cavalry in some rough enclosures and mud walls which would have offered some protection from a Highland assault. Argyll's men were now in the position where Mar's right wing had originally advanced from. Mar had formed up in similar fashion, but now outnumbered his enemy by 4:1. Both sides waited. Mar appears to have not sent word to any of Hamilton's force that Argyll was now trapped between them and that any Jacobites that could be brought back to the field at this stage would mean that Argyll was surrounded. There was an hour before dark and Mar's men were eager to fight, but Mar was not and waited; Glenbucket is reputed to have shouted out, 'Oh! For one hour of Dundee.' No such spark emerged from Mar and eventually as dusk fell, Argyll made a feint towards Mar's position and then headed west to Dunblane, leaving Mar in possession of the field, but it was no victory. Mar headed south to Ardoch. The battle could have even been fought the next day, for Argyll returned to collect his wounded and a great store of weapons he gathered from the field – Mar and part of his force watched, but did not interfere.

Argyll had lost 377 killed including 23 officers, 153 wounded and 133 prisoners, but he had won the battle – he had stopped Mar's army getting past him to the south. In addition, he lost fourteen colours, 1,400 weapons and four cannon. Mar lost sixty killed, ninety wounded and eighty-two prisoners and six cannon, 1,000 weapons and the six bread wagons near the Allan Water that had been their complete supply train. Mar had also lost the battle, the rising, and the greatest chance since Bonnie Dundee was killed of regaining the throne for the Stuarts.

The unlucky 13 November contained one more unpleasant surprise for the Jacobites. The Mackenzies had held the castle at Inverness for the Stuart cause with a garrison of around 600 men, 300 from their own clan and 300 from the MacDonalds of Keppoch. Eventually, having been besieged by 2,500 men from the clans of Fraser, Forbes, Rose, Munro and Grant, they were forced to surrender though most of the Mackenzies fled by boat, abandoning all of their baggage to avoid a confrontation with their arch rivals, the Frasers. From the Jacobite side the major penultimate act of the '15 rising was over. And all the time these events were occurring in his name, what of James? The Old Pretender's courage, unlike that of his father, could not be questioned. He had not wanted to sail away from Scotland in 1708 when events turned against the French fleet – he was prepared to land anywhere on Scottish soil if Forbin would have taken the risk and landed him. Perhaps, on reflection, those instructions not to risk any harm coming to James were a coded signal from Louis to his commander not to land James unless there was a Scottish army to meet him. What if the plan was for the French to make a show to frighten the British into reacting? This way, the French would get what they wanted without risk of losing anything, and with a safe heir with which to repeat the exercise

Memorial clan stone on Sheriffmuir.

The memorial to the clan MacRae at Sheriffmuir.

later. An expedition where one ship is lost to capture – and the same rations consumed by the men whether on land or sea – amounts to very little overall expenditure in the grand scheme of international politics, and if it makes Britain keep sixty warships and 20,000 men at home in case of invasion then it ties up a huge part of the British army and keeps twenty regiments away from mainland Europe. So with his job of making a show of force done, Forbin could return home with James still alive to be used again as a threat to the British throne when Louis XIV wanted to support him in another invasion. Whether in reality this was a French attempt to mount a full-scale invasion, or whether it was an attempt to appease James and provoke a reaction from Britain, we will never know, but with no Scottish rising for James to bring his French troops to, it was never going to succeed, and Forbin was surely warned of this by Louis before any embarkation took place.

Regarding French support, the faint letters within the writing on the wall were already beginning to appear for James in 1713 when, as part of the Peace of Utrecht, James was forced to leave France and reside in Bar-le-Duc, which at that time was in the independent territory of the Duchy of Lorraine. However, with Louis XIV gone, Orleans was not prepared to risk any venture likely to further damage the French equivalent of the English exchequer, the 'Caisse d'Emprunts', so Orleans deliberately kept James from any hint of what his real plans were. James, frustrated by this French game of chess (in which he was the pawn and not the king), was forced to make his own arrangements so that he could learn for himself how Mar and the rising were progressing. It was not only bitterly cold in Scotland but in France too, and road transport and shipping had been disrupted. Following repeated attempts on his life, James travelled in disguise and, having made arrangements for his own safe passage, he sailed for Scotland in mid-December aboard a small brig with just eight guns. It was the correct ship for the mission: James needed something small and fast to avoid the many British naval patrols that were not only on the lookout for smuggled wine and brandy, but any news of a possible rival candidate for the throne who might be hidden among the contraband. Back in London, the talk of a major Jacobite rising and the events in Cornwall as well as to the north had every ship on alert. It should be noted that after the Union, contraband smuggling of wine and brandy increased to the point at which the Excise men could no longer control the flow of illegal contraband into England via Scotland. James eventually landed at Peterhead on 22 December 1715, a remote port almost at the tip of north-east Scotland. Within a few days of his arrival, he had contracted a virulent cold and was unwell for some days, spending five days in bed, and was forced to wait until 2 January 1716 before setting out on the week-long journey to Perth to meet with Mar and his army. James does seem to have been unlucky with illness; at the start of the 1708 expedition he was gravely ill with measles and was still suffering from the disease when he joined his ship for the journey. On arrival, James viewed his followers – his army now stood at less than 5,000 men, almost half what it had been just two months before. The Government had not been as idle as the clans would have liked, for while their numbers dwindled, the government army grew. The usual plague of desertion had swept through Mar's ranks and Mar had even warned James that he feared their army being outnumbered by the growing Government army and their strategy of sending troops north now that the rebellions in England were clearly over. Argyll had been reinforced with some new, heavier artillery, and in December three regiments of dragoons arrived in Glasgow, with 6,000 Dutch troops arriving later in the month, to give him a very strong force. Seeing the desperate straits that the Jacobite army was now in with Argyll closing in, Mar decided to try and slow Argyll's advance by burning villages between Stirling and Perth, before on 30 January, leading the Jacobite force north towards Perth. By 4 February the Old Pretender knew that this expedition was not going to succeed and he wrote a farewell letter to Scotland and sailed from Montrose on 5 February for France, a country he was not allowed to enter. There were further campaign moves as the Jacobite army evaded the Government patrols and the clans returned to their glens. Then in July 1717, in a show of clemency, the Indemnity Act 1717 had the effect of pardoning all those who had taken part in the rising, with the exclusion of the whole of the Clan Gregor – including Rob Roy MacGregor, the infamous Highlander immortalised in Sir Walter Scott's book *Rob Roy*. George I eventually pardoned Rob Roy on hearing all of the facts behind his misfortune, the circumstances which originally led him into the debt which caused his family's decline.

Conclusion

Once again the Jacobites had thrown away an opportunity to exert real pressure on the incumbent monarch. When the rising began, George I was not popular with the people and for the first time since James II abandoned his throne, there was widespread support throughout England and even in some ranks of the army for the Stuart line to return. A properly coordinated rebellion, with risings in the south-west and the north of England coinciding with a rising in Scotland, would have stretched the already reduced remnants of Marlborough's great army to breaking point. If the French had supported James at this time with good generals, quartermasters, and the arms they had requested in 1708, then it is difficult to see how the Stuart advance on London could have been stopped. Coordinating such a countywide strategy is very difficult, but there was little in their way to prevent a proper invasion, which, if it had been handled properly, would have obtained more valuable support than it did in its disorganised state. Having failed to coordinate their strategy and get James at the head of the rising by the time of Sheriffmuir, Mar still had a glorious chance to take control of Scotland, to which either French or Spanish forces could have been landed in safety. With Argyll on his knees and with 10,000 men within a day's march of the moor, Mar chose on two consecutive days to avoid battle, making no attempt to crush his weaker opponent. The Government troops, when they found themselves in those positions of power, did not slacken their hold on the net and always chose to close in on their opponents.

The 1719 Rebellion

After arriving back in France, James went to the city of Avignon, which in 1716 was still governed by the Pope, and from there in 1717 he moved to Italy, residing at Urbino. Back in Scotland Argyll had garrisoned the country with no less than twenty-nine brigades of foot soldiers or regiments of dragoons. His aim was to garrison those towns or passes which would be on any Jacobite commander's mind to either take or march through. Thus, with the country subdued and the key centres under Government control, Argyll handed over his title of Commander in Chief to General Cadogan on 27 February 1716. The threat of a further Jacobite uprising was ever present, but with James now in Italy the Government knew that it would be far more difficult to lead an invasion fleet from so far afield without running into either difficult weather or one of the many British fleet patrols. The British spy network was also highly skilled and had contacts in most of the western European capitals. This network uncovered a plot in 1717 in which Protestant Sweden, under the leadership of Charles XII, was planning to invade Scotland with an army of 12,000 men in retaliation for the losses of Swedish territory to Hanover in the Great Northern War, which had raged since 1700, embroiling most of northern Europe. Sadly for James, the discovery of the plot and the subsequent arrest of those suspected of involvement brought the whole scheme to an end. A year later, however, James began to receive overtures of support from a new front, albeit a fading power.

Spain had been in decline for over half a century, but still held sway over an enormous empire, although those territories were being slowly lost to the ever expanding British Empire, where the increasing dominance of the British Navy was sweeping all before it. This repeatedly brought Spain and Britain into conflict, particularly in the Mediterranean Sea, and the loss of Gibraltar as part of the Peace of Utrecht continued to gall the Spanish court. Spain was looking for a way to put pressure on the British at home and once more the idea surfaced of creating a rebellion which would force her government to bring ships and men back home in order to defend her sovereignty. In 1715, the Duke of Ormonde had fled Britain following the failed Cornish uprising, revealing that he was guilty of supporting the Jacobites. Whether he had been guilty is questionable; he did have a proud military record for his country, having served with distinction under William of Orange before rising to Commander in Chief of the forces, succeeding Marlborough in 1711. Following the arrival of George I and the removal of Tories from their prominent positions of office, Ormonde found himself out of favour. It therefore seems that it was his replacement by prominent Whigs and the political isolation of his Tory associates and some of his Jacobite friends that drove him to openly support the Stuart cause. After a short time in France, Ormonde moved to Spain and soon he was introduced to a new ally in the form of Philip V's chief minister, Cardinal Alberoni. The two men plotted an elaborate scheme to put James on the throne. The theory was the same as previously undertaken by the French: a large invasion fleet would carry men, arms and money and it would invade Britain, while, to coincide with the landing in either Cornwall or Wales, a rising would begin again in Scotland.

On 8 March, James arrived in Spain and almost immediately the preliminary force set sail for Scotland with two ships under the command of the Earl of Marischal, who had naval command, and the Marquis de Tullibardine, who had the military command, secured only after a great deal of argument, which was to continue throughout the campaign. On board the two ships were 307 Spanish foot soldiers and a considerable quantity of arms, ammunition and money for the clans. James's hopes rested on the success of this advance force in raising the clans before the main Spanish fleet arrived. On 19 March, Jacobite sympathisers in France also set sail for Scotland and the appointed rendezvous on the Isle of Lewis. Accounts vary as to the size of the main Spanish force but it consisted of at least 5,000 men (perhaps as many as 7,000) aboard a fleet of twenty-seven ships which had set sail from Cadiz on 7 March with the Duke of Ormonde aboard. Once more it was natural forces that were to take over, and, as the fleet rounded Cape Finisterre on 29 March, they were struck by a ferocious storm. The Spanish fleet was scattered and the ships limped into various ports along the coast to make repairs before returning to Spain. Meanwhile, James' two ships had sped on and on 13 April the expedition landed at Eilean Donan Castle on Loch Duich, one of the Earl of Seaforth's residences. The Spanish ships unloaded their cargo of men and munitions, including a quantity of 2,000 muskets for the expected Highlanders. With few recruits to meet them and a paltry force of their own, there was nothing for them to do other than to make the castle their base and await the expected clan rising. Several hundred Highlanders had marched to meet them – the clan Mackenzie, the clan Macrae, and Rob Roy Macgregor arrived to support their king – but this was hardly an army. The Jacobite command then received the news that the Spanish fleet had been scattered and that their planned invasion of southern Britain had been abandoned. Tullibardine was all for the force dispersing while the command, together with the Spanish troops, returned to Spain to try again with a fresh armada and more men. But Marischal would have none of it and as naval commander he sent the two ships back to Spain – there was nothing more the command could do. Considering the small size of their force, they had to raise more men, and so, leaving just a platoon to guard their stores and munitions in the castle, the main body of Highlanders marched west to raise more clans to the Stuart banner.

However, the Government had received news of the Jacobite activity in the Highlands and was already planning their military campaign. Reinforcements were sent to the Inverness garrison and five Royal Navy ships blockaded the end of Loch Duich. While in the Highlands, on 9 May 1719, James married by proxy Clementina Sobieska, the daughter of James Sobieski and his wife, who was the granddaughter of King John III of Poland. This marriage was to have important consequences for the future of the Stuart cause as the couple went on produce two sons: Charles Edward Stuart in 1720, and Henry Benedict in 1725. Thoughts of his future, though, were far from James's mind as his position became perilous in early May. Early on 10 May the British Navy sent in three small warships towards Eilean Donan Castle: HMS *Enterprise*, HMS *Flamborough* and HMS *Worcester*. Captain Boyle called upon the castle to surrender, which it refused to do. These three ships bombarded the castle and having met little resistance, Captain Boyle sent in his

Eilean Donan Castle, destroyed by the Royal Navy.

ships' boats filled with marines and sailors to storm and secure the castle under the cover of dusk and a furious cannonade. The garrison of forty-four – of whom forty-two were Spaniards – surrendered with little resistance and was captured together with 343 barrels of powder and fifty-two barrels of musket shot. The prisoners were put aboard the *Flamborough* and were taken to Edinburgh. With the area around the bay secure, the navy set about searching all of the surrounding dwellings. They discovered more powder and food supplies and systematically destroyed everything that they could not use themselves. The castle and its outbuildings were charged with a considerable quantity of powder and everything was raised to the ground. The castle remained a ruin for over 200 years before being rebuilt between 1912 and 1932 into the 'chocolate box' residence seen today.

Despite the lull before the Government ground forces were ready to advance west, the Jacobite commanders, who had been out among the mountains and glens to drum up support, failed to return with the significant rising predicted. The thousands of the '15 just four years before were echoed with just hundreds now. Lord George Murray, who was Tullibardine's younger brother, arrived with a small number of men and Locheil returned with 150; Seaforth returned with the 500 he promised, but it was still a paltry force. All of these men had regrouped in Glenshiel, but they had already realised that the Government net was closing in around them, and that with the rebellion already foundering, if they were going to escape to raise a rebellion in the future, then they were going to have to fight their way out.

Heading out from Inverness on 5 June, the Government force under General Wightman, who was a veteran of Sheriffmuir, was not strong. Wightman led a small army of just one regiment of dragoons, 180 men at most; a similar number of Highlanders loyal to the Hanoverian Whigs; and around 850 foot soldiers, mostly Dutch infantry, and also some artillery (four small coehorn mortars), which were to play a significant part in the forthcoming battle.

The Highland clans rally to the Stuart Standard, 15 mm Essex Miniatures army.

Front rank Government regiments in 28 mm, painted by Alison Browning.

Pulteney's 13th Foot firing by platoon. (Courtesy of the Lace Wars)

The dominating bastions of Edinburgh Castle, never captured by the Jacobites. (Courtesy of Rachel Saunders)

Above left: A Highlander's equipment from the front, including his musket. (Courtesy of the Lace Wars)

Above right: A Highlander's equipment from the back, including his targe. (Courtesy of the Lace Wars)

Dillon's Irish Picquets. (Courtesy of the Lace Wars)

Highlanders take cover in a field, front rank 28 mm, painted by Jonathan Worton.

Swarkestone Bridge near Derby – the closest the Stuarts ever got to London.

Derek under the Rebel Tree at Clifton where the Highlanders were buried in 1745.

Bonnie Prince Charlie by Ramsay 1745. (Kind permission of the Earl of Wemyss and March)

Cobham's 10th Dragoons with sword and carbine. (Courtesy of the Lace Wars)

Carlisle Castle captured in the '45 rebellion by the Jacobites, who later surrendered to Cumberland.

Cumberland's army lands at Aberdeen – a 28 mm demonstration game by the Border Warlords.

A mannequin of Charles Edward Stuart in the Jacobite room at Derby Museum.

The Jacobite front line at Culloden marked with blue flags.

Cumberland's Government army in 15 mm, an Essex Miniatures army.

Wightman advanced steadily and by 9 June was at the head of the valley, close to Loch Clunie. On the following day he was marching down between the ever increasingly steep hills towards the pass of Glenshiel, the narrowest part of the valley, where the River Shiel carved out a deep watercourse for itself (it is now spanned by a modern road bridge).

From 9 June, close to this point in the valley, the Jacobites had been aware of the approaching Hanoverian force. Murray had a string of outposts along the valley and these retreated, always keeping at least half a mile ahead of the approaching Government troops, and providing the Jacobite command with constant updates. In this narrow valley, where the Jacobite army rested, the mountains on either side rise to over 1,000 metres (almost 3,500 feet) and they seem to press down upon anyone looking up from the valley floor. The steep sides are striated by a succession of streams and cascading waterfalls which have cut vertically into the sides of the mountains. Over time, these tumbling waters, eagerly rushing to join the river below, have exposed rocks and loosened stones, which makes them perfect for piling up on the banks of streams to make temporary defences. These defences could not have been shaped with timber and soil, as one would expect for field defences on fields or pasture. The soil there is thin and peaty, with shrubs of heather and moss intermingled with boulders and rocks which are strewn everywhere, having fallen from the heights above for many millennia. Apart from abundant forestry, it is easy to imagine the rebel force lifting the many loose stones to form barriers in which to shelter, ready to receive the Government force when it came into range. The Jacobite command had a twenty-four-hour period in which to prepare their defences, and with a force of between 1,200 and 1,600 they had plenty of man power to undertake this exercise. When completed, the men on the hillside sheltered in their trench (presumably a doctored

Murray's isolated first position at Glenshiel, 1719.

watercourse), which was lined eastwards by a newly raised stone parapet. The road that led down into the valley was also barricaded in line with these entrenchments.

Wightman later reported that his enemy amounted to 2,540 men, which seems a little high given the few clan numbers that reported in when the army regrouped at the beginning of June. Either way, with such a strong defensive position, the Jacobites should have been more than a match for Wightman's smaller force of regular soldiers. The majority of their troops were spread in a line up the side of the mountain, with just Murray's men taking a covering position on the south side of the river on a prominent hill with a commanding view of the valley. The Government troops appeared working their way along the valley and keeping close to the road, presumably in order to aid the movement of their small mortars, which were the only artillery present at the battle. It was around 2 p.m. that the armies first had full sight of one another, and they were initially deployed as shown on the map.

The Jacobites, having been in position for some time, waited for Wightman's advance. Wightman held up his approach once he could see the Jacobite positions, about half a mile from their prepared positions, which Wightman noted were well 'dispositioned for defence'. Indeed, the Jacobites had all the advantages: they outnumbered their enemy, they had steep slopes which they could climb to rain down missiles on those below them, and they were entrenched, blocking Wightman's route to the sea and any rendezvous with the Royal Navy. One final irony was that it was James Stuart's birthday and he could have wished for no greater present that day than a victory to reignite the campaign and allow a second Spanish fleet to be sent.

Map I Battle of Glenshiel 10 June 1719

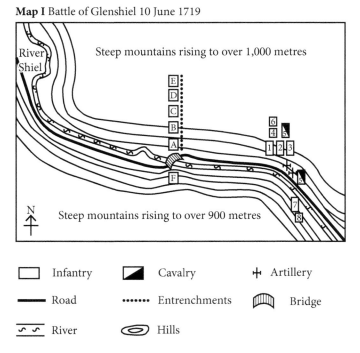

The author has proportioned the Jacobite force led by Tullibardine at 1,500 in total, split as follows:

A. The Spanish foot soldiers under Nicholas Bolano, 300 men

B. Locheil's clansmen, 150 men

C. Glengarry's clansmen, 250 men

D. Macgregor's, McKinnon's and Seaforth's clansmen, 350 men

E. Seaforth's picked clansmen, 300 men

F. Lord George Murray, 150 men

Wightman's army is listed in some reports as being 1,286, which would make the proportions as follows, and this does balance to the known numbers of the smaller units taking part while allowing the three Dutch foot regiments to be of equal size.

1. Montagu's foot soldirs, 240 men

2. Ruffel's foot soldiers, 240 men

3. Amerongen's foot soldiers, 240 men

4. Colonel Harrison's foot soldiers, 50 men

5. Dragoons, 180 men

6. Lord Strathnaver's foot soldiers, 56 men

7. Clayton's foot soldiers, 200 men

8. Munro, 80 clansmen

The battle opened between 5 p.m. and 6 p.m. when a hail of mortar shells landed on the hill that Murray was defending and against which Clayton's and Munro's men now advanced, using the mortar attacks to cover their approach. Alone and without any proffered support, Murray was forced to retreat, cross the River Shiel and into the defensive position offered alongside the rest of the army. This turned out to be a grave mistake and one which could have been avoided. Had Tullibardine given some additional troops to Murray then he could have seen off the Clayton and Munro attack and advanced himself, and, having got inside the range of the mortars, enfiladed Wightman's men from the southern bank of the river. By deciding to hold fast, Tullibardine allowed Wightman to concentrate all of his mortar fire onto their topmost units of the line, which were Seaforth's men, who were simultaneously shot at by muskets from Montagu's and Harrison's regiments. With what seems undue haste, the clan units began to retreat up the mountain to escape, first Seaforth's men, followed by the amalgamated unit led by the MacGregors, who, in turn, were then closely followed by the Glengarry clan. In a matter of minutes the Jacobite left had simply 'gone', leaving just over half of the original army close to the foot of the valley.

The Spanish under Bolano offered to charge, but this offer was declined by Tullibardine, who suggested that they should look to escape together and regroup elsewhere to continue the struggle. With that, it seems that all save the Spanish unit took the attitude of 'every man for himself' and the whole army fled north and up the mountains, with the

The steep watercourses which scar the sides of Glenshiel.

The view the Government troops had at Glenshiel, 1719.

The route of the Government forces at Glenshiel, 1719.

Coirein nan Spainteach, the mountain climbed by the fleeing rebels, so named after the Spanish who spent the night up there.

Spanish eventually bringing up the rear, having continued to shoot at the approaching men of Montagu's regiment. The Jacobites, dressed in light plaids and used to mountain climbing as it was their home soil, made light work of getting away from the pursuers, and as it was late when the battle began, it may well have been getting dark by the time the Spanish reached any kind of shelter in the rocks above them, by which time the rest of the army had vanished. The Spanish spent a cold night on the mountain which they had reached by nightfall and they duly surrendered the next day. As prisoners they were taken to Edinburgh where they were reunited with their comrades captured at Eilean Donan Castle, and eventually, following negotiations with Spain, they were returned home.

There are two significant points to note in relation to this battle. The deployment map above is contrary to many interpretations, which put the Spanish troops in the highest position because of their retreat up the mountains before capture the following day. The accounts of the battle clearly state that the second wave of fire from the government mortars was concentrated on the Jacobite left, which was the highest point of the Jacobite line, and that it was Seaforth's men that fled first. The other Scottish clansmen on the left also fled, following Seaforth, and leaving the Spanish alone in the centre. And as the Jacobites all ran 'in headlong flight over Scour Ouran and up towards the top of the mountain', it is clear that they must have been closest to it, otherwise they would have been climbing over the Spanish regiment to get away and the mass would have been an even bigger target for the shooting government troops. The other thing to question is why the Jacobites abandoned so strong a position when they outnumbered their opponents and neither side had taken any significant casualties. This point of note may have been answered by local tradition. According to people living today in the glen, the battle was over so quickly because the bursting mortar shells set fire to all the heather and grass around the Jacobite entrenchments. Being blinded by acrid smoke while being hit by mortar shells dropping into their trenches, would have made the Jacobite position impossible to maintain. Even Wightman commented that the casualties were light, as he lost only twenty-one men killed and 121 wounded – and most of those from Montagu's regiment who had led the main assault across the hill towards the defenders positions. The losses on the Jacobite side were reported to be no more than 100 killed, though nearly all of the officers and many of the men had been wounded. For their pains, three places where the Spanish camped that June night are now named after them. The origin of the peak Sgùrr na Ciste Duibhe ('the Peak of the Black Chest/Coffin') is less obvious; some say this is because of the black ravines that cut through the mountain making it particularly dangerous to walkers. Others link it back to the battle saying that the Spanish hid a black chest there when fleeing from the battle.

Conclusions

This third rising once more epitomises all that could go wrong with an attempt to restore the Stuart monarchy. The main invasion force failed to make the British coast due to a vicious storm at sea that wrecked the fleet. The clans failed to rise in sufficient numbers to provide a strong enough army to threaten England and when in a position to beat the Government army, the Jacobite command was not skilled enough to win the victory necessary to bring more clans to their triumphant banner. To James, who was waiting in Spain, the news of the loss of the fleet, closely followed by news of the defeat at Glenshiel, was a hammer blow. Alberoni still toyed with plans to refit the fleet for a fresh expedition to Britain, but he knew that this was a vain hope as such a refit would take months and already he was losing the War of the Quadruple Alliance and his funds were, as ever, failing. This war that had begun in 1718 saw Britain and France allied together with the Dutch Republic, Savoy and the Holy Roman Empire to defend the Peace of Utrecht and prevent Spanish attempts to regain some of their lost territories. With any peace agreement likely to insist that James be banned from Spanish soil, the Stuart heir quickly gathered his entourage and set sail for Italy, where he landed in September 1719 and where he at last met his long-awaited bride. James was shattered by the successive failures of three expeditions in eleven years and settled down to a quieter court life in Italy, where he and his family were well received and socially accepted. Eventually, on 23 December 1743, James appointed his eldest son Charles Edward to be Prince Regent. Britain had by this time been at war with France for three years, this time over the Austrian succession, and Louis XV was thinking of resurrecting an old plan. If he could create trouble at home for the British then they would have to reduce their armies on the European mainland and as the British were currently winning the war against the French, Louis needed to do something quickly. King Louis XV's generals had even been beaten by George II himself, who, with his son the Duke of Cumberland, had won a resounding victory over the French at Dettingen on 27 June 1743.

Government garrisons, like Stirling Castle, were built to survive a siege.

6

The Young Pretender
1720 to 31 December 1745

Charles Edward Stuart, having been born on 31 December 1720, provided staunch Jacobites with a means of prolonging their hopes of a Stuart dynasty, and if not a Stuart monarchy then a separate Scotland. In reality, the odds on either of these dreams becoming a reality lengthened with each year that passed. By the time that Charles Edward Stuart was appointed to be Prince Regent in December 1743, there had been twenty-four years of comparative peace and so many changes in the way that Scotland was governed that even the most hardened of the Highland clans questioned whether a rising in support of a Stuart pretender would be worth the risk.

The Commander in Chief in Scotland, General Cadogan, who had taken over from Argyll, ran the country with brutality and there was a great deal of looting and destruction, not only from Jacobite sympathisers but from staunch Whigs too. Many complained about the uncouth behaviour and wanton destruction that the troops billeted on the towns meted out to property, irrespective of who it belonged to. Despite Cadogan's controls, there were skirmishes in 1721 at Coille Bhan and Glen Affric as clans fought among themselves or refused to pay taxes levied upon them. In 1724 Cadogan was succeeded by George Wade, who was not only a soldier but also a sound strategic planner. Upon taking office, and on his first visit to the Highlands in 1724, he found them in 'a state of anarchy and confusion' and more importantly virtually inaccessible to any of his troops. In the sixteen years that Wade was in command, he built a staggering 240 miles of military roads, of which many have either been built alongside, or had the surface replaced by modern tarmacadam. In addition to the road system, he constructed new, modern, defensive forts, which gave their names to the places where they stood, such as Fort William, Fort Augustus and Fort George near Inverness. Rivers proved no obstacle and as well as the many small hump-back bridges to cross tributaries and deep gullied streams, he built thirty bridges over major rivers, including the five-arch bridge over the Tay at Aberfeldy that is still in use today. These roads allowed a much quicker deployment of men than had been possible before and the garrisons could police local areas more effectively as they were able to respond to any local dispute or clan incident without the need to send for masses of reinforcements. These forts played a similar role to the Norman motte and bailey or the castles of Edward I in Wales.

In 1727 George I died and was succeeded by his son, George II; this time there was no hint of a rising to protest at the German monarch who had been born, like his father, in

Hanover. Britain's expanding trade routes, the stability of the government under Robert Walpole (the first Prime Minister in all but name), and the commitment George II showed to Britain rather than Hanover, all contributed to a smooth succession. This was partly helped in Scotland by George I allowing General Wade to re-establish the Independent Highland Companies, which had been disbanded in 1717, allowing, according to some, 'the lawless situation to run riot'. The first three companies to be raised were of 114 men each and were commanded by William Grant of Ballindalloch, Simon Fraser the 11th Lord Lovat, and Sir Duncan Campbell of Lochnell. Three smaller companies of just seventy-one men each were commanded by Colin Campbell of Skipness, John Campbell of Carrick, and George Munro of Culcairn. Wade was a most thorough commander, tightening up the discipline and training of these new units, and emphasising to their captains that any irregularity within their financial or military actions would be severely dealt with. In a review of 1738, Wade decided that the six companies he had at his disposal should be strengthened into ten and that they should be amalgamated into a single regiment. This restructuring took place in 1739 and the 43rd Highland regiment was born – later, in 1748, they became the 42nd when a renumbering of the regimental roll took place. Their name as the Am Freiceadan Dubh, or Black Watch, has endured ever since their formation and there is a whole range of reasons as to why they should be given such a name and why it should stick. The most likely has to be the fact that they were seen at the time as traitors by their own countrymen because they spied on the other Highland clans, hence 'black', or evil, watchers. Indeed, the adjective black is used elsewhere to mean evil, as in the term blackleg, for instance, where it is used for those people who go against the majority within an amalgamate union or club. Wade's skills seem to have achieved the desired effect as the Highlands, for the most part, remained tranquil.

In 1740 the War of the Austrian Succession began when Frederick II (later known as Frederick the Great) invaded Silesia in order to amalgamate his isolated Prussian territories into one complete Prussian state. France was allied with Prussia and supported the attack on Austrian Silesia. Britain was allied with Austria, and so once more Britain was plunged into a European War where her regiments were transported to the Continent and marched into Europe. This time, however, there was far more to consider as the British monarch was also still the Elector of Hanover and this meant he had much closer borders to the question of Prussian expansionism than his British coastline. Things came to a head for Louis XV on 27 June 1743, when, with George II in personal command, the British and their allies defeated the French at the Battle of Dettingen. With the war going badly, Louis harked back to his great-grandfather Louis XIV and approached the Old Pretender about another attempt at regaining his crown. James declined, but his son Charles Edward, the appointed regent, at just twenty-four years old, was enthusiastic to try and succeed where others of his line had failed before him. Flushed with the over-confidence of youth and convinced he could triumph and that his ancestral people would flock to him, he agreed to the plan and travelled in secret to France to join the French fleet assembling at Dunkirk for an invasion of England. The French plan was to form two fleets: the first one would be a small squadron under Admiral Jacques Aymar de Roquefeuil, which would sail from Brest and monitor any patrolling British warships. If all was clear, a signal would be sent to the main invasion transport ships at Dunkirk so that they could set sail for Maldon in Essex. This eastern estuary was a perfect place to land as it was well away from any large centres of population – it had famously been the landing site for a Viking force, which had defeated the Saxons there in 991. This scheme had been planned by the French ministers of war and was to be headed by Marshall Saxe, a most able commander, who would have around 12,000 men under his command. However, once more the British spy ring was fully aware that an invasion was being planned and although Britain's standing army at home was very small, 7,000 of the available 10,000 men were deployed to defend London and South East England. The plan went wrong when Roquefeuil failed to accurately locate the British fleet until it was on him off the coast of Dungeness on 27 February 1744 and their main invasion fleet was already at sea en route to the Essex coast. Roquefeuil retreated while the British Admiral Norris pursued right into the teeth of a gale. It was such a sudden and violent storm that it prevented Norris from attacking, but it scattered the first French fleet and severely damaged the invasion fleet, where twelve transports sank, many with great loss of life. It was a week before the damaged French ships were able to limp back into the safety of their own ports. The result was the instant abandonment of the expedition, and what remained of Saxe's force was marched into Flanders to reinforce the French army there. For almost a year, Charles Stuart sat, waited and brooded in France, even as his father had done some thirty years earlier, and the same questions ran around his head: 'Would the French help again?'

The network of Jacobite sympathisers was as active as the Hanoverian spies and Lord Clare, the commander of the French Army's Irish Brigade, was able to introduce Charles to a group of Irish exiles who had ships based at ports along the French coast (which they normally used for carrying slaves to the West Indies). These were groups of privateers, who for the right price were willing to take anything to anywhere, so if the Prince could raise the money, he and as many men as he could muster could be taken to Scotland. On 11 May at the Battle of Fontenoy, the French army soundly defeated the British army led by the Duke of Cumberland. With the British fully committed in Europe, a Jacobite rising would have had a better chance of succeeding. It may be that Louis XV was fully aware of Charles' intentions and may have assisted financially in ensuring that Lord Clare secured two ships for the prince. In mid-June, heavily disguised, Charles went by boat down the Loire from Nantes to St Nazaire, where the 16-gun frigate *Du Teillay* waited. The ship was captained by Anthony Walsh, who was the grandson of the captain who had rescued James II, Charles's grandfather, after the defeat in Ireland in 1690. Walsh was ready for the prince and sailed at once for La Belleisle to await the arrival of the second ship to accompany them. This was *L'Elisabeth*, a full 64-gun French man-of-war. Charles and Walsh waited and eventually, almost two weeks later, *L'Elisabeth* arrived. On board was Lord Clare, with 2,000 muskets, 500 broadswords and 100 marines, who presumably had been recruited with Louis XV's permission. On 5 July the two ships sailed, but just four days later, off the coast of Cornwall, they encountered HMS *Lion*, a

60-gun British man-of-war. There followed a fierce sea battle, which lasted long enough for the *Du Teillay* to make a complete get away, but *L'Elisabeth*, whose captain was killed, and the *Lion* were both so badly damaged that they had to limp back to their home ports. For Charles this was a disaster; he had lost all the men and arms that would have given his attempt to regain the throne some credence. He arrived in Scotland at Eriskay on 23 July before reaching the mainland at Loch Nan Uamh on 25 July. Unsurprisingly, Charles was not greeted with any enthusiasm by the few clan chiefs that had turned out to greet him and he was advised to go home.

He is reported to have retorted that he 'was home'. Seeing the difficult position he was in, Charles wrote to Louis XV asking for assistance, while at the same time sending messengers carrying the lighted cross that called for the clans to rise to his calling through Scotland. In anticipation, he raised his standard at Glenfinnan on Loch Shiel on 19 August with around 1,000 clansmen. In the time between Charles landing and the raising of his standard, the Government became aware of his arrival, but the war in Europe left them few resources at home, just as Charles had hoped. All of the forts and key castles, including Edinburgh and Stirling, were garrisoned for the Government, and Lieutenant-General Sir John Cope, who was now the Commander in Chief of Scotland, marched north with a small army of around 2,000 foot to deal with the rising. A planned Jacobite ambush at the Corrieyairack pass was avoided by Cope, who was forewarned of the plan by his intelligence network, and instead he marched north to Inverness to establish a base from which to deal with the insurrection.

The Glenfinnan Monument to Charles Edward Stuart.

Sadly for Cope, this played right into Charles's hands and with no army within three days march, the rebels were free to march south down the centre of Scotland – the route to Edinburgh lay open before them. The next Government outpost on their march south was Ruthven Barracks at Kingussie, which they reached on 29 August. Although the garrison was small, it was able to repulse the Jacobite attack, and without artillery and with little firepower the Highlanders could do nothing against the solid walls of the elevated barracks and marched on the next day. On 3 September, having travelled via Blair Castle and passed the sites of Killiecrankie and Dunkeld, Charles arrived and took Perth, where he was greeted with fresh recruits. With the army now around 2,000 men, he appointed Lord George Murray and the Duke of Perth to be joint Lieutenant-Generals. Cope, hearing at Inverness of the Jacobite intentions, began a march east with his men towards Aberdeen, with the intention of sailing from there to Edinburgh. Charles, after the experience at Ruthven Barracks, bypassed Stirling Castle, where any assault without substantial artillery was out of the question, and with an ever swelling army, arrived to the west of Edinburgh on 15 September. The garrison was brought out of the city, and Colonel Gardner, with two regiments of dragoons, the town guard and the Edinburgh regiment, deployed his men at Corstorphine west of Edinburgh. Next day, 16 September, this force was reassembled at Coltbridge under the command of the newly arrived General Foukes from London. The troops were now much closer to the city and were drawn up in the fields to the east of the bridge, thereby blocking the route into the city. This force was approached by a handful of the prince's horse, who were reconnoitring the city's defences, but on seeing the dragoons, they advanced and fired their pistols. The dragoons, without returning fire, bolted, careering into their own foot behind them before fleeing the field, closely followed by the now unprotected infantry. The town capitulated the next day and Charles proclaimed his father King James III, with himself as regent. Once more, the impregnability of the castle meant that it remained a bastion of the Government surrounded by a sea of jubilant rebels. At the same time, Cope and his army had arrived at Dunbar, east of Edinburgh, ready to march to stop the Prince's party. Hearing of Cope's advance, Charles took his men out of the city to meet the Government's first real challenge to his army and by 20 September both armies were in position near Prestonpans.

Cope lined up facing south, with his back to the sea, but with a wide area of marshland to his front offering considerable protection from a direct assault. The Jacobites deployed facing Cope but standing on high ground and well out of cannon range – both were excellent defensive positions, so neither army wanted to risk assaulting the other. It was a stalemate, so as night fell the two armies remained where they were. Among the Jacobite command, not for the first or last time, there was much debate about whether to attack or not with the dawn light. Murray knew that a frontal uphill charge across a marsh would be a disaster and they would be shot to pieces by both musket and cannon fire and he insisted that they should not attack a prepared enemy. As the debate grew in intensity, a local farmer's son, a Lieutenant Anderson, spoke up and convinced Murray and the others that he knew a sheep track which led through the marsh and which would lead them onto the flank of Cope's army.

Prestonpans from the Jacobites' first position in 1745.

The rather forlorn Prestonpans memorial, which is surrounded by roads.

The probable night route taken by the Jacobites at Prestonpans.

At around 4 a.m. the entire Jacobite force, in a narrow column, followed Anderson's lead and crept quietly through the marsh to take up a position by dawn which can be seen on the map.

Charles's army was hastily deployed and as each clan or unit came onto the field, they assembled in the morning mist, awaiting their comrades, as per the map, in total there were around 2,500 men. The whole army was to fight on foot and almost all were Highlanders; it is unlikely that any were mounted men and they had no artillery with them at all. Once they were all assembled, the order to advance was given and with the typical mixture of screams, taunts, chants and wails, and to the accompaniment of the bagpipes, the Jacobite units advanced across the level farming fields of Prestonpans.

Map J Battle of Prestonpans 21 September 1745

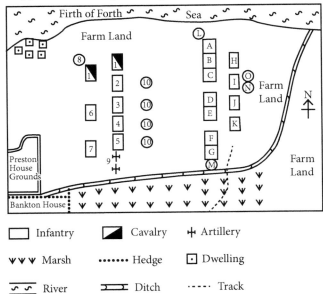

A. Clanranald

B. Glengarry

C. Keppoch

D. MacGregor

E. Duke of Perth

F. Appin

G. Locheil

H. Atholl

I. Robertson

J. MacLachlan

K. MacDonalds of Glencoe

L. Duke of Perth

M. Lord Murray

N. Lord Nairn

O. Prince Charles Edward Stuart

Cope's army numbered almost the same as the Jacobites – around 2,400 men – and was formed up as per the map when the Jacobite advance began. How many of the units were in position is questionable. Evidence suggests that Cope had started to move his line from its east–west alignment to a north–south one the night before. It is certain that he deployed 200 of his dragoons and 300 of his infantry as pickets, spreading them across both his frontage and his flanks, and these would have been closest to the enemy when the Jacobite charge began. It is also certain that some of the regiments were still deploying when the Jacobite attack struck and the artillery was only just in line to fire once, by which time most of its gunners had already fled in fear.

1. Hamilton's dragoons

2. Murray's regiment

3. Lascelle's regiment

4. Guise's regiment

5. Lee's regiment

6. Whitney's dragoons

7. Gardiner's regiment

8. General Cope

9. Colonel Whiteford's artillery

10. Pickets – made up from companies of the eight main regiments above

By having a quarter of his men scattered from their units and on patrol all night, Cope drastically reduced his overall firepower. As we know, the musket is most effective in massed ranks and due to the dispersion of his men, coupled with their hasty recall to reassemble, there would have been confusion and disorder as the wail of the pipes and the cries from the advancing Highlanders penetrated the early morning mist.

Due to an unforeseen marsh in the centre of the battlefield, the central Jacobite advance slowed, which meant that their two wings got ahead of their centre and crashed into the left and right wings of the Government line, routing it almost immediately. This allowed the two triumphant wings to turn in on the Government centre, which was hit simultaneously by the central units of the Jacobite line, which had by then crossed the rough terrain and hit home. Debate as to whether the battle lasted as long as ten minutes or as little as five minutes still continues, but it was certainly over in less time than it takes to tell. With his Government army destroyed, Cope fled south towards Berwick, as did many of the dragoons. Many infantry were killed when trapped against the walls of the Preston estate; in all around three-quarters of Cope's army was killed, wounded or captured. The Jacobites lost in total around 100 men, many from the first few scattered volleys that the Government infantry managed to get off before the Jacobite charge hit home. Like the dragoons, most of the Government foot did not wait to engage, they simply fled without reloading, looking for any way of escape. The day was just dawning, but it belonged to Charles and in triumph they returned to Edinburgh, restocked with weapons, ammunition, and provisions taken from their prisoners. The news of the victory moved those wavering clans and support for Charles now poured in; the French had also heard the news and it rekindled ideas in Louis XV's head about helping Charles to regain his throne. In October Charles's army grew to 5,500 men, and for the first time he had some cavalry of around 500 horse, mostly of the light skirmishing type, but excellent for reconnaissance and harrowing the enemy. Murray organised these clan bands of brothers into balanced units and gave them proper training, as well as ensuring that the administrative side of the army worked efficiently. Meanwhile in England, the aged Wade, who was now seventy-two, gathered his troops at Newcastle upon Tyne, and the Duke of Cumberland, who was recalled from Flanders, was given instructions to concentrate his forces in the Midlands to prevent any Jacobite surge towards London. Across England and Wales all the militia units were called to arms, and in the Highlands loyal clans formed a new regiment – Loudon's – and a whole series of new independent companies were formed. With both sides in this civil war recruiting strongly, the campaign became a game of cat and mouse as the Jacobites (who would always be outnumbered unless significant French troops arrived to support them) looked to strike out for London, the heart of the Government, knowing that if they could capture the capital, they would win the war with Charles ready to ascend the throne.

With the Jacobite army fully prepared and as well trained and as well armed as possible, it broke into two separate forces which left Edinburgh on 31 October. Charles and Murray led one column south via Kelso and Jedburgh, while a second column led by Perth and Tullibardine travelled by way of Moffat and Peebles. On 15 November, Carlisle surrendered after a short siege, and a fortnight later, on 29 November, Manchester was taken without a shot being fired in its defence. Alas for Charles, the same thing happened in 1745 as in 1715 – very few people rose to welcome a Stuart claimant for the throne. Two hundred men did join at Manchester, named the Manchester regiment, but there were precious few other men willing to join the march south. While the Jacobites marched south, Wade sent two regiments of foot and two of dragoons to Edinburgh to reoccupy the city and strengthen the defences should the Jacobites turn back. On 16 November Wade left Newcastle to head south with the rest of his men, planning to turn west and to cross the Pennines and so attack Charles from the rear. The atrocious weather at the time meant that the roads over the mountains were impassable and Wade was forced to return to Newcastle without encountering his enemy. On 1 December, learning that Cumberland was at Lichfield with 2,000 horse and 8,000 foot, Murray, with the light horse, headed towards Wales, thought by the Government to be a hot-bed of Jacobite support. The ruse worked and as Cumberland headed north-west to Stafford, Murray doubled back and met up with the rest of the army, which had by now reached Derby.

It was there, while the army rested and regrouped, that a string of conflicting information arrived which caused division among the Jacobite command. News that Wade was again advancing south-west towards them and that Cumberland was now hovering to the north-

The memorial cairn at the Crewe & Harpur Inn at Swarkestone.

west meant that overall they were outnumbered by around three to one. Some good news also came in and that was that a small group of French soldiers, together with further money, arms and cannon, as well as some trained artillerymen, had arrived in Scotland. However, this was offset by no news of any sizeable French force preparing to invade southern England. The decision among the council of war to march into England had only been passed by a majority of one, whereas the decision taken at Derby to return to Scotland was almost unanimous. Only Charles believed they should continue south to London with only 125 miles to go, at most a seven-day march. Given the three things against the Jacobites – the failure of any English uprising to support Charles's claim; the lack of French support in the south of Britain; and the fact that there were two armies bearing down upon them – retreating north was strategically the right thing to do. Charles was furious but bowed to the majority, yet in spite of the logic of the council's decision, he would not trust his generals properly again, especially Lord Murray, and this was something which would haunt him later in the campaign.

On 7 December the Jacobite army commenced its retreat, retracing its steps to Manchester, Wigan, Kendal and then Penrith, close to the Scottish border. Cumberland, with just his mounted men, began the pursuit, while Wade tried to intercept the rebels at Wigan, but he failed to get there in time due to the winter snows on the Pennines. By 17 December the Jacobites had almost reached Penrith, but Cumberland had almost reached the Jacobites and Murray, with the rear-guard, took up a strong defensive position in the rural hamlet of Clifton, today no more than a small village. In 1745, as today, there were many walls, hedges and enclosures and it was a strong position, but Murray, sensing the strength of Cumberland's advance guard, called on Charles for reinforcements, claiming that he would be easily over-run without additional troops. For once Charles complied and immediately sent two units of Highlanders back to assist Murray, who was then able to secure his position, as the map shows. The Jacobites waited, very well positioned to ambush the advancing Government troops as twilight fell, but Cumberland was a canny solider and he was not going to walk into a Jacobite ambush.

Map K Battle of Clifton Moor 18 December 1745

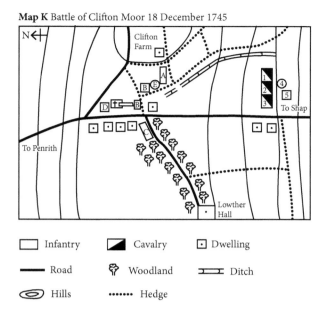

☐ Infantry	◩ Cavalry	⊡ Dwelling
▬ Road	🌳 Woodland	⊐⊏ Ditch
⬭ Hills	•••••• Hedge	

Murray had around 1,000 men split into four units:

A. MacPherson's Highlanders
B. Roy Stewart's Edinburgh regiment
C. Glengarry's Highlanders
D. Appin Stewart Highlanders
E. Lord Murray

Cumberland's men were all mounted units: three full strength dragoon regiments and a unit of rangers who had been destined for America, but were requisitioned by Cumberland when he returned from Flanders. These rangers were travelling on horse but normally fought on foot.

1. Bland's dragoons
2. Kerr's dragoons
3. Cobham's dragoons
4. Duke of Cumberland plus his 16 Hussar bodyguard
5. Georgia rangers

At around five in the evening, Cumberland ordered some companies to remain mounted in reserve and he ordered the majority of his dragoons to dismount and to advance alongside the road, not down it. It was already beginning to get dark, but over the next hour, the dragoons advanced several times to probe the rebel defences, but each time, after a brisk fire-fight, they were pushed back. After such an exchange between

MacPherson's men and Bland's dragoons, the Highlanders, who had fallen flat on seeing the flashes of powder from the dragoons' fire, rose as one and charged the dragoons before they could reload; this action, being fought among the hedges and the long ditch on Murray's left flank, drove the dragoons back towards their reserves up the hill, with the Scots killing some of them in their pursuit.

Murray immediately halted his men for fear of them being hit by their own comrades who were shooting from the right flank into Cobham's dragoons, who had advanced in similar fashion to Bland's, but on the left of the road going north. Murray withdrew MacPherson's men back behind the hedges, and it seems that somehow in the dusk those on the right had seen the success of the MacPherson attack. Accordingly, after Cobham's and Kerr's men also paused to reload, the Glengarry and the Appin men counter-attacked and at point of sword drove those two dragoon units back towards their own lines. Murray knew it was time to retreat and the Jacobites retreated to into the night. The battle had raged for almost an hour and although there were casualties on both sides, the Hanoverian dragoons had come off worse, losing around sixty men compared to forty or less of the Jacobites. This was a resounding success for Murray, buying him the time he needed to get the Jacobite army away north before Cumberland could bring the rest of his army up to catch them. The rebels broke camp and marched on north, pausing briefly at Carlisle. Murray left the Manchester regiment of 200 men, together with a further 200 non-clan troops, with instructions to hold the castle for as long as possible. The Jacobites then marched on, crossing the River Esk and onto home soil for so many of the army on 20 December. Free from pursuit, the rebel army reached Glasgow on Christmas day and planned the campaign for the New Year.

Cumberland occupied Clifton around 6 p.m. the same evening, but the Jacobites had swiftly flown their hedge-lined nests, leaving Cumberland to gather his forces the next day, ready to march further north. Was Clifton a battle or a skirmish? It was larger than many Dark Age battles, but smaller than many battles of the English Civil War – the importance comes from the date. Some say Sedgemoor in 1685 was the last battle on

Fields to the right of the lane into Clifton across which the dragoons advanced.

The hedges where the Jacobites drove off the dragoons at Clifton, little changed since 1745.

English soil and there were certainly many thousands involved. For most wars fought across Britain, Clifton is large enough to be deemed a battle, as it was fought with formed regiments and cavalry squadrons, involved at least 2,000 men and lasted a lot longer than many other battles that have been fought in these isles. Clifton is certainly not the last skirmish fought on English soil, as this occurred at Goudhurst in Kent in 1747, between a gang of smugglers and a force of local militia.

A day behind Charles's retreating army, Cumberland arrived at Carlisle on 21 December and as the town and castle refused to surrender, he commenced siege operations against it, bombarding it with heavy cannon. Eventually, on 30 December the Jacobites asked for terms, but despite being given none other than 'they would be reserved for the King's pleasure', they decided to surrender. They had held out for ten days, which had bought the rest of the army valuable time to get well away, but the punishments meted out were brutal. Some were immediately hanged at Carlisle, but others waited in squalor for weeks before being executed. The treatment of all the officers was worse: they were all transported to London to be hanged, drawn and quartered as traitors. Cumberland, his initial job of seeing the rebels out of England done, also returned to London, leaving General Hawley to pick up the Jacobite trail north. Despite the loss of Carlisle, the year ended on a high for Jacobite morale. Across the whole country there was another rumour of a French invasion in the South East of England, which once more caused panic in society London. More tangible was the fact that at Inverurie, near Aberdeen, Lord Gordon with 900 men had defeated MacLeod's independent company, who were fighting for the Government, causing many casualties among the latter's 500 men and wiping it out as a fighting force. This news helped to convince more recruits to join the rebel army and by 31 December Charles's army had swelled to 9,000 men.

7

The Last Campaign,
1 January 1746 to 19 September 1746

The Jacobite army was now at its strongest since Sheriffmuir thirty years earlier and it was vital that it was used to its full potential. Although siege warfare was not their forte, on 1 January they began to besiege Stirling Castle, one of the most impregnable fortresses in Europe, let alone in Scotland, with a force of Highlanders ill-equipped for siege warfare. In their ranks was the Duke of Perth, who had arrived from France as commander of the Royal Scotch Regiment. Under the treaty by which the Dutch had capitulated to the French, the Dutch were not allowed to take up arms against them. Under such terms, the Government was forced to stand down the 6,000 Dutch troops and to send for Hessians to replace them. Meanwhile, General Hawley had concentrated all of his forces at Edinburgh, where, with Wade's reinforcements, he now had three regiments of dragoons and fourteen of foot: a sizeable force of close to 8,000 men in total.

If Charles's plan was to bring the Hanoverian troops out into the open, besieging Stirling Castle certainly worked. Hawley marched out of Edinburgh on 14 January to relieve Stirling, but Murray's spies were on the ball and he was aware of their intentions. Leaving just 1,000 men to continue the blockade of Stirling, Murray marched the bulk of the Jacobite army to intercept Hawley's advance, but was taken aback by the cautious way that Hawley advanced; whether this steady approach was because Hawley feared an ambush because of the speed at which the rebels had destroyed Cope's army, or whether he did not want to move too far away from his base at Edinburgh is not certain. Uncertain of Hawley's intentions, Murray could not risk his army disintegrating to look for food and shelter for the night and so he decided to take the initiative. Learning that Hawley had made camp at Falkirk, he determined to seize the high ground to the south-west of the town and draw Hawley out.

The short daylight of winter was already drawing in when Murray's advance units began to reach the summit of Falkirk Muir on 17 January 1746. There is much conjecture as to whether Hawley knew the Jacobites were extremely close to Falkirk or not. Some accounts speak of him returning late from a luncheon at Calendar House where he had been deliberately delayed by Lady Ann; others speak of his dismissing their close proximity as a mere patrol and not the whole army, so he was only able to react at the last minute when he realised that the whole Jacobite army was upon him. What is clear is that the Jacobites had just gained the high ground before the first of Hawley's men and therefore the Government

Impregnable Stirling Castle – the Jacobites never got near to capturing it in all their rebellions.

The rough scrub atop Falkirk Muir, seemingly unchanged since 1746.

troops were at a disadvantage from the start of the action. Hawley's failure to have proper troops stationed on the summit of the moor and on all of the approach roads towards Falkirk determined the course of the battle that was to follow. Once again, how many were involved is debatable. If Murray had all the men available, barring the 1,000 left to besiege Stirling, his force should have been around 8,000 men, but most sources put the number at between 5,200 and 6,500 men. This was considerably less than he should have had and given the list of clans present and the desire of Murray to keep the army together, the higher figure would seem the most accurate. Hawley left Edinburgh with 7,000 men, so, as there is no intervening action, one must assume that this was the size of his force before deployment; but again, differing interpretations have put his force at between 6,370 and 8,100. The map shows their positions just before the dragoons charged at the foremost Jacobite units on the hill; while the cavalry were facing the enemy, all of the Government troops should still have been marching south, and would have only faced the Jacobite lines once they had reached their position in the line. The artillery became bogged down on the edge of escarpment in very soft ground indicated by a marsh on the map.

Map L Battle of Falkirk Muir 17 January 1746

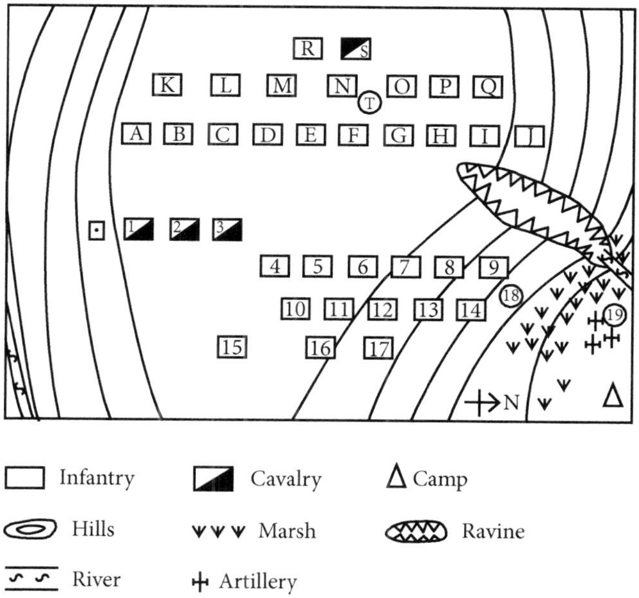

The Jacobite army was as follows:

A. Macdonalds of Keppoch
B. Macdonalds of Clanranald
C. Macdonalds of Glengarry
D. Farquharsons
E. Mackenzies

F. Macintoshs

G. MacPhersons

H. Frasers

I. Locheil Camerons

J. Appin Stewarts

K. Atholl brigade

L. Ogilvie's

M. Ogilvie's

N. Gordon's

O. Gordon's

P. MacLachlan's

Q. Drummond's

R. Irish Picquets

S. Elcho's

T. Lord Murray and Prince Charles

Hawley's Government army was as follows:

1. Hamilton's dragoons

2. Ligonier's dragoons

3. Cobham's dragoons

4. Wolfe's regiment

5. Cholmondeley's regiment

6. Pulteney's regiment

7. Price's regiment

8. Ligonier's regiment

9. Royal regiment

10. Blakeney's regiment

11. Munro's regiment

12. Fleming's regiment

13. Battereau's regiment

14. Barrell's regiment

15. Glasgow militia

16. Edinburgh volunteers

17. Howard's regiment

18. General Hawley

19. Artillery – stuck and unable to shoot

Whatever the reason for Hawley's delay, the daylight was fading fast. enhanced by the heavy and stormy winter weather, and the Government forces were still marching towards the enemy when some of the Jacobites were already formed up on the level ground at the top of the moor. Hawley was not aware of the true situation developing on that southern part of the moor and in trying to retrieve that knowledge and so regain control of the situation, Hawley sent his three dragoon regiments to secure the summit. By the time the dragoons were actually riding uphill to engage the rebels, it was around four in the afternoon and the storm, which had threatened for some time, now began to blow directly into the dragoons' faces. Seeing the rebel line ahead, all three of the dragoon units charged, but the Jacobite infantry held firm and loosed a volley of their muskets at around ten yards and killed eighty of the horsemen, driving back Hamilton's and Ligonier's dragoons in shock. Cobham's dragoons did charge home on the MacDonalds of Glengarry, but in what were clearly rehearsed tactics they kept low, avoided the dragoons' swords and stabbed the horses from below to bring both man and horse down. The other two unscathed MacDonald units charged the remaining dragoons, who turned and fled back down the hill. Some of the routing horsemen careered into the Glasgow militia, who are reported to have deliberately fired a volley into them for their action.

With the successful Jacobite charge on the right acting like a modern 'Mexican wave', the remainder of the Jacobite front line rose and charged. The Government regiments of foot were hardly formed, let alone in a position to shoot effectively, and the rain put an end to any hopes of an effective firefight. The first volley (of which the number of misfires is estimated at 25 per cent) failed to halt the Jacobite advance. The most southerly regiments at the front of the line, and the first to receive the charge, began to panic, which, according to a private of Barrell's regiment, spread like an infection, with the whole front following. Every regiment save Price's, Barrell's and Ligonier's had ceased firing; most infantry had fled save those on the extreme right of the line, protected from a charge by the ravine. Cobham's dragoons, the remaining horse, rallied and tried to regain the hill, but were

The Highlanders rout the dragoons – recreation of the Battle of Falkirk, 1746, in 15 mm.

driven off by the French-Irish Picquets who were protecting Charles and Murray. The atrocious weather, the onset of night, and the difficulty of the terrain in such conditions forced Hawley to withdraw what remained of his force to Linlithgow and then back to Edinburgh. He abandoned his guns and all his tents and equipment, having lost around 400 men, of whom some were killed, many were wounded and around 300 were captured. With no more than 120 killed or wounded, this was a resounding victory and an embarrassment for the Hanoverian forces. Unfortunately for the Jacobite cause the weather and the long winter night afforded Murray no time to regroup his forces and follow up his victory. This highlights a major weakness in the rebel forces, as there was no reliable cavalry force to follow up a victory and turn a beaten enemy into a broken one. Ironically, the French cavalry were some of the bravest in Europe and if the French had sent some to aid Charles, the rising may have had a very different outcome. If the Jacobites could have harassed and pushed Hawley's army to destruction, their position in Scotland would have been far more secure. It would also have bought them time to communicate with Louis XV and show that the time was right for a French invasion. Despite the building of a modern housing estate, a canal, railway and hospital, much can still be seen of the battle site, particularly the summit and higher parts of the moor together with parts of the ravine.

As expected, the continued Jacobite siege of Stirling Castle achieved nothing and in typical fashion, the Highlanders started to desert and return to their northern homes, causing Murray to advise Charles to abandon the siege and head north to the Highlands for the winter to regroup, ready to fight in the spring. The tension between Charles and Murray intensified and only with reluctance did Charles agree to head north, once more moving further away from London. On 29 January the Jacobite army began to break the siege and on 1 February, again in two separate columns, the clans and Murray headed north as they had hoped. While the rebels had pondered their future strategy, Cumberland had been busy making plans for his spring campaign and he arrived at Edinburgh on 30 January to take personal command.

On 4 February Cumberland began the slow pursuit of his quarry, but he was not intending to follow their central route through the Cairngorms and on to the Great Glen. Instead, he was going to head east to Aberdeen so that he could keep in contact with the Navy and receive supplies and reinforcements as required. Meanwhile in the Highlands, Loudon strengthened the defences of the strategic port of Inverness against the Jacobite retreat towards him. Cumberland's progress was almost instantly halted on 6 February when his army was held up at Perth by more atrocious weather, but good news arrived on the same day when 5,000 Hessian reinforcements at last arrived to replace those Dutch regiments who were ineligible to fight. Cumberland issued orders that these Hessians should garrison Perth, thereby blocking the route to Edinburgh should the Jacobites turn to march south again. While bad weather delayed Cumberland, the Jacobites, who were maybe ahead of the storms which affected the Hanoverians, made good speed. The first column, thanks to their captured artillery train, succeeded in besieging and capturing Ruthven Barracks, allowing the defenders safe passage to Perth. Leaving a small garrison to occupy the small, but strategically important, hilltop bastion, the

The steep drop into the ravine on Falkirk Moor.

The Falkirk 1746 memorial.

The snowy wilderness of a Highland winter drove many clans to starvation point.

second column continued towards Inverness. By 16 February the second column was just a few miles south of Inverness. On receiving intelligence that Charles was staying at Moy Castle for the night, Loudon attempted a night raid to capture the prince and end the war in one fell swoop, but by careful defending the attack was beaten off and Loudon returned empty-handed to Inverness. Two days later, seeing the size of the army that was now approaching his meagre force, Loudon abandoned Inverness and retreated further north to Dornoch. With the key port of Inverness and the top of the Great Glen now in their control, the Jacobite army halted and consolidated its position. Cumberland reached Aberdeen on 25 February and maintained his position for six weeks, deciding to fully muster his army and retrain it ahead of the forthcoming spring campaign, when he knew a decisive battle would have to be fought to stop the Jacobite rising. The armies were camped just over 100 miles apart.

Although the Jacobites controlled the head of the Great Glen there were still occupied Government garrisons along the valley. In early March Murray sent an expeditionary force down the glen to deal with these potential threats and besieged Fort Augustus for two days before a lucky shot hit the central magazine and blew most of the fort and garrison apart. One bastion corner still remains to be seen as part of the former Benedictine monastery, now luxury holiday apartments.

Flushed with success, the rebels took a formidable siege train with additional guns from Fort Augustus, and continued south towards Fort William at the southern end of the Great Glen. The exultant clans of Cameron of Lochiel and MacDonald of Keppoch, who were leading the advance against the forts, were the sworn enemies of the Campbells, who were defending Fort William, and they saw the siege as a chance of revenge, even taking time to write to Charles to inform him that they were going to declare war on Clan Campbell. The siege lasted from 20 March until 3 April, but the Jacobites could not repeat the lucky strike they had achieved on Fort Augustus. Captain Scott held fast to his task, aided by the Royal Navy, which supplied the fort with food, powder and ammunition by ships through

The remains of Fort Augustus have been incorporated into the later abbey, now a resort centre.

Loch Linnhe. Both sides exchanged many cannonades, doing some damage to each other, before Scott succeeding in knocking out completely one of the main Jacobite batteries. Eventually, after two weeks of bombardments, the garrison launched a sally which led to the capture of several Jacobite cannon and their mortars and ruined their casting forge. A day later a second such sortie knocked out the remaining Jacobite guns and now lacking firepower with which to carry on the siege, the Jacobites abandoned their works and started to march north back up the Great Glen. While this Jacobite expedition was only partly successful, Murray led an operation against Loudon at Dornoch and defeated him, taking 300 prisoners in the process, while those Hanoverian supporters that escaped fled still further north. But March was to end on a bad note for the Jacobites. On 25 March a French ship named *Le Prince Charles* carrying £12,000 and much needed supplies for the Jacobite army was forced into the Kyle of Tongue to escape from her pursuer, the British frigate HMS *Sheerness*. Despite managing to unload the money, the crew were surprised and attacked the next day by Captain Mackay at Drum Nan Coup.

Mackay was the son of the chief of the Clan Mackay, who were loyal to King George II, and after a brief fight, the crew and the Jacobites sent to escort the supplies were defeated and captured along with the money itself. This combined loss of men, munitions and money was a major blow to Charles's cause and deprived him of valuable resources which would have gained him more time now that the campaign season was about to begin again. With no more money to buy food or pay his men, Charles was committed to fighting as soon as possible before the already dwindling army totally dispersed. With news of the defeats at Fort William and Tongue, the Jacobite command sent out messages on 8 April to all of the men in outlying posts, recalling them back to Inverness ready to begin a major offensive. In contrast to the pressurised Jacobite command, Cumberland seemed calm

Tongue Bay, where the *Prince Charles* landed £12,000. (Courtesy of Alan Rowan)

and assured as he steadily laid his plans. When in early April he was satisfied that the weather had improved sufficiently to start campaigning again and that his men were ready for a fight, Cumberland led the army west from Aberdeen on 8 April, heading straight for his cousin Prince Charles and the Jacobite army at Inverness. Cumberland's strategy of keeping close to the coast for supplies paid extra dividends when the army came to cross the River Spey on 12 April. The river was guarded by a sizeable Jacobite force of 2,000 men, including all of the Jacobite cavalry, the Lowland regiments and over half of the army's French regular infantry. With the river fast flowing and waist deep, it should have been a perfect place to attack the three columns of Government troops as they crossed, but the Jacobites were under orders to fall back rather than engage. While Cumberland's men were approaching the river Commodore Smith, commanding the naval squadron supporting the army, allowed a ship to close in and broadside the Jacobites waiting on the western bank of the Spey. To mighty cheers from the red-coated ranks, the Jacobites retreated to Inverness and the red columns forded the river and marched steadily on.

When news of Cumberland's approach reached the Jacobite command on 13 April, plans were made to rendezvous at Culloden House on the edge of Drummossie Moor, east of Inverness. While Cumberland's consistent progress bought him to Nairn on 14 April, the Jacobite supply infrastructure collapsed due to the illness of Murray of Broughton, the prince's secretary. The responsibility for ensuring the army was fed fell on John Hay, who was simply not up to the task. As Charles's army gathered on Drummossie Moor, the carts of oatmeal (with which Charles was paying and feeding the men since the loss of his additional money) failed to appear. The result was that hundreds of Highlanders were off seeking food rather than being fed and rested for the battle to come. Contrary to George Murray's wishes, Charles gave Colonel O'Sullivan orders to draw up the army on the moor, which was rough with heather, shrubs, small marshes and pools, but was generally flat. Therefore no advantage would be given to either side and it was certainly not typical terrain for a Highland charge – the Jacobites' main weapon. Responding to Murray's concerns, Charles did send Brigadier Stapleton (of the Irish Picquets) and Colonel Ker to examine the ground Murray preferred, which was some hills on the other side of the Nairn. However, although they reported the ground most favourably, Charles would not consider moving, saying that they would not have time to remove all of their baggage and supplies from Inverness and would lose it to Cumberland before any battle could be fought. As 14 April drew on and it became clear that no attack was forthcoming, Charles was informed that 15 April was Cumberland's birthday and that his army would be celebrating, which was why the Duke was waiting before attacking – he wanted his birthday celebrated first.

The seeds of a plan developed in the Jacobite command foe a night march and a dawn attack on the British camp. Even Lord Murray approved of the plan, though only because he saw the moor chosen as no place for Highlanders to fight, so even a precarious raid was better than waiting on the moor. Plans were laid and the Jacobites set off, Charles personally thanking Murray for agreeing to the dawn attack. From the start it was a disaster, with the front units getting well ahead of the middle ones, who were slowing down all behind them. Some men, seeing this as a chance to find food and shelter, went off into the darkness and did not return with the light. After several hours, it was clearly not going to be a success and, rather than risk further confusion in the dark, Murray overruled the prince and ordered a retreat to the moor.

At dawn on 16 April around 5,000 men (out of what should have been an army of 7,000 men) collapsed, exhausted and starving, on the edge of Drummossie Moor, most having not eaten for a day with very little, if any, rest. On Charles's return to the moor, he fully believed that Cumberland would not move that day and gave orders for the men to rest as he set to ensuring they would be fed that day. With no pickets posted, the news that Cumberland was approaching caused panic in the rebel ranks. Charles himself took command and drew up the battle plan and unit deployment, but he was slow at dealing with the enclosures on the Jacobite right flank and the MacDonald clan began to dispute where they had been placed. There was a strict rotational etiquette among the clans as to which of them had the right to the coveted position of far right in the front battle line, which went back to the battle of Bannockburn in 1314. Such a place and at such a time was hardly the moment to have a dispute as to who was going to stand where and for the sake of the prince, the MacDonalds moved to the far left of the front line, promising to make a 'right out of the left'.

Cumberland had not altered his approach to the matter in hand since the campaign had started, as repetitive as the drums that his men marched to: he resolutely kept on closing on Charles and his army until he had them where he wanted them, on terrain which was more suitable for his men than for the Jacobites. Cumberland had clearly learnt three vital things, presumably from studying the reports of the historic and current rebellions. The first point is that the Jacobite artillery was for the most part ineffectual – only the lucky shot at Fort Augustus had caused any serious damage to a Government regiment or strongpoint in over sixty years. In contrast, at Glenshiel the mortars had wreaked havoc among the entrenched Jacobite positions, winning the battle by driving the defenders out of their positions. The second weakness was that the Jacobites had very little cavalry – if you got behind their lines they were vulnerable as the strength of a Jacobite force was going forward not in defence, and horsemen could exploit a weakness in the line or pursue a retreat to make sure that it became a rout. The third and final point was that if a Government foot regiment held firm, supported by its other regiments to the side and rear, the Jacobites could not break in to the line. Regarding this latter point, there is much debate among historians as to whether Cumberland, when he had the army for six weeks at Aberdeen, drummed into them a new bayonet drill, specifically designed to deal with the Highland charge. This bayonet drill was that each man, instead of bayoneting to his front (as per the existing manual), bayoneted to his right and so into the vacant shieldless area beneath the weapon arm of the attacking Highlander. This theory works if all Jacobites were right handed and all were using targes (shields), but some were using two-handed axes and others were using clubbed muskets and charged as a moving morass rather than a neat, disciplined line with their right arms stretched high and their shields held close to the chest and stomach. The new bayonet drill theory works in part, but not completely. Platoon firing was the standard British way of shooting muskets; if there were six platoons in a regiment then one platoon at a time would fire, going down the whole line, including all three ranks, and by the time the last one had fired the first would have reloaded. While this platoon firing worked in

Map M Battle of Culloden 16 April 1746

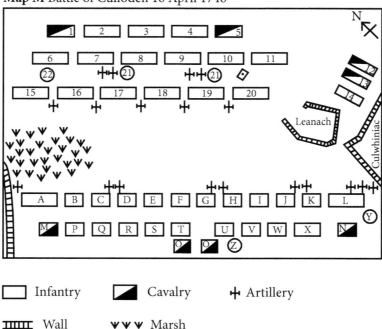

Infantry	Cavalry	✛ Artillery
Wall	ⱽⱽⱽ Marsh	

Europe, where battles were fought with parade ground tactics, it did not work against the Highlanders, who closed the ground so quickly with their charge that the platoon firing did not stop them. Stuart Reid advocates in his book *Cumberland's Army* that the change was not made in the direction of the bayonet drill, but in the combined use of the bayonet and how the regiment fired their muskets. Reid maintains that after the first volley was fired by the whole regiment, the front 'charged' their bayonets (levelled at the approaching enemy) to keep the Jacobite swordsmen or axemen at bay while allowing the second and third ranks to keep firing at point-blank range into the enemy.

The other great advantage that Cumberland had at Culloden was that he had between 7,000 and 8,000 men, most of them infantry, so outnumbered his cousin Charles by a ratio of three to two. Although there were only three regiments of dragoons, for the first time there was a detachment of the Royal Artillery Regiment, which meant properly trained bombardiers and fireworkers, and they had eighteen pieces of ordnance, twelve 3-pounder guns and 6 coehorn mortars, all light enough to move quickly in the difficult Scottish terrain. The carefully placed Government army was in three lines and was deployed as follows, with the calculations as to how many men were in each regiment.

1. Kingston's dragoons, 100 men
2. Pulteney's regiment, 400 men
3. Battereau's regiment, 360 men
4. Blakeney's regiment, 300 men

5. Kingston's dragoons, 100 men

6. Howard's regiment, 400 men

7. Fleming's regiment, 360 men

8. Bligh's regiment, 400 men

9. Semphill's regiment, 400 men

10. Ligonier's regiment, 320 men

11. Wolfe's regiment, 320 men

12. Kerr's dragoons, 300 men

13. Cobham's dragoons, 260 men

14. Argyle's men, 200 men

15. Royal regiment, 400 men

16. Cholmondeley's regiment, 400 men

17. Price's regiment, 300 men

18. Scot's Fusiliers, 360 men

19. Munro's regiment, 400 men

20. Barrell's regiment, 340 men

21. Coehorn mortars, 60 men

22. Duke of Cumberland, aides and personal bodyguard, 20 men

The Jacobite army was far weaker than it should have been, and at the start of the battle some men were rejoining at the rear, having been awoken by the gunfire, or returning from foraging the night before. Better managed, the prince could have commanded almost as many men as Cumberland fielded. Instead, through mismanagement, the prince had at most 5,500 men, but probably nearer to just 5,000, and their deployment was not as measured, and certainly not as planned, as the Government army opposite them. Eventually they deployed in two lines as below, most of them clan regiments where the lairds or the laird's sons would lead from the front. Most of the Jacobite army was infantry and the cavalry they did have was in very small units, mostly just eighty or 100 strong, certainly not strong enough to break through a line or defeat an enemy cavalry unit. For once the Jacobites did have some artillery, with a range of small pieces and with some experienced French crews, but they were short of the right calibre of shot to suit the cannons they possessed.

A. MacDonalds of Glengarry, 500 men

B. MacDonalds of Keppoch, 200 men

C. MacDonalds of Clanranald, 200 men

D. Chisholm, 150 men

E. Macleod, 120 men

F. MacLean, 290 men

G. Farquharson, 250 men

H. Chattan, 350 men

I. Fraser, 400 men

J. Stewarts of Appin and MacLean's, 250 men

K. Camerons, 400 men

L. Atholl men, 500 men

M. Highland Horse and Baggot's Hussars, 100 men

N. Fitzjames's Horse, 80 men

O. Mixed Horse units as reserve

P. Irish Picquets

Q. Duke of Perth

R. Glenbucket

S. Kilmarnock

T. John Roy Stewart

U. Lord Lewis Gordon

V. Lord Ogilvy

W. Lord Ogilvy

X. French Infantry

Y. Lord Murray

Z. Prince Charles

Artillery, 50 men

At about 1 p.m. the small Jacobite guns opened fire, to be met with a far more effective barrage from the Government cannons and mortars. In the confusion of the Jacobite deployment much time had been lost deciding what to do about the enclosures on their right. In the end they were ignored, but this afforded Cumberland the chance to use them, and his left flank set about occupying them under cover of the artillery exchanges. Such was the accuracy with which the Royal Artillery was hitting the Jacobite right wing that Cumberland was content to let it continue, the Atholl men, the Camerons, and Stewarts and Maclarens suffering the worst of it. The clan regiments receiving the casualties without the ability to reply were far from content and questioned with Murray why they had to continue suffering casualties from the barrage. It may have been that as much as fifteen minutes had passed, some reports say thirty minutes, before Murray got word through to the prince, who ordered the charge. This order, though, was also miscommunicated and the charge did not go off as one full line; the right units (who were already straining at the leash to be let loose to silence the guns which were shooting at them) went off first and they were closely followed by some of the centre front line units. In a staggered charge the line began to close on the redcoat line ahead of them, but when Price's and Scot's Fusiliers in the centre of the Government line fired their first volley, the Jacobites veered right into their own men. This meant that a quarter of Charles's army was heading straight for the two regiments on the left of the Government line – Munro's and Barrell's. This bunching of the Jacobite right restricted their ability to shoot their own weapons and as they closed in for the impact they were hit with grape shot from the cannon, musket volleys from Munro's and Barrell's regiments, and, as a final shock, they were enfiladed by Wolfe's regiment, which had been brought up to the Leanach enclosure. In spite of the

The remains of the enclosures upon Culloden.

Cobham's 10th Dragoons in pursuit. (Courtesy of the Lace Wars)

The Atholl memorial gravestone at Culloden.

losses suffered, the Highlanders took the cannon ahead of them and crashed into Munro's, Barrell's and Semphill's regiments in the second line. There was a ferocious hand-to-hand struggle in which Reid's hypothesis stands up, because despite being engaged in melee the Government infantry continued to fire. So close were these regiments that both Semphill's and Wolfe's regiments, by firing into the melee, were causing casualties to both the rebels and their own men, until the order came from General Huske, commanding the second line, to 'give them the bayonet'. The casualties being inflicted on the Jacobite right were increased when the Campbells emerged from the enclosure and joined in the flank attack on the already trapped Highlanders with their own bayonets and swords.

And what of the Jacobite left? When the centre and right of the Jacobite front line charged obliquely to the right, they left the MacDonalds facing three red-coated regiments about to shoot at them and with no flank protection on either side they were totally exposed. Worse still, ahead of them the ground was marshy and difficult to charge across, meaning that they would receive several volleys from at least two (maybe three) regiments before they closed with their enemy. Despite being at a great disadvantage, the MacDonalds thrice advanced in order to try and draw the redcoats to shoot at long range, but the redcoats stood fast to their training and would not be drawn to fire. While the MacDonalds tried to tempt the volleys to their front, the battle on the right was already over. The Jacobites who had charged were in retreat and the rest of the army also began to retreat in a series of controlled withdrawals so as to prevent a rout and the massacre that would ensue if they were caught by the dragoons; the Ogilvys' Forfar men even formed a withdrawing square to foil the dragoons from attacking. At the rear of the rebel army there was suddenly a threat to Charles himself, when the dragoons broke out from the enclosures on to their rear right flank and they were crowded into a small space. In haste, Fitzjames's horse and some of the mounted Highland reserve rode up to block the dragoons' advance. Neither side moved to attack one another, but the few minutes that passed in stalemate gave sufficient time for the remaining troops on the right side of the prince's army to retreat in order.

The Government army was now advancing slowly, shooting at groups of the enemy, bayoneting any wounded or any individuals in retreat that they overtook. On the left flank the MacDonalds were aided by the French and Irish and despite being outnumbered, they held their ranks well, aided surprisingly by one cannon which had arrived late and had swung into action from the rear. This lone gun shooting in support of the retreating men ahead of it did such damage that no less than four cannon and a mortar were brought forward to silence it. The French, Irish and the MacDonalds were the last to leave the battlefield. The whole bloody encounter had lasted almost an hour, of which the first quarter at least had been an unequal artillery duel. Cumberland now unleashed his dragoons for the role they were intended: to keep the enemy running, killing as many in the pursuit as possible. Cumberland would bring a finality to this rebellion that had been missing after the '15 and '19 risings.

Cumberland lost between 50 and 100 men killed and around 300 were wounded, many from Barrell's regiment, some of which were clearly caused by Wolfe's regiment shooting into the melee directly in front of them. The Jacobites lost at least 1,250 men killed, with a similar number wounded and 376 prisoners being taken, of whom only 154 were Scottish, the rest

The author at the central cairn on Culloden Battlefield.

Ruthven Barracks, ruined since the end of the '45 rebellion.

The Bay of Loch Nan Uamh, where the final naval action took place.

being regular French and French-Irish soldiers. In the aftermath a further 120 Highlanders were executed and 936 transported to the colonies, similar treatments to those meted out to the prisoners taken after Sedgemoor when James's army had triumphed over Monmouth. The military campaign had effectively come to an end. The clans had scattered so Charles called for them to gather at the ruins of Fort Augustus; however, the majority who could regroup had gathered at Ruthven Barracks, where there were around 1,500 awaiting the prince's instructions. The prince sent a letter to the Highland chiefs, inviting them all to 'look to themselves' as the Stuart rising was officially over. On hearing the news at Ruthven, Murray sent a letter, dated 1 April, to Charles tendering his resignation of office and heavily criticising the prince's management for the last few months of the campaign and his choice of battle site. Clearly the letter had been started two weeks before Culloden, with Murray adding his footnotes, which referred to the defeat, while at Ruthven. The clans dispersed and made their own way home, looking to find shelter and protection from friends and family as time and fortune allowed. Few would escape the purges that would follow.

There was still one last combative action of the rising to be fought. On 30 April 1746 two thirty-six-gun French privateers arrived in the bay of Loch Nan Uamh, the very place Charles had landed just a few months ago. The ships brought brandy, powder, weapons and gold for Charles's campaign, but it was too late. On hearing that Charles was not on hand, the captain of the French ships, the *Mars* and the *Bellone*, wanted to leave with all his supplies intact for the prince. The arrival of three British ships changed his mind and, having off-loaded their cargo, the ships engaged the three Royal Navy vessels in a long and damaging battle which the French ships won. The next morning they sailed for home with Lord Perth, Lord John Drummond, Lord Elcho and others who had accompanied Charles. Charles had separated from these men earlier and spent months criss-crossing the Western Isles of Scotland, often evading capture by minutes, while he sought a ship for France. On 16 June 1746 Flora MacDonald became the heroine for the Stuart cause when she helped Prince Charles on the Isle of Skye, assisting his escape by dressing him as a woman; this part of his escape is one of the best known facts about the whole of the prince's life. It would take until 20 September 1746 for Bonnie Prince Charlie to board a boat that would ensure his escape back to France.

By the time that Charles escaped, Cumberland was long gone. Having achieved his first objective of putting down the rising, he regrouped at Fort Augustus, which remained his headquarters until the middle of August. There he wrote to the Prime Minister, advising him that his second objective was 'to destroy utterly the spirit of rebellion in the Highlands' and that he had handed over command to Lord Albemarle and General John Campbell before returning to England. Phase two, from Cumberland's perspective, was the harrying of the glens and the destruction of the property and the homes of the Jacobite chiefs and their clansmen. The burning was widespread. Castles, homes and in some cases every property within a glen were destroyed – those clans who had supported the Stuarts were now paying a heavy price. Cumberland was right – the clans' spirit of rebellion was broken and the clans did not rise again.

Footnote

In 1759, at the height of the Seven Years War (1756–1763), France was being humiliated all over the known world by the skill of the British armed forces on both land and sea. The result was that Louis XV, almost in desperation it seems, tried once again to encourage the 'Young Pretender' to invade Britain. At a secret meeting in Paris, a plan was put before Charles involving a French army of 100,000 which would end Britain's involvement in the Seven Years War at a single stroke. Such a victory would also force Britain to hand back all of the territorial gains she had made thus far in the war. Charles was reputedly drunk and late for the appointment and showed very little interest in the plan or in raising the Highlanders again. The French abandoned the thought of using Charles or the Stuart cause and the draft plan continued until two naval defeats to the British Navy at Lagos and then Quiberon Bay further weakened Louis's navies and destroyed any chance of an invasion.

Conclusions

The '45 rebellion is unusual in many ways. The main campaign was fought from September until April when normally a campaign would be fought from April until October. Fighting over the winter caused logistical problems for the Jacobites with regards to keeping the army fed, dry and warm when on campaign without it dispersing widely, looking for shelter, the moment it was stuck in the open. For the Government, they knew that fighting in wet weather with an army that relied on musket fire made them vulnerable to the Jacobites, who favoured hand-to-hand combat as quickly as possible, so halting the deadly redcoat volleys. On most occasions the spies for both sides did an admirable job of keeping their masters informed of their opponent's troop movements, yet incredibly the armies managed to bypass each other several times, seemingly ignorant of how close they were to each other.

The army that successive Jacobite commanders led into battle had changed little from the army that John Graham, the Marquis of Montrose, that great champion of the Royalist cause in Scotland, had led in a blistering campaign in 1644–45. He led a small but determined army which pulled off a string of sensational victories against overwhelming odds while marching at an unrivalled pace against his enemies through at times an atrocious Highland winter. Montrose used the terrain coupled with the icy steel of his men to out-think and outfight his opponents and in doing so spread fear through his enemies. He fought and won the Battle of Inverlochy, for example, when outnumbered two to one in just seven ferocious minutes, slaying half of the enemy in the ensuing rout. There are undoubted parallels to the armies that Dundee and Murray would lead and the battles that they would win, but sadly for the Stuart cause the outcome for the Jacobites would be the same as for the Royalists 100 years earlier. The Jacobites could only win battles if they played to all their strengths every time, and they could only win the overall campaign and put a Stuart back on the throne if they won every battle and convinced the people of England that a Stuart king was a better option than a Dutch or German one. 1715 was their best chance and through a lack of strategic military and political planning, what should have been a coordinated rising became a series of mismanaged campaigns. The reason that Cumberland succeeded where the other British commanders had failed is because he was the first commander on either side to mastermind a complete plan of campaign. He also stuck methodically to his plan and came up with a style of fighting to counter the Jacobite strengths. The old adage of 'know your enemy' was certainly reflected in Cumberland's approach; he had clearly studied and learned from the previous failures. Cumberland also knew that once your opponent is down you have to finish him off; you cannot let more blood be spilt because you allowed the beast to rise again and create another rebellion. The Stuart risings were akin to the Hydra of mythology – every time the head of one rising was removed, another one grew – but Cumberland was determined that all of the heads would be removed this time. One cannot forgive the brutality and the destruction of the clans' way of life that followed Cumberland's victory at Culloden, nor the lame evidence that the Jacobites had sworn to give 'no quarter' in their orders – something that there has never been any evidence for. One can understand why in a different age such brutality was applied, but even for the time the late 1740s were made unforgivably hard for many of the innocent victims of the '45 rebellion. Worse still, they paved the way for the Highland clearances that would follow. No one doubts that the clan way of life could not last forever, but these remote people who had their own language and long-standing customs should have been allowed to develop their changing society themselves, not have it burnt into their homes, their glens and their mountainsides.

Like the majority of the Stuarts, Charles Edward had some fundamental flaws in his character and like his ancestor, Charles I, his stubborn streak would emerge to the detriment of his final campaign. Unlike Charles I, who proved to be an able field commander, Charles Edward possessed no military prowess and would ignore experience for favouritism, believing in an almost childlike way that his Highlanders were invincible. He increasingly ignored the advice of his more experienced generals, which ultimately led to their final and crushing defeat.

The Stuart risings were doomed for a whole range of reasons, some of which were military, but just as many were religious, political and socio-economic ones. On the occasions where they were briefly in control of Sheriffmuir, Derby and Falkirk, the Jacobite command failed to exploit that brief moment of advantage and instead of learning from their mistakes, they went to repeat them time and again. The final time the Jacobites lost was because they fought when simply everything was against them – they were tired, outnumbered, the terrain was against them and they were led by someone who was really only out for himself. In many ways each of the Stuarts is a true Shakespearian tragic hero. There was so much that they could have done to have ensured that the people and Parliament were with them long before they ever lost power. Had James II taken that flexible approach at the outset, the Stuarts would not have wasted the next sixty years trying to get their power back, destroying many thousands of lives in doing so.

Rules for Recreating Battles of the Jacobite Rebellions

Across the spectrum of tabletop wargaming, each period of history has something that sets it aside from all of the others, making it unique and thereby providing the gamer with a new set of challenges to overcome. The Jacobite period of history is no exception, spanning as it does almost sixty years of history. This was a time where warfare changed from the old reliance on a balance between 'pike and musket', to the new era where each man, via the use of the newly invented bayonet, became his own pikeman, able to ward off, if properly formed up, the more deadly and mobile cavalry. Properly formed troops therefore could be hard to break down. The Jacobite army, however, still fought in their traditional Highland manner, a tactic employed for more than 1,000 years, which consisted of a great charge delivered at high speed directly into the enemy ranks with cries and whoops of bloodcurdling terror. As we have seen, this was effective against raw untrained recruits and even against tired or ill prepared troops, but against properly prepared ranks of infantry on flat terrain, the bravery alone of the Jacobite charges was not sufficient to defeat their opponents.

There are several advantages that the Jacobite period has over other Continental wars at this time. Foremost is the fact that all of the battles were fought in the British Isles and so a variety of modern maps are freely available to allow gamers to follow and refight the campaigns in detail. Secondly, while much larger battles involving many thousands of troops were taking place on the European mainland, the battles at home involved much smaller numbers of men, which means that the gamer does not require as many figures to either recreate the battles or to refight the campaign. Also, the troops within the respective armies were colourful and contrasted one another well: the red ranks of the British forces, the red and blue of the French and the white of the Spanish contrasted well with the individual colours of the Highland weave that some of the Jacobites wore and were in even starker contrast to the semi-naked, shirt-clad tenants who made up a fair proportion of the Jacobite ranks. We know that even the tactics were at odds with one another, as the Highlanders relied on their blood curdling charge to break the enemy ranks, whereas the armies of Europe deployed their neat ranks of lace-clad troops with parade ground precision and fought a war of attrition in almost chess-like symmetry, tactics that left thousands of dead on every battlefield. Finally, the war allowed for small-scale naval actions between ships of the French and Spanish navies as they vied with the British squadrons valiantly blocking their attempts to bring material support to the Jacobite cause.

As the reader will now appreciate, the greatest challenge to anyone writing a set of rules for this period is how to recreate these battles in miniature so as to allow for the sharp contrasts between the fortunes of the armies in the battles documented in the previous chapters. Apart from at the last and decisive encounter, Culloden, the Jacobite army had the advantage, with the ability to cross difficult terrain, charge at an effective pace, take a higher proportion of casualties than Government troops and still continue to fight. Even when they took heavy casualties, such as at Killiecrankie, they were still capable of hitting the opposition with a frontal assault of such force that it could disintegrate. How else does one account for the superb way in which Hamilton, at Sheriffmuir, fought a strategic withdrawal, beating off no less than twelve cavalry charges in the process and losing fewer men than his assailants? Therefore, the rules have to give a working rigidity but with some inbuilt flexibility that gives the Jacobite army the chance of achieving success without being biased in their favour. Thus, the rules have to allow for the British to be caught unawares, perhaps on difficult terrain, or prevented from using their firepower by inclement weather. If the Jacobites were caught in a firefight then they would suffer heavy casualties, but if they were able to avoid the devastating volleys as they charged home, then they could inflict a murderous toll on the Government ranks in melee. If the Government troops stood firm on good ground, the Jacobites would be unlikely to break the line. What follows then is a tried and tested set of rules, entitled 'Raise the Clans', which allows these two distinctly different armies to come together in conflict with each side capable of beating the other.

Figures and Scales

The choice of figures and the variety available for this period has never been greater and is increasing all the time. Compared to other battles of the eighteenth century, where tens of thousands of men were deployed in each army, the majority of the Jacobite battles were fought between armies that were well below 10,000 men – even at Culloden there were only around 15,000 men in total. Figures are commercially available in a range from 28 mm down to 6 mm. In the larger scale, regiments would tend to be represented by around twenty figures, with a ratio of men to figures of between twenty to one and thirty to one. Regiments of this period were often woefully below paper strength and the Jacobite units could range from eighty to 800 in strength. If using 6-mm or 10-mm figures, a gamer can collect an army of thousands of figures so that many of the battles can be fought on a ratio of four to one or less. The use of smaller scale figures does make the gaming area more expansive, allowing large, flowing flanking movements and more tactical defensive manoeuvres to be undertaken, something which is not always possible with the larger sized figures if the table is less than 8 by 6 feet. Unless one is lucky enough to have a room to dedicate to the hobby, most people are restricted to the size of their dining table, but bear in mind the bigger the gaming area one can get, the more varied and rewarding the military action becomes.

In addition to the figures there is a good variety of scenery, including buildings, available. The model buildings are usually made from resin, and generally come ready assembled and sometimes painted, depending on the manufacturer and the budget the gamer has at their disposal. There is always the option of scratch-building one's own pieces to match particular structures that were present during a campaign. Other materials for recreating a battle in miniature include trees, walls, hedges, pools and rivers, which are all available from a wide range of manufacturers, details of which appear in the appendices. Most gamers will already have collections of these typical geographical features with which to dress their tabletop and as long as the bases of the trees blend in with the table colour, there is no need for further outlay. The best way to appreciate the variety of armies and scenery is to attend a wargaming convention. Hundreds of these events are held every year all over the world, details of which can be found in all of the monthly magazines that are published on the hobby as well as online. Details of some of the major shows are to be found in the appendices. A convention will have a whole host of traders, covering between them every aspect of the hobby, some of whom will be putting on demonstrations and participation games to introduce different gaming periods to new players, thereby allowing the enthusiast to try out a new period of history before any financial outlay.

Models available for the Government troops will be marching, charging, loading and shooting their muskets and as regular troops they look the part when assembled in their neat ranks performing parade ground manoeuvres. The same is true of both the allied Protestant troops that fought for the Government and those French and Spanish troops sent by their Catholic monarchs to support the Jacobite claim. The Jacobite figures tend to be much more fluid in movement and many castings are available with them running and shooting while on the move. The figure manufacturers have correctly captured the styles in which these troops fought: some men carry the Lochaber axe, some swords and targes and others bows, muskets and pistols. For a realistic Jacobite unit, a good mix of figures in a variety of poses and positions gives the look of a more disorganised unit and reflects the variety of weapons and clothing worn by the clans supporting the Stuart cause. The scale of the figures to the actual men involved depends on the budget of the gamer and the space available to set up a battlefield terrain but most players use around twenty men to one figure, which is what these rules have been developed for, with fifteen figures on the tabletop representing a 300 man dragoon regiment. For street fighting and for ship to ship battles then the scale is one to one.

The 'Raise the Clans' Rule System

Here follows a set of mechanics and tables which allow players to both recreate in miniature the battles that have been described in this book and to create their own fictitious encounters, either by agreed design or by accidental encounter through a fully executed campaign. The aim of this system is to provide the players with a rule structure that is both swift to play and recreates in a realistic manner the type of warfare which typified these scattered series of wars collectively known as the Jacobite rebellions. All that the players will need are some measuring implements – recommended implements include a retracting rule or a standard 12 inch ruler, and a protractor for working out curved moves and angles of fire. The players will require some standard six-sided dice and some ten- or twenty-sided dice to generate scores from 1 to 10 (0). To assist the speed at which the game can be played once the players have read through the rules a number of times, and also to save the gamer from thumbing through this rule section when playing a game, a two-page quick reference sheet has been compiled which contains all of the main tables and this has been included in the appendices on pages 183 and 184. It is recommended that these two pages be photocopied, placed back to back and laminated to give the players a sturdy and durable play sheet, a procedure for which the author readily gives his permission.

Dice

Dice are used throughout the rules to bring an element of chance to both the movement of troops and to the damage caused by both artillery and musket fire. The rules will refer to a particular die which will need to be thrown at a specific time – a six-sided die will, for example, be referred to as D6. Both a D10 and a D20 generate scores from 01 (1) to 00 (100) and are used to give a much greater range of numbers than when using the more common six-sided die. It is the flexibility offered by these dice that allows for a much more expansive set of tables, creating more accurate results than simply counting the number of sixes that have been thrown. In addition, as most rolls are made for whole units this speeds up the overall moving and shooting actions within a game move, especially compared to some systems where a D6 has to be thrown for every single figure involved and in some cases several times per move. This is not only time consuming but it can also generate freak results where if the majority of dice happen to settle as a six, casualties can be caused which are way out of proportion to what we know happened historically. The chances of causing casualties here are scaled based upon the casualties caused in battles of the period and then proportioned down to the scale of the troops. The dice thrown within the *Raise the Clans* system are designed to provide a slight deviation from the predetermined tables, ensuring that those small 'chance' elements of war are reflected within the conflict of the game.

   Despite trying to cover every eventuality within the depth of this rule system, complex situations will occasionally arise which are unique either to that battle or to a particular situation within that battle and they can seem tricky to resolve. This is true for all wargames, which is why the larger tournaments always have umpires to administer on any unusual circumstance that has arisen. Common sense must prevail and if all else fails then the issue can be resolved with a simple D10. It is worth saying at this point that the author has recreated many battles from different periods of history and it is uncanny, in spite of giving the generals a free hand to fight the battle in their own way, how the recreation on the table top has mirrored the original battle.

Scale

All the distances are given in inches to allow moves and ranges to be quickly measured and they are designed for 20-, 25- and 28-mm figures. If players are using 15-, 12-, 10- or 6-mm scale figures then simply use centimetres as the distance instead of inches, so that whereas a 28-mm horseman might move 12 inches on the table, a 15-mm or 6-mm one will move 12 cm – these distances work equally well with all the smaller scale of figures. Each figure is assumed to carry a sword or knife with which to defend themselves at close quarters if their principal weapon has been lost. Musket-armed infantry are known to have clubbed the butt end of the musket into an opponent if the bayonet is lost or broken off.

Troop Types and Base Sizes

It is important that all of the troops are based to match, one common type with another. For instance, light troops should be on bases that allow them to be more dispersed than regular troops. The short table below lists all of the basic troop types and the size of base that one figure should occupy; because of the accuracy required, the size given is for one wargame figure in millimetres (mm). To aid the speed of movement on the table a regiment of twenty men would not all be based on individual bases; instead allow for two lines of ten men, with four bases of four men, one base of two men and two bases of one man. Thus the unit can stand in a ten man line, two ranks deep. It could also be in column with a two man line, ten ranks deep, or combination thereof.

Troop Type	Frontage	Depth	Notes
Regular line infantry	20 mm	25 mm	Standard for all Government troops and militia
Highland infantry	20 mm	25 mm	Includes all Catholic units from France and Spain
Light infantry, rangers	25 mm	30 mm	Very few were used in the Jacobite wars
All cavalry	25 mm	50 mm	Dragoons, Hussars and Lifeguards
Officers/mounted	30 mm	50 mm	Includes bodyguards and individual personalities
Aide de Camp	25 mm	50 mm	For all types of mounted battlefield messengers
Artillerymen	20 mm	25 mm	Includes engineers, horse holders, so forth
Artillery/wagons	Special	Special	Bases made to fit the different size of models

All armies will have generals and sub-generals running through the chain of command while under them would be the regiments, which will each have officers, standard bearers as well as the drummers and fifers to beat out the orders. The clans will have standard bearers, pipers and their own family clan hierarchy, which can be represented on the tabletop by a small group of figures in a mixture of poses providing a neat cameo. Some generals had small personal units of bodyguards – the Duke of Cumberland, for example, had sixteen Austro-Hungarian/German troopers – which would be represented by a single wargames figure; both of these troop types would be classed as individuals for movement purposes. All senior officers above regimental level are also important as they have a direct effect on the morale of a unit. If you already have troops based for this period then there is no need to rebase them; the most important thing whatever rule system you are using, is that both of the armies are based to the same principles.

Compass Point Marker

It is much simpler to write complicated orders, detail the more intricate moves and determine long range artillery shots if the table has a small marker in a convenient corner of the battlefield that shows the compass points. A simple one can be made in a matter of seconds using a spare piece of card, with the points clearly marked with a large point marker pen so that wherever it is located the players can clearly see which side of the table equates to which direction. This is particularly important when the weather comes into consideration, as it should do in all battles; the presence of the wind and rain can have a dramatic effect.

Setting up the Battlefield

If the battle about to be fought is part of a campaign then the terrain layout will be governed by the location upon the map where the armies have met – see section below on creating such a campaign. The miniature scenery should be placed upon the table to reflect that location before the relevant armies are deployed and the player whose army arrived first has the choice of where to deploy first. Sometimes, though, a game will be set up from scratch and so the terrain will need to be created randomly to give the miniature armies a realistic battlefield to fight over. On average there will be between six and twelve pieces of terrain in place, which can be simple and common features such as hills, woods, fields, walls, buildings, rivers, marshes and cliffs, or more complex items such as mountains, villages, ravines or castles. Twelve may seem a lot, but remember that many features can be layered: woods, walls, buildings and pools can all be placed on top of hills, for example. The first thing to do is work out how many square feet the battlefield covers; thus a 6 foot by 4 foot battlefield would equate to 24 square feet. For every 2 square feet there should be a terrain feature, the rest of the battlefield being flat and representing flat grasslands, moor, plain or heathland, depending on what kind of country the armies are moving in. It could be the rolling or flat agricultural land of Derbyshire where the Jacobites decided to turn around and retreat north, or the rugged Scottish Highlands where the Jacobites decided to retreat – these differing landscape elements need to be taken into consideration.

In this example there would need to be twelve pieces of terrain, each player generating six pieces each in alternate moves and placing them where they will. For example, player A may throw and receive a hill, and then a wood in his next turn, which he might decide to place upon the hill. If two or more rivers are selected then they must be allowed to meet up, irrespective of how many pieces of terrain have been chosen. All rivers must either flow to the table's edge or into a cave or a pool. A generation table has been provided, by which players are able randomly to choose the terrain for their battlefield by simply making a percentage roll for each piece of terrain and placing the appropriate model upon the table. No terrain piece should cover an area of more than 1 square foot, and rivers should be no wider than 6 inches. Note that all forests are twice as dense as woods. Players must decide at this point which hills can be climbed, charged up and down (clearly steep hills and cliffs cannot be charged up or down by every type of troops), which rivers can be crossed without the aid of a ford or bridge and so forth, so that everyone is aware of any restrictions that might be placed on their troops before sides are chosen and deployment of those troops begins. These terrain elements and what is possible are all about common sense.

Roads always create something of a dilemma as their quality, and whether they aid movement or hamper it, needs to be decided upon. One reads of guns sticking in the quagmires that many of the unpathed roads became after wet weather, whereas if they were baked hard by a long, dry summer then they would be perfect to march along though the potholes would be a hindrance to any wheeled vehicles. Having worked as a re-enactor in an artillery regiment in the English Civil War Society, the author knows that even on rough terrain a small 3-lb or 4-lb cannon can (if properly drilled) be quite easily manhandled by a gun crew over hedges, walls and dragged along to positions some miles away by hand on drag ropes. Once again, therefore, it is important to take account of the impact of the weather and the quality of the roads before the battle commences.

Terrain Generation Table

Score Terrain piece and relevant considerations

01–05   Castle which can be manned and defended by forty figures and ten cannon, counts as solid cover.

06–10   Walled field which contains crops from April until September, ploughed field during the other months.

11–15   Hedged field which contains crops from April until September, ploughed field during the other months.

16–20   Farm, with three buildings and adjoining walls which will make it completely enclosed, is hard cover.

21–25   Low hill which impedes all uphill movement by 25 per cent; downhill move increase by 25 per cent

26–30   Broad river which is not crossable except by a bridge or a recognised ford.

31–35   Pool of still water. If two such pools occur next to each other this becomes a loch or lake.

36–40   Village, which consists of six buildings with a mixture of hedges and walls around them, is soft cover.

41–45   Rolling grassland, no effect on troop movements

46–50   Moor, barren and windswept with small clumps of bushes and scattered trees.

51–55   Moor, barren and windswept with small clumps of bushes and scattered trees.

56–60   High hill with a cliff on one side which cannot be traversed; uphill movement reduced by 50 per cent.

61–65   Rolling grassland, no effect on troop movements.

66–70   Wood, if two woods occur next to each other these areas become an impassable dense forest.

71–75   Low hill which impedes all uphill movement by 25 per cent; downhill move increase by 25 per cent.

76–80   Marsh, can only be crossed by light foot troops and at a half of normal speed.

81–85   A stream through grassland which is no barrier to troop movements.

86–90   High hills with a narrow valley running through it – a river may pass through this valley.

91–95   High Hill, if two high hills occur next to each other these become an impassable mountainous area.

96–00   Coastal area with a sea inlet or a loch which can be navigable by ships with up to forty guns.

Cover on the Battlefield

Many of the above features will provide troops moving or fighting on the battlefield with some form of shelter. This cover falls into three types: soft, hard and solid. Solid cover is provided by those stalwart fortresses such as Stirling or Edinburgh castles, or the new Government strongholds such as Fort George and Fort William, which were designed to hold out against a siege and were so strong that only an army equipped with an uninterrupted supply line and the very latest siege train would be capable of attacking it with any degree of success. Such indomitable bastions are so strong that any attempts to assault them would be a complete waste of men and resources. Far more relevant are the terrain features to be found as one passes along on any day of the year almost anywhere in the country: hedges, woods, low walls, high walls and fences, scattered farms and dwellings. These are categorised according to how much an obstacle they are and how much protection they might give to any troops sheltering behind it from missile attack or from a direct frontal assault. These different types of terrain are classified as follows:

Soft Cover	Boats, carts, fences, hedges, limbers, timber dwellings, wagons and woods.
Hard Cover	Brick buildings, dykes, forests, ships, stone walls, ruined castles and towers.
Solid Cover	Castles and Government forts in solid repair, manned and provisioned for defence.

Deploying the Armies

Once the terrain has been positioned onto the battlefield area it is necessary to decide which player has which side of that battlefield to deploy their armies upon. If it is not part of a campaign where the arrival of the troops determines the dispositions then the simplest way to decide is for both players to make a single dice roll and the player with the highest score deploys first. However, that player also gets the benefit of choosing which side of the table to deploy upon.

Alternative methods of deployment now follow because a game is much quicker to set up if both sides can deploy at the same time. The first and most hazardous for both players is where a D10 (or two D10 if it is a large army) is rolled, with the number indicating which unit is to be deployed upon the table first. In this method both players start in the left hand corner as they look at the table and they then work to their right. This provides both players with an equal disadvantage, as neither player is likely to end up with their troops starting where they would like them to be. This method works well if a solo game is being played where one person is commanding for both sides, perhaps getting familiar with the armies, the rules, or trying out new tactics in advance of a tournament. The second and most common method of deployment is for both players to draw on a separate piece of scrap paper a simple plan of the battlefield showing the main terrain pieces and where their units are to be placed in relation to that terrain; they are indexed by the number of the unit from their respective army list. Both players agree a time limit to prepare this map, say five minutes, and then once both players have finished they place their maps on the table and deploy their troops accordingly to match their sketches. These drawings should be able to take account of any questions that arise relating to the deployment of either side. The third way is one that I have developed using the numbered tiles from a game called 'Rummikub' (produced by Spears Games), which is available at most toy shops. The game contains a series of cream tiles, in four different coloured sets, each numbered 1 to 14. These are perfect for representing the unit numbers on an army list and placing the tiles face down where a unit is to be placed, which saves the time of drawing the sketch maps. The two blank 'jokers' are also placed upon the table so that the opponent does not know exactly where all the units will be going. Once both sides are completely deployed the tiles are replaced by the actual figures. Once all of the troops are deployed, orders can be written and the game is ready to begin.

Classification of Troops

We have the advantage with this period that the quality of some of the troops is known and therefore, as the armies that the players use will have been prepared in advance, there is no need when recreating actual battles to have the random generation of a unit's quality. Sometimes it is desirable to add a little variety to a game and to reflect the inconsistent quality that can befall certain regiments within an army, especially if a fictional encounter is being played out. Therefore, players may choose to grade some of their troops to set them aside from the rest of the rank and file. If this option is chosen, then for each army players pick three units of their own to be classed as elite troops, which will have better fighting ability and also higher morale. However, to counter this advantage each player must also pick two units that are not as skilled and which are unused to the horror of a battlefield. They are raw units and so have a lower morale factor and will be less reliable in battle. These units are noted by the player for later reference, but they need not be declared to the other players until their attributes come to be tested as the game unfolds.

Game Moves

The four 'Ms' govern the order of events for each move in a historical battle: Movement, Missiles, Melees and Morale, but before any of those four can be executed, battlefield orders have to be written.

Orders

These fall into two types: firstly, standing orders for the overall army for the forthcoming battle; and secondly, any special instructions for any individual unit which the player has singled out to perform a specific action. The former type of order might be 'all regiments in the second line to hold their position irrespective of what happens to the front line'. This is straightforward, so no matter whether the front line advances or retreats, the second line is to remain as a defensive formation. The latter would be more complicated in nature, such as giving instruction to a dragoon regiment to 'ride away on the right flank of the battlefield and take up a position in the farmhouse on the ridge and fire upon the enemy flank'. No matter what the dragoons find, they have instructions to capture and hold the farmhouse; if they find it occupied and a fight ensues then it is the results of that action and the morale of the dragoons thereafter which will determine if they carry out their general's instructions to the letter. Finally, certain musical drum-beat commands would have been memorised on the parade ground and these can be used by the general to override all existing commands in place. However, these would probably only be used once it is clear what the outcome of the battle is going to be; these three army commands are the 'general advance', the 'general retreat' and the 'engage enemy with a wholesale charge'.

So it is clearly in the initial writing of orders for an army that the real skill of the players is tested. The player will try to guess their opponent's strategy while at the same time expanding their own game plan. Unlike the all-seeing tabletop general that towers over the table surveying everything with an all-encompassing eye, real generals would not have that advantage, which is why orders have to be written in advance. Yes, in the main, the general would have been on horseback and they would have tried to find an elevated position within their own lines to survey the battlefield, but this would have still been limited. The general has to issue orders for the army as the battle lines are being deployed, and if those orders need to be superseded later, then an aide de camp (a battlefield courier for a general) needs to be sent with the appropriate new order before the miniature regiment can begin to carry out those new instructions. To complete this process naturally takes some time – at the very least a few minutes, sometimes much longer – and in that time the battlefield could change and just carrying a message to the regiments could be fraught with danger. If the courier is killed then a fresh order needs to be sent. To assist the gamer Appendix 1 on page 181 is a pre-prepared order sheet, which may be reproduced for your own use. Orders should always be concise and specify the direction required and any specific terrain features involved. Among friends who play regularly it may not be necessary to write orders for all units' each move, instead only writing down crucial manoeuvres such as feigned retreats, charges, or, as in the case of the Government artillery at Culloden, firing the cannon upon specific targets. Remember that during a game, regiments within the army will have their orders overturned as their own morale changes and impacts upon the way that they behave, often against their general's wishes.

Normally, in addition to the overall commander of an army there would be a series of sub-commanders who were responsible for different elements of the army: a captain of artillery, for instance, and a captain of horse. The rank of these men would depend upon the size of the army and the campaign that that they were in, and we know that at Culloden Cumberland had four senior major-generals or captains with him. This is why on the table top it is essential to have these key personalities represented; their presence with a unit can allow the player to change their orders and so react to an enemy action threatening your position. They can raise morale, giving nervous men more courage and reluctant men the conviction to charge. An officer's presence, while being of benefit, also brings an element of risk, and later in the section on missiles we will see how we account for this personal risk upon the battlefield and the effects it can have on the game.

Sequence of Play

Each move of play during the game will involve a set of activities which have to be carried out in a specific order; this ensures that the charges, the shooting of muskets, the melees, any resulting morale tests, and the removal of casualties all follow one another in a logical order. The sequence for these is as follows:

1. **Declare charges**: These should always be written as an order before a move to reflect the regimental commander being given the order to seize the initiative to exploit a weakness in the enemy's position. A charge must be made with the intent to attack an enemy unit, not simply to move fast across the battlefield, and a charge can only be declared as long as the orders do not violate any orders given by the general. The enemy unit that the charging unit intends to attack will recognise this initiation of a charge and they will then have to make a decision for themselves as to how they respond. In addition, the player who wishes the unit to charge must himself take a morale test for that unit to see if they perform the charge required.

2. **Responses to charge declarations**: Counter charges or actions to hold and receive a charge are then noted in response to point 1 above and any relevant morale tests are immediately taken.

3. **Movement**: All movements are now carried out simultaneously by all players, including the first distances of any charge moves and compulsory moves noted down from the previous move's morale tests. Any units encountering each other, or clearly ending up occupying the same space, have their distances measured at the same time, with the unit or individual moving the furthest occupying the space first and the units then line up against each other as appropriate for either a melee or for avoidance as per their orders. It is possible that they will end up facing each other and engage in a firefight, shooting at each other until one side either breaks or attempts to charge home.

4. **Artillery shooting**: All long-range weapons, cannons and mortars, shoot first. These weapon calculations are now made with the player of the shooting unit deciding at which point within the move his troops will shoot. This can be any time that the target unit is in range and reflects the trained eye of the artillery captain, who would shoot his artillery pieces at the optimum time to cause the most damage to his target.

5. **Musket and other weapon shooting**: All short-range missile weapon calculations are now made, with the player of the shooting unit deciding at which point in the move his troops will shoot; again this can be at any time that the target unit was in range. Now that both elements of shooting have been calculated, all the shooting casualties from this move are removed.

6. **Melees**: Any units that are in hand-to-hand combat, either by design or by accidental collision, now have their combat casualties calculated. If a melee occurs by accident then the combative units do not get the benefit of charging factors unless they were already in motion from before. Note from point 4 above that any figures which were lost to artillery or small arms shooting on the way into this melee should be removed before the melee is calculated as they cannot count as combatants. Finally, after the melee has been fully calculated, any resulting casualties are removed, and appropriate models placed.

7. **Morale**: Once all the casualties have been removed, any units involved in actions arising from steps 4 to 6 above need to take a morale test.

8. **Compulsory actions**: If any unit has to make a compulsory move as a result of the above morale test then this is noted on the order sheet ready for the unit to be moved as part of the next game move.

This sequence is then repeated each time for every game move.

Movement

Due to the regimental parade ground tactics, the speed of regular infantry is quite slow and needs to be reflected in the rule system. This inability to cope with the speed of the Jacobite charge coupled with deploying on poor terrain is what on some battlefields handed the initiative to the Jacobite forces. Cumberland sought to gain the upper hand by forcing the Jacobites to fight on his terms. This table reflects the distance that each figure, normally as part of a unit all performing the same action, will move while in formation over the battlefield terrain during a game move – there is also a manoeuvre section which covers the re-formation of a unit in order to face a different direction or move around difficult terrain. These distances may well be modified depending upon the type of terrain that the figures have to traverse and also the type of weather conditions that are prevailing at the time of the battle. The following table lists the basic troop types and how far they move; in some cases a dice is thrown to complete that movement, which adds an element of chance as to just how far a unit could move. At first this may seem unrealistic, but having walked Killiecrankie, Sheriffmuir, Clifton Moor, Prestonpans and Culloden, all have different degrees of difficulty – Sheriffmuir in particular is a mass of floating sphagnum and one lurches rather than walks the battlefield. This simple dice mechanism reproduces the uncertainty of what is underfoot. The 'manoeuvre' column is used for all wheels, about turns and changes of formation except for the expansion and contraction of ranks, which is explained below.

MOVEMENT TABLE					
	Distances in inches				
TROOP TYPE	Normal	Manoeuvre	Charge	Retire	Rout - O/O
Infantry - Line	4	2	2 + D6	3	8
Infantry - Column	6	3	6 + D6	4	8
Light Infantry	8	6	8 + D10	6	8
Light Cavalry	16	10	16 + D10	12	20
Heavy Cavalry	12	6	14 + D10	8	20
Naval crew	6	6	6 + D6	6	8
Jacobite foot	8	4	8 + D6	6	10
Jacobite Horse	12	8	10 + D6	6	20
Artillery - manhandled	2	N/A	N/A	2	8 No Guns
Artillery - limbered	6	N/A	N/A	N/A	10 With Guns

The above distances only account for moving on easy ground in dry conditions; varying types of terrain and a spell of inclement weather can cause an even slower rate of movement. The following military actions or instances alter the above distances. Note that all movement is dependent upon there being sufficient space to move the figures into the required location. If units are given orders that cause space to become overcrowded, with insufficient room to place the figures where planned, then the unit that arrived first has priority, followed by the second unit and so on. Any units involved in such congestion count as disordered (i.e. in disarray) until the situation has been remedied and they can resume their normal desired formation. Such disorder affects the shooting ability and the overall morale of the unit until it has spent at least one complete move as a re-organised unit. Any unit shooting into such a congested area shares out the casualties inflicted by taking the losses from the unit closest to it, and then the next closest and so forth.

Special Movement Considerations

Type of move, action or terrain	Effect
Crossing small ditches, hedges, low walls	½ M to cross for infantry, no penalty for cavalry
Crossing larger ditches, hedges, walls	1 M and is only possible for infantry
Embarking/disembarking	½ M for all
Bogs, marshes, rivers, swamps	½ M for the duration of time in that terrain.
Sand – beaches/estuaries	½ M for the duration of time in that terrain, only infantry may cross
Streets between houses	-All troops normal moves
Uphill move on steep hills	-2 inches for mounted; ½ M for all other troops
Through woods	-2 inches for infantry; ½ M for all mounted troops

• Mounted troops are not allowed on cliff paths or in forests; they must dismount and lead their steeds as if foot.
• Any unit which routs goes into open order (O/O) and the figures are spaced half an inch apart to reflect the fact that they have lost their disciplined shape and are now disordered.
• Artillery is not allowed in woods, forests, marshes, sandy estuaries or to try and cross other difficult terrain.
• Artillery takes a full move to unlimber or limber and cannot fire during those actions.
• If any terrain affects movement such as crossing marshes, crossing rivers, climbing over walls, etc., then any movement penalty incurred remains until the unit has completely left that area of terrain.
• Troops cannot cross any major water-based terrain features, save by ford, bridge or boats.
• Interpenetration is only possible when one light or dispersed unit passes through another light or dispersed unit, and all units involved will be disordered until they have emerged from their mingled situation.
• Units may only charge in an attempt to contact an enemy unit. If the first move of this charge fails then they may continue for a second move to try and contact the original

enemy or a newly appeared enemy target. The charging unit is allowed to veer by up to 2 inches to either side of their original frontage within that movement without any movement penalty. However, if at the end of the second move the charging unit has failed to contact an enemy unit, then it is disordered and must spend a complete move reforming. At the end of the reforming phase, as long as the unit has not been forced to defend itself (which it is allowed to do but only in its disordered state), it can face in any direction the player requires and is ready to move again the next move.

• No unit may charge for more than six moves during one day of battlefield activity, i.e. three complete two-move charges

• A unit may expand its ranks at the rate of two figures per flank per half a move.

• A unit may contract its ranks at the rate of one figure per flank per half a move.

• A unit while moving forwards may make an inclined move and veer up to 2 inches to either side of their original frontage within that movement without any movement penalty.

• A regular infantry unit, which is not in melee, may turn a rear rank around to form a hollow square or rectangle. This takes one move to complete and the rest of the unit must remain stationery, but the non-moving ranks may shoot their muskets.

• A unit may retire, stepping back while facing the enemy and remaining in good order, but this is at half the normal move speed and such a unit cannot wheel or charge. The front rank may continue to shoot and the unit does not become disordered.

• A mounted unit advancing may wheel up 45° with no movement penalty.

• Stand means that a unit will prepare itself for holding the ground it is on – it cannot advance or retreat, but it can reshape itself into the required formation.

• Individual personalities, aides de camp and generals do not incur any movement penalties for turning, wheeling and so forth because they are not a unit and so have no movement restrictions.

• Units in fog, swamps and storms are allowed to make unseen movements by recording them on paper after removing the figures from the table. If the fog they are in is moving as per the random movement chart then this needs to continue to move on the table and details of where the units are within the fog must be maintained.

Random Movement

In some battles instances will occur where a random method of determining where a unit moves is required. It may be that a battle is being fought at night, or during inclement weather such as in a snow storm or in dense fog, weather which we know which would be perfect for a Jacobite ambush. The Battle of Cromdale in 1690, for example, was fought both at night and in fog. The following table can be used to reflect this random action, but this is only for units that have orders to move or are moving as a result of a morale test. A D10 is thrown once their movement distance has been determined and then the appropriate deviation, if applicable, is actioned. If a unit stumbles towards dangerous terrain such as a sheer cliff drop, a loch, lake or a river of unfathomable depth, then the unit will not enter as it is deemed to have that much common sense. Instead it will skirt along the aforementioned terrain feature until they come once more to clear terrain, when another dice roll will be made.

Score Action

1–3   Unit moves forward 25 degrees to the left

4–7   Unit moves as instructed

8–0   Unit moved forward 25 degrees to the right

If it becomes necessary to determine a more significant deviation, or to determine from which direction fresh troops may be entering an existing affray, then this can be achieved by using the following table (the compass point marker comes into use here). This would only be used in extreme circumstances, perhaps in the case that a unit has been routed and finds itself in open territory and is not sure which way to run. It is based on the points of a compass and with a direction marker on the table it is very easy to use.

Score Action

1   Unit is moved the full available distance for that unit in any direction by the opposing player

2   Unit moves full available distance north

3   Unit moves full available distance north-east

4   Unit moves full available distance east

5   Unit moves full available distance south-east

6   Unit moves full available distance south

7   Unit moves full available distance south-west

8   Unit moves full available distance west

9   Unit moves full available distance north-west

10   Unit is moved any distance up to the maximum for that troop type in any direction by their own player

Weather Considerations

At the Battle of Falkirk, we saw how the weather was responsible for three things which affected the Government troops: firstly, it slowed the speed at which the infantry could march, slowing their arrival on the battlefield; secondly, the ground was so sodden that the cannon became trapped in the mud and most were later abandoned; and finally, once on the battlefield the rain greatly reduced the effectiveness of their musket fire so that hardly scathed Jacobite units were able to charge home. Rain is the most crippling type of weather as it makes anything other than well-drained fields and the best of roads difficult to walk upon. Ploughed fields become a morass of clinging mud, while persistent rain can cause both rivers and lakes to flood roads, making any strategic advance impossible if the means to cross such a river in spate are removed. The author was lucky enough to see at first hand just how dramatic a rise in water level can be over a very short space of time within the Scottish Highlands. While on holiday at Loch Awe, near Oban, in 1988 a severe squall appeared from nowhere, filling the valley with violent winds and torrential rain in the space of just fifteen minutes. The downpour occurred over the valley and lasted for

		GEOGRAPHICAL GENERATION TABLE				
Score	01-12	13-25	26-37	38-50		
Terrain	Water - inland	Coastal area	Lowlands	Highlands		
01-10	Brook	Sandy beach	Farming	Hill - Cliff 1 side		
11-20	Small Pool	Mudflats	Dyke & Ditch	Large Castle		
21-30	Stream	Estuary	Pasture	Loch		
31-40	Marsh	Weed bed	Orchard	Moor		
41-50	Shallow River	Cliff	Wood	Ridge - 1 steep side		
51-60	Deep River	Sea loch	Forest	Valley		
61-70	Loch - oval	Sand dunes	Loch / Lake - round	Forest		
71-80	Loch - long	Quicksand	Settlement	Gorge		
81-90	Saltmarsh	Rocky beach	Fields	Tor		
91-00	Sea loch	Port	Heath	Stone Tower		
Score	51-62	63-75	76-87	88-00		
Terrain	Mountain area	Settlement	Industry	Agriculture		
01-10	Deep Valley	Mine / Quarry	Timber	Cereal crops		
11-20	Pass	Church	Timber	Root crops		
21-30	Cliff path	Large castle	Stone	Orchard		
31-40	Marsh	Farm	Stone	Cattle		
41-50	Summit	Hamlet	Coal	Sheep		
51-60	Ravine	Burgh	Coal	Cattle		
61-70	Scree	Village	Mine - Iron	Cattle		
71-80	Arête	Town	Mine - Copper	Sheep		
81-90	Gorge	Stone Tower	Mine - Silver	Horses		
91-00	Loch / Lake - oval	Caves	Mine - Gold	Deer		

around two hours. In that time, as the rain fell like 'stair rods', the loch rose by around two metres; every little stream flowing into the valley became a raging torrent, and the rain poured off the mountain sides into the loch. Such was the ferocity of the deluge that whole fields alongside the loch, complete with fences and stone walls, which had been perfectly safe to walk across only an hour before, were submerged. It is not only the ground that is affected: vision is impaired as the clouds descend and communication is lost as the noise of the wind and rain combine to distort sound. Regiments of men with no shelter and open to the elements would be drained by such conditions and would surely lose their fighting spirit when marching through hostile territory and unforgiving terrain.

While it is not compulsory to use weather in wargames – many gamers simply ignore it – for the sake of accuracy in the majority of conflicts, and certainly to give the Jacobites an even chance in recreating their successes, the weather should be taken into account. Falkirk we have mentioned, but an even clearer example comes from one of the most famous battles of them all, Waterloo. If the summer storms had not soaked the battlefield for the day and night before the battle, Napoleon's cannons would have had a far more devastating effect on the British lines than they did. The sodden ground meant that instead of the solid iron cannon balls bouncing through rank after rank and regiment after regiment, many buried themselves in the soft ground where they first landed. They did cause some casualties, but the lack of the ongoing bounces into the men that lay beyond was significant in reducing British casualties.

As with terrain, different types of weather have a greater effect on some troop types when compared to others – there is a random weather generation table below which can be used to provide the required weather for a battle. This is based upon the type of terrain that the battle is being fought over, reflecting the microclimates one often encounters in the British Isles, but the information links as readily into a campaign as into an individual battle. The following factors only come into effect if the weather is played and when generated from the table. Note that if this weather table declares that wind is present, the direction can be determined using the random movement table above. Note that once wind is generated and one is rolled on a D10, the opponent chooses the direction; if ten is generated then the dice-thrower themselves chooses. The wind, however, will blow from the same direction for the whole game so a throw does not have to be made every move. The wind will also be important in sea battles, see below. All of the following types of inclement weather will have some effect on the battlefield. Although all of the known Jacobite battles were fought either in the north of England or in Scotland, it is possible that a campaign will place

WEATHER GENERATION TABLE						
Overall Terrain	**With Wind**			**Without Wind**		
	Storm	**Rain**	**Fine & sunny**	**Mist**	**Rain**	**Warm & sunny**
Marsh or large wetland	1	2-3	4	5-6	7-8	9-0
Coastal area - all	1	2	3-4	5	6	7-0
Lowlands Agriculture	1	2-3	4-5	6	7	8-0
Forests - large	1	2-3	4	5	6-7	8-0
Moors and upland plateaus	1-2	3-4	5	6	7-8	9-0
Hills - rolling	1	2-3	4-5	6	7	8-0
Mountains	1-2	3-4	5	6-7	8-9	0
Water - inland lake or loch	The weather is as per the terrain that surrounds it					
Settlement - major town	The weather is as per the terrain that surrounds it					
Sea for naval actions	1-2	3-4	5-6	7	8	9-0
If a "Storm" then re-roll	5 or less will be snow and 8 to 0 hail and thunderstorms in November to April; all other times just rain and thunderstorms					
If "Mist" then re-roll	7 or less will be fog in November to April, just mist in May to October					

Jacobite armies at least as far south as Derby and even nearer to London. If this is the case then for any battles below a line from Chester in the west to Lincoln in the east, add a +2 to the weather generation dice roll. Simply note the predominant terrain feature and throw a D10, then read across the table for the resultant weather.

For example, let us consider the Battle of Glen Shiel, 1719. Glen Shiel was a battle fought in a valley in the Scottish Highlands, with high mountains on three sides. A player throws a D10 and rolls a 6, which means 'mist'; as the battle was fought in June, a check on the chart shows it is definitely summer mist and not a dense fog, which would affect the troops more; even so artillery accuracy is affected by the poorer visibility.

Weather Effects on Troops

Mist   All troops move at normal speed but artillery have -1 on all dice rolls

Fog   All troops move at half speed and any missile over a 6-inch range causes half casualties rounded down, and artillery cannot fire at any target beyond a 6-inch range

Hail   All troops move at half speed and no missile shooting is allowed at all

Rain   All troops move at half speed and all missile casualties are reduced to a quarter rounded down

Snow   All troops move at half speed and all missile casualties are reduced to a quarter rounded down

Wind   All smoke is blown away from the battlefield and visibility is good +1 on all artillery dice rolls

Fine   All troops gain +1 inch on all movements – this applies to the current battle only and not to a campaign move

Storm   All foot moves at quarter speed and no missile shooting is allowed at all; all cavalry must dismount and horses must be led moving at only half the normal foot speed for regular infantry

Fatigue

Often forgotten in wargame systems is the draining effect that combat has upon troops. At Killiecrankie, for instance, the Government troops stood to attention in blazing heat while the Jacobites sat and rested above them on the hillside, ensuring that the Government troops would be drained both physically and mentally by the time the Jacobites charged. In contrast, the Jacobite army attempted a night attack on Cumberland's army (the night before what was eventually the Battle of Culloden), and their shambolic night march weakened the tired army still further, and meant that they had little time to rest before the battle began. The following standard deductions should be applied after a pre-determined number of game moves and apply to all units to reflect the weariness of the men and their horses and their inability to respond to the needs of their commander at the speed that they would wish.

After 10 moves -1 inch from all foot and -3 inches from all horse movement

After 16 moves -2 inches from all foot and -5 inches from all horse movement

Missiles

As we saw in the earlier chapter on the weapons of these campaigns, while there are a variety of artillery pieces there are only a few missile weapons available to the infantryman – the musket, pistol and occasional bow for the foot, and the pistol and carbine for the cavalryman. While the reports that some of the Highlanders still carried longbows may well be true, they would have been in such small numbers that they do not warrant being segregated as a separate unit on the wargames table and therefore do not require a separate table within the wargame rules to reflect their shooting and damage to an enemy. The Jacobite tactics meant that their chance of success all hinged in the initial charge, because they would shoot their muskets, then discard them; shoot their pistols, then discard them; and finally charge in with their swords, targes and axes and in some cases improvised weapons. This meant that if the initial charge failed to break the opposition ranks, they had no back-up plan to recover the situation. They had no firearms left to reload and so inflicted long-range casualties and were therefore vulnerable to the drilled musketry of the Government ranks. This of course is exactly what happened at Culloden. On the table below there are specific factors which cover these Jacobite actions. All forms of small arms shooting is calculated on the shooting table below.

Note: In all types of shooting it has to be the logical target that is shot at, which is

	SMALL ARMS SHOOTING TABLE									
	Short Range up to 6"					Long Range 6" - 12"				
	Carbine / Musket / Pistol					Carbine / Musket				
No of Figs	First Volley open terrain	First Volley at soft cover	Other Volley	At Soft Cover	At Hard Cover	First Volley open terrain	First Volley at soft cover	Other Volley	At Soft Cover	At Hard Cover
1 to 5	0.6	0.3	0.3	0.2	0.0	0.3	0.2	0.2	0.1	0.0
6	0.8	0.4	0.4	0.3	0.1	0.4	0.3	0.3	0.1	0.0
7	1.0	0.5	0.5	0.4	0.1	0.5	0.4	0.4	0.1	0.0
8	1.2	0.6	0.6	0.4	0.1	0.6	0.4	0.4	0.1	0.0
9	1.4	0.7	0.7	0.5	0.1	0.7	0.5	0.5	0.1	0.0
10	1.6	0.8	0.8	0.5	0.2	0.8	0.5	0.5	0.2	0.1
11	1.8	0.9	0.9	0.6	0.2	0.9	0.6	0.6	0.2	0.1
12	2.0	1.0	1.0	0.6	0.2	1.0	0.6	0.6	0.2	0.1
13	2.2	1.1	1.1	0.7	0.3	1.1	0.7	0.7	0.3	0.1
14	2.4	1.2	1.2	0.7	0.3	1.2	0.7	0.7	0.3	0.1
15	2.6	1.3	1.3	0.8	0.3	1.3	0.8	0.8	0.3	0.1
16	2.8	1.4	1.4	0.8	0.4	1.4	0.8	0.8	0.4	0.2
17	3.0	1.5	1.5	0.9	0.4	1.5	0.9	0.9	0.4	0.2
18	3.2	1.6	1.6	0.9	0.4	1.6	0.9	0.9	0.4	0.2
19	3.4	1.7	1.7	1.0	0.5	1.7	1.0	1.0	0.5	0.2
20	3.6	1.8	1.8	1.0	0.5	1.8	1.0	1.0	0.5	0.2

normally the nearest enemy straight ahead, or the unit that is most threatening to the one shooting.

Small Arms Missile Factors to take into Consideration

• One rank shoots if Jacobite troops are shooting while charging, one and a half ranks if in a defensive position.

• Two ranks shoot if Government and if Spanish, Dutch, Irish or German troops in foreign or mercenary service.

• Three ranks shoot if French troops.

• One rank shoots for all carbine volleys and one in ten dragoons must be a horse-holder and cannot shoot. Carbine shooting counts as other infantry volley, but not a first volley, as dragoons skirmishing were not as effective as a regular line infantry unit giving fire by ranks or companies.

• Any first volley would normally be delivered against troops either in the open or behind soft cover as any shooting against hard or solid cover would be unlikely to cause casualties and so be a waste of a prepared volley.

• A Jacobite first volley when charging an enemy will always be at long range; the only time a Jacobite first volley would be at short range would be if they were behind cover in a defensive position which they planned to hold.

• Jacobites may fire one round of pistol shot within a game; this counts as a short-range first volley, and would normally be straight after the musket volley when charging. Jacobites that are holding a defensive position may hold their pistol fire until they are attacked.

• Jacobites that are secure in favourable terrain may choose to defend such a position and use their muskets as regular troops would have done, reloading and shooting rather than shooting and discarding them in a charge.

• Target units which move across the line of fire as opposed to toward the shooting unit count as being in soft cover.

• Units which are dispersed as opposed to being in neat ranks count as being in soft cover.

• Government regular troops may shoot once per move if moving forward or retiring, or twice in one move if completely stationary.

• Only half of all Jacobite troops are classed as carrying pistols.

• Troops may only shoot out of a wood if they are within 2 inches of the edge of that wood.

• All missile ranges in woods are reduced to half.

• Any unit armed with missile weapons may shoot up to 45° from their frontage.

• All shooting is simultaneous so a casualty in the shooting phase is allowed to shoot during that move, but no casualties from shooting count in any subsequent melee.

• Carbines are shot only when the dragoons are fighting on foot as infantry, they are not shot from the saddle.

• A unit may shoot over the heads of up to two ranks of their own side as long as they are on higher ground than their own troops and their target unit is not within 6 inches of their own unit.

• After ten moves of shooting all men within that unit have their number that is eligible to shoot reduced by 10 per cent in all further shooting calculations. This is to reflect those men who have damaged or lost their scouring sticks (ramrods), some of which will have been left in the barrel and shot at the enemy. Similarly, it covers men who have run out of powder or shot and can no longer fire and men who are simply paralysed by the fear and shock of the encounter and can no longer keep up with the required musket drill.

• It is almost certain that at Culloden Government units enfilading the flank of the Jacobite attack also hit their own units who were engaged in melee with the Jacobite line, a term known today as 'friendly fire'. If such action occurs then casualties are split evenly between the target units involved, with any 'odd' number of casualties being determined by a dice roll to see which unit lost the additional casualty.

• A unit that is in melee at the start of a move cannot shoot during that or a subsequent move until the melee is completed or is broken off by other means.

Example 1 – Small Arms Shooting

A unit of twenty Highlanders is charging towards a unit of sixteen Government regular infantry who are stationed behind a simple low hedge which counts as soft cover. As explained previously, when charging home the Jacobites were renowned for firing their muskets at long range to try and draw their enemy's return fire, before discarding their own muskets to charge in with their close combat weapons. Therefore, on our shooting table we look for twenty at long range against soft cover, which gives us a factor of 1.0 for the first volley, so they have caused one casualty figure and no dice roll is required as there is no part decimal to be accounted for. The Jacobites also fire their pistols, but we only count half of them as carrying them, so we have ten pistols at close range and first volley against soft cover, which is a factor of 0.8. So, as this is a part decimal the Jacobite player rolls a D10 and needs to score 8 or below to cause a casualty. The player rolls a 3 and has caused a second casualty. The Government regiment of sixteen has lost two model figures from the Jacobite shooting. As it is in simultaneous moves, the Government player shoots with all sixteen men and as it is the first volley and open terrain into which they are shooting it is a factor of 2.8. The player rolls for the 0.8 factor and utters a mild curse as they roll a 9, which being above the 8 means that there are no further casualties and, like the Jacobite player, he has caused just two in total. But the Government troops are stationery and allowed to shoot twice in a move. The player now has to check the 'other' volley column as his most advantageous first volley has already been shot. For the second volley the factor is 1.4 and rolling this time they roll a 3, meaning that two casualties have been caused. To summarise, the Government troops have lost a total of two and the Jacobites a total of four, leaving the Government troops with fourteen men and the Jacobites with sixteen. We will continue this example and find out what happens next when we come to the section on melees.

Artillery

For the majority of the Jacobite campaigns the cannon on both sides were of small calibre, which meant that the pieces were light and could keep up with the movement rate of the rest of the army – there are examples of both sides abandoning artillery pieces when the weather conditions were against them. Even if they were of small calibre, cannon and mortars were an integral part of the army and made telling contributions in some of the confrontations.

To reflect the difficulty of accurately hitting a target, a random element has been built into the mechanics of the artillery shooting table which allows for some deviation of shot. There are also factors which can increase the chance of hitting the desired target; for example, a bonus occurs if the cannon are continually trained upon a single target, which allows for the accuracy achieved when gunners learn to hone in on a target after earlier misses.

ARTILLERY SHOOTING TABLE						
CANNONS - ALL CALIBRES						
Range	**Close Range up to 10"**			**Effective Range 10" - 40"**		
Target is in open ground						
Government	1 Gun	2 Guns	3 Guns	1 Gun	2 Guns	3 Guns
	1.0	2.0	3.0	0.5	1.0	1.5
Jacobite	1 Gun	2 Guns	3 Guns	1 Gun	2 Guns	3 Guns
	0.5	1.0	1.5	0.2	0.5	0.8
Target is in soft cover						
Government	1 Gun	2 Guns	3 Guns	1 Gun	2 Guns	3 Guns
	0.8	1.6	2.4	0.4	0.8	1.2
Jacobite	1 Gun	2 Guns	3 Guns	1 Gun	2 Guns	3 Guns
	0.4	0.7	1.0	0.2	0.4	0.6
Target is in hard or solid cover						
Government	1 Gun	2 Guns	3 Guns	1 Gun	2 Guns	3 Guns
	0.4	0.7	1.0	0.2	0.4	0.6
Jacobite	1 Gun	2 Guns	3 Guns	1 Gun	2 Guns	3 Guns
	0.2	0.4	0.6	0.1	0.2	0.3
MORTARS 15" - 35" ONLY						
Target is in	**Open or soft cover**			**Hard or solid cover**		
Government	1 Gun	2 Guns	3 Guns	1 Gun	2 Guns	3 Guns
	1.0	2.0	3.0	0.5	1.0	1.5
Jacobite	1 Gun	2 Guns	3 Guns	1 Gun	2 Guns	3 Guns
	0.5	1.0	1.5	0.2	0.5	0.8

ARTILLERY HIT LOCATION TABLE	
D10 Result	**Action**
1	Gun misfires - A throw of 1 twice running and the cannon explodes
2	Shot overshoots centre of target by 6"
3	Shot falls short of centre of target by 6"
4	Shot falls short of centre of target by 3"
5	Shot overshoots centre of target by 3"
6	Shot falls left of centre by 3" from the firing cannon
7	Shot falls right of centre by 3" from the firing cannon
8 - 10	shot hits in the centre of the target from the firing cannon
Each time artillery shoots at the same target +1 on the dice roll	
Artillery shooting at a static target e.g. a building +2 on the dice roll	
A moving target always counts as a fresh target	
· If a target moves between 4 and 8 inches -1 on the dice roll.	
· If a target moves between 8 and 12 inches -2 on the dice roll.	
· If a target moves further than 12 inches -3 on the dice roll.	

Artillery Missile Factors to take into Consideration

• Each time an artillery piece shoots at the same target +1 is added onto the dice roll.

• If an artillery piece is shooting at a static target +1 is added onto the dice roll.

• A moving target, such as a distant cavalry regiment, is always classed as a new target.

• If a target moves less than 4 inches no penalty on the dice.

• If a target moves between 4 and 8 inches -1 on the dice roll.

• If a target moves between 8 and 12 inches -2 on the dice roll.

• If a target moves further than 12 inches -3 on the dice roll.

• There is no penalty for a unit advancing towards shooting cannon; however, if a mortar shoots at troops advancing towards it then there is -3 penalty on the dice roll.

Example 2 – Artillery Shooting

A D10 is rolled for each cannon shooting, thus for a three-cannon battery a player would roll three D10. The three scores are noted and the relevant impacts noted; the best way is to place the relevant dice at each location so that the casualties can be determined. Then the player looks along the line relevant to where the hits have landed. Our Jacobite player wishes to shoot his two cannon at a unit of stationary Government dragoons who are approximately 30 inches away across the table, conveniently sat upon a hill and so in open ground, presumably awaiting the order to charge and exploit any Jacobite weakness. The player rolls D10 twice, throwing a 9 and a 7. This is the first time that this artillery has fired at this target and so there are no other factors to consider: the 9 and the 7 are the scores. The measurement is taken from the mouth of the cannon to the centre of the dragoon regiment, with the 9 as a hit in the dead centre of the unit. The location for the hit of the 7 is 'right of centre by 3 inches' and by measuring we find that this shot has not landed on the dragoon unit but it has in fact hit a mounted officer. The Jacobite hit of one cannon on the dragoons in open ground gives a score of 0.5; the player then rolls to see whether he has succeeded in killing a dragoon figure and he rolls a low 2 so he has succeeded as it is under 5. However, in addition he must also roll for the stray shot which just missed the dragoons but hit the associated officer. There is a separate table below for the potential loss of personalities. The player rolls to see whether he has killed an officer; if he is successful then their enemy's flexibility as a vital part of the army is temporarily removed. The player rolls a 6 and reads that the officer is wounded and has to retire for five moves in order to get a field dressing applied to his wound before he can return to action.

As the game moves are simultaneous, the shooting can technically take place at any time during the game move. The casualties should be calculated when it would have been most advantageous for those shooting, which would normally be either when the enemy was at its closest point to the shooting unit, or while the target unit is still in sight before perhaps going behind some kind of cover. This gives the individuals within the unit the freedom to pick the optimum moment to shoot when their commander gives the order to 'give fire'. Any troops with missile weapons are only permitted to shoot at a target if they had a clear line of sight during the move. It is permitted for a unit that shoots during a move to still defend itself in hand-to-hand combat if it ends up in a melee after it has shot its weapons.

British troops can shoot twice in one move as long as they have remained stationary, annd can choose to let their muskets fire at the optimum moment so they may have to settle for either shooting twice, one shot at long range and one at short range if they are being charged, or they could choose to hold their fire until the very last moment if it was to be their first volley.

Note that all regular troops, including foreign regiments, fighting for the Jacobites, and allied units fighting for the Government use the Government line when calculating casualties caused from shooting.

You will note that no distinction has been made in the rules between the types of missile fired from cannon during these Jacobite battles. Smooth bore cannon would be loaded either with a solid 3-, 4- or 6-pound cannonball depending on the calibre of the piece, as these solid cannon balls (also known as round shot) could travel almost a mile. They caused damage by the speed of their passage, hitting and bouncing through the ranks of men, knocking them down like skittles. These cannonballs were designed for hitting the enemy at a long range and causing as much destruction as possible, sometimes bouncing through one unit and on into a unit behind. For much closer targets the same cannon would be filled with a mass of small solid balls, like musket balls, in a pre-prepared bag or sometimes a thin tin case, which were known as grape shot or canister. These smaller projectiles were designed to scatter on leaving the mouth of the cannon and were used when the enemy was at close quarters, where the densely packed bodies of men made an easy target. Because the artillery crews would use the most advantageous ammunition for the situation they were in, it is therefore assumed that the player would also load the most effective missiles and so this has been pre-planned into the artillery shooting table above.

The mortar was a smaller device than cannon which shot a pre-lit shell into the air, flying over intervening obstacles to land onto the troops from above, when, in theory, it exploded. This is why the mortar ranges are very specific and they cannot alter their

28 mm Jacobite artillery. (Courtesy of Tim Hewitt)

ammunition nor fire at anything closer to them – there always has to be a minimum range for a mortar to fire successfully at a given target. For this reason, only artillery pieces shooting at greater than 10 inches are required to throw on the artillery hit location table; anything under 10 inches is assumed to be canister at a line or round shot at a column, which would both be devastating at such range.

Risk to Officers and Generals

The battles of Killiecrankie and Sheriffmuir both show what happens when a personality who is key to the ongoing performance of his army is removed, whether that is, as in the case of Bonnie Dundee and Clanranald, by being killed in action, or through an injury which renders them incapacitated for a period of time. Although thirteen years after Culloden, the Battle of Quebec in 1759 saw both of the opposing generals killed along with three of their senior officers. The French commander Montcalm was wounded and died in the retreat, while Wolfe (himself a veteran of Culloden) was the British general who had pulled off an incredible victory after leading his army up precipitous cliffs the night before the battle.

The procedure for working out what damage has been caused to a personality figure is very simple and it is the same table for both missile fire and hand-to-hand combat. Each time an overall commander, general, sub-general, clan leader, aide de camp or messenger is directly involved in any direct combat then a D10 is thrown and the result noted. It is normal for the player hitting the target to make the resulting dice roll, but sometimes that player will ask the player whose personality has been hit to make the crucial roll.

Score Action upon personality

1–2   Killed outright, will have a negative effect upon any unit he was attached to, see morale table.

3–4   Badly wounded, leaves field immediately and is incapacitated for D10 weeks if this is a campaign battle.

5–6   Slightly wounded, retires for a field dressing for 5 moves; is killed if hit again in this same battle.

7–8   Hat blown off, no wound, but nervous and remains behind any unit he joins causing -1 on their morale.

9–0   Becomes fearless believes it is his lucky day and gets +1 on all dice rolls concerning morale for the rest of the battle.

With all of the shooting completed, all casualties are removed at this point to ensure that the correct numbers of figures are left in place, ready for any melees that may occur or second shooting volleys from any regular troops that did not move. Some players like to put casualty models down at this point to show how many men have been lost and where they have fallen so that the ebb and flow of the battle can be followed.

Melees

A melee is formed when one unit goes into hand-to-hand combat with another. This can be two single units against each other, or a combination of several units and some individual personalities all piled in together. In essence it will normally be the neat ranks of the regular troops being hit by a sprawling mass of charging Jacobites, who will chop with their swords and axes and push with their shields against the disciplined ranks until one side either breaks or withdraws. Occasionally one side will withdraw to regroup before charging again, although this tactic is more likely to be performed by cavalry units.

Infantry Melees

Melee combat will continue for a minimum of two and maximum of three moves so long as one side has not been eliminated or broken before that time due to either failing a morale test or being wiped out. The only other way to extract a unit from a melee that has not been concluded is to choose to take a morale test. Any individual personality involved in a melee is not restricted to fighting for a maximum number of moves and can, if they have the space available and are not hemmed in the sprawl of the melee, step back from the melee with no restriction on movement and proceed elsewhere on the table top. If one unit has been pushed back twice in the first two moves then the melee ends at that point and that unit will break and rout, running away from their victors for two full moves, after which the fleeing unit can attempt to rally to see if they halt from routing and regroup. If

A dragoon and infantry melee into its second move.

after three moves neither side has pushed the other back twice, then both sides retreat away from one another with a full 'retire' move, still facing their opponents. Those units will then take a further move to re-form from their disordered state, if necessary repositioning themselves to face a new direction. These moves are compulsory. Any unit attacked while making these moves can defend themselves, but they will count as disordered in combat until they have a move in which to reform properly.

Cavalry Melees

The actions of mounted troops in melee are different, depending on whether they hit a regular formed infantry unit, a loosely formed infantry unit or another mounted unit. If they hit a prepared regular infantry unit in line then the melee is calculated over three moves as above. In this instance, if the cavalry push back the formed infantry twice in succession they will cause the infantry to break and rout as explained in the infantry melee above. If after two moves the cavalry have taken more casualties twice running then they will break in rout for two moves and will have to take a morale test to see if they will rally. If after three moves neither the cavalry nor the infantry have gained the upper hand then the cavalry will retire for a full move in order to reform; however, the infantry will reform their line where they already stand though they can change formation if required when reforming.

Against all other opponents, if cavalry win the first round of a melee in the first move, they pass through the first rank to encounter the second rank of that unit. If there is no second rank then they break out of the rear of the unit they have ridden through and can either attack the rear of that enemy unit or alternatively push on towards any new target ahead of them. They would still count as charging if they had only made one charge move up to that point. If they are not charging then they can still advance a full move and count as advancing in any subsequent new melee. If the first unit they hit had a second rank then the first line of horsemen would fight the second rank of that unit, and the second line of horsemen would then attack the first rank behind the horsemen's first line. At the point at which this second move of melee starts, all units involved will be classed as disordered as the four ranks are intertwined with each other.

MELEE FACTORS TABLE			
Event	Factor	Event	Factor
Attacking enemy in the rear	+ 4	Attacking fortifications / solid cover	- 8
Formed infantry line against irregulars	+ 2	Attacking hard cover including ships	- 5
Surprising the enemy	+ 2	Receiving a fanatical Highland charge	- 4
Advancing, but not charging at all	+ 2	Routing troops	- 4
Advantage of ground, uphill of enemy	+ 2	Attacking soft cover including small boats	- 2
Attacking enemy in the flank, each	+ 2	Disordered troops	- 2
Charging over level terrain	+ 2	Fighting while in bogs / marshes	- 2
Fighting a disordered enemy	+ 2	Pushed back last move	- 2
Horse against disordered infantry	+ 2	Receiving a Highland charge	- 2
infantry armed with formed pikes pre 1700	+ 2	Shaken troops	- 2
Infantry charging	+ 2	Untrained troops	- 2
Opposition is artillery or naval crew	+ 2	Using bayonets pre 1700	- 2
Won last round of melee	+ 2	Fighting with improvised weapons	- 1
Horse Charging uphill	+ 1	Fired at by Jacobite pistols this move	- 1
Horse Charging down a steady hill	No change	Retiring troops	- 1

Melee Factors to take into Consideration

• Surprise attacks are ones that emerge from caves, fog, forests or smoke or from being hidden by terrain.

• Only the front rank of a unit in melee counts as fighting in the relevant calculations, though if cavalry break into a unit then the second rank may come to be taken into account as per the moves outlined above and for both sides.

• In battles before 1700 some units carried pikes and any of these in a second rank are allowed to count in melee. This only applies to formed Government troops and not to the Jacobites wielding a variety of weapons.

• Troops charging into contact who overlap an enemy unit on either or both flanks may continue their move and use up the remainder of their allotted move distance and so attack the enemy unit from one flank, or both flanks, as well as from the front. The overlapped defending unit may turn figures to engage with the new attack, but only if they are not already engaged in a frontal activity.

• Units that shoot during a move are also allowed to defend themselves if attacked but may not manoeuvre.

• If a unit charges into a formed unit, the impetuousness of the charge and the steadiness of the formed infantry will count for the first two moves of a melee if neither side has pushed the other back after the first contact round. If a charging unit is pushed back after the first round, or a formed infantry unit is pushed back after the first move, then they each respectively lose that melee advantage when the next factors are calculated.

• The side winning a melee, if it has lasted less than three moves, must follow up its success and chase the routing enemy unit, even though it is also disordered. If the unit has been destroyed then it will carry on into the next available enemy unit. If the commander does not want this pursuit to happen then a morale test must be taken.

• As with all rules systems common sense must prevail – distinction must be kept between a charging unit and an advancing unit, as these are separate. The different types of charging factors are listed separately because it is more difficult for horses to charge downhill and keep a disciplined line than it is to charge up a gentle hill.

Example 3 – Melees

Let us return to our earlier example (1) of the Highlanders charging towards the Government redcoat line. From the initial exchange of shooting the Jacobite unit fell from twenty men to sixteen, while the Government unit fell from sixteen to fourteen.

MELEE TABLE RESULTS						
Final Score	0 - 07	08 - 13	14 - 19	20 - 25	26 - 30	31 - 35
Casualties	0	1	2	3	4	5
Final Score	36 - 40	41 - 45	46 - 50	51 - 55	56 - 60	61 - 65+
Casualties	6	7	8	9	10	11

The Government troops have the benefit of being formed behind a hedge, which although it counts as soft cover and offers some inconvenience to the Highlanders, does not stop them crashing through to engage the redcoats.

To calculate a melee and its impact upon each unit involved we have to work through a series of steps. The process commences with a count of each figure involved in the melee for each side, with all cavalry counting as two – thus ten cavalry would be 20 figures. In this case we have sixteen Jacobites and fourteen Government troops to start with and to this we add on all relevant factors from the melee factor table above. Thus the Jacobites get +3 for charging, but also a -2 for attacking an enemy behind soft cover, giving them a score of 17. The Government have 14 points and then they get +4 for being formed infantry against irregular troops, but then a -3 for being charged by fanatical clansmen, giving them a score of 15. To these scores is added the number generated by the roll of one D6 each. The players roll simultaneously and the Jacobites add 4, while the Government troops add 6. The final scores end up even at 21 each. They then consult the melee result table to see what damage they have inflicted on each other. The table shows that for 21 points three casualties are incurred. There was no push back from either side so the melee will continue into its second move with neither side having pushed back the other.

Melee Result Compulsory Actions

Casualties are equal	Both sides remain in the same positions and continue as long as it is not third melee round
Lost one more casualty	Pushed back by 1 inch, victors following up
Lost two more casualties	Pushed back by 2 inches, victors following up
Lost three more casualties	Pushed back by 3 inches, victors following up

If a unit loses more than three casualties then they have to take an immediate morale test.

The results for all other circumstances, especially those relating to cavalry, have been explained in the melee section above. All of these actions as a result of a melee are compulsory and no other movement actions are permissible unless a morale test result supersedes the above.

Extraordinary Events

Note: There will be times when circumstances or situations on the battlefield will create a dilemma which no player or perhaps even an umpire will have seen before. Remember to be reasonable: muskets cannot be shot through solid buildings, heavy cavalry cannot leap solid stone walls ten feet high. So common sense comes into play; simply apply the most logical remedy to the unit/s involved and then if the players cannot agree, call on the 'Gods' and let a duel of the dice decide what prevails.

Removing Casualties

All those figures that have been killed through melee actions are removed from play at this point, normally back to their storage box. Although casualties are removed because they can play no further part in the battle, the numbers should be recorded if the game is part of a campaign, when they should not all be seen as dead. To calculate the overall effect, apply the following rule: one-third of the casualties have indeed been killed and can play no further part in the campaign; a further third are severely wounded. Dice for each one on a percentage basis – a throw of 66 or under means they are dead, 67 or over and they survive and will be ready for action in two months' time as long as they have a safe settlement in which to recover. The final third are classed as slightly wounded and will all recover in one months' time, again as long as they have a safe settlement to recover in. Once recovered, all these men can be drafted back into the armies on campaign when units local to them are mustered, or when an appropriate army on campaign passes within a day's march.

Morale

This is the mental ability and confidence that a unit has; it has to be just right in order to carry out its commander's wishes. If the morale of a unit is too high it may go and attack the nearest enemy unit and upset the player's plan. If the morale of a unit is too low, it may run away at the crucial time, again upsetting the general's plan. Morale is the single most important element of an army. It is crucial in the history of military conflict and histories tell us of great fortitude where forces vastly outnumbered managed to hold out against all the odds to emerge triumphant. In some battles single regiments took 50, 70 and in the American Civil War even 90 per cent casualties, and still carried on fighting. It is important to note that generals and other personalities do not take morale tests. A unit tests morale at the appropriate time in the game move when any of the following events have come into play and specifically relate to that unit. If it has already tested morale for one of the events in a move, then it does not test for the same event again in the same move, though it may have to face a different situation later and have to take a further test at the end of the move.

Reasons for a Morale Test to be taken
- To instigate a charge, to determine whether the charge will commence now that the order has been given.
- If a charge is declared against a unit, then that unit tests to see how they will respond.
- Each time four or more figures are lost in one move.
- In order to try and rally from a rout after losing a melee.
- To try and withdraw from an ongoing melee.
- Once a unit gets below 40 per cent of its original number then it must test at the start of every move.
- If an allied unit routs and passes within 8 inches of the testing unit.

- Uphill of a disordered enemy unit below and within charge reach.
- Downhill of an enemy advancing towards a unit, not behind a defensive position or at least soft cover.

All morale tests commence by the roll of a D10 and to this randomly generated number are added and subtracted all of the relevant factors from the morale factor table below. The final number is then cross-referenced to the morale results table and to the relevant situation that the unit is being tested for; there are three different elements. As long as the final score is within the parameter stipulated then the unit will perform the action required by the player making the dice roll. If not then the unit will behave as dictated by the table and there are no exceptions. If at any time a Jacobite unit generates a high score then there is a chance that they will become fanatical, either charging, counter charging or even just running at their nearest enemy unit in an uncontrolled charge. A general, clan chief, or commanding personality can have both a negative as well as a positive score when influencing a unit, so their presence can be used to either calm down or inflame a unit as required, which is particularly useful if a unit is in danger of going mad with battle lust, risking upsetting a general's battle plan and in need of calming down. As stipulated above, once committed a unit will charge for two moves and will end up disordered if it does not encounter an enemy unit in that time.

MORALE FACTORS TABLE			
Event	Factor	Event	Factor
Advancing	+ 1	Being charged by fanatical clansmen	- 3
Artillery shooting in support	+ 1	Routing	- 3
Each secure flank	+ 1	Disordered	- 2
In soft cover	+ 1	Downhill of nearest enemy	- 2
Winning current melee	+ 1	Enemy to the rear	- 2
Won last melee	+ 1	Government cavalry below enemy	- 2
Already charging	+ 2	Government cavalry charged while stationary	- 2
Clan unit already fanatical	+ 2	Jacobites charged by horse	- 2
In hard cover	+ 2	Losing 4 figures in one move	- 2
Jacobites fired upon by artillery	+ 2	Losing current melee	- 2
Nearest enemy retreating	+ 2	Lost last melee	- 2
No casualties suffered to date	+ 2	Outnumbwered by at least 2:1 in current melee	- 2
Uphill of nearest enemy	+ 2	Poorly trained or militia regiment	- 2
Government cavalry uphill of their enemy	+ 3	Surprised	- 2
Within fortifications / large building	+ 4	Being charged at by clansmen	- 1
In solid cover	+ 10	Each 2 figure casualties suffered	- 1
Other senior officer with unit	+ 1 / - 1	Each routing unit within 12"	- 1
Sub-general with unit	+ 2 / - 2	Enemy to the flank	- 1
Clan Chief with unit	+ 3 / - 3	Fired upon by artillery	- 1
Commander in Chief with unit	+ 3 / - 3	Retiring in the face of fhe enemy	- 1

Morale – Definitions and Elements to be taken into Consideration

- Note that all regular troops, including foreign regiments, fighting for the Jacobites and allied units fighting for the Government use the Government line when calculating morale results.
- Routing is when a unit turns its back on the enemy and runs away as fast as possible from all enemies.
- A unit that routs to the edge of the allotted battlefield makes one more attempt but if that morale test fails then the unit is deemed to have left the field of battle for good.
- A unit that fails three morale tests in a row, even if not engaged in melee or suffering other battle effects, will retire for two moves in good order while still facing the enemy. Once those moves are completed it is free to move forward again, but would have to take a morale test to make any of the critical moves listed above.
- A unit that is behind cover and does not want to pursue an enemy unit that it has repelled does not have to follow up unless the player commanding the unit wishes it to do so and only if it is specified within the orders for that unit.
- Any factor that has an optional plus or minus factor means that the general has the option of which to apply.
- Any unit which falls below 50 per cent of its initial strength and started with less than ten figures must rout off the table.

				MORALE RESULTS TABLE				
	To Charge			Response to being Charged			All other situations	
core	Govt Foot	Govt Horse	Jacobite	Govt Foot	Govt Horse	Jacobite	Govt - all	Jacobite
14+	Yes	Yes	Yes - fanatical	Countercharge	Countercharge	Countercharge & become fanatical	Obey orders	Charge fanatically at nearest enemy
1-13	Yes	Yes	Yes - fanatical	Countercharge	Countercharge	Countercharge & become fanatical	Obey orders	Advance 1 move forward
'-10	Yes	Yes	Yes	Hold & fire twice	Countercharge	Advance & fire	Obey orders	Obey orders
- 6	Advance, fire once	Advance - no charge	Advance, fire once	Hold & fire once	Retire 1 move	Hold & fire	Obey orders	Obey orders
- 3	Shaken - No movement	Shaken, no advance	Stand	Fire & retire 1 move	Retire 2 moves	Fire & rout	No advance	No advance
0-1	Shaken - Retire 1 move	Shaken - Retire 1 move	Shaken - no movement	Rout	Retire 3 moves	Rout	Retire 2 moves	Retire 2 moves
<0	Shaken - Retire 2 moves	Shaken - Retire 2 moves	Shaken - retire 1 move	Rout	Rout	Rout	Rout	Rout

Example 4 – Testing Morale

A Jacobite clan unit currently moving forward across a ridge wishes to charge a unit of dragoons who are slowly approaching them from further down the hillside. Neither side is charging at present. The Jacobite player throws his D10 and scores a 6; checking the factor table the Jacobites get +1 for already advancing and +2 for being uphill of their nearest enemy. They also receive a -1 as they were hit in the previous round by a shot from the Government artillery. This gives them a score of 8; however, the clan chief is also with the unit and his personal command is so strong that he can either add or subtract 3 to a total morale score to either excite a unit to charge or to calm it down from being too eager to charge. As the chief wants to charge he adds his 3 to the aforementioned 8. Checking the morale results table, the unit with 11 goes fanatical and charges down towards the dragoons. The Government player does not want to involve his dragoons in a melee as he was hoping to get them behind the enemy flank, and they have orders not to engage. So the dragoons now have to respond to the Highlanders' aggression and the player throws a 9. They have no plus factors at all save the fact that they were moving forward (advancing) which gives them +1. They do have some minus factors: -3 for being charged by fanatical Highlanders, and -2 for being downhill of the enemy, which brings them down to 5. There are no other factors applicable and so on consulting the table in 'response to being charged', a 5 means that the Government horse will retire for a move, which takes the dragoons away from the charging Highlanders for this move. A further test will need to be taken next move as all charges last for two moves.

Disorder

A unit can become disordered for a number of reasons; when this happens the fighting ability and the morale of that unit can be adversely affected because it is no longer a coherent body of men moving and fighting together. The causes of disorder are as follows:

- Crossing larger ditches, hedges and high but climbable walls, embarking or disembarking from boats.
- Fighting in marshes, woods, forests or other difficult terrain.
- Fighting inside a settlement with a maze of streets and buildings.
- The third and any subsequent rounds of melee actions.
- An allied unit interpenetrating with any of its other allied units.
- While in the process of re-forming for one move after a melee or rout has ended.
- Suffering 50 per cent or more casualties in a single move, whether from missiles, melees or a combination thereof.
- If attacked by an enemy unit which has surprised it, perhaps coming out of fog, cave or building/s.
- If engaged in melee by an enemy unit while in the process of changing formation.
- Assaulting high walls and fortifications, entering a breach made by an artillery bombardment.

Ship to Ship Battles

The Jacobite rebellions provide the gamer with the benefit of both land and sea battles, all encompassed within British territorial waters. A complete set of naval wargame rules would provide enough material for a whole book in itself and indeed there are dedicated wargame systems available for sea battle enthusiasts that delve into every minutiae of commanding a fleet from every period of maritime history, from Ancient Greece up to the Cold War. For our purposes, given that the naval encounters in these uprisings were small, the following tables, together with a ships master sheet in the appendices (see Appendix 2), will give the players a simple but a comprehensive set of mechanics with which to resolve any ship to ship encounters and these could easily be used for larger sea battles as part of a campaign if required. The principles are very simple: apply the size of the ship in the game to the nearest size of ship on the table below. Each ship has factors which apply to it – these are listed on the table below and should be written at the top of the ships master sheet before play starts. This master sheet is very simple to complete and also allows a record of each move and the damage both inflicted and sustained to be recorded.

At the start of each move orders are written for each ship, just as if the captain was on the deck bellowing out his orders as the crew manned their guns and ran up the ropes to adjust the sails. The key thing for the player is to always stipulate every move four simple things: whether his guns are primed to fire or reloading; if loaded, whether they will fire at an enemy's hull or rigging; what speed the ship will be moving at; and whether they will sail straight or bear to port or starboard or a combination thereof. The key elements and factors to understand are:

- Guns per ship – how many it carries in total.
- Batteries per side – how many D10 it rolls per side firing and all ships' cannon takes a full move to reload.
- Hull points – how many hits it can sustain before sinking – a ship normally surrenders if half of these are lost.
- Hull points per battery – how many cumulative hits takes out one battery.

NAVAL RULES TABLE											
Size / Type of ship	Guns per ship	Batteries per side	Hull Pts	Hull Pts per battery	Rigging Pts	Speed in cms			Short range	Medium range	Long range	Damage pts caused
						Slow	Part	Full	0-8 cms	8-16 cms	16-24 cms	
Gun Ship of the line	74	4	40	5	24	4	8	12	5-6	7-8	9-10	3
Gun Ship of the line	60	4	40	5	21	4	8	12	5-6	7-8	9-10	3
Gun Ship of the line	48	3	24	4	18	5	10	15	6-7	8-9	10	2
Gun Ship / Privateer	32	3	24	4	15	5	10	15	6-7	8-9	10	2
Gun Ship / Privateer	20	2	16	4	12	6	12	18	7-8	9-10	N/A	1
Gun Brig / Privateer	12	1	8	4	9	8	16	24	7-8	9-10	N/A	1

A French privateer being broadsided by a British man of war.

- Rigging points – how many hits it can sustain before it just drifts – it normally surrenders if all of these are lost.
- Speed in cm – how far a ship moves is determined by how much sail it has and the wind direction.
- Ranges in cm – what number needs to be thrown on a D10 at the appropriate range to score a hit.
- Damage points caused – if a hit is caused then this is how much damage that hit has done to the target vessel.

Each ship has a finite number of hull and rigging points. Every time the number of hull points per battery is achieved, the vessel loses the ability to shoot that battery – if all of these are lost then it sinks. If rigging is damaged, and one-third has been lost, the ship can only go at slow or part speed; when two-thirds have been lost then the ship can only move at slow speed.

Once again, our compass and random direction need to be brought into play as the wind direction needs to be determined, a crucial factor as a ship cannot sail directly into the wind and cannot go above 'part' speed when sailing within 90 degrees of the wind. A normal protractor is ideal for this measurement and can also be used for determining turns to port and starboard – each 10 degrees being a 1 cm movement space.

Sieges

The history of our world is littered with battles, but there have been many more sieges than open conflicts in the field. The majority of British castles have been besieged time and again in their long history, and now stand as ruined monuments to their bygone days. There were very few successful siege actions by the Jacobites during the rebellions – Stirling and Edinburgh castles both remained in Government hands throughout all of the campaigns. All of the other siege actions where a side surrendered were due to overwhelming odds, such as at Ruthven and Inverness, where no shots were fired. The only really successful Jacobite siege action was at Fort Augustus, where it was a fluke shot that destroyed the whole fort. To allow this to be replicated on the table-top then the artillery shooting table from above is used; every successful hit destroys one square inch of the defender's walls. After every ten successful shots a percentage dice roll is made, with two ten-sided dice. If a score of 5 per cent is generated then a pre-named part of the defences has been destroyed (this could be a gateway, a door, an enemy battery on the walls and so forth). This may seem a slow, cumbersome process, but it reflects the lengthy time that the Jacobites wasted at Fort William and Stirling Castle, where the artillery was just not up to the job. The Government artillery, with its better statistics, will therefore destroy more of any defended building and they will destroy a key pre-named part of the defences if they throw below 15 per cent on a percentage roll.

Cover

The protection offered to troops can either be natural, such as a hedge or woodland, or planned and constructed defences. Any foot troops can take shelter behind walls or hedges, snuggle down into ditches or move into buildings, and some mounted units may also be able to take advantage of larger walls and buildings depending on the size of the terrain. The number of people that can be protected is equivalent to how many figures would fit behind an object or into the space available inside a building. Thus if a small cottage occupied a base area of 4 inches by 2 inches, this would equate to 8 square inches, sufficient to protect eight figures. It is assumed that at need forces would close ranks to get protection or to hide from the enemy. This mechanism can be used for all infantry units, while one cavalryman and one horse would be considered to occupy 3 square inches in total. Cover can be destroyed either by men smashing at it with axes or swords or by artillery firing directly at it. Damage is caused as follows:

Soft Cover	Can be destroyed at the rate of 1 square inch per move per one figure involved: thus six figures would clear 6 square inches in one move; artillery destroys 2 square inches per hit
Hard Cover	Can be destroyed at the rate of 1 square inch per four moves per one figure involved: thus twenty-four figures would clear 6 square inches in one move; artillery destroys 1 square inch per hit
Solid Cover	Can only be damaged as per siege conditions

Fire and Smoke – Optional Rules

Smoke is created equivalent to the size of the area of terrain that is burning. Thus if a cottage on the table was 6 inches by 4 inches by 3 inches high, then the smoke will be of that volume.

This smoke will move according to the direction of any wind that is blowing and obscure units and terrain as it drifts behaving like fog on the weather table. If there is no wind in the game then the smoke moves in accordance with the random movement table, representing its erratic movement in eddies created by the heat from the burning cottage. Fire will not start in an area of wet terrain such as a pool, marsh or river. In addition, if there is no wind at all then every time an infantry unit lets fly a volley, or an artillery battery shoots, smoke will be created equivalent to half the size of the unit shooting, which will last for three game moves before dispersing. Any units shooting through smoke or charging through smoke count as disordered.

Street Fighting

The vast majority of battles will be fought across open terrain, but as we have seen both Dunkeld and Preston were fought in the narrow streets of a settlement. While the initial exchanges might be from volleys of formed troops approaching barricades or buildings, those troops will soon become separated into small groups or even individuals. To determine casualties in this type of situation, instead of shooting as a group, all shots are taken individually and thrown for on the following table. The number in the box is the relevant number that needs to be generated on a percentage dice roll, a D100, to cause one casualty; and the more sheltered the intended target is, then the harder they are to be killed. For example, if a dragoon shot with a carbine at a Highlander running across a street, he would need to throw under 31 (the number on the table for the relevant circumstance), meaning that he needs 30 or under to have scored a hit. Artillery shooting is calculated in the normal manner as it is capable of damaging buildings and any troops concealed inside. It may be necessary for the players to keep separate records of how many men are hidden in which building for a full-scale battle such as Preston.

INDIVIDUAL TARGET TABLE					
Figure Firing using	Range	Target is in ...			
		Open - stationary	Open - moving	Soft Cover	Hard Cover
Carbine	0 to 12"	<41	<31	<21	<06
Flintlock musket	0 to 12"	<41	<31	<21	<06
Matchlock musket	0 to 10"	<36	<26	<16	<06
Pistol	0 to 5"	<51	<31	<21	<06

Organising a Campaign

Like any gaming subject, when players think about a campaign then the matter of budget comes into play and how much time, scenery and figures are available. For a simple campaign covering a small area then a feud such as between the Camerons and MacDonalds with cattle rustling and homestead burning can be played out. It is more like a Wild West campaign than anything else in Britain, with rocky mountains and forests replacing deserts and mountain creeks. All that is needed is a detailed ordnance survey map of the area, and castles which are perhaps now ruins can be reinterpreted as habitable. For a more comprehensive campaign, a travelling road/route map of Scotland and northern England will provide all of the basic information necessary to begin, with the forces deployed relevant to the month and year that the players wish the campaign to start. To aid the players with some campaign ideas, there is a summary of 'what-ifs' at the end of this chapter. There is a commercial board wargame available which provides everything needed to re-fight the 1745 rebellion, but the pieces could be used for any of the earlier campaigns with a little adaption. The author does not know if the game is still available new but second hand ones do appear at conventions from time to time; it is called 'The '45' and it was produced by Decision Games.

Conclusions

The spectacular scenery of the campaigns, the colourful uniforms of the regular troops and varied clothing of the Highland troops and the contrast between a modern European government-controlled army and the old-fashioned, quasi-medieval tactics of an army fighting for a cause, all combine to make the Jacobite wars a fascinating period to wargame in. This can be further enhanced by the gamer if they choose to run a campaign whereby they remove the natural events which conspired to thwart so many of the attempted Jacobite risings. These alternative scenarios are summarised below within the year that they happened to provide the enthusiast with some ready-made campaign scenarios.

1689   Bonnie Dundee is not killed in the Battle of Killiecrankie and the Jacobite army is swelled by the recruits arriving at Blair Atholl Castle. The Jacobites go on to win the Battle of Dunkeld and have an army of 10,000 to support James II's rising in Ireland. This forces William III to face two major rebellions on two fronts, while the threat of a French invasion of England could open up a third front.

1692   The French invasion fleet is not destroyed at the Battle of Cap de la Hogue by Admiral Rooke and the French-Irish army of 16,000 men is landed in England or Scotland together with James II.

1708   The French invasion fleet of thirty ships and with 6,000 men aboard is not driven off by Admiral Byng and successfully lands in Scotland. This combines with a similar force of clansmen that flock to the cause, thereby giving James II's son James Edward Stuart (The Old Pretender) a force of 12,000 men who were well armed and sufficiently provisioned to invade England. With Marlborough's forces stretched upon the continent of Europe, this would be the war on two fronts which the French were consistently aiming for.

1715   The Jacobites in England hold out long enough at Carlisle to allow the victorious Mar to follow up his advantage at Sheriffmuir and invade England with a significantly larger force looking to combine forces with their comrades in Preston.

1716   With the Royal Navy already at war with Swedish privateers in the North Sea and Baltic channels, the Swedish Government agree to aid the Jacobites and send an army of 10,000 men on a fleet of thirty ships to be the mainstay of a new Jacobite rebellion. This is in retaliation to the concessions made to Hanover, and thereby the new British monarch, in new European treaties.

1719   The Spanish invasion fleet is not scattered by a series of storms and they land with 5,000 men in Cornwall. At the same time, the Highland clans rise in significant numbers on learning that the Spanish have landed on British soil and begin a march on Edinburgh.

1744   The large French fleet which assembled with 10,000 men ready to invade the British Isles is not hampered by a series of Channel storms and succeeds in landing its troops as planned, in the Thames estuary and in Scotland. Had this happened then the famous '45 of legend would have been the '44 and a very different outcome may have transpired as the British forces in 1744 were heavily committed in the campaign in Europe, exactly as Louis XV wanted.

1745/6   There are a whole host of possibilities in these years for any gamer playing Charles Edward Stuart to exploit, and the majority bring with them the possibility of a greater success than occurred in reality.

A. Both of the two ships which convey Charles Edward Stuart to Scotland arrive, giving the Bonnie Prince both more money and a good quantity of arms with which to pay and equip his recruits. More men flock to the prince than originally to begin the uprising as the news of his gold spreads.

B. The Jacobites do not turn around at Derby and instead push on to London – their army growing at a small rate means that they would have an army of around 6,000 by the time they reached London, and being so close to the capital there is a chance that French support might materialise if Louis XV is convinced that the Jacobites can succeed and replace the Hanoverian and Protestant George II with a Stuart king who would be beholden to Catholic France.

C. Although the Jacobites do turn around at Derby and win the battle of Falkirk, this time they follow up their victory and harry Hawley's retreating army, bolstering their own force with captured weapons and equipment, enabling them to continue the campaign.

D. The vessel *Prince Charles* safely lands and delivers the 11,400 English guineas, which is met by the Jacobite escorting detachment, allowing the prince to pay and buy better rations and equipment for his men prior to Culloden and stave off clan desertions to their homes.

E. After Falkirk and the subsequent arrival of Cumberland's army, Lord George Murray is allowed to choose the field of battle and so avoids the unfavourable terrain of Culloden, and instead picks ground much more suited to the Highland style of fighting. Murray also ensures his men are rested and ready to fight by avoiding any high-risk night time manoeuvres, giving them the best chance of winning where the speed and brute force of his men will count above all else in his army.

1759 Charles agrees to the French plan to invade Britain but only if they invade England and not Ireland or Scotland. Dissension in the latter two countries, with some surviving Jacobites keen for revenge for Culloden, leads to a rising in Scotland aided by Irish Jacobite supporters. Despite defeat at the Battle of Quiberon Bay the French manage to gather together twenty-five ships and 8,000 men which they land in Devon.

The Border Warlords Falkirk Battle at WMMS 2014. Showing the author, Tim, Sam and Alan.

Acknowledgements

I am eternally grateful to those people that have accompanied me and helped me interpret the many varied sites I have visited over the years, and not least on my long trips from the Midlands and Mid-Wales to the Scottish Highlands. Alan Hewitt has accompanied me on many expeditions and our friendship extends as far back as our first attempts as wargaming back at KEGS in the early '70s. Alan's approach as a questioning academic who is always ready to challenge any written source as well as my own interpretations is always welcome and will always be so. We are now joined in our interpretations by Alan's son, Tim, whose own military knowledge expands with every visit. Tim is also a seasoned wargamer who readily challenges rule mechanics and the reasons behind the results obtained, and why, as the rule designer of a historical period, I am looking for such results. Similar thanks go to my good friend Derek Crawford, my companion on many a long journey to a remote landscape. His help in interpretation is just as challenging as Alan's and his knowledge of the different types of wood is particularly useful when examining old weapons. My thanks too for the support of my dear friend Annie and her ever-faithful dog Rosie, both of whom accompanied me on my first long battlefield tour of Scotland, some ten years ago now; sadly, Rosie has moved on and is now chasing golden rabbits, as big as sheep apparently, on some enormous battlefield moor in the sky. My thanks to my son-in-law Ed and my daughter Sabrina, who are now established as photographers in their own right and who now help me with each of my book projects, with advice on photography in general, and who take responsibility for the close-ups of the figures when we have a photo shoot. Imogen, my youngest daughter, is the ancient historian of the family and her knowledge of the way army lists function, and her ability with maths, make her the perfect foil for checking all my wargame tables and army lists.

My thanks also to for my dear friend Sam for his rule reading and play-testing, and also to his partner Alison, who is an accomplished figure painter and whose work is captured in some of the photographs. They have also accompanied me on many battlefield walks and hopefully the work we have done together will appear in a new book before too long. Like Alan above, Adrian and I go right back to KEGS days, which for me started in 1969. Adrian is a historian, re-enactor and leading entomologist, and when battlefield walking, has been known to focus in on the fauna to determine where the armies stood. Without his help and encouragement back in the early '70s I doubt if I would have ever become so heavily involved in military history. Adrian has been an avid gamer and has

Above left: Sabrina, Ed and Imogen – my family support team.

Above right: Alan studies a map ready for the afternoon detective work.

play-tested many rule ideas, and like all of my close friends, his friendship and help is greatly appreciated.

There is a memorial to the Jacobite army just outside Derby at Swarkestone Bridge, which crosses the River Trent. The river was the last major obstacle that the Jacobites had to cross before the road was open all the way to London. That memorial cairn is in the grounds of local public house and I am most grateful to the management of the Crewe and Harpur Inn, who have kindly given me permission to include photographs taken from their garden – it is an excellent spot to sit and ponder what would have happened if the Jacobites had pushed on to London. My thanks to my dear friends Louise and her daughter Emma, who gave me tremendous support as we researched our way around Preston on a bitterly cold day in March, and for their help with the photographs at numerous other historical sites.

Turning slightly more to the academic side, I must thank Vanessa for her personal insight into the Battle of Killiecrankie and the great kindness she extended to Annie and myself when we were visiting. My thanks to Mr Steadman at the Wemyss and March estates, who has kindly allowed me to reproduce the portrait of Prince Charles Edward Stuart, painted by Allan Ramsay in Edinburgh 1745. I would like to acknowledge the copyright and reproduction, which was with the kind permission of the Earl of Wemyss and March at Gosford House.

The National Trust staff at Kedleston Hall were fantastic when I arrived on a day in the winter when they were not officially open, and let me in to take a picture of the very rare original coehorn mortar abandoned there by Lord Ogilvy's clan at the commencement of their retreat from Derby. As a member of the National Trust for thirty-six years, I am very grateful for all the help they have given me over the years.

I am most grateful for the wonderful assistance of Lucy Salt at the Derby Museum, who has allowed me to reproduce a photograph of the room in Derby where the fateful decision was made for the Jacobite army to return to London. The museum has a detailed Jacobite section and the city boasts a statue of Bonnie Prince Charlie looking forlornly towards London. Lucy and Andrew Bamford are also members of a re-enactment association known as the 'Lace Wars', which is Britain's premier eighteenth-century living history organisation, made up of a number of groups recreating military and civilian life during the turbulent and fascinating era that I cover in this book. The Lace Wars Society specialises in the period 1740–1760 and in particular the 1745 Jacobite Rebellion. They stage events throughout the year at historic sites in the UK and Europe. They currently have members recreating infantry and dragoons from the forces of George II, the Highland and Lowland Jacobites, and detachments of the Manchester Regiment and Irish Picquets. Clients include the National Trust, English Heritage, and Historic Scotland, as well as local museums and private houses. Their events can vary from mock battles with infantry and cavalry to small regimental living history camps. They are a family friendly group open to both new and experienced re-enactors – more information can be found on their website, www.lacewars.co.uk.

When working on any project there are times when something special is required – luck or a miracle – on more than one occasion I have been blessed by a stroke of fortune and in the writing of this work, serendipity struck again. While at Dornie on the west coast of Scotland in March 2014, I made the acquaintance of another author, Alan Rowan, who writes on climbing the mountains of Scotland. Due to some inclement weather I had been unable to capture the image I wanted of Tongue Bay and time restraints meant that I had not got the chance to revisit. Luckily, Alan already had such a picture and thanks to his kindness that picture is now within this work. More information can be found on Alan's work at munromoonwalker.com, so called because Alan's speciality is climbing the Munros at night. Emma at Preston Museum was also a great help with small but important facts about the town's role in the '15 Jacobite rising and the museum is looking to include some local events in 2015 as the town celebrates the 300th anniversary of the battle.

While travelling the mainland of Britain I have had many small but invaluable snippets of information which have allowed me to drive up the correct lane, or find a convenient place to park in order to get the best photograph, and so a big thank you to all those public spirited people from across Scotland and the north of England who made my battlefield research so rewarding.

A big thank you to the team at Amberley Publishing, who ensure that all the small but essential elements of a book that combines both military history and wargaming are met to provide the reader with a complete guide to a unique period in not just British but European history, so thanks to Louis, Emily, Sarah, Eleri and Campbell.

Finally, a big thank you to my mother, who in her own career long before the advent of a PC or laptop was an RSA3 shorthand and typist – I only wish I was that quick across the keys! When the chips are down and the deadline looms ever closer I am grateful to the hot meals and drinks provided at regular intervals to keep me going, while every available flat surface in the house seems to have a detailed map of a different part of Scotland spread out upon it. I know you would like to help more than you are able to do, but you are and always have been a wonderful mum.

In case there is anyone I have forgotten, an extra thank you goes to you.

Martin Hackett 2014

Army Order Sheet

my			Commander		
anding Orders for the battle					

Move	Unit	Orders	Target	Result	Duration / Notes

Naval Order Sheet

NAVAL RECORD SHEET:		SHIP'S NAME:			
Ship's Guns & Batteries		Commander			
Hull Points record		Rigging Points record			
Port Batteries record		Starboard Batteries record			
Move	Ship's Speed	Ship's Directions and orders	Guns Port	Guns Stbrd	Target ship, hull or rigging
1					
2					
3					
4					
5					
6					
7					
8					
9					
10					
11					
12					
13					
14					
15					
16					
17					
18					
19					
20					

ARTILLERY SHOOTING TABLE

CANNONS - ALL CALIBRES

Range	Close Range up to 10"			Effective Range 10" - 40"		
Target is in open ground						
Government	1 Gun	2 Guns	3 Guns	1 Gun	2 Guns	3 Guns
	1.0	2.0	3.0	0.5	1.0	1.5
Jacobite	1 Gun	2 Guns	3 Guns	1 Gun	2 Guns	3 Guns
	0.5	1.0	1.5	0.2	0.5	0.8
Target is in soft cover						
Government	1 Gun	2 Guns	3 Guns	1 Gun	2 Guns	3 Guns
	0.8	1.6	2.4	0.4	0.8	1.2
Jacobite	1 Gun	2 Guns	3 Guns	1 Gun	2 Guns	3 Guns
	0.4	0.7	1.0	0.2	0.4	0.6
Target is in hard or solid cover						
Government	1 Gun	2 Guns	3 Guns	1 Gun	2 Guns	3 Guns
	0.4	0.7	1.0	0.2	0.4	0.6
Jacobite	1 Gun	2 Guns	3 Guns	1 Gun	2 Guns	3 Guns
	0.2	0.4	0.6	0.1	0.2	0.3

MORTARS 15" - 35" ONLY

Target is in	Open or soft cover			Hard or solid cover		
Government	1 Gun	2 Guns	3 Guns	1 Gun	2 Guns	3 Guns
	1.0	2.0	3.0	0.5	1.0	1.5
Jacobite	1 Gun	2 Guns	3 Guns	1 Gun	2 Guns	3 Guns
	0.5	1.0	1.5	0.2	0.5	0.8

ARTILLERY HIT LOCATION TABLE

D10 Result	Action
1	Gun misfires - A throw of 1 twice running and the cannon explodes
2	Shot overshoots centre of target by 6"
3	Shot falls short of centre of target by 6"
4	Shot falls short of centre of target by 3"
5	Shot overshoots centre of target by 3"
6	Shot falls left of centre by 3" from the firing cannon
7	Shot falls right of centre by 3" from the firing cannon
8 - 10	shot hits in the centre of the target from the firing cannon

Each time artillery shoots at the same target +1 on the dice roll

Artillery shooting at a static target e.g. a building +2 on the dice roll

A moving target always counts as a fresh target

. If a target moves between 4 and 8 inches -1 on the dice roll.

. If a target moves between 8 and 12 inches -2 on the dice roll.

. If a target moves further than 12 inches -3 on the dice roll.

Distances in inches

TROOP TYPE	Normal	Manoeuvre	Charge	Retire	Rout - O/O
Infantry - Line	4	2	2 + D6	3	8
Infantry - Column	6	3	6 + D6	4	8
Light Infantry	8	6	8 + D10	6	8
Light Cavalry	16	10	16 + D10	12	20
Heavy Cavalry	12	6	14 + D10	8	20
Naval crew	6	6	6 + D6	6	8
Jacobite foot	8	4	8 + D6	6	10
Jacobite Horse	12	8	10 + D6	6	20
Artillery - manhandled	2	N/A	N/A	2	8 No Guns
Artillery - limbered	6	N/A	N/A	N/A	10 With Guns

SMALL ARMS SHOOTING TABLE

No of Figs	Short Range up to 6" — Carbine / Musket / Pistol					Long Range 6" - 12" — Carbine / Musket				
	First Volley open terrain	First Volley at soft cover	Other Volley	At Soft Cover	At Hard Cover	First Volley open terrain	First Volley at soft cover	Other Volley	At Soft Cover	At Hard Cover
1 to 5	0.6	0.3	0.3	0.2	0.0	0.2	0.2	0.1	0.1	0.0
6	0.8	0.4	0.4	0.3	0.1	0.3	0.3	0.1	0.1	0.0
7	1.0	0.5	0.5	0.4	0.1	0.4	0.4	0.2	0.1	0.0
8	1.2	0.6	0.6	0.4	0.1	0.5	0.4	0.2	0.1	0.0
9	1.4	0.7	0.7	0.5	0.1	0.6	0.5	0.3	0.1	0.0
10	1.6	0.8	0.8	0.5	0.2	0.7	0.5	0.3	0.2	0.1
11	1.8	0.9	0.9	0.6	0.2	0.8	0.6	0.4	0.2	0.1
12	2.0	1.0	1.0	0.6	0.2	0.9	0.6	0.4	0.2	0.1
13	2.2	1.1	1.1	0.7	0.3	1.0	0.7	0.5	0.3	0.1
14	2.4	1.2	1.2	0.7	0.3	1.1	0.7	0.5	0.3	0.1
15	2.6	1.3	1.3	0.8	0.3	1.2	0.8	0.6	0.3	0.1
16	2.8	1.4	1.4	0.8	0.4	1.3	0.8	0.6	0.4	0.2
17	3.0	1.5	1.5	0.9	0.4	1.4	0.9	0.7	0.4	0.2
18	3.2	1.6	1.6	0.9	0.4	1.5	0.9	0.7	0.4	0.2
19	3.4	1.7	1.7	1.0	0.5	1.6	1.0	0.8	0.5	0.2
20	3.6	1.8	1.8	1.0	0.5	1.7	1.0	0.8	0.5	0.2

NAVAL RULES TABLE

Size / Type of ship	Guns per ship	Batteries per side	Hull Pts	Rigging Pts	Hull Pts per battery	Speed in cms			Short range 0-8 cms	Medium range 8-16 cms	Long range 16-24 cms	Damage pts caused
						Slow	Part	Full				
74 Gun Ship of the line	74	4	40	24	5	4	8	12	5-6	7-8	9-10	3
60 Gun Ship of the line	60	4	40	21	5	4	8	12	5-6	7-8	9-10	3
48 Gun Ship of the line	48	3	24	18	4	5	10	15	6-7	8-9	10	2
32 Gun Ship / Privateer	32	3	24	15	4	5	10	15	6-7	8-9	10	2
20 Gun Ship / Privateer	20	2	16	12	4	6	12	18	7-8	9-10	N/A	1
12 Gun Brig / Privateer	12	1	8	9	4	8	16	24	7-8	9-10	N/A	1

APPENDIX 4

MELEE FACTORS TABLE

Event	Factor	Event	Factor
Attacking enemy in the rear	+ 4	Attacking fortifications / solid cover	- 8
Formed infantry line against irregulars	+ 2	Attacking hard cover including ships	- 5
Surprising the enemy	+ 2	Receiving a fanatical Highland charge	- 4
Advancing, but not charging at all	+ 2	Routing troops	- 4
Advantage of ground, uphill of enemy	+ 2	Attacking soft cover including small boats	- 2
Attacking enemy in the flank, each	+ 2	Disordered troops	- 2
Charging over level terrain	+ 2	Fighting while in bogs / marshes	- 2
Fighting a disordered enemy	+ 2	Pushed back last move	- 2
Horse against disordered infantry	+ 2	Receiving a Highland charge	- 2
Infantry armed with formed pikes pre 1700	+ 2	Shaken troops	- 2
Infantry charging	+ 2	Untrained troops	- 2
Opposition is artillery or naval crew	+ 2	Using bayonets pre 1700	- 2
Won last round of melee	+ 2	Fighting with improvised weapons	- 1
Horse Charging uphill	+ 1	Fired at by Jacobite pistols this move	- 1
Horse Charging down a steady hill	No change	Retiring troops	- 1

MELEE TABLE RESULTS

Final Score	0 - 07	08 - 13	14 - 19	20 - 25	26 - 30	31 - 35
Casualties	0	1	2	3	4	5

Final Score	36 - 40	41 - 45	46 - 50	51 - 55	56 - 60	61 - 65+
Casualties	6	7	8	9	10	11

INDIVIDUAL TARGET TABLE

Figure Firing using	Range	Target is in ...			
		Open - stationary	Open - moving	Soft Cover	Hard Cover
Carbine	0 to 12"	<41	<31	<21	<06
Flintlock musket	0 to 12"	<41	<31	<21	<06
Matchlock musket	0 to 10"	<36	<26	<16	<06
Pistol	0 to 5"	<51	<31	<21	<06

MORALE RESULTS TABLE

Score	To Charge			Response to being Charged			All other situations	
	Govt Foot	Govt Horse	Jacobite	Govt Foot	Govt Horse	Jacobite	Govt - all	Jacobite
14+	Yes	Yes	Yes - fanatical	Countercharge	Countercharge	Countercharge & become fanatical	Obey orders	Charge fanatically at nearest enemy
11-13	Yes	Yes	Yes - fanatical	Countercharge	Countercharge	Countercharge & become fanatical	Obey orders	Advance 1 move forward
7-10	Yes	Yes	Yes	Hold & fire twice	Countercharge	Advance & fire	Obey orders	Obey orders
4-6	Advance, fire once	Advance - no charge	Advance, fire once	Hold & fire once	Retire 1 move	Hold & fire	Obey orders	Obey orders
2-3	Shaken - No movement	Shaken, no advance	Stand	Fire & retire 1 move	Retire 2 moves	Fire & rout	No advance	No advance
0-1	Shaken - Retire 1 move	Shaken - Retire 1 move	Shaken - no movement	Rout	Retire 3 moves	Rout	Retire 2 moves	Retire 2 moves
<0	Shaken - Retire 2 moves	Shaken - Retire 2 moves	Shaken - retire 1 move	Rout	Rout	Rout	Rout	Rout

MORALE FACTORS TABLE

Event	Factor	Event	Factor
Advancing	+ 1	Being charged by fanatical clansmen	
Artillery shooting in support	+ 1	Routing	
Each secure flank	+ 1	Disordered	
In soft cover	+ 1	Downhill of nearest enemy	
Winning current melee	+ 1	Enemy to the rear	
Won last melee	+ 1	Government cavalry below enemy	
Already charging	+ 2	Government cavalry charged while stationary	
Clan unit already fanatical	+ 2	Jacobites charged by horse	
In hard cover	+ 2	Losing 4 figures in one move	
Jacobites fired upon by artillery	+ 2	Losing current melee	
Nearest enemy retreating	+ 2	Lost last melee	
No casualties suffered to date	+ 2	Outnumbered by at least 2:1 in current melee	
Uphill of nearest enemy	+ 2	Poorly trained or militia regiment	
Government cavalry uphill of their enemy	+ 3	Surprised	
Within fortifications / large building	+ 4	Being charged at by clansmen	
In solid cover	+ 10	Each 2 figure casualties suffered	
Other senior officer with unit	+ 1 / - 1	Each routing unit within 12'	
Sub-general with unit	+ 2 / - 2	Enemy to the flank	
Clan Chief with unit	+ 3 / - 3	Fired upon by artillery	
Commander in Chief with unit	+ 3 / - 3	Retiring in the face of the enemy	

Useful Addresses

Wargame Shows

In a year there are now hundreds of wargame conventions, or 'shows' as they are commonly known, all over the world: the United Kingdom, the United States of America, and Europe have all seen growth in weekend events. These exhibitions bring together thousands of likeminded people to play competitive games, put on demonstration or participation games, or to shop gaming items. Many of these shows have become established as annual events and have been running as near as possible to the same date and at the same venue for decades. They are eagerly awaited by gamers and traders alike as old acquaintances and friendships are renewed, battles are fought and new armies purchased and discussed. The magazines below often contain adverts for forthcoming events and within a year there are bound to be one or two shows within your area. There is no better place to compare and contrast the different types of figures available – the variety of armies and scenery seems almost limitless and really brings a miniature battlefield to life. There is insufficient space to list all of the United Kingdom shows let alone those across the rest of the world, so an internet search engine is the place to browse for forthcoming events if a magazine is not available to you. So well established are some of the conventions that although I cannot put forthcoming dates down here for them, I can advise that the following shows are always in the same month as listed and they represent the major shows within Britain in any given year.

Crusade is held in Cardiff in January; WMMS is held in Wolverhampton in March; Salute is held in London in April; Britcon is held in Manchester in August; Claymore is held in Edinburgh, also in August; Colours is held in Newbury in September; the World Championships is held in Derby in October; Warfare is held in Reading in November; and Wargamer is held in Birmingham in December. In addition there are two shows a year in Newark entitled Partizan and these two events, normally held in spring and summer, are also well worth visiting. When the actual event is imminent, advertisements will appear within some or all of the magazines listed, informing the reader exactly what is going to be on at the show, what traders will be attending and there will usually be a map or a set of directions to make sure that locating the venue as easy as possible. If you have never been to a show, then give one a go; people I have taken who have never been to one before, even if they only have a passing interest in history, have been amazed and inspired by what is on display. They really bring history to life.

Magazines

The publications listed here are an excellent way for the reader to keep right up to date with the latest products available from the advertisers as well as any forthcoming events and the latest rule systems and ideas to evolve within the hobby.

Miniature Wargames with Battlegames, Atlantic Publishers, c/o The Editor, Miniature Wargames, 17 Granville Road, Hove BN3 1TG. Web: www.atlanticpublishers. com. These two long established magazines merged in 2013 and still produce an excellent, independent monthly magazine, which covers every facet of the hobby, now over thirty years in production. This magazine always covers a range of different wargame periods in each issue, and covers a wide range of topics within the hobby. It contains regular review columns on books and figures and has a specific science-fiction and fantasy section each month. There are numerous adverts from suppliers across the hobby and details of forthcoming events.

Wargames Illustrated, Unit 4C, Tissington Close, Beeston, Nottingham NG9 6QG. Web: www.wargamesillustrated.net. This wargames magazine is now approaching its twenty-seventh year in print and continues to deliver an inspiring issue each time. The magazine covers an abundance of wargame periods, but with each issue having a themed period examined from different angles, and coverage of some of the more obscure periods of warfare. There are regular review columns as well as numerous adverts from suppliers to the hobby and details of forthcoming events.

Wargames, Soldiers and Strategy, PO Box 4082, 7200 BB Zutphen, Netherlands. Tel: 00 31 575 776076. Web: www.wssmagazine.com. This wargames magazine is a bi-monthly publication which covers a wide range of historical periods in each issue. Sometimes articles are linked to a theme within an issue which can make it a useful reference point in the future, and there are also some articles which link from one issue to the next. There are in-depth reviews and also advertisements for wargaming products.

Shops

Although the days have long gone when every town had its own independent toy or model shop selling models, balsa wood, plastic and metal figures, there are still some places where they survive. If there is not a dedicated model shop selling figures, you may still find a model railway shop, where at least the necessary paints, brushes and landscape scenery can be obtained; Kidderminster, for instance, has two such shops, perhaps influenced by the Severn Valley Railway being based there. Luckily for the gamer, a few independent gaming shops do still survive and their details are listed below.

The Games Shop, 6 Wellington Street, Aldershot, Hampshire, GU11 1DZ. Tel: 01252 311443. Web: www.the-online-games-shop.co.uk. This shop has been established for many years and has always been a leading independent games centre. They stock a wide range of historical and fantasy figures and games covering all aspects of role-playing and wargaming. They also stock a wide range of rule books, paints, scenery and an extensive range of board games.

Sanda Games, 4 Albert Place, Donnington, Telford, Shropshire, TF2 8AF. Tel: 01952 676722. Web: www.sandagames.co.uk. Sanda have been established for many years and have a good range of both historical and fantasy figures. They also sell scenery, paints, role-playing games, rule systems, military books and some board games. They have a gaming table on site and can provide a painting and mail order service for customers as well.

Shire Games, 41a Parliament Row, Hanley, Staffordshire, ST1 1PW. Tel: 01782 287270; Fax: 01782 285741. Shire has been established for over six years and they have a good range of board games and some historical figures as well. They organise regular events and tournaments where people can try out new board games to see if they like them, and this attracts enthusiasts from across the United Kingdom. They also provide a mail order service for customers.

Spirit Games, 98, 114 and 115 Station Street, Burton-on-Trent, Staffordshire, DE14 1BT. Tel: 01283 511293. Web: www.spiritgames.co.uk. This shop has been established for many years and has an extensive range of historical figures and board games, including both a second hand and a discounted section. There is also a whole series of sections devoted to the different fantasy figure manufacturers, providing a myriad of figure choices for both the wargamer and role-player, and the and role-playing systems that go with them.

Wayland's Forge, 2 Fletchers Walk, Paradise Circus, Birmingham, West Midlands, B3 3HJ. Tel: 0121 683 0075. Web: www.waylanddsforge.co.uk. This is an Aladdin's cave of gaming products, including a large section of second-hand items and a huge range of board games. There is a collection of military books, and a large selection of historical figures in a range of different scales. There is also an excellent selection of fantasy role-playing books, associated figures and different rule systems.

Suppliers of Figures, Scenery and Storage Products

The United Kingdom contains the largest number of companies manufacturing wargame figures in the world and naturally the majority of the companies listed below are based there. Unless you have seen the figures, either at a wargames show or as part of someone else's collection, the author would recommend examining the figures online through the relevant company's web site. The majority of these websites allow the gamer to see the variety of figures available from a given manufacturer and to see just how good they look when painted up or in their raw metal state. Every reader of this book and every gamer will have their own interpretation as to which figure company produces the style of casting that to them reflects the way their armies would have looked. Some people like to bring great variety to their armies by using as many different figures from as many different companies as possible, thereby bringing a great range to the height and build of the figures within their army, and so reflecting the infinite variety of the human frame.

Other people prefer to have a complete army from one manufacturer to give continuity. The great advantage for the collector is that today there is a greater range of figures in a greater range of scales available than ever before.

Battleboards HQ, 36 Grove Avenue, Weymouth, Dorset DT4 7RJ. Tel: 01305 77635. Web: www.battleboards.co.uk. This company, formed in 2010, produces a series of wargame terrain boards in two shades – desert sand and grass green. Each board is around 600 mm square and 40 mm thick, but as this book is written the size of these boards is going to change slightly, so they will be slightly different to those shown in some of the photographs within this book. For commercially made terrain, these boards are incredibly detailed, so much so that you can see the swirls in the water where troops have crossed a river through a ford. As well as the basic boards, a range of hills, buildings and terrain features will also be available to match the base boards.

Baccus 6 mm, Unit C, Graham House, Sheffield, S3 8AS. Tel: 01142 724491. Web: www. baccus6mm.com. As the company title suggests, Baccus produce just 6-mm figures, and although they do not produce a specific Jacobite range, they do produce seventeenth-century Scots and a whole range of early and mid-eighteenth-century figures which could easily represent the armies required. This scale allows simple conversions to be done through painting alone.

Eagle Figures, 6 The Larches, Ormesby, Middlesborough TS7 9DG. Tel: 07985 029871. Web: www.eaglefigures.co.uk. Eagle Figures produce a comprehensive range of true 28-mm figures for the Seven Years War, one of their specialist areas, which covers troops from both Britain and France as well as the other European nations including Hanoverians. This is an expanding range under new ownership and they produce figures which are suitable for some of the more obscure troops that fought in the rebellion. They also produce civilians and some later militia troops and very rarely available correct Hungarian troops for the War of the Austrian Succession.

Essex Miniatures, Unit 1, Shannon Centre, Shannon Square, Thames Estuary Estate, Canvey Island, Essex, SS8 0PE. Tel: 01268 682309. Web: www.essexminiatures.com. Essex produces an extensive range of 15-mm figures, and the often neglected equipment, tents and encampments to support an army on campaign. Both Government and Jacobite armies are available in their 15-mm range, and some packs contain variants so that the groups of similarly armed figures will look fluid and not like automatons when assembled into units. Essex also makes the Lowlanders, Highlanders and the regular troops that fought on both sides. They have an excellent range.

Front Rank Figurines Ltd, The Granary, Banbury Road ,Lower Boddington, Daventry, Northamptonshire NN11 6XY. Tel: 01327 262720. Web: www.frontrank.com. Front Rank produce true 28-mm figures for all periods of the various Jacobite risings and with close to 300 castings in a wide range of poses, including casualties. There is also a comprehensive range of artillery pieces including the effective coehorn mortars as well as battlefield carts and civilian personalities. Front Rank cover the period more than any other manufacturer at time of publication. There are late seventeenth-century peasants and regular troops for the Sedgemoor and Boyne campaigns and the War of the Spanish

Succession range covers the '15 and '19 risings. For the '45 there are both Highlanders and Lowlanders, and figures within their Severn Years War and French-Indian Wars ranges also allow the gamer to cover some of the more obscure units from the '45 rebellion (specifically the Georgia Rangers and Cumberland's bodyguard of mounted hussars).

Hinds Figures Ltd, 99 Birchover Way, Allestree, Derby DE22 2QH UK. Tel: 01332 559025. Web: www.hindsfiguresltd.com. This company specialises in selling complete painted armies or units ready for the wargamer to use in all scales. Armies can be painted and based to order so as to comply with a specific rules system or a specific manufacturer. They also provide newly painted figures and carry a huge range of second-hand painted and unpainted figures, books, models and accessories. They also have their own figure range, Hinchliffe Models, an extensive range of 25-mm figures which covers all the major conflicts of history. The artillery models from this range are some of the finest pieces of ordnance available to gamers anywhere and there are a whole series of vignettes across different periods of history to give extra detail to armies.

Instant Armies, The Smallholding, Clifton Road, Netherseal, Derbyshire DE12 8BP. Tel: 07758 451 853. Web: www.instantarmies.co.uk. As the name suggests, this company supplies painted figures ready for the wargamer to use in all scales. They have an extensive range of new and second-hand painted figures available in units, or whole armies or individual units can be painted to order, either from a specific manufacturer or to meet a particular rules system. They stock tens of thousands of both painted and unpainted figures in all scales and sometimes have associated scenery and models in stock as well.

Magnetic Displays, 6 Lumley Crescent, Skegness, Lincolnshire, PE25 2TL. Tel: 01754 761383. Web: www.magneticdisplays.co.uk. As the name suggests, this company supplies the magnetic sheets which are cut and adhered to the bases of the figures and the boxes in which those figures will be stored, thereby protecting figures as much as possible from the rigours of moving them either around the gaming room or to exhibitions and competitions elsewhere. Magnetic Displays also produce a range of generic resin scenery and they have a wide range of brushes, paints and accessories, including a base texture product which can be applied to the bases of the completed models, blending them into the scenery over which they will fight.

Miniature Figurines c/o Caliver Books, 100 Baker Road, Newthorpe, Nottingham, NG16 2DP. Tel: 01159 382111. Web: www.miniaturefigurines.co.uk. Established for many years, 'Minifigs' make an extensive range of 15-mm figures. The 15-mm range has many packs available covering all the British and other European armies, but do not produce any specific Jacobite figures, though again casting from other ranges such as the English Civil War range provides some good basic figures.

Newline Designs, 32 Royal Crescent, South Ruislip, Middlesex, HA4 0PW. Tel: 01895 814713, Mob: 07743 266066. Web: www.newlinedesigns.co.uk. Newline are a company that have just started to produce some figures for this period in 20 mm – it is a new range at the moment but they are looking to expand in the near future.

Parkfield Miniatures, 21 Lincoln Park, Amersham, Bucks, HP7 9EZ. Tel: 01494 725631 or 01494 432389. Web: www.parkfieldminiatures.freeservers.com. Parkfield produce true 25-mm figures and although they do not produce a Jacobite range as such, they do produce some French-Indian War figures which have a number of castings which would serve as Government troops and they do produce a good range of around forty figures for the Glorious Rebellion period.

Pendraken Miniatures, 1 Easby Grove, Eston, Middlesbrough, TS6 9DL. Tel: 01642 460638. Web: www.pendraken.co.uk. All Pendraken figures are in the 10-mm scale, and they produce a specific range for the Jacobite rebellions, including the regular troops that fought for both sides. They also produce a specific range for the War of the League of Augsburg, allowing the gamer greater flexibility in troop styles as in this scale a conversion can be achieved through painting alone.

Reiver Castings, Unit A16, Stonehill, Shields Road, Gateshead NE10 0HW. Tel: 0191 4690745. Web: www.reivercasting.wordpress.com. Reiver figures are a large 28 mm and they produce a comprehensive range for all of the early Jacobite rebellions up until 1719. They produce Monmouth Rebellion, The Irish Rebellion and specific Scots for the '15 and '19. They also have a good selection of field defences, artillery pieces, wagons and pontoon bridges.

Warrior Miniatures, 14 Tiverton Avenue, Glasgow, Scotland G32 9NX. Tel: 0141 778 3426. Web: www.warriorminiatures.com. Warrior only produce a small range of twenty figures in true 25-mm scale, but they are specifically for the Jacobite period and they have starter pack deals. They also produce a few 15-mm figures.

Bibliography

As the reader will appreciate, the information available on this period varies greatly. Some battles are documented in great detail, and yet different interpretations come up with different troop dispositions, and even a different axis as to whether the battle was fought east–west or north–south. Accordingly, I have based my interpretation of the battles within this book not only on the primary and secondary written material, but also on the evidence of site visits and the examination of the relevant topography to see for myself where the relevant action was most likely to have been fought, allowing, of course, in certain places for urbanisation. The websites used to confirm details passed down through oral tradition are not listed, due to volume.

Barnett, C., *Britain and Her Army, 1509–1970* (Allen Lane, 1970)

Barthorp, M., *The Jacobite Rebellions*, Osprey Men At Arms Series No. 118 (Osprey Publishing, 1982)

Baynes, J., *The Jacobite Rising of 1715* (History Book Club, 1970)

Black, J., *Culloden and the '45* (Alan Sutton Publishing Ltd, 1990)

Brooks, R., *Cassell's Battlefields of Britain and Ireland* (Weidenfeld & Nicholson, 2005)

Burne, A. H., *The Battlefields of England* (Greenhill Books, 1996)

'Call to Arms', *Re-enacting Directory 2004/5* (Beta Print, 2004)

Castleton, R., *King Arthur* (Routledge, 2000)

Childs, J., *The Williamite Wars in Ireland, 1688–1691* (Hambledon Continuum, 2007)

Daiches, D., *Charles Edward Stuart: The Life and Times of Bonnie Prince Charlie* (History Book Club, 1973)

Douglas, H., *Jacobite Spy Wars* (Sutton Publishing, 1999)

Falkus, M., and J. Gillingham, *Historical Atlas of Britain* (Book Club Associates, 1981)

Fairbairn, N., *A Traveller's Guide to the Battlefields of Britain* (Evans Brothers, 1983)

Featherstone, D. F., *War Games Through the Ages, Volume Two 1420–1783* (Stanley Paul, 1974)

Funcken, L. & F., *Arms and Uniforms 2 – Eighteenth Century to the Present Day* (Wardlock, 1972)

Funcken, L. & F., *The Lace Wars*, Volumes 1 and 2 (Wardlock, 1977)

Grant, C., *From Pike to Shot, 1685–1720* (WRG Publication, 1986)

Guest, K. & D., *British Battles* (Harper Collins, 1996)

Gush, G., *Army Lists 1420–1700* (WRG Publications, 1984)

Gush, G., and M. Windrow, 'The English Civil War', *Airfix Magazine Guide* 28 (Patrick Stephens Limited, 1978)

Hackett, M., *Lost Battlefields of Britain* (Sutton Publishing Ltd, 2005)

Harrington, P., *Culloden 1746*, Osprey Campaign Series 12 (Osprey Publishing, 1991)

Harrison, I., *British Battles* (Harper Collins, 2002)

Hill, J. M., *Celtic Warfare 1595–1763* (John Donald Publishers Ltd, 1986)

Kamm, A., *The Jacobites*, HMSO 1995 (NMS Enterprises Ltd, Scottie Books, 2000)

Kinross, J., *Discovering Battlefields of England and Scotland* (Shire, 2004)

Kinross, J., *The Battlefields of Britain* (David & Charles, 1979)

Kinross, J., *Walking and Exploring the Battlefields of Britain* (David Charles, 1988)

Lenman, B., *The Jacobite Cause* (Richard Drew Publishing Ltd, 1986)

Low, S. J., and F. S. Pulling, *The Dictionary of English History* (Cassell & Co., 1911)

MacDonald, D., *Slaughter Under Trust, Glencoe 1692* (Robert Hale Ltd, 1965)

Marren, P., *Grampian Battlefields* (Aberdeen University Press, 1990)

McLynn, F. J., *The Jacobite Army in England 1745* (John Donald Publishers Ltd, 1983)

McCorry, H., *The Thistle At War* (National Museums of Scotland, 1997)

McOwan, R., *Stories of the Clans* (Lang Syne Publishers Ltd, 1985)

National Trust for Scotland, *Culloden* (National Trust for Scotland, 2009)

Norris, J., *Gunpowder Artillery 1600–1700* (The Crowood Press, 2005)

Prebble, J., *Culloden and Glencoe* (Folio Society, 1997)

Reid, S., *Eighteenth Century Highlanders*, Osprey Men at Arms Series No.261 (Osprey Publishing, 1993)

Reid, S., *Culloden Moor 1746*, Osprey Campaign Series 106 (Osprey Publishing, 2002)

Reid, S., *Cumberland's Army, The British Army at Culloden* (Partizan Press, 2006)

Reid, S., *I Met the Devil and Dundee, the Battle of Killiecrankie 1689* (Partizan Press, 2009)

Reid, S., *Like Hungry Wolves, Culloden Moor 16 April 1746* (Windrow & Greene, 1994)

Reid, S., *The Last Scots Army 1661–1714* (Partizan Press, 2003)

Reid, S., *Wargaming with Jacobites 1745* (Partizan Press, 2013)

Reid, S., *Cumberland's Culloden Army 1745–46*, Osprey Men at Arms Series No.483 (Osprey Publishing, 2012)

Russell, C., *Eighteenth Century Army Lists* (Cheltenham Wargames Association, 1988)

Robinson, R. E. R., *The Bloody Eleventh, History of the Devonshire Regiment* (Sydney Lee, 1985)

Sapherson, C. A., *The British Army of William III* (Partizan Press, 1987)

Sadler, J., *Scottish Battles, From Mons Graupius to Culloden* (Canongate Books, 1996)

Schofield, V., *The Highland Furies, The Black Watch 1739–1899*, Volume 1 (Quercus, 2012)

Selby, J., *Over the Sea to Skye* (Hamish Hamilton Ltd, 1973)

Sinclair-Stevenson, C., *Inglorious Rebellions, The Jacobite Risings of 1708, 1715 and 1719* (Hamish Hamilton, 1971)

Smurthwaite, D., *Battlefields of Britain: The Complete Illustrated Guide* (Mermaid Books, 1984)

Tabraham, C., *Scottish Castles and Fortifications* (Edinburgh HMSO, 1986)

Tomasson, K., and F. Buist, *Battles of the '45* (William Clowes & Sons Ltd, 1962)

Further Reading

Such is the interest surrounding the Jacobite rebellions, especially as the question of an independent Scotland has appeared on the political agenda, that more information is coming to light on this fascinating period of British history and more people are wanting to look into it. On a March day in 2014 at the Glenfinnan monument, no less than twenty vehicles arrived in one thirty minute period, indicating a clear interest out there among the general public. Indeed, there is now so much information available that a separate book could be written, or in some cases now has been written, on every facet of the campaigns: the armies, the uniforms, and even each individual battle sites. In this book, the author has looked to give the reader sufficient insight into the period to go and visit the sites for themselves and to begin wargaming the period, but please do not stop there, dig deeper into the specific areas which are of interest to you.

GONE

An Anthology of Crime Stories

Edited by

Stephen J. Golds

RED DOG
UK

Published by RED DOG PRESS 2022

First Edition

Hardback ISBN 978-1-915433-15-2
Paperback ISBN 978-1-915433-17-6
Ebook ISBN 978-1-915433-16-9

www.reddogpress.co.uk

CONTENTS

Introduction

Contributors Biographies

Disclaimer:

Don't be alarmed. The stories in this anthology have been written by authors all over the world. Author choice of UK or US English has been preserved.

GONE
An Introduction

I often (maybe too often) think it isn't the things we have that make us who we are, but the things we don't have. The things we lack. The things we've lost. More importantly, or detrimentally, it is the things that are missing. That are gone. Each of us carrying the weight and the scars of people and things long gone, or the holes of things that were never really there in the first place. When you stare at your reflection in the mirror every morning it's always those absent things staring back at you. Not enough money for the rent. You didn't get that salary increase your boss promised you a year ago. Your ex-lover left and took your pet parrot Marjorie with them. You get my point. We are driven, too often, by our needing and wanting for what is gone.

Now close your eyes and think of a famous true crime case that has stuck with you since the very first time you heard about it.

Chances are you thought of one of the following: Jack the Ripper, D. B. Cooper, The Zodiac Killer, The Isabella Stewart Gardner Museum Art Theft, the disappearance of Jean Spangler… Maybe you thought of another high-profile case. It doesn't really matter all that much. What I'm trying to say is —all of the crimes that lurk constantly in the shadowy parts of our mind have the central theme of 'gone'. We're fascinated with criminals who commit crimes and then seemingly disappear. Here one moment and then gone. It's the main reason these crimes are still so high-profile decades after they were committed. I've been obsessed with these kinds of stories my whole life. Constantly falling down pitch black rabbit holes of unsolvable true crime.

And what of crime fiction you ask? If it's possible for a single word to epitomize and encapsulate a whole literary genre, the simple word 'GONE' surely does it for crime fiction.

Go ahead and think about the last piece of crime fiction you read or the last crime movie you watched.

She's gone.

He's gone.

They're gone.

It's gone.

So many stories branching out from this one singular haunting word.

Gone *is* the definition of crime fiction.

And, right now, you're holding thirty of the best Gone crime stories all in one anthology. Stories written in every single sub-genre of crime fiction, from the cosy to the hard-boiled. From the literary to the pulp. You're about to embark on one hell of a ride. Get a good grip on the steering wheel and fasten your seatbelt. I know you're going to love all of these stories as much as I do.

It's been a massive privilege putting this international crime anthology together. A big thank you to every single writer involved who let me share in their literary talents. Red Dog Press for always taking risks with this author who often acts like a mad dog chasing cars. Another big thank you to YOU the reader. What is a writer without a reader?

I'd also like to dedicate this collection to my mother, Tina Golds who gave me the idea for the anthology and who taught me that the most interesting questions in life have infinite answers.

And now that this short introduction is over with—I'm gone.

Stephen J. Golds ~ Japan — July 2022

A NIGHTMARE ON ELM LANE

by

Richard Chizmar

MY FATHER and I started digging the day after school ended.

I had just finished the seventh grade at Edgewood Middle School and was looking forward to a summer of fishing, bike riding, and playing Magic the Gathering with my friends. If I was lucky, I might even run into Katy McCammon at the creek or the swimming pool and finally summon the courage to ask her out to the movies and to get ice cream. Charlie Mitchell had bet me twenty bucks on the last day of school that it wouldn't happen. I was determined to prove his fat ass wrong, even if it meant crashing and burning with Katy. After all, I would have the entire summer to get over it.

My father had just finished his millionth year of teaching upper-level science at the high school and evidently had other plans for the first week of my summer vacation.

"I'M HOMEEE," I announced and flung my baseball hat on the foyer table.

"Don't let the door—"

The screen door slammed shut behind me.

"—*slam!*" my dad finished from the next room.

I walked into the family room, flashed a sheepish grin at my mother, who was reading a magazine on the sofa, and shrugged at my father, who was kicked back in his recliner watching the Orioles on television. "Sorry…I forgot."

"You forget one more time, you're gonna be sorry," he said, a hint of a smile betraying the tough-man attitude. My dad was a lot of things—a terrible singer in the shower, a horrible driver, often embarrassing in public, an ace Scrabble player—but tough wasn't one of them. My mom always called him a Disney Dad.

I plopped down on the sofa and started taking off my shoes. "Who's winning?"

"Don't ask," my dad grumbled

I laughed and made a face at my mom. She rolled her eyes. My dad was also a lifelong Orioles fan with, how shall I say this, unusual views regarding baseball managerial strategy. He believed in three-run home runs, double steals, and two out bunts. Sometimes all in the same inning.

"My God, what'd you boys do tonight," my mom asked, wrinkling her nose. "You stink."

"Played whiffle ball at Jimmy's," I shrugged. "Then went down to the park.

"You boys catch any fireflies?"

"Yeah, Mom. We all ran around and chased fireflies and stuffed them in an empty jar. Then we played hide-and-go-seek and tag and did a sing-along. What are we, five years old?"

She swatted me on the shoulder. "Don't be a smart aleck."

I grabbed my arm and pretended to swoon.

She laughed. "Go put your shoes on the back porch and take a shower. You're making my eyes water."

I jumped to my feet and gave her a salute— "Yes, ma'am, Janet, ma'am." —and headed for the kitchen and back door.

My father's voice behind me: "Don't call your mother by her first name."

I opened the back door. "Sorry, Henry, won't happen again."

I heard the squawk of the recliner as my father released the leg rest and got to his feet in the next room. I hurriedly tossed my shoes on the porch, slammed the door, and took off for the back stairs...

...just as my father, all five foot eight and hundred-fifty pounds of him, scrambled into the kitchen, nearly slipping in his socks on the linoleum floor and landing on his ass. "I'll teach you not to backtalk your parents!"

I bounded up the stairs, giggling, and locked myself in the bathroom.

"You're lucky today's the last day of school, you little communist!" my father bellowed from downstairs.

I TOSSED the wet towel on the floor next to my dirty clothes and climbed into bed. The sheets felt cool on my bare legs. I used the remote to click on the ten-inch television on my dresser and found the Orioles game. They were losing 8-3 in the bottom of the seventh. It was going to be another long season.

My dad stepped into the doorway. "Hey, I know tomorrow's your first full day of summer vacation, but I need your help for a few hours."

"Help with what?" I asked, dreading the answer.

"I have a little project for us. Won't take long."

"Oh, boy," I said, remembering the last little project. My dad had come home one afternoon with blueprints for a fancy tree house. We'd spent almost two weeks sawing boards and nailing them into place in the old weeping willow tree in the back yard. When we were finally finished, it looked more like a rickety tree-stand for hunting deer than it did any kind of a tree house, and it had cost my dad over three hundred and fifty bucks in materials.

My father laughed. "Now you sound just like your mother. Get some sleep, Kev. I'll see you in the morning."

I RUBBED sleep from my eyes and walked across the patio to the picnic table tucked in the far corner. There were two shovels and a pick-ax leaning against the table, and a couple pairs of work gloves and a sheet of what looked like complicated directions sitting atop the table.

"Not more blueprints," I grumbled.

"They're instructions, smartie pants," my father said from behind me. "How do you expect to do a job correctly if you don't have instructions to follow?"

I resisted the urge to look over at the weeping willow tree.

"You get enough to eat?"

"Yeah," I grumbled.

He picked up the instructions and work gloves. "Grab those tools and follow me."

I cradled the shovels and pick-ax in my arms and followed him into the back yard. He walked past the back-stop I used for pitching practice, past the two-tier bird bath my mom loved so much, underneath the drooping branches of the weeping willow tree, and stopped just short of the vegetable garden that lined our back fence.

"You can put them down here."

I dropped the tools onto the grass. "Okay, now can you tell me? What's the big surprise?"

My father smiled, spread his arms wide, and turned in a slow circle. "This is where our brand-new goldfish pond is going."

"Goldfish pond?" I wasn't sure I had heard him correctly.

"That's right," he said, pointing. "Twelve by six foot pond there, complete with miniature waterfall. Rock garden there. Couple of nice benches there and there. It'll be a thing of beauty when we're done."

This sounded like a lot of work. "Mom know about this?"

"Course, she does. Whose idea do you think it was?"

I knew better, but wasn't about to say so. "How long is this gonna take?"

He tossed me a pair of work gloves, started pulling his on. "Don't worry, Kev. I only need your help with digging the hole and laying down the liner. I can handle the rest."

I breathed a sigh of relief. Not to be a jerk about it, but I *was* thirteen years old and it *was* summer vacation. I had a lot of important stuff to do.

"We've got two days to get that done. After that, the pump and circulation kit will be here, couple days after that, the live plants and fish." My dad was grinning like a kid in a candy shop. He got a little nutty about things like this, but I sure loved him.

I slipped on the work gloves and picked up a shovel. "Well, what're we waiting for? Let's get digging."

He slapped me on the back. "That's the spirit."

A COUPLE hours later, Mom brought out glasses of lemonade, and my father and I sat in the shade of the weeping willow and took a much-needed break. We were dripping with sweat, and despite the gloves, we both had blisters on our hands.

"Not bad," my father said, taking a long drink and eyeing our progress.

The kidney-shaped outline of the pond was complete. Chunks of sod and dirt were piled off to the side on sheets of clear plastic. Later, when we were finished digging for the day, we would take turns filling up the wheelbarrow and humping loads to the driveway where we would shovel the dirt into the back of my father's pick-up. I wasn't looking forward to that part of the job.

"How deep do we have to go?" I asked.

"Thirty-six inches from end to end."

I looked at the hole. It was maybe six inches deep in most places.

"Take a few more minutes," my father said, putting on his gloves. "Finish your lemonade."

I watched him pick up a shovel and start digging. I sat there in the shade and drank my lemonade and thought about Charlie and Jimmy and the rest of my friends. They were probably down at Hanson Creek right now fishing. Or playing ball at the park. Or betting quarters on the shooting games at the arcade. Or...

My father slung another shovelful of dirt over his shoulder, grunting with the effort. I finished my lemonade and hurried to his side. I figured I had plenty of time for fun and games later on.

"YOU POOR BOYS," my mother said, watching us struggle to grip our forks at dinner.

She had made my father's favorite, beef stroganoff, and even though we'd worked up quite an appetite, the blisters on our hands made eating a slow process.

"I told you we're fine, honey," my father said. "Few blisters never hurt anyone."

I stuffed another bite into my mouth and nodded agreement. I felt strangely happy and proud of myself. I felt content.

"Well, maybe you should take a break tomorrow and—"

"No way," I said, my mouth still full. "We need to finish digging, so we're ready for the pump on Thursday."

My father beamed. "That's right."

We finished our stroganoff and wolfed down two slices of chocolate cake each for dessert, then we all moved to the den to watch the start of the Orioles game. I was in bed and snoring by nine-thirty. It was my last peaceful night's sleep.

WE WERE up and digging by eight the next morning, energized by a big breakfast and a good night's rest. Dad brought out a radio, and we listened to callers complaining about the Orioles' lack of pitching, hitting, and coaching for the better part of an hour before switching over to an oldies rock station. We were making decent progress on the hole. I figured we'd be moving dirt right up until dark tonight, but we would definitely finish. We were determined.

By late-morning, my father was working his way in from one side of the hole while I attacked the other side. The plan was to meet in the middle, and then use the tape measure to see how much deeper we needed to go. The work was methodical and mindless, but oddly satisfying.

A Led Zeppelin song was playing on the radio when my shovel hit something solid. I wasn't surprised. So far, we had unearthed about a million rocks of various shapes and sizes, an old toy truck, a rusted-out lid from a Speed Racer lunch box, and a few tangles of copper wire that my father said was probably left over from when the house was first built. I had even found a keychain in the shape of a miniature horseshoe with an old key still attached to it. I'd stashed that in my pocket to show my friends later. Maybe it opened a treasure chest somewhere.

I looked down and saw something small and pale in the dirt. Then, I saw another one. Maybe three inches long.

I lifted my shovel for a closer look—and my breath caught in my throat. I'd never seen one before in real life, but I had seen plenty enough on television to know what I was looking at.

They were bones.

"Umm, hey, Dad."

The volume on the radio was loud, so I called again, "Dad, I think you should take a look at this."

This time he heard me and came right over. "What's up, Kev?"

I raised the shovel to give him a better look. He squinted in the morning sun, then reached down and picked up one of the bones. "Huh. Probably the previous owner's dog or cat."

He dropped the bone back onto the shovel and hopped down into the hole next to me. "Where'd you find it?"

I pointed out the spot with the tip of my shoe.

He carefully dug a wide circle around it. "I saw this on a National Geographic special about dinosaurs." He dropped to a knee and started sifting through the dirt with his hands.

"Jurassic Park on Golden Elm Lane," I laughed.

"Bingo," my father said, holding up another bone for me to see.

"Kinda gross, don't you think?"

"Just part of nature, son. You're the horror movie freak, how can you think…" He didn't finish his thought. He knelt there, perfectly still, his shoulders suddenly rigid.

"What's wrong?"

He leaned closer to the dirt.

I tried to see around him. "What'd you find?"

My father stood and turned to me, a strange expression on his face. "Let's take a break and go inside and cool off."

I moved to the left to try to see around him. He moved and blocked me. "Kevin—"

"What is it, Dad?"

He let out a long sigh. "Put your shovel down. Carefully. I'll tell you in the house."

"Tell me now," I begged, laying down the shovel on the grass and peeking behind my father into the hole.

Several slender, pale bones lay atop the pile of dirt.

June sunlight glinted off something shiny encircling one of the bones.

It was a dirty gold ring.

BY DINNERTIME, there were three police cruisers parked in front of the house and a police van parked across the street. The back yard was swarming with officers and detectives. Some of them investigating the hole and bagging evidence, others just standing around, talking.

I sat on the patio and watched everything. All of my friends had stopped by at one point or another, but my mother had shooed them away with the promise that I would call them later that night. Most of them spent the evening texting me and watching from across the street, their bikes parked on the sidewalk.

A police detective had interviewed my father and me, first in the living room, and then again as we showed him what we'd found in the back yard.

He'd asked us a lot of the same questions two or three times, almost like he didn't believe us. When the other cops showed up, he quickly finished with us and got to work with the others.

Both my mom and dad must've asked me at least a dozen times throughout the day if I was all right. Each time I reassured them I was fine. The truth was I was more than just fine. I was excited and anxious to find out even more about what was going on.

I eavesdropped on every conversation I could. I offered policemen drinks and made other excuses to talk to them. I even used the zoom on my phone camera to try to get a glimpse of what was going on over by the hole.

Finally, around the time it started getting dark and two policemen started setting up portable lights, I climbed the weeping willow and perched myself inside my tree house. I couldn't see much from up there, there were too many branches in the way, but I was comfortable enough and could hear a lot better.

Around nine o'clock, I heard a cell phone ring somewhere below me.

"Sharretts," a voice answered, and then there was a long pause. "Make sure you check with Henderson first. He left here fifteen minutes ago."

I recognized the voice now. It was the detective who had interviewed my father and me earlier in the day. He obviously didn't realize I was in the tree above him, listening. I knew this because of what he said next.

"That all depends on what Cap says. I think they're gonna GPR the whole damn back yard in the morning."

Another pause.

"Three skeletal right hands so far."

I realized I was holding my breath.

"That's right. No other remains. Just the hands."

I could hear his footsteps moving away from the tree.

"Someone's checking on that right now. Okay, talk soon," and then there was just the muffled chatter of the policemen below and the soft whisper of a breeze in the weeping willow.

A short time later, I crept down from the tree and went inside. I hurried to the bathroom to pee—I'd been holding it for what felt like forever—and realized that I still had the horseshoe keychain in my pants pocket. I knew I should probably go back outside and give it to the police. It could be important evidence.

Instead, I went to the kitchen and ate a snack and used my phone to look up what GPR stood for: *Ground Penetrating Radar.*

They were going to X-ray the back yard tomorrow. They were looking for bodies.

I WAS too tired to call my friends back that night, so I called first thing the next morning. I started with Jimmy.

"My mom says you can maybe come over tonight, but just you, not the rest of the guys."

"Awesome. My mom said she saw the story on the news last night. They had pictures of your house and everything. Golden Elm Lane is famous!"

I'd watched the same news story this morning during breakfast. It felt weird seeing my house like that. Not a good weird either. It was almost like they were trespassing or something.

"What are they doing now?" Jimmy asked. "They find any more skeletons?"

I walked over to the window and looked outside. "A couple vans showed up a little while ago…"

I told Jimmy what I'd overheard the night before about GPR and how there was a guy in regular street clothes pushing something that looked like one of those portable golf caddies with three wheels back and forth across my yard. A cop in uniform walked alongside him, carrying a clipboard and a fistful of little red flags attached to wire stakes. Every once in a while, they would stop and the cop would take a knee and plant one of the little red flags in the grass, and then they would move on again.

Jimmy was fascinated— "It's just like a freaking movie, man!"—and made me promise to text him a photo from my phone. I told him I would. I didn't say a word about the other thing I'd overheard while sitting in the tree house: about the police finding three right hands. Just like with the keychain, I hadn't even shared that information with my parents yet. I didn't know why, but I'd kept that to myself.

FIRST THING in the morning, the police had asked my parents to make sure everyone stayed clear of the back yard, so I was forced to watch from my bedroom window. I pulled my desk chair close and cracked the window a few inches, but I still couldn't hear much. To make matters worse, the weeping willow blocked a good portion of my view. I was flying blind today.

I sent Jimmy a blurry picture of the cops operating the GPR machine and did my best to keep up with my other friends' text messages. I ate a ham and cheese sandwich and Doritos for lunch and skimmed a couple articles in the new issue of *Gamer's Monthly*. I almost fell asleep twice after lunch and took the fastest bathroom break known to man for fear of missing something important. I counted four red flags sticking out of the ground. No telling how many more there were behind the tree and around the hole we'd dug.

The hours dragged on. I started thinking about sneaking outside for a closer look. I even considered sneaking up into the tree house again. What were they going to do, arrest me?

I had just about convinced myself to go for it, when there was a knock on the door behind me. I turned and both my mom and dad were standing there.

"Hey, Kev," my dad said. "Got a minute?"

They walked into the room and sat on my bed.

"Did they find something else? Did they—"

My dad put his hands out. "Whoa, slow down." He glanced at my mom and continued, "We just finished speaking with one of the detectives, and we thought we'd share with you what he said."

"If anything we say upsets you," my mom said. "Just say so and we'll stop."

I looked from my dad to my mom and back to my dad again. "Just tell me!"

"This stays inside the house, Kevin. It's family talk, not for your friends. Got it?"

"Got it," I said, nodding and sitting on the edge of my seat.

"According to the detective, they've found skeletal remains from at least three different people in the back yard."

No duh, I wanted to say.

"They've also marked some additional areas they plan to search later this afternoon. The detective told us the lab ran some tests on the bones we found and they came back as more than twenty years old, so fortunately they know we had nothing to do with this."

I hadn't even thought of that. "Wow, we could have been suspects!" I blurted, putting an immediate frown on my mom's face. Wait until Jimmy heard about that.

"They also pulled property records and discovered that the sole owner before us of 149 Golden Elm Lane was a man by the name of Walter Jenkins. By all accounts, he was a friendly, well-liked man with no complaints against him and no arrest record. He was retired from the Navy and worked at the hardware store in Dayton. He was widowed when he was in his sixties and moved to a nursing home about ten years later. That's when we bought the house and moved in."

"Is he still alive?" I asked, my mind working.

My dad shook his head. "Died six years ago. Didn't have any children and no living relatives nearby."

"So, if he didn't do it... who did?"

"That's what the detectives are trying to figure out, Kev. Detective Sharretts said they might have a few more questions for us in the days to come, but mostly they'll be looking around for folks who knew Mr. Jenkins back when he lived here."

"You know some of the world's most famous serial killers were normal and friendly on the outside, right?" I asked, remembering some of the books I'd read. "They weren't all weirdos like Dahmer and Gacy and—"

"You hush now," my mom interrupted, getting up from the bed. "No more talk about serial killers. Get yourself washed up and help us prepare dinner."

"But, Mom..." I whined, looking at my dad for help.

He stood up from the bed. "You heard your mother, Kev. Let's go."

So much for help. I groaned and followed them downstairs.

THAT NIGHT, I dreamed Walter Jenkins was chasing me.

The house was dark, and Jenkins was old and wrinkled, but incredibly fast and strong. No matter where I ran or hid, he kept finding me. He had a hideous grin and an evil laugh and a long, wicked-looking knife. He wanted my right hand.

Terrified and cornered, I crept into the basement.

"Come out, come out, wherever you are," he called in a gravely, sing-song voice.

I sat perfectly still in the space between the washer and dryer, afraid to breathe. I had piled several dirty towels on top of me. I couldn't see a thing.

"I know you're down here," he said, and I could hear the shuffle of footsteps getting closer.

"C'mon now, Kev, I'm not going to hurt you."

The footsteps stopped right in front of me. I felt a whisper of cool air as one of the towels was removed from on top of me.

"I promise I won't hurt you."

Another towel gone.

"I'm just gonna kill you!"

The last towel was snatched away, and I saw that evil grin and long, shiny blade slashing—

—and that's when I woke up in my dark bedroom, sweaty sheets clenched in one hand, my other hand the only thing stopping the scream from escaping my mouth.

"DUDE, YOU'RE like a celebrity," Doug said. "Everyone's talking about you."

Charlie rolled his eyes. "I wouldn't go that far."

"Don't be a douchebag," Jimmy said and punched Charlie in the shoulder. "You're just jealous."

"The day I'm jealous of gay boy Kevin here is the day you get to bang my sister."

"Already banged her," Jimmy said, pushing off on his bike. "And your mom, too."

Charlie's chubby face went red. He jumped on his bike and started chasing Jimmy down the trail. "Take it back! Take it back!"

Jimmy just laughed and kept on peddling.

It felt good to be with my friends again, instead of locked up inside the house. The police had left a couple days ago, and even the news crews had stopped coming around.

"So, they have no idea how they got there?" Doug asked for at least the fifth time that morning.

I shook my head. "It's a big mystery."

"You mean a nightmare," he said, and then his eyes flashed wide. "A nightmare on Elm Lane!" He hooked his hands into claws and started slashing at me. "Maybe Freddy Krueger did it!"

I laughed and pushed him away.

"My dad says they should check out the folks who own the house in back of you," Doug said, still giggling.

"Police already did that. The current owners and the previous two owners."

"And?"

"And nothing, I guess."

Doug grunted and looked around for Jimmy and Charlie. "It's hot as piss. Wanna go get a Slurpee?"

"Sure."

Doug put his fingers to his mouth and whistled. Thirty seconds later, we heard a returning whistle from deep in the woods. A few minutes after that, Jimmy and Charlie came racing down the trail, both of them red-faced and sweating. We all set out for 7-Eleven.

THE FOUR of us sat on the curb outside the store and drank our Slurpees and opened our packs of baseball cards. Charlie and Doug got into an argument about who was a better third baseman, Manny Machado or Kris Bryant, and that turned into a pebble fight until Charlie plunked Doug in the eye. Jimmy and I were content to sit back and watch the spectacle and drink our Slurpees in silence.

A car pulled into a parking spot nearby, but none of us paid it any attention.

"Hey there, boys," a voice called. "Hot enough for you?"

We all looked up. Mr. Barnett from down the street was leaning out his car window, the stub of a cigar poking from his mouth. It smelled like cat shit.

"Sure is," Jimmy answered.

Mr. Barnett looked at me. "Kevin, you're quite the celebrity these days, aren't you?"

Doug gave Charlie a smug look: *I told you so.*

"I dunno about that, Mr. Barnett."

"I saw you and your dad on the news a couple times, walking around in the background. Pretty exciting stuff, huh?"

I nodded, but didn't say anything. Mr. Barnett was the first grown-up to use the word exciting to describe everything that had happened. Of course, all us kids thought it was exciting and cool, but the only words I'd heard other grown-ups use were horrible and terrifying and dreadful. But Mr. Barnett was like that. He wasn't like the other adults I knew. He always drank too much at the neighborhood block parties and shot off too many fireworks on the Fourth of July and my mom was always complaining that he was breaking the speed limit on our street.

"Sooo…the police find anything else that hasn't made the news or the papers?"

"My parents aren't really telling me much," I said. "They're afraid I'll have nightmares."

Mr. Barnett's face tightened, and I could tell he didn't believe me. "So, they found the remains of three hands, and that's it?"

I nodded again, worried my voice would betray me.

"You know I asked my father about the guy who used to live in your house," he continued, "and my father knew him."

Now he had my attention. "He did?"

"Said he was a nice enough fella but kept to himself. Said he even had a photograph of him somewhere, from an old Veteran's Day parade."

I thought about telling Mr. Barnett that he should have his father call the detectives, but I didn't. I had finished my Slurpee and just wanted to get out of there.

"Well, boys, I better run. Kevin, Jimmy, tell your folks I said hello. Looking forward to the cookout on the Fourth."

"Yes, sir," Jimmy said.

I waved as he pulled away.

We all got up, tossed our trash into the can, and mounted our bikes.

"That was weird," Doug said.

Jimmy shook his head. *"He's* weird."

"No, that's not what I meant. He pulled up and talked to us and left without even going into the store."

Jimmy thought about it for a moment and shrugged. I thought about it the whole way home.

14

THAT NIGHT, I heard something in the back yard.

A thunderstorm had rolled in after dinner, dumping nearly an inch of rain and dropping the temperature by twenty degrees. My mom had opened all the upstairs windows, and I had fallen asleep earlier to a chorus of crickets and bullfrogs.

But something else woke me up.

I wasn't sure if I had dreamt or imagined it, but I got out of bed and went to the window.

The back yard was cloaked in darkness, the weeping willow a towering shadow against an even darker backdrop. A lonely bullfrog croaked somewhere in the weeds and I could hear the muffled barking of a dog from the next block over.

I was just about to return to bed when I saw it: a shadow breaking away and moving independent of the other shadows around it. The shadow was in the shape of a person.

And then I heard it, the same sound that had woken me earlier: a *thump* followed by another *thump*, and then the sound of two feet landing on soggy grass.

Someone had just climbed over the fence in the back yard and jumped to the other side.

I SAT on the front porch and watched the sanitation guys emptying our trash cans into the back of their truck. I wondered if they ever found anything valuable in the garbage. It seemed like such a cool job.

I hadn't told anyone about what I'd seen and heard the night before. First of all, I wasn't one hundred percent sure I hadn't dreamt the whole damn thing. My head was still fuzzy. Second of all, I didn't want to worry my parents. They were tense enough with everything that was going on. I'd even heard my mom after dinner last night blame my dad for picking that spot for the goldfish pond.

The street was quiet today. No police had come by the house for almost a week, and the news people hadn't been by in even longer. It had been an exciting adventure while it lasted, but I was glad life was getting back to normal.

"Caught you daydreaming, didn't I?"

I looked up and saw our mailman, Mr. DeMarco's, smiling face.

I laughed. "Guilty as charged."

He stepped past me onto the porch, stuffed some mail into the box, and plopped down next to me on the stoop.

"I'm getting too old for this job." He took a handkerchief out of his pocket and wiped the sweat from his face. As usual, I caught a faint whiff of his cologne. It was the same stuff my father used to wear. Blue Velvet or something like that. He looked over at me. "You doing okay, partner?"

Mr. DeMarco had been asking me that ever since it all happened. He said finding dead folks in your back yard was no joking matter, and I shouldn't hide my feelings if I was struggling. Mr. DeMarco was cool like that. All us kids loved him. He was old, had to be at least sixty, but he would still toss his mailbag under a tree some days and play whiffle ball or kick ball with us. Other times, he'd treat us all to fudgesicles if the ice cream man was making his rounds.

"I'm doing good," I said.

"Any plans for today?" He glanced up at blue sky. "Looks like it's gonna be a good one."

"We're going fishing down at the creek. Just waiting on Jimmy to finish mowing his lawn."

He got to his feet with a groan. "Now that's a great way to spend a day like today. Even if they ain't biting."

"Oh, they'll be biting all right," I said, grinning. "We've got our secret bait."

He squinted at me. "Lemme guess…cheese balls?"

"How'd the heck you know?!"

Mr. DeMarco tilted his head back and laughed. It was a good, happy sound.

"I know because that's exactly what my friends and me used for bait in that exact same creek fifty years ago! Those fatty carp love cheese balls!"

I laughed.

"As a matter of fact," he said, face turning serious. "I told that police detective pretty much the same thing when he asked. Me and my friends used to run this neighborhood just like you and yours. Fishing, kick the can, racing our go-karts down Golden Elm."

I imagined Mr. DeMarco cruising down the road in a go-kart. Then, I thought of something I'd never thought of before.

"Did you and your friends know Walter Jenkins?"

Mr. DeMarco nodded. "Sure did. Even raked his leaves and cleaned his gutters once or twice. Me and Kenny Crawford, God rest his soul. Told the detective that, too."

"What was he like?" I asked.

"He was a good man, Kevin. Don't you listen to any of the rumors going 'round." He paused, thinking for a moment. "Mr. Jenkins reminded me a lot of my own father. That's how highly I thought of him."

I nodded and was about to respond—when a loud whistle sounded from somewhere down the street.

I whistled back and jumped to my feet. "Gotta go, Mr. DeMarco."

"Summer awaits, Kev. Those carp won't wait forever!"

LATER THAT night, I sat by my bedroom window and watched over the back yard. After nearly two hours of seeing and hearing nothing out of the ordinary, I returned to my bed and was asleep within minutes. I didn't have any bad dreams that night.

TWO AMAZING things occurred later in the week.

The first happened on Thursday morning while I was eating breakfast on the back patio with my mom. My phone buzzed in my pocket. I went to take it out and my mom said, "Uh uh, no phones at the table, remember?"

I put my hands out proclaiming my innocence. "I was just gonna turn off the ringer. Geez."

"Don't you geez me, mister."

I smiled and switched off the ringer on my phone—and saw the text.

I thought I was going to faint right on top of my plate of French toast.

The text wasn't from Jimmy or Charlie, as I had expected.

The text was from Katy McCammon.

Kevin, I'm having a pool party this Sunday at 2. You should come. Lemme know. Katy ☺

I placed my phone beside my plate and read the text a second and third time from the corner of my eye. Then, I broke the world speed record for eating French toast and dumped my dishes in the kitchen sink. I yelled goodbye to my mom and ran down Golden Elm Lane as fast as I could to show Jimmy.

The second amazing occurrence happened on Friday evening, just before dinner. My dad and I were watching a *Seinfeld* re-run when the phone rang. My mother picked up in the other room. A moment later, she came in with the cordless phone pressed against her chest.

"It's Detective Sharretts," she said in a low voice, handing the phone to my father.

"Hello?" My father mostly listened, every once in awhile punctuating the conversation with an "uh huh" or a "no kidding" or an "okay."

After several minutes of this, he finally hung up. "Well, that was interesting."

Stone faced, he walked back to his reading chair and sat down. Turned up the volume on the television. Stared silently at the screen.

My mother *("Honeyyy!")* and I *("Dadddd!")* erupted at the same time.

He cracked up laughing.

"Tell us what he said!" I begged.

It took another thirty seconds for my father's giggling to wind down, then he filled us in. "Detective Martin said they have a person of interest in custody."

My mother clasped her hands together. "Thank God."

"A former resident of Dayton who moved away a long time ago," my father continued. "Evidently, he admitted to everything. The detectives are going over his story to make sure it all adds up, but Detective Sharretts thinks it will. In the meantime, they at least have him on a weapons charge, so he's not going anywhere..."

I HAD a hard time falling asleep on Saturday night—I kept telling myself: *In fifteen hours, you'll be looking at Katy McCammon in a bikini; in fourteen hours, you'll be sitting in Katy's back yard with all the cool kids; in thirteen hours...*—so I found an old movie to watch on television. When the credits rolled at one a.m., my eyes were finally getting drowsy.

That's when I heard the footsteps. Not outside in the yard, but inside the house this time.

I held my breath—and heard it again.

A creak on the stairs. Getting closer.

My entire body broke out in cold sweat.

It's just Mom coming back from getting a drink of water, I thought. *She has trouble sleeping.* But I knew better. My mom hadn't woken in the middle of the night in forever, not since she'd started taking sleeping pills. And forget about my father, he slept like a bear in hibernation.

Another creak and the whisper of a footstep on hardwood floor. Someone moving slow and stealthily. Someone creeping.

The house was silent for the next minute or two, and I was just beginning to believe I'd imagined the whole thing, when I heard a quiet *thump* from down the hallway, from the direction of my parents' room. And then I heard a second *thump*. Like something heavy hitting the floor.

I snatched my cellphone from the end table next to my bed and pulled the covers up over my head like I used to do when I was a little kid and afraid of the monster that lived inside my closet. I punched in the security code and keyed in 911, but I didn't press SEND.

My bedroom door creaked open.

Even underneath the blanket, I could hear someone in the room breathing.

Something unnamable—no, it had a name; it was *terror*—stopped me from pushing SEND, stopped me from leaping to my feet and trying to flee.

It's Walter Jenkins and he has a knife.

My heart was beating so hard that I couldn't hear the footsteps shuffling closer. I couldn't hear the breathing growing more labored.

But nothing was wrong with my nose—and that's when I smelled it.

The faint scent of cologne. Blue Velvet or Blue Ice or whatever the hell it was called.

Now I knew who'd buried the hands in my back yard all those years ago.

Now I knew whom the keychain belonged to.

He wanted it back.

DIRTY LAUNDRY

by

Trevor Wood

A WOMAN walks into a room. That's how it always starts isn't it? Could be a bar or an office. Probably not a bedroom. Too soon for that. But eventually. Maybe.

She's usually tall, a looker, alluring but unavailable. Nearly always blonde too. Whereas the lawyer or, as in my case, the tec (I use the abbreviation to show that I'm a professional) is the opposite: medium-build, handsome in a run-down kinda way and available at the drop of a casually-tilted fedora. To be honest I'll take that description—it's more than fair, especially given the way I look now. Like I've spent the day sleeping in a whisky vat. Though that's her fault. Well, mostly.

I'll reverse the normal order of these things by giving you the case for the defence first.

Whatever you've read about de(tec)tives, private eyes, gumshoes, investigators (we all have our favourite terms but I'm sticking with tec) you can forget now. Especially if, like me, you're English. Maybe our Yankee friends over the pond have a different experience but on this side of the Atlantic tecs are as rare as clients who pay their bills on time. And right at the bottom of the crime-fighting food chain.

Forget about murder investigations, you're lucky if you get a missing person—though that's no sinecure. Most missing persons don't want to be found and have left their situation for a very good reason—their families are godawful people and they never want to see them again. Sometimes I'm amazed that the people left behind even bother to look for their absent wives/husbands/sons/daughters when it's obvious they haven't given a fuck about them when they were there. Usually it's something to do with wanting money from them. Money that they're not particularly keen to pass on to you when presented with an invoice.

If it's not missing persons, it's cheating partners. That's it; there are almost no other cases. The latter option though is one area I have a lot of experience in. Take my wife—everyone else has. *Boom-tish.* You might detect a bitter tone because after lying on her back for most of the neighbourhood, she eventually landed on her feet and left me in a beat of her non-existent heart. She took my kid and I took to the bottle.

You can picture me properly now, can't you? Short, stocky, dishevelled and utterly alone apart from the half-litre bottle of cheap blended whisky in my jacket pocket and a heart full of simmering anger. I'd bet you didn't see me sitting on a rooftop ledge though. (I'll come to that.) All that's missing is the hat and the wisecracks.

I looked better before Melody Gould walked in.

It had been another quiet week. Who am I kidding? It had been another quiet year. I was thinking of bunking off and going to the beach; if I was going to spend the day staring into the distance, I may as well be looking at the sea. Then she appeared in the doorway. Blonde, tall, lithe, dressed to kill, with a skirt short enough to raise an eyebrow. Straight from central casting and just my type (not that I generally have the luxury of a choice.)

She was clearly expecting a different set up. A waiting room, maybe even a receptionist. She stopped just inside the door and looked back at the name on the glass.

"Are you Hurt"

"No, I always look pained. It's a shitty world."

Okay, it's my standard gag. You can't have that surname and not use it, and it's good to relax the clients from the get go.

She didn't laugh.

"You're a detective?"

"Guilty as charged."

She took a step back and for a moment I thought she might leave. Which, in retrospect, would have been a blessing for everyone.

"Take a seat," I said. Me and my big mouth.

Even then she hesitated, but I stood up and indicated the chair on the other side of the desk. She took the hint.

"You're not what I expected," she said, crossing her legs smoothly as she sat, an electric buzz shooting straight under the desk from her nylons.

"I try to defy expectations. For example, I already know how to whistle, no advice required.'

Nothing. Not a glimmer. To be fair she was a lot younger than me and probably had no idea who Betty and Bogie were.

But then she surprised me.

"You're not very smart, are you? I like that in a man."

She'd seen Body Heat. And could quote from it. I was impressed. Unlike her, I smiled.

"What else do you like?" I replied. "Shallow, ugly, tired? I got 'em all."

This time I got a smile.

"You don't look tired," she fired back and the smile grew bigger. I was blinded by it.

"You know Ned Racine is a lawyer, not a detective."

"Of course I do. It's my favourite film," she added.

I should have shown her the door right there and then, but I was already bewitched.

"You have good taste." I paused, breathing in the smell of her perfume that had subtly worked its way across the room. "Though I hope you don't want me to kill your husband?"

This time she frowned.

"No," she said. "I want you to save him. Franco said you could help me."

PERMIT ME A digression. I'm the one whose sitting on a roof ledge, so it's the least you can do. I didn't climb up here just to admire the view.

I've made it clear there was never much work to go around and most of it was dull, unless you have a thing for taking long lens photos of out-of-shape middle-aged couples fucking—think Jake Gittes in Chinatown before he's approached by the real Evelyn Mulwray. Like I said, it always starts with a woman walking into a room. Even if you're Jack Nicholson.

So, a tec is always looking for new income streams if he's going to stay in business, particularly if he's been landed with a large dollop of spousal maintenance and child support. Diversify or die! Or if you're really unlucky both. Though back then I didn't want to die.

My occasional third specialty was Reputation Laundering. You may not have heard about it. It's new and like most things these days you can blame it on the internet.

It started out by chance. I was sitting in my favourite greasy spoon, the imaginatively named Franco's, devouring a bacon sarnie and reading the paper when the owner, yes, he's called Franco, sat down opposite me.

"It's quiet this morning," I said.

"It's quiet every morning."

It was true. I used to be surrounded by customers nursing hangovers, desperate for a full fat wake up call. That day there were none.

"Enjoy the sandwich, it could be your last one."

I looked up to see he wasn't smiling.

"I'm just waiting for a client to pay his bill. I'll settle my tab next week, promise."

"It's not that."

I breathed a sigh of relief. I'd exhausted my credit in pretty much every eating joint in town, and if Franco kicked me out I was going to starve. My wife had done all the cooking so I never learned. Why keep a dog and... Forget I said that.

"What is it then?"

"It's being named the worst restaurant in London."

That did seem harsh. Don't get me wrong, the bacon sandwich wasn't great, but it was edible. And instead of those little sachets of sauce that always end up on your shirt, Franco's had authentic bottles of Heinz Tomato Ketchup on every table—the real thing, not watered down like some.

Franco placed a laptop in front of me and brought up a popular review website.

Franco's was never Premier League, more like steady lower division. Until a barrage of one-star reviews suddenly appeared. Scathing wasn't the word. Brutal was. They tore apart the food, service, décor, cleanliness, you name it, they hated it. Franco tried to up his game, but the floodgates had opened and the terrible reviews poured through them. Even Gordon Ramsey would have labelled it a lost cause. He even got them when the place was closed down during the last lockdown. Which was when he knew for sure most weren't genuine.

He was being trolled by persons unknown—though a reasonable guess would have been the middle-class wanker who'd not long opened a nearby organic vegan brunch place just down the road.

Some of the local papers picked up on it and ran stories like 'I Found a Dog Turd in my Omelette.' No wonder the punters now flocked elsewhere.

"Can you help me?" Franco looked desperate. He must have been to ask me for help.

"Me?"

"Make it go away. Maybe find out who's doing it and warn them off."

The idea of me warning anyone off was laughable. I'm twelve stone wet-through and would struggle to frighten a nervous lamb with an anxiety disorder. This was so clearly not a case for someone like me.

"Free breakfast for life?" he suggested.

"I'm your man."

A WEEK LATER I'd put a plan together. I had plenty of time on my hands. The adulterers and the runaways had stopped for the school holidays. I'd done some reading up and discovered Reputation Laundering. It's big in the States and South America which inevitably means it will make its way over here sooner or later. Keeping it simple, it's a way for people to remove old stories floating around on the internet that don't paint them in the best possible light: drug cartel bosses who want to go straight, corrupt businessmen who have been asked to run for political office, that sort of thing.

I managed to make things a little better. Initially by making them worse; penning a variety of clearly libellous remarks in the comments section in the various papers running the stories. With the help of a friendly notary and a dodgy lawyer friend we threw up enough chaff to silence the guns. It's amazing what a threatening letter from a lawyer can achieve. Rather than remove the many dubious comments it was easier for the papers to take the stories down. We even got a lot of the original reviews removed, thanks to notarised letters from the reviewers stating clearly they'd been paid to make up their comments and had never eaten in Franco's in their lives. It took me ages to write them. My breakfasts were secured though Franco was a little dismayed to find that lawyers and notaries like to eat free too. Clearly word got round as my laundering sideline became a nice little earner with no downside. Until Melody Gould walked into my office. I told you how it always starts.

MELODY SANG A fine tune. Though I guess it now looks like she played me like a worn-out fiddle. She noticed my cigarettes on the desk and asked me if she could have one, gently holding my hand still when I lit if for her. She had all the moves, even down to the smoke rings she blew out of my office window as I watched. She wasted no time in telling me that she loved her husband—a lucky loser who went by the name of Keiron. They'd been married for three years and had been trying and failing to have a family. Putting myself in Keiron's position I imagined that he'd tried at least once a day and twice at weekends. Eventually they'd done some tests and it turned out she couldn't have kids. She didn't go into details and I didn't want her to. No one wants a goddess with clay feet. Adoption was their only option but there was a problem. Keiron had history.

I used to have my notes from that conversation in a file. I burnt it in a waste bin earlier today and have just scattered the ashes off this roof and watched them float down to the ground, which seemed ominous even to a dullard like me. I still remember every word though. When Keiron was nineteen he'd been arrested for assaulting a child in Liverpool. Some kid had kicked his dog in a park and he'd slapped him. Melody reckoned the kid deserved it and I couldn't help agreeing. I love dogs, humans not so much. Unfortunately a witness took the story to a journalist. Keiron was in a local band, a minor celebrity, and the story got picked up by most of the local press. He was arrested but never charged—the kid's mother had supported his story, apparently telling the police that her son was out of control and if Keiron hadn't slapped him she would have. I think now someone had paid her off.

Anyway, point being there was no criminal record to worry about, but the stories were still out there on the internet. Melody was convinced the adoption agencies wouldn't let him anywhere near a kid if they saw them and she really, really wanted them gone.

"Franco tells me you can make such things disappear," she said. At the time I was grateful that he was spreading the word. Now, I'd like to strangle him.

"For a price," I said.

"Whatever it takes. You can't put a price on having your own kid."

"Cash?"

She hesitated, holding my gaze to try and work out what kind of man I was. She guessed correctly.

"I need every penny I have if I'm going to have a family. How about in kind?" I raised one eyebrow. I'd been practicing it in front of the mirror. It looked pretty cool.

"How many instalments?" I asked.

"That's negotiable. Why don't you buy me a drink first?"

It was the 'first' that hooked me. I accepted her offer with unseemly alacrity.

We went to a quiet bar around the corner, sank a few short ones, and then took a room in a cheap motel that rented rooms by the hour. In my defence… who am I kidding, I have no defence. I told you I was shallow.

I wonder now if she'd done her research. I'd never been the quietest of guys when I'd had a drink and many a bartender had heard my tales of woe. Maybe she knew I was an easy lay, too easy. More importantly, maybe she knew I was more sympathetic to the cause than I should have been. I hadn't seen my own kid in two years. Otherwise I might have done my homework properly.

To be fair, I did check her I.D and a quick Google search backed up her story about Keiron, arrested but then released and never convicted. At the time I thought I'd got the deal of the century. It was one of the easiest clean-ups I'd been involved with. There were only a handful of stories, all from years ago and only on the local papers' websites, nothing in the nationals who were far harder to get to. A handful of fake court-orders ordering them to remove the relevant URLs and a month later they were gone.

I didn't come across Mrs Gould again for two years. Ironically, it was in a news story I stumbled across on the internet accompanied by a picture of Keiron Gould, his wife and a young boy, Adam. I only really noticed it because of the headline above it. I glanced at the picture and did a double take. Then another one. A quadruple take I guess. His wife's name wasn't Melody, it was Cathy. She wasn't the same woman who had come to my office. And Keiron had just beaten their recently-adopted son to death.

I GLANCE OVER the edge of the roof and raise a glass to the people far below going about their daily business with no idea of the shit that's about to rain down on them. Top of the world, ma!

I've never really done guilt before. I've made mistakes sure enough, my ex-wife could give you a long list and probably still has the bruises to prove most of them. But guilt had always felt like a reach until I read that story. It burnt what was left of my heart out. It felt like the kid's death was down to me. No one else. Well maybe two other people and the law was dealing with one of those.

Two years too late, I did my research. I spoke to the real wife, Cathy, once. It was a short conversation. She clearly knew nothing about her husband's past and when I asked her if he had another wife tucked away somewhere she set her dog on me. I still have the scars, but I wear them with twisted pride, I earned every last one of them. A friendly bent cop (every tec has at least one to turn to) got me a copy of Keiron Gould's sealed court records. He had a lot more previous than I'd been led to believe. He'd been in all kinds of trouble as a teenager, most of it violent. A lot of it involved his younger sister, who went by the name of Melody. She was his sister, not his wife. Some fucking detective I am.

It took me three months to track down Melody Gould during which time I burnt the candle at both ends, blazing through enough whisky to keep a battleship afloat and seeing that poor kid Adam's face every time I woke up screaming. I pounded on her door on a daily basis. She refused to let me in—possibly because she could smell the fumes from a mile away. But the only quality I really have in common with the great tecs of the silver screen is doggedness, so I persevered. She had to go out eventually. When she came back home, I was sitting on her sofa. She didn't seem surprised.

"Come for a second instalment have you?" she said.

I shook my head. I really wasn't in the mood, and anyway, I wasn't the only one who looked like shit. She'd aged ten years since I'd last seen her.

"Pity. It's been a while. And you've more chance of that than an apology."

She was faking it. She was as damaged as I was. I'd had a good look round in her absence. The place was a tip. Dirty dishes piled everywhere, bottles overflowing from the bin. Just like home. The lounge, where I'd waited for her, was a slight step up, just a couple of ashtrays crammed with dog-ends and something that looked like dried up cat shit in one corner. I was perched on the edge of a chair, not risking my trousers on the full seat. She stayed on her feet.

"Why d'you do it?" I asked. I didn't want to spend any more time there than I had to. Do what I'd come there to do.

"Nice to see you too," she deadpanned. "He's family. Simple as."

"He's a fucking psychopath. He killed a kid."

"He was unlucky. Only hit him once. Kid cracked his head open on the kerb."

Before I knew it I was on my feet. In her face.

"You think your brother was the unlucky one?"

"Not his fault. Nurture not nature. He learnt from the best. Our so-called father used to beat the shit out of us until Keiron got big enough to stop him."

"And yet you helped him get a kid."

She tried to back away. I grabbed her arms and pulled her towards me. She stank of fags, booze and something else. Fear maybe. I could feel her shaking, though that could have been the booze.

"I thought he'd changed," she muttered, turning her head away from me. I grabbed her chin with one hand and turned it back.

"You thought." She was starting to gabble, she might even have pissed herself. I was beyond caring.

"They were supposed to get a girl. He'd have been okay with a girl. It's always been boys he's had a problem with. His stupid wife changed her mind at the last minute."

"So it's her fault?"

She reminded me of my wife, never taking fucking responsibility for anything, talking to me with the same disdain, a permanent scowl on her duplicitous face.

"Well?" I said.

Eventually she shook her head.

"Not really. She didn't know about his past."

"Down to us then."

"Doesn't really matter now. Dead is dead. Kid came from a broken home anyway, the year he had with Keiron was probably the best of his life."

I didn't buy her act. Like me, she'd fallen to pieces since that first meeting and the look in her eyes as I reached for her throat told me she was as haunted as I was by what we'd done. She never really tried to stop me as I squeezed the life out of her. Sometimes it ends with a woman walking into a room.

We'd both fallen a long way since that first fateful meeting, but there's always further you can go. You might be able to erase your mistakes if they're online but not when they're firmly embedded in your head, tattooed on the back of your eyelids in permanent ink. Impossible to escape from that.

So now there's one last fall to come, just as soon as I've emptied this bottle.

Bottoms up.

Author's note. I had only just started writing this story when I heard that an actor from one of my favourite films had died and it morphed into something else. I hope he would have enjoyed it.

RIP William Hurt 1950-22

AULD BRIDE

by

Judith O'Reilly

I NEVER WANTED to come back. Deep down, I knew I shouldn't and yet, I came here anyway.

THE QUAYSIDE WAS colder than I'd imagined possible as I clambered off the boat. A wind sweeping in from across from the North Atlantic with one intent, to blow the marrow from my bones and leave them hollow. Even in my thermals and goose down jacket, I shivered.

Everything was arranged. They'd told me a chap called Malcolm would be waiting for me. And sure enough, as I looked to the end of the quay, the headlights of a black SUV flashed on and off. I raised my hand in greeting. By rights, I should have started walking towards the car, and yet I stayed rooted to the spot, staring at the cliffs and the churning sea flecked with white foam. The stone houses some way up the road. And I thought about every time my father had warned me this island was not for me. Nothing good ever came out of this place. *Except you, my darling,* he'd say. And whatever happened, I was never to go back. *There's nothing there for you. Are you clear about that, Elodie? Absolutely, Daddy,* I'd say.

I knew the story, of course. My mother had died when I was six months old. A fever, he said. Bereft, my father swaddled me up, packed a suitcase, and left on a supply boat one dawn. His own parents long since dead. He told no other soul he was leaving.

And throughout my childhood, even into my early twenties, I never wanted to go back to the island. Never curious. Until my father died, and I saw the job advertised: Marketing manager, Auld Bride Whisky Distillery: £60,000, six weeks holiday, accommodation provided. *Only suitable for someone happy at the idea of remote island living*, it warned. I liked the outdoors and the occasional whisky, and the job would be a massive step up from being a marketing assistant. But it wasn't the money, so much as the idea that took hold. Because my father shouldn't have done what he did. He shouldn't have gotten ill, and he shouldn't have died, and he certainly shouldn't have left me. And this right here was his punishment, because now I was standing where he said I shouldn't ever go. The recklessness of it thrilled me.

Then again, he'd only ever wanted the best for me.

And there was still time to change my mind. As the engine of the boat roared into life again, as the captain's mate unwound the rope from the metal cleat embedded in the concrete, and tossed it down into the well of the boat, I considered retreat—calling for the captain to take me back with him.

But, as if he suspected as much, Malcolm was right there in front of me. His calloused hand over mine, taking the case from me with a grunt, swinging my rucksack onto his own back, and it was too late. No going back anymore. Instead, I watched as the boat pulled away, picking up speed as it cut through the choppy water, lifting and falling, sea birds wheeling in the air above as it headed back to the mainland.

I cursed as I hurried to catch up. Shona was waiting to meet me, he said. Everyone was waiting to meet me.

HER ARMS WERE wide as I pushed open the door of the distillery. It made me hesitate. Did she mean to hug me? My father was not a tactile man, so Shona's warmth made me panic. I stumbled, almost falling at the threshold and Malcolm's strong fingers gripped my wrist to keep me upright. Smiling at my reticence, she lowered her arms.

We had never met. Only talked on Zoom during the interview when I'd confessed that I'd been born on the island. But now she spoke with the warmth of someone who had known me a lifetime. "Elodie McKenzie, come home to us." And a cheer went up from the workers.

I couldn't help myself then. I grinned. Who doesn't have that reaction when they're cheered? But then, I didn't know what it was they were cheering.

I lost track of how many hands I shook, how many tearful hugs the women gave me. *Dougie's child*, I heard more than once. I felt a flush of pleasure that my father was remembered here. And sadness that he couldn't see he'd been wrong not to come back. And, if I'm honest—and why wouldn't I be now—there was anger there, too. That he'd kept me away so long.

I should have run then, of course. But I had no idea what was to come.

LATER, IN HER office, a peat fire blazing in the hearth, Shona sat me down in a leather armchair, placing a whisky glass in front of me. With some ceremony, she reached for a bottle and poured both of us a drink. Her eyes narrowing as she watched me take my first sip. They were amber I realised, the same colour as the whisky she'd poured, and the flames from the fire flickered in them.

"What do you think, Elodie McKenzie, child of Douglas and Moira McKenzie, grandchild of Fraser and Anne McKenzie?"

That was new, my father never discussed his family. The people here would know more about my own heritage than I did. A moment of disquiet before the taste of the whisky hit me.

Over the years, I had tasted various whiskies. A Laphroaig after a country walk, a Talisker on a date. A whisky cocktail in a nightclub. And each and every time, it was as if voices whispered to me but I couldn't make out the words. But this whisky was the truth. I heard all of it, and understood what it had to say to me. That it was the rain that fell from the sky. And the barley that grew through me and around me. I'd yet to swallow it, but knew the heat that had passed over it, because I was that heat. And I was the peat and the smoke, and the oak cask around it. The noise and the silence of the years of waiting. Knew that the whisky was me and I was the whisky.

Swallowing down the fire of it, I struggled to catch my breath and the whole time Shona talked, and I thought it was to give me time to come back to myself.

The Auld Bride distillery was a ghost distillery, she told me. There'd been 'aquavite' brewed in a monastery on the island as early as the 16th century, with a distillery opened by the laird in 1701. Business was good, but tastes change and the distillery closed in 1994. That was the year my father left the island. Was that the reason for his bitterness? That the island first took his wife and then his living when the distillery closed its doors? Shona was still talking as I zoned back in. Three years ago, a bottle of the 1912 Auld Bride came up at auction and fetched £56,000. I blinked then. For one bottle, I queried. Shona nodded. My eyes went to the bottle we'd been drinking. I could have sworn it too was a 1912.

"We're going to do it again, Elodie," she said, turning the bottle away from me an inch. "With your help." She pulled out a smaller flask from a drawer. But when she poured this and lifted the glass to the light, the liquid in it was crystal-clear. "In the oak barrels, it turns to Auld Bride. It's a different creature without the ageing." I went to take the glass from her, but her hand stayed mine. "Tomorrow," she said.

I NEVER DID get to the accommodation I'd been promised with its stove and its views over the sea. Apparently, the roof was leaking. Instead, Shona took me home with her. It could have been awkward, but she made it seem like the most natural thing in the world.

I dragged myself into the bed and slept for twelve straight hours. The next day I came down to salted porridge and a pot of tea you could stand a spoon up in. And then Shona drove me back to the distillery. It was raining, but even so people lined the road. Each man, woman and child straining to see into the car.

I panicked then, I admit. But Shona patted my knee. Said not to worry. The islanders were pleased to see me. It was a mark of respect.

And what could I do but trust her.

The morning passed slowly. They told me the landline and internet connection had gone down, so I'd little to do but wait in my dusty office for a tour of the distillery. Shona had promised to come for me at twelve, and I hoped the tour would inspire me with ideas for a marketing campaign. Truth to tell, I also hoped it would reassure me. Malcolm had bolted the huge distillery gates behind us as we drove in and now islanders stood six deep outside them. I could catch the low thrum of their murmurs even through the leaded window.

I called to Fiona, the elderly secretary outside my office. What was happening?

But she waved a hand. Shona was sorting things. She'd said the same about the lack of signal on my phone. But I must need another cup of tea? I'd shrugged okay and went back to the bookshelves I'd been idly scanning.

That was when I found the *History of Whisky*. It was at the back of the lowest shelf in the darkest corner. I sneezed as I pulled it out and carried it across to my desk. Something told me not to let Fiona see it, so I met her at the doorway when she brought me tea in a bone china cup, a triangle of sugared shortbread balanced on the saucer. *So kind,* I said.

I closed the door and went back to the book on my desk. Turning the book's pages with care, the tea forgotten.

Auld Bride Whisky.

It was a short enough entry and much as Shona had told it. The monks. The distillery and laird. The geography and geology of the island that helped lend the whisky its distinct flavour. Then I turned the page. An addendum on the superstition of the Auld Bride.

"Originally, this author understands the whisky was known as 'Auld One's Bride'. According to legend, no fisherman could catch so much as a sprat in his nets, and the crops had failed year after year. The islanders were starving when the local laird summoned the Devil. They made a pact. The Devil would help them brew unforgettable whisky they could trade for gold. In return for which, every generation of islanders must drown a girl of the Devil's choosing in an oak barrel full of clear spirit. The girl to become his bride in Hell. Witnessed by each and every islander, the laird signed his name in blood. The first bride the devil chose was his youngest daughter."

My mouth dried and I stood up from the desk. My father had left this place for a reason. Because he knew the evil here. And the islanders had laid the perfect snare. There'd never been a job for me. No picturesque cottage with a stove and windows overlooking the sea. If anyone ever enquired, they'd say I'd never arrived, and that I must have thought better of it. I had no father and no mother to search for me. My London friends would wonder and then they would forget me. I'd be gone from this earth and no tears wept for me.

I was chosen.

I HEAR THE scrape of the gates over the cobbles now, the islanders streaming through. Malcolm already stands outside the door. When I finish writing this, I'll leave these pages pressed between the pages of the history, and hide the book again as best as I'm able. As they pull me to the open barrel, I'll fight them harder than they expect me to fight them. Fight against the drowning and the Devil.

I expect to lose

WHERE IS SHUMI?

By

Awais Khan

HER MOTHER HAD warned her about venturing too far into the fields. All it took was one misstep to lose one's way. She wasn't even in the fields anymore, though. She'd made the mistake of following an old ox, thinking it would guide her back to civilization, but the silly old thing was only looking for water.

There was none to be found.

The sun was high in the sky, and Shumi felt like the last of the water inside her was bleeding out in the form of sweat.

"Stop sweating," she muttered to herself, but like always, her body rebelled against her. Everywhere she looked, there was only yellow sand and brown shrubs, the green leeched right out of them. Her stomach rumbled, but there was nothing to eat except the old ox, and as much as she'd seen her father butcher animals, she didn't think she had the strength to bring down a grown ox, not to mention anything to kill it with.

"You're a strange one, Shumi," her mother always said to her. "God knows what we'll do with you."

She had no need to worry, for Shumi wasn't long for this world. Just a few days ago, she had started bleeding, and although the flow today wasn't as bad as it was yesterday, she didn't think her body had anymore blood to give. Between that and the sweat, it was a surprise she was still walking. She'd bundled up a wad of muslin in her underwear to prevent the blood from leaking out, but she could feel the familiar sticky wetness now, and her heart quailed. What if she bled to death here? How would anyone find her? The old ox looked like it didn't belong to anyone.

Shumi looked around, but was met by a wall of heat. Her vision blurred, but she kept following the ox. Surely, it would take her to where there was some water. She'd heard from Abba that animals had better noses than humans. They butchered their own animals because they didn't have the money to buy meat from the local butcher, and her father always patted the animal and whispered to it before sacrificing it.

"They're living things too, Shumaila. They deserve to be treated with respect."

No, Shumi would not entertain any further ideas of killing the old ox. Abba would be most displeased.

Just as she was about to lose heart and collapse, she spotted some hills in the distance.

Strange... they didn't have hills in their village. She'd only ever seen hills once when they had travelled to Quetta. She couldn't be in Quetta, could she? It was hundreds of miles away!

Upon closer inspection, she thought that they looked less like hills and more like caves. Caves she had been warned about. Restless spirits of the dead haunted these caves, spirits that had not found peace.

"Spirits of bad people," Ama Ishrat, the old storyteller, would tell anyone who listened. And people did listen to her. "Murderers, rapists, wicked little girls that ran away and got married against their parents' wishes. The caves are the devil's playground."

Everyone avoided the caves because there had always been unexplained disappearances and the caves seemed like the only place where the spirits might linger.

"They come for wicked girls who are up to no good," Ama Ishrat said. "They feast on their unborn foetuses, and then bathe in their blood."

Shumi shivered as a new realization hit her. She was bleeding, which made her fair game. How could she have been so stupid? She slapped her palm against her forehead like she'd seen her mother do whenever things went south. She turned around, ready to run in the opposite direction when she heard it.

A sound... no, a tune really. A very mournful tune from a flute. The ox grunted, its head swaying to the music. Oddly, Shumi wanted to do the same. Despite her heart galloping in her chest, urging her to run, run far, run fast, she felt compelled to turn around. Don't do it, Shumi, her mind screamed at her. But when had she ever listened?

She turned around just as the music stopped.

"ONE SECOND HERE and the other second gone. Poof. Like dust," Ama Ishrat remarked, shaking her head. "It has happened to more girls than I can even begin to count. Poor Shumi. Only nine."

"I don't suppose her menses would have begun yet, Ama," one of the younger midwives said, sitting on her haunches in front of Ama Ishrat. "Who would want anything to do with a girl so young?"

Ama Ishrat shook her head, dunking a chunk of jaggery in her tea before sucking on it. "Nine is old enough for the monsters of this village, Jamila. Both human and other."

"Other?"

A small crowd had gathered around Ama Ishrat, the women sitting on the earthen floor, their silver jewellery clinking as they adjusted the *chaddars* on their heads. The men stood in a semi circle, some of them pretending to not be interested in what had happened, but it was hard to ignore it. No matter how hard they tried, Ama Ishrat had their attention.

Ama Ishrat knew how to work a crowd. Her eyes rolled back as she clutched her chest. The piece of jaggery rolled to the floor, immediately snatched up by one of the younger children. Her body contorted as she had one of her legendary fits. "They've taken far too many of our daughters," she gasped. "But they still want more."

The crowd gasped. "More?"

Ama Ishrat shook her head, her dupatta sliding from her head, revealing her henna-dyed amber hair. 'Let them take Shumi. If we stop looking for her, maybe they will stop taking more of our girls. Shumi is with them now. Let her be. Save the rest.'

Rasheeda lay on a charpai under the shade of a *shisham* tree, her kameez soaked in what must be days of sweat. She was exhausted beyond belief, but when she heard Ama Ishrat asking everyone to stop searching for her little Shumaila, she rose from the bedstead. With her legs shaking, she stepped forward towards the crowd. That *kuti* Ishrat had been fooling the villagers with her theatrics for decades, but no more. Rasheeda couldn't let her capitalize on her Shumi's disappearance. She brandished a finger in her direction. 'Don't you dare take my daughter's name, *haramzadi*. How dare you call off the search?'

Ama Ishrat's eyes swivelled back and narrowed before she let out a wail. "She won't rest until all your daughters are taken. She wants them all taken by the Others! *Haye*!"

Before Rasheeda could react, she felt her knees give way and the world go dark.

GIRLS HAD BEEN vanishing from Meetha village for decades, to the point that it was now considered a way of life.

"At least they don't take our sons. We can always have more daughters, but our sons are far more precious," most people said.

Rasheeda despised those words. Birthing a daughter was no different from birthing a son, so why should loving one be? Shumi had torn her way out of the womb, so much that the midwife had to use a hot needle to sew Rasheeda back together. Still, Rasheeda knew that she would do anything for her daughter. If only she knew where she was.

It had been three days since her daughter had disappeared. One moment she was running after the goats and the next she was gone. Rasheeda had only gone to check on the chicken karhai she was cooking and tend to Baby Farhana. One thing led to another and it wasn't until the evening that she discovered that Shumi had vanished. Her beautiful little girl. At nine, she was still too young to attract the attention of men, but who could say in this day and age? She'd heard stories of babies stolen from their cots only to be abused and discarded in the fields, so how could a nine-year-old fare any better?

She took deep breaths. She couldn't let her mind go in those dark places. Her Shumi was a spirited girl. A fighter. She'd sooner throw rocks at a man than let him do anything to her. Still, she'd seen her limping about a little recently, as if she had something wedged into her shalwar. Surely, she couldn't be having her period. Rasheeda hadn't had hers until she was twelve, but she'd heard of girls as young as eight starting their periods.

She ought to have been more attentive towards her daughter. Rasheeda put her head in her hands. Everything hurt. Her husband had been out looking for Shumi with her, and was now passed out on the charpai next to hers. They'd wept, screamed, bashed their heads against the walls, but none of that had brought Shumi back. With a rising sense of dread, Rasheeda realized that the villagers too had given up on her daughter. The women had stopped visiting with gifts of porridge and *lassi*. The mention of Shumi still brought pity in their eyes, but everyone in the village was busy, and nobody seemed to ever have enough money. Her husband, Fahad, worked in the neighbouring city as a secretary's assistant, but even with his seemingly superior salary, they barely made ends meet.

Rasheeda refused to believe that ghosts had spirited away her daughter. That was an old midwives' tale. And Ama Ishrat had been peddling this nonsense for decades. That didn't make it true, did it?

They said the spirits resided in the caves outside of the village. Rasheeda had never been there. Nobody had. Ama Ishrat said that the very air of that place was tainted and that the music from the caves had lured many people to their deaths. This is what Rasheeda had never understood. How could there be music when there was nobody alive there?

"Spirits are much more alive than us, you silly girl," Ama Ishrat had once chastised her. Rasheeda hadn't bothered asking again.

They had scoured every inch of the village for Shumi, but it was as if she'd vanished into thin air. Rasheeda had hoped to find a footprint, a dupatta... anything to indicate her daughter had existed, but it seemed like the earth had swallowed her whole.

Spirits or no spirits, she knew what she had to do. Deep down, she'd always known that she'd have to go there in the end.

To the caves.

SHE DIDN'T WAKE Fahad. If she were to die, at least he'd be there for the kids. Sure, the bastard would remarry instantly, but at least the children would still have a father. Rasheeda continued this banter with herself as she stole through the village square in the middle of the night. She couldn't wait until morning. Her strength might fail her by then. At night, everyone was asleep, so nobody could talk her out of this suicide mission.

She realized she didn't care. All she cared about was finding her daughter.

"Maybe you'll find her body there," a voice in her mind piped up. Raseeda quelled it immediately. There were many things she was willing to endure in this world. Burying her own daughter was not one of them.

"Who do you love most in the world?" Shumi had asked her once.

Burdened with the responsibility of a new baby while having to cook and clean for four others, Rasheeda was unimpressed by the question.

Perceptive as ever, Shumi had rephrased her question. "Which of your kids do you love the most?"

In those days when Farhana was newly born, Rasheeda's patience lasted all of a few seconds. "I love Farhana the most right now because she needs me the most," she had snapped back. "Are you happy now?"

She remembered how much her words had wounded little Shumi, but there was no way she could take them back. The worst bit was that she was so tired that when she saw those fat tears sliding down Shumi's face, she didn't care. Not a jot. She went back to nursing Farhana.

Rasheeda blinked back the tears that blurred her vision now and pushed ahead. "I love you the most, Shumi," she whispered. "Please come back."

She walked until the muddy roads turned into fields which then turned into fine desert sand. She walked until her feet ached just as much as her heart. She walked until she heard music in the air.

The sound made her stop dead.

It was pitch black around her. In her haste, she'd forgotten to bring a torch or Fahad's cell phone which had a built-in torch. The darkness in villages wasn't like the one in cities. It was all encompassing… absolute. Rasheeda stood very still, her ears straining to catch the direction the music was coming from. Up ahead. It had to be. She rushed ahead, not caring that her shalwar was snagging on the bushes. She abandoned her dupatta when it caught against a thorny shrub. To hell with it, she thought. She was probably going to die anyway. Strangely enough, the music didn't scare her as much as she thought it would. At this point, nothing could.

The music steadily grew stronger as she walked on, and before long, she thought she could see pinpricks of yellow light in the distance. How bizarre, she thought. Who was foolish enough to play music in the caves at this time of the night? If this bastard was hiding her then so help him God, because she was going to kill him.

Her feet sank in the sand as she marched towards the caves, all fear of the spirits forgotten. There never were any spirits. That was all nonsense. She was almost at the foot of the cave, when she stopped short. Along with the sound of the flute was a familiar voice. "Stop playing this bloody flute. I've told you a million times we cannot just put a girl on a truck and send her to the city. There is only one road leading into the village and it is watched at all times. Now that the villagers are starting to get busy with their own stuff, we can move her." There was a pause before the same voice spoke again. "Stop playing this flute, *kanjari ke.*"

Rasheeda's blood went cold before it rushed back to her head. For a moment she felt like she would explode. The nerve of that *haramzadi*. She rushed inside to find the strangest scene playing in front of her: Ama Ishrat sitting on the floor with a bearded man who was playing the flute with his eyes closed while an old ox stood chewing the cud in the far corner of the cave. Ama Ishrat seemed to be caressing the head of someone sleeping in her lap. With a cry, Rasheeda realized who it was.

"Shumi!" she cried.

Ama Ishrat and her partner looked up. There was only a moment's confusion on Ama Ishrat's face before she broke into a toothless smile. "Look who we found! Your Shumaila. Someone seems to have drugged her but she's safe. Look!"

In retrospect, Rasheeda knew she should have taken Ama Ishrat at her word and left with Shumi, but at the time her mind was choking on anger. "You *haramzadi*," she said, advancing on the two people, not caring that the man looked young and strong enough to fell an ox. "All this time you've been spreading stories about those spirits while you kidnap girls. Do you sell them? Huh?"

The music had stopped. The man was looking up at her nonplussed.

To her credit, Ama Ishrat didn't let her smile slip. "No, my *beti*, you are mistaken. I personally came here to look for Shumi—"

Rasheeda held up a hand. "That's for the Jirga to decide what you were or weren't doing. For now, give me my daughter. I can't believe you've been spreading all these lies all this time. There never were any spirits at all. Just you."

Shumi appeared to be drugged because she didn't so much as move.

Ama Ishrat was still caressing her head. Rasheeda wanted to slap her hand away. "Just give me my daughter."

The music started up again.

Ama Ishrat slapped a palm against her forehead. "For the last time, Bashir, stop playing the flute."

"But, I'm not. Look at me." Bashir held up his flute.

For the first time, Ama Ishrat looked scared. "Then who is playing the flute?"

The sound appeared to be coming from somewhere deeper in the cave.

Rasheeda closed her hand around Shumi's wrist just as she heard Ama Ishrat scream.

THE FALL OF MAN

by

Charles Ardai

GENE LEVITT LIVED twenty-three stories up, in a penthouse apartment at Eastgate House. His bedroom was next to his mother's, so he tried to be quiet when he opened the window by his dresser and climbed out onto the terrace. He reached back inside for his scotch-tape dispenser, a marker, and four sheets of paper from a notepad. Then he looked around his room—at his knapsack, at his computer with his half-finished term paper in it, at his fish tank—and pulled the window shut behind him.

It was early in the morning and it was chilly. Gene shivered in his thin pajamas as he knelt on the stone tiles. He laid out three sheets of paper side by side and, copying from the fourth, wrote a few lines on each with the marker. He printed carefully but quickly. The tremble in his arm only partly from the cold. When he was done, he capped the marker and laid it aside.

Along the wall of the terrace there was a row of metal plant boxes. Gene dug a hole in the soil of one of these, crumpled the fourth sheet of paper into a tight ball, and buried it as deep as it would go.

He knelt down again and fumbled open the buttons of his pajama top. The air slid in against his chest, pricking up gooseflesh. Gene took the top off.

He folded the three pieces of paper twice each, until they were the size of playing cards, and addressed them: *"To Mom," "To Robert," "To Eden."* Then he pulled off long strips of tape and wrapped them around his upper arms. Under each band of tape he pushed one of the folded pieces of paper.

The third he taped to his chest.

Finally, he stood.

For a moment he was silent and still, his hands balled into fists, the thin, pale muscles of his arms straining against the tape. Then he slid his thumbs under the waistband of his pajama pants and let the pants fall to his ankles. He stepped out of them, climbed up on one of the plant boxes, and onto the rim of the terrace wall.

From there, the breeze felt much sharper. It swept over him teasingly, as though it knew that too sudden a shiver would be enough to make him fall. He took a few deep breaths to steady himself.

Then he crossed his arms over his chest, closed his eyes, and took one big step forward.

"EDEN, COULD YOU come in for a minute?"

Eden released the intercom button, pushed her chair back, took her pocketbook down from the shelf above her desk, and walked across the hall. Sharon's door was closed. Eden raised her hand to knock, then dropped it to the knob. After a moment, she eased the door open just far enough to look in.

"Come in. Please."

Sharon sat facing the door, her elbows on her blotter, her tented hands supporting her forehead. "Eden, you knew Eugene." Sharon spoke without raising her head, without looking at Eden. "You were close to him."

It was almost a question, but not enough of one that Eden felt she ought to answer. Instead, she stared at the wall-to-wall carpet and picked at a cuticle.

Sharon looked up and noticed that Eden was still standing. She pointed to an empty chair.

"Thank you," Eden said. "I heard about what happened." She let her hands drop to her lap. "I'm really sorry. He was a sweet boy. You must be devastated."

Sharon *looked* devastated. Eden thought she looked as if she didn't know what she was doing here. What's the use of nine-to-six, review in July, promotion imminent, when your son's gone and jumped out the window? Eden wasn't supposed to know that's what had happened, not officially, but everyone knew.

"Very much so," Sharon said. "It's hard to believe he's gone."

Eden nodded. Gene had been a nice kid, bright and lonely and sincere. No trouble at home, as far as she knew—but she hadn't really known him, had she? Only from his visits to the office, when he had come in after school or during one vacation or another, and more recently from tutoring him in some of his classes as a favor to Sharon. Going over *Great Expectations* with someone was a far cry from actually knowing him, and the one real overture he'd made, such as it was, she'd nimbly ducked.

"We're trying to understand why he did it," Sharon said. "We thought he might have said something to you."

There was no veiled accusation in Sharon's words, but Eden still felt uncomfortable being brought into it. Of course he hadn't said anything. If he had, she'd have told Sharon. "No, I'm sorry," Eden said. "He didn't. We only talked about his schoolwork, really."

"How was he doing?"

"Fine. He was having a little trouble focusing on his term paper for his history class, but it wasn't a big deal. And the other class, he was getting all As."

"That was the English class?"

"English, yes."

Sharon shook her head. "Eden, we're trying to figure this out. I mean, why he would do it. He was happy."

"Apparently not." The words came out thoughtlessly before Eden could hold them back.

Sharon looked more hurt by the truth of it than by Eden's saying it. "No. Apparently not."

"I'm sorry, Sharon. I didn't mean that. He must have had a reason, but reasons that make a lot of sense to a teenager… I mean, maybe he had a fight or something."

"I don't think he was the kind of kid to get into fights."

"Okay, I don't know," Eden said, "but something. He did badly on a test, he read a book that depressed him. It could have been anything. Whatever it was, he didn't say anything to me."

"Eden," Sharon said, "there are two reasons I had to ask you. First, because he talked to you more openly than he talked to either his stepfather or myself. Because you're closer to his age than we are, and he liked you."

Eden tensed at this. It was how Sharon had gotten her to tutor Gene to begin with: *you're closer to his age, he'll listen to you.* Not that Eden had minded doing it, but her boss' son, how could she have said no, even if she had wanted to?

And *he liked you*—sure he liked her. He'd been moony-eyed over her since she started working for his mom when he was thirteen and she was fresh out of NYU with her useless literature degree and her dream (every English major's dream) of writing short stories for *The New Yorker*. Not a problem, just your standard crush, even sweet in its way, but three years later it had made tutoring him just the tiniest bit awkward. But still, she did it, and it was fine. He was fine.

"But the second reason," Sharon continued, "is that he left you a note."

"A note?"

"Yes." Sharon swallowed heavily. "It was taped to his chest."

"What do you mean he left it for me?"

"There was one for me, one for Robert, and one for you." Sharon lifted three pages from her desktop and passed them to Eden. They were photocopies. The bloodstains from the originals were reproduced as black spots. Each sheet had two words that had been typed at the top by the police.

On the first, the typewritten words were "TO MOM" and the carefully printed words below said:

EZEKIEL: Behold, I am about to take the delight of your eyes away from you at a stroke; yet you shall not mourn or weep nor shall your tears run down. Sigh, but not aloud; make no mourning for the dead.

The second said "TO ROBERT" at the top, and below that was written in big letters:

PROVERBS: Do not rejoice when your enemy falls

The last was addressed "TO EDEN", and it said:

NUMBERS: The maiden was very fair to look upon, a virgin, whom no man had known...
He who blasphemes the name of the Lord shall be put to death; all the congregation shall stone him.

Eden found her hand was shaking, even after she set the pages down again.

"Oh my God," she said.

"You see why I hoped you might be able to explain."

"These are... these are from what he was working on for his history paper," Eden said. "They were doing this unit on the Bible as a historical document."

"What do they mean?"

"I don't know," Eden said. She picked up the first sheet of paper again. "I mean, this one... He didn't want you to be upset, didn't want to hurt you." She pointed to the second page. "It was your husband he was angry with."

Sharon shook her head and Eden almost missed seeing a shade of anger in her eyes. "No. I don't believe that."

"I understand," Eden said softly.

"No, you don't," Sharon said. "Eugene never was angry with Robert. Resenting Robert was a pro forma thing with him. He wouldn't let himself admit he loved Robert, to honor his father's memory. But really, he did love him. He was starting to. There was nothing bad between them."

"But he calls Robert his enemy—"

"He didn't mean it," Sharon said. "I mean, look what he called you."

Eden was shocked by the casual hostility. *The maiden was very fair to look upon, a virgin, whom no man had known.*

"What does yours mean?" Sharon demanded, her voice rising, strained. "Why did he write that?"

"I don't know," Eden said. She reread the quote. It seemed wrong somehow, incorrect, and she stirred her memory until she knew why. "It's actually two separate quotes," she said. "The first line and the second are from different places. They—" Eden covered her mouth with her hand.

"What is it?"

A scene suddenly played out in Eden's mind, unreeling in slow motion. A session about Andrew Marvell's "To His Coy Mistress." Afterwards, Gene had given her a book he had wanted her to read. It had been a copy of *Cyrano de Bergerac*.

I've read it, she'd said. He had looked disappointed. *Open it*, he had said.

"Eden?"

She put her hands to her temples. "The first line is from Genesis. The second's from Leviticus. Genesis Leviticus," Eden said. "Gene Levitt."

"I don't understand," Sharon said.

It had been a cheap paperback edition, a used copy, well thumbed, and at first when she saw the black cursive on the title page she didn't realize it had been written to her rather than to some previous owner of the copy, decades earlier. It had said, *For E.* And then, beneath that, in tidy ballpoint penmanship, a quote from the play: *And why not? If you love her, tell her so!* She'd smiled, reached out to ruffle his hair, and he'd caught her hand and pressed it to his lips.

He who blasphemes the name of the Lord shall be put to death.

She had tilted her head, pursed her lips, and said, *You practicing to be a French swashbuckler, kiddo?* And he'd stammered: *I—I—* He'd let her hand drop and rotated the old paperback on the table between them.

And that's when she'd kicked herself for not twigging to his meaning sooner. Ah, God. He was even looking at her like a puppy dog, like a goddamn Hallmark-card puppy dog. *That's very sweet*, she'd said, even though it wasn't, because now she had to put him off, and he was Sharon's son. But that's puberty for you—you heap your silk shirts on a table for a girl and sometimes all you get is a heap of shirts. *Let's not get out over our skis here, bucko. One of the girls in your class would love to get a copy of this book, I promise. Seriously. Maybe someone named Emily or Eloise? You won't even need a new copy!*

He'd nodded and looked down at the table and blushed like a three-alarm fire. How long had it been since she'd seen puppy love in all its fury? *Come on*, she'd said. *I'm eight years older than you are.*

What's eight years? he had asked earnestly.

Half your life? she'd said.

But I love you, he had insisted.

No, she had said firmly, *you don't.*

How many times had she come over after that? Six? Seven? And he had been fine each time. Intense as always, but never another word about the incident.

She'd never actually taken the book home.

"He—He—" Eden couldn't keep the tears out of her eyes or her voice. She could barely speak. "He meant himself," she tried to say.

"I don't understand," Sharon said again. "This stuff about the virgin, the blasphemer— What did he *do* to you?"

"He didn't do anything!" Behind her eyes, a parade of images went past again and again, like children on a carousel. "He didn't do a thing!"

"Then why did he write that note?" Sharon said. "What does it mean? If it's Genesis, why did he say it was Numbers? Eden, if you understand, you have to tell me!"

Eden shook her head violently, which was all she could do. She did understand. Why was it Numbers? Because it wasn't the words that mattered, not really, it was the numbers, the verse numbers. She knew what they were without even having to check. The first line was Genesis 24:16, and the second was Leviticus 24:16. And that was his message, his explanation, his cry — because she was twenty-four, and he was sixteen.

RABBITS

by

M.E. Proctor

THERE'S THREE OF us kids on Claw Ridge Farm. I'm Jake, I'm twelve. Lily is two years behind, and Simon, better known as Shoes, because he always loses them, is four years old. Then Mom and Dad, of course. There's more family spread out in the county. Our name—Purcell—is on many buildings. Sometimes, when I drive around with Dad, running errands, it's like the entire place is populated by my relatives. It's not a pleasant feeling. A big fist pushes on my chest, trapping air in there. I have to close my eyes tight to avoid seeing all the signs. *Purcell Lumber. Purcell Hardware. Purcell Plumbing. Purcell Sod & Soil.* I haven't seen it on a church or a hospital yet, but I know there's a cousin that's a pastor and another that's a nurse. There are Purcells everywhere I turn. And they all know who I am. Maybe they also know what's going on in my head.

LILY CAME INTO my room last night because she heard me scream. I was having the nightmare again. She shook me awake.

"It sounded terrible, Jake." She put her arms around me. "I don't want you to go to the hospital. I don't like it when you're not here."

"Was I loud?"

"I think we're okay. With the storm and all."

A thunderstorm made the glass in the windows shake. The crash of thunder was deafening. Hail like nails rolling on the metal roof. "You heard me over this racket?"

Lily and I shared part of the attic, with a thin plywood partition between us.

"I wasn't asleep," she said. "I hate storms. I was counting between the flashes and the booms. Can I stay with you tonight? I'll bring my blanket." She smiled. "I think I could sleep, and you wouldn't have a nightmare."

"Sure. Bring a pillow."

It was a little tight, and I was embarrassed, because of the cold sweat from the bad dream. Lily was soft and warm. She smelled good too, from that apple shampoo she uses.

"Do you remember what the nightmare is about? Do you always dream the same one?"

"I don't know, Lil," I lied.

I lied to her like I lied to Mom and Dad. Like I lied to the doctor who made me stay in the hospital for two days *in observation*. I was so afraid I would have the dream when I was locked in there, and they would know what it was about that I did not sleep at all.

THE NIGHTMARE IS always the same. In the beginning I'm in our yard, then the view changes, and I don't recognize anything. I try to remember when I wake up, and I can, up to the point when I'm so afraid I think I'm going to die.

I'm in the dream with nobody I know from real life. One person I see clearly. He's tall, with dark hair and kind eyes, and if he could be with me the entire time, I wouldn't be scared. I wouldn't scream. Sometimes, he waves at me. At other times he makes a sign with his hand to follow him. We're close enough to touch. Then the terror comes. I don't want to be afraid in the night again, but I want to know where he'll take me.

I know he's my brother.

Not little Shoes all grown up, no, he's my older brother. The brother who isn't here. The brother I'm not supposed to have.

The brother I'm supposed to have forgotten.

There should be four of us on Claw Ridge Farm.

I know his name, but an invisible curtain hides it from me when I'm awake. In the dream I call him by his name. I have it right here now, like these things you see from the corner of your eye that disappear when you look at them straight. I will be in class, or biking to school, or sitting at the dinner table, and I'll be so close to remembering his name that I'll stop whatever I'm doing. Then the feeling goes away and I want to scream. That would send me to the hospital for sure.

Recently, I've been seeing my brother when I'm awake. Like camera flashes, and it seems that I remember more and more. In these memories, he looks a lot like me, like I am now, but taller. In the memories, I'm not twelve years old, I'm much smaller. The clearest image is the two of us standing by the rabbit hutches stacked against the barn. We don't have rabbits on the farm now.

This morning, I ask Mom when we stopped raising rabbits.

Her back is to me. She's doing the dishes. She doesn't answer. She puts plates away. Maybe she didn't hear me. Then she says: "You remember the rabbits, Jake?"

"Vaguely," I say. "They were white and I gave them lettuce."

She's hunched over the sink, scrubbing at something. "You wanted to help with farm work, but you were scared of the cows. The rabbits were more your size. And the chickens."

"The chickens were all right, but there was that nasty turkey that attacked me. I think he was waiting for me, and he saw me coming from a mile away."

"That was Mean Arthur," Mom says. "He attacked everybody. It wasn't just you he was after."

Mean Arthur is no longer in the coop. "Did we eat him?" The thought grosses me out, even if that crazy bird was my enemy. I think of cannibalism. The winners in battle eating the hearts of the losers.

"Your aunt Clara fried him. None of us had any. Even your dad couldn't bring himself to have a bite." She shakes her head. "Mean Arthur. We should have let him die of old age."

"That was after the rabbits," I say, trying to get her back on the subject.

She stares out the kitchen window. "Why the sudden interest, Jake?"

"I don't know. I looked at the barn and I thought about them."

She gets on her knees and rummages in a bottom drawer. I hear the clank of the cake tins.

"Why isn't Shoes feeding the chickens? He's having it way easier than I did. Doesn't he have chores?"

"You're absolutely right," she says. "Go boss him around."

LILY SLIPS INTO my bed again tonight. There is no storm and I'm not even a little asleep yet. I should tell her to scram. This is getting awkward. Before I can remind her that she has her own bed, she delivers her news.

"You're going back to the hospital, Jake," she whispers.

"No, I'm not. What are you talking about?"

"I heard Mom and Dad. They're very upset. I think they've been fighting."

I lean on an elbow and switch on the flashlight I use to read under the covers. I need to see my sister's face. Is she telling a tale? I've heard it enough, from one or another Purcell—*The Craw Ridge kids have too much imagination.* It's usually blamed on Mom's side of the family.

Lily's little triangular face is serious, her clear eyes are big. She shields them from the light and I click the flashlight off.

"What did they say?"

Lily has a talent I envy. She's the quietest walker I know. Even the creaking staircase doesn't make a sound when she goes up or down. Maybe she floats above the steps.

"I went down for a glass of water. They were in the kitchen. Mom was at the table and she'd been crying, I could tell. Her eyes were red and swollen. Dad was pacing, you know like he does, and talking with his hands. He said it had to stop. That they'd let it go long enough. Mom said something about rabbits and a guy named Arthur. I couldn't make sense of it."

A thin cold finger caresses my spine and I shiver. "They talked about me?"

"They talked about me first," Lily says. "Dad asked if I knew about the rabbits. Do we have rabbits, Jake?"

"No. Please, Lily, what did they say?"

"Mom started crying. Dad said you had to go to the doctor to get this fixed. Mom was scared. She said *no* many times, and that you didn't have the nightmares anymore, and that the pills worked."

I took the pills for a while after the hospital, but they made me sleepy all the time and I couldn't read or do my homework. I would read two lines and forget what it was about, and have to start all over again. It drove me crazy. After that, I pretended to swallow them.

"Dad said he would call the doctor and take you to the hospital. Mom was crying really hard. Dad said it was a curse and he looked angry. Mom said it was not important and to be patient. Dad said he'd been patient enough and he used bad words, and Mom ran to the den. She had her head in her hands. Then Dad left. He slammed the door, and I heard his truck leave."

I heard the truck too. A few minutes ago. I didn't think anything of it.

"I would never get angry because of rabbits." Lily sits on the side of the bed. "They're cute."

I don't know what I triggered with my questions but it was serious enough for Mom to tell Dad about it. I won't go to the hospital again. I'll fight. They can't make me.

"What about the doctor?" Lily says. "I'll run away with you."

My fierce sister. I tug at one of her braids. "We'd be caught before lunch time, silly."

I could go hide somewhere. Be out of sight for a while. Long enough for Dad to change his mind about the hospital. Since school let out, I've had this idea in the back of my mind to look for the places I see in my dreams. It's probably stupid. Dreams are not real. They're puzzles with pieces that don't fit.

"Go back to bed and try to sleep, Lil. There's no storm tonight."

"YOU'RE UP EARLY," Mom says.

"It gets too hot later to do anything outside. Clay and I are building a camp in his grandpa's field. His dad said he had boards and tools we could use. It'd be neat if we could have it done this summer." The words are coming out too fast. Mom's going to stop me. Tell me to wait for Dad. I see it coming.

Sure enough, she takes a step toward me. "Jake, I think you should ..."

Lily runs in, laughing, a tornado in pink sneakers. She grabs my backpack and starts raiding the pantry. Apples and energy bars. Bottles of water. Mom and I stare at each other across the kitchen table.

"Come on, Jake, let's go." Lily takes my hand and pulls me toward the door.

I hold Mom's gaze for an instant.

"Be back for lunch," she says. I catch the hint of a smile.

Dad's truck is in the driveway. He must be in the barn.

We take the path down to the creek at a run. It's the way to Clay's parents' farm. When we're safely out of sight from the house, we stop to catch our breath.

"Where are we really going?" Lily says. She's bent in two with her hands on her knees, gasping. "You can thank me, by the way."

"That was well done, Lil. I was about to get nailed." I adjust the backpack on my shoulders. "Let's go around to the north pasture."

That's where my dreams begin. The cluster of pines at the end of the field.

I sit on my heels to take in the view. The dark mass of the house is above us, on the ridge. The barn is halfway between us and the house.

In my dreams, the barn is lit by the setting sun that paints the rabbit cages a violent orange. The pine trees are taller than they are in reality, their straight trunks varnished black. My brother leans on one of them.

I close my eyes to focus on the memory of the dream.

I walk toward my brother and he motions for me to come closer. It must be fall because dead leaves crunch underneath my sneakers. Little kid shoes fastened with Velcro.

I open my eyes, and touch the pine tree. The bark is rough and flaky, with the heat of the morning sun underneath. It feels alive.

In one version of the dream, my brother turns and walks deeper into the trees. I follow him. The barn no longer visible.

"Is this place in your dream, Jake?" Lily whispers.

"It is, but then it changes, and I don't know where I am anymore."

I start walking in the direction my brother took, Lily follows closely behind. I pull out my phone to look at the compass. East. We soon leave the cover of trees. We're on grazing land. The cows don't pay us any attention. A row of pecan trees and a barbed wire fence mark the end of the field. I squeeze under the fence, then hold up the wire for Lily. We're off our land now, in a stretch of forest that's part of a natural preserve. I hike and bike in there with my buddy Clay, but we always stick to the well-marked trails. There are snakes, bobcats and deer, wild hogs too, and it's big enough to get lost. I keep going straight, through brush and fallen trees. It doesn't look like the forest of my dreams. It's rougher and messy.

"I don't want to get lost, Jake," Lily says.

"We're not going far."

I shiver. It's an echo of words heard long ago. I remember a broken-down shed. Was that in my dream or is it a memory?

A few minutes later, another piece of the puzzle falls into place.

We're on the edge of a marsh. The reeds were brown and dry, now they are green and fluffy. The water is glassy and reflects the blue morning sky. Dragonflies skim the surface for bugs. Something jumps out of the water and falls with a flap. The long neck of a blue heron swivels. He stares at me, arrogant and cool, eye make-up like the picture of Cleopatra in my history book. I think of the snakes that must swim in these shallows. And the alligators.

Lily takes my hand. "It's pretty. Have we arrived?"

On the right, a big fallen tree is half-submerged. "I think we have to go that way."

I climb on the tree trunk and help Lily get up.

We slide on the other side and slip under the lower branches of a massive magnolia, and there it is. What's left of the shed. The roof is pierced, the door is off the hinges, vegetation poking through the cracks of the rotting planks.

"I'm not going in," Lily says. "Imagine what's living in there. Yuck."

I pick up a fallen branch and bang it on the side of the shed. The wildlife doesn't want to meet me more than I want to meet them. I peek inside.

I've been here before.

With Charlie.

The realization is so sudden I stumble and fall to my knees.

"Jake, you okay?"

"Just put my foot down wrong."

I was here with my brother. With Charlie.

I step into the shed, holding the branch like a sword. It smells musty, of decaying leaves, with a whiff of something sweetly rotten. I see a pallet with a moldy blanket, a crate, cans so rusty I can't guess what they once contained, a couple of shelves, a metal box on one of them.

Charlie's voice in my head: "Look."

I use the branch to pull the box from the shelf. It falls to the ground and snaps open.

Newspaper articles and handwritten pages. A plastic syringe.

The box is the size of a cookie tin. I gather the documents and use one of the sheets to pick up the syringe. I drop the box in my backpack.

"Let's find a place to sit and have a bite, Lil."

She doesn't need more encouragement to clamber over the fallen tree. I can tell she doesn't care for this place. We walk back to the cow pasture and sit under an old oak. The cows gathered by the pond give us a lazy look. Lily curls up with her head in my lap. She's asleep in five minutes.

I open the box and start reading the yellowed press articles. Four girls murdered in Barwin County. The police have no clue. A business card is stapled to one of the sheets. Olivia Rezki. Deputy Sheriff. A phone number written on the back of the card.

The terror strikes as it does in the nightmare, opaque darkness in bright sunlight. One minute, I'm reading Charlie's notes. The next, pain cuts through me, from neck to tailbone. I see the blade that's hacking me to pieces. It's large and silver. Too big for a hunting knife, pointier than a machete. Then it's over. The pain is gone and I feel the heat of the sun on my face. I wipe away tears I didn't know were running. Lily's head weighs on my leg. I hear the cows tearing and munching grass. I hear the shrill cry of a mockingbird, and the sound of a tractor behind the trees.

I pocket the business card and put the papers back in the box.

"Wake up, Lil."

DAD ISN'T HOME. If there's a hospital visit in my future, it won't be before tomorrow. I have to make the best of today.

"I'm going to the library," I say.

"I was hoping you could keep an eye on Shoes," Mom says.

"I'll do it," Lily says.

I'm out of the door and on my bike before Mom can protest.

The library is deserted. Chloe Jenkins is behind the desk. She waves at me—I'm a regular—and gets back to her studies. She told me she had the perfect summer job. She could do her school work and still get paid. I sit at a table in the far back, next to the reference books. With a bulky World Atlas open in front of me, I call the number on the card.

Clicking sounds.

"Olivia Rezki."

"Uh, hi. I'm Jake Purcell."

"Yes? What is it about?"

She has a nice, deep voice, with a slow way of talking that makes it sound warm.

"Do you know my brother, Charlie Purcell?"

"Should I?"

I tell her about the box I found in the shed with the articles, the notes, and her card inside. She asks about Charlie.

I peek around the corner. Chloe is still buried in her papers. "Charlie is gone. I mean, like he never existed, but I know that's a lie." I'm aware of how confusing I must sound. Panicked. She'll think I'm nuts.

"It's okay, Jake," she says.

I swallow and I'm sure she hears it through the phone. "I'm scared. The pills, and, uh, the hospital." God, it's getting worse. I dig my nails in my palm to stop the shaking.

"Where are you, Jake?"

Her voice makes me want to cry. I can't cry.

"The Barwin Library. It's on the corner of …"

"I know where it is," she says. "I'm an hour away. Can you wait for me? I'll meet you in the parking lot. I drive a silver Toyota pickup."

I call Mom to tell her I'm still at the library. There's that big book I want to look at that I can't borrow. I've been lying a lot lately. It's like everything, I suppose. The more you do it, the better you get at it.

I ask Chloe where I can find old newspapers. They're on the computer. She shows me how to search and print what I want.

"You have to pay for the copies," she says.

OLIVIA REZKI GETS out of her truck and lights a cigarette.

"You're younger than I thought," she says.

I point behind her. "There's a picnic table under the trees over there."

I tell her everything. The nightmares, the bits of memory that cut like broken glass. She doesn't interrupt. The box is open on the picnic table. The syringe is on top of the papers. I put it on the table and give her the stack of documents.

Olivia doesn't bother with the newspaper articles. She knows what's in them. She reads Charlie's notes. I watch her light another cigarette and forget about smoking it. The ash falls on the table.

She folds the pages and sits straighter on the bench.

"Is it true?" I want to believe it isn't. That Charlie was even better at telling tales than Lily and me. I want to hear her say that the person who killed the girls has been caught and is locked up somewhere.

"You called me." She spits the words.

"Because I found your card. Why did Charlie have your card if you didn't know him?" My voice cracks.

"I dropped my card left and right, hoping somebody would talk." She notices the cigarette ash and wipes it off the table. "The FBI swooped in. We had nothing. I worked the case for a year, then I transferred to San Antonio PD. The murders stopped." She lights a fresh cigarette. It's the last one. She crumples the pack and sticks it in her jeans' pocket. "It's been years, but I haven't forgotten the Barwin girls."

My hand shakes when I give her the copy I printed from the computer. Two columns of text and a picture of a burned building. "Charlie is dead. I thought it was the sunset that painted the rabbit cages orange. It was the fire. He was in the barn. It burned to the ground. It's been rebuilt since."

She scans the article. "How long have you had these dreams, Jake?"

"Over a year. It wasn't bad in the beginning. I would wake up and not know where I was, but it wasn't scary."

Olivia exhales a cloud of smoke. She taps a finger on the barn article. "How old were you at the time?"

"Five. It says there that Charlie was fifteen."

"You didn't have nightmares before last year?"

I shake my head. "I don't think so. I was sick for a long time. I couldn't talk, or something. A fever, I think it was. I missed a lot of school. I'm caught up now, but it was hard going."

She smiles. "The mind is a strange thing."

The way she looks at me makes me uncomfortable and I focus on the windows of the library. Chloe is moving inside. She's closing the blinds against the afternoon sun.

"What about the syringe?" Olivia says.

"I don't know. Medicine. Like I got at the hospital."

She leans on the table. "Look at me. You're a bright kid, Jake. The dreams, the memories that are coming back. You saw a lot of things that your mind couldn't understand." She knocks on the side of her head. "Something in there is working damn hard to make sense of it all."

"It's a puzzle with the wrong pieces."

"Not wrong, jumbled." She sighs. "Your parents love you very much."

That does it. I can't stop the waterworks. She gives me a tissue. It's humiliating. I hear the train blaring as it clickety-clacks over the Main Street crossing. A few more puzzle pieces fit together. I don't want to see the picture they make. I should have taken the damn pills as I was told. None of this would have happened.

Olivia waits. She's very patient.

"I won't have the nightmares anymore? If I say the words aloud?"

"I don't know."

I feel the terror rising. The flash of the blade. The flames. I bury my face in the backpack to stop the scream that's building inside.

Olivia reaches for me across the table. "It's in the past, Jake. It can't hurt you."

I know where the terror comes from. I know the fear is not my own. It's the girls' fear when they see the flash of the blade. I saw it happen. I saw… I bend over and puke. There isn't much. All I've had today is water and a cereal bar.

"Charlie wanted to end it," Olivia says. "He didn't want to be arrested."

The nausea settles. I put a hand over my eyes.

I'm in the barn. The smell of gasoline is strong. Charlie sits cross-legged on the dirt floor. He tells me to get closer.

"It stinks in here," I say.

"It's the tractor. The fumes. I just drove it outside." His kind eyes are smiling. "Sit." He opens a paper bag and extracts a candle and a lighter. "You want to light the candle, Jake?"

I struggle with the lighter. It flickers at the third try and I put the flame to the wick.

"Good job." Charlie puts the candle on the ground. He rolls up his sleeve and gets other objects from the paper bag.

I've seen him do this before, in the shed in the woods. I enjoy watching. The bubbling in the spoon and the needle sucking the liquid. I usually look away after that. Charlie says it doesn't hurt but I think it does. I always wrap my arms around his waist and put my head on his chest to hear his heart go fast as a train.

This time, he doesn't let me. He unwraps my arms. "I want you to do something for me, Jake."

Anything. I'll do anything for Charlie.

I take a deep breath. How much time has passed? Olivia's like Lily in a way. She can be really quiet. I bet she wouldn't make the staircase creak.

"What will you do with the box?" I ask.

"Destroy it. Nothing good can come of it. You and I know the truth. Your parents too, I believe. They worry about you. About what you saw and what you remember, and what it does to you. They're trying to protect you." She shrugs. "Protect the family." She closes the box and stands up. "I'll take you home. We'll have a talk. There are no more secrets."

That isn't true.

CHARLIE FILLS THE syringe. "Listen carefully, Jake. This is important." He smiles. "Promise, you'll do exactly as I say. Raise your hand, say *I promise.*"

"I promise."

He gives me the lit candle. "Hold it so I can see what I'm doing. When I say *Go*, take the candle and put it in that can on the work bench. You see it?"

"Yes."

"Don't let it go out, okay?"

"I won't." The smell of gasoline is making me sick.

"I know I can trust you. Put the candle in the can, go back to the house, and get in bed. I'll be there soon and we'll read a story together."

"But I want to stay with you!"

Charlie raises a finger in warning. "You promised, bud. Give me a kiss. Okay, hold the candle straight."

Go.

I'm at the kitchen door when I hear the explosion. Flames curl like crashing waves over the roof of the barn, and flow in a scarlet river out of the door and the hatches. It's so beautiful I cry in joy. A bright orange flood washes over the rabbit hutches.

I realize what I'm seeing and I scream.

I scream till I have no voice anymore.

RETIREMENT PLAN

by

Ted Flanagan

The Night with The Gambler and the Gambler's Kid

"THE HEART IS a mystery to itself, that's why you can't trust it," Monty said, the pistol in his right hand, pointed sight-down toward the Cadillac's floorboards. "It's neither good or evil. It just is, and once you know what's in someone's heart? Then you've got him by the balls, man or woman. Kid, are you listening to me? This is the first rule."

He passed the pistol to the man in the passenger seat, a hair-gelled body-builder type the old men had ordered him to groom for bigger and better. The kid took the pistol and eyed it as one might a tissue sample in a lab.

"Yeah, yeah, I hear you. Evil, good, rules. Jesus, Monty. How old is this piece?"

"It's mature."

The kid said: "Look at that rust. I know this thing's going to end up in some river when we're done but, I have to ask: you find it in one, too?"

"It'll fire."

"I'll pull the trigger, you got my word on that. Not sure we can count on the boom after."

Monty exasperated now. He thought, these fucking kids the old men keep sending me are exhausting. Why this kid? Why now? Tonight's errand was his own fault in the first place, he had to admit that. He'd cut the guy too much slack, never should have let Gedden get so deep on all the gambling losses. See a man betting BC to cover the spread against Clemson? That there is a cry for help. Maybe the old men sent this kid as punishment. Maybe they thought he'd gone soft.

Monty himself didn't know the answer to that. He added it to the list of mysteries he carried with him, riddles seemingly without solutions.

He pointed at the gun. "I never had one jam on me yet. That's why I only use revolvers. You want to know, when the time comes, so does the fun. Another rule."

The kid tucked the pistol into a side pocket of his black leather jacket, identical to Monty's, but uncreased, smooth at the elbows, a nod to the new and unknowable, of the way things reveal themselves only when the time dictates and not a moment earlier. "You and your rules."

ROUTE 9 WESTBOUND in the gloam, dusk here and gone but no true darkness yet in its place, the sky above the city a bruise healing from the outside in. Monty thought this new kid, asleep in his new coat, drooling against the window, filling the car with a miasma of wet leather and Axe body spray and with his hair gelled like that, Monty thought he looked like the Big Boy restaurant mascot. Big Boys long gone, of course, ironic, Monty thought, what with this kid here.

Streetlights flashed across the hood and into Monty's eyes in a metronomic beat. Wet tire whine lulled him into a state between sleep and not sleep. Expansion joints at the road's asphalt borders kept the beat—*thumpclick, thumpclick, thumpclick.*

Monty envied the kid. He used to be able to sleep before jobs. No matter the thing—cracking a safe, deadbeat leg-breaks, juror encouragement. The hits. He'd always been able to sleep. Now, job or not, he was awake, slept irregularly in fits, in the recliner, in his car, in a diner, in an empty parking lot, at the movies. The urge hit, he dozed. Time meaningless, like everything else.

He heard the guy on NPR say it was a matter of age. That his body had slowed its production of adenosine, the stuff that builds in your bloodstream until ten o'clock at night. That's the magic time the man said, this scientist. Ten o'clock and bam, time for bed. That was the hell of it, this scientist had said. Aging didn't mean he needed less sleep. Quite the opposite. He needed it now more than when he was the kid's age. Sleep was just another thing that betrayed him, one more way his body could no longer deliver.

Monty had the urge to talk, disliked the kid and his peace. He slammed on the brakes then stomped on the throttle. The Cadillac CTS-V rocked, a child's toy shaken by an unseen hand.

The kid woke up, rubbed drool from his bottom lip.

Monty looked over at him. "I used to have trouble sleeping before a job, kid. Don't mean a thing".

"We there yet?"

"Never ask if we're there yet. Don't blow your wad too early. If you're going to do this job for a long time, you got to know how to manage the flow."

"No way I'm doing this job much longer. I'm going to make a couple scores then I'm out."

"That's what I said, fifty years ago. What are you in a rush for? The old men sent you here because they got stuff lined up for you. You been chosen, my man. What could be better than that?"

"This isn't for me. I got other plans."

Monty smiled. "Like what?"

The kid shrugged.

"Come on, partners don't keep secrets," Monty said.

"I'm a DJ."

"A what? Like, for weddings and shit? You play the chicken dance and lead conga lines? My niece got married last year, DJ at her reception wore a different hat for each song, drank so many white Russians that he eventually pissed himself and passed out into his slice of the cake."

"None of that shit. Clubs and stuff. I'm known all over the South Shore already."

"Oh yeah? You got a name?"

The kid looked out the window and away from Monty. "I don't want to tell you."

"Why?"

"You won't understand."

"That's not fair. I'm a very understanding guy."

"I got a feeling for these sorts of things."

"Tell me the name," Monty said.

"No."

Monty pulled the black sedan into the breakdown lane and threw it in park. He turned to face the kid. "Look, we're about to go clean up this thing for the old men. Big rule, the devil's in the details. I need to know who I'm working with. One more time. Please. Pretty please. Pretty please with a hit of X on top. What's your DJ name?"

The kid huffed. "Fine. DJ Rayza. They call me DJ Rayza. Okay? You happy? Can we go take care of this guy now?"

He smiled, dropped the car into drive and stood on the gas. "Not good, Rayza. Never cave under questioning."

The Day Before

RAYZA CRASHED UNTIL almost lunch, showered and drove over to Loreen's for a couple Boston Crème donuts and an ice coffee. He found Kelly out back on a butt break. He stood with her by the purring HVAC unit, and she smoked while he ate.

"They call you yet?" she asked.

He shrugged. "They want me to go out to Worcester tomorrow, work with this guy of theirs. I met him last night at Pepe's. Old school. Weird dude, like goofy, but you mention his name to anyone who knows, and they go quiet. Freaks me out. You got to be a special kind of heavy to make the people I was talking to go quiet. But you talk to him? I don't know. This isn't the right word, but the only one that comes to mind is that he's sad."

"My uncle still has a spot for you on his lot, you want."

"Selling used cars? I'd rather deal with a million weird old dudes."

"It's just a gig until you can make the DJ thing work."

He scuffed his feet in the gravel lot. Above them, egrets circled and dove. A jet not-near-but-not-far shot into the sky, a big passenger place climbing out of Logan Airport. Dark-bellied clouds loomed over the Dollar General across the street and over the power lines and pine treetops across the road. The leaves had flipped, and the breeze went silent. Triple deckers lined the road like terra cotta soldiers, immobile and pock-marked with dirt, chipped paint, and missing shingles on the rooves like tooth-absent mouths.

"I know what your uncles are telling you, and I know you think you need to follow in some fucking ghost's footsteps, but you're not the kind of guy, Ryan. You don't have to do this."

"You check on that other thing yet?"

She shook her head. "I'm not that late, just a couple days."

"We talked about this. Avoiding the test isn't going to fix the problem."

"Problem?"

He crumpled up the donut bag and lobbed it into a nearby Dumpster. "You know what I mean. If there are decisions to make, not taking the test isn't going to make those decisions go away."

"I'm so sorry to inconvenience you."

"That's not what I said."

She dropped her cigarette on the ground and mashed it with her heel. She gave Rayza the finger and turned to walk away. "Break's over anyway."

The Night with the Gambler and the Gambler's Kid

THEY'D DRIVEN FOR an hour when Monty made the announcement. "We got to make a stop."

"It's three in the fucking morning. What stop?"

He scratched the bridge of his nose, traced along the thin scar that bisected a freckle cluster between his eyes. "Just a stop. Have to pick up some equipment. It's relevant."

"I know I haven't been at this long, but only equipment I know of for collecting a debt is pain."

Monty nodded: "There are all kinds of ways to administer pain."

THEY DITCHED THE Cadillac in favor of a beat-up old Ford F-150 connected to a trailer on its hitch. They were in the backyard of a low-slung compound in Leicester. Mud everywhere. A stack of gutters on the ground below the gutterless roofline. Cars without wheels, cars without doors, cars without doors and wheels, scattered in the scrub and dead trees dotting the fenced-in yard. Woodsmoke curled from a narrow metal chimney above the gap-toothed fence around them.

The kid didn't want to get in. "How old is this piece of shit? Same guy sell you that gun?"

"Like that perfectly fine piece, this thing is also older than you, kid. Made back when quality was important. And don't call it a piece of shit. My buddy owns it and he's doing us a favor. The man's sensitive about his stuff."

"I'm going to need a shower after this."

THE DRIVE TOOK half an hour and ended at the top of a hill covered in low trees and whip ivy along a quarter-mile gravel driveway. At the end of it, the largest house Rayza had ever seen stood dark blue against the black sky. The house was vast and unlit. They parked behind a carriage house a hundred yards from the main property. Rayza was surprised when Monty walked to the front door and tapped a few numbers into a keypad outside, then a beep and the door popped open. They stood in a large foyer edged by a curving staircase that spun up into the darkness of the floor above them.

They remained on the first floor and moved in silence to a room in the far back, an open space filled with rubber balls and gym equipment. In the ink-dark floor-to-ceiling windows that surrounded the room, Rayza could make out the distant red lights atop the surrounding hilltops, marking water and cell towers for planes.

Monty turned on the recessed lights and stood in front of an empty wheelchair in the far corner of the room. It was tall and motorized, with a high-backed chair and a joystick and tablet attached that made it look like the errant cockpit for a fighter jet.

Rayza jiggled the joystick and looked at the expensive weights and machines. "I know we're not stealing a kettle bell or something, right?"

"This is how we apply the pain."

"Where's the guy? Shouldn't we be pulling him out of bed? Tie him up in the garage or something? Tell him he needs to come up with the money he owes the old men?"

He laughed. "You watch too many movies, man. You want to get pinched, be Timmy Toughnuts, go ahead. Not me."

"That another rule?"

"Should be," Monty said. "You want to really hit a guy where it hurts, hurt his family. Forget any notions of chivalry or fair game. This is a business, not a sonnet. This chair belongs to Gedden's daughter. She's four. She has one of those, what do you call it, muscular wasting diseases. This chair is her lifeline. Without it? Well."

Rayza held up his hands. "Keep me out of this bullshit, man, whatever you got planned. I don't mind breaking a leg or whatever, but I'm not going after any kids."

"We're taking the chair. This guy, he'd let us cut off a pinkie rather than pay the old men. But taking his daughter's chair? Trust me. I been doing this a long time. He'll come around."

"Why'd we even bring the guns, then?"

Last Month

RAYZA DROVE HIS Camaro to Ingersoll Pond and planned to smoke a joint and try to put some distance between the day and the previous night's argument with Kelly. She wanted him to do something with his life, had bigger plans for herself than working at the coffee shop forever. She said she didn't care whether he followed the family business or pursued the DJ thing, she just wanted him to find a direction. He knew that was a partial lie. She knew his family history, wanted nothing to do with it. Kelly believed in making your own mistakes, he knew, and she'd let him make his own, if that's what it came to. Still, she pushed the DJ thing whenever the topic arose.

His phone rang and the familiar voice on the other end erased any mellow from his high.

"We need to talk. Overton Tavern, half an hour."

The line went dead.

His plans would have to wait.

The old men would not.

RAYZA TORE THE bar pizza to shreds while he waited for his audience. He felt the anxiety in his guts—the old men didn't call on whims. Young guys like him dreamed of getting the call to come see them, until they did, and then the dread began. Going into these meetings could end in two ways, only one of which saw you walk out on your own two feet.

You could never know whether you'd somehow offended the old men, he knew. He turned over in his mind the job with Monty the night before. Had they done something wrong, broken some unknowable etiquette, exposed themselves or the old men to the law? Would he be walking out of here, or rolled in a piece of plastic sheeting, bound for a defunct New Hampshire quarry?

The place absorbed light—dark bar, dark stools, dark paneling, dark ceiling, dark souls, dark night, dark day, dark like a black hole, gravity itself unable to escape. The door to the basement—dark brown and pocked by errant dart throws—almost pulsed in the intensity of his gaze. Behind that was… what? His past. His future.

Mickey Dunham emerged from behind the door and beckoned. "Just don't cough on none of them's faces."

"I wasn't planning to," Rayza said.

"Don't get wise with me. Liam ain't been feeling well, so just keep the crud in your own nose son."

He led Rayza down a narrow, unlit staircase with minimalist treads and steep risers, too steep, backtracking and spiraled in loops and switchbacks, two stories down. They came to a cement landing, devoid of any furniture or furnishing, with a single bare bulb hanging from the ceiling and a metal door at the far end.

"Maeve, this is himself," Mickey said.

Maeve stood before the door like a Praetorian guard. She was a short woman in her fifties with a hard chin and grey eyes. She nodded, and waved Mickey back up the stairs. She said nothing until they'd heard Mickey far above them, open and close the door.

"Ryan McGuiggan?"

"Everyone calls me Rayza."

She shook her head. "No one here will be calling you that. Before we go in, a couple rules you'll need to obey. There aren't that many, but they are enforced with great enthusiasm."

He nodded.

"First, do not speak until spoken to. And if I might add a caveat, in general try to speak as little as possible. Second, when explaining yourself, don't. Explanations will only make a bad situation worse or, eminently less desirable, turn a good situation bad. Lastly, Liam is on home oxygen and can be hard to hear, so pay extra attention to him, and Mr. Finlay's… outbursts… are amplified these days, what with some of the issues the old men have been dealing with. I say this only so you won't be startled into doing something stupid like laughing. Also, don't make Red get up. His sciatica has been acting up all year. Remember Lonnie O'Brien?"

"Tommy Murray's guy from Swampscott? Nobody's seen him in like a year."

Maeve cocked an eyebrow and said nothing.

"Oh shit, yeah, okay, I understand."

She looked at Rayza a moment longer, then went into the room and closed the door behind her. Five minutes later she opened it, waved Rayza inside, then stepped out and closed the door behind her.

The Night with the Gambler and the Gambler's Kid

MONTY LIKED FISH and chips at Hooley's for breakfast after a job. They'd turn on the taps and fryers just for him if the old men called ahead. He left the cell phone on the table between them and sipped at a beer and stared hard at Rayza. "What? You not hungry?"

"It's nine in the morning."

"Thirsty?"

"You old guys are a mystery to me."

"Your old man didn't drink in the morning?"

"I never met him. He was always gone."

"How'd you catch on with the old men, they didn't know your pops? Usually, they're one degree of separation kind of guys when they take someone on, and even then."

Rayza looked at Monty, knowing what he said next would change it all, had seen the power of a name, the power of a name even when the person who held the name hadn't been seen in decades, even when the person who held the name had never even met his own son.

"He was a McGuiggan."

Monty put the beer down and looked at the kid, like seeing him for the first time. "No shit? That explains a lot. You should have told me earlier."

Rayza shrugged. "What are we doing tonight? Is this really the job? I know this thing isn't glamorous, but I needed the money for new gear. But what'd we do? Stole a little girl's wheelchair? What the fuck are we anyway?"

Monty dashed down the bitters at the bottom his glass, rapped the table for a refill. "Can't think of it like that, kid. Guy had it coming. Degenerate gambler who's worth a hundred times what he owes the old men, just doesn't want to pay."

"So, we punish his little girl?"

"You don't know much about people, do you Rayza?"

"I know what's fucked up."

Hooley himself laid down a coaster and another pint in front of Monty, then disappeared behind the kitchen doors.

He took a sip. "Rules are all we have, kid. Even in this line of work. In fact, if people followed the rules, you and I would have to work straight gigs. Can you imagine? Me with a nine-to-five, you without your disco."

"DJ."

"DJ. Sure. Whatever. But that's the thing. Rules. And Mr. Richie Rich back there, he didn't play by them, and the *worst* thing, the thing that made it so easy to run off with his little girl's hundred-thousand-dollar wheelchair, is that he could so easily just pay up. He was being slow with the money because he felt like Brooklyn should have won that game, like the old men had gotten to the refs and let the Celts win."

"Didn't they?"

"Beside the point. And officially? No. Regardless, the rules say, the house always wins. That's the thing he didn't understand. The whole enterprise is geared toward one result—guys like our new friend always lose out in the end, but they still want to play, demand it, like a sickness, like someone with a deadly disease refusing the cure. Or turning down a vaccine in the middle of an epidemic just to prove some point nature couldn't give a shit less about. Nature will do what nature will do, and the opinions of man don't matter one bit."

"So, in this philosophy of yours, what are we? Nature's leg breakers?"

"We are the mechanism that keeps the natural order. There's no conscious thought other than to rebel, so that's where we come in. We are the consequences of his actions. Without us? Chaos, my friend. Fucking chaos."

Rayza scratched his chin, checked his six, then leaned closer to Monty. "My mother damn near shit herself when she heard I was coming out here. She doesn't want me anywhere near the old men, or anyone like them. But what are you going to do? Economy is a mess, no work out there, even if I wanted it."

"There are a lot of reasons not to do this job, kid. But it *is* recession-proof. It's amazing to me how people find money under the right methods of encouragement, even when there doesn't appear to be any money to be had."

"You think this guy will pay?"

Monty laughed. "My guess, five minutes after we left his empty therapy room, wire transfers were already being arranged. Even gamblers love their kids. In a life where they've disappointed everyone else, the kids are the last ones they still give a shit about. I'm not even going to take the chair off that trailer unless we don't hear anything by lunch. But we will."

Last Month with the Old Men

RAYZA LOOKED BACK at the door as Maeve closed it behind him. The basement of the Overton was filled with crates of booze, empties, a forlorn pool table propped up on its side over in the corner. A felt-topped poker table sat in the middle of the dank space, covered in food wrappers and set beneath a haze of cigarette and cigar smoke drifting in horizontal planes beneath the single bare bulb hanging above.

Three men sat arrayed around the table. None of them so much as looked in Rayza's direction when he entered the room. He took the advice and kept quiet.

"Cock! Balls!" A man in a high-necked wheelchair spat the words, as if spitting out a poison.

"Finlay, godammit you about scared me to death," said another man to his left, a pale wraith, more a suggestion of humanity than physical presence. A nasal cannula pumped oxygen into his nose while he chain-smoked Parliaments. An overflowing ashtray rested in front of him on the table.

"Must be nice, not to have no afflictions."

"I'm not saying you don't suffer—"

"Bastard! Bastard!"

"All I'm saying is, sometimes it would be nice to have a sit down without you shouting all the time."

"You're a heartless prick for a guy with no lungs," Finlay said.

A third man, short and round, barrel-chested with freckles and a flattop of red hair riven by chaotic streaks of gray, pounded his fist on the table. "You over there. You the McQuiggan?"

Rayza took an unsure step forward. "Me?"

"No kid, the other guy standing over there. Yes, you."

"Cock! Balls!"

"I'm Ryan McQuiggan. I think you knew my pops."

Red nodded, exchanged a look with the other two that Rayza knew carried a weight he could barely comprehend.

"We knew your Pops," he said.

"It was a sad day when he…" Liam began. "Well, it was better before he…"

"No one is happy he's gone, kid," Finlay said. "And that wasn't your fault, but you're his son. Some debts don't end when… When someone gets gone."

"Debts?"

"We have a little problem, and we been watching you, and we know you're the man to fix it. We want to send you out to Worcester. We got a guy out there named Monty Devlin."

"Monty has worked for us for a lot of years," Red said. "He knew your Pops. We want you to go work for him."

"So, I'll be part of his crew," Rayza asked. He prayed his tone did not betray his feelings about this, his feelings that the last thing he wanted was to be part of a crew, let alone with this guy he didn't know in a city far enough away it might as well have been the Moon.

Liam leaned forward in his chair, closed off a nostril and blew a plug of mucus onto the floor. "You're not joining his crew. We've got one last job for Monty, but he's been slipping lately. Getting sloppy."

"Costing us money," Red said.

"Which is the most unforgivable part of the whole deal," Finlay said.

"It's time for Monty to…"

"Cock! Balls!"

"Get gone," Rayza offered.

"Get gone," Liam agreed.

"You want me to—"

"We want you to work one last job with Monty, then administer the retirement plan," Finlay said.

"Monty is the worst kind of crook," Red said, with a sidelong look at the others at the table. "The kind that don't know when to move on."

The Morning After the Night of the Gambler and the Gambler's Kid

THEY HAD THE chair back to the house by 10 a.m. The gambler's wife met them at the door, bags under her red eyes and dried tear streaks on her cheeks.

Monty was magnanimous as he guided the chair back in through the back door while the wife looked on. "Look what we found! Good as new!"

She wrapped her bathrobe tighter around her waist, violently silent.

"This could have gone a lot worse," Monty said.

Rayza slapped his hip in anger. "People could have gotten hurt."

"You think no one got hurt?" she said.

Monty tried tact. "Mrs. Gedden, the world is a dark place at times. Let's all just be happy this little kerfuffle got worked out and we can all get on with our day."

"How long until you come back? A month? Two? What will you take next time? The Rothko in the hall? The Cobra in the garage? How about Jerry? Why not take him? Do us all a favor."

"We didn't cause this!" Rayza was surprised by his own volume.

Monty pulled his partner's elbow and eased him toward the back door. "Kid…"

Aileen Gedden's face went blank, sanded smooth of any emotion, only something less than disgust remained. "Do something else with your life. Anything else. My husband will be gone soon, but there will be many more like him for you, an ocean of them, so many more you'll drown in the fucking flood of them. What a future. You want to become like your partner here? Still doing this in your sixties or seventies, a relic with nothing to show for it except a smooth delivery and high blood pressure? Still robbing people, breaking legs or whatever else it is you do?"

"There are rules," Rayza said.

"Fuck your rules," she said, cool like someone stepping on a snail. "And fuck you."

AT THE BUS station where they'd left Rayza's Mustang, Monty left his car running while Rayza took his time getting out. Sun peaked above the rotating silver globe that sat atop a pole next to the terminal. Mercury himself was welded into the globe, and Monty's head throbbed every time the morning glint reflected off the lightning bolt heel and into his eyes.

"You haven't said a word since that woman slammed the door in our faces."

"I haven't felt right since we ate at Hooley's. Hard to talk when I'm nauseous."

"She left out an important rule."

"Which is?"

"If you want to play big boy games, be prepared to pay big boy prices. And, a corollary: always know who you're marrying."

"We're way down on Maslow's scale."

"Maslow? He that guy from Somerville, the guy with the fentanyl?"

"Something I heard in school, the semester I did at Bunker Hill. The higher on the scale, the better your life is. Or something like that. I didn't really listen. Maybe I should have. You ever think of getting out?"

"To do what?" Monty said. "Sell insurance? Take up Pilates?"

"Anything. Didn't you ever want to do anything?"

"DJ!"

"Never mind."

"Look, kid, I appreciate the sentiment. If there were something else I could do, I would, but for now, I wait."

"For what?"

Monty shrugged, answered the steering wheel. "A heart attack? Maybe cancer? Or maybe the old men get tired of me, send someone up here to pop me. Doesn't matter. When you come on this planet, there's an expiration date on your ass, but you don't know when that is. That's the thing I always loved about the life: Someone else sets the rules and you decide whether you can live within them or not. Simple as that. In the end, the only choice you have is whether you're willing to pay the price. Otherwise, you find yourself chewing on the barrel of a pistol, and the only question left is, who put it there: you, or someone just like you?"

Rayza tossed the revolver on Monty's lap before he got out.

"You don't want to keep it? It's got at least one more job left in it before it's got to go for a swim."

Rayza shook his head. "I'll find my own."

"The old men should have something lined up for us on Wednesday, although they've usually called me by now."

He nodded. "Call me."

"Stick with me, kid. I'll learn you the rules."

THE QUAIL, THE GROUSE AND THE RABBIT

by

Mark SaFranko

IT STARTED OUT QUITE simply, as most complicated messes will. She'd been working as a server at Lavoy's restaurant, The Quail And The Grouse, on the Delaware River for eight or nine weeks when the owner first took notice of her. He always seemed frantically busy, which would explain why he hadn't said anything to her earlier, but eventually they began having little conversations here and there, about mundane subjects from the weather to the weekends, and before she knew it, they were a little more than just employer and employee.

Lavoy was always cordial—even nice—to her, which was good, because elsewhere things weren't going so well. Kelsey had broken up with Jason six months earlier, and her new roommate, Gretchen, after promising to abide by the terms of the apartment lease, which they both held, had recently bailed too. Kelsey couldn't afford the rent on her own, and she didn't have any other roommate candidates to help her out. She'd floated the idea past some of her fellow servers at the Quail, but none were interested or in the same fix as she was. She was already a couple of months behind on the rent and didn't know what she was going to do.

"How's it going there, Kelsey?"

The lunch rush had died down, business was slow, and she happened to be placing dinner settings when Lavoy walked by. And that was how it had really started, with just those few words.

"It's been better—if I can be honest." She laughed, in an attempt to keep it light.

"Tell me about it," he said. He plunged his hands into his trousers pockets. His tone was so genuine, so sympathetic, that she jumped at the invitation.

She explained her living issue, and Alex Lavoy seemed to be listening, *really* listening. He nodded and walked away, and she thought nothing of it, except that maybe she shouldn't have been so open because some people will hold your vulnerabilities against you. The next Thursday, however, when she was on the evening shift, he approached her when she was waiting on an order near the chef's station.

"I was thinking about your situation," he said.

She felt herself go red in the face. She'd hoped that he'd forgotten all about it by now.

"You can always move in with me temporarily, until you get back on your feet. My place is on Anderson Avenue, near the park. There's lots of room. You'd have a whole wing of the house to yourself. I could use a little friendly company. It seems a shame to be living in a humongous house by myself when I can help out one of my employees."

Then Lavoy walked away. Kelsey was stunned. *Was he for real?*

She spent the rest of the night obsessing over the conversation. She knew from hearsay that Lavoy was divorced, and that he'd owned another restaurant nearby before selling it and buying The Quail And The Grouse. *Was he interested in her personally—as a lover? Why not just ask her out then?* What was also strange was that she judged herself nothing but average in the looks department, and she wasn't one to shy away from the truth. She wasn't the kind of girl who got hit on constantly, like some of her college friends or even some of the other servers at the Quail, like Inez or Jennifer. Lavoy was a nice-looking man, if a bit older. He was capable of better than her. None of it made sense.

For some days afterwards Kelsey didn't see him. None of the other Quail workers talked about Lavoy much because he wasn't a particularly hands-on owner, the kind who hovered and made you feel uncomfortable. He was more of an elusive presence flitting across the background, coming and going at odd times, which was the way most of the chefs and servers liked it, even if his lack of predictability was sometimes less than ideal.

When Kelsey finally bumped into him again, he asked, "So—did you think over what we talked about?"

"Yes," she answered. She'd been chewing on it from the moment he'd brought it up, and if he was serious, she couldn't think of a better alternative to her present circumstances.

By the following weekend she had broken her lease and moved her stuff into the big house on Anderson Avenue. It had only taken the greater part of a rainy Monday, which she had off from the restaurant.

AT FIRST THE arrangement worked. Kelsey only saw Lavoy in passing, and they rarely exchanged more than a pleasant word or two. He was always out, either at the restaurant or attending to other business. The place was everything he said it was, if a little antiseptic. It looked barely lived in and smelled of newness. The presence of Lavoy's ex-wife couldn't be detected at all—no photos, no clothes, no nothing. All Kelsey knew was that he'd been single for over a year, and he never mentioned his ex.

She unpacked her belongings and set up her bedroom. It was as if she were living in the house alone. After a week or so, Lavoy knocked at her bedroom door one evening.

"Everything okay? You've managed to settle in?"

He was smiling and dressed in his usual uniform, khakis and golf shirt.

"Oh—yes! Everything's great. And thanks again for this—for helping me." Kelsey's heart was pounding because she still didn't quite understand her position here. But she was young, only twenty-four. Maybe she just didn't understand how things worked.

"Don't mention it. I always like to extend a hand to a good worker… Have you eaten?"

"No," she said. That day, she hadn't even thought about it. She had resolved to be frugal until she climbed out of the red—she still owed money on her old apartment—even if it meant cutting out a meal or two here and there. Besides, not eating helped keep her weight in check.

"Care to join me for Chinese takeout?"

She was starving, but she couldn't help but think of her tight finances. Lavoy must have read the uncertainty in her face.

"Don't worry—my treat."

"Oh. Okay—well, thanks."

She still wasn't convinced. Did it mean she would have to sleep with him or something like that as payment? It wouldn't have been so bad, she reasoned, though it might make things around the house and restaurant a little awkward if it didn't work out. Frankly, the thought of some type of extracurricular—personal—relationship with Lavoy had already crossed her mind, and she'd decided that she would go along with the program, whatever it was. You never knew what it might lead to. She was, after all, wide open and available, and so, presumably, was he.

Dinner at the long dining room table turned out to be just that and nothing more—moo shu pork, shrimp with broccoli, and wonton soup, washed down by a couple of beers. The conversation was about nothing and everything. As he ate, Lavoy seemed hardly aware of his new housemate.

"Okay," he said, pushing himself away from the table. "I'm beat. And I have to be up at six tomorrow morning to meet with a plumber at the restaurant. That sewer line in the basement backed up again… Anyway, thanks for joining me."

"Can I clean up?"

"Don't worry, I'll take care of it. Enjoy your night off."

And that was that. Kelsey needn't have worried at all. It didn't appear as if Lavoy was in the least romantically interested in her. She went back to her side of the house relieved—and also a little disappointed.

LAVOY'S APPARENT INDIFFERENCE to Kelsey's presence made it all the more baffling when he came to her two months later and informed her that she was late paying her half of the water bill.

"Really? I'm sorry!" she exclaimed, not even realizing she was in the arrears. "How much is it? What do I owe?"

"I slid it under your door a week, ago, remember? Your share is fifty-three dollars."

She didn't remember seeing a notice of any kind, but she had to concede it wasn't out of the question she'd somehow overlooked it. Bills weren't something she necessarily had any desire to look at. But fifty-three dollars? She hardly used any quantity of water. All she ever did was take showers, and they were brief at that.

"Let me get my checkbook…"

She was flustered. She wheeled around to the desk and pulled it out of the top drawer. She quickly filled a sheet, tore it out, and handed it to her landlord.

Lavoy looked at it. "Thanks," he muttered before walking away.

Well, that was *weird*. There'd been an undertone of something new in Lavoy's demeanor—annoyance, aggression. But why? She shut the door and sat on the bed. Jesus, she hoped that he wouldn't try to cash the check immediately, because she didn't think she had the funds in her account to cover it. She was still trying to make good on her debt on the previous apartment. Her paycheck from the Quail wasn't issued until Friday, and it had been an uncharacteristically bad month for tips. Maybe she should have told him to wait before taking the check to the bank…

Days later there was another rap at her door. This time sharper. It was late in the evening, and she was wiped out from an overtime shift at the restaurant and just about to crawl into bed.

"That check you gave me for the water bill? It bounced," announced Lavoy, his arm holding up the doorjamb. The expression on his face was hard and flat-out exasperated.

"Oh, no—I apologize!"

"Weren't you aware you didn't have enough money in your account to cover it?" There was an unmistakably accusatory tone in her boss's voice that she hadn't heard before.

"I guess I wasn't," she lied. "I must have not been paying attention… My bad."

"Now *I'm* going to have to cover the service fee."

"I—I'll pay for it."

"Please don't let it happen again, okay?"

"Okay…" She searched her landlord's face. "Did I do something—something else—to upset you?"

Lavoy didn't answer. He walked away, and Kelsey shut her door and locked it. She was quaking from head to toe.

What in the world was going on?

THE CURIOUS THING was that Lavoy never approached Kelsey at work, never criticized her, and, in fact, sometimes let slip that she was doing a good job. But at home on Anderson Avenue, things were much different. Soon he had a new beef—the electric and power bill. Kelsey was late paying that, too. Then it was the actual rent. She'd somehow been under the impression that she owed only a certain percentage of the total, but now she realized she was mistaken. Her obligation was fully half of the mortgage Lavoy paid each month. If she wasn't part owner of the home, she wondered, why did she have to pay so much?

Like a prisoner, she sat in her room mulling everything over. In the beginning she was convinced that Alex Lavoy had wanted to *help* her. But now she understood that it was a delusion. He really wanted someone to help *him* with his monthly nut, despite the fact that she'd seen no indication whatsoever that he was in even the least financial distress. But there was even more. She had begun to wonder whether his real intention in inviting her to move into his house was to *torture* her. But did that make sense, any sense at all? He didn't even *know* her, for God's sake, not even a little! But what else was she supposed to make of it? Perhaps she'd been a bit naïve in assuming that Lavoy was a generous sort who would allow her to cut a few corners when it came to her debts, but still, he had to understand that she wasn't exactly rolling in the green, didn't he? Why else would she be working at the Quail?

Before she finally drifted off to a queasy sleep that night, she arrived at the uneasy conclusion that something else was going on here, something she didn't grasp at all, and that the only way she would understand what it might be was to ask Lavoy again.

But she already knew that he wasn't going to tell her.

"KELSEY! YOU OWE me rent! I can't keep carrying you forever! This is out of hand! You have to pay up!"

She lay huddled under the covers, Lavoy's complaints of the night before tolling in her head. What he didn't know was that, because she was trying to make up all of her debts to him, debts that had mysteriously accumulated to a preposterous level, she'd stopped paying her credit card and other bills. She simply didn't have enough to make good on everything she owed.

She still didn't understand how it had happened. She desperately wanted to escape Anderson Avenue now, but she had nowhere else to go. Her father had died when she was little and her mother was struggling too. Her only sister was married and already had three kids and no financial wiggle room at all. None of her few friends were in any position to help.

There was no one to turn to. And Lavoy kept coming after her.

"You owe me... you owe me... you owe me... When are you going to pay? When, Kelsey? This isn't why I threw my door open to you, so you could take advantage of me at every turn! Goddamn it, Kelsey!"

Their battles over what she owed became a daily ritual. It had reached the point where she couldn't stand to see him. One day she walked into the Quail and straight into Ali Harkness's tiny office off the back of the kitchen.

"I can't do it anymore. I just can't do it…"

Ali was the schedule supervisor. Looking after the day-to-day operations and reporting to Lavoy. She glanced away from her computer screen and at Kelsey, who was standing in the door.

"What?"

"I can't do it anymore. I quit. I'm resigning right now…"

Ali was confounded. "I don't get it… I thought you were—"

Like everyone else at the Quail, Ali Harkness had made the assumption that Kelsey was in some kind of intimate and therefore protected relationship with the owner, Alex Lavoy.

She smiled. It was a smile of congratulations.

"I could tell that you've been distracted lately, but… You don't have to work anymore, is that it?"

Kelsey shook her head, violently.

The schedule supervisor didn't understand. No one but Kelsey and her landlord could possibly understand. It was no use trying to explain.

Kelsey herself didn't fully know why she'd quit, and what she was going to do. If she owed all kinds of money, the last thing she should have done was dumped her job.

Mentally, emotionally, she felt as if she was walking on very thin ice. She wasn't 'distracted,' as Ali had mistakenly put it—she was falling apart and barely functional.

Back at Anderson Avenue that night, she waited for the inevitable, and it came late, around eleven o'clock. Lavoy's banging at her door was insistent and furious. The look on his face when she opened up was frightening.

"I heard the news. So—you got another job?"

"No."

Lavoy's ire morphed quickly into consternation. "No? Did you come into an inheritance? How are you going to pay what you owe me if you're not working?"

Kelsey was petrified. She said nothing, but merely stared at her tormentor.

"You realize that you can't just go on living here and leeching off of me, don't you?"

"Yes," she admitted, but it didn't mean she had any alternative in mind. She had a flash of herself living on the street.

"How do you propose to handle this? You have no income at all now. If you think you're just going to sit here and waste time and drain me like some kind of parasite, you've got another think coming, girl!"

"Why did you do this to me," said Kelsey quietly, deciding suddenly on a different tack. "I've done nothing to you, nothing at all."

"*Do what to you?* I didn't do anything to you! I generously opened the door of my home to you. All you had to do was keep up your end of the bargain and you couldn't do it. Whatever happened is your fault. I didn't 'do' anything to you. You're crazy."

"No—this is—you—you're gaslighting me."

"I—*what?*"

It wasn't going to work. He wasn't going to listen. There really was no hope for her.

At that moment, a bulb lit up in Kelsey's brain.

"I have an idea."

Lavoy wasn't amused. "It had better be good."

"It is. Please... *please* listen."

"Talk."

"I can take care of everything here—in the house—until I find a new job to allow me to pay you back."

"But you had a job, a good job, and you quit. I don't get it."

"Listen, please. I can take care of everything—seriously, I can."

"Everything... like what?"

"I can keep the house, I can cook, I can—I can do anything you want me to do... I can give you sex, if you want it."

"No, I don't want that. Why would I want sex with you?"

"All right then, forget that. I can do everything else you need me to do until I get back on my feet."

Lavoy looked skeptical. "Well, maybe. But on a short-term basis only. It can't go on forever, do you hear? You owe me. *Money.*"

"I promise," she said.

SHE SLEPT. IT was a deep sleep, as if she had been drugged. When she woke, she felt as if she were underwater: something seemed to have happened to her mind overnight.

She heard the front door slam and Lavoy's BMW start up and fade out of the driveway. After lying there for what seemed like hours, she limped out of bed and took her time dressing. When she slipped her sneakers on, she momentarily had trouble remembering how to tie the laces. Nothing like it had ever happened to her before. She didn't give a thought to eating or drinking, but instead got into her Kia and drove over to the Petco at the strip mall where she sometimes bought groceries. There she purchased a live rabbit, which was handed over to her in a large cardboard transport box by one of the clerks.

"What are you going to do with him," asked the cashier, a young woman with blue hair and several rings in her nostrils. She seemed concerned by something in Kelsey's dazed demeanor.

"Oh—he's going to be a pet," she answered dreamily.

"Please be gentle with him. He's a sweet boy."

"Okay…"

"You forgot your credit card," the cashier called after her, before running out the door to hand it over.

Kelsey nodded and walked off with her cardboard box.

"It's okay, baby," Kelsey reassured the rabbit as she drove back to Anderson Avenue, even though the animal was surprisingly placid.

When she got to the house, Kelsey placed the container on the kitchen table, pulled the sharpest knife out of the block, and slit the creature's throat where it sat. Its blood spurted everywhere, and took a long time to sop up. Then Kelsey skinned and gutted the carcass and tossed all of the unwanted parts into a trash bag that she tied up and carried to the bin on the side of the house.

Afterwards she drew a bath in the master bathroom—Lavoy's private lavatory—and luxuriated in it for an hour or so. Her mind a pure blank. She didn't have to think about anything, because she already knew what she was going to do.

After climbing out of the tub and getting dressed, she went about preparing dinner: apple walnut salad dressed with balsamic vinaigrette, French bread, grilled asparagus, and the centerpiece, slow-roasted rabbit. All of her dishes worked out to perfection, as if she had laid plans for them days in advance. She'd seen enough complicated cuisines, from pheasant to duck, prepared at the Quail to understand how to go about it...

When Lavoy came in at six-thirty, it was all there waiting for him on the dining room table: a scrumptious dinner and a tall glass of wine.

"Okay... Well, it's a start, I guess. But you owe me for..."

He was in his typically nasty mood. He began to reel off a list of Kelsey's obligations but she wasn't listening. She watched him sit and quaff the wine, which was one of his finest vintages from the stash in the basement.

"What the hell?" he bitched when he caught sight of the Caymus label. "You shouldn't be opening my wine—you know that, don't you? Who the hell gave you permission? You're going to have to replace this bottle—if you can."

He was irate all over again, but Kelsey merely giggled in response and took a seat at the other end of the table. She'd crushed enough Xanax and mixed it with the Alsatian Riesling to bring down a bull elephant. It was the last time Alex Lavoy was going to complain about anything.

Nevertheless, he went on bitching through the first mouthfuls of the freshly slaughtered rabbit.

"Hey—this isn't half bad. I see you stole my chef's secret recipe. But I have to tell you that it's not going to soften me up when it comes to what you owe me..."

Kelsey's smile widened. She nibbled on a crust of baguette as she watched her landlord and former boss slowly begin to run out of steam. He blinked, then blinked again, as if he'd begun to finally understand that something was happening to him, but he couldn't put his finger on what it was.

"I hate you, Alex," Kelsey said quietly. "I fucking hate you. You made my life a chamber of horrors, but it's all over now..."

Lavoy worked his jaws as if he'd never opened his mouth before, but he couldn't do it. Kelsey herself still felt as if she were submerged, as if what was happening right before her eyes was nothing but a weird waking, even comical, dream. And maybe it really *wasn't* happening, she couldn't completely discount that. She remembered once reading you were the only person who could verify your experience, that there was no way to prove what you saw and felt and thought was anything but your own imagination at work. Maybe that's where she was now.

Just the same, she said it again: "I hate you, Alex. I fucking hate you..."

Lavoy tried to shake his head back and forth, but he could only do it in exaggerated slow motion, which made Kelsey laugh out loud, because his struggle was so funny. There was one last angry flare of light in his eyes before it went out altogether.

When his forehead smacked into the plate of unfinished rabbit and vegetables, Kelsey dropped her napkin and took her time getting up from the table. She went into the garage and took the hatchet off the wall from among the other garden tools.

"You pathetic... *thing*," she whispered at the inert form of Alex Lavoy.

She yanked him by the arm and he flopped onto the floor like a sack of potatoes. It took a good deal of grunting, but she succeeded in rolling him onto his back, then splayed his limbs over the parquet until he looked like a giant flying bird.

Then she knelt next to the body. She could hardly believe that she'd let him sucker her so easily; in the end, for all of his bluster and bullying, Lavoy had been nothing, a pushover.

With her fingers, she located the big arteries in his neck, felt them pulsing with sleepy life. She hoisted the hatchet over her head and swiftly brought it down on the soft spot between his clavicle and jaw. The flesh gave easily, and not a sound came out of the victim's throat. It was already over, but she went on hacking away until Lavoy's head rolled five feet away from the rest of his corpse.

This time she didn't bother cleaning up. The way she figured it, there was no point. Instead, she took a quick shower, put on a set of fresh clothes, grabbed the keys to Lavoy's BMW, and walked out of the house. After a moment's hesitation, she turned and locked the front door behind her.

SHE DROVE FOR a long time—hours, then days—stopping only to refuel, visit the ladies' room and buy food and drinks out of vending machines. Most of the time she hardly knew where she was and didn't care, but somehow, she made her way south, which had also been in the back of her mind. If she had to be on the run, it made sense to do so where she could be outdoors if she had to abandon the car...

Eventually she got tired—very, very tired—of driving. She found herself on an old Florida highway whose asphalt was cracked and white lines were faded and broken. At mile marker 36 a flag read "Kiosk #11". She glided into the parking area, which was deserted at this time of night, and steered all the way to the dense jungle at the far edge. Another road, this one much tighter and darker, spooled off the main lot. A yellow sign read "No Vehicles," and another warned that it was unlawful to harass the crocodiles, but she nosed the car in anyway, traveled another fifty yards, and cut the engine.

She looked up. The sky a vast canopy of twinkling lights. Everything up there—planets, asteroids, constellations—seemed much closer to the earth than it did back in Pennsylvania, where she could hardly see anything at all.

She let her head drop back onto the seat. It was as good a place to spend the night as any she'd encountered so far on her journey. What she needed was a good, long slumber, then she'd continue on her way—to somewhere…

"Kelsey. How are we today?"

She recognized the voice. It belonged to Mister Freed, her old piano teacher. He always referred to her as "we".

They would start with something simple, an Irish folk ballad or an exercise from Bach. Her mother would always retreat upstairs to her bedroom, and wouldn't appear again until the end of the lesson. The check she'd made out—for forty dollars—always sitting right there on the stand, waiting for Mister Freed to pick it up and deposit it in his breast pocket.

After Kelsey played the first piece, he would begin to instruct her in a soothing voice. "Nice, but you mustn't forget the slurs. You don't want it to sound like you're pounding on a typewriter—right? Otherwise, it's very good… Now, let's try it again, shall we? Slurs this time."

And when she would touch the keys, fingers trembling, Mister Freed's hand, with its short black hairs that seemed to stand straight up, would begin its slow journey up her bare leg to her forbidden center, where it would linger throughout the performance, moving here and there, making her feel frightened, then upset.

The mystery that lingered was why she never cried out or said anything to her mother about what Mister Freed did to her. She didn't know. She didn't know anything. She was six, maybe seven years old. How could she know anything?

When her mother came downstairs to see Mister Freed off, it was as if nothing at all had happened. And maybe nothing had. As far as she knew, no one had ever found out what Mister Freed had been doing to her or any of his other students. One day he disappeared, and she never saw him again. She sometimes wondered, even now, where Mister Freed had gotten to…

But what had happened between them had landed her in the hospital, not once or twice, but three times. And still her mother never knew why. In the end it was something Kelsey could never talk about.

She remembered the voices in the hospital too. Oh, they were terrible, those voices. Always telling her what to eat, what to wear, what to think, what to *feel*.

It was a miracle she escaped those voices, but they kept letting her out of the ward, even when she felt she wasn't ready to leave. She would be better, the doctors persuaded her, it would just take time.

Just as Kelsey's eyes were about to close, there was an explosion of white in the rear-view mirror. She didn't even bother to turn and look: she'd been expecting something of the sort all along, even if it was nothing but a dream.

She heard one of those voices now, squawking at her, bellowing orders, but it was impossible to know what it wanted her to do, so she just sat there and waited.

The police vehicle was followed by another, then another, in a long, curling train. Within seconds the strips of lights on the roofs of the cars ignited, creating a field of giant fireflies in the night. And the voice went on squawking.

Really, it was just like a dream, wasn't it? And she was still dreaming.

Before the posse could get to her, she flung the door open and bolted straight into the belly of the Everglades. She ran and ran and ran, as far as she could, until there was only her, and the swamp, and that beautiful sky above.

THERE WERE MANY theories for what happened to Kelsey Davidson: an unfortunate encounter with a crocodile, or an alligator, or a hungry panther, or maybe even a bear—but they never did find her, or even a single shred of her clothing.

THEY'RE GOING TO LOVE YOU IN GERMANY

by

Gabriel Hart

"ACTUALLY YEAH, DR. Marvin, there is one more thing… could you recommend… uhm, prescribe anything for anxiety?"

It was my plan to go in there for one thing and leave with another, not to make the appointment all about drugs—not that he gave me any reason to worry; for some reason, I just felt suspicious all the time. *Actually, Dr. Marvin, could you prescribe anything for chronic guilt?* is what I should have asked. Whatever he could give me to turn my brain off. Something to make my thoughts disappear; because all too often, whatever it is I'm thinking of, it's like it's actually happening. I had to board a plane to Germany the next day, and I didn't want to go into hysterics, convinced we'd be free-falling at the slightest dip, the mental torture measuring the aftershocks of turbulence, thinking it would all lead to something final, something fatal.

"Sure, sure," said Dr. Marvin. "Trouble sleeping, problems at work, that sort of thing?"

"Yeah, it's just like, all the time, really… Just, like, really bad thoughts, you know?" I say, averting eye contact for no good reason.

"No problem, Cameron. I'm going to write you up a prescription here," he said, grabbing his white pad and blue pen. "How does 10mg of Trazodone sound?"

I had no idea what that was, so his question seemed presumptuous. I was immediately flushed with the fear he assumed I'm some veteran pill-head, that he's testing me, that if I knew exactly what it was, he'd put me under some kind of medical or even legal scrutiny.

"Oh, what's that, exactly?"

"So, Trazodone is kind of a multi-purpose anti-depressant that also works as a sedative. I know you didn't say you were depressed, but anxiety is often a result of depression, of something more buried, maybe. Sometimes we need to just turn off those thoughts so we can think straight, focus on getting well again."

"Yes, yes that sounds perfect, a sedative," I said, too much.

"Sure, okay. Now, thing is with Trazodone—you don't take it as needed, like say, Valium or Xanax…"

I squint my eyes, tilt my head, a totally campy move *hmmm, interesting, I am totally unfamiliar with those particular medications.* Internally I scolded my overacting, riding the motions of my unnecessary performance.

"With Trazodone, you'll take one right away when you get home, then another tomorrow when you wake up," said Dr. Marvin. "It's a medication that has to sort of 'build-up' in your system before you reap the benefits." He assured me the sedative element would take effect within the same hour of consumption, yet only directed to be taken once every morning, and, only if needed, once at night as a sleep aid. He sent me off with the note to redeem at the pharmacy, my last detail before my American rock n' roll band departed to Europe for a three week-tour—a plane trip I'd barely remember since I tripled up on my dose. Frightened to fly, weary at the responsibility of orchestrating eight imbalanced band mates, I wasn't taking any chances.

"MAKE YOURSELF AT home in Hamburg, this will be your headquarters for the next three days," said our driver, Stephan, stepping out of the black Sprinter van to help with our luggage. Ahead of us: a long eight flights to the top floor of the legitimized squat, a towering brick tenement. "You'll be staying in the attic, but it's very nice, very spacious, but we are also very crowded at the moment with more refugees." We assumed he was referring to people like us—other wayward musicians cutting swathes through his country. "Very little of them speak English, so do your best to be welcoming."

"Germans?" I asked.

"Haitians," he said. "After the gig tonight, there will be at least four or five asleep in the attic with you, but they know you're coming…"

WE LEARNED LATER: no matter what strangers we'd bunk with, we'd be too wasted to care. Germans get you drunk when you arrive to the show, during the show, then make sure you had little to no recollection of the show by the time you leave; the thrill to test American exuberance.

Upon our return, the eight flights of stairs would test us further, each stair spinning with every step, leading us to strange floors, doors that were not the attic. Finally stumbling into our quarters, I made it even more difficult for us. *Nobody turn on any lights* I whispered. *Nobody say a fucking word, just go right to your sleeping bag so we don't wake these guys up.* Rather than be grateful for our host's hospitality, I felt guilty we were there; I mentally criticized us, the way we spread out our sleeping arrangements instead of making a respectful use of space—a flagrance that relegated me between two Haitian men deep in slumber, their snoring a declaration of rest better earned than mine.

I laid myself down, only to stare at the rafters for an hour, surrounded by the men's invasive nasal emissions flanking me. I gave in, grabbed three Trazodone out of the orange, white-capped bottle, and within five minutes the Haitian's snoring in stereo faded like whispering static.

BACK IN THE states, it moved so fast. Cameron, your friend is giving us his house, you don't mind moving back to Orange County *said my girlfriend, a demand rather than question I was hypnotized to abide by; after decades of renting instability, I knew I had to agree. It was a shit or get off the pot time for her and I, a fork in the road of our romance; if we didn't think bigger, commit to some grand sacrifice, we may never find our foundation.*

She took my hand to show me into the house she'd never been in. I was relieved to see everything inside had changed, no trace of our teenage debauchery in the Hellhouse, now legitimized for the Joneses. Remodeled, there were added levels, a staircase beyond a threshold. You didn't tell me there was a basement *I said.* Why would I tell you, I've never been here, *she said.* Do you want to go down there?

Right then, a flood... no, a tsunami of memory, carrying something huge, coming unglued from the deep ocean bottom yet impossible to dilute.

No, no I do not want to go down there. It's not supposed to be there. *Have you ever constructed a lie so well, protecting a conscious decision you made, that you successfully suppressed not only the remorseful decision you made, but forgot all about the lie you created to protect it?*

Well, now you have to go down there. This is your house now. You can say somebody really bought the farm, *she said, her voice fading behind me as I descended the stairs. Pitch black, but of course I knew my way: once to the bottom, I just walk straight, there's that other threshold, barricaded with furniture, one couch on top of another, a coffee table for extra inconvenience of my climb over. Then, I go right, a long hallway, another staircase, darker still, I know my way, I could do this all backwards— I actually did twenty years ago, when I not only vowed to never return, but forget he ever existed. We'd kill him from the Earth, we'd kill him from our minds, no one would care if he died. And as I climb down the ladder, down this little furnace shoot, I am burying myself through time, excavating the crime we committed—telling myself it never happened, because it didn't, you know… yet, I can't prove what never happened until I can see clearly, that there are no remains from him, because none of him remained, we ran too fast to remember. I'm running towards it now, that deepest spot where nothing happened. I'll know it when I see it, the life no longer living. Wrapped in blankets as a bandage for our wounds, he took advantage. Now I'm sliding all over the floor of the slippery slope, what do they call the escalator that does down, the de-escalator? No one could de-escalate our plan's ramping up. We had to put him down. I ask myself if I know what's it like to kill somebody and I say* nope *because I never did.* Oh, why do you have this memory, then? *It was then I pled the 5ᵗʰ. I must see it with my own eyes to prove it's all a myth, no further questions then. We never questioned him—he cemented his intentions on that irreversible night, unmistaken.*

That's when I see him.

But is he *still a* him *when his manhood has shriveled, rotten? His anatomy shrunken into calcified muscle, hugging bones exposed; a mouth wide open:* were you asking a question? Perhaps a tardy admission? *The rats in this cellar have eaten the clothes of the skeleton in our closet, someone who's been forgotten, but me, everybody knows. So everyone can see the look of secrecy, remorse, emergency, I must emerge from this subterranean, subhuman, even if it kills me—anything is better than a lock with no key. Just live my life inside, a forever closed mind, but my girlfriend is outside, still upstairs where it's now night, surrounded by flashing lights of the cops she called when I didn't return, she was more afraid to come down here than I was, more paralyzed by fear; and maybe that's the irony, our most common of ground: our refusal to budge, above or below, this multi-teared burial mound. If I ascend, I'll be turning myself in. If I remain, I'll be turning on myself, inside out; radiating regret, a magnet. I begin to wish I were remains, just like what's his name here, who will never be forced to confess; his consciousness set free, finally. But when the living kills, the living dead, there's never true escape, no home to*

return to, only evasion—you're your own free-range prison; your own judge, jury, and
subsequent life-sentence.

IT TOOK CAMERON'S eyes some time to adjust to the darkness, his depth
perception lightening the blackness into heavy greys, though nothing quite
took shape until a sliver of sun came over the horizon, nearly stopping his
heart when he saw he lay next to a black man wrapped in blankets, his eyes
closed, a healthy body, fully-fleshed. Cameron began hyperventilating; after
convincing himself he wasn't facing the corpse of the Puerto Rican he killed
as a teenager. He then assured himself he was merely decades into prison for
killing that same victim. Because where else—why else—would he be
bunking with a black man? He scolded his racist thought, a typical American.
He reached over, tapping him on the shoulder.

"Hey, who are you?"

The Haitian stirred. "Mwen pa konprann…"

"What is this?"

The Haitian propped himself on his elbow, grabbing a knife from under
his pillow, a force of habit accustomed to thieves in the night. "Med! Idyot!"
He pointed the blade at Cameron.

"I'm sorry, fuck! *Fuck!*"

His bandmate Katie rubbed her eyes, awoken from the commotion.
"Cameron? What's going on over there?"

"Katie, what is this?" Cameron squeezed his temples.

"What is what?"

"Where are we? Am I in trouble?"

"No, you're with your band, your friends…" said Katie, her voice trailing
off, trying to be reassuring, but came across concerned instead. "We are in
Hamburg, in Germany, sweetheart."

"Why'd you take me here? What are you doing to me?" Cameron's heavy
breathing made hard questions even more difficult.

"Uhm, nothing? We are going to play a show tomorrow night, downtown
Hamburg. Downtown, where all the strip clubs are."

"Oh, for my last night?"

"Your last night… What do you mean, Cameron? You're freaking me
out."

He'd said too much. He couldn't let them know that *he knew* they were going to turn him in to the police, under the guise of playing a "show," where he'd be a dancing monkey—his final performance before he'd be the monkey in a cage.

"If you guys were really my friends, you'd just level with me—that we're here to turn me over to the German Secret Police…"

"Cameron, what? You're like, in the wrong era entirely…"

"I'm not in the wrong! Not then, not now!" He spoke a mile a minute, not getting anywhere, backtracking, confused, should he pander? "I mean, its considerate of you to take me to another country, so I won't damage my reputation in the States immediately, but they'll find out back home soon enough—why don't we just go home and rip off the band-aid?" Cameron paced around the room, throwing his arms around, over-animated; if this was his last day of freedom, he no longer cared how crazy he looked.

Katie woke up Ben, Cameron's bass player and best friend.

"Ben, something is wrong with Cameron. He's having like, a weird break."

Ben stirred. "That's fine. Show's not until tonight."

"No, like a fucking *psychotic* break—look!"

She pointed to Cameron, arguing with two Haitian refugees who appeared furious with him. *"You think I don't know how you guys fit into all of this: the paid guards who make sure this all goes according to plan, sleeping on either side of me so I won't escape?"*

"Cameron! What the fuck, man?" said Ben. He realized he should calm himself first if he aimed to diffuse his friend. "Why don't you come over here, tell us what's going on."

He broke from the Haitians, walked to the center of the room, pointed at Ben and Katie. "This is as far as I'm walking, and this is far as I'm talking. You think you're gonna get a confession out of me? *You're fucking crazy.*" His eyes were big, jaundiced, webbed by red veins like he didn't sleep, like he may never sleep again. The rest of their group had awoken, yet were silenced in shock, confused by the erratic developments. Staring back at them, the armed Haitian returned the knife underneath the pillow, yet maintained his optic daggers; while the other rolled his eyes, wondering if he was ever going to get a good night's sleep in Hamburg, the sanctuary city granting him and his brother asylum, when this room resembled an asylum of another kind; an unsettling resettlement.

Cameron's head whipped to the exit—no one was guarding it—the Haitians were crawling back into bed. He ran to the door, Ben sprinted after him.

"Don't let him leave!" Katie screamed, which Cameron heard as he was turning the knob, confirming they were keeping him here against his will, that Katie was possibly the one in charge. Ben grabbed Cameron's biceps from behind, retracting his hand from opening the door, *restraining him like a fucking cop*, thought Ben, ashamed; scared for his best friend, worried he'd have to use even stronger force to subdue him. "I don't want to hurt you, Cameron, but I might have to if you don't chill the fuck out," he hissed, stern.

Cameron weakened. He broke into sobs, breathing heavy, hesitant into Ben's ear: *I just don't want anyone to look at me, I don't want to look at anybody, please…*

"Do you want to go to the van, downstairs, outside?" said Ben. Relieved by the sensitivity, he moved Cameron's head in front of his for direct eye contact.

"Am I allowed to?"

"Yeah, of course you're allowed to," Ben heard himself speak to him like a child.

"No one is going to drive me away?"

"What? No, not until tonight, when we go to play the show, at the club."

Cameron thought: *There is not going to be a show tonight,* careful not to say it out loud.

BEN PROCURED THE keys from the driver, Stephan, told him Cameron needed to be alone, was too hungover, or something. "Ah, he's got Road Burn, huh?" Stephan said, laughing. "I've seen it happen towards the end of tour, but never the first night, yikes. Okay, you're in charge of the keys—Cameron probably shouldn't have them."

"Agreed," said Ben. "Thanks. And I'm really sorry about the chaos upstairs, I feel bad for those two guys…"

"Trust me, they've seen much worse," said Stephan.

CAMERON WAS ALREADY outside at the van, waiting impatiently to sequester himself. "Here, let's get you in here," said Ben, swinging open the side door. Cameron climbed right into the van's loft, enough room for one person to sleep. "Good, man… Please, sleep as long as you can, all right?"

"What's that supposed to mean, like sleep forever?" Cameron barked, visualizing another nefarious subplot *Now I can't sleep because they're going to poison me.*

"Uh, no? We'll wake you up at like, 5 p.m."

"Yeah, and then what?"

"And then we are going to have a totally killer night playing music for Germans."

Cameron laughed to himself, nearly amused how delusional Ben was. "Yeah, right."

"Can I get you anything, man. Want a water?"

Interesting, this must be my last request. Suddenly, Cameron no longer cared.

"Yes, you can do something for me."

"Anything, what?"

"I just need to talk to you. Here, come in."

Ben obliged, lounged onto one of the van's bench seats so could face Cameron behind him. "What's up, man?"

"I think I might have killed someone…"

AN HOUR LATER, Ben arrived back upstairs. When he opened the door, he saw his group re-animate from their pow-wow on the floor. *What's going on? Is he okay?* Ben didn't say much at first, no words could make it past his gritting teeth, his glare. He motioned them all to the table where they all took a seat.

"Man, I don't know what's going on. Cameron is convinced he killed someone when he was a teenager, and he's just now remembering it, or something?" Ben explained, though unable to process.

"Like, what, he had a bad dream?"

"No, I don't think he even slept last night—neither does he, and whatever he's going through seems rooted in some real terror he can't shake. He was like, bawling his brains out with remorse, kept saying sorry, sorry, that he was so sorry."

"Did he give a name?"

"No, he refused to say who it was, that if he did, it would be him confessing. But that's why he thinks he's here—that we've kidnapped him in a van to turn him in, that we took him away from America so his family would never know. None of it makes sense. He's delusional, like fully immersed." Ben shook his head.

"He gave you no details of what he thinks he did?"

"He said when he was a kid, him and some other friends poisoned some guy who took advantage of one of them, sexually I guess, then buried him under the foundation of some house, like, under a basement?"

"There's no way they could've gotten away with that…"

"Well, he's deathly afraid they might have. I mean, how do you even tell whether something is repressed memory or pure delusion?" said Ben. "Whatever the case, he's seriously not well right now. I don't know what to do."

"What was he like when you left him?"

"He wanted me to wrap him up in a bunch of blankets, then kind of push him in the corner of the van loft. He said he was going to try sleeping, but he made a weird production out of how he wanted me to like, tuck him in, wrap him up really tight?"

"Okay, that's really weird…"

"Yeah, he kept saying to hide him, for everyone to forget he's there."

Katie shivered. "Oh my God, he's like, reliving it?"

"I… have no idea."

"Well, you did your best. We're doing our best."

"I guess…"

THEY ALL FELT the same way: that it seemed to take a lifetime for the clock to strike 5 p.m. that day, when Ben said he'd go back down to wake Cameron up in the van, giving them two hours to resettle, get ready for their show. But when Ben returned to the van, when he re-entered through the side door, when he climbed onto the backseat to stand himself up into the loft, he reached his hands across to push on Cameron's back, so much softer than before; his hand kept going into the pile of scrunched up blanket with nothing stopping him, because Cameron was no longer there.

"Fuck, no fucking way… *Cameron, you fucking asshole,*" said Ben, heart accelerating, pulling all the blankets away, revealing nothing, no body at all.

He uh, went to the store or something he thought, but dread immediately choked his faith, anything logical became incongruent with Cameron's behavior.

Ben ran back up the eight flights of stairs, opened the door, slammed it behind him. "Uh, Cameron's fucking not there…"

"What?"

"Gone."

THE NINE OF them, including the driver, were down at the van within five minutes: circling the outside of the vehicle, army-crawling underneath, looking beneath the seats, ransacking the loft. "Ben's trying to call him, so listen for his phone, look for his phone, we need to find Cameron's phone, he's not picking up, I think Ben's on his fifth try," said Katie. "Wait, here's his bag." She reached into a crevice in the loft behind a pillow, pulled out his canvas knapsack. Her eager hands dove in, rummaging, getting frustrated until she dumped out its contents onto the seat, spreading it all out for optimal view.

"There's no phone here, but there's his medication," she said, holding up the orange, white-capped container. "Did anyone know Cameron was on medication?"

"What, no? What is it?"

She squinted her eyes, sounding it out: *Traz-o-done?*

Ben grabbed the bottle, typed it into his phone, scrolling in focused silence. "Okay here it is, an anti-depressant…"

"Anything else?"

"Sedative… wait, one second…" Ben scrolled down, finding Trazodone to be a rather popular medication. He scrolled further, finding it was also synonymous with America's recent rash of mass shootings and teenage suicides. Ben read out loud to the group, rattling off headlines like *Another School Shooting, Another Psychiatric Drug: Trazadone, the real suspect,* articles confirming over thirty-seven public massacres where the assailant was on the trendy, overprescribed medication. *Two potentially serious side effects of Trazodone are hallucinations, mania, and psychosis.* "Fuck, this is really bad," said Ben, cutting off his stream of doom-scrolling.

"What should we do?" said Katie.

"Fuck, I... don't know. We're obviously not playing the show. Let's you, me and the driver take the van, scour the area. The rest of you stay here in case he comes back, comb the immediate grounds if you can."

The three of them jumped in. Stephan turned the key, the rest saluted solemnly outside the windshield, mouthing the words *good luck.*

Ben squinted his eyes, a detail recalled. "When I left him in the van, he said one more thing as I shut the door: *'You play the song. It's all in the song.'*"

"What's that supposed to mean?" said Katie. Ben didn't mean to ignore her—he was too focused leaning under her seat, grabbing their merch box from underneath. Methodically, he filed through their CDs, grabbed their first album with "The Cops Hate Rock n' Roll," the hidden song after track twelve. He scraped the shrink wrap off with his fingernail, opened the jewel case, stuck the CD into the van stereo, hit the track skip button eleven times. Through the speakers, the forgotten—and otherwise forgettable, unassuming, stupid—twelve-bar rockabilly song filled the van, Cameron's slurring vocals adopting a haunting air, now that Ben and Katie were paying close attention to the lyrics:

Well, the cops hate rock and roll, so they'll never find it here
The fate of the man who stole my innocence, supplied the fear
I slipped something in his drink stronger than any alcohol
If you need some higher proof, well, his name was Ignacio

When he began to puke, I knew revenge was on the way
And in a way, it was cute when he tried apologizing late
But in that final silent moment nothing came out of his mouth
I rolled him up and buried him so far underneath that house

BEN AND KATIE forced eye contact in over-bitten symmetry. *I mean, that doesn't really mean anything, right? I don't like this... It's just a song? Why is it there then? This feels fucked up—like, too specific, can't make this up—fucked up.* They jogged their memory back to that night in the studio: he had been getting drunk all day, could barely speak by the time he told them all to leave, that he needed privacy.

When the album came out, no one in the band even knew the song was on there—it was buried after the end of track twelve ran for a minute of silence—until fans started circulating the secret song everyone just assumed was Cameron's drunken studio piss-take.

"Goddamn… what do you think?" Katie leaned up to Ben in the passenger seat.

"Uhm, well, if he killed someone when he was a teenager, there's not a whole lot we can do about it right now. Right now, after reading that stuff about Trazadone, I'm more worried that, like…"

"He could hurt himself or someone else today?"

"Yeah, exactly."

Stephan pulled the van over. "Give me one second, I'm getting a call from the house." His eyes squinted with worry: *"The what? Oh, the guy's knife? You looked all over the attic? Okay, yeah… this could be bad…"*

"What's the deal?"

Stephan hung up. "That was your bandmates. Apparently one of the refugees had a hunting knife underneath his pillow before Cameron left the room, and now it's gone."

THE KNIFE WASN'T gone—it had merely changed hands, and it was now going on its own little (de)tour of Germany, charged with renewed intention, because Cameron was a killer now, and killers need a weapon. He was so far ahead of them, on a different path from where they'd ever consider heading. While they fruitlessly scoured the red-light district of Hamburg, congested in rush hour traffic, Cameron was already ten miles outside of the city.

After throwing his phone into the Elbe River, he found a nice grassy knoll along the autobahn where he stuck out his thumb, capturing the eye of every driver through their windshield as they accelerated faster, frightened, *something's not right in that man's eyes,* until one charitable motorist pulled over. Cameron ran for his life to their car, damned if he was going to let this one go, marveling how true it was, what everyone told him, how *they're going to love you in Germany.*

IN BARCELONA

by

Megan Taylor

ACCORDING TO THE guidebook, the city was more than a place, it was a state of mind. But when Jo tried to explain this to Laura, she stopped fussing with her bra-straps, and glared at Jo. "Have you gone insane?" she asked.

She couldn't believe Jo was still planning on going. "There's no way you should be out there alone," she said. "Haven't you heard the stories? All that stuff about criminal gangs… Jo, you won't be safe."

As Laura spoke, the baby lolled from her breast. *Milk-drunk*, Jo thought, except her nephew's gaze was even more unsettling than her sister's. He had freakish, little old man's eyes, and Jo couldn't tell if he was searching out her deepest secrets or looking straight through her, like she wasn't there at all.

"And won't it only make you lonelier?" Laura kept on. "Won't it make you miss him more?"

"Maybe," Jo said. "It's what I need. A whole new scene…"

She was momentarily distracted, considering the sadness that had recently settled over her apartment, but she'd promised herself she wouldn't dwell. "It isn't even five full days," she said more brightly. "You'll hardly know I'm gone!"

But Jo's attempt at a chirpy defence did nothing to convince the baby. He was huffing back towards his mother's breasts, and Laura's shock had segued into a familiar expression of 'concern'—her grey eyes narrowing, neat mouth pursed—and frankly, Jo was tired of that face. She'd been seeing it for months.

Although Laura was meant to be the calm and sensible one, whenever Jo mentioned Ben, the air between them would tighten, and earlier, when Jo first brought up his change of heart, her sister's control had briefly slipped.

"What did you expect?" she'd snapped. "He was never going to leave his wife."

Jo had turned away, like she was turning now, and through the window, the sky was the same grubby-dishrag-grey, the rain still falling. It had been an exceptionally poor summer.

But this time, gazing at the silvery panes, Jo found herself returning to the guidebook's promises, and "it'll be okay," she murmured. "Besides, I really need some light."

AND NOW JO'S standing in a pool of pure gold light, on the landing outside her *atica* apartment. The sun pouring over her from a skylight in the sloping roof, the floors below, quiet. Double-checking her keys, and shutting the apartment's door, she imagines layer after layer of peace, both rising and descending.

She's made it, despite Laura's doubts, and the similar, if simpler, concern of her colleagues. Although she didn't mention Ben—she's never mentioned Ben at work—they grew high-pitched with worry when Jo revealed she'd be travelling alone.

"Watch out," they told her. "It's so easy to get robbed."

And Laura had been right about the stories. There were numerous tales of friends-of-friends who'd had their pockets picked as soon as they'd stepped off the plane. Apparently, the thieves were professional tricksters, who often worked in pairs. One of them might collapse, feigning a heart attack, while another swiped your Euros and passport, though their distraction techniques weren't necessarily that extreme. Annie from Accounts knew a girl who'd been mugged among the basic bump and spill of a takeaway coffee.

But Jo has travelled all this way, all by herself—*I'm here, I'm really here*—and so far, she seems intact. Wearing a bum-bag strapped high across her chest, as the guidebook suggested, she managed to negotiate the airport and find a taxi without experiencing any medical emergencies or a single splashed hot drink. Fairly certain the cabbie didn't rip her off, and when she arrived at her holiday-home, the owner's son was there to show her around, exactly as arranged, and the apartment was more than she'd dared to hope for.

Occupying the old block's highest floor, its clean, pretty rooms opening onto an unexpected gift of a roof-garden. With its terracotta tiles, deep, comfortable loungers and exotic-looking plants, the terrace is a whole other magical living space. Every angle offering a spectacular view of shimmering towers and fairy-tale spires, and when Jo first stared out over the balustrade, she'd found herself wishing she could fly.

"Our beautiful city," the owner's son had pronounced unnecessarily, and he'd sounded equally proud as he went on to describe, in impeccable English, the metro and the shops and the recycling rota. His enthusiasm didn't wane until he was about to leave, when "You're alone?" he'd blurted, a cloud passing over his youthful face. "Please, take care, I warn you. Look after all your things."

And that, along with the garden's spell, has made it hard for Jo to drag herself out. But she can't allow her nerves to overwhelm her, not after making it this far—*not now I'm truly here*—and turning towards the quaint cage surrounding the lift shaft, she realises there's no need to negotiate the control-panel. Through the bars, as if it's been politely waiting, the lift's already here.

It's the first time Jo will be using it. It's too small to accommodate more than one person, and when she arrived, she offered to climb the stairs while the owner's son took her suitcase up. He'd argued, but she'd insisted. It was only six floors, no trouble at all. She'd meet him at the top.

Jo's generally known for her consideration, for putting others first. Often described as 'a nice girl', but though she'll smile shyly, taking the compliment, sometimes it makes her wonder. Is there an underlying implication that she's too deferential, too trusting? Guided more by fear than self-respect…

After the owner's son stepped inside the lift, there was a moment on the stairwell when her heart had floundered. She'd been about halfway up, approaching the third floor, when the timer-lights twanged off.

The darkness engulfed her, swallowing everything except her quavering breaths and the lift's whining as her suitcase went on rising away from her, disappearing, up and up.

But it wasn't her vanishing things that disturbed her. For a second, Jo felt as if the shadows were seeping inside her, merging with her panicked thoughts, and she'd almost screamed—

Ben!

Instead, blind and stumbling, she'd scrambled on, feeling just as chased by the things she'd hoped to leave behind as she was by the tumbling dark.

But somewhere between the fifth and sixth floors, the stairwell flooded bright once more. The pale stone of the steps reappeared, and the lift was quiet, stilled. The owner's son, having made it to the top, had switched the lights back on. And by the time Jo reached him, she was wiping her flushed, wet face as if ridding it of nothing more than sweat, her panic disguised in apologetic giggles.

"I'm fine," she told him. "It's all okay." But inwardly she'd been resolved; she'd never take the stairs again.

And now, beyond its cage, the lift looks charming, like an antique cabinet or wardrobe… Jo doesn't know why she's paused before it, one hand hooked limply to the metal gate. The lift's still waiting patiently, and she can see that it's empty. There's a long, thin window embedded in its narrow, wooden door, and if someone was skulking inside, she'd surely glimpse their bulk. And besides, what choice does she have? She's not risking the stairs, that flooding dark. Just thinking about it makes her shudder.

Shaking her head, she draws back the gate, and reaches for the door's smaller brass handle. But when she opens the lift, the urge to scream returns.

A face is staring back at her.

It has huge, glistening eyes, and damp, blotchy skin. There's frizzy hair sticking to its forehead in sweaty strings, and a strange pouch roped awkwardly across its breasts—

Jo's looking at herself.

The lift has a mirror on its back wall—that's all—an old-fashioned frosted looking-glass. She needs to get a grip.

Stepping inside, she forces out a smile, and though her reflection only grimaces, she shuts both the gate and the wooden door determinedly. Stabbing the lowest button and then releasing her breath as the mechanism catches and the lift rattles into life.

And now Jo is going down, and down. Through the window, she watches the stripes of the passing floors. Somebody must have turned the stair-lights on, but there's no sign of anyone waiting. Nobody's looking back.

She concentrates on keeping her breathing steady, wiping her moist hands on her blouse. Beyond the earthy scent of her body, she can smell the layers of polish scrubbed deep into the panelling, and she forcibly reminds herself how picturesque this is. *Like a lift in a Victorian dolls' house…*

But the idea doesn't make much sense. Jo's never seen a lift in a dolls' house, and despite the heat flopping through her limbs and messing up her hair, she's far from doll-like.

Still, isn't this better than the stairs, the darkness? She hasn't ever experienced claustrophobia, and she's hardly likely to give into anything like that now. Except—

As she breathes in the polish, still trying to admire the burnished wood, she's no longer thinking about miniature houses. She's reminded of a coffin.

The lift jolts—clanking to a stop.

Jo flinches. "No," she murmurs—but then she sees.

Through the narrow window, the lobby's gleaming, and *I'm here*, she thinks again, *I'm here, I'm here*, and close to ecstatic, she snatches the lift's handle and wrenches open the gate. And then she's rushing across the marble tiles and spilling out through the heavy entrance door, plunging headlong onto the street.

JO'S BEEN WALKING for over an hour. Now and then, she reaches out to cradle the bag bumping against her chest. Its soft beatings like a second heart, but though she's keeping it settled, safe and close, she can't pretend she isn't lost.

Despite the owner's son's meticulous instructions, she's failed to find the nearest supermarket or the metro station. This part of the city's meant to be simple, laid out in squares, but Jo feels like she's walking in circles. Although the streets are wide, the balconies layering the blocks on either side are starting to hem her in, and she can't tell if the big black table parasols on every corner belong to different cafes, or if she's passing the same one again and again.

Then, out of nowhere, the buildings give way, revealing an eye-watering stretch of blue, blue sky, and a swathe of lush green grass. There are bushes, resplendent with fat, bright flowers, and the open arms of trees.

Jo has somehow stumbled across a park, and she feels swept into a kind of Technicolor dreamland, strolling through it. Birds flit like tiny rainbows from branch to branch, their tropical-sounding trills rippling through the heat.

Several other people wander the paths, and Jo reminds herself to stay alert. It's not just thieves she needs to worry about. Along with its passage on pickpockets, her guidebook described how some ongoing battle for independence has recently led to an additional surge in crime. But Jo hadn't really understood the politics, skimming through that section on the plane.

And right now, the heady sweetness of the flowers is distracting. Meandering between the laden bushes, Jo wonders if the park's her first hint of the city as a state of mind, and the strangers around her look harmless; most appear to be sleepwalking. No one seems to notice she's there.

Jo's reluctant to leave the park, but to her relief, once she's stepped through the gates on the other side, the grid of streets has been replaced with cobbled, story-book alleyways that curve and split and scurry off. And as she follows them past intriguing, cave-like bars and past churches – so many churches – she recognises an ancient, crumbling wall, and then a distinctive stone arch. She's ended up in the Gothic Quarter.

Ben had shown her pictures on his laptop; he'd been particularly keen to visit… But Jo mustn't think about Ben, she promised herself. Despite the shade of the ever-narrowing streets, the heat's intensifying. Verging on oppressive.

Sensibly, nearly as sensible as Laura, Jo stops at a cafe. She's ushered to an outside table by an incredibly pretty girl, who smiles as she brings Jo iced water and black coffee and a generous wedge of moist, yellow cake.

On the table to Jo's right, there's a tired-looking, sunburnt family, British tourists, like her.

But as she's considering striking up a conversation, "What about the bank?" the woman says, and her tone is shrill. "Can't the bank help? Does it have to be the embassy?"

Shielded behind his mirrored shades, the man doesn't reply, and their ice-cream-smeared toddler ignores her too, smacking his highchair with his fists. Jo suspects he's working himself up towards a full-blown wail, and she thinks of her nephew, and then of her sister again, guiltily remembering she hasn't called or texted like she'd promised. That honestly isn't Jo's fault; although she dutifully checked with the provider before she left, her phone's refusing to connect to the network, just as it's stubbornly holding onto English time. She ought to be an hour ahead, or behind; she can't remember which.

"John, please," the woman's saying, then the man's leaning forward, cutting her off with a throaty growl.

"I told you. Why do I have to keep telling you? We're not going through this again."

The toddler starts to cry.

Trying not to look as if she's eavesdropping, Jo nibbles her astonishingly delicious cake, contemplating the contrast of Laura's world, where everything's so calm and carefully managed, including her sister's husband, Greg.

Jo can't imagine Greg snapping. He's quieter than Laura, and even more practical. He's been fastidiously restoring their Edwardian semi, and during Jo's last visit, she saw he'd added a custom-built shoe-rack to their newly parqueted hall.

When she first arrived, before she'd been forced to explain what had happened with Ben, Jo had popped a pair of knitted booties at the end of the rack, slipping them in after her brother-in-law's brogues and her sister's sensible pumps. She'd thought it would be funny seeing them lined up like that. *Daddy Bear, Mummy Bear, and Baby…* Except as soon as she set them down, Jo's vision had smeared. Suddenly irrepressibly sad.

To Jo's left, there's an older, good-looking couple. The man is handsome in a swarthy, black-and-white film kind of way, and the woman's laughing, shaking out a tawny mane of hair. But when the woman takes the man's jaw in her confident hands, Jo turns away. She doesn't want to think about Ben's wife.

It's then she feels something crawling across the nape of her neck. Where her skin's exposed, it's bristling, and she immediately recognises the sensation. Jo is being watched.

Someone's watching her from inside the café behind her. She knows it; can feel it. At least one pair of curious eyes…

Jo tries to keep chewing, but never mind the heat, her mouth's turned cold, and the yellow cake's becoming an inedible mush. As slowly and as casually as she can, she glances back over her shoulder.

For a moment, the café's windows flare. They're gold and then black, jostling with silhouettes—

But just as quickly, Jo's vision clears, and now there's nothing behind her but pre-occupied customers and busy, pretty waitresses. Nobody's looking at her at all.

HEADING BACK, JO gets lost again. It's nearing dusk, her blouse is ragged with sweat, her shorts are chafing, and she's longing to lie down. Imagining curling-up on her roof-garden among its friendly plants, but first she needs to find her apartment block, and even then, before she's safe, she'll have to face the dreadful choice between the stairwell and the coffin-lift.

Stop it, Jo tells herself. *You can do this—aren't you doing this? Aren't you here?*

And isn't getting lost meant to be an essential part of any proper foreign adventure? Besides, if she needs it, there's a map folded small inside her bag, along with the guidebook, both handily pocket-sized.

Except she isn't supposed to get either out, not on the streets; everyone, including the guidebook, has advised her. Such accessories will only emphasise her tourist status—bewildered and vulnerable—although isn't the bum-bag a massive clue in itself? Jo's wondering if she should start wearing it underneath her top when she sees a man standing in a doorway up ahead.

He's still several feet away, and huddled in the spreading shadows, but as she closes in, Jo makes out a broad torso, the suggestion of straggly hair, and the orange wink of his cigarette. She attempts to quicken her pace without appearing to, trying to recall further advice.

Always walk with confidence and purpose. Walk as if you're crystal-clear about where you're going. As if you know completely who you are…

Jo isn't sure if that's quite right, but as she passes the man, she sees that he's hunched over, busy with his phone. He doesn't glance up even when she stumbles, and after she's moved on, the skin on her neck remains just skin. There's no sense of a trailing gaze.

As Jo keeps walking, it occurs to her she might be in a bubble, separate and protected. As if she's floating underneath the balconies, and then she's bobbing past other men. They're collected in muttering groups, here and there, along the pavement, but not one of them turns as she approaches. Still, Jo tries to stay grounded. Obviously, it would be a mistake to become complacent, especially since the evening's deepening with each step.

The sky's soon a velvety indigo, but as Jo's gaze returns to the street, she begins to laugh. It's another small miracle, like coming across the park, the way she's suddenly *here*, exactly where she wants to be. Those black café parasols belong to her street corner, and it's like the whole beautiful city's been playing hide-and-seek with her. *Hey, Jo! Peek-a-boo!*

Once she's reached her block, she clicks on the lobby-lights before pressing the heavy street door closed, and then stands for a moment, feeling the weight of the apartments above her, their coolness and their quiet. Her footsteps jar, echoing as she knew they would, when she crosses the marble floor.

She gazes from the mouth of the stairwell to the lift, lurking behind its cage, and then in a rush, she's tugging open the gate and the door, shutting herself in without glancing at the mirror.

And after jabbing the highest button, she shuts her eyes as well. If she keeps them closed the entire way up, then maybe everything will be okay.

But through the dark in her head, the lift sounds too loud. She can hear the age in the machine—there's something distinctly pained about its clanking and whining—and then, between its heaving groans, she hears something else.

Please, Ben. I'm sorry…

It's Jo's own begging, wheedling voice. *Please, Ben, please,* as if everything's happening all over again.

She opens her eyes as the lift clatters to a stop. But though she's reached the top, and she's yanking at the doors and scrambling out, Jo goes on feeling trapped. Surrounded by a terrible rushing silence, still waiting for Ben's reply.

THE NEXT DAY, there's no way Jo will shut her eyes. Standing, blinking, in the sunshine streaming through the skylight, she can't fathom why she thought adding her own darkness to anything would be a good idea. She's also switched on the landing's lights, having already reconsidered and dismissed the steps again. Peering into the stairwell, the clammy air unfurling back at her had been too like shallow breaths, and though the lift remains her only option, she's come up with a basic plan she's praying will help. She'll simply count the floors.

She can't let her exit delay her any longer, not when there's so much to explore, and with the morning practically over. Waking late after a long, unsettling night, riddled with dreams about Ben, she eventually stirred in her double bed, and ran her hands over the mattress, imagining his shape.

Later, out on her roof-garden, Jo had started feeling better. How could she not, surrounded by all those thriving feathery palms and fleshy succulents? With the city beyond them reduced to a glittering toy-town, she might have lingered all day, snacking on the dusty, but weirdly moreish crackers she'd found in the kitchen, if the pigeon hadn't turned up.

When the bird first fluttered onto the terrace, Jo had been delighted. It appeared more elegant than the pigeons at home; its mauves and browns softer, its bobbing neck gracefully thin.

But when it cocked its head towards her, the bird's gaze, both blank and uncannily beady, had struck Jo exactly as her nephew's had. It was time for her to go.

INSIDE THE LIFT, Jo looks around deliberately, telling herself there's nothing menacing about the mirror's smoky glass or the panelling... There's a number set above the door she hasn't noticed before. Someone to call in case of faults, she assumes, emergencies, and it would, she supposes, be reassuring, except her phone's still refusing to connect.

And now, as she descends, she's thinking about all the calls and messages she might have missed. Thinking helplessly of Ben.

Why is he always in the lift, with Jo? Even if he'd relented and come away with her, they'd never have fitted in together. Nonetheless, she imagines him pressed close, and forgets to count the floors.

And as the lift keeps falling, her nightmares return. Once more, Ben's above her, and he's inside her, and at first, everything's beautiful—he's so beautiful, gazing into her.

"I love you," he says, and she can feel the weight of his emotion.

But then, Ben's underneath her. Below her, slipping down and down, and he isn't looking anymore. Nobody can see—

And the second the lift hits the ground floor, Jo's out and running.

JO HAD INTENDED to brave the metro, to begin her tour with the astounding basilica, the main attraction in this city crammed with astounding attractions. Even in pictures, she found its fantastical towers dizzying, and Ben had explained how it was still being built. *A dream that never ends...*

Instead, Jo simply walks, allowing her feet to guide her. Perhaps she'll stumble across one of the surreal houses with their melting balconies and mosaics? But this time, when the blocks give way, she finds herself swept onto the city's main tourist drag.

The road is wide, but filled with tacky souvenir stalls and overflowing bars. As Jo struggles to keep moving through the crowds, the warnings become a mantra rambling round and round her head.

Watch out, look after all your things. Watch out, Jo, watch out…

Everyone else appears focused on one another, or the street performers. Puppeteers and flamenco guitarists and a long row of living statues. Jo finds the 'statues', which seem to be mainly giant, spray-painted angels or demons, particularly unnerving. There's no sign of their real eyes behind their oversized masks, and the tourists taking their photos look so vulnerable, recklessly waving their phones.

And yet, despite the jostling, Jo remains untouched. No one bumps her, or even brushes close, and maybe the skin of her bubble is thickening? But rather than feeling relief, Jo pictures herself trapped inside it, shouting soundlessly.

Then, thank God, the throng thins out. Jo glimpses creamy columns and a haze of blue—the promise of the sea.

EVENTUALLY, SHE FINDS an empty lounger. There are bodies everywhere.

After slipping off her sandals, she gingerly rolls up her shorts, trying not to feel self-conscious about the pallor of her thighs. Most of the people, around her, are the same burnished brown as her lift. Beyond them, the sea's an expanse of cool-looking glass, and Jo wishes she could swim. But her costume's back at the apartment, and anyway, there's nowhere to stash her bag.

Surely, it's safe to take out the guidebook here? Other people are reading, though they're mostly chatting or eating or playing together, sharing picnics and beachballs and sunscreen.

Jo lies back and waits to be charged for the lounger. There are several men weaving between the sunbathers, hawking their wares in heavily accented English. "Mass-sage," they call. "Ice-cold water," "Very best beer!"

But nobody approaches Jo, and as she flicks absently through the guidebook's pages, their cries fade in and out, not so different from the tide. The heat's becoming liquid too; Jo's face is dripping, her eyes sticky, longing to close. But she knows how unwise it would be to fall asleep; she'd lose track of all her things.

Still, on the verge of dozing, Jo considers her bubble again. Perhaps it's nothing new. Hasn't she felt a sense of separation since she started seeing Ben?

In the early weeks, the secrecy was exciting. Jo would feel spy-like, evading her friends' invitations with vague stories about mild illnesses and late nights at work. Much of the time, nobody, including Jo, knew exactly where she was.

When Ben didn't come sneaking over to her place, he'd arrange to meet in deadbeat pubs and desolate restaurants or tucked-away hotels. Jo often ended up in parts of her hometown she'd never known existed, and there was more than one occasion when she'd found herself propping up the wrong empty bar, waiting for hours alone.

It was probably inevitable the thrill would start wearing off, although Jo isn't certain when that happened. It might have been when her friends gave up calling, or when she could no longer reel her feelings in and confessed everything to Laura.

Jo must have been ridiculously naïve to hope sensible Laura, with her new house and husband and her weird, wise baby, might empathise. Instead, her sister, the only person she's ever truly trusted, has become the single person in the universe who no longer thinks Jo is a good person.

"Who even *are* you?" Laura asked her once.

Jo has wondered too.

Except that's all over now. *Everything's changed*, Jo reminds herself, and the sunlight's also transforming. It's growing heavier, a molten weight between her lashes, and those circling voices have become hypnotic. "Ice-cold water... Beer..."

But you're here, Jo thinks. *Come on, stay here...*

Only it's impossible; she's exhausted, and the heat that's surrounding her, like another bubble, is continuing to build.

JO'S BACK AT home, preparing dinner, and though Ben's standing right beside her, she's doing her best to tune him out. He's telling her, again, that the timing's wrong; he can't come away—and yet he won't leave her kitchen. He just keeps talking on and on.

"I'm sorry," he's saying. "I can't, not now. But soon, I promise..."

Jo goes on slicing onions, trying to focus on their silvery slivers. Eyes stinging, vision blurring, and she doesn't want to slip.

"Jo," Ben says. "You know how much I want to be with you. You know I love you too."

Jo shakes her head, although, yes, she knows. Not only has he told her repeatedly, hasn't she seen it? Those unquestionable moments when Ben looks down at her, straight into her, his emotions deepening his gaze…

But, *too*, Jo thinks. He loves *her* too.

And though his hand is warm, she scarcely feels it brush her neck, as she can't connect with her falling tears. While they speckle the chopping board like miniature stars, she's in another universe.

JO WAKES WITH a start. The late afternoon sweeping over her in a fiery rush, and for a moment, she's blinded.

She wipes her damp eyes. Every part of her is sweating, and her thighs burnt an angry red. *Stupid*, she scolds herself for falling asleep, and then, in a panic, she remembers her things. But the guidebook's nestled at her side, and her bag's still clinging to her chest, her purse tucked away, inside it. It's all miraculously where it's supposed to be, and everyone else on the beach appears distracted. The families are packing away, gathering up their towels and toys and toddlers. When a baby starts mewling, Jo's tempted to close her eyes again, but a different crowd is moving in—a laughing party crowd.

They take over the loungers, passing bottles back and forth, music competing from their phones. They aren't much younger than Jo, but they all seem absurdly attractive and happy, and Jo reaches hastily for her sandals, ignoring the bite of their buckles against her tender skin.

Walking away, she allows her sore feet to lead her into the shallows, and the water, threaded pink now, is as soothing as she'd imagined. It laps silkily over her sandals and between each toe, and with the laughter fading behind her, she draws in a long breath. There are gulls scattered like pale, thrown pebbles against the melting sky—everything's beautiful—and the loneliness that hits her is another wave, far colder, rushing in.

ON HER WAY back, Jo stops at a restaurant. She's eaten nothing since her breakfast of crackers, and she's also overwhelmingly thirsty, parched inside and out.

Her sunburnt skin has tightened, each step's a sting, and it's an enormous relief when she's eventually seated. She had to glare at the waiter before he acknowledged her, and Jo's tired, she realises, of feeling like a ghost.

After downing half a pitcher of water, she begins to feel more solid. She takes in the restaurant's age and candlelight, the shadows dancing between its alcoves and the low, grey ceiling beams. The air's dense with the scents of ancient stone and rich tomato sauce, and after ordering tapas, Jo takes out her guidebook again. Determined to ignore the other tables, all those gilded couples, smiling and holding hands.

She treats herself to cava too. It's crisp and clean-tasting, and makes her instantly light-headed. The sensation's vaguely bubble-like, though its distancing effect puts her wholly at ease, and when the words begin to squirm across the guidebook's pages, nobody notices when Jo giggles. *And at least I know I'm here.*

As soon as her meal arrives, Jo tucks in. There are fluffy, spiced potatoes, and bowls of squid in cream, and tiny, curling, salty fish, all Ben's favourite dishes...

But that doesn't matter now. Nothing matters. She orders another sparkling glass.

JO'S ALMOST LOOKING forward to getting lost. She's enjoying the purpling sky and the evening's gentler warmth, and nobody's about to rob or attack her; they can't touch her. *The city*, she remembers, *is a state of mind*, and as she wanders, her sunburn numbs, and the balconies seem as carefree as bunting. But though she could keep walking forever, her apartment block's no longer hiding. She finds it easily.

The lobby lights are already on, and that might have felt welcoming, except as Jo stares across the gleaming floor, her tipsy flush evaporates; her sense of belonging disappears.

The lift's cage is bound, as if in ominous gift-wrap, in bright-striped tape, and though Jo doesn't understand the sign propped up against it, its message is starkly clear. The lift is out of order.

Grounded on the ground floor, she thinks, but she can't even fake a giggle now. Shuffling closer, she sees that the wooden door is shut tight behind the bars and tape, and that a padlock's been clamped to the gate. Everything's sealed. There's only one way up. She'll have to take the stairs...

At the thought, Jo tastes acrid anchovies, and cream, gone sour. She's afraid she might be sick.

But it isn't just the entrance hall that's shining. The stairwell is also illuminated, and under the circumstances, maybe the timer's been disabled? Perhaps the lights will burn all night.

Gathering herself, Jo sucks in a shaky breath, and then, without looking back, she starts to climb. *Only six floors...*

She's panting by the time she's reached the first, and her heart's jumping, and as she whisks past the empty lift shaft, she can't help glancing towards the thick, black shadows contained behind the cage's bars.

Her footsteps clamour against the next flight, though the lights stay on. There's no reason to panic, nothing to make her picture Ben.

Ben, in her kitchen, telling her *no, not yet*. He's sorry; she'll have to go alone.

And nobody knows how alone Jo is. There, on the steps, with the lift's pulleys silenced, she has never been so alone.

But as she reaches the second floor, though her sunburn's flaring and her heart's still beating wildly, she doesn't allow her pace to slow. This time, she's determined she won't look through the cage into the dark.

Except she can't stop herself, and on the third floor, it's even worse. Behind the bars, the black's rolling like oil. It seems about to surge.

Again, Jo tries to tell herself she's okay. She's nearly back at her apartment, and her roof-garden's waiting. All those magical, thriving plants...

For a short while, picturing the terrace genuinely helps. She makes it, perhaps, to the fifth level before the lights go out.

And now the shadows from the lift shaft have erupted, there's nothing for Jo but darkness, and Ben—*there's Ben*—

Blind and helpless, she attempts to keep going, and though she's stubbing her toes on every invisible step and smashing into the clammy walls, she doesn't fall. *I will not fall*—

And suddenly Jo's reached the top.

She's on her floor, the final floor. There's nowhere else for her to go. The skylight's a gauzy square, and by its thin glimmer, she's just about able to see the rough outline of her apartment's door and the well-like hole of the lift shaft.

I'm here, I'm here. I am still here...

But the gate to her cage has been left open, and unable to stop herself, she's turning to that space where the shadows are thickest, imagining creatures struggling up through the oil. There's a sense of straining, and then "Who even *are* you?" Laura's hissing, and "I'm sorry," Jo's saying, "I'm sorry..." Unless those words belong to Ben –

A part of Jo tries to stay on the landing with the skylight and her apartment, and the garden, beyond it, but she isn't there. She's back in her kitchen, and though Ben's fingers are warm, stroking her neck, her hand's stiff with cold and white-knuckled, tightening around the knife.

And suddenly, Jo's moving, raising her arm, her vision clouding as she swings. But through the clouds, there are flashes of silver, and then she's tumbling forwards, and the silver's streaked with red.

But it's Ben who's falling. It's Ben who's sinking down, and down... No longer lost inside her shadow or in the spreading mess she's made.

And now that she's seen—as Jo's finally seeing—exactly what she's left behind, the skylight and her door have completely disappeared. There's only one way through. The cage is ready, the gate wide open, and there's no choice but to keep going back, back to where Ben's still waiting below her.

"Here I am," Jo whispers into the lift shaft. "I'm here, at last." And then she steps out into the dark.

EYES THE DEEPEST BLUE

by

Stephen J. Golds

[...ALSO, MORE BREAKING news this morning: the husband of Kate Haines has reportedly been found dead in a hotel in Shinjuku, Tokyo, Japan. Kate Haines was the Boston lawyer who went missing during the couple's honeymoon in Honolulu, Hawaii — September of last year. We have since learned U.S Marshals were searching for Nick Haines in connection to...]

Two Days Previously

THE KID BEHIND the cash register cast a flickering glance over the photograph, the translation card, and shook his head dismissively. Nodded at the space over Nick's shoulder to the line of customers gathered there.

"No. No, no, please, look properly. Look again." Nick thrust the photograph of his wife up into the guy's line of vision, stammering out the words on the laminated translation card once more.

"Kono josei mita kota ga arimaska? Have you seen this woman? Please, *please."*

The clerk shook his head again. Leaned back and away. Mumbled something about speaking no English. Nick cursed, stepped aside as an old man in a shirt and tie pushed towards the counter with a four pack of beers, bitching underneath his breath in broken English. Nick paid no attention. Stood gazing down at the picture of his wife. The photograph, the last he'd ever taken of her, on their honeymoon. It had become frayed over the last year. Worn around the edges. Creased. Exhausted. Nick supposed he appeared the same way to the people around him. He couldn't remember the last time he'd given a damn about how he might look. When he'd last shaved. His jacket radiated stale sweat and he'd been wearing the same shirt and slacks since he'd gotten on the plane at Daniel K. Airport two days ago. Or was it three? He didn't know. He hadn't slept and the time difference had him all fucked up. Turned around and confused. It didn't matter though. Nothing mattered anymore but finding Kate.

Under the harsh lights of the convenience store his eyes darted and danced over the photograph taking in every minute aspect of his wife. Her bright face. The crooked smile with the slightly chipped tooth. The dimples. The small turquoise butterfly tattoo on her slender shoulder he'd run his tongue and lips over as they made love the morning of the day she disappeared. The slight fading of colors in the picture had done nothing to dim Kate's beauty. Her eyes still stopped his heart. Eyes the deepest blue. Eyes so blue they were almost black. He nearly grinned at the photograph. Her smile always highly contagious. But she was gone. The grin died stillborn. He wanted to scream out, a man long ago awakened from a nightmare into a reality much worse. He swallowed the scream back down his throat. Sighed hard, slipped the picture back into his breast pocket next to his heart, and pushed his palms painfully into his eyes. Pulled the bottle of pills from his side pocket, unscrewed the cap and dry swallowed a couple. Then he turned around and shuffled out of the store into another night-damp and neon-soaked street of downtown Tokyo.

Kabukicho, Shinjuku, was Tokyo's red light district—the Lonely Planet Guide he'd grabbed at a Narita airport bookstore on arrival had told him. Of course, he'd gone to the Japanese cops first. They were less help than the cops back home and in Hawaii had been after Kate disappeared from their hotel. Even the Feds finally believed Kate had simply drowned or changed her mind about the marriage and left him. The only time the authorities had ever shown any kind of interest in really solving the case was in the first few months, when they wanted to pin it on Nick. Case closed. And they would have if over twenty witnesses and security footage at the hotel hadn't backed him up.

The Japanese cops stuttered, stared, fidgeted and clucked their tongues. Speaking a language Nick couldn't understand. They pushed a dozen different forms in front of him with a ballpoint pen. He lost his temper, threw the papers in the air and left.

Completely finished with the authorities in two countries now.

After, he'd caught a taxi to Kabukicho and had remained there. Renting a small room in a cheap business hotel above an inconspicuous and dim noodle shop.

Something on the air, in his guts told him, no, shrieked at him, he was on the right track *this* time. Kate was *here*. He could feel her there. Screaming out his name. Being held against her will in one of the faceless, neon pulsing buildings. The buildings with their own photographs of women, their faces blacked out, pasted to the exterior walls as some kind of crude advertising billboard. Breasts exposed, short skirts hiked all the way up their thighs. The images causing guilt-laced arousal and disgust simultaneously whenever Nick examined them for any likeliness of his wife.

After leaving the last convenience store, he let himself drift aimlessly like a ghost within the riptides of swarming pedestrians for a little while, then stepped out of the crowds into the darkness of an alleyway at the side of the street. Slid the folded piece of paper from the pocket of his slacks, needing to feel it between his fingertips again. To convince himself once more it was real. The print-out of an anonymous email he'd received in Hawaii four days ago. He'd read the damn thing so many times he knew it by heart. A single sentence.

'I'm so sorry your wife is alive in the basement of a whorehouse in Tokyo. X.'

AT FIRST, MOMENTARILY, he didn't know if he should believe it. Could believe it. Calling his parents from a payphone in the departure lounge of the airport, they'd told him it was just another crank. Another hoax pulled by some sicko. Told him to leave Hawaii. To give up the search. It had been a year. Accept she was gone. Come to terms with it. Grieve. Move on. Too many people had been hurt. Too many others had questions needing to be answered. The Press. The Feds. The Cops. People wanted to know why he'd quit his job. Emptied their joint bank accounts. Fled Boston. That was the word his own parents had used; *'Fled'*. He was wanted by the cops in Hawaii. They begged him to come home. Said he needed 'mental' help. Counseling. Therapy. He hung up on them. He was alone.

It was the way the sender had apologized in the brief email that had convinced Nick. *'I'm so sorry.'* Something in those three words had sped up the maddening ticking clock in his skull. Something that had made him rush from the public library he'd made his headquarters in downtown Honolulu.

Quickly selling the old Ford Bronco he'd been living in, traveling around in for the last eight months. He gathered every last cent he had and he had ran. He didn't flee. He wasn't running away. He was running towards Kate. Towards her. For Nick, she was all there was and all there ever would be. He couldn't live the rest of his life with the rotting wound of her absence never healing. The daily irrevocable fact that she was gone wrapped so tightly around his throat like a noose. He couldn't breathe. The utter and complete pitch-black of unknowing. That's what his parents couldn't understand. No one could understand. There was no coming to terms with it. No moving on. No acceptance. There never would be.

IN THE ALLEY, back against a pile of stacked plastic beer crates, his eyes swung slowly back and forth over the greasy piece of paper repetitively, murmuring the words underneath his breath as though it were a Hail Mary— a mantra—and then he slipped it carefully back into his pocket. Pushed the plastic bottle to his mouth and gagged down more of the pills he'd been steadily upping the dosage of for the last few months.

'I'm so sorry your wife is alive in the basement of a whorehouse in Tokyo. X.'
Kate was alive.
Kate was here.

KABUKICHO WAS A madman with a split personality. Nick struggled to become aquatinted to both. Worlds apart from the red light districts of Hawaii he'd frantically ripped apart searching for his wife in the months after her disappearance, following up on every last tip, sighting or rumor. In the daytime, the place was a dull grey wash of commercialism. The scents of miso soup, popcorn, exhaust fumes and green tea a fusion jabbing at the back of the throat. Game arcades blasting inane tunes. The flow of heavy traffic a constant rattling hum in the background. Cracked pavements streaming with shoppers, clusters of laughing school kids and rushing businessmen. Most establishments seemingly waiting in eager anticipation for the hungry darkness to take a chokehold of the streets.

As the night fell like a heavy Fall rain, the place scurried to life like a cockroach infested kitchen. Traffic roared. Music blasted, rattling the fillings in the back teeth. Kanji neon lights flashed, pulsed, blazed, blinded. The senses assaulted. Concussed. Battered into submission. Touts touted. Hawks hawked. Pushers pushed. Hookers hooked. Looped announcements over a speaker somewhere slurring warnings of rip-off bars and credit card fraud in English and Japanese were drowned out by a woman faking high-pitched orgasms on repeat from another. Young women posed outside pink neon illuminated doorways dressed up as high school girls, rabbits, French maids, and leather clad dominatrix, unenthusiastically chanting the same words over and over at passers-by. "Asobou! Play with me! Asobou! Play with me!"

The last few nights had been the same. Repetitive. Nick wasn't sure if it was the pills or the atmosphere of Tokyo's underbelly. Jarring. Disorientating. He felt as though he were being slowly asphyxiated. Drowned. His breath stinking and ragged. He stumbled up to groups of girls waving Kate's photograph and the laminated translation card. The women placed their hands to their lips, shaking their heads. Avoiding eye contact. He staggered, culture-shocked and punch drunk, down the three main strips trying every group of women, every seedy storefront he came across. None of the girls would talk. Seemed scared. Not of Nick, but frightened if they were seen speaking with him. Their eyes darting everywhere but Nick's face. The strange foreigner. He felt as though he were being watched. A sickening feeling of rusty acupuncture needles to the spine. He snatched glimpses of greasy characters standing apart from the crowds. Watching. Waiting. Predators. Pimps. Security. Nick didn't know. Paranoia prickled his flesh akin to a fever sweat. Mouth cotton-ball dry. He popped pills like breath mints attempting to zone himself out. Trying to appear casual. Just another drunken tourist. Pausing, he fumbled with a pack of cigarettes and finally got one lit. The blue smoke drifting demented in the toxic neon. He took a right into another alleyway, telling himself he'd try a street over. The vaporous stench of piss and garbage in the alley was overpowering. Nick's head swam. He gagged and ditched the cigarette. A figure stepped out in front of him from the darkness blocking his way. He startled. Clenched his calloused fists.

"Sex?"

It was an older woman awash in shadow. Dyed blonde hair and a halter neck top cut low, revealing a deep scar of cleavage. Face intensely, darkly lined. Not Japanese. A foreigner like him. A cluster of raw sores around her mouth wept glistening in the lone street light. Dark bruises or makeup or both smothered around her eyes.

"What?" Nick stuttered.

"Sex and massage?" She grinned faux-shy, teeth chipped and nicotine yellow. Casting quick, cautious glances around them both.

"You speak English?" Nick said.

"Yeah, I speak English. You want sex and massage?"

"Where are you from?"

"Columbia, you know? I've already got hotel room, over there," she pointed to a dimly lit small building with a purple neon sign flashing erratically above what looked like a security door further down the alley. "We can kiss, shower together. Sex and massage. I can suck you. Ten thousand yen. Hotel charge extra. Hotel tax, you know?" She grinned again. Her eyes were black, worn stones embedded cruelly in her face. Nothing alive moved in them.

"No, no, I'm sorry. I just want to talk with you," Nick reached for the photograph and card in his chest pocket and the woman took a few steps back. Wary. "No, wait. Please. Have you seen this woman? She's my wife. She's an American like me. She's thirty years old."

On hearing the word wife, the woman seemed to completely lose interest in Nick. Her shoulders sagged. Looking blankly through him down the alley for the next potential customer. Nick momentarily felt like a ghost again. As though he'd been dead since Kate disappeared and was still desperately trying to communicate with the living.

"Please, just take a look at the photograph."

She took a few more steps back. Turning away from him slightly.

He pulled a few crumpled cash notes from the inside pocket of his leather jacket, held them out. The woman snatched the bills and the photograph out of his fingertips before he'd even seen her move towards him.

She frowned down at the photograph, sucking at her swollen bottom lip. "Yeah. I see this woman, maybe. Six, seven months before. When I first come," she said tonelessly, squinting down at the photograph.

Nick's breath left him. He tapped at the picture frantically, "This woman? You've definitely seen her?" He wheezed.

"*Maybe*, I say. I don't know. Her hair was color black, cut very short like boy. Not blonde and long like in photograph, but this," she scratched a long, sharp, blood-red fingernail against the turquoise butterfly tattoo on Kate's shoulder. "I remember this. This butterfly tattoo. And her eyes. I remember very blue. Very beautiful."

"It was an American woman? You're sure."

"I don't know. This woman they call her 'moku moku'."

"Moku moku? What does it mean?"

"Muda. Mute. She never no speak. Nothing. She adicta. Trouble."

"Adicta?"

The woman tapped at her forearm with a finger. Syringe sign language. Nick cursed. That cold beating started to throb behind his eyes. He gripped at his knees, sucked in the dirty air. Trying to calm himself. The woman giggled and tutted.

"Where did you meet her?" He asked as he unscrewed the pill bottle and shook a few quickly onto his tongue.

She tutted again. "I can't remember. Always they move the women. Customers bored same girls, same girls, same girls. They change. Always moving, always changing. They sell us on. Each time cheaper, cheaper, cheaper. Each time worse, worse, worse. I am here eight months only. Now put out on street like dog. I'm still the best, you know? They don't cut me like some. Hey, you waste my time. You want fuck or no?"

Nick breathed slowly. Wiped a sick sweat from his face. Tried to compose himself. "Did you see her around here? Nearby here? Please."

She thrust the photograph quickly back at his chest, "I say six or seven months ago. Now? I don't know. You go to hotel with me now?"

"Please, are you sure? I need to know. I'll pay more," he pulled out a few more crumpled bills and she wrenched them away like a starving animal accepting scraps. She looked him up and down. Examining. Scrutinizing. "You come with me to hotel. Private place. I tell you much more."

"Okay," Nick said. He followed her further down the alley. Her perfume stinging his eyes. The echoes of her high heels hitting the concrete like gunshots. His heart beating so damn fast he wondered if he was having a heart attack. Trembling. Mouth dust dry. The Columbian placed two fingers in her lips and let out a shrill whistle and giggled again, this time there was something nervous in it. That feeling like rusty needles aching in his spine again. Nick brushed the sensation away. Kate's photograph scorching hot through the cotton of his shirt and into his flesh. Throbbing like a heartbeat. *Kate. Kate. Kate.* Her name over and over. He would take her away from this fucking place. Far away. Save her. Make everything better for her again. He didn't care what it took. They'd get over all this shit together. He should've protected her. Should've been there for her. He would never leave her side again. Everything would be okay. Everything was going to be alright once they were together again.

It was only as they got closer to the hotel Nick realized the woman had quickened her pace away from him. The hotel wasn't a hotel at all. It looked as though it was some kind of Chinese medicine store and it was closed. Graffiti scrawled shutters pulled down. Two of the upper windows smashed-in.

Pain exploded at the base of his neck. He tumbled hard into the rusted shutters. Angry voices cursing in indecipherable tongues. Metal shook and rattled. Fists rained down. Fireworks flashing in starless skies. A heavy blow to the face. Another. Another. His nose ruptured, sending brutal currents of pain to the center of his brain. He thought he heard the Columbian woman giggling again. Shrieking something in Japanese. He swallowed blood. On his hands and knees. The concrete hot and damp. Slick. Two or three sharp kicks in the side put him on his back. Something inside his rib cage snapped like the overwound string on a guitar. Shoes scraping over pavement in a mad, frenzied dance. Hands tore at his pockets. He held his fist tightly over his breast pocket. Begging them not to take Kate away from him again. Take the money, but please just leave Kate. Leave her alone.

A voice bellowed from the other end of the alley. A world away. Another kick snapped his head back.

"Yes, you fucking were, Nick."

"Okay, so what if I was talking to the waitresses? They're the waitresses!"

"Not waitresses. The waitress. Just one. Her."

"Come on! She was just being nice, Katie."

"Every time I turned my back, or went to the bar or something, she was sniffing around you, shoving those gross plastic tits in your face, acting like some kind of fucking bitch in heat. Did you tell her we were on our honeymoon?"

"No, come on, that would've just been weird."

"No, it wouldn't have. I bet you just loved the attention, didn't you?"

"Do you want me to tell everyone I meet that we're on our honeymoon? Hi, I'm Nick, we're on our honeymoon. Hi, I'm Nick, I'm on my honeymoon. Hi, I'm Nick, we're on our honeymoon. You want me to sound like some kind of fucking Stepford Husband now that we're hitched, that it?"

"You were fucking flirting again!"

"Oh, please. No, I wasn't. You're drunk, Katie. I told you we shouldn't be drinking so heavy."

"I know I'm drunk, but I also know you're a piece of shit who fucks everything that walks or crawls. I know it! Know it all too well!"

"I married you, didn't I? When are you going to forgive me and forget about my mistakes? It's like you want to punish me all the time."

"It was my best friend, Nick!"

"Do we really need to have this conversation again? On our fucking honeymoon too."

"I want to be on my own for a little while. I really need to think. I'm going out for a walk."

"On the beach? Now?!"

"Maybe. I don't know. But I want a little space."

"Are you serious? It's pitch-black out and you can hardly walk straight. Don't be crazy."

"I'm fine. You can stay here and call that little whore up for room service."

"Go and fucking sober yourself up then, Katie!"

A door slammed.

Kate.

He coughed up something boiling, swallowed it back down with an aftertaste of blood. Rubbed at his breast pocket, sighing deeply at the outline of her photograph. They had left him with that at least. His fingers slowly found their way to the cool metals of his Rolex and his wedding ring. Still had those too. The pockets of his jacket had been torn open. Billfold and cash gone. He cursed, prodded at his nose and hissed. Cursed again. Broken. Couldn't open his eyes. Swollen. Stuck shut with blood. He used his index finger and thumb to pry them open. Tender as hell. Yellow light on dim. A single unslept in bed. A desk. A television. A chair. Slumped in the entrance of his motel room. He couldn't remember how he'd gotten back there. It didn't matter. He pushed himself up the wall slowly. Locked the door and pulled the chain across it. Agony to move. Every muscle and joint screamed. Touching the ribs on his right side made him scream through gritted teeth. Breath coming out in a jagged, wheezed panting.

The Columbian had recognized Kate. That hadn't been a con. He was sure of it. He'd seen it in her eyes. Recognition. Real recognition. Kate *was* here. Knowing that he was finally a few steps closer to her was worth a thousand beat downs and every last red cent.

He undressed slowly, dropping his clothes to the floor and staggered into the shower. The water flowed warm and soothing and pink down the plughole. He let it run over his body for a long time before he attempted to wash himself.

THE TIME ON his Rolex Submariner illuminated twenty past eleven. Too much damn time gone. Wasted. He yanked on the same damp, blood-stained clothing. Groaning and hissing with each small movement. Avoiding the reflection in the mirror above the sink, he swallowed a handful of pain killers with the remnants of the other pills and the half-drunk bottle of whiskey next to the bed.

After, he wrapped the empty liquor bottle in a moist bath towel and stamped on it. Picked through the broken shards. He examined the jagged neck, pushing the pad of his thumb against the sharp points. Stabbed at the air with it and then slipped it into his side pocket. It wasn't perfect, but it was better than nothing. This wasn't home. There were no guns in this country, but he wasn't about to let anyone else steal anymore of his time. He pulled the last rolls of bills from their hiding place underneath the mattress, and counted them out on the duvet. Five hundred thousand yen. He didn't know what that meant in dollars, but he did know it was the very last of his cash. It was return to Boston with Kate or bust-out. He wasn't leaving without her this time. He swore it to God and the empty hotel room.

BACK OUTSIDE ON the street another light rainfall had thinned the crowds. Puddles reflecting illuminated street signs and storefronts made the whole place a twisted hall of mirrors. Nick's head throbbed. The pills had him hyperaware and coasting simultaneously. He wiped a trickle of something warm from his upper lip and tried to enter one of the first places he came across. A narrow, white plastic-looking building on the corner of the block. A luminous sign shaped like a pair of lips pulsed out its name—*The Love Palace.* He shoved his way through the PVC garbed girls clustered outside the doorway and plunged through the entrance. Bass thick music pounding, shadows and cigarette smoke permeated. A coatroom to the left. An elderly woman hunched behind something akin to a bank teller's cage on the right. A sumo wrestler with his hair tied in a top-knot and obese frame barely contained within a tight-fitting tuxedo flanked by a wiry, younger man with gold chains and a punch-perm stood in front of an extra set of interior doors blocking his way. They grappled him, shoving him back out the entrance hard onto his ass. The broken bottle neck jabbing painfully into his hip. The girls scattered, tittered, tutted and giggled.

"I'm an American. I'm an American looking for an American woman," he pleaded with the two men.

They sneered. Cursing at him in words Nick didn't understand and didn't need to.

"Japanese customer only. No foreigners here," the sumo wrestler held out his meaty arms crossed in front of his chest in an X gesture, then turned around and shuffled back into the smoky, sickly sweet aroma of the club laughing.

Punch-perm grinned around the cigarette he was lighting. Nick noticed the pinky and ring finger on his right hand were missing. Just smooth, fleshy stumps. He spat on the concrete and spoke in perfect English, "Why did you come to Japan if you want to fuck American girls? You should go back home, huh?" He helped Nick back up on his feet. A car honked its horn repetitively down the block.

"I'm looking for someone," Nick said.

"This club is just for Japanese; you can only come in here if you have a Japanese friend with you. You have no Japanese friends with you, so you need to go to the place with the foreign girls. Foreigners can go inside okay there."

"You have foreigners in there?" Nick pointed back into the doorway.

"No foreigner girls here. Just Japanese. Japanese kyabakura, you know? Hostess club."

"Where are they? The places with American girls?"

"The foreign places are the cheapest or the most expensive clubs in Kabukicho. You need to go up or you need to go down. Depending on what you like. What you want to pay," punch-perm shrugged, blew smoke at the night sky. "What happened to your face, American? You look like Bruce Willis! Die Hard, huh? I love American Hollywood."

Nick ignored the question, asked his own, "How do I find them? The places with American girls?"

"Don't worry," he sniggered with a grin like a broken bottle. "They will find you."

"Wait, please, have you seen this woman?" Nick pulled his wife's photograph from his breast pocket holding it up to the moldy yellow light of a street lamp.

Punch-perm frowned at the picture, waved the hand with the missing digits in front of Nick's eyes, "I've seen too many like her. Looking for women around this place can sometimes get you in trouble." He bowed very slightly, "Good luck, Die Hard, you will need it." He tossed his cigarette into the gutter and turned back inside.

THE NEXT PLACE Nick tried was a small basement club a Nigerian tout dressed as a New York rapper guided him to with the promise of "cheap white pussy and cheaper drinks."

Electric blue lighting. Wall-to-wall mirrors and a stifling atmosphere pregnant with cigarette smoke and perfume greeted him like a hammer blow to the synapses. He limped past two businessmen bickering at the bar and slid into the booth nearest the door. Scanning faces. His eyes stung. Couldn't see his wife. That old feeling of bitter disappointment crushing inside his guts. He clamped his throbbing eyes shut. Massaged his brow. More time wasted. He swallowed another handful of pick and mix pills.

Girls were scattered around the room, two to a booth. Blondes. Eastern European features. They looked happy enough. Dressed in stilettos and tight, bright dresses. Pouring drinks and fawning over the drunken Japanese clientele. At the far end of the bar a redhead was over-enthusiastically singing *Fantasy* by *Mariah Carey* on a karaoke machine. Nick was about to get up and leave when two of the women squeezed into the booth either side of him blocking his departure. One held a bottle of champagne and the other dangled three champagne flutes from her fingers.

"No, no, no. No champagne for me, please. I was just leaving. I was supposed to meet a friend, but it looks as though I've made a mistake and have the wrong bar. Very sorry," he waved his palms in front of himself in the international gesture of no. One of the women poured the champagne and the other started rubbing at his thigh playfully as though they hadn't heard a single word he'd said. Their hungry eyes locked onto his and smiling with teeth glowing florescent in the blue hazy lighting. A ruddy faced, white man wearing a green Fighting Irish baseball cap and a black polo shirt sat across the room on his own grinned at Nick and raised a bottle of Budweiser in salutation.

"Stay with us a little while, please. We haven't spoken to anyone interesting all night, especially foreign man," the champagne pourer looked as though she was in her early twenties, but had the voice of a fifty-year-old heavy smoker. Russian accented.

The one on Nick's right side moved her hand higher up his thigh to squeeze his prick. The human contact made him ache. He closed his eyes briefly and thought of Kate. The last couple of months, whenever he thought of his wife, the memories were restricted to the photograph version of her. He found himself willing the static image into some kind of fraudulent reanimation. It felt profane and Nick despised himself for struggling to remember her and how she really was. He wasn't even sure which of his memories of Kate were genuine or which ones were the guilty creations of his own desperate, tortured mind.

He could feel the red-faced man across the room watching him intently. He pulled the girl's hand away and dropped it onto the fake leather seating. She pouted across the table at her friend, but said nothing. Nick pushed the glass of flat looking champagne away and placed Kate's picture in front of the Russian girl on his left.

"I'm looking for this woman. Have you seen her?"

She sipped at her drink, crossed her legs high and croaked out a tired bark of laughter.

"Are you some kind of policeman?"

"Do I look like a cop?"

"No, you don't, but you are acting like one, yes? An American cop on vacation, yes?"

"What happened to your face? Someone beat you bad?" the one on the right asked in a polish accent. Nick ignored her, keeping his focus on the older Russian.

"Have you seen this woman or not?" he said.

"Why you waste our time? We should go to another table. We want fun talk. Drink the champagne, it's so yummy. Let's have fun. Party, party, party." She held out the glass to Nick and he slapped it out of her hand. It smashed on the tabletop and the girls pushed themselves quickly out of the booth, shrieking and squawking towards the barman. Two skinheads appeared from behind a black curtain. White. Probable Russians. Little Putins on steroids.

One of them grabbed Nick by the lapels of his jacket, dragging him out of the booth towards the cash register. The strength of the man shocked and awed Nick.

"You fucking pay, man. You fucking pay now."

Nick grappled with the thick, tattooed fists biting down on him. His feet slipping on the tiled flooring. Another girl started warbling *TLC's Waterfalls* on the karaoke machine which had been turned up to its full volume. The speakers vibrated. Sound distorted. All the patrons appeared to have found things of fascination at the bottoms of their glasses. All heads down. All eyes unseeing. Un-witnessing. Except the guy in the green baseball cap. He was still watching intently. Amused. The blue lights flickering gleefully in his dark eyes. Thick lips turned up slightly at the ends in a near sneer or smile. Thug number two sucker punched Nick hard in the guts and he collapsed onto his knees, inhaling desperately. Lungs burning. Hand in the pocket of his jacket squeezing down on the neck of the broken bottle. He didn't want to use it, but it was starting to look as though he would be forced to. Hurting people had caused his search in Hawaii to get out of control. More difficult. Fucked up. He didn't want that to happen again. Not in Japan where everything was already complex. Alien. Not when he was so close to finally finding Kate.

Two pairs of scuffed army boots were joined by a pair of brown, expensive looking loafers. Harsh, murmured conversation. Nick kept his head down, choking for oxygen. Fingers wrapped even tighter now around the broken neck of Jim Bean. He twisted his body slightly towards the door. Glanced at it. Seemed far away. The boots moved out of his line of vision. The loafers remained. Nick was pulled to his feet by invisible hands for the second time in an hour and moved gently out of the door. He released his grip on the makeshift knife in his jacket pocket.

OUTSIDE NICK COLLAPSED on the damp steps leading back up to the streets and sucked in the bitter night air. Pop music from the bar still vibrating sickly through the soles of his feet. He vomited.

"What's the matter, kid? You don't like Russian broads or something?"

Nick squinted up at the large silhouette casting a thick shadow like an oil slick over him. The bones in his neck cracked audibly. The guy in the green Notre Dame cap was smiling down at him.

"Thanks for helping me get out of there." Nick nodded.

"You look like you've been getting a raw deal of it lately, judging by your face. Your nose is broken. In case you didn't know it. Besides it weren't nothing. Those little pricks know not to fuck around with me. Bring a lot of business their way. Fucking Russians though, am I right or am I right? Pricks."

"You're not wrong. You're an American too?"

"Certainly born one. Chicago, but I haven't been back there for a long, long time. The world is my playground now. Name's Grover. Grover Cleveland." He stuck his hand out to shake and Nick took it. The man's palm was dry ice. The grip too tight.

"Grover Cleveland? The twenty-fourth president? You giving me a fake name?" Nick squinted at the man.

"The twenty second *and* the twenty fourth president. Besides, Does it really matter if it's my real name or it ain't? We're all strangers when we die anyhow."

"No, I guess you're right. It doesn't matter. Name's Nick. That's my real name though."

"I wouldn't doubt it for a second, Nick. Pleased to make your acquaintance, pal."

"Pleased to meet you too, Grover Cleveland."

The man with the fake name readjusted the baseball cap on his head, wiped the sweat from his face with his forearm and started up the stairs. "Come on, Nick. Let's go and get a real fucking drink, shall we?"

Nick glanced at his wristwatch. Twelve fifty-five. "I'm sorry, I appreciate you helping me out and all, but I don't have the time."

"Nice watch, that's a real Rolex, right?"

"I'm sorry. I've really got somewhere I need to be."

"Oh, I don't doubt that for a second either, buddy. However, you're in one of the biggest red-light districts in the whole wide world, and it looks to me, kind of like you don't know a pussy hole from a sushi roll. I think, just maybe, you're in desperate need of a tour guide, my friend."

Nick used the metal stair railing to pull himself groaning to his feet and followed after Grover clutching at his side.

GROVER GULPED DOWN his third Sambuca, slammed the glass down on the bar, and nodded to the barman for the same again. He gazed at Nick with eyes red raw from alcohol or heartbreak.

"I fucking knew I recognized you," he wiped at his mouth with a paper napkin and chuckled. Nick sipped at a beer, lit up his fifth cigarette and checked his wristwatch.

"Your wifey, she ran off on your honeymoon and you took a baseball bat to a whole bunch of whorehouses in Honolulu or some shit, right? I saw the news. You even made the Japan Times. Just a small column. I keep track."

"My wife didn't run off," Nick spat, fist drained white on the beer bottle.

"All right, buddy. Jesus. Don't get all testy now. I'm just saying what the news was saying is all," Grover shrugged. Chuckled again.

"She's here. I know it," Nick said, stubbing his cigarette out in the ashtray. Orange sparks flew.

"How could you know a thing like that? She's probably still in Hawaii shacked up with another asshole. Looky here; I go to Hawaii all the time on my buddy's private plane and, each time, leaving gets that little more harder. Paradise on earth. Pussy to die for. What the hell makes you believe she's here in Japan of all places? The whole things for the birds." He licked his blue-tinged lips.

"No, I know she's here. Know it in my heart. I don't know why Japan. None of it makes any sense. And I got this email. Here, see," Nick unfolded and smoothed out the printed email on the sticky bar top. He read the words out loud in a voice that wavered and croaked, "I'm so sorry your wife is alive in the basement of a whorehouse in Tokyo. Kiss."

"Who sent that to you?"

"I don't know. It was anonymous. But if I got an email like this saying she was in Timbuktu, I'd catch a plane there."

Grover scoffed.

"Well that ain't a kiss."

"What do you mean?" Nick shook pills into his palm and washed them down with warm Heineken. Lit another smoke. His hands trembled.

"I'm so sorry your wife is alive in the basement of a whorehouse in Tokyo. X. See, the X mark? It ain't a kiss mark like you think it is. It's the name of a club. Club X. A very special kind of club catering to a very special kind of clientele."

Nick coughed up beer and smoke. "What?! Have you been there?"

"Sure, a few times. Not really my bag, but what sells sells."

"You've got to take me there now."

"Woah, woah, buddy. You need to forget about all this. Go home. Move on with your life. I'm trying to save you from a lot more fucking pain here. I'm trying to be a nice guy. Trying to get some good karma over here."

"Just show me where the place is."

"Doesn't work like that, buddy. You need to be a member or accompanied by a member to *even* get a foot in the door. They got security up the fucking wazoo. Then there's the entrance fee, that's two and a half thousand fucking bucks a head. For thirty fucking minutes! This ain't your usual cathouse is what I'm trying to say here. We're talking fucked up VIP cathouse."

"Are you a member?"

"I'm a member of a lot of places." He shrugged. "That's part and parcel of being Grover Cleveland."

Nick slapped the last two rolls of cash on the bar. "There's over five hundred thousand yen there."

Grover raised his eyebrows, took off the baseball cap and wiped at his bald and scarred head with another napkin. "I can see that, but it's still a no. There are some places that shouldn't be gone to."

"You're a fucking member!"

"Like I said before, that's something else entirely, buddy. I felt bad for you, so I'm trying to help you out."

Nick unclasped the Rolex from his wrist, held it dangling in front of Grover's face for a moment and then pushed it into the man's moist palm. "So help me! Take me there now. Get me in. That's all I want. All I need. Please, I'm begging you."

Grover threw another Sambuca to the back of his throat and licked his lips again. Something reptilian flashed in his eyes for a split second.

THE RAIN CAME heavy like tears from the eyes of screaming children. The streets dead. Haunted. The dark blue of early morning birthed like a premature infant.

Nick stood swaying, glaring at the three story building in front of him. "What the fuck is this, Grover? It's a fucking parking garage."

Grover laughed heartedly. The sound of it carried booming out into the silence like a dysfunctional car alarm.

"Don't be so god damned naïve, buddy. It just *looks* like a parking garage. You think places like this survive operating out in the open? It's kind of like that secret VIP bar they got in DisneyLand. Sort of like an urban legend but not. Come on," he waved Nick to follow him up to the empty cashier booth. They both peered through the cloudy Plexiglas. The booth was sparse. Just a phone and a paper calendar on an empty desk. Grover waved into a single security camera above their heads and grinned teeth stained bright yellow by spotlights. He held up two fingers in the peace sign and then fingered a code into a security lock embedded in the structure next to the window. Then an electric whining as a small alcove slid open to reveal a pneumatic tube and a cylindrical container. Nick watched as Grover counted out the bills and pushed them into the tube.

"Watch this shit. Gets me every time. So fucking cool. Wish I could pay for everything this way. The future is now."

There was a harsh sucking sound as the capsule disappeared down the tube and into a hole in the wall. "Thing reminds me of my ex-wife," Grover elbowed Nick. Nick wiped sweat from his eyes. Heartbeat jacked. Reached for the pills in his side pocket. Shook the container. Empty. He cursed and tossed it.

After a few moments there was another high-pitched electric whine as a thick metal door to the side of the men automatically unlocked and creaked ajar. Red light the color of emergency sirens leaked out like a splash of blood. Music. He knew the song. *Schubert—Ave Maria*. One of Kate's favorites, it had been played at their wedding. He closed his eyes and was dancing with her again. Her white wedding dress underneath his fingertips. Eyes the deepest blue.

"Wakey-wakey, Romeo." Grover bowed and waved an arm theatrically towards the door. "All the answers to your needless questions await. Welcome to Club X, buddy. I tried to warn you. I really did. This ain't a Honolulu whorehouse. Remember I tried."

Nick stumbled up to the door. Breathless. Hyperventilating. Bathed in scarlet. The door clanked shut and automatically locked behind them.

"How do we get out later?" Nick asked.

Grover looked like the devil in the spotlights. Drenched in crimson and full of sin.

He shrugged. "Well, we won't be leaving this way, buddy."

A long, wine-red corridor led steadily down to another door. Nick staggered and limped along quickly, his palm pressed to the hot, smooth wall for support. A sweet smell like almonds on the air crawled down his air passages to settle at the back of his throat. In his lungs. He vomited into his hands again as he elbowed open the second door onto darkness and light. He remembered once going to a night aquarium show with Kate when they'd first started dating. The huge tanks of brightly colored tropical fish lit up blue as the only source of light. The audience moving slowly in the darkness, peering through the glass at the beautiful flailing creatures. It was so damn similar he thought. Except the smell. The stench. Medicinal aromas mixed with the stink of blood and semen.

Small groups of people, shapes made grotesque by jerking movements and gestures, crowded in front of murky glass windows. He turned around to look for Grover but saw only dark twisted shapes resembling monsters from childhood nightmares.

He pushed his way a little closer to the nearest window. Hand palsied, shoved deeply in pocket. Fingers tight around the bottle shard. Trembling hard enough to make his teeth chatter. Swaying on tiptoes trying to get a better look at what it was the audience were so enraptured with.

Ave Maria reaching crescendo. Inside the aquarium, blood and shit puddled on the light blue floor tiling. A pink and blurred shape convulsing. Nick wiped the sweat from his burning eyes. Blinked. Gagged. Through the glass—a naked thing like a broken store mannequin sprawled on a surgical table writhing. Little more than a torso. Its arms and legs removed at the joints. Amputated. Crudely wrapped in rotten brown bandages. Breasts gone, puckered, pink scars. Mouth cut into an everlasting grin. Nick gagged down vomit again and forced his face closer to the glass.

The thing's shaved, scarred, and scabbed head lolled semi-consciously towards the audience. Nick caught a glimpse of what remained of a shoulder—a small turquoise butterfly tattoo.

It opened its swollen eyes, catching his. Eyes the deepest blue. Eyes so blue they were almost black.

Nick screamed.

THE RAT

by

Noelle Holten

"HE'S GONE. HE'S gone. He's gone…" rocking back and forth, cross-legged on the floor, I dabbed the back of my hand at the blood dripping from my nose and lip. The crashing of the front door slamming into the wall caught me off guard again. Fear took its familiar choking hold of me. I scrambled across the wooden floor, squeezing my aching body behind the chair, forcing my fist into my mouth. Biting down.

"Jess! Jess! Where are you?!"

My shoulders slumped, the coiled tension leaving my body. It was Cara, my sister-in-law; a friend, not a foe.

Pulling myself up, I turned my face towards the shadows, teased my sweat dampened hair forward until it hung over my face. I didn't want her to see what he had done to me. What he had done to me again.

"Oh my god, Jess! What happened?" She rushed over and gently lifted my chin, tilting my face towards the light. Her fingertips warm. "Where is he? I'll fucking rip his balls off." She hissed through gritted teeth as she glared around the room, free hand balled into a fist at her side.

"He's gone…" The words fell stilted from my mouth like broken porcelain.

"Right then. We're calling the police. They can nab him if he has the nerve to show his face back here again." She turned away from me towards the landline. I grabbed at her. Flailing.

"No! No police… please. I just want to forget about it. He won't be back."

"What the hell, Jess? Why are you *still* protecting him?"

The tears locked tightly inside finally rushed out of me. Quickly. Silently. Tears of upset, tears of sadness. Tears of frustration. Cara didn't understand. She never would. She had the perfect marriage. A husband who adored the ground she walked on. Spoiling her with gifts. Flowers. Tenderness. Love. Kindness. Making her feel... special. My mother had raised a decent man.

"Hey. I'm sorry. Don't get upset. When Debbie called me, I panicked—didn't know what to expect... here..." She pulled a tissue from the box on the table and held it out to me.

Debbie lived next door and couldn't keep her mouth shut if her life depended on it. I sometimes forgot how thin the walls were. She must have heard the argument and instead of coming to see if I was okay, she'd rung Cara. I suppose I should've been grateful it wasn't the police.

Wiping at my eyes, I noticed my tears had mixed with the blood around my mouth and nose and was starting to drip onto the floor.

"Fucksake." I brushed past Cara and grabbed a handful of tissues. "What a mess."

Cara glanced around, taking in the room. The overturned chair. Shattered porcelain. "It's not too bad, I'll tidy it—you just sit down. I'll make us a cuppa first and then start cleaning this place up, okay?"

I hadn't been referring to the room. The broken vase, the spilled tea on the rug in front of the fireplace, or even the shattered picture frame. I let her make her own assumptions. I hadn't the energy to argue and she wouldn't have listened even if I did.

TEN, OR IT could've been fifteen minutes later, Cara returned to the room with two mugs of coffee, and a half-eaten packet of biscuits tucked underneath her arm.

"How are you feeling now? We should really go to A&E." She looked me up and down quickly, the pity evident in her limpid eyes.

"I'm fine. It's just a bloody nose. And a headache. I need some pain killers..." I stood up too quickly, my head spun. I grabbed at the arm of the chair for support.

"Sit back down. I'll get them. Where are they? Bathroom cabinet?"

"No. Second cupboard right of the sink." I aimed a trembling arm towards the kitchen and prayed she hadn't heard the panic in my voice.

Cara headed towards the kitchen but turned in the doorway, looking at me with that same mournful pity again. "I've told your brother. Don't be mad…" Then she was gone.

Why couldn't she just leave things well enough alone. Tommy will be out looking for him now and just stirring up more shit. I hope he doesn't come over. The look in his eyes will break me, and the shame, guilt, embarrassment, and pain will crash to the surface again. I don't need my big brother here. This isn't a playground fight where he can defend me. He won't understand that I just want to forget… move forward and put this awful chapter of my life behind me.

I didn't notice Cara come back into the room until I heard the rattle of a small bottle of pills being shaken in front of my face. I took two pills, gulping them down with a mouthful of coffee.

"Where did he go? Do you know?" Cara asked, as she lowered herself into the chair beside me. The squeak of leather and hiss of air being released from the cushions a welcome distraction.

I shook my head emphatically. Immediately regretted it when a sharp burst of pain tore from my cheek to the top of my forehead. Answering her through gritted teeth as I rubbed my temple. "I've no idea. He won't be back though…"

"His van is still outside. 'Course he'll be back. But don't worry. I'm not leaving, and Tommy said he'll come by later."

*Fuck…*Just what I needed.

"I'm really tired. You can go. I'm just going to have a nap." I began to tuck my legs under me on the couch. Cara grabbed at them.

"Jess. You can't sleep. What if you have a concussion? I really think we should call an ambulance or take you to A&E."

"No! Will you just leave it, Cara? I don't need to go to the hospital. I don't even have a concussion. It's not like… like… this hasn't happened before… I just need to be left on my own…"

I fingered the sore split in my bottom lip as I lied. Lying to Cara, but mostly lying to myself.

Cara sat back, eyes wide staring at me, and I regretted getting so angry, but she just didn't get it. I needed to be alone.

There was a long silence in the flat—a roar of deafening nothing.

"I'm only trying to help…" Cara finally murmured.

143

"I know." I reached out and touched her hand. "I didn't mean to yell, but really, I just want to forget about today... He's gone... and he'll never touch me again." I lied again and the atmosphere fell once more into a void of all the things we couldn't say.

CARA WAS NEVER comfortable with silence, and instead tried to occupy her time by tidying up. Every now and again, I noticed her looking at me from the corner of her eye, but I just stared straight ahead. My gaze locked on the window, on the white van outside with PETE'S PEST CONTROL and a picture of a giant rat painted on the side. Reminding me of my wedding night...

The day I became Mrs Flanagan was both the happiest and saddest day of my life. I should have listened to my mother. Pete and I had met in a bar and dated for eight months before he proposed. I was twenty years old; he was thirty and I was smitten. Never had a man loved me so much—he took me out, bought me little gifts, called me day and night telling me how much he loved me.

Love bombing. That's what they call it. But back then, I didn't know that. I thought, naively like all new lovers tend to be, it was just his way of showing how much he loved me. Turns out I wasn't the only one he bombed with his love.

We had said our vows, proclaimed our love and he'd kissed me with such passion, I beamed when he said 'I do'. However at the reception something had already started to change. I thought he was just tired but there was a definite distance. A coldness. I chose to ignore it. I drank champagne, chatted, and danced until my feet could take no more. Seems so foolish now.

After the reception, on our way through the hotel lobby, Pete had said he needed to use the restrooms and he'd meet me back in the room, but I didn't want to go into the honeymoon suite on my own. I wanted to walk in as husband and wife, so I hung back in the lobby. Waiting for him. My husband. I was staring out of the big glass windows overlooking the beautifully manicured front lawns of the hotel, when I caught a glimpse of a woman in a red dress heading to the toilets. She had dropped something and as I got closer, I realised it was her key card. She'd need that. I headed towards the toilets but when I entered the ladies, no one was there. Every cubicle door stood wide open and vacant. I'd just leave the key card at reception, I thought as I fixed my hair in the mirror and put on a fresh coat of lip gloss.

I should have stayed there. Staring in the mirror, at the reflection of a bride. Eyes so bright with hope and contentment. And love. But I didn't.

The woman in the red dress was coming out of the gents as I left the ladies, giggling as Pete grabbed her arse from behind before he spotted me. I couldn't speak. I just stared at the pair of them, waiting for some kind of an explanation. My mind screaming at me it wasn't what it seemed. But it was. I'd just married a cheater. A cheating rat.

"What the hell is going on?" My voice broke. I threw the key card at the woman's feet. She didn't stick around. She picked up the card, shrugged her shoulders at Pete, and brushed by me as if nothing had happened.

"Now don't get your knickers in a twist, Jess." He walked towards me, palms out. "She just went into the wrong toilets is all, and we were having a little laugh about it..."

"Do you think I'm an idiot? You grabbed her arse. I fucking saw you! Do you do that to a lot of random girls?" I turned to walk away, and he grabbed my arm. His fingers pinching into my flesh. "Don't touch me!" I tried to wriggle free, but he squeezed tighter. The pain forcing me into motionlessness.

"Are you calling me a liar? Do you seriously think I'm such a bastard that I'd cheat on you? On our wedding day? What kind of man do you take me for?" He shoved me hard backwards against the wall and stomped towards the elevators. I saw a concierge watching from down the hall and bowed my head.

Maybe I had seen it wrong. Maybe it was all innocent, Pete had always been a total flirt—was I being a jealous wife? "Pete! Wait..." I dashed after him as fast as my wedding dress and heels allowed. "I'm sorry. It just took me by surprise... of course you wouldn't do that to me." I was embarrassed I'd even thought it and wished I could've taken back my accusation.

He held the elevator doors open looking me up and down slowly. His mouth like a hard scar gouged in his lower face. A winter coldness in his eyes. I didn't see it at the time, but it was the first red flag, one of many, that I shouldn't have ignored. But I was young, newly married and in love.

FINGERTIPS ON MY shoulder. "Earth to Jess. Hey! You okay? You were miles away. What were you thinking about?"

"Uh. Nothing. Sorry—just... never mind." I didn't want to talk about it.

Cara nodded as though she understood. "Where should I put this? Is there enough room in the kitchen bin, or should I use the one out back?"

She held up the dustpan of broken things she had collected and then poured them into a plastic bag.

"I'll do it." I went to take the bag from her hand, and she pulled away.

"Don't be silly. I'm already standing." She headed towards the kitchen and then called out. "This one's full. I'll take them both out the back."

I swallowed down frustration like a bitter pill. "Cara! Will you just stop! Leave them both in there and I'll sort it out later. Look, I know you're only trying to help, but I'm tired. Give me another hour and I'll be right as rain and needing to keep myself occupied, okay?"

When she returned to the living room, hands in the air and brow furrowed, I regretted shouting at her again but my eyes still pleaded with her to just go. To give me space.

"I just want to help. What is going on, Jess?"

Had I gone too far?

"I told you. I'm shattered and my face is killing me. I can feel it swelling. That ibuprofen hasn't done a thing…"

"It *does* look like it's swelling up, but if you won't let me take you to hospital, I don't know what to say. How about I make us something to eat… I saw some soup on the stove I could reheat that and…"

"Don't touch that fucking soup!" I jumped up, bumping Cara on the shoulder as I pushed past her on my way into the kitchen, grabbing the pot off the burner and dumping the contents down the sink. I began scrubbing frantically at the pot, my hand aching from the pressure as I pushed down and scraped the bottom of the pot.

"Jess! What the hell are you doing? What is wrong with you? You're acting hysterically." She grabbed at my arm and used her other hand to wrench the pot from my grip. Water splashed over her shirt. She sighed, placed the pot on the counter.

"I'm worried about you," she said, dabbing at her blouse with a stained tea towel. "It's soaked through." She sighed again and turned away from me, starting to walk towards the stairs.

"I'm just going to grab one of your tops, all right?"

Fuck.

I raced past her and blocked the stairs. "You can't go up there…" My legs shook as Cara cocked her head and frowned. "There's some clean clothes in the back room."

"I need the loo." She placed her hand on her hip. "Do I have to piss in the back room as well?"

My hands were trembling and I slid them both into the back pockets of my jeans. Out of her sight. "I'm sorry. It's just a mess up there. That's where the fight started. I just didn't want you to see."

Cara reached out and rubbed my shoulder. Her touch warm and tender, but also patronising. "Sweetheart, I've already seen it a few times before. Why don't we give it a quick tidy and then you can put your feet up. I'll wait with you until Tommy arrives—you look exhausted, but until I'm sure you're not concussed, I'm not going to let you sleep."

I stepped aside and let her pass. Watching her as she made her way up the stairs. She turned, pointing to the left. 'There's a basket of clean clothes here, I'll just grab a T-shirt'

I bit down hard on my lip, opening the split in the flesh wider. All I wanted was for Tommy to come and take her home. Then I could do what needed to be done and after that, rest. Lots of rest. So fucking tired.

IT FELT LIKE hours, but there was no scream. No shouting. Nothing from Cara, except the flush of the toilet. I looked up when I heard her footsteps. She stood at the top of the stairs and stretched; her blouse bundled in her hands.

"I'll just pop this in the hamper. Two secs." She turned and headed in the direction of my bedroom. Everything moved in a thick mist. Slow motion. I scrambled up the stairs. The pain in my face returned, and I caught a glimpse of the raw injuries across my cheek and jaw in the mirror on the landing as I yelled for Cara to stop. But it was too late. She had already entered the bedroom.

"Oh my God, Jess! What h-h-happened? He's… Pete's… Oh my God."

I stared past her at the body of my husband slumped on the floor. Soup or blood or both splashed across the walls like paint. The mug, I'd served the soup in, smashed to small pieces, looking like the white teeth of rats scattered across the floor around him.

Then Cara's hands on my shoulders, shaking me. Softly at first, then harder. I couldn't speak. Pete's eyes were wide open, mouth a bitter grimace and his hands locked in an odd position as if he was reaching out… for me.

"Jess! Tell me what happened." She was leading me out of the room, towards the bathroom. I heard the water running from the tap and then something cold brushed against my hand. "You're in shock. Drink this."

She directed my hands towards my mouth, and I gulped the water down slowly, knowing that the moment the last drop touched my lips, I would have to explain.

When the water was drained, the plastic cup dry, I looked Cara in the eyes, and told her what happened.

I KNEW HE was drunk and angry as soon as I heard the back door slam. The bellowed shouting. It was how it always started.

I was still in bed, exhausted from another restless night. My insomnia had returned with a sick vengeance. I pulled the duvet over my head and ignored him. Pleading silently for him to just stay downstairs. Begging for this time to be different. But my silence was a mistake. One I would be forced to pay for.

He stamped up the stairs. Screaming out the words 'lazy bitch' over and over again like a mantra. He ripped the duvet from the bed exposing me. Trembling so hard, it was as though I was in the midsts of a deathly fever.

"Where did you fucking put it, you bitch? Get up and find me those boxes, I have a big job coming up and I need it. I fucking want it now."

"I'm so sorry. I'm sorry. I don't know what you're talking about?" I rubbed at my eyes feigning sleep, sat up and reached for my dressing gown. Buying time. I knew what he was talking about, but he called me dumb all the time so that's how I acted. Sometimes it calmed him down. Other times it didn't.

"The fucking rat poison—the boxes from my dad. Stop messing me about, you dumb little bitch." He growled the words through gritted teeth. Spittle flew from his mouth.

"I'm sorry, I'll go look now. No need to get upset. No need to talk to me like that." He hated when I talked back.

"Get out of my face and find those boxes or there'll be real upset…" He headed towards the desk, the makeshift office in the corner of the room where he worked on his invoices.

I wrapped my dressing gown around me and slid my feet into my slippers. "Have you checked the shed?"

"Of course I fucking did. Are you deliberately trying to wind me up?" He wouldn't even look at me, and I'm glad he didn't, as a smirk suddenly broke out across my face. It was like a flower kept in a damp, dark place had finally blossomed. It felt beautiful.

"Okay, I'll have a look around. Are you hungry?"

He grunted as he shuffled through the invoices. "Yeah. I'll have some of that soup. In a mug, not a bowl. And make sure it's not too hot."

He'd always been a fussy eater. I used to love cooking, until his demands became ever more annoying. His bread had to be sliced a certain way. His food separated on the plate— God forbid if his potatoes touched his meat. I had made a large pot of his favourite soup and baked a fresh batch of crusty rolls for tea last night and hoped he would want the leftovers today.

I was humming when I got to the kitchen. Turning the knob on the oven to medium heat and grabbing a spoon to stir in the special spice I'd be adding today. I opened the cupboard under the sink, pulled on the plastic gloves I used for washing up, pushed aside the bottles and grabbed the last box of rat poison from Pete's dad. I had dumped the others. This poison had been discontinued in 2006 because it contained strychnine, but his father had never destroyed his overstock and Pete still used it occasionally. And I was so glad he did.

I only had one shot. I was banking on the greedy bastard taking a big slug of the soup before the piece of shit realised what I had done. I still hadn't figured out what I was going do afterwards, with the body, but that wasn't going to stop me.

I dumped half the box of poison into my granite mortar, picked up the pestle and began crushing the pellets into a fine dust. Holding my breath. When I was done, I stood back, arms outstretched and dumped the contents into the boiling soup. Stirred until the powder blended with it completely. I ground some black pepper in and then ladled the warm soup into his favourite mug. Removed the gloves, chucking them in the bin—I'd get rid of them properly later, and carefully picked up the mug of soup to take upstairs to my dear, soon to be dead, husband.

He was sitting on the bed, talking on his mobile phone when I entered the bedroom. I stood in the doorway, trying to steady my shaking hands, while I waited for him to get off the call. I didn't wonder who he was talking to. I already knew. It was another woman— another new piece on the side.

"Okay, doll. I'll see what I can..." He turned around and glared at me. "I gotta go. Speak later." Tossed his mobile on the pillow. "You spying on me now?"

I just bowed my head. He needed to drink the soup. I wasn't going to do anything that would make him angry now.

"Here, drink it before it goes cold." I placed the mug on his desk. He eyed me strangely. Shit. Did he suspect something? Maybe I should have questioned him more about the telephone call. Acted jealous. But he reached for the mug and took a big swig from it.

"Oh, I found that poison you were looking for." His face went red and then drained of colour. "Good soup?" I began backing away as his body started to convulse, soup sprayed all over his invoices and the wall. He staggered to his feet. Shit. I turned and stumbled towards the bedroom door when I felt fingers claw deeply into my shoulder. Then he shoved me with such force into the door I heard the cartilage and bones in my nose splinter. Blood sprayed from my nostrils everywhere, I nearly slipped on the now slick wooden floor.

Pete did slip. Fell on his back, right where he dropped the mug of poison. His breathing became harsh. Raspy. His body shaking. I just stared at his chest, willing him to die fast. Not because I wanted him to be out of his misery quickly, I just wanted him dead. Gone out of my life forever.

And then as if by magic, the convulsions stopped. His choked breathing ceased. He lay there frozen in a macabre position, like he was climbing an invisible ladder. But there'd be no stairway to heaven for Pete. He'd be speeding down the highway to hell. Ironic really, considering how he so loved AC/DC

"That was it. After that I went downstairs, smashed a few things to release the tension, sat on the floor and tried to figure out what I was going to do next. Then you arrived." I told Cara.

SHE LOOKED AT me blankly for what seemed a lifetime before she pulled her mobile phone from her pocket.

"What are you doing?" The pitch in my voice rose with panic. I tried to grab the phone from Cara's hand, but she pulled away, and held her other hand out.

"Stop it Jess! We have to call the police. What were you going to do? Hide the body? What about when people called looking for him—his sister? His mother? His employees? Think about it. Do you want to be looking over your shoulder for the rest of your life?" She started dialling. "You can tell them all about the years of abuse. You just snapped. We'll sort this out." She turned away and spoke to whoever was on the line.

"Okay…" Prison wouldn't be so bad. At least he was finally gone, and he'd never hurt me… or any other woman again.

I slid down the wall. Maybe she was right. Maybe we would figure it out, but my eyes kept swaying to the long, sharp piece of broken porcelain on the floor next to my dead husband and back to Cara speaking hysterically into the phone.

THIS CRUEL MAKER

by

John Bowie

I KEPT THE notion of love alive by pushing it away; well clear of my splintered ricocheting thoughts. The four cold hospital walls were built to hold people like me, but I was already bound by a damaged mind; barricading me in, wrapping me tightly in a self-fulfilled echo chamber made of blood, dishonour and regret. Tenderness was also there with me, kept at an arm's length, I wouldn't let it get too close. Love's wings were too fragile to fly by me now. They'd be crushed in an instant if they dared; left to be carried on a dying man's breath, drifting over oblivion's vanishing point.

It helped to know it was still out there: love. Now pushed to a distance, but still beating. Knowing it existed was enough for the fragments that remained of me.

Through the amnesia, I somehow knew this was all I deserved. To know love, without feeling. First hand, slightly glanced; a final touch of fading warmth in a world of dying embers.

Earth's circadian rhythms forced to give in, submit to my tailored, drug-induced pulses and comatose patterns. Flickers of reality came at me like a run of grainy old films. My mind came close to being awake each day in the early hours after the staff had gone and left my room. A lucidity triggered by the click from the hospital room door as the last to leave locked up. The unsympathetic clicks of that heavy door birthed a universe on the ceiling above my stagnant bed, with a lone flickering light my only sun, and a waning fan the waves and wind of my new mind's auditorium.

With each cycle, I took that stage.

Through the slow opening crack of a weary eyelid, I could see galaxies beneath the peeling flakes of the ceiling. Up to infinity. Surface imperfections and scars transformed into unexplored deserts and mountains rippling over the tired plaster's undulations and morphing tones.

I was everywhere and nowhere. Like a dull pain, only there if you give it attention.

With no memory of what had come before, or aspirations of what could be, memories of voices heard throughout my days in the hospital brought slices of solace, empathy and a glimpse of my buried personality, now lost or wiped clear for good. I could interpret my feelings, measured against other peoples' sounds and voices in my room. Paint pictures. Seeing all their houses, lives, loves and objects of importance. All that made them tick.

These lives were as confusing and without rationale to me as my own predicament. I was a blank disc, at least with them I had something to work with: a daily input. Without them, I was on a treadmill, an overlapping tired disintegrating track, with no appreciation of the start or end of the song. An endless nagging bridge section. They gave point to the journey itself; in vicarious experiences, borrowed, stolen and trespassed on.

I became a cover song to their lives, replaying them, reimagined puppets to that empty auditorium.

Often, as the door clicked and my fluorescent sun flickered and beamed overhead, I felt they, the workers, doctors and nurses about me, were indeed the real trapped ones. Not me. Because they had a chance and weren't embracing it. I was a dead stone in these deep brassic waters and wasn't going anywhere but down.

I knew I was done for. Destined to eventually sink, drifting slowly to the sea bed, to rest forevermore undiscovered. It seemed, despite seeing me every day and witnessing the futility of all our journeys they still chose to tend to my being, stuck on repeat, going nowhere.

Each day brought a penultimate final round of stabs, pills and adjustments before the door closure. As each nurse, porter and doctor left me for another night, so I could explore that ceiling canvas overhead. With it came a twitch in the corner of my mouth. A smile, almost. And no one to see it, to be able to claim that recovery or progress in me. To tick the form on the clipboard, get a gold star and a meat factory bonus.

Maybe that was the point—they didn't wish either: my recovery, or their own recognition. All, mere zombies, trapped in the dog machine, one rung up the ladder from me at best. Why else work in a position only two grades better than my own, locked away from humanity. Slightly better than my own position they nursed and tended to like it mattered: in a coma.

After they left, the seconds were like aeons in my head as my eyes creaked half-open to that sorry peeling grey ceiling.

Time.

Time.

Time again.

Cyclic. And…repeat.

No change, they'd say in the mornings that followed these nights of ceiling exploration. Without witnesses to that attempted smile, I was lost.

So, they kept increasing my dose, delaying my waking further into the blackness and the minutes after they'd gone from my room. And further from the chance at witnessing my struggled signals.

My mind would keep digesting these cycles of events heard, felt and eavesdropped on throughout the days. And as I lay prone, these other souls continued touching me with glimpses into their lives that tentatively crossed the borders of my nightmares, dreamscapes and chemical fuelled madness.

Or was it soberness that brought the madness?

As I might have said, I didn't know what I was: a man drugged to sanity… Or, a sane man drugged to insanity.

Everyone strikes that self-medicated balance. Now, I was prescribed past free will on the matter. Without a choice. The bed walkers around me… they had a choice, but didn't take it.

My balance belonged in others' hands, on clipboards and targets to be met, failed, topped up and adjusted until the system or I broke, or I simply died in the bed.

After they left my room they returned to their own lives. I could not to my own, beyond the ceiling and eavesdropping from a deep sleep, I didn't know what life was anymore. Or worse, had any desire to find out. Something deep inside kept a tight lid on that too. Wrapped up tight, with the love.

Hate was there too. Boxed away, not so far from touch.

These people held me, dosed me and prodded at me like a piece of steak and yet didn't instil any anger behind my eyes. Just curiosity, pity and care simmered and boiled there. Most of all, that curiosity of, who was I that they should devote their vocations to? Why me, and my soiled sheets as they slowly fused to my skin.

I had little or no memory, identity, a past or future to hold on to. And still, they tended to me like I was worth saving and caring for. Yet, also at the end of these days, they triple-locked that heavy steel door on their way out like I was something to fear.

A monster.

Why keep the beast at all? Feeding it by tubes and with those images of your lives in passing… Why should I care if the doctor is unhappily married and he hasn't noticed true love in the tired nurse constantly tagging along by his side yet? Or that poor porter, or cleaner, with a rich gangster brother that never calls. The ideas and things here can make us fat whilst wasting away. Living through them. Travelling in others' shoes without moving. Living without risk or time limit on moments, which is no life at all.

Amnesia held me like a wounded lover. And sooner or later, as they do, it would leave.

What I gleaned about myself was from these interpretations and moralistic judgments over what I'd heard. Noises from these strangers rattled around me and were absorbed during the day as they busied about my bed, arms, head and veins. As if servicing a car with no wheels, with barely enough fuel to tick it over and a windscreen splattered with a thousand miles of off-road detritus.

I was quite a picture, I'm sure.

With my coma-carers, came that retrained empathy and an innate sense of right, wrong and hope: as much as a damaged young child, and as little as a dying veteran on a battlefield after the final tank has left.

I couldn't remember my own name, but I could remember the sound of war. And through the bombs and bullets in my head, it was these strangers, working around me that I felt for most of all. I was next to nothing. Only through these people was I barely something. A naked pulse. A dancing feather in the wind before earth's last thunderstorm that would ground me forever.

THE HOSPITAL PORTER was more of a skivvy and was bitter with it. I'd heard him talking to himself as he cleaned, dusted and moaned like a furious grimy bastard; covered in all matter of strangers' shit. He battered around my room like a drunk looking for his car keys. His frustrations echoed and bounced off the walls and landed in my dreams with rata-tat-tat. It was a sorry game of squash with my mind the echoing court.

He was involved less with cleaning, mainly focussing on the moaning. He farted. Often surprising himself, loud—like a shotgun. He didn't like the surprise of his own involuntary actions, or the smell. Apparently… that was someone else's fault too. His anger with his own flatulence was easy for him to vent at. He wasn't in a coma, strapped to a bed and forced to breathe in a cloud of a stranger's shit particles, wondering why the dreamscapes had turned strangely farmyard related.

He'd made it very clear, life was a chore imposed on him. And he was left as king of the dead flies and wastebaskets… not to mention those bedpans. Don't get him started on those: stink bells, he called them. And true clangers.

He said, no one else had time for his rages, rants and unqualified opinions on life. I did, but couldn't say. To me, they were distilled magic.

Across the canyons of my coma, I felt those chips on heavy shoulders weighing him down. Long hours for fuck all pay, he'd rant on. As well as clanking my bed in enunciations, like it made a difference—those clunking exclamations by brush handle. Capital letters of hardwood against the steel of the frame.

Clunk. Clack.

He didn't know it, but someone very close by was listening to him. Cared even. Someone listening as he dusted the bluebottle carcasses from the flaking window ledge into a shaky palm, and described the action like it was the highlight of his day. Naming each one as he dropped them one by one into the basket. A wing at a time, with the dull rustle of fat dead flies against cheap plastic liner; it was quite unique. Ugly to some, maybe, but to me it was beautiful. Like a small twig breaking in an untrodden Autumn forest.

Crack.

"And I'll tell you another thing, sleeping baby," he'd go on, to only me and the tired furniture. There never was: an… other… thing. It was purely a signal he had more than realised time was up. And it was time to empty the slop bucket and, "get da fuck outta Dodge."

He either loved to hate his predicament, or, had lost all sense of love and was wrapped in something he loathed. Whichever, I felt it and it told me something of myself I'd forgotten or lost. Loving hate. Or, hating to love.

The opportunities for closeness were limited where the porter had landed himself. For me too. And maybe I related because that had been me before the bed ride to nowhere. Or, maybe right now and these moments were the whole point in my being; to still draw breath.

I knew all too well this existence was my deserved reality, before the bedsores set in and they increased my dose so even the remunerations became second fiddle, and the dark echoes took over centre stage.

I took all in, all I could. Drank it down with thirst: flies, rants and bellyaches.

The porter had an end of shift mantra: if only his bad-assed brother was there to silence them, he'd mutter. Over and over. As the shift ended for him, a story opened each time within me. Nearly every night the same. He called out to his brother. Sang his praises. This gangster brother from the big city. The one that didn't suffer crap. Not from no one. His name: Max Ballard. Something like that. Strong. A name and a brand. Could've been a superhero. Or, a villain. Instead, it would seem this brother bashed heads as the porter bashed bed frames. Extorting money—taking no shit from anyone. Whereas the porter was left to shovel it up. And with each fractured skull, this absent criminal brother highlighted all the shit and piss this porter brother was left with; to mop the floor and lap up life's left overs and waste. Like the weaker timid sibling around a dinner table frenzy.

Hence the chips on shoulders; pulled down with the lead weights of fraternal envy.

The grass was always greener, easier, richer for the other brother. Of course. Why else than for the porter to go into this caring profession, what better reason than to cancel out the moralistic floors of the other brother. A gangster.

I admired the sad, underpaid brute with heavy shoulders and dead bluebottles for friends, devoted to the worry of others, stained tissues, dust, stains and worse. He was some kind of saint and creating balance.

Words charged from him like an angry priest, hatred soaked prayers or pleas for help from an absent brother with a mop. Where the other brother wielded a shotgun; widowed wives and robbed sons' lives from mothers.

Words of the porter on his brother were muttered, safely spoken out of earshot of this demon that he implored, admired, missed in whispers by my bed. He could have just made the call, but I guessed he never did or would. To do that would be to risk upsetting that balance. And the other brother would never shift his life towards the porter's, and so the porter would be tipped on a fulcrum to be criminal. And that just wouldn't do. So, for now he didn't... make that call.

I sensed he was safest here. With those treading life's waters like the other staff.

Maybe this brother was a demon, to be feared. A monster too, like me.

He reached out with words of longing, knowing his brother would never respond back. He spoke out safely from another person's cell, my own, and from the corridors of this forgotten asylum.

Like wails of an estranged child. I guessed he felt better as the tears rolled, knowing the existence of a parent, but with the absence of a comforting touch anywhere nearby. And still, used to the estrangement—the tears needed no reply. A reminder of being together, even whilst apart.

Why had the porter been left to rot, like me, in this peeling tired room?

He worked hard and banging my metal bed frame was the pinnacle of his daily grind's worth. I really did... feel for the angry bastard.

I often smiled, in my head—out of sight. Rattle away, I'd think, across that infinite blackness.

Rattle. Away.

The porter's frustrations at his employment and brother often built up to a crescendo, with that *clankity-clank* around my room and bed frame. Cleaning it almost every other day—as much as a comatose man's dwelling should be. Or, so it seemed to the eyes of my virtual captors. I suspected it was cleaned more for those who transiently entered than for me trapped inside for good, or bad, to the end.

There was no cure here. Not for me or the porter.

I wished I could tell him just that: 'Walk the fuck out, don't look back. Unlike me, you don't have to be here. Escape, breathe and live.' He wasn't taking any real breaths inside the asylum. Breaths gave life, but not inside this place, it only took them away.

Another night came and he was back and I'd missed him. He clattered and bashed that bed frame more than ever.

Bang, clank and *crash*. It was a fine chorus.

From my pillow and a still face, I gave another invisible smile. Both corners of my mouth twitched. If only he'd witnessed it, his purpose may have been made in that moment. And he'd step outside, breathe and leave.

Be gone from here.

Live.

I FELT THE doctor's gaunt mass at the bed end. He talked coldly like a mechanic with a car he had no desire to run. A nurse by him gave much away too. Making sounds as if the clipboard he held was an empty chocolate box and she hadn't been offered one.

Both sounded lonely and I could feel the distance, despite them being close enough to see the clipboard he held. They took turns reading from it. Summing up my existence in scribbled and smudged pencil lines, scrawled numbers and spurious sounding drug brands. Most of all they recorded my time on the clock. Time in. Time left. Before changing gear with another brand to distort this time. The pencil scratch was the real God in here. Its lead, lightning bolts shaping my evolution with a stroke.

It wasn't their fault. They did what they felt they deserved and for me, what I was due too. The God of the hospital would speak. The drugs, spikes and vials would come. And like me when it dulled, blunted or broke it would be replaced. God was in its act. Not in it its being.

The nurse asked him, why the dosing-up so much? And given my condition or lack of it? Each time she was quickly dismissed, as if she didn't know what she was talking about. The fact was her challenges proved she did know enough. He knew and so did she that my dosing was to keep me in this stasis.

She changed tack, blunt: instead, she queried why I was kept on ice like that: immobile, mute. Frozen.

There are people outside the asylum, the doctor explained, that wanted me out of action whilst they found out what they wanted to find out. And maybe if they didn't, they just needed time to make it up, something to stick. She quickly piped up asking, what would happen after that… when the powers that be got what they needed to stick?

I didn't know who I was or what I'd done, but I was sure it was their empty cause. A powerless doctor pushing drugs that weren't in the interest of healing and a nurse whose true care came from testing the authority and decisions above her. Rather than the compassionate care, you might expect—human to human.

Yes, I was sure they were lost too. Like the porter. I was as sure as I was definite of the sadness in them. It rang, resonated within me also.

They should both hold hands, walk out together and forget all about me. After all, I had.

A NEW NURSE was introduced into my world and she was tired before she'd started, working relentlessly without thanks. She was barked at in my room like she was a dog, and as if she'd worked there her whole life, dropped countless balls, and so deserved spite.

I sensed her strength from my place.

Across that sea of my drug-induced coma, her being there, in my room, cracked through the blackness like lightning. Without opening my eyes, I could see cherry red hair, a cheeky smile against the odds and giant green Irish eyes.

She regularly had something to say. But unlike the others, who blamed the world for their predicaments, what she did say was only for me—in order to save herself. Beyond reason, I could tell my recovery somehow mattered to her. With the others, I was invisible, an obstacle or symbol of their lack of touch with a real-life—whatever that was. It seemed, with me and her in the room together, I was her life and sole importance.

Love's safe distance drew dangerously closer.

She read prose to me, extracts from the same piece each night, lover to lover. A patchwork quilt of desire and memory. Tender fragments that became one. She whispered into my ear:

Against the decaying wall of existence is the weary faces of many women,
an eternity of them, waves upon waves of endurance between them.
Tired and insulted by experience,
on paths made more uneven by the men encountered en-route.

One of them looks between a small gap in the stones of the giant wall,
uncertain, after all they've suffered, if she wants through
to the other side.
To touch the hand of God: This Cruel Maker.

She broke up the lines and sections, pleading for me to recover.

As if she knew me. I wondered if she was a real nurse at all. Maybe she was an angel that had flown down to push me one way or the other—love or hate—life or death. With this last gift of love either way. Her words continued, like honey:

When their struggle stops,
journeys are complete,
and God finally sees them,
the crowd of women turn away,
as the wall that once separated them crumbles.

The sounds of their marching become the waves.
Their sighs, now the winds.

Leaving God to question which side of the wall he was on.
And why it was there in the first place.

A breath in my ear:

God is now made weary too…
by the experiment; failed.

She touches then grips my hand, waits for a pulse from my wrist, then continues:

Will they ever return to face the creator?
Or instead, take the hand of their lovers,
Sailing headlong into the sun.

Her sweet voice the purest nectar.

Drugged up, I couldn't taste it, but felt better, somewhere inside, just knowing it existed. That sweetness. And her touch too… When she stroked my hand, wrist, arm and hair. I was numb to it physically—but inside a fire burned again. And that black sea of my coma was set alight as if a match was thrown to the oil slick on its surface, as optimism burned, floated, then was gone.

Ethereal notions, like paper boats sailing on a savage sea towards a relentless burning sun.

I HEARD THEY had a visitor. Someone checking up on me.

They didn't give much away but what they did was to sentence me to oblivion. The visitor, a man in a black suit with an ID card, had stoked the fires of resentment, my inconvenience to them and the sheer chore that my care was to the asylum, the institution and its staff.

I was a dead weight to most of them, but one.

Where was my nurse, my angel?

I wept for the honey-toned green eyes from a distance. The same distance I once pushed love to willingly, it was pushed away when I now wanted it, needed it… And looked to pull it nearer.

I wished that if they did rid themselves of me, it would be worth it and they'd be reborn. Make something of themselves. Sad but true; I knew it wouldn't be the case. I wanted them all to take a chance whilst they still had the choice; to sink or swim. Breathe or suffocate.

I was sure to sink in the morning, to die. And the sting wouldn't be the fall or extinguishing of those last thoughts. It would be that Green Eyes wasn't there to catch me, even if only one last time. To whisper so softly that she hated the distance too—wanted me.

Medical lexicons had concentrated against me and their differences had aligned. Now, all there was left in my sphere of damaged perceptions were the chief physician, his cohorts and this common enemy they saw firmly in me—the demon laid bare. A sleeping monster to be euthanised.

I now saw the beast as if disconnected from it and on their side. As if I was ready to join in and throw the switch myself.

My cherry-red Irish nurse wasn't there as they riled themselves up like a pack of hungry wolves encircling a wounded sleeping animal. I feared they'd locked her out, up or worse. Knowing she cared for the person inside this dead shell. When they'd been treating and working around me: the object.

That notion would have woken me: of her influenced and harangued against her will, all for me. If it wasn't for the lorazepam, I might have roused a fight-back. I knew deep down the fight wasn't just. And my new fate was deserved. I was a vulnerable evil target to them, a beached shark with a child's leg in its belly.

I didn't deserve a chance.

They confirmed to themselves I hadn't been treated here after all. Just subdued. And that the man in the black suit had come to tell the chief Physician that it was time: to switch me from *silent*, to *off*.

They walked around my bed after this visitor had left. He'd left a heavy sentence over me, then was gone. Leaving the nurses, doctors, the porter and a few others all pondering, pacing and considering what had to be done with me. All key stakeholders were invited in, passing judgement on this, me, the prize in the bed. A sacrificial goat to die with their frustrations and resentment.

I felt like a voodoo doll to all their ailments, excuses to themselves, failed marriages, shitty friends and enemies. And I was about to get stuck with their needles threefold. Down to the bone and stuck in my joints.

I hoped, at least, they'd feel some release.

A tube was ripped out and my food, nutrients and fluids went with it. I felt pain but couldn't cry out. Not for another hour and by then they'd be gone and the door locked again— maybe for good and with my remaining full lung about to expire.

Where was she? My nurse and saviour. If only for a moment, I'd love to hear her speak those lines again...

Still, they talked. Considered action. Inaction. Whichever weighed easiest on their conscience. Up until now, their voices had been all the sustenance I craved, before. But it had turned. Words tainted to poison. A death sentence. Their spoken lines held a mirror to my unmoving face. The more they spoke the more I found out about myself and where we'd ended up was hellbound.

"I'm going to up the dose on the bastard."

"Why, doctor?"

"He's a killer."

"How many?"

"You couldn't tell to look at him now, could you? It's true though."

And there it was, with last night's voices opening a curtain to my future. To be drugged into eternity, and just as I was getting a handle on reality. The nurses' love had strengthened my fingers as I held onto the edge of an abyss in my dreams, about to find hope enough to pull myself up.

Now, nothing else mattered.

Last night, the walls felt weaker as my mind soothed in her prose. I felt close to opening up now, to the right person. If only they'd try. I'd tell them of those kills. The visitor in black had painted them all and me bad. They were that way already—those kills.

In the end, at last, maybe that other word that I'd pushed away did get a look in, delivered by an angel. That one word I used to keep at a safe distance. And now, I'm left to roam what is left of my mind. In the darkness. As that single word leads the final chorus in a lingering trinity:

Love, honour… and regret.

Tomorrow, they looked to drug me up and gas me to hell. Burning all their lives' regrets with me. Until then… I'll wait for the click of the door's lock, haunted by those delicate sweet words and emerald green eyes. So, I can take flight just one last time. Before I'm gone forever.

Fly with me.

BELLA

by

B F Jones

July 1941
Who put Luebella down the Wych Elm?

February 1943
Who put Bella in the witch Elm?

May 14ᵗʰ 1939
"You're a witch aren't you Bella? No? Let's say that you are anyway. Do you know what happens to witches, Bella?"

She shakes her head frantically, not that she's listening, just panic climbing through her, and the revulsion at the thought of the thick cloth they have rammed into her mouth slowly making its way down her throat and choking her.

"No?"

She shakes her head again, her brown eyes on them, feeling the perspiration running down her temples, the tears running down her cheeks. All that moisture, all that salted water. Humans are sixty percent water. If you kick water, does it feel pain?

"We cut their hand off."

VAN RALT LAUGHS at the lightening of terror in her eyes, suddenly hazel. A pretty woman. Almost beautiful. Different to what they had thought, therein lied their problem. He had desired her briefly, he always desired them. All of them. He had mentally undressed her, focusing on her breasts for a bit—that softness, a very slight droop. He should have known then that she was not in her twenties. And he had understood too late, annoyed at being fooled, he'd taken extra pleasure at stuffing her mouth with the thick cloth, hoping to break her uneven teeth in the process.

Van Ralt points to Mossop who quickly extracted a small machete out of his satchel and passes it to him.

"No, no," said Van Ralt. "You do the honours. It's your fault, isn't it? So this is your punishment."

Mossop grabs the slender arm. Flinching for a second at the sight of the cheap-looking metal band on her ring finger, perhaps wondering if she had children.

I AM WATER.

I am water.

I cannot feel pain. I am the clear water of a translucent stream, the moist trickle licking parched mountain rocks, the sea that I will never navigate.

I can feel no pain.

No pain.

She closes her eyes and the little face of her boy moves behind her eyelids, in bright odd colours, flashing but un-erasable. She scrunches her eyelids closed just like she did when she was a child and thought there might be a witch under her bed.

Now she's the witch.

Witch.

"GET ON WITH it already."

The order is barked by the scary man that Mossop has seen kick a dog to death and strangle a woman, so he pushes his thoughts away, uses the remnant of his fading inebriation to gather some strength and lets the blade fall on the smooth pale skin with a neat chopping sound.

The noise that bursts from Bella's throat raises every single hair on Mossop's skin.

She dies quickly after that, they didn't need to do much, just let her suffocate on the taffetas whilst her arm poured blood quickly swallowed by the earth.

It's Van Ralt's idea to stuff her inside the tree after noticing it was hollow and climbing it with surprising agility. He grabs her under her armpits and heaves her up while Mossop holds her legs, blood splashing onto his suit, noticing the common, sensible flat shoes, wondering how him and Van Ralt got everything so wrong, wondering how he even managed to get there, knowing his life will never be the same.

March 2nd 1941

THEY KNOW THEY might get in trouble, and that they shouldn't be there, but they gather courage from each other, and from the rumbling of their stomachs. The prospect of anything but yet another helping of potato soup motivating them to go over the knackered fence easily.

"That's a lovely part of the woods isn't it," ventures Peter, unleashing his dog, encouraging him to go find a rabbit or two. Tom doesn't like it here and would have rather stayed home with Ma—he'd always rather stay home with Ma and Pa. They've been crying so much lately, and Ma has been wasting away and he doesn't like being apart from her, but the boys always come and drag him out. Last week they had found a bottle of gin from somewhere and Tom had been sick the next day.

"Come on Tom, come along. It's all safe here, we're just looking for a bit of dinner." Tom catches up to them eventually, finding his friends at the bottom of the large tree Peter was climbing.

"That's a Wych Elm," he says, to no-one in particular.

"We don't care lad, what tree it is, as long as there's a nest or two." James laughs and licks his lips in anticipation, almost hearing the crackling of fresh eggs frying in a pan.

"Bloody Hell!" The curse, which Pete learnt from his father, recently returned an invalid, comes from the top of the tree. "Bloody Hell!" Pete repeats, pulling at something the boys can't make out immediately. He comes down from the tree, holding the skull by the last of its mucky brown hair.

"BLOODY HELL!!" they all exclaim, taking in the hollow eyes, the nasal cavity, the uneven teeth, a couple of them broken halfway. Tom sits down on the parched ground, his head against his knees, rocking slightly. James sits next to him, pats his back awkwardly.

"It's okay buddy, it's okay. It's just one of those things." The boys all agree not to tell anyone and they put the skull back in the tree, place it back on the rest of the skeleton they know will haunt their dreams. They don't talk much on the way back, just intermittently telling the dog to stop barking and Tom to stop crying. They go home and eat potato soup and don't sleep much that night.

January 6th 1940

JAY TUCKS THE boy in, reads the story, sings the song, trying his best to do what she would have done, wondering again and again where Isabel is. What happened? She wouldn't disappear for no reason. She wouldn't leave him. She definitely wouldn't leave the boy.

He'd watched her for seven years, boiling her underwear and sheets whilst crying herself to sleep at night. He watched her cry again, pain and joy as the long-desired infant shot out of her two weeks early, onto the kitchen floor. He was the one that had wrapped the slippery little thing in a flannel rag, tied the umbilical cord with his shoelaces before cutting it, still shivering to this day at the memory of the spongy wetness of it. She wouldn't have left them.

"Good night, sleep tight," he singsongs as usual, and kisses his son on the forehead, as usual, not knowing it would be the last time.

Jay dies that night, natural causes they say, broken heart they think, and the boy goes into foster care, first for a few months, and then moves in with his aunt Aida who later relocates somewhere in Europe; and that's an entire family swept off that part of the world, a microcosm of love turned into a lonely tombstone in a graveyard and the fading memory of a woman who just vanished one day, never to be found again.

March 9th 1941

TOM HASN'T SLEPT in nights. The dark circles around his eyes have been concerning Moira who uses her kindest quietest voice to try to get the boy to talk. Her and John have been so concerned by their son's behaviour. Already frail and sensitive, his older brother's death had almost destroyed him with grief, and lately he'd become increasingly shaky, worried—the slightest noise making him start and the twilight making him cry.

"It's those boys he is spending time with," she had said one evening, lighting a rare cigarette, ignoring the look of disapproval on his face. "They're bad news."

John had nodded in agreement, but argued that those boys were all that their "sensitive" son had in way of friendship, and as rowdy as they were, they also always made sure Tom was included in their games. And his friend Peter had given Tom his old bike, a gesture his father would be forever grateful for—not being able to afford such extravagance lately.

On the fifth night of hearing their son waking up crying, they both walk into his room and demand that he tells them what is going on. Tom finally breaks the promise he made to his friends, and the words pour out of him as he feels his whole body filling up with the relief of not holding such a big secret anymore. He tells them about trespassing, the search for eggs, the tree and the skull in there. About how Pete had lifted the skull and cursed, and how he'd cursed more when he realised there was a whole body in there and how they all ran away screaming, and he says how sorry he is for not telling them sooner, and curls up in Ma's arms to cry all the tears of this scary wild world that he will never fully get.

February 21st 1946

NURSE RITA TUTS gently at the cantankerous man sitting by his bed. His robe is half open and he hasn't bothered putting underwear on. She can't help but peek at the man's penis, sitting defeated, deflated, stuck to his left thigh. She's slightly fascinated by penises. She hasn't slept with anyone yet. Her and Andrew were engaged to be married and, aside from the "accidental" wandering of their hands during their most passionate kisses, they had saved each other for after the wedding. But there had been no wedding for Rita, who never saw Andrew alive again, and the memory of their embraces had been replaced by the feel of his cold skin under her lips, and life had become the same grey as the forehead she had kissed.

She peaks again, and wonders if she'll ever be ready for someone else, she feels Andrew's death has wiped her clean of any inclination to be in a relationship, whether carnal or romantic.

"Mr Mossop, let's wrap you up, it's not warm around here." And she gently wraps the man in a light blanket. Her eyes meeting the mix of sadness, fear and disillusion in his.

"Did you know you were talking again last night Mr Mossop? Something about a tree. You said it wasn't her! Not her in the tree!" Rita chuckles softly. "God knows what it can mean. I wish I knew more about dreams so I could find out and understand what mine mean too. Don't you Mr Mossop? What strange things our brains are."

May 14th 1939

SHE WALKS QUICKLY up the street, the hem of her skirt almost touching the ground, glad for it and for the sinful shoes it hides. No classy woman would be caught dead in them. But is she classy? She's beautiful, they always tell her that. She could have married above, become aristocratic. She's got the looks for it—the curl of her honey hair, the milky skin, straight nose, the slight defiance of her chin, the pink lips hiding the overbite and disorderly teeth she always feels self-conscious about, making her a rare smiler. She only smiles liberally to her husband and boy, her two loves.

"My two loves!" she regularly exclaims, opening her arms wide, flashing her crooked smile, hugging them both.

The two men look at her and she doesn't really like that—people are dangerous. Men are cruel, especially lately. There was that story in the news about that young teenager and she could never finish reading it because too many tears got in the way, and it was probably better that way. Better not to know.

The men greet her: "Evening Madam, can you tell the moon is about to rise?" and she nods back, not sure what to answer, raising her chin, forcing herself not to increase the speed of her steps. Even when they start walking on each side of her. Even when they say they have been waiting for her and she should come with them, even when the panic in her throat rises as one of them uses her nickname and says that he reckons she wouldn't mind a nice drink of gin somewhere, even when she can feel the arm of the larger man clasped around her waist as they direct her towards the club hidden behind a plain house door.

Inside it is warm and the atmosphere oozes luxury and she can't help but enjoy it all. The dimmed lights, the plump velvet seats, the perfect tartness of the gin. Things used to be like that. She hates how things are now and she hates the two men sitting on each side of her making increasingly unpleasant conversation as they get drunker and ask a lot of questions.

She decides to talk as little as possible, drinks her gin slowly. They talk about things she doesn't understand, people she doesn't know and demand information she hasn't got, swears she hasn't got. She swears no-one gave her a folder and she was just coming back from visiting her dying aunt, and then one of them takes a crumpled picture out of his pocket and compares her to it and nods to the other.

The other, the bigger one, spits on the floor and calls her a waste of time. Growls she's a little cunt and tells her she deserves a good beating for wasting their time. The younger one tries to calm him down and she hears him muttering in his ear, catching snippets of sentences imploring him to let the poor sod go. But the larger man brushes him away, stands up next to her and places a heavy hand on her shoulder. Digging his fingers painfully through the fabric of her dress and into the flesh. He barks at her to get up, and the trio stumble out of the pub and towards the woods while everyone else looks away, knowing better than to say anything, as the three people become shadows and then disappear into the night.

TWO STREETS DOWN, Luebella waits, the clicking of her heels on the pavement echoing in the quiet street. In her hand, a small folder she hasn't opened. She would like to, very much so, but she knows how risky it is. If they found out she'd read it they'd kill her. She heard the rumour about Anna J. who was found strangled. Was it because she looked inside the folder? She paces slowly, humming a cheerful tune to try and dissipate how gloomy she feels.

As the night falls, she feels rage and disappointment mounting in her chest, causing her breath to become shorter. Ragged. First they forced her. Out of her town, out of her candour, out of her knickers. And then, just when she's starting to enjoy the thrill of her "job", to look forward to the nighttime escapades, they blatantly leave her high and dry. She's got used to the nice perks. All she has to do is meet at the agreed destination, generally a quiet street not far from a clandestine pub, hand out a folder full of useful information, and get wined and dined by a stranger or two, sometimes unzipped out of her dress, always after enough gin that she no longer cares. She really wants some gin now, she's been sober almost a week and can feel the need, the void gnarling at her insides, so she decides to wait a little longer.

After another 10 minutes a man turns up. He isn't the kind she is used to. She curls her nose at his appearance, a dark brown stain mucking his suit.

"My partner was injured," he blurts out, noticing her inquisitive eyes, quickly introducing himself, saying the agreed sentence, reassuring her that he is indeed the person she had been sent to meet.

"He'll pull through thankfully, but you have to excuse my appearance, my dear," he adds, looking at her long and appreciatively, taking a picture out of his pocket that he raises to eye level, nodding to himself and extending his arm for the folder that she extracts out of her bag and passes on to him.

She walks back home, disappointed, thirsty, takes her heels off and rubs her feet before going to bed. Tomorrow is her birthday, she will be twenty-four.

March 6th 1941
Small Town Makes Grim Discovery.

Human skeletal remains have been found in a hollow tree one mile into the Hagley Woods. It hasn't yet been possible to confirm the gender or identity of the person whose life mysteriously ended in such circumstances, however the coroner has estimated the body had been concealed within the tree for approximately 18 months to 2 years. Police are currently investigating missing persons' records in hopes of finding a possible match.

March 3rd 1941

THE TWO POLICEMEN have sealed off the area, casting as wide a berth as possible from all the onlookers, thirsty for morbid details, as if the war wasn't enough for them. Langdon shakes his head in dismay. *Why are we, as humans, so despicable? And who are you, madam? Is there anyone looking for you?*

That same morning the pathologist had established the body belonged to a woman of "childbearing age" and that she had probably died due to asphyxiation, a conclusion they had reached after the coroner had extracted the remains of what appeared to be a dark blue taffetas lodged deeply in the woman's unusual protuberant jaw and from between the crooked teeth.

In the meantime, the policemen had looked into what little survived of the woman's garments — a long plain skirt, and a pair of simple flat leather shoes.

"Dora wouldn't be caught dead in these," muttered Langdon, immediately regretting the uncharitable thought as he bagged them as evidence.

August 21ˢᵗ 1939

A FEW MONTHS pass before Luebella is called in for more work. She reluctantly turns up to the agreed location, her previous experience still hanging unpleasantly in her mind, the man covered in blood, the way he'd looked at her, and the way he'd dismissed her. But this time around, the man, going by the name Van Ralt, is on time. He apologies on behalf of his associate. "He's a brute, my dear, but he did save my life, so I'll have to let him off." He roars with a hearty laughter that screams at her ears and fills the entire pub. He clicks his fingers in the air for more Champagne for the gorgeous lady.

Later on, when she's glazed over and swaying, he brings her home, where he slumps on his back demanding she service him. He calls her a little witch and growls she's a little cunt the entire time. She wakes up groggy, the aftertaste of semen and shame in her mouth. Slips back on the dress he'd taken pleasure in ripping of off her body and runs out of the house, down the street and down another. She runs until she is home.

LUEBELLA DISAPPEARS ALTOGETHER that week. It's easy to disappear. So many people have recently. *What about that woman in the spring who never returned to her husband and little boy?* She'd read about it in the paper—there had been some articles initially, a large picture of a beautiful woman—classy, slightly severe, looking straight at the camera. She'd followed the case with interest at first, but the articles had become smaller until they disappeared, and she'd forgotten all about the beautiful woman, been distracted by other news, other disappearances, other horror all around. Been drowning her sorrow in gin and cheap wine, hiding under her grimy covers like she did when she was a little girl and worried a witch was hiding in her wardrobe.

"You little witch, you little cunt, all women are witches, they all deserve punishment". Van Ralt's words echoed in her head as she packed everything that mattered into her small bag, alarm bells ringing every time she thought of his face, of how he'd tried to strangle her before passing out. She ran out again and disappeared into the woods, leaving no trace of her young self in the town or even in the next couple of towns. She simply vanished and was soon forgotten about, along with the other war casualties.

"She simply vanished," is what Van Ralt related to Mossop and the others the following day after her disappearance. Would she compromise them? There was always a risk. Generally the women are too terrified to disappear or disobey, but there was always the off chance. They searched for her for a short while but gave up after a week, presuming her dead, and got a new one.

March 26th 1941
Police Asking for Information in Relation to Town Square Graffiti

Over the past three nights, the town has been defaced with graffiti painted in bold red strokes asking the following: "Who put Luebella down the Whych Elm?" The police believe the graffiti has a connection to this month's discovery of the skeletal remains of a woman inside a Wych Elm in the Hagley Woods. If you have any information with regards to this name, please do come forward.

March 27th 1941
Hollow Tree Body Identified

In light of the recent graffiti appearing all over the town, it has been established that the body in the Wych Elm is of one Ms Luebella Jessops that went missing in the summer of 1939 and who was since presumed dead. The police have confirmed the case might have been an isolated case of witchcraft that ended up in accidental death and have now closed the investigation.

Luebella tosses the paint pots behind a holly bush and pulls her large mac back on, the smell of turpentine on her hands making her gag. She puts the hat and sunglasses back on and gingerly climbs the bus steps, her feet not used to the broad flat shoes she's wearing. Wouldn't get caught dead in them she smiles, then panics, wondering if she's jinxed herself. She rides the bus to the station and then jumps on the first train to nowhere, hoping her ploy works. Hoping to never, ever be back.

October 1943

MOSSOP HASN'T BEEN feeling well lately. Three years in the institution haven't made him feel any better. Maybe even worse. The nightmares have been fiercer, louder, longer. The nights have been a river of blood escaping from a severed arm, muffled screams and supplicating hazel eyes meeting his. They've been large red-blood letters asking about Luebella. 'You're a witch Bella, aren't you?' Van Ralt's words waltzing in his forever-ringing ears. Whatever happened to Van Ralt? 'You're a witch Bella, aren't you? You're a witch Bella, aren't you?' And the machete closing on her pale skin. And the guttural, animal sound coming out of her. And the hazel eyes. The hazel eyes. The hazel eyes.

June 1943
New Graffitti Appears

Two years after the Wych Elm case closed, new graffiti has appeared throughout the town, with a slight variation on the initial one, and the message reading "Who put Bella in the witch Elm?" The change in the name or the spelling of the word witch isn't enough for the police to re-open the investigation and they believe this can be attributed to a copycat or a resident wanting to stir up unpleasant memories.

February 1946

NURSE RITA RAISES the sheet over Mossop's face, a single tear pearling at the corner of her eye.

"Ah, Mr Mossop. You were a quirky one. I guess I'll never know who that Bella you talked about so much was." She rests her hand on his chest for a few seconds. "Rest in peace if you can, Mr Mossop." She starts tidying up—soon the room will be occupied again. She gathers Mossop's belongings; it doesn't take long. She finds the notebook concealed under another book inside the bedside table draw. It reads the same sentence over and over again.

I put Bella in the Witch Elm
I put Bella in the Witch Elm
I put Bella in the Witch Elm.

THE SCENT OF AUTUMN

by

Nils Gilbertson

Ryland Pierce

SOMETIMES DEATH PRODUCES something wonderful, like the earthy-sweet scent that emanates from decomposing leaves in autumn. Wonderful, not in a philosophical sense. Not in the sense there is beauty in death as it is a necessity to appreciate the fullness of life. I speak of the beauty in the act itself—decay, decomposition. Rotting, bloated flesh peeling from bone. The sour fragrance of returning to whence we came. But even when we go, we are never gone.

He hadn't been dead the last time I'd checked on him. Hard to say what did it. The trap biting down on his leg was no picnic, but the way the TV portrayed them crushing bones and amputating limbs was fiction. Could've gotten free if he'd kept his head. But, like most, he'd panicked. The dehydration likely did the job. It'd taken its sweet time with him, his stages of dying progressing slowly as the seasons. I watched as though they were as inevitable as the progression from fall to winter. The pleading was over now. Only cold skin and dead eyes like marbles. And the smell, *oh*, the smell. I inhaled deep and smiled. My lips were cracked and my mouth was dry from the bitter autumn chill. I took my time gathering snot and saliva, watching the forest tremble in the breeze. Once I'd gathered a cheek-full, I spat on the corpse and turned back towards the cabin.

Myra was dishing up supper when I got back. We ate in silence for a while.

"He dead yet?" she asked.

"Uh-huh."

"You gonna bury him or leave him there to rot?"

"What's the rush?" I asked. "Ain't nobody venturing back there."

"I heard the bank's gettin' suspicious and'll send more fellas to poke around. Don't like their man going missing. 'Specially not with the heat they're putting on us to sell."

"Let them come," I said. I let the soup scald my tongue.

THE MAN WHO came was tall and lean, an overcoat draped over him, leather gloves like an extra layer of shiny dark skin. He removed one to offer a shake.

"Wes Timmons," he said.

"You with the bank?"

He grinned. "I'm a private investigator. I've been hired to track down a fella called Don Ritter, a land surveyor who worked for Hillside Bank & Trust. May I come in?"

I grumbled but Myra came to the door and nodded.

"Right this way."

She showed him to an old wooden chair and poured three cups of coffee from the percolator. He glanced around at the decent state of the place like he was expecting much worse.

I took the seat across from him. "I don't—"

He cut me off with a subtle movement of the hand. "There's no need, Mr. Pierce. I've read all about your dispute with the bank. You ask me, what they're doing to you folks and your land is criminal. A damned disgrace."

"But here you are on their behalf," Myra said, handing him a coffee.

He smiled. "Ma'am, I got a kid with more health problems than an inbred mule and a wife with a taste for the finer things. You find me a fella who puts the good of the world before the good of the household, and I'll show you a fella who can't tell his ass from his eyelids."

"So, if you think the bank's no good, what're you here for?" I asked.

"Good thing for us, Mr. Pierce, is that they don't know how much I loathe them. Keep your enemies close—am I right?"

"Uh-huh."

"They hired me to figure out what happened to poor old Ritter. After all, he was only doing his job. Bastards want me to dig around your property and see if I stumble over any bodies." He peered through the window towards the hills and the naked trees, shedding the last of their color before hibernating through the long, dark months. "My mother used to send me out here each summer to stay with my uncle and his family. He taught me how to hunt, fish," he paused. "But it wasn't about that. It was about the quiet. I learned the importance of quiet out here. And, I'll tell ya, it's a hard goddamn thing to find these days."

I drank my coffee and wished it was something else. "You got a point to make?"

"You're a fella who thinks more than he talks. The world could use more of you, Mr. Pierce." I couldn't pry my eyes from his blink-less stare. "I've been doing this a long time. I'm good at it, and the bank trusts me. Driving through these hills, I had a thought about how we can make some cash off them, given what they've put you through."

"How's that?"

"I tell them I got a lead on what happened to Ritter, keep stringing them along, say I'm gaining your trust, but got a bad feeling about what you've done to that fella."

"And what if I did do something to that fella?"

"Sir," he said, "I don't give a damn if you ripped his guts out through his nostrils." He looked at me in a way that almost made me believe him. "You keep letting me come around, give me something now and then to show to my client to keep them paying the bills. Same time, I'll make sure no real investigation goes anywhere. And you get a cut of my payment."

"What if the bank decides you're doing a shit job and calls the cops?" I asked.

He chuckled and sipped his coffee. "Cops? Banks don't trust cops, especially in hick towns like this, where they assume the chief of police is your cousin or drinking buddy."

I felt my wife behind me. "What d'you think, Myra?"

She snorted. "I think folks like us don't get far trusting folks like him."

He stood up and did a spin as though to show he didn't have a piece on him. Then he nodded to the gun rack in the corner. "I trust you, ma'am."

My eyes met Myra's and she nodded.

"What sort of cut do we get?" I asked.

"Fifty percent sound alright? And, I assure you, the bank pays well."

"What's the catch?" Myra asked.

He grinned and raised a finger. "Only one. I'd like to see him first."

Myra and I weren't sure whether to act dumb or laugh his ass out the door. We sort of snorted and exchanged glances—surprised by his bold request. He sipped his coffee and waited to explain.

"See," he said, once he could tell we didn't know what the hell to do with ourselves. "For the rate they're paying me, the bank demands details. And I don't want to give them details unless I'm sure they won't be contradicted by happenstance. For instance, if I claimed I spotted Ritter's ripped up and bloodied coat out in these woods, I'd be in a tough spot if he turned up the next day in one piece. See what I mean?"

"Guess so."

"It's good for me to see the whole picture if we're going to go into business together. Besides, suppose you got him dead out back somewhere. You show me the body. What's my move? Run to my car without a shred of evidence beyond my word, drive the two hours back to town, then two hours back with a posse? I can't imagine you letting me borrow your phone to call it in." He'd finished his coffee and nodded to the percolator for more. "All hypothetically speaking, of course. Ritter's probably off on a bender somewhere. Rumor has it, he's a drunk who smacks his wife around. Good riddance. Hell, I'll help you bury the son of a bitch if it puts your mind at ease."

My eyes met Myra's before finding their way back to him.

"All right. Let's go."

THE WOLVES MADE it to him first. They went for the meaty parts, not that he had much left on him. I watched Wes Timmons squirm and try to hide it.

"You did this?" he asked.

"I did nothing."

I watched him swallow hot spit and felt the wind, like God's whispers, numb my cheeks.

"It's a funny thing," I said. "What *nothing* can do to a man—a fool of a man who put his foot in the wrong spot. He was once nothing, now he's nothing once more."

The investigator looked as though he'd be ill.

"But let's not go down the rabbit hole of thinking about *nothing*," I continued, the trees like an army behind me. "Don't do no one any good.

All of this—*everything*—came from *nothing*. Why we got such a damn problem with *nothing*?"

He opened his mouth, but I stopped him.

"Don't answer that. Smell it. Smell *him*."

I inhaled death and he tried to mimic me. But, with a crack and a rip, he dropped, his chest staining yellow leaves a syrupy crimson.

I closed my eyes and when I opened them Myra was beside me, rifle slung across her back.

"I love that smell, Myra."

"I know you do, Ryland."

I tried to block the rest out, let death fill me with life. As I inhaled, I felt an overwhelming awareness of everything.

"You know we couldn't have trusted him, right?"

I nodded. "You reckon we'll see snow soon?"

Daisy Ritter

HER HANDS WOULDN'T stop trembling and it took conscious effort to steady them enough to pour another slug from the bottle. The house was a mess. Dishes were piled high in the sink and empty glasses drew sticky white circles as she peeled them from the liquor-stained coffee table. She kept the shades drawn. His dirty laundry was still reeking up the place from a corner in the hall. She didn't dare go near it. A soiled reminder of all the things he'd done to her—that she'd done to him. She took a drink and considered that, under the circumstances, her misery was appropriate, expected by onlookers and well-wishers, even if unexpected by her.

Her heart quickened when she heard the smooth engine in the driveway. She peeked out at the familiar burgundy Mercedes and, on instinct, turned to the mirror to fix her hair. She smiled weakly. The bruises on her cheek and eye socket had evolved from dark purple to yellow and were now almost gone. She washed down the lingering shame with the drink.

A knock on the door and she opened it for a handsome man in a dark gray suit. "Hello, Mr. Adler."

He removed his hat. "Ms. Ritter, may I come in?"

She nodded and glanced out at the street before shutting the door behind him.

"Can I get you something?" she offered.

He eyed the half-empty fifth. "I'm all right." He stepped towards her. "Are you?"

She tried to turn away from him but he grabbed her and pulled her close. She relented and nestled into his chest. "I—I can't get his face out of my head."

"I know, darling, I know."

She tilted her head back and kissed him and then shoved him away. "*Do you*, George? *Do you* understand? Jesus, I know it was *our* plan. I know I agreed to have you send Don out there to survey those lunatics' land—I know it was *my* idea to have you mark the map to make him wander too far onto their property." She paused. "But why didn't *you*?"

"Excuse me?"

"Him beating the shit out of me for years wasn't enough for you to do it on your own—take care of that son of a bitch and tell me it was an accident?" Quiet tears, tears she was used to, wetted her cheeks. "For all the times you've said you loved me—said you'd leave your wife for me if my husband was out of the picture—why couldn't you have taken care of him on your own and left me in ignorant fucking bliss? Don't I deserve at least that?"

"Daisy I—I never would've—I couldn't—unless you wanted me to…"

He tried to pull her towards him again but she collapsed onto the couch. He joined her and they embraced. Her arms slung around him, she said, "I know we did the right thing, George, I'm glad the son of a bitch is gone. I am. But I didn't think I'd feel this way after—I thought it would be easy. I thought when he was gone, he'd be gone. But he's not. He's still here with me. Still tormenting me."

He kissed her on the mouth. She wrapped her legs around him and he pulled up her dress and started undoing his shirt. Her tears had stopped but she felt them drying, salty and sticky, on her cheeks as he kissed her face and neck and chest. She closed her eyes and felt the quiver in her breath and the strained curl of her toes and tried to capture and bottle the feeling of aliveness brought by each thrust before it ended and everything was once again cold and dark and brutal.

They shared a cigarette after.

"It'll be all right, Daisy," George said. "The important thing is that pathetic excuse for a man will never lay a hand on you again. Try to find some solace in that."

"Okay, George." She paused. "You sure the cops won't put it together? They've been 'round asking me plenty of questions 'bout all sorts of things, about you and some others fellas at the bank."

He shook his head. "As long as you stick to the story as we discussed, you won't get any trouble, darling. You remember the kids when we were growing up here who ate glue and could barely read? They're the cops now. Still, they're smart enough to know messing with the Pierce's isn't worth it. We had to send a fella out, of course, to keep up appearances. But, I promise, nothing will come of it." He chuckled. "Poor fella might never come back either." He checked his watch, stood up, and started getting dressed. "I'm sorry to run out, dear, but I've got to get home."

She sat up, covered only by a thin blanket. "You don't have time to talk about what's next?"

"What's next?"

"You know, between us?"

He leaned down to kiss her on the cheek. "Things are too hot right now, darling. You knew we would have to wait until all this blows over. We've got to let things cool down, see if the PI can track down the body. Go from there." He grinned. "Besides, what's the rush now that he's gone?"

Linas Timmons

A MAN IN a busted-up Oldsmobile watched from down the block as the burgundy Mercedes purred around the corner, out of the humble neighborhood towards downtown. The heater was dead and the November chill was setting in, and he blew into his hands and pulled his beanie down over his ears. He figured there'd be snow soon.

He checked the photos and made sure he got a clear shot of Daisy Ritter's and George Adler's faces. It wasn't a slam dunk—the bank exec overseeing the dispute with the Pierce property visiting the wife of their missing land surveyor—but he'd seen and heard enough around town to piece it together.

Linas hadn't liked his cousin's plan from the start. Sure, on paper, it was sound. From his work with the bank, Wes knew all about George Adler's affair with the surveyor's wife. So, when he got the assignment to poke around the Pierce place, dig up what he could, Wes knew it was a fool's errand. He'd also spent enough summers with Linas and his pa in those hills to know you don't fuck around with the Pierce's and their land. A sharp investigator, Wes saw right through it. But rather than blackmail his client for the knowledge of the affair, he'd wanted to make a deal with the Pierces. *Talk about mutually beneficial,* he'd said to Linas over a few beers. *I can bleed those fucking bankers dry and Adler won't question a thing, as long as whatever I tell him helps with his cover-up. I throw a chunk of it to the Pierces, and they get away with murder. Hell, don't get away with it, profit from it. I win, Adler wins, Daisy Ritter wins, the Pierces win. Who loses? Don Ritter? He was a piece of shit wife beater. The bank losing cash for a phony investigation? Fuck the bank—the bank's nobody.*

It made a hell of a lot of sense. But some folks don't think like that. Linas had tried to find the words to warn his cousin, but he'd never been good with words. All he could muster was that he ought to tag along in case things went sideways. Wes had grinned. *You at my hip with that rifle of yours sounds like the exact sort of thing that'll set these people off.*

Linas surrendered to the memory of his pa taking him and Wes out one summer when they were boys learning to be men. He remembered feeling free out in those hills—hunting and fishing with the only man he'd ever looked up to and the only true friend he'd ever had. In the end, family was all there was, and his cousin was the last one left.

The shivering cold and the dark gray sky stole him from the memory and reminded him Wes hadn't returned from his trip out to the hills that morning. He checked his watch. Still a couple of hours away from the time they'd agreed he'd head out there if Wes hadn't made contact. *The reception is shit out there,* Wes had said. *Last thing I want is us passing each other on my way back and you end up out there come dark.* Linas recalled the horror stories parents in town would tell them as kids to keep them from poking around the Pierces' 40 acres of undeveloped hillside. Passed down tales of shots fired and limbs blown off in booby traps. The shunned family was rumored to never step foot off their property, although their occasional appearance at the hardware store refuted this. But fact became intertwined with fable as it tends to do. The fair warnings of danger turned to ghoulish tales of incest and abduction and torture and human sacrifice that occurred out in those woods. As a boy, that stuff had scared the shit out of Linas. But after the carnage he'd seen in Kandahar, trigger-happy hillbillies didn't get his heart rate up. His shriveled soul didn't have any room left for fear. He didn't even know what fear was anymore, a foreign concept to a man who had nothing left to lose.

He looked down at the pictures of Mr. Adler and Mrs. Ritter. They were the ones who started it all, who'd sent Wes out there in the first place. Not to mention that same damn bank had foreclosed on his ass when times got tough a few years back. But there'd be time enough for them later. The hills beyond town beckoned. He felt the scoped Browning in the trunk.

Ryland Pierce

I SAT ON the porch sipping whiskey and watched the last shreds of sun bleed through the trees before night blanketed the hills. I basked in the death all around me. The forest held such beauty because everything was always dying. An unending cycle of birth and death and rebirth as the seasons came and went. The whiskey stung, as all good things do. At my age, I tried not to lean on the bottle too much, but after inhaling the sweet scent of death, it was the only thing that could let me down gently from the high. And two corpses in a few days had me like a tweaker on payday. What a gift it all was.

The heat of the liquor warmed me and burned a hole through the veil separating the material self from something beyond—a metaphysical realm in which death and life were the same. I pulled a buck knife from my coat and sliced an apple as I pondered the consoling fiction. The liquor after a kill insisted there was something else in me—a spirit—like an ancient, primitive man who, eons ago, had died and decayed to dirt and sprouted again as corn which was harvested and distilled to liquor and now ran through my veins. I felt him. I heard his whisper in my soul that he was never gone, only recycled back into the same cosmic dance. I thought of my decomposing entrails feeding the soil that would grow the food that would nourish the living. I smiled and could hardly wait.

Soon the bottle was half-empty and the apple core was soggy and brown and I still waited for Myra to emerge from the trees. She'd gone for firewood in anticipation of the coming freeze. She ought to return before dark, but her delay didn't worry me. Our families had been in those hills so long we could navigate them deaf, dumb, and blind. The trees were a symphony of chirps and rustles and whistles. It was cold, but I could tell from the smell that the freeze was still a few days off. I always hated when the snow came. It dulled the aromas.

I closed my eyes and listened. I sensed her close by but there was something else out there. I picked up the rifle that leaned against the porch railing and steadied it across my lap. I felt the primitive instinct of the man in my veins demanding that I fight or run, but I knew it didn't matter.

The sound came shortly after a prick of light in the distant trees. An unfamiliar crack ripped through the hills before giving way to a sonorous thud. Then silence. I waited, but only more silence. I put the glass aside and took a long drink from the bottle. I didn't wonder who fired the shot or whether more would follow. It didn't matter. Whichever of God's creatures emerged from those trees was a pure manifestation of fate. I didn't budge or put rifle to shoulder. Instead, I took a long inhale of the last vestiges of autumn and contemplated, in death, all the lives I would live, the people I would feed, the veins I would poison as others had poisoned mine. I knew, if more bullets flew, nothing but beauty would come of it.

DRIVER

by

Sebastian Vice

"Nothing records the effects of a sad life so graphically as the human body"
~ Naguib Mahfouz, *Palace of Desire*

THE MIDNIGHT WIND ripped through Rick's clothes, his hands caked with Henry's blood. Maria's gravestone littered with last week's dead flowers, today's half-wilted. He leaned against the cold quartz and tied off his left arm.

"If you're out there, darling, I tried, I really did." The air burned his lungs and he pictured Maria's face on their wedding day. A white dress, her smile a candle among nightmares, who moved with the grace of a broken angel. "I was a hell'va racecar driver, ya?"

He filled the syringe and tears flowed. No more racecars. No more pretty girls with the blue ribbons at finish lines. No more beautiful gasoline. No more songful engines ringing in his ears. Only low-rent, degenerate pimps too cheap to supply condoms. Only chandelier people, the type who swirled fancy wines and sucked expensive cigars at lavish dinner parties. The upper-class degenerates who popped barbiturates while ranting about the scourge of marijuana.

Rick inserted the needle and pushed down on the plunger. "I guess the whole world is like blood smeared over cracked mirrors."

It began to snow as Rick drifted off. The snake bite was like Maria's first kiss.

A FEW DAYS after release from prison in '68, Rick's first client was like a stripper on Broadway, a tapestry of broken promises painted on a yellowed canvas. She wore a cashmere coat and an evening gown, dolled up like a geisha girl, but the makeup couldn't hide the gash on her cheek, or the wound on her chin. Truman Capote was right, Rick thought, Americans hate non-egalitarian beauty.

Kleopatra finished the joint and flung it out the window, her *Chanel* overpowering the atmosphere. "How lovely, darling. Henry got himself a new whore."

"Close the window. There's a draft."

She lit a *Pall Mall* and inhaled. "What's yer story?"

"I drive."

"Ya musta messed up bad to get in with Henry." She dangled the cigarette between her fingers. "A natural born loser if I ever met one. And sweetheart, I've been to Hollywood."

Rick stared out the windshield. "And that means what to me?"

"The world's one big whorehouse, driver. Ya face looks like a hangover. What broke ya?"

"How 'bout we have a nice *quiet* ride, okay?"

"Wife?"

"No."

"Kids?"

Rick slapped the dash. "Hey, whadd'I say?"

"You must have some story. They all do. And they all spill their guts. The johns—"

"Ya gonna psychoanalyze me now? Ya Sigmund Freud? I ain't a cheap trick, and I ain't yer john."

"Mine? No." She cracked the window again and winter flooded the car. "I ain't Freud, nor Jung, nor Skinner, or whomever the hell else, but I sure as hell don't need a degree in psychotherapy to see right through you."

Rick started the engine. "The window. Close it."

Kleopatra took another drag. "The real question, the one that keeps you up at night, the one which haunts your waking nightmares, and the answer that alludes you is—" She paused. "Guess."

"No."

She twirled her gold engraved lighter. "What shattered you? You don't belong here. What series of—"

Rick gestured to a payphone down the block. "Shall I call Henry?"

WHEN RICK GOT started, a pimp named DJ Sparkles said in 1966 Henry got in on the numbers racket. The bosses got wind Henry skimmed too much from the top.

"Henry ain't smart, Malone," DJ Sparkles said. "Afta da bosses got hold'a his ass, that dumb prick drank outta straws fer bout a year." He laughed licking his joint. "Dumb bitch tried shakin' me down few months back, ya feel? He pissed his pants when ma gals smack'd him about. *Golden Shower Henry*. Dat's his new name 'round here."

A few months later, societies elites started hitting up Henry. Oil men, politicians, diplomats, anyone on the right side of capitalism.

"You really want know why they didn't bury him?" Howard McIntyre asked, puffing on a pre-Castro Cabana, sipping a glass of 1937 Glenfiddich, his yacht swaying back and forth. "To send a message. Few years back, José Miguel Battle, the man himself, in the flesh, told me Henry's a billboard now." He puffed harder and Rick's eyes began to water. "The Italians tell folks that too. *Billboard Henry*."

"Mr. McIntyre, if I may ask another question?"

"Howard," he said. "You did my family right, by all means."

Rick itched his scabbed knuckles. "Half the girls die, or if you'll excuse my language, end up reproductively fucked. Doesn't this—"

"Whores, mere objects to society." Mr. McIntyre poured himself another glass and offered one to Rick. Rick declined. "It's not my daughter, or the daughters of my kind. It's hookers, pal. Strung out and broken. Ya think anyone cares? The pimps? The cops? The politicians?" He downed the scotch and poured himself another. "I know you ain't green, pal. Your eyes don't lie, nor your knuckles."

"With all due respect," Rick said. "These are human beings."

"Hey, listen, look, I got nothin' against prostitution. I've gotten my fair share of fellatio when the old bitch goes away. It's an honorable profession if you ask me. With that said, besides you, and maybe some goodie-goodie feminist types, ya think anyone *really* cares?"

A BLACK WIDOW cracked Kleopatra's face. "You lost someone you loved, eh?"

He gripped the steering wheel. "Lady, I will call—"

"Henry don't give a damn. He's paid well." She took another drag, then another, and flung the butt out the window "Wanna know about me?"

"No."

"You're a puzzle, driver. I like puzzles."

"I don't."

She lit up again and fresh smoke clouded the car. "No one dies a virgin, honey. Life fucks us all."

Rick shifted into drive.

IN THE WINTER of '72, Rick's '62 Cadillac Sedan idled waiting for his latest client. Blood soaked through his knuckle bandage, and he yanked open the glove compartment, grabbing a roll of gauze and tape. Needles spilled on the floor.

He wrapped his knuckles taut, and stuffed the blood caked rag in his glove box along with the needles.

The girl was blood smeared over a cracked mirror, the crucifix hung around her neck like an albatross, bones pultruding through skin. Broken dreams and shattered promises sucked air from the car, as though she had *Born to Lose* tattooed across her face from conception.

The rearview mirrored dead eyes and quivering lips. A stranger looked back and Rick couldn't tell whose eyes were whose.

Leaving suburbia, Rick sped down a carless highway, knuckles throbbing and head spinning.

"What's your name?" The girl asked.

"Driver."

"No, no, not your occupation. Your—"

"Driver."

She leaned forward, tears welling up in her eyes. "Can you make this easier on me? Please?"

Rick glanced in his rearview. "I'm your driver this evening, and the appointment's in thirty."

The girl gazed out the window. "Oh, okay. I see."

Girls like her came from families who played *The Convent Game*. Simple rules: Shuffle them to convents for a few weeks, tell congregations, or other interested parties the poor darling's in a hospital, or visiting relatives, or temporarily ran away, or hooked on reefer. Tell them anything, absolutely anything, except she got pregnant out of wedlock.

The Convent Game: a revolving door of girls returning to the same convents with the same stories, and the same rationalizations. Maria used to joke the word immorality was selectively applied to sexuality. Take an envelope from the mob? You're corrupt. Fuck without being married? You're immoral.

The rearview's crucifix a flashback of the parade of priests visiting Maria as cancer ravaged her body and decayed Rick's soul.

The oils.

The holy water.

The incense.

The robes.

The Last Rites.

And the crucifixes. The endless crucifixes.

"Mr. Malone," Father Vincent would say. "Has Maria atoned for all her sins?"

"Guilt her," Rick said, "And ye'll leave here on your back."

"Mr. Malone, my son, you seem troubled."

Rick balled up Vincent's collar. "Did Jesus die so altar boys could suck yer filthy pecker?"

Vincent tried pushing Rick away. "A preposterous accusation. How dare you?"

"I know 'bout you. I know 'bout the last three congregations you worked."

"You don't know—"

"I know you were at The Vatican when they turned Jews away."

"You go ta Hell."

"Guilt her, and I'll deliver you there." His eyes pierced the priest's, he let silence echo through the hall, he could almost feel the priest's heartbeat. "We clear?"

"Crystal."

"Good." Rick pushed the priest away. "Now get the hell outta my sight."

Incense burned, and they'd chant scripture in mechanical Latin. A dead language, read by dead eyes, interpreted by dead mouths, for an almost dead woman.

"Ricky," she'd say after they'd leave. "Could I trouble you to read some in English?"

Rick would nod, caressing her paper hands, the wedding ring dangling from the bone.

"And Jesus said unto him, verily I say unto thee, today shalt thou be with me in paradise" (Luke 23:43).

Rick memorized Luke 23:43. Something in those eighteen words, arranged just right, brought a strained smile to her face. He read it eyes glazed over, mouthing the words, its resonance deafening.

"Another, please, Ricky?"

A fired boiled in his gut.

"Darling?" she'd ask. "More? Please?"

"And God shall wipe away all tears from their eyes; and there shall be no more death, neither sorrow, nor crying, neither shall there be any more pain: for the former things are passed away" (Revelation 21:4).

Maria wept enough salt to create a second Dead Sea.

"It's alright darling," Maria caressed his arm. "I know you can go on without me, baby. You're stronger than you know. You were the best thing in my life."

He'd melt in the chair, every muscle became rubber, every tension loosened, and for a moment, the world evaporated. Back and forth, she touched him as a mother should. Her touch was like his first hit of heroin almost a decade ago.

"Promise me you won't give up your dream," she'd say. "Promise me you'll be a famous racecar driver. Please, Ricky?"

Rick covered his eyes. Turned away.

"Ricky, baby, you'll be okay. Hey, listen, remember when we met Paul Newman? I never saw you smile so much." She let out a laugh. "And who can forget Steve McQueen? Think he still hates Newman?"

Rick shrugged.

Maria clutched at Rick's arm. "In time, promise me you'll find someone who loves you like I do."

Rick hung his head. "We promised never to lie to each other."

"Do it for you, and if not you, do it for me, sweetheart." She placed the wedding ring in his palm. "Find someone, Ricky, and touch her with your beautiful, gorgeous, giant heart." She paused, gasping for air. "And darling, please, for her, stay clean."

Rick fled the room. He collapsed in the hall.

RICK LIT UP a Chesterfield King. "Hope you don't mind?"

"Your car," the girl said.

"My rudeness was uncalled for. My apologies."

"I got a bruised rib," she said. "And last year my jaw was wired shut."

Rick offered her a cigarette. She declined.

The engine idled at a stoplight and Rick gazed out the window. Too many memories to correlate, and too many girls with the same story, stuttering like the needle on a broken record player.

The nights left Rick with fantasies of what could have been, of what should have been. Between the upstairs neighbor slapping his wife, the stench of marijuana next door, and hookers hitting him up for blowjobs every time he came home.

He took respite in the mental images of making Henry's head a canoe.

He'd walk into the office, no hellos or goodbyes, just a single shot to the head. Or maybe he'd unload all six to prevent an open casket. The office was on third floor, perhaps a fall would do him good. Perhaps turn him into a running torch.

He'd awake in cold sweats and caress his wedding photo, a time when dreams were vivid and futures were filled with racing sponsorships. Dreams of being a big-ass winner, in a big-ass town, driving a fast-ass car. Dreams of making love till dawn while snow blanketed a lakeside cabin.

In prison, inmates talked about a forest of forgetting. Where trees had no memory, where animals didn't judge, people didn't scorn, and rivers washed away sins. Alone in his cell, Maria's voice was all he sang. On the outside, a forest of forgetting might be nice.

He vowed to save up for that.

"Aren't we gonna be late?" The girl asked, staring at the green light.

Rick stepped on the gas and pulled into a Walgreens parking lot.

"I don't do this," he said. "But what's with the crucifix?"

"Do what? Ask questions?" She chuckled. "*Now* you're curious, huh?"

"What I do, and given your family, well, it's a little…I—"

"Family said I had to do it. And, well, you know, they know best, right?"

Rick's father smashed beer bottles over his head, and his mother told him she prayed for a miscarriage. Before she died from cirrhosis of the liver, she muttered: *disappointment*. At fifteen he was homeless. At seventeen he couldn't find a useable vein in either arm, and barely one in his legs. On his twentieth birthday he got the call his father hung himself. There was no inheritance. Just bad blood and bad genes.

Rick shrugged. "Blood, water, thickness and all that Jazz. Yeah, never resonated with me."

"I'm an embarrassment to the family. They don't like my decisions." Tears flowed down her cheeks. "But hey, it is what it is, right?"

It is what it is. How Maria died while Rick squealed tires to pay medical bills.

It is what it is. How funeral bells rang while cops busted his nose with a phonebook as he coughed up names.

It is what it is. How guards laughed as inmates ran a train on him.

It is what it is. A phrase for when bodies forget souls' have given up. Or maybe it's the other way around.

"I know you're staring at the crucifix, driver. Ya Catholic or somethin'?"

"What's your situation?"

"You want the truth?"

Rick glared at her in the rearview.

"Well, shit, driver," she said. "The Leave-It-To-Beaver story is I was messin' 'round with some country boy, and you know what they say about teen girls, right? We're all too dumb to use rubbers." A chuckle choked from her frown. "A story flag saluters accept. It fits the American narrative of a life going wrong, no?"

"And the truth?" Rick asked.

"I'm no good at Geometry. Hell, driver, I'm downright terrible at it. But I have this math teacher who agreed to 'help'. At first a few suck jobs, then, ya know, one thing led to another and he wanted more. So here I am. Oh, and he comes from a country club family, and, well, I don't. So there ya have it." She stared out the window and shrugged. "Why I'm tellin' you? Who knows? You're just a driver, right?"

"Rick"

"Pardon?"

"The name's Rick and my wife was Catholic."

"Was?"

"Was."

"What happened?"

194

"Nothing good."

"I bet ya loved her very much." She rested her head against the glass and rubbed the crucifix. "I'm Elizabeth. I try to be Catholic."

"Maria would'da liked you."

"Yeah?"

Rick took a long drag. "She um, well, wasn't all that different from you." He paused. "Family outcast and all that."

"That doesn't sound good."

"On the contrary. For a few years she helped me forget." He took another drag. "Elizabeth, most of my life has been defined by violence, humiliation, and degradation. I guess I just… I dunno."

"I bet you have a good heart, Rick."

Rick chuckled. "Maria said as much too. But she don't see me now."

"But I do."

Long pause before shifting into drive. "Okay, no more time to waste. Sorry for bending your ear."

She smiled like Maria used to. "It's quite alright."

IN 1968, THE first day a free man, Rick arranged carnations on Maria's grave before reporting to his parole officer. The room sweated bourbon and reeked of stale cigars. A haze hovered above.

"Rick Malone, right? Cigarette?" Henry Johnson asked.

"Yes sir, but I don't smoke."

Rick sat as Henry thumbed through Rick's file, chaining cigarettes, and slamming glasses of Johnnie Walker. "Hell'va a deal from the D.A, Rick." He let out a cough and hawked mucus into a bucket. "Yes indeed. Hell'va deal. Hell'va file."

"Sir, imma play it straight, I promise. I'm a changed man." Rick opened the newspaper. "I've even got leads on work, ads for cabbies, limousine drivers, a few garages are—"

"To hell with all that." Henry poured another glass. "Got something better."

Rick flipped to the ads. "I have a dozen or so circled. I can show—"

"Rick." Henry slammed the glass down. "Did you hear what the hell I said?"

"Sir, with all due respect, I think—"

Henry threw the file across the room. "You sold your rehabilitation story to the parole jerkoffs. Good for you." He slammed his fists on the desk. "You people. A bloodstain on American society I gotta mop up. People don't change, pal. Sell that bullshit somewhere else."

"With all due respect, if you'd look, you'd see lots of ads for—"

Henry cracked a window. "You'll drive, alright? Special kind'a driver. I'll set things up, give you the time and place, and you be there, alright? I take seventy percent, you get the rest."

"I ain't a wheelman no more. A cabbie? I can do that. And I know cars. In prison, I brushed up on manuals. I'm sure a garage—"

Henry leaned over. "Listen here. You do what the I say, or I make one phone call and yer sweet little D.A deal becomes null an' void. Back to the can for hard time. Time so hard you'll think ya got hit by a train." Henry dangled an unlit cigarette from his lip, sweat drenched his forehead. "We clear?"

Rick clenched his fist. "Yes sir."

"Good, I'll call you in a few days." Smoke poured from his nostrils. "Now get the hell outta my office, ya white trash piece of shit."

Rick pointed at the window. "Talk like that to me again, and I'll jam your head through the goddamned window."

Henry bolted up and threw the glass at Rick. "How bout I call the D.A?"

Rick flexed his meaty hands towering over Henry. "My wife and dreams are dead." He could feel Henry's breath as he let the words linger. "Feel what I'm gettin' at?"

Henry crashed in his chair. "Just wait for my damn call."

A FEW DAYS before Rick met Elizabeth, Rick kicked open Henry's door. "She's dead, ya maggot."

"The whore?" Henry asked, puffing on a Cohiba. "Say what ya will bout that pinko Castro, he knows cigars."

"Ya listening to me? Another dead girl." Rick flung a photograph of mangled body parts at Henry's face. Then another, and another. "But I found someone reputable."

Henry puffed harder. "Doin' thinkin' now, eh Ricky? That's fresh."

"I pick the provider. We clear?"

"Or, perhaps I call—"

Rick pointed to the window. "Remember what we talked about?"

Henry grabbed a shotgun. "You people don't know yer place. I don't know what's worse. You or the goddamn pigs I gotta deal with."

"I know the church you and your wife attend. St. Boniface Cathedral, downtown, 7:30am, every Sunday." He took out an envelope and slid it across the desk. "And I happen to know that every Friday you meet a sexy blonde bombshell. I even talked to her. Washed up French model turned prostitute, no? Mole on her left cheek?"

"Hey, fuck you and fuck yer dead wife."

"I happen to know she's also mob connected." Rick paused. "She don't much like you, say's yer a bit rough. Perhaps I tell her to let the mob know you been slapping her around?"

Henry slumped down in his chair. "What's the provider's name?"

"Eat shit, that's her name. Just tell me where and when."

"We done?"

"Almost," Rick said. "You're gonna gimme the shotty, then you're gonna take the beatin' we both know you deserve."

RICK PULLED UP to the clinic and killed the engine.

"She's good, right?" Elizabeth closed her eyes, clutching the crucifix. "Please, Lord Jesus, let her be good."

Images of Maria banged around Rick's skull.

Elizabeth rocked back and forth. "Hail Mary, Full of Grace, The Lord is with thee. Blessed art thou among women, and blessed is the fruit of thy womb, Jesus. Hail Mary—"

"The way I see it," Rick turned to face her. "You can enter the clinic, and a few hours later I drive you home, or in about fifteen minutes, a bus'll take ya to a train station. Catch ma drift?"

A few days earlier, sandwiched between a church and an adult bookstore, Rick met Dr. Rita Wilson at her family practice.

The night before, she slipped a folder under his door with a note:

Mr. Malone,

You need someone reliable.

We should meet.

My number's inside.

Half confession, half resume, the dossier revealed Dr. Wilson didn't pump the women full of Lysol or plant poison. And, somehow, despite the odds being against her because of where she grew up, she graduated top of her class at Johns Hopkins.

Catholic paraphernalia littered her office like children's toys at the county morgue.

"Surprised I'm Catholic?" Dr. Wilson asked.

Rick thumbed through the file. "Impressive, sure."

"Look, if it needs to be done, it needs to be done right. And with care." She lit a *Newport*. "I don't like what I do, it goes against everything I believe. But it is what it is, ya know? And what's the alternative? These med school dropout jerkoffs? Or, worse, the ones with suspended licenses and fat malpractice files. Not sure which class of degenerate is worse."

Sirens blared in consistent intervals. A gunshot rang out. A woman cried for help. This should have startled them. This should have made them run, but before entering the clinic, Rick had stepped over a body, and before that, drove past a stop sign with three bullet holes, and before that, a car bomb illuminated a side street.

She took a long drag. "They market this to us, ya know." She exhaled through her nostrils. "Gotta love the slogan: *Alive With Pleasure*. He let out a cackle. "This whole crazy world is—"

"You reliable?"

Her face hung like the slow ticking of a grandfather clock. "Last week a woman came into my practice—a sweet, precious thing, something God made, a fever of one hundred and three. She damn near died'a heat stroke. You know what I found? A rubber catheter in her cervix." She took another drag and exhaled. "Let that sink in. And every week I see hatchet jobs like this. These people are like children fumbling with chainsaws." She puffed harder. "And, every week I grow more and more goddamn sick of it."

"How'd she turn out?"

Dr. Wilson stared at the wall, as though the nicotine stains would divine answers. As if the Virgin Mary mural would reveal God's unvirgin plan. "Told her she couldn't have children. Too much cervical damage." She closed her eyes. "Slit her wrists the next day."

"Sorry to hear that."

"Yeah," Dr. Wilson said. "All too common. Shall I continue explaining why I do—"

"No."

"Who'da thunk we'd be outlaws?" She cracked a window, a cool breeze flooded in. "Folks like us always return to the streets. Our souls are tethered to it, rusted chains we hate, then learn to love." She paused. "At least I get a 9-5 paycheck."

"Are you reliable?"

"What's yer favorite color?"

"Don't have one."

"Food?"

"Whatever Maria made."

"Who? Oh, never mind." She said, "And did you choose to love her cooking? Or did it choose you?"

"Look. Time's valuable. Are you—"

"You know Rick, let me tell you somethin'. It don't matter I went to Johns Hopkins. It don't matter I graduated in the top of my class." She exhaled a cloud of smoke. "People never see the white coat. You know what they see?"

"Someone who talks too much?"

"Hardy-har." She extended her arm and rubbed it. "This. That's it."

"Listen lady, I—"

"The point, Mr. Malone, is the outlaw lifestyle chose us, not the other way around. You don't have to like it. You can downright hate it. I know I do. But it likes you. It likes me. Ya feel?"

"You contacted me, said you were reliable. Another time, another place, I might entertain such philosophical ramblings, but right now, I need someone who will do these girls right. How'd ya find me anyway?"

"The streets sing your name." She laughed lighting up another Newport. "The streets say yer a failed race-car driver, they also say you were about to make it big, say ya had a lovely wife too. Boy oh boy, life sure took a left turn off a cliff." A car backfired, or maybe it was another gunshot. "How many times has yer soul broke? Has it shattered yet? Will all the king's horsemen and all the king's men—"

Rick lit up a joint DJ Sparkles had given him.

"Word 'round these parts is Thomas Richardson's doin' time in the ICU because'a you." A smile shattered her face. "Ya took care of what I couldn't. For six months I been tryna put that evil prick outta business."

After the third girl died from Thomas "Lysol" Richardson, Rick called 911 after turning his face into hamburger. And there was Martin Johnson, and Cynthia Morgan, operating out of warehouses caked with mold, using blood rusted instruments. Cynthia would shoot heroin before washing up, and Martin would slam vodka during procedures. Both babbled about *The Doors* and *Janis Joplin*. Both danced around like Woodstock junkies. Both ended up in body bags at the bottom of a river.

THC hit Rick, and he closed his eyes. "I don't suffer incompetence."

"Ma time's endin'," Dr. Wilson said. "Rumor has it this will all be on the up and up." She tossed Rick *The New York Times*. "Been followin' the *Roe v. Wade* case?"

"I've heard," Rick said. "But, right now, are you reliable?"

"Bring 'em to me. I'll do 'em right."

"Ma'am, for yer sake, I hope so."

"Ma'am? I'm movin' up in the world. Streets never say you's a gentleman."

"I ain't."

Rita patted her St. Jude statue. "You'll not find anyone better."

RICK PRODUCED A crisp one-hundred-dollar bill. "Maria said to keep this for a rainy day."

Elizabeth waved it away. "I'm okay."

"Whatever choice you make, clinic or bus, I'll be here, understood?"

Elizabeth slammed the door and approached Rick. "Thank you."

"Okay, sure, off you go."

"No, really, you're the first person to care." Her hands trembled and shivered with the wind. "You were a, well, I guess, the only person who ever listened, and in your own way, touched me with your heart."

Rick turned away. "All right, no worries, off you go now."

"Thank's again."

The girl began walking away. Rick slapped the dash. "Damn it, hold up."

"Why?"

"Most days I feel like a ghost, Elizabeth."

"Me too."

Rick scribbled down numbers on a pad of paper. "This is an account number. Take it to any *Wells Fargo* branch, and you'll have just over four-thousand dollars. Maybe you could use it for, I dunno, a fresh start? New life?"

"Rick," Elizabeth teared up. "I can't take this."

"Maria would want it." Rick's hand shook as he lit another cigarette. "For a guy pushin' fifty? Doin' what I do? Ma time's pretty much passed. You need to take this."

"Rick, I—"

"Please." His eyes bled desperation. "You *need* to take this. Maria *needs* you to take this." He reached into his pocket and removed Maria's ring and kissed it. "This too."

"Rick, I…can't."

"Elizabeth, please. Take it."

"Okay." Elizabeth stuffed the paper and ring in her pocket. "Kindness is in short supply these days. I… well… I just—"

"Get goin' now. Bus'll be here in less than ten, and you're already late. But I'll be here." He took a long breath. "Yeah, I'll be here."

"Thank you, Rick." Tears rolled down her cheeks. "May you find peace someday."

THEN SHE WAS GONE

by

Sharon Bairden

20th December

SILENT NIGHT, holy night

"I'm going to kill her, so help me God"

All is calm, all is bright

'Where's my mummy? I want my mummy. Mummy, mummy…" cries fill the hallway. Suffocating me.

Round yon Virgin, Mother and Child

"Muuuuuummy," her voice rising to a crescendo.

Clutching at the side of my head. I try to drown out her voice. Allow my fingers to wind themselves into my hair. The tugging brings pain. It is welcome. A distraction from what is unfolding behind closed doors.

Holy infant so tender and mild

Her words morphing into screams now. Sharp. Stabbing. Needles piercing my brain. I wish her gone. I wish me gone.

Sleep in heavenly peace

"Sleep in heavenly peace, that's a fucking joke," I want to fill my lungs and scream my pain out into the world but what's the point? Nobody will hear me. My screams will only mingle with hers to fill the empty void of the house we share. Me and her.

Us.

Two.

I want it to be one.

I want it to be NONE!

Outside, the carol singers fall silent, before launching into the next verse, turning the air rich with Christmas spirit. Me, I've gorged myself with bitterness, shattered dreams and an agonising realisation I'm trapped with no way out. Filled with a desire to burst out my front door and bludgeon every last one of those carol singers to death. Maybe then people would know what it's really like for me.

I don't. Of course, I don't.

I stay where I am, and give in to my legs buckling under the pressure of being me. I crumple to the floor like a puppet released from my strings and stuff my fist hard into my mouth to muffle my own frustrated shrieks.

Still, she keeps screaming.

The night fills with the sound of Christmas. Behind my front door, resentment seeps from the walls and swallows me whole.

I try to stand up. Can't. I want to sink into the floor and disappear. To be gone. Forever. To be free from the smothering responsibility of her.

It's my first Christmas on my own with her and I really don't think I'm going to make it.

21st December

SAUCHIEHALL STREET IS swarming. I'm standing in the midst of the crowds, panic rising in my belly. I steal a glance at my phone. 1.25 p.m. I've been gone an hour already; I didn't realise the bus would take quite as long as it had. Should have gone for the express bus, or the train. But money was tight. Every penny is a prisoner these days. Just like me. From out of nowhere a little hint of excitement bubbles up and almost masks my panic. A small voice whispers *This is what it feels like to be free.* But I'm not free, I know I'm not, this is all just an illusion, pretending on the outside to be like everyone else around me. Normal. I'm not normal. I'm not free. I'm trapped. She'll be ok on her own, it's only for a few hours, isn't it? She'll be fine? Won't she? She's had her lunch, fed and watered, she'll be fine. I won't be gone *that* long. If I say it often enough, does it become justification?

She was fine the other night when I left her by herself. It was just for an hour. 60 minutes. That's all. I wasn't that far away. Just at the pub. I mean, I had to get out. I needed a break, is it so wrong to want some freedom in my life? Is it terrible to need some escape from the relentless, thankless drudgery of it all? I didn't ask for this, this wasn't the life I chose for myself. Nobody asked me if I wanted to be left alone with her, nobody gave me a choice. So surely there's nobody out there that can begrudge me a little bit of time to myself. *Me time* that's what they call it. They tell you it's good for your mental health, *me time,* yes that's all it is. I can hardly ask for a sitter, can I? I can hardly go chapping the doors of strangers to ask someone to look after her. What would they think? She'll be fine, I'll not be gone long. I repeat it five times under my breath, reassuring myself; justifying my choices. *The medicine will help,* the voice whispers in my ear.

The crowds on the streets seem to have a life of their own, a pulsing mass of bodies move as though unseen hands direct them. I've never felt so alone. I drop my eyes to the pavement and push my way through without even realising the direction I am going in. Abruptly I come to a halt and lift my head. I'm outside of Lauders on the corner of Sauchiehall and Renfield Streets. The smell of stale beer and the raucous laughter of the customers from inside is intoxicating. It draws me closer to the door. So very tempting. *Just one.* My fingers tighten round the purse in my pocket. The money inside is for presents, for food. Things that will make Christmas feel just a little bit normal.

Just one little drink. It won't hurt, will it? She'll be sound asleep. She's safe, the door's locked, she can't get out and nobody can get in. She won't even notice I'm gone.

I nudge open the door and hesitate on the threshold as though waiting for permission to step through a portal to a better life. The rush of warm air on my cheeks is welcome. I'm chilled to the bone.

I lift one foot in front of the other, ready to take that step over the threshold when a group of hideous Yummy-Mummies veer towards me. All I see are tits, teeth, and designer clothes. A cloud of expensive perfume threatens to choke me.

They are laughing.

I stop in my tracks.

Laughing at me?

"Come on Sylv, we need to get a shift on, I need to get back for the schools getting out. You and your liquid lunches," squeals the woman leading the pack.

I fade into the doorway. The other women braying like hyenas as they pour out the door past me. I'm invisible. Gone. Not here. Women like them don't see women like me. I don't even exist on their radar. No tits and teeth marking me out as one of the beautiful ones. Christ, I hadn't even brushed my teeth this morning and I can't even bring myself to think of the grubby grey bra holding up my saggy tits. I find myself carried out in their wake back onto the street, like they were placing me back in my rightful place, outside looking in.

Then they were gone, and I was still here. I am still me. She is still at home. Alone.

The crowds around me blur now as I wipe my eyes with the back of my hand. It's even busier. People swarm around me, jostling and jolly, agitated and angry—they flow this way and that, back and forth, in and out, round about. All ways. Everyway. I'm losing myself and nobody cares. Not one person stops to ask me if I'm okay. Season of goodwill, my arse. They're all going somewhere. Purpose to their lives. They are someone. Me? I could be anybody. Anything. Nobody. Out here, I'm drowning in waves of indecision, stay or go? Make Christmas special or turn and run for the hills? I know what my choice would be.

I don't make it. Of course I don't.

I make myself still, I breathe real deep and I ground myself. I can feel my feet firm against the ground. Take another deep breath, ignoring the mutters of irritation from people trying to get by me. I want to scream out loud, "Look at me, I'm here, I'm real!" but I don't. Instead I steel myself, put my head down, and move with the crowds. Invisible. But I need to do this, it's Christmas, and we need one small shred of normality in our lives. She needs some normality in her life. I will do this. This year.

Basket in hand, I sweep the shelves. I don't pay much attention to what I pick up, as long as it's shiny, it doesn't matter what I buy, she doesn't know any better. Once wrapped in last year's wrapping paper, it will all be much of a same to her. But it's what I need to do. I need to give her a Christmas day. She deserves that much.

22nd December

I STAND AT the window, gazing out at the neighbouring houses. I wonder if anyone else feels like I do tonight. Night-time has engulfed the street save for the twinkling lights of neighbours' decorations. I guess they probably don't feel the same. I pull the curtains closed. Glance around my own living room. The worn and tired furniture, wallpaper peeling at the edges, the ancient cheap tinsel stuck onto the wall failing to add any cheer. No sparkling fairy lights here, no Christmas movies playing in the background. A solitary Christmas card balanced precariously on the mantelpiece, above a gas fire long ago condemned by the gas board. Look at the card closely enough and you will see the Sellotape barely holding it together. Like me. Holding on by the skin of our teeth.

I choose to ignore the soft sobs coming from her bedroom. When she is quiet, it's so much easier to drown her out. She's been like this since teatime. Whiney, whinging and bloody irritating. Apparently, she didn't like what I put down in front of her for dinner. Why is she always so bloody ungrateful? I'm doing my best… the very best I can do on my own. If only he hadn't gone.

It had all been so different before, it doesn't even feel like that long ago. Back when things were good, the three of us together, muddling along in our own way. Family. But then he left. And she blamed me. All my fault as usual, everything is always my fault, isn't it? Bastard. Wherever he ended up and I hope it is hell, he'll be blaming me too. I know he will. But it wasn't my fault. It was all down to him. He changed. He wasn't the same man he used to be. Oh, of course, he denied it, but I knew. I'd watched him change into someone nasty and spiteful. I couldn't do right for doing wrong. Neither could she. We both bore the brunt of it. Of him. So yes, it's for the best he's gone now. I try so hard to convince myself.

My eyes turn to the front door, my escape route. I could nip down to the pub. Just for one little drink, maybe two? I'll be okay there, nobody bothers me in there—it's not that kind of place. Just one wee drink. It will calm my nerves, settle me down. Help me sleep. Nobody will ever know. The neighbours' curtains are all drawn now.

I drag a brush through my hair. I don't bother with make-up. It's not like I'm trying to impress anyone, there's no point in that. I mean who would want me with her in tow. I just want some *me time*.

Her cries are just a whimper now, as I push open her bedroom door. Her eyes squint as the light from the hallway bathes her in a stark white light. She shrinks back into the covers. Cowering. Her reaction irritates me. Why is she so afraid of me? All I've ever done for her is to look after her, everything I've sacrificed for her. My whole life. Me.

Hush little baby, I croon as I move towards her. Holding the spoon out to her mouth, careful not to spill one single drop.

She resists at first. I fix her with one of my stares. She knows better. Her jaw falls slack, her eyes resigned, and she swallows.

"Good girl," I whisper, as I back out of her room, pulling the door closed behind me.

She's asleep in minutes. I checked. Of course I did—I'm not some kind of monster.

I slip on my trainers and rummage around in my jeans pocket. The crumpled-up note is still there. Ten pounds saved from Christmas shopping. A couple of drinks won't hurt, will they? If I tell myself often enough, it will become the truth.

I slip out the front door and the night-time swallows me whole.

I'm gone.

23rd December

THE HOUSE IS quiet. Still and for that I am thankful. A couple of drinks turned into four. Five? Six? I can't remember. Unable to move my head, my hands tentatively grope the bedsheets around me. It's only me. Thank Christ for that. At least I hadn't been stupid enough to let whoever it was who bought me those extra drinks come back home with me.

My mouth feels like the bottom of a bird's cage and the taste is just as disgusting. I need water, but I can't bring myself to move. A sudden cramp in my belly changes that and I leap from my bed making it to the toilet just in time.

The bathroom tiles are cold. I lie on my back while the room comes into focus and my body embraces the chill. Above me on the ceiling, memories play out like a bad movie, the cracks like the interference on the old black and white films of my childhood. Happier times. Happy memories. Fun. Love. Laughter. When I was glad to be there. When I didn't wish to be gone.

The tracks left by my tears sting my cheeks. The past is gone, and this is the present. My present and my future. Another wave of nausea creeps over me. I vomit and this time I don't even attempt to make the pan.

I'VE BEEN WATCHING her sleep for the past couple of hours now. And yes, I checked she was still breathing. I didn't give her that much medicine, only enough to allow me to get a quick nap after I was sick. Just lying there, she looks so peaceful. At rest even. Not for the first time, I long for things to be different. Is it so wrong of me to wish that we were just like every other mother and daughter out there? Why can't we be snuggled up on the sofa watching Christmas movies and overdosing on chocolate? There's nothing wrong with that. It's not like I'm asking for the moon, is it?

She stirs.

"*Mummy.*" The word slips from her lips. Oh, Christ not again, please don't let her start again. Reaching deep into my soul, I search for some empathy, for some kindness. I find a little nugget tucked deep inside. My hand strokes hers; hers are so tiny and fragile inside my big, ugly clumsy hands.

"Ssshhh," I whisper. She opens her eyes and smiles up at me. My heart sings.

24th December

I WAKE UP, not with my usual feeling of dread, instead I feel a strange long forgotten feeling of contentment. Last night had been good. Really good. For the first time in a long time, our house had felt normal, like I imagine all the other families out there at this time of year, smiles on our faces as we curled up on the couch watching Christmas movies. I hadn't even had to fight with her to go to bed and she had slept like a baby the whole night. I honestly can't tell you how good it felt to be like a normal mum and daughter just being together.

It doesn't last though, it never does.

Today normal service has resumed.

Today she is sullen. Nothing pleases her. Not even her favourite breakfast. Cereal gets tipped over the floor; toast mashed into the carpet. I give up. She can go hungry. I tried. She decides she wants to go out. I say yes, perhaps the fresh air will tire her out. So, I wash and dress her. Well, I try my best. She wants to do it herself, even though she can't, and I can't possibly let her go out wearing a summer dress in the middle of winter. That causes a strop. So, we compromise, she gets to wear the dress and I bribe her with chocolate—*well at least she has eaten something*—to put on her favourite jumper. I force the hat, scarf and gloves on while melted chocolate dribbles down her chin. I wipe it off roughly with the cuff of my jumper and ignore her indignant protests.

I've just wrestled with her to get her shoes on and got my jacket on when she announces that she doesn't want to go out after all.

"It's too cold," she whines, and plonks herself down on the bottom stair. She's stubborn and there is no amount of cajoling that will force her over the doorstep. So, I give into her again. Always me making the sacrifices. I put on the television for her, and I try to tidy up a little. She won't settle. She's like a little shadow following me from room to room. Questions come fast and furious.

"What are you doing? Why are you moving that? Don't touch that, it's mine? Where has he gone? Why isn't he here? He should be here? Why did he leave us? You made him go. It's all your fault and I hate you…" It's at this point that she goes into a full-blown meltdown, her fists raining blows down on me. Of course, she's not strong enough to do me any harm, but it doesn't matter, those mean little punches build and build in their intensity, until something inside me snaps, and I slap her. Hard. Right across her face. The faint outline of my handprint rises on her cheek. Then she is quiet. Her eyes accuse me. I should feel shame, I should feel sorry. I feel neither, I just feel relief. The silence is golden.

I push her into the bedroom and slam the door shut.

I hate her. I can't take anymore.

I play Christmas music loud enough to drown out her tears, I put her dinner on a tray and leave it in her room. I don't even care if she eats it or not. Christ, I don't even care if she chokes on it. I wish she would.

Before I go to bed, I leave out milk and biscuits for Santa Claus and a carrot for his reindeer. It's good to keep the old traditions going don't you think?

25th December

I'VE BEEN UP since 4 a.m. with her. Helping her unwrap her presents. All for her. None for me. Well, it's not like she can go out and buy me anything is it? I remind myself it's about the giving and not receiving. All very well until you are the one who does all the giving all the time and receive nothing back in return. And I mean nothing, not even a smile, a hug or even a thank you. No, all I got was a tantrum for my troubles. It's a wonder the neighbours haven't called social services before now.

This is the last time I will ever do this.

I'm done.

I'd pushed her out of the living room and slammed the door in her face. My back against the door, I ignored her cries. Screams at first, slowly giving way to soft sobs.

Outside the voice whimpered: *"Mummy, mummy, I want my mummy."*

Something snaps inside me. My decision made. I step out and take her by the hand.

"Mummy, are we going home now?"

I feel calm now. "Hush," I soothe, as I lead her into the bedroom. "Lie down, I'll tuck you in."

She resists, a little.

I force her onto the bed and tuck the covers tight around her, like a shroud.

Closing my mind against the struggle.

I pick up the pillow, place it over her face and push down. "Hush now, sleep, please sleep."

A minute… two… three… four.

The struggling stops. She is still. Gone.

I collapse to the floor. Relieved. Calm.

THE RATTLE OF the letterbox forces me out my thoughts. I have no idea how long I've lain there.

A voice barks through the letterbox: "It's me. Are you there? Is everything okay?"

I force myself to my feet and stumble to the door, unlatch it and peer out. The blue uniform of the carer is instantly recognisable.

"How's things, love? I've missed you both this last week. I got the message from the office cancelling your visits all week. Is everything okay?"

She doesn't wait for my reply; the words keep spilling from her mouth. "I thought I'd just pop round and see how you were both doing?"

"Hush, I've just got her off. She's had a bad day. I think she'll sleep well now."

The carer gives me reassuring smile. "You're doing a grand job. I don't know how you have coped this last year. What with your dad dying so suddenly like that."

My face flushes. *Please don't start talking about my dad, that's all in the past now,* I silently beg her. She remembers my dad; she was here for him too. Until he died in his sleep. But she didn't know him before he changed, before he became spiteful and nasty. He had to go. I couldn't take it anymore; I couldn't take him anymore.

My big ugly hands twitch as my brain reminds them of the pillow...

This carer had been kind then. She sent me a card when Dad went. A lovely sympathy card. I bet she wouldn't have sent it if she knew the truth. If she knew it really was all my fault. I wonder if she'll send one this time. I wonder if she will have sympathy now.

She's pushing herself forward. I want her to stop. I can't stop her. That would be rude. She would think it was strange. She would think I'm strange, her being so kind and all that.

"It's not easy," she's saying to me. "Your mum will know you're only doing your best love. Underneath it all, she's still in there, she's not gone. The dementia only masks her identity, but she's still there inside and she knows you care."

If only she knew. It's too late now, she's gone.

I try to smile. "Please don't wake her," I whisper as I let her in.

AND THEN HE WAS GONE

by

Ailsa Cawley

MONDAY MORNING AND Janie was off to work. Exactly as she'd return—in the dark. It was winter and the sun wouldn't start to rise for at least another forty minutes. She felt him there as she did every day. Every moment as she left the house. Walking far enough behind her to duck into a doorway or pretend to be tying a shoelace if she turned. The flesh on the back of her neck prickled with it, the knowing, warning her today she was yet again not alone.

Later he'd be there following at a pace right on schedule, ducking and diving. Revelling in his own cleverness. Perceived cleverness. It was wearing and yet he never acknowledged this was what he did. Nothing in his demeanour to show he was doing it. Out of the corner of her eye she'd witnessed him on many occasions and yet he still denied it.

If she finished work early she'd do the shopping. Likely struggle onto a heaving bus, by then in rush hour, always with eight or nine heavy carrier bags. He would be following her then, too. And after she'd been in half an hour, he'd waltz through the door smirking at her and always saying the same thing: "I tried to get back sooner so I could help you home, but I must have missed you again."

Janie had tried to confront him about his endless following of her. At first, she'd been convinced it was just some weirdo from the estate they lived on. He'd laughed and said she was imagining things. Had said she thought too much of herself. She was too self-important. Too spoiled. Her suspicions were confirmed when he had to work late and nobody was following her from the bus stop. No tell-tale tingling screaming she was being watched. But the most important thing to prove her suspicions was when she went out to empty the bins ready for the next day's collection. A neighbour, Ann, had struck up a conversation about the weather, and the usual everyday things neighbours talk about when her expression had suddenly changed as though she'd recollected some unwanted, bitter memory.

"Why do you stay?" she'd asked, clapping her hand over her mouth, as though it had betrayed her.

Janie had felt her mouth go dry. "Why wouldn't I, Ann?"

The conversation had developed quickly, comfortably as though they'd always been friends and Ann had confirmed Tom, her husband, was indeed following her every single day. She'd once said to him that if he wanted to follow her then he should see her to the bus stop like a normal man, or meet her on the way home and help her carry the shopping, but he'd simply laughed in her face and denied he was doing anything. For a while she'd started questioning herself. Her own sanity.

Thanks to Ann, she knew she wasn't imagining it all. Yet, she still couldn't see how to stop it, unless he finally admitted it. Which he would never do. She knew all this, but still couldn't summon the strength to leave. To get away. Run.

AFTER SAYING GOODBYE to Ann, Janie had sat on the living room floor sorting through the laundry, tears rolling down her cheeks. After a little while, she'd decided to put the kettle on and make sure the kitchen was tidy. It caused ructions if there was a single thing out of place, and she hadn't the energy for an angry exchange tonight.

Things seemed to be escalating recently, but she was sure he'd never do anything. The rest of his family were quick to get physical, but he always seemed to condemn them. More so in private than public. She was starting to wonder what on earth she'd got herself into. Their house had to be run so similarly to his parents that she wondered if he was afraid of displeasing them, had no imagination or just thought it was the only way to be.

SHE'D SENSED HIM suddenly at the kitchen window and turned, shocked by his appearance there, instead of at the unlocked back door next to it. Janie had just decided to keep her new knowledge to herself and at least she knew she wasn't losing her mind. But, she thought something would have to be done about it. This could not happen for the rest of her life. Though how to stop it and who to ask for advice was more difficult. She'd think about that tomorrow.

Tom looked around the kitchen, his smile less than pleasant. "Dinner?" he asked.

"I didn't make any. You said you were finishing anywhere between seven and nine so you'd grab something at work," Janie said.

"So, you didn't bother? Which means I have to go to the chippy again?" he goaded her.

"It'll take half an hour to cook something and we'll eat then." Janie knew she sounded like she was trying to reason with a toddler and moderated her tone before an almighty row broke out.

"Don't worry, I'll go and get us *both* something, eh?" He rolled his eyes. Obviously expecting that she'd not emptied the bin, he had kicked it over and looked more annoyed when nothing fell out onto the floor.

LATER, JANIE WONDERED why she hadn't picked up on these signals. Yet, it was like having a leaky tap. If it's not loud and consistent you don't tend to notice. She sighed, picked up the bin and noticed that it was marked from the boots he always wore.

Fifteen minutes later he breezed into the kitchen. Two carrier bags in his hands. Huge smile replacing the earlier frown and what she could only describe as a 'tantrum'. And yet, she was careful. After dinner she was curled in the armchair as he took away the plates. As he passed, he leaned in to kiss her forehead. She had to force herself not to duck.

Returning and sitting on the sofa, he kept watching her as he first sipped and then necked his lager. Lifted his arm and indicated to Janie to sit next to him. His fingers dug into her shoulder.

"No tantrums Janie, eh? You know we always sit together of an evening. That's being a couple." He spoke slowly, deliberately. Explaining to the stupid child he considered her to be. They were ten years different in age and he felt it necessary to give her advice on how she should act, be. Had this only begun since they'd lived together? She couldn't recall. Janie was hoping he was having work problems that would soon go away. He seemed to be very stressed at work, recently.

"I know. I just thought you looked comfortable and didn't want to shift you after a tough day." Janie was amazed at the lie tripping off her tongue, as she realised she didn't want to sit next to him. She felt unsafe around him. Was it just the chat with Anne? Or was it how she felt deep down?

It got to about ten thirty and Janie found herself stifling a yawn.

Tom looked at her, indulgently. Infuriating her. 'I suppose you need to get to bed. You do need to get more sleep. You're not looking your best right now. I can't have people thinking you're neglecting your appearance since we moved in. But if I want to I will wake you later. I don't actually care if you are asleep so you might as well give in, okay?' He challenged.

"We were told to leave it for the week. It's only been two nights," Janie replied. Stunned that he'd seemed to have forgotten.

"They always say that, but nobody does," he scoffed.

He actually means it, Janie thought.

He doesn't even know the full story, Janie thought as she'd told him that she'd had an infection and that was all. They'd thought that she'd been pregnant when she went to the GP surgery. The doctor was a straight talking woman, who'd put her hand on his chest when he tried to barge into her room. She'd helped Janie to lie down and looked her directly in the eyes.

"Does he know?" she asked Janie

"He knows I might have been, but that's it. Why?"

"I suggest you say you were mistaken. Missed periods are common. I've known men like him. Lie." The doctor was emphatic. Janie nodded.

"We can't save the baby, now, but that's probably best for many reasons. You need rest after this. He doesn't have to know at all."

Janie felt the tears sting and let them course down her cheeks. She gasped in pain. The doctor apologised and rubbed her arm, soothing her gently. She'd stilled her hand on Janie's arm.

"It's definitely gone. You do have an almighty infection, I'd not be surprised if it was from him. You need to rest. We'll make sure he understands."

Janie nodded. Silently naming her child and knowing she wouldn't meet it. Her.

He'd seemed to understand and go along with things and now... now he'd moved the goalposts again. This happened too often. Yet Janie didn't know how to change it or what to do. She was buying a house with a man who day by day was becoming the image of his father. A man who she knew instilled fear in his wife. Who decided exactly what happened in his house—unquestioned. A man who she knew wanted his family to emulate him. She knew she couldn't endure this forever.

Except the wedding was booked. The dread lay on her shoulders like a cloak weighted with stones. It made her feel as though she was going under. She'd manage. Maybe she just needed to get on with it, like most people were suggesting. Her friend had suggested she got out now. But there was already a mortgage round her neck. A noose that was tightening by the day.

Janie managed to fall asleep remarkably fast, considering the thoughts spinning around her head. It was the nightmare that pulled her back from the deepest sleep in a long time. She'd felt like she was suffocating. Then she heard the voice.

"Bitch. You bloody bitch. Think you can tell me what to do? Say no to me?" It was Tom. This was really happening.

Janie tried to squirm off the bed and get away. But he was too strong. "No, don't. Please. No!"

She kept repeating herself, hoping the words would penetrate his head, or heart, if one existed. The light from the hall cast more than enough glow into the room. He'd moved a mirror so he could see himself as he kept forcing himself into her. Occasionally muttering, "That's what you want really, you lot." Tears coursed down her cheeks and her throat was hoarse from telling him no she didn't want this. It had spurred him on. It was easier to zone out, surrender, tell herself it would be over soon.

Eventually, soaked in sweat he climbed over her, onto his side of the bed. She'd tried to move away as far as she could. But pain stilled her. Somewhere inside the fear was dissolving into sheer anger.

She thought he was asleep and slowly rose to get to the bathroom so she could clean herself up. The bruising had begun and there were scratches blooming. The bleeding had started again, too. She got herself some more pyjamas from the hall cupboard. The others he'd torn from her. If they were salvageable, she'd never want them near her again.

As she eased herself into bed she heard him speak, voice low, warning.

"Don't ever say no to me, again, Janie. You wouldn't be able to take me if I lose my cool."

Without thinking Janie replied, anger cold and hard.

"You do that to me again, and I will kill you as you sleep. So you had better sleep with one eye open." She'd heard him gasp, before he sighed deeply as though already asleep and was sleep talking.

THE NEXT MORNING Janie was in a lot more pain than the previous night. But she was damned if he would know that.

She'd whistled and sang as she made her tea before leaving. Janie put on more makeup than usual. Extra blusher to cover her pale cheeks. She took her lunch from the fridge and opened the door into the concreted backyard of the small terraced house.

It was crisp outside, a mild frost having settled overnight. The cobbled lane glistening like sprinkled diamonds. The street was always slippery along the side of the house, so she crossed the lane, then the main road—determined not to fall.

She'd left a few minutes early, but if he was following her today, she didn't care. Janie even turned in challenge, although she knew he wasn't there.

AT THE BUS stop the queue was building. This bus was always pretty busy and there were still a few minutes left before it's arrival.

There was a butcher's shop looking on to the bus stop. The butcher waved at Janie every morning. Today was no different, she thought. Until suddenly the man came dashing from the shop and asked her if she was okay and after scouring the street asked her if she knew 'the feller' was following her around. Janie nodded, and before she could reply he said, "You want him gone, love." Raising his eyebrows at her. Again, she nodded, not sure what to say. She usually bought her meat there and said she'd pick up dinner, tonight.

Janie's anger was burning. The butcher, a virtual stranger could see what he was. Yet, why wouldn't he? He was able to see the bus stops that she used from his shop, so he was perfectly placed to notice. What do you say to someone who knows, *someone else who knows,* she thought, remembering her neighbour and their conversation. How many people knew what he was like? Yet, realistically what could they do?

A sense of shame and anger washed over Janie, making her breathless with the feeling of going under. From every angle she felt trapped. She glanced back at the butcher who waved.

THE BUS SQUEALED to a halt, spraying dirty grey slush across the path and anyone too close to the edge of it. A few splashes hit Janie's black trousers and she felt sick as memories of last night peppered her mind. She showed her bus pass, and the driver looked at her.

"You alright, love? You've gone a bit pale," he said.

"Fine thanks, just cold. But I'll soon warm through." She wasn't sure if she was reassuring him or herself.

She'd found her seat, and settled in by the window. It was still dark enough to not see clearly, and mixed with the salted spray over the windows, outside images were blurred. In about twenty minutes she'd get to the bit of the journey that was pleasant. The part of the journey that for her spelled hope. As soon as the bus passed the factory on her right—a big sprawling factory that had been instrumental in making munitions and now made tanks and machinery, although everyone said it wouldn't be there forever. But what was?

Janie looked to her left, eyes training the ground for the signs she needed at the moment. There they were. Just poking through the virgin snow, right next to the flats that towered above. Their shadow was cast in another direction and now, as the sun rose properly, the carpet of crocuses heralded a beginning. A new beginning. One Janie wanted so badly, but couldn't find a way to bring about.

How do you leave someone who is getting more terrifying by the day? When you know they have the capacity to destroy you and anyone around you? Her friends had recently overheard a call he made when she was at their house for a girls night. Threatening to drag her home if she wasn't through the door in ten minutes. She was thirty minutes away in a taxi. Her guts had turned to water as he yelled and screamed. Her friend had taken the phone from her—a landline so there was no kidding where she was even if she'd wanted to. She'd asked what his problem was. He'd seemed to calm down, but he'd blamed her. Handing the phone over for sympathy, he'd screamed later.

How had this all come about? One thing she felt she did understand was why none of his relationships had survived. It's never his fault, his mum had said. He was just 'unlucky' and he was 'a nice lad, who got taken advantage of'.

Janie felt like she dreamt her way through the day, everything on autopilot. Apart from the pain, she'd felt nothing, thought nothing. Apart from the moment the lady at work brought her a cake over saying she was losing a lot of weight recently. She accepted it almost tearfully, and guiltily. As if he would know. The monitoring of her as if she was unable to manage herself had to stop. But getting out would be harder, so much harder than getting in had been. How do you solve a problem that's so all consuming?

SHE LEFT WORK almost on time, missing her first bus by seconds. She'd still catch the butcher as he was kind enough to open the door if people got off the bus. Maybe she'd just ask the man for a knife and do the job herself. Knowing unless she had to, she'd not actually go that far.

The bus was hot and sticky within minutes. She'd been able to see steam rising off the people getting on as it began to rain. The stench of sweat, dirt and food mixed together making her nauseous. The blood was still flowing from her and she was sure everyone could smell it, as she could. *This is not going to be the sum total of my life.* Becoming a domestic drudge, his fucking mother, and some terrified woman who watched her words, actions and thoughts. She felt as though she was melting inside. He'd already destroyed any bits of joy she had and was picking at her. She felt like every time the wounds he made were scabbing over he picked at them again, so only a deep scar would be left. A ghost self.

Well, that's not going to be me. I can't wait to see what he does. I will die. That thought terrified her so much she'd decided to find a way out. Whatever that entailed.

ON THE RIDE home, Janie always looked out to see if she could catch sight of the river as it curled in and out of the various places that it had been tamed into over the years.

Tonight it flowed quickly, the rain having come down hard today. Again she thought she'd do something. If the river fought back, then so could she. In her own way.

An older man was standing by the bus stop, though he didn't get on. He seemed to be watching her. He was well camouflaged in the strange light. His coat was a heavy winter coat and he wore a cap on his head and a jaunty scarf tied around his neck. Strangely, it didn't creep her out as it should have done. He'd raised his hand in acknowledgement of her scrutiny and embarrassed at being caught staring, she'd mirrored his wave. More of a salute than a wave, she thought.

As the bus pulled away Janie was compelled to look back, feeling like he was watching. But he'd gone, already. There seemed to be a familiarity to him, yet there couldn't be.

Her bus stop arrived suddenly and she dashed from the seat, pressing the bell so he didn't whizz by.

She'd climbed down and turned, looking behind her at the wasteland where she sometimes walked. Desolate some people called it. It was where an old factory had stood, before being raised to the ground. Very little grew there. The occasional bush stood out vividly on the grey-brown landscape. It looked as though it ended suddenly, and you'd fall off the earth.

With a sigh, she'd turned towards the butcher's shop. She needed to pick up the meat for dinner. *Or that'll be another thing.* It's not like there's nothing in, he just wanted certain things on certain days with no deviation. Unless one of his good friends suggested it, then it was a different matter. Then, he became Mr Moveable. Anything could be done differently to keep in with buddies, and their opinions became his.

They'd gone out with them a few weeks ago. He'd outdone himself then. She'd always felt measured against his friends' girlfriends. He'd proven that what he said was rubbish, was in fact truth. On returning he'd scrutinised her, closely. Suggested, as his nails dug into her arm, that she 'try' wearing green contact lenses and dye her hair black. She'd refused and he'd said she was a bore. She'd neither wanted to, nor felt it right to become someone else's carbon copy to satisfy his fantasies. But last night, still playing on her mind, had now cemented her thoughts that they were not going to last.

Someone had to give. Someone had to go. Permanently.

"YOU'RE LOOKING CHIRPIER than this morning," said the butcher as she closed the door.

"Well, Pete, I can't let my life go lower so I'm just hoping it's on the up," she'd replied with a smile.

"Have you kicked him out, then?"

Janie raised her eyebrows at the mental picture of that.

"Hope?" repeated Pete.

"It's all I've got right now. I'll come to a decision," she hedged.

"Have you seen him?" Pete's face looked hopeful.

"Who?" Janie was anxious, looking around her.

"Not him. The Auld fella. I saw you looking across the wasteland there, I assumed you'd seen him. You wouldn't be the first."

"I don't know who you mean. I didn't see anyone. I just walk there sometimes. Anyway, I'd better go, Pete. You know…" She tailed off. You can't really say *or the shit'll hit the fan* without garnering the pitying or scathing looks from people. Something clicked in Janie's mind. It's him or me. It buzzed like a swarm of angry bees all the way up the hill and into the empty house. Him or me, him or me, him or me. It's not going to be me she decided.

HOW SHE WAS making it come about was beyond her, but she knew it was time to fight back or die trying. The thought didn't scare her anymore. Should have worried her, but didn't. She'd thrown the meat in the fridge, rammed other things into cupboards. Ran upstairs to the bedroom. Tore the bedding off the bed, seeing the blood stains on the sheets. Her anger spilled over into an elongated animal growl, clearing the fog in her head.

Janie found an old CD and shoved it into the player. Volume up loud, she sang. Every song was one of leaving, escaping or breaking away. Nothing soppy to make her cry or cave in. Janie was almost shocked at the vivid images of murder that danced in her mind. Almost.

She went downstairs to the kitchen and started to make dinner. Knowing his physical strength outdid hers, she considered the offer for him to disappear that she'd received the other week. Yet, she wasn't sure she could do anything to help. It wasn't like you could kill someone here and not be noticed. You couldn't sneeze without the street knowing you had flu!

Tom burst through the door. Eyes piggy and red-rimmed.

"Don't want anything to eat I feel like sh…" he dashed for the bathroom. Staying there some time.

"Whatever we ate last night was off." Janie felt his breath hot on her face when he finally returned.

"Well, I'm not ill. Maybe it's whatever you're taking at the gym?" She didn't normally comment and he stormed off. She closed the door until she was about to take her dinner through. Almost dropping her plate in shock.

The plants on the window lay shredded on the floor, soil sprayed everywhere. The books on the shelf torn to shreds and he'd barged past her, barrelling up the stairs, throwing her a mean glance as he went. Janie could have cried at the mindless destruction he'd wreaked, but she wasn't going to give him the satisfaction of that. But after finishing her dinner, she set her plate on the table and began cleaning up the mess that selfish bastard had made. As she vacuumed the soil from the floor she smelled something. Burning? Had she left the oven on? Dashing into the kitchen she seen Tom, standing with a small metal bin in which he was burning something. His eyes gleamed as he'd looked from bin to her. It was balanced on a piece of wood on the breakfast bar, and was filled with paper with her own writing on it. She suddenly realised that he was burning the story she'd been writing for the last two years. Stepping around, he advanced on her so quickly she found herself against the wall in seconds.

"Be careful how you speak to me," his mouth twisted horribly in a grin.

"Get to fuck," she spat without even thinking, and saw his hand sailing toward her. Whether he was slower, or she quicker, she managed to duck out of the way as he punched the wall. Her heart was banging wildly, but he'd pushed too far.

She'd run upstairs and locked the door. Knowing he'd not break the lock or he'd have to explain it.

Calmly, slickly, he crooned.

"Come on, Janie. There's no need to be silly. Come out."

"Go to the gym, you're always saying you don't have time." She tried to keep her voice calm. "Maybe you're right and dinner last night was bad." She was terrified.

"Sure? I could do with working the gut ache off." Anger forgotten already he added, "I had to show you." Then, all sweetness, he went down the stairs.

Janie went to tidy up the ashes and dishes. She'd make sure she was in bed before he returned. Probably drunk, pumped, nasty.

"I fucking hate you," she said to the empty room.

She'd opened the cupboard where his gym potions and powders were. So much stuff he shovelled in and she was sure it wasn't all vitamins. Knew it wasn't. She'd seen too many dodgy conversations and the moods if the matey chats weren't to his liking. She used to worry, once. Now, Janie was numb.

LATER, HE RETURNED, still being sick. *Sweating like the pig you are.* She couldn't feel sympathy after all he'd done. She'd smiled at the satisfaction of him being ill as she'd told him often enough that the junk he took would react with his body. Smothering the mirth, she went back into the bedroom, she was borderline hysterical wanting to laugh at his timely pain. Janie knew that she wasn't herself, but now she had changed. He'd stumbled off into the spare room and was curled up on the single bed. Silently, she'd walked downstairs. She missed the stairs that she knew made a noise, or he'd want to know why she was going downstairs. Needing to know every move. As always.

Janie closed the kitchen door behind her quietly. Five minutes peace and a cup of coffee, she thought.

Almost time. The streetlamp in the lane made her eyes catch a shadow, but turning she saw a face at the window. Janie withdrew the bolts and turned the key. She'd opened the door and motioned for the guest to come in.

"He's upstairs," she said in answer to the unspoken question.

He'd nodded.

"Won't take long," the man replied. "Then me and him'll be done."

"Like I get a say in his shenanigans," Janie snorted.

"Janie, what the fuck's going on down there? Who've you let in? A fella I can hear." Tom bellowed. He started to make his way down the stairs. Making more noise than necessary.

Janie carried her cup through to the living room, knowing he'd thunder through here, anyway.

He stopped, hand on his stomach. Obviously in pain, but trying to live the hard man part he wanted to portray.

"Bellyache, pal? You're looking like you're in pain. I've brought you some more of the powder. Might ease things a bit, eh?" He'd stepped towards Tom. A conciliatory gesture, hands open and smiling.

Tom's face softened, then he looked at Janie.

"It's just a pain killer. I've taken a bit more the last day or so. But it'll stop. I think you could be right, it's something in the gym powder I got the other day. So, he's been helping me." He'd nodded towards the man in the living room.

The man who'd waved at Janie from the bus stop. Up close he looked older, yet his smile was knowing. He took off the coat he wore. It looked like an army relic. A long coat, brass buttons. Like her Grandad's army greatcoat.

"A nice glass of water, son. That's what you need. Then a good long sleep. Nothing to worry about after that." He'd sounded mocking, yet nothing showed on his face.

He started to unfold a piece of material and placing it on the floor. It looked like a thick painters dust sheet. He eased Tom down onto it.

"Sit with me, son, I ain't as young as I was, these days. Late night messages, well I've almost given up on them." He'd sat to the side of the material. He'd looked at Janie, motioned her to move back. She'd done so, but wasn't sure why.

Tom's voice began to slur as he drank the water, encouraged by the old man to have more, then a little more. His face softened and he obviously knew the old man, who he called Bobby.

"Shall we go for a ride in a bit? I've got the car and we'll see where we end up, eh?" He'd nodded at Tom as though he'd already agreed to it.

Tom was so spaced, he'd agreed. Janie knew he didn't know what he was agreeing to.

"I'll help you, son. The auld fella always solves problems and helps, doesn't he? Good boy."

Janie smirked at the thought of him being so pliant and childish.

"Can we keep him like this?" she'd chuckled, quietly.

"Janie, once we leave, things will change. Don't you worry. Do you remember seeing me earlier?" he'd asked seriously.

She nodded.

"What about on the wasteland the other day? Remember that? Our conversation?"

"Yes, did you really mean it?" Janie asked, feeling her mouth open a little.

"We can stop it, if you tell me right now. But if not, this is your last sighting of this piece of shit," Bobby spat.

"Will it come back on me?" Janie worried.

"There's only a few people have used my services and I've never been caught yet, love. The Auld Fella goes unnoticed every time."

Tom choked a little, his head lolled forward and he lifted his arm trying to point aimlessly at Janie.

"I'll sort you after I've been out with my friend," he'd growled at her.

"Just do it. The sooner the better," Janie said. She couldn't take any more of this, and didn't care if it did come back to haunt her. If she caved now and pitied him, she'd pay as always.

Bobby nodded.

"You're making the right decision. A rabid animal always bites. There's nothing in here to come back on you. The old factories used to use Thallium, it's added to his magic powder." He put a hand on her arm, squeezed gently. It was remarkably cold though reassuring.

He'd wrapped the cloth from the floor around Tom, like a floor length cloak.

At Janie's confused expression he remarked

"The cloth will stop the light from showing him up so well. I'll take him now. Last chance to change your mind." Bobby looked at her intently.

Janie shook her head and decided that even if Tom returned later she was going in the morning.

Bobby helped him to his feet, turned him towards the door and told him: "Say bye-bye to Janie and tell her that she's not to worry."

No reply, just a dismissive wave of his hand.

"What will you do with ..." she nodded towards Tom.

"All over the world there are secrets hidden in the earth, one way or another. It's best this is another thing that's hidden away." He'd spoken calmly. "Have a good life love." He smiled gently, but his eyes remained cool.

Janie nodded and the door closed behind them quietly.

THE NEXT MORNING Janie slept late and Tom hadn't returned. Means nothing she told herself.

But she had hope.

Her day off and she did the usual things. A bath, a walk and a new book. On the walk, she passed the butcher's. Pete waved her inside.

"Are you alright? I might have overstepped the mark yesterday," he said

"No, you didn't, honestly," Janie replied.

"I saw him last night in the street." He shook his head.

"Oh, right. Did you?"

"Aye, but he was coming away from yours and he was a bit off his head if you ask me. Talking to nobody, you know. I think he's lost it love. Should just get yourself away."

"On his own? I thought he was out with… friends. But what do I know?" she laughed.

"You haven't had any unexpected visitors have you, Janie?" asked Pete, worry in his face.

"Good God no! Chance would be a fine thing! You know how tightly he runs things. He just didn't come home last night. But I'm sure he'll get back sooner or later."

She smiled and left the shop after buying her usual amount of provisions.

I WAS BEING totally truthful, thought Janie. There were no unexpected visitors at all. Just a very much expected and planned visitor. And she was about to tell nobody. Especially now that her terror was gone. Maybe she should feel good, but all she felt was relief and freedom. She had no guilt either as she didn't actually do anything. She didn't add the poison to the powder. Nor did she mix or feed it to Tom. He did it all himself. The tainted powder in the cupboard was gone as was the glass he'd used. Gone. All gone. Freedom had definitely begun. She hadn't brought anything in or taken anything away. Sometimes the rubbish took itself out. With only a little help.

It wasn't only the coldness of his touch that Janie remembered about the old man, or the way his eyes held no warmth towards Tom. Those things alone wouldn't have troubled her. What did bother her, just a little was the fact that when she had looked into the mirror, she'd seen herself, seen Tom, yet the Auld Fella was not reflected there too. But she'd seen him, hadn't she?

SHE HAD TO call the police and as the only person who said they saw him was Pete, the butcher, it was assumed by everyone that he'd gotten mixed up with drugs and wandered off into the night after going to the gym. Janie didn't say he'd been home, or about the mysterious visitor.

Everyone except Janie was sorry that the seemingly amiable Tom had disappeared. Janie put up the front of a devastated fiancé.

Six months later in her desolation, she sold the house and moved away from the area. Free from him and his family, she began again. The only thing she had kept wondering about was the man's striking resemblance to her long dead grandfather. Along with the same sweet smell of tobacco he'd left behind him that night.

THE NEWMANS

by

Chris McDonald

VANESSA NEWMAN WAS an unknown quantity.

She'd lived in Holland Park, in a quiet cul-de-sac in an upmarket part of town, for nearly fifteen years. During that time, she'd had very little to do with her neighbours.

When Dave at number thirty-four had pulled out all the stops for the Royal Wedding street-party over a decade ago, everyone had offered to do their part. Lesley at forty-five had brought enough food to feed an army; Tom at number two had cancelled a paid night of DJing in a club in town so that his equipment and showmanship could be used for the good of the community. Everyone had showed up.

Everyone except Vanessa, that is.

Similar story when Paul's mum died. Everyone had knocked on the door of twenty-one politely and offered their sympathies and a shoulder to cry on. Not Vanessa, though. Her shoulders had remained dry.

Same when England had reached the European Championship Final in 2021. Karen had put on a big do that not even the inevitable loss on penalties could dampen. They'd commiserated long into the night, ending with a euphoric version of *Three Lions* on the street. Vanessa's voice was not amongst those of the drunken choir.

There were rumours about Vanessa. Rumours that started off akin to a soft Spring breeze. Fun rumours neighbours uttered to each other with no fear of being overheard. And if they were, so what? It was light-hearted. They'd say it to her face, probably, if she ever bothered to show it on the street again.

Then, the rumours grew darker, becoming a storm of black clouds and gale force winds. Wives would scold husbands as they'd relayed what they'd heard from their brother's son's girlfriend's hairdresser who had done Vanessa's hair a decade ago. The words were extreme. Unsubstantiated.

But, if you thought about them hard enough, long enough, they *could* match up with your idea of Vanessa.

Her house was the one at the end of the road; the one with the well-maintained flowerbeds, the polished car in the driveway and the recently painted blue door. All of these tasks were completed by hired hands, presumably, unless Vanessa was toiling in the middle of the night.

Scaffolding hugged the house like a jealous spouse.

It painted her a certain way—that she knew her own mind and had her shit together; though this was a veneer.

Inside, you'd be forgiven for thinking that no one lived there. It was clean; spotless in fact, but lacked any form of personality. In the living room, there was a small TV, and only one cushion on the grey three-seater sofa had any sort of groove in it. There were no pictures on the walls, no mirrors, no vases full of colourful flowers.

This theme of emptiness, of a life going to waste, continued into the open plan kitchen and into the hallway.

UPSTAIRS, VANESSA WAS in her bedroom, ironing some clothes. Every single item was black. Whether for fashion or function, it was hard to tell— Vanessa wasn't keen on conversations. Hadn't been since 'the incident'.

She slipped a pair of trousers off the ironing board, folded them neatly, and had just placed them into a drawer when the telephone rang.

She didn't have a mobile phone, as there was no one she wanted to contact and no one she wanted to contact her, but the landline had been a compromise with her elderly mother.

'What happens if I get sick or have a fall?' she'd asked, and Vanessa had acquiesced. In the ten years since, she'd neither fallen or contracted an illness of any kind.

The old hag will outlive us all.

That's what Mike, Vanessa's ex-husband, had said once.

Vanessa had slapped his arm playfully at the time. Things hadn't lasted very much longer after that, though not because of his mischievous comment.

Vanessa marched down the stairs and into the kitchen, where the phone was, and checked the caller ID to find that it was withheld.

Probably some scam call, she thought.

"Hello," she answered, holding the phone between her ear and shoulder while she leafed through the growing pile of envelopes on the worktop.

"Hi, mum," the bright voice said.

"Fuck off," Vanessa shrieked, and slammed the phone into its unit. Her hands quivering, she stared at the phone like it might explode into a million pieces any second.

It didn't.

Instead, it did something worse.

It rang again.

Vanessa considered letting it go unanswered, but knew that she should nip this in the bud, otherwise she'd dwell on it for days to come. She snatched up the phone.

"Now you listen here…" she started, though was interrupted.

"Mum, calm down. I know it's been a while since we spoke…"

"But… But…"

"But nothing. I hated how we left things, and felt like the time was right, you know?"

Vanessa moved into the living room and sat on the arm of the sofa, hardly believing what she was hearing. They spoke for a few minutes; Vanessa in a daze as she listened to her daughter's voice. A voice she thought she'd never hear again. She listened intently as her daughter pleaded with her to hear her out. She felt as though she was having an out of body experience, as if she was a fly crawling along the ceiling of the living room and watching herself break down into great, wracking sobs as she said goodbye.

Families argue all the time.

Most reconcile quickly, though some feuds can linger for days.

Weeks.

Months.

Years.

Eternity.

So why the extreme reaction from Vanessa?

Well, the phone call was certainly an odd one.

A bolt from the blue.

Physically impossible, one might say.

You see, there's no way in hell Vanessa Newman just spoke to her actual daughter on the phone because she'd murdered her only daughter ten years ago. To the very day.

HERE AND NOW, Vanessa sinks back into the sofa and thinks back to *that* night.

Chloe Newman had been heading out for a night on the tiles with friends. Her and Vanessa's relationship had always been fractious, and things had been coming to a head. That night, as she came down the stairs, Chloe had said something withering to her mum—or that's how Vanessa remembered it anyway—she had been on a new medication in an attempt to finally deal with the depression that had been growing inside her like an unwanted foetus for years. As Chloe reached for the door, Vanessa had smashed her over the back of the head with the iron poker she'd been using to help stoke the fire into life.

Chloe had immediately collapsed to the floor, blood gushing from the nasty wound that had split open the back of her skull. She was dead in minutes. Vanessa had slumped down on the floor and watched her die.

After, panic taking a chokehold of her, Vanessa had wrapped a *Bag for Life* around her dead daughter's head to try and stem the blood pouring onto her tiled floor. She'd dragged her out the back door and into the trees that backed on to their house.

She'd spent the night digging a makeshift grave and burying her only daughter in the mossy, worm-ridden ground.

Then, there'd been blood and alibis to deal with. Chloe's friends had got in touch the next morning to ask what had happened to her, and Vanessa had shot the question straight back at them, claiming her daughter had left the house the previous evening, ready for a night on the lash.

She'd rang the police and played the worried mother. A missing persons case had slowly unfolded and then, as these things often do, died away again due to lack of public interaction and dwindling police budgets.

Her husband, Mike, had never given up.

He'd bankrupted himself and his business in an effort to get to the bottom of his only child's disappearance. He'd gone from being the life of the party to a man who looked double his age; shoulders stooped from the weight of the world resting on them.

On the sofa, Vanessa gave herself a shake and scolded herself for dwelling. The obvious answer was that the person who had just phoned was not her daughter. Except, she *had* known some personal details and mentioned things that only Chloe and Vanessa could know.

Vanessa rose, and walked to the kitchen.

Guilt had been eating her since that moment a decade ago. She'd stopped leaving the house, stopped taking an interest in much at all. She'd considered ending her life on more than one occasion, but found living to be an even greater punishment.

Now, though, the phone call had changed her mind.

She opened the medicine cabinet and pulled out the boxes of tablets she'd been saving. She popped each blister pack, letting the little while tablets bounce playfully onto the gleaming marble worktop.

When she was satisfied there were enough, she turned on the tap and poured herself a pint of water, which she used to wash the first three tablets down with.

Then three more.

And another trio, and another, until all the tablets were gone.

Then, a new panic set in.

What happened if the tablets didn't do their job?

The pile had looked like enough on the worktop, but seemed a measly number in hindsight.

She started for upstairs.

Her hand glided along the polished banister as she trooped up the steps. She bustled into her bedroom and flung open the wardrobe doors on Mike's long-discarded side. When he'd left her, he'd gone without most of his earthly possessions, such was his haste to leave her behind.

She pulled out his rack of ties and spilled them onto the floor. Picking two up, she knotted them together and pulled tight. She gave them a testing tug, and it felt secure. She repeated the process a number of times, until she had a makeshift rope of about the right length.

She bundled it up and carried it over to the bedroom window. The one that overlooked the street. She parted the blinds with a finger, and peeked out.

The cul-de-sac was silent and unmoving.

Just like she'd hoped.

She'd fallen in love with the long, vertical windows when they'd viewed the house. The expanse of glass had allowed swathes of sunlight to flow in and brighten the place, rousing her early in the summer months. Now, it was about to come in handy for a very different reason.

She opened it and stepped tentatively out onto the wooden planks used by the builders, one hand on the cold steel scaffolding beams to keep steady.

She took a deep breath, looped one of the ends of her tie-rope around the steel beam and peered over the edge.

It was a long drop, but she didn't feel anything other than relief.

The guilt. The shame. The blood on her hands. It was all about to disappear.

She slipped the silky noose around her neck, moved to the edge of the ledge and, without further thought, stepped into thin air.

Thirty miles away, Georgina hung up and immediately dialled another number.

"Done," she said.

"Meeting point. Thirty minutes," the man's voice replied, before hanging up.

Georgina pulled the battery off the back of the phone, removed the SIM card and snapped in half, just as she'd been instructed. She put the fragments in the front pocket of her jeans and stamped on the phone with her heavy winter boots, smashing it to pieces.

She grabbed a black duffel coat off the hook by the door and left her small apartment behind.

The streets were busy with well-heeled men and women striding towards their next port of call—dinner with friends, a first date, *another* business meeting with deals waiting to be done.

Georgina barely took any notice. She was thinking about the deal *she'd* made.

Two weeks ago, a stranger had approached her in a bar. He'd bought her a drink, but had very quickly made it clear he wasn't trying to take her to bed. He hadn't been unattractive, but he was old enough to be her father.

Instead of trying to chat her up, he offered her a different type of proposition. All she had to do was make a phone call, and he'd give her five grand.

She called bullshit, but he swore he was serious. He fed her some information about what she would have to say, who she'd have to pretend to be, and then slipped her the burner phone with the two numbers she would need.

That's when she knew he was serious.

They'd parted ways and she'd looked forward to earning the easiest lump sum of money she'd ever have.

She had plans.

Big plans.

Plans that could be shaped and moulded by 5K.

The streets emptied as she approached the docks. The sun was setting and casting a crimson glow across the still water. Huge concrete warehouses were silhouetted against the ruby sky, erupting out of the ground like manmade mountains.

Warehouse 17 was the one she needed.

She'd scoped it out a few days ago to make sure she knew where she was going. And for possible escape routes should shit go south.

Arriving at her destination, she peeled back a length of chicken wire fencing and crawled underneath. The knees of her jeans grew muddy and she narrowly avoided touching a used condom with her hand.

She cast a suspicious glance around to make sure she hadn't been seen sneaking in, and then made her way to the shadows.

Warehouse 17 hadn't been used in decades, from the looks of it.

Only shark-tooth imitations of glass hung from the window frames, long smashed. The cracked and broken fragments crunched under her feet as she approached a loading hatch with no door.

The darkness inside was almost total. She fumbled in her pocket for her phone. Pulling it out, she flicked on the torch, though it barely made a dent in the black.

She breathed deeply, telling her self the guy had approached *her*. Offered *her* the money. She'd have done it for a hundred quid. And she hadn't asked questions. She hadn't asked for his name or given hers. There was safety in anonymity. No reason for him to renege or change the deal now.

The guy who approached her was straight up, she convinced herself, as she walked through the door.

As soon as she had, the 'straight up guy' who had been hiding inside the doorway blew her brains out.

MIKE REGARDED THE angel he had just felled.

The ivory skin.

The halo of blonde hair now soaked with blood and brain matter.

The wounded expression on her face.

He bent down beside her and picked up a filthy syringe from the floor, its needle bent and rusted. He sunk it into the girl's forearm a number of times, and dropped it again.

It would be a while until she was discovered, and when she was, they'd assume she'd been a worthless junkie. There'd be no investigation for a junkie, even with a bullet in her head. The police couldn't afford to waste precious resources on an addict.

He smiled, before walking across the warehouse and tossing the gun through a glassless window. A quiet plop told him his aim was true, and that in a few minutes the weapon would be nestled nicely on the seabed.

He turned back to the doorway, stepped over the dead girl and made his way into the heart of the city.

THE NEXT MORNING, he woke up hungover.

After doing what he did, he'd gone to a bar and drank late into the night. He'd imagined at the time that he'd looked very *noir;* dark jacket, flat cap, lowball of whiskey in hand. He'd taken a corner table by the rain-splattered window, watching as the lights of the city battled the darkness.

Now, he was filled with shame.

What he'd done had been planned for a long time.

He couldn't prove it, but he *knew* deep down that Vanessa had murdered his beautiful daughter. His wife had always been volatile. After Chloe disappeared, she'd lived her life on a precipice. All he had to do was give her a little shove into the abyss, though not by his own hand.

His plan had been solid, and when he'd approached the girl in the bar, he had meant to pay her what he'd promised. But the thought of shifting five grand for almost nothing had choked him for two weeks. His flat was so small he could practically lie in bed and boil the kettle at the same time. He had bills to pay; bills that were seemingly rising with every fucking breath.

So, he'd amended his plan—keep the money and kill the girl.

Simple.

And it had been. But the shame was still there.

He got out of bed slowly, and made his way to the small living room. He flicked on the television and was startled by what he saw.

A reporter with a thick Mancunian accent —Jessica something or other—was standing in front of his old house. She was saying words but they barely registered. Something about a cost-of-living crisis and the despair that is forcing normal citizens to extreme measures. Once she was finished her diatribe, she turned to a neighbour who, from how glamorous she looked, had used most of the night to get ready for her fifteen minutes of fame.

"Vanessa Newman was a pillar of the community," she was saying. "It was a shock. A total shock. To see her hanging there…"

The neighbour trailed off with mascara tracks running down her cheeks. Her performance was so over the top that Mike actually laughed.

He turned the TV off and sat back.

It seemed his plan had worked. Albeit quicker and more efficiently than he'd ever dreamed it.

He'd figured Vanessa would be driven to do something stupid by the phone call. He'd just figured it would take a couple of days more than it had.

His phone (his actual phone—no burners here, no sirree) buzzed on the small oak coffee table. He answered, and faked a dramatic cry as his friend told him of Vanessa's passing.

"No, I've not seen the news yet," Mike said.

"What a fucking tragedy," he yelped.

"I have to go," he said through crocodile tears.

He threw the phone back on the coffee table and flicked over to a re-run of Frasier.

Six months later, Mike sat in the big house in Holland Park.

He'd loved this place before his divorce, though he'd since rid it of any notion of his ex-wife and replaced it with the festering wounds of an alcoholic.

Crumpled beer cans littered every available surface and empty litre bottles of vodka clunked together as Mike shuffled from one room to the next in a fog.

He'd thought that the money he'd inherited from Vanessa's untimely passing might have soothed him. That his small part in her demise might somehow blunt the agony he felt when he thought of Chloe; of what he imagined Vanessa had done to her.

But it hadn't.

If anything, he felt emptier.

His thoughts lingered on his poor daughter as he snatched the brown paper bag up. Money could get you anything in this city, and it had got him a new gun.

He set it on the side of his chair and scrunched the bag up, tossing it over his shoulder.

He hated this place.

The house with its lingering memories.

The cul-de-sac and its gossiping inhabitants.

Yeah, he'd give them something to gossip about alright.

He picked up the gun and shambled towards the door. He pulled the drawstring of his dressing gown tight, and shoved his feet into his slippers, before leaving the house.

He walked down the driveway, patting the soft top of his little red convertible. He kept going until he stood in the middle of the narrow road that linked the houses together.

He pulled the trigger, firing a shot into the air.

That would get their attention. They'd dine out on this story for months.

Years, even.

He saw curtains twitching.

Faces appearing.

Uncomprehending eyes gazing out.

Mike raised the gun ceremoniously, opened his lips and stuck the barrel in his mouth.

His finger didn't linger on the trigger for more than a second.

And then, he was gone.

THE LAST CONFESSION OF ERIC PHILLIPS

by

Steven Kedie

ERIC PHILLIPS STOOD over his wife's grave. His whole body aching like a rotting tooth. Feeling every one of his advancing years. Today was worse than most. It was pouring down with rain and he had the flu. Shivering—sweat and rain pouring down his cheeks—running through the rough stubble speckling his lower face. In good times and bad. In sickness and in health, he'd said that the day he married her. He meant it then and he meant it still.

He'd been visiting Lynne's grave once a week for the last twenty-six years. Never missing a week.

She'd passed away at fifty, too damn soon. They'd had twenty-six good years together. Years filled with laughter and friendship. Eric knew he should be grateful for those. He had acquaintances, men who didn't seem to like their wives much at all. He'd never understood that.

They'd had tough times. He and Lynne. What couple didn't? He'd not pulled his weight when Lauren, his daughter was born. Truth be told he'd not been sure how to. Eric was tough. A tackle that could rattle your soul, as a football teammate once described him. But that baby girl had scared the shit out of Eric. All tiny hands and angry cries. Face red as she wordlessly demanded her needs be met.

Lauren was fourteen when Lynne died. The hardest thing Eric had ever done was look his daughter in the eye and tell her that her mother was gone. Harder than holding Lynne's hand as she passed. Harder than all the appointments, harder than watching the cancer snatching the light away from his wife's face.

Twenty-six years together.

Twenty-six years since she'd gone.

In all the hours by Lynne's grave, Eric had told her about his life. All of it. Every decision, every mistake. Each conscious choice. He'd hidden nothing, hoped she'd understand. Wherever she was. He'd kept her up to date with news from family and friends. Mainly, he'd talked about Joseph.

Lynne would've loved Joseph.

Eric had never felt the way he felt on this particular visit. Never felt so sure he would be joining her soon.

JOSEPH PHILLIPS WALKED quickly down the hospital corridor, his trained eye taking in all the details. Not just the signs directing him to Ward 19, but the height and hair colour of the mid-fifties porter who pushed a frail woman in a wheelchair, or the people queuing in the small newsagent near the canteen. Sometimes he felt like his mind had not switched off since he'd completed his police training three years before.

Ward 19. He pressed the buzzer and waited.

A nurse looked through the thin window before opening the door slightly, "Can I help you?"

"I'm Eric Phillips' grandson."

The nurse opened the door fully. "Last room on the right."

"Thank you," Joseph said, stepping inside.

Outside his grandfather's private room, he took a slow breath before knocking. "Room for one more?" he asked as he entered.

"Hello," his mum said, as she forced a smile. Lauren Phillips stood up from the red plastic chair she was sat on and hugged her son tightly. Joseph leaned down and kissed the top of her head.

"Okay, Joe?" Eric asked.

Joseph took in his grandfather slowly. He didn't look as frail as Joseph had expected, but he seemed smaller than usual and the pyjamas hung loose from his body.

"The main thing is you are."

Eric shrugged. "That's for the doctors to say."

"And what do they say?"

"Cancer."

A small cry escaped from his mother as Joseph kissed the old man's sandpaper-like cheek.

He walked around the bed, shook off his coat and placed it on the back of the chair he then sat on.

The three made small talk about the awful parking and the awful weather.

Joseph answered questions thinking of a thousand things he wanted to ask but somehow wasn't able to form the words.

Eric turned to his daughter and said, "Why don't you go and get some food?"

"I'm not hungry."

"You need a break. Sitting here looking at me won't do you any good."

Lauren wanted to protest, but she was too tired, too drained to argue. She picked up her handbag, attempted a smile, "I won't be long."

"No rush," Eric said as she left the room.

Joseph went to speak but Eric raised his hand, indicating a request for silence. Seconds ticked by... Seven, eight, nine... Eric making a show of listening for something.

"Shut the door properly," he finally said.

The tone of the instruction meant Joseph didn't question why.

As he shut the door, Eric said, "Bring your chair closer."

Joseph moved it closer to the bed and sat down.

"What's going on, Grandad?" His voice was low, unsure why the room's atmosphere had changed.

"I'm dying, Joe," Eric said, matter of fact.

"We need to hear what the doctors say." We haven't got time for all that,' the old man said, dismissively. "I need you to do something important. Whatever you're feeling: sadness, grief, anger, put it to one side. Understand?"

Joseph nodded.

"Seven. Six. Eight. One. Repeat it."

"Seven. Six. Eight. One."

"Again."

"Grandad, what's—"

Eric raised his hand. "Again."

Joseph repeated the sequence.

"Go to my house and go up into the loft. Be careful, it's a mess. There's a pile of boxes in the middle. One's got your nanna's dresses in. The top dress is green. Take the dresses out. Don't," he stressed the word, "lift the box. Inside is a safe."

Voices came from the corridor. Eric stopped talking, his eyes fixed on the door. The muffled voices disappeared and Eric continued, "What's the code?"

"Seven, six," Joseph's words caught in his dry mouth. He coughed, trying to keep the noise down. "Eight, one."

Joseph lifted a jug of water from the top of the cupboard by the bed, pouring some into a plastic cup. He downed it in one.

"In the safe, you'll find cash," Eric said. 'More than you're thinking. Thousands." Eric looked his grandson dead in the eye and said, "Hide it."

"Grandad, I'm a police officer."

Eric ignored him.

"Hide it. Don't involve Ellie. And not on my boat."

"What's going on?"

"Joe, I know you've got questions, but I need you to get this into your head very quickly: we don't have time. I promise I'll explain everything. But not until that money is hidden. Do you understand?"

Joseph nodded.

"Code?"

"Seven, six, eight, one."

"Good."

"What about Mum?"

"Go."

Joseph's head was spinning as he pulled his jacket back on. "Tell Mum I got a call from a lad at work about going out tonight and you made me go. I was upset and you said a night out with my mates is what I needed."

Eric nodded this time.

"I'll be back tomorrow," Joseph said. He kissed his grandfather goodbye. The old man whispered the four numbers to him again.

THE CORRIDORS WERE a blur on the way to the car park. Faces slid by featureless. Joseph stepped through the automatic doors at the front of the hospital and made himself stop. He needed to think. He took several deep breaths, slowed his thoughts. The smell of smoke curled into his nostrils. He looked at a group—a mix of patients and visitors—passing a lighter around, then taking long drags on cigarettes.

He walked quickly to the dirty yellow ticket machine, removed a thin ticket from the back pocket of his jeans and followed the instructions, reading each message on the screen twice to keep actions present in the here and now. He paid, went to his car, a double beep signalling it was unlocked. Got in and started the engine. The radio burst into life, Morrisey singing about Hector being the first in the gang with a… The song died, silence appearing instantly as Joseph pressed the *Off* button.

Another car appeared, the hassled looking driver staring at him, wanting his space. Joseph put the car into gear and drove to the mechanical orange barrier at the exit.

Driving away from the hospital, Joseph tried to concentrate on each act: checking his mirrors, assessing the lorry to his right, letting that cyclist move out around the parked bus. The problem was his brain kept firing the same question at him: *What the fuck is going on?*

JOSEPH PARKED OUTSIDE his grandfather's house.

The house was a standard thirties semi-detached that was starting to show its age. When his grandfather died, someone would have a proper renovation project on their hands. Wraparound extension, walls knocked down, all the mod cons. Play catch up with the other houses on the cul-de-sac. For now, though, the house still looked like it did when Joseph had lived in it as a child.

The box room had been his room for the first nine years of his life. A single bed covered in a Spiderman duvet, a small box of toys, a bookshelf with football magazines and sticker books piled on a thin wardrobe. He could picture it all now, clear as the day he left it when he and his mother moved to the flat.

Joseph let himself in and went upstairs to his old room. Eric had a rowing machine in here a few years ago but it was completely empty now apart from an L-shaped metal bar that had been placed against the wall. Joseph used the bar to open the loft hatch and carefully unfolded the ladder on the inside down.

He climbed up.

Apart from a few of streams of light coming in through a gap in some roof tiles, the loft was dark.

Joseph took his phone out and turned on the torch. The illuminated view showed him the mess his grandfather had mentioned. Piles of boxes, an old Christmas tree, a clothes rail that had coats covered in binbags hanging from it. A box with the word *Books* scribbled on it. Joseph wondered, knowing his grandfather's simple and tidy ways that dominated not only the house below but the barge he kept on the local canal, if all of the chaos was designed to cover the fact there was a safe hidden in here.

The floor creaked as he stepped off the ladder and into the loft, adjusting his body position to allow for the sloped roof. He slowly moved towards the pile of boxes labelled *Lynne's Clothes*. The smell of mildew and dust was like a hand gripping at his throat.

He awkwardly tried moving boxes with one hand, his phone in the other. Quickly gave up, propping the phone up on top of a box, the bright light shining towards the wall adjoining the house next door. Although that meant part of where he was working was dark, using both hands allowed him to work faster.

Meticulously, he cleared a small path through the mess and found the box with the green dress. He removed all the dresses carefully until the box was empty apart from an eighteen-inch square safe that was padlocked shut.

Seven.

Six.

Eight.

One.

Joseph's fingers moved each number into position and then he pulled down on the horseshoe shaped lock.

Click.

The door opened.

HIS GRANDFATHER WASN'T joking, he was staring at thousands.

Joseph jumped as his phone started to ring.

Ellie calling.

His girlfriend of four years.

He quickly tried to shut off the torch and answer it before the neighbours heard a noise coming from the loft.

"Hi babe."

"Hi."

"Just wanted to make sure you were all right. How's your grandad? Is he okay?"

"No, he's got cancer. The doctors don't think he's got long."

"Oh, babe. I'm so sorry. That's awful. What can I do?"

"I don't think there's anything you can do, or anyone else, but thank you."

Joseph heard a television start playing somewhere in the neighbour's house.

"Where are you? You sound weird."

"In my grandad's loft."

"Why?"

Joseph paused, thinking over how much he should reveal.

"He wanted me to try and find an old ring of Nanna's but I can't find it." The money pulled at his attention again.

"I'll be home in a bit," he said. "Look, I'm kind of sat at a funny angle right now and my leg's going numb. Can we talk later?"

"I love you."

"Love you too."

He hung up. The room went pitch black.

JOSEPH GOT A supermarket *Bag For Life* from the pantry under the stairs, carried it back to the loft. Dropped the bundles of cash in it and then covered the safe over again. It took time to get it all cleaned away, but he knew when his grandfather died, whoever came up here next—an estate agent, a willing buyer, his mother—would question an open and empty safe.

He carried the bag of cash downstairs into the dining room. Pulled the curtains closed, shutting off any view into the room from the street or the houses opposite. Then he poured the cash out on the pine dining table and started to count.

Sixty-four grand.

JOSEPH DROVE HOME in a daze.

The money was wrapped in clingfilm at the bottom of the *Bag For Life*, with two towels and a few different sets of his grandfather's clothes placed on top. He didn't expect to get stopped but if anyone looked in the bag, he wanted to be able to say it was stuff to make his grandfather feel comfortable in the hospital.

On the way back to the flat he'd recently moved into with Ellie, he thought about the lie he'd told her: *An old ring. I can't find it.*

"Shit," he said aloud.

Instead of going home, he drove to his mother's. Her small Fiat was parked on the road outside the tight terraced house. Joseph parked up behind her, jogged up the garden path and let himself in.

"Hello," he called down the hallway.

His mother appeared at the living room door. Face patchy, eyes raw from crying.

"I thought you were going out," she said.

"That wasn't true," Joseph admitted. He ignored the shock on her face and said, "Grandad wanted me to look for a ring of Nanna's in his loft. He wanted to have it with him at the hospital, but he told me to not say anything because he didn't want you going to the house to try and find it. He thought you might find it too upsetting."

Joseph stopped talking, aware this lie could run and run. All that mattered was his mother and Ellie had the same story now.

"Oh," was all his mum offered.

"How are you feeling?" Joseph asked.

"Numb."

"That's understandable."

"I knew he wasn't well, but I wasn't expecting the scan to reveal he was this ill. They think he's got weeks, if he's lucky. He must've hidden how sick he is for months."

Joseph hugged his mother and she cried into his chest before she pulled away and wiped at her eyes.

"What time does visiting start tomorrow?" Joseph asked.

"Ten."

"I'll go for then," he said. "I'm on shift later."

"I'll come too."

"Let's split the day out," Joseph said quickly. 'Not overwhelm him."

His mother nodded. "That's a good idea."

A shock of guilt ripped through him like a lightning bolt.

"ARE YOU GOING to tell me what's going on?"

Joseph sat opposite his tired looking grandfather.

"Where's the money?"

"Inside an old cricket bag at mum's, underneath the pads and whites. The bag's under my old bed. That bag's not been touched for years. Mum's not moving it any time soon."

"Alright."

"Grandad, this is pretty difficult. I need more information. I don't need months of police training to know that money is not legit, but now you've got me hiding it. Yesterday I got a call saying you didn't have long left to live. Instead of dealing with that, I'm running around like I'm in a Guy Ritchie film."

His grandfather's hand shook as he lifted a mug of strong tea to his lips. He put the mug down and shifted his body position to get comfortable.

"It's a long story."

ERIC PHILLIPS LOOKED at his grandson, knowing the boy's life was about to change forever. He took a moment to get composed, and surprised himself when he blinked away a warm tear.

"Before I start," the old man said, coughing a couple of times. "Do you have a detective at work you can trust? I know I'm not making much sense," he added. "But I'm asking you to trust me, like you've always done."

After some thought, Joseph said, "The boss, Lennon. He's a good copper. Again though, why?"

Eric ignored the question. "I've known I've been dying for a few months. Not through tests or anything. Just known in my heart. My body hasn't been right. You get to my age; you understand some things you never thought you would. Death being one of them."

He reached for the mug of tea again, sipped from it. It was going cold.

"I'm not afraid of dying," he said. "I haven't been since your nanna died. I don't know if I believe in Heaven or the afterlife, but if there is a small possibility I can see her again, I'm happy to die and take my chances."

He put the mug down.

"The last few months I've been thinking about what kind of man I've been."

Joseph's instinct was to say 'the best' but instead he stayed silent, letting his grandfather work through his thoughts.

"I've not been perfect. I've made mistakes, but I've tried to do my best. Especially by your mum and by you."

Eric felt Joseph's hand wrapped gently around his.

"Have you heard of the Maguires?" he asked.

Joseph tried not to audibly sigh with frustration that the conversation was jumping in several directions. He wanted to try and keep it on one path.

"Of course. They're one of the biggest crime families in Manchester."

"What do you know about them?"

"Two brothers, mid-forties. Old school gangsters. Run drugs, guns, girls. Bit of extortion. Legitimate businesses across the city as fronts. Enough people scared of them that we never quite get stuff to stick. They spread just enough money around their local area that people think the streets are safer with them. It's story as old as time. What's this got to do with the cash in your loft?"

The old man told him everything.

AS JOSEPH SCANNED his pass and the electronic lock on the door to the CID office buzzed loudly, his mind raced through series of flashbacks of his life with his grandfather. The football matches, the hours sailing his barge. A memory of the time in Year Eight when he asked for advice about how to handle the group of kids who were picking on his friend, Gary. He could still remember being on the barge, slowly cruising along the water as his grandfather listened intently, before saying, "You ask them to stop. If they don't, you tell the teachers. If they still don't stop, deal with it with more force. If you get in trouble, I'll be there. But you must try the first two ways first." Joseph did as he was told but the bullying didn't stop.

One day during breaktime, Joseph walked up to the biggest kid in the gang—a fat lad called Nathan. Joseph could still see his face now, laughing with the other boys who'd been pushing Gary into tables and throwing his bag onto the school roof. He waited until Nathan turned to face him.

"What the fuck you want?" the bully spat.

Joseph punched him and he punched him hard. His fist connecting perfectly with the boy's jaw twice. Just like his grandfather had taught him.

The fat kid hit the ground and Joseph had leaned over him and said, "Touch my friend again and I'll be back."

He never needed to go back.

Now, Joseph was outside Detective Sergeant Lennon's office. He knocked twice and was called in.

"Phillips," Lennon said, before acknowledging Joseph's lack of uniform. "You not on duty today?"

"Not yet, Sir."

"What can I do for you?"

"It's my grandad, Sir. He's dying of cancer. He doesn't have long left. Days maybe. He wants me to bring a detective to the hospital to talk to him. A last confession, of sorts."

Lennon sat up straight in his chair. Something in the way P.C. Phillips was delivering his words made him realise this was not some old man's last daft request.

"What does he wish to confess to?"

Joseph told him.

Lennon moved with purpose to the office door. He opened it and addressed a detective sat across the office. "Barnes, in here."

Detective Sean Barnes joined Lennon and Joseph. Lennon shut the door and returned to his chair.

"Barnes, this is P.C. Phillips. He's going to take you and Tony to see his grandad in hospital. The man is dying. You're there to conduct an interview so take whatever recording equipment you need and make sure Phillips isn't in the room when the interview happens. If you get this right, today might be the day you get to arrest Donovan Maguire."

DETECTIVE BARNES FACED Eric. His partner for this little field trip to the death ward was Tony Scholes, who chose to lean on a grubby magnolia painted wall, his face wearing a constant, practised bored expression.

Barnes set up his recording equipment on the meal tray that was attached to Eric's bed. He checked the sound quality and said, 'Interview with Eric Phillips,' before stating the date and time. He then asked the old man to confirm some details. Eric cleared his throat.

"My name is Eric Phillips. I'm in Wythenshawe hospital. I'm of sound mind and fully aware I'm possibly dying soon, in a short number of days maybe, due to cancer. I've requested this interview to take place to confess to numerous crimes and provide information that may assist police in further arrests."

"Thank you, Eric." Barnes said. "Let's start with why you've asked us to come here. Your grandson, Joseph Phillips, who is a Police Constable in the Manchester police force, has stated you have information regarding Donovan and Cameron Maguire."

"That's right," Eric confirmed.

"How have you come about this information?"

"Years of working for them."

"Doing what type of work?"

"I've done a few different things, but it mainly involved getting rid of guns and moving drugs up and down the country."

Barnes shifted in his seat and Scholes nudged himself off the wall.

Eric eyed both men. "Should I start at the beginning?"

"Please."

"My wife, Lynne, and I met when we were twenty-four," Eric said. "We were married within six months. We didn't have a lot, but we worked hard and managed to get a house. I worked my way up to shift supervisor at an industrial rubber place in Trafford Park. Lynne worked on the tills at Tesco."

He took a drink of water, trying to soften his dry lips.

"We tried for kids straight away, but it didn't happen. Not for years, not until we were in our mid-thirties, and then we had Lauren, Joseph's mum. Joseph who works with you."

Barnes nodded.

"I ran a Sunday football team and Lynne and Lauren would come and watch. Lynne was a runner in those days and would do half marathons and things like that. She was fit, and healthy and for those years when it was the three of us, we had a good life. We weren't fancy or well off, but we were happy. Then, when she was fifty, Lynne died of cancer. Lauren was fourteen at the time."

More water.

"I know you're wondering how all this fits with the Maguires. It does, I promise."

"Take your time," said Barnes.

Eric put the drink down.

"Our lives changed when Lynne died. I know that's obvious, but they really did. The path we were on just eroded. Lauren went very quiet, in herself. Very nervous. It was tough. I didn't know what to do, how to cope. I was in bits. I threw myself into my football team. When I was there, I was surrounded with funny lads who talked all the time. I focused on them. On Sunday mornings it meant I focused on the ball and the players, not on the fact I'd buried the love of my life. If football wasn't on, I'd be on my boat. I had a barge. It was peaceful, quiet. That's not to say I abandoned my daughter. I didn't. I really tried. I just didn't know what to do. She was a fourteen-year-old girl and I was a fifty-year-old man. We had two things in common: our surname and Lynne's death."

Eric paused, blinking away the tears forming in his eyes.

"A year after she died, I was made redundant."

A couple of tears escaped and ran down his cheek.

"You're doing well," Barnes assured him.

"Twenty-two years at that company. Went in one morning, home by lunchtime. One month's pay as a thank you. Nothing really…" His voice trailed off to a long silence.

"When you take a man's livelihood away, you force him into making difficult choices," he said. "I tried to get work, but I wasn't employable. My age. My technology skills. Well, I didn't have any. I was a widowed father of a teenager. I had responsibilities outside of whatever work I'd find. I was honest about that. Some firms didn't like that I had to be at home straight after finishing time for my daughter."

Scholes pulled a chair next to Barnes and sat down. Barnes confirmed the action for the tape.

"I decided we needed a holiday, so I booked us a caravan in North Wales. There were lots of families on the site. Teenagers, Lauren's age. Big group of them. It was good for her. She made a friend or two. I let her go off, have a bit of freedom. I watched her with these kids. She smiled a lot. Laughed. I didn't know at the time, but she had a thing with one of the lads. A one-night thing. She got pregnant. Sixteen, she was. Just a child herself."

Eric coughed.

And coughed.

The cough grabbing hold of him and shaking him violently for a full minute.

"Sorry," he said.

"It's okay," Barnes said.

After a few deep, wheezy breaths, Eric continued. "Joseph came along. Strangely, it brought us closer together. I did everything I could to help her. Some dads would've shamed her for getting pregnant. I didn't. I tried to show her how to do the things you need to do with a baby. Truth is, I didn't know myself."

Cough.

Cough.

"We muddled through. Lauren was great. She worked at night and I'd look after the boy. She trained to be a nursery nurse. Grafted. But it wasn't enough. That boy deserved more. He deserved stability. So did his mum. I took what work I could. Did some gardening, bit of delivery work. Anything for a bit of cash. But a stable job on the type of money I'd been on at the rubber place never came."

Eric looked at the detectives. "I'm a man. I wanted to provide for my family."

A pause.

"And that's when what happened, happened."

"What happened, Eric?"

"Noah Dunne."

"Who's that?"

"He played for my Sunday team. Seventeen he was. Good player. Winger. Grew up on the Harkness Estate. You know it, I guess?"

Every copper in Manchester knew it.

Knew the Maguires started out there.

"Noah Dunne was one of those kids. On the edge of everything. Needed guidance. Needed a good group around him. He wanted more from his life than his family knew how to give him. I liked him, kept an eye on him. I'd get him to help with training the younger kids at the club. He was football mad, but he had a switch that got him into trouble often. He struggled with the right choices. I'm not making excuses for him. He was seventeen, not seven. Anyway, one day he was in our changing rooms on a day when there was no game. I'd left something there, a pump, I think it was and, anyway, I went to get it and found him on a stepladder messing with a ceiling tile."

Eric stopped and closed his eyes, opened them again slowly.

"I'm sorry," he said. "I get so tired."

"No rush, Eric. You're doing great."

252

"I asked him what he was doing there? Didn't take a lot to get it out of him. Think he was relieved I'd caught him."

Another cough, followed by eight in quick succession.

"He was hiding a gun."

Both detectives' senses heightened, Scholes shifted in his chair and leaned forward.

"It didn't take much more for him to tell me what was going on. He was a tough kid but he was scared, in over his head. The Maguires had used the gun in a robbery of a warehouse. They would've been early twenties then. On the way up. A security guard had been shot in the leg. They'd told Noah to get rid of the gun. He'd not been at the robbery."

Another violent coughing fit. Deep and painful.

"It was a test really. He'd been around them his entire life on that estate. This was their way of seeing if he could make the cut. I knew that boy. He didn't want that life. Not deep down." Eric shrugged his thin shoulders. "But he thought it was his only option."

Eric went quiet for a few seconds, tiredness etched on his face.

Gently, Barnes asked, "Can you remember what happened next?"

"Yes."

"And what was that, Eric?"

"I got rid of the gun."

Barnes paused, before asking, "How?"

"In the canal. I got on my barge and sailed out towards Warrington. On a quiet stretch, I just dropped it off the side. Then I went to see Donovan Maguire." The old man paused, gasped and then let out a long, wounded breath. "I'm sorry. Would you mind if we took a break?"

A NURSE COMPLETED checks on Eric and he ate a bland hospital meal before he was ready to resume his confession. Barnes started the recording equipment again and confirmed the time and date, and that the same people were present, before saying, "Eric, before we had a break, you told us you got rid of a gun used in a robbery by the Maguire brothers. We are going to need details of dates and anything about the robbery you can remember."

"I know you'll have questions and I can answer them," Eric said. "But this is just the start of it all."

"Okay," Barnes said. "Why don't you carry on telling us what happened when you went to see Donovan Maguire?"

"It was funny really. I'd heard about these hard, scary brothers. Donovan especially. Old school gangsters in the making according to all the rumours. Running the estate with an iron fist. I knocked on his front door and said "I think we should have a chat." He just let me in. I didn't feel scared or nervous. I was giving myself options being there. I was straight with him. Told him I'd got rid of his gun and he was to leave Noah out of any future ventures. That boy wasn't cut out for the things Maguire wanted from him. That wasn't fair on Noah and, frankly, wouldn't be good for Donovan long term. Then I offered him a deal."

"What kind of deal?"

"That anything he needed moving or getting rid of, he was to come to me. I was a stand-up community man with a daughter and a grandson. No one would look at me twice. I told him I'd want paying. It's madness when you think about it. I remember he said, "And what can you offer?" and I said, "A barge." He laughed at me, but I was firm with him. Told him how no one checks barges. Not for people like me. We go up and down canals, waving at joggers and drinking tea, having the time of our lives. No one ever thinks about what's on our boats."

Barnes and Scholes shared a look.

"So, I started moving stolen goods and drugs for them. And getting rid of weapons. As the brothers got higher up the chain, I got busier."

Barnes spoke. "Eric, this is quite the story. As I said, we are going to need to check the details. Can you remember dates? Did they ever share with you what the guns were used for? Was it in robberies or murders? And you mentioned being paid for these acts. This is a big thing for you to be confessing to. Can I ask, is this just to get it all off your chest before," Barnes paused and adjusted his tone slightly, "forgive me for being so blunt, but before you die? Apart from the story, what evidence do you have that all of this even took place?"

"Well, I wrote a lot of it down, the dates the different guns were delivered and what type of guns they were. In the end, I stopped getting rid of them and hid them," Eric said. "They're on my boat."

IT WAS JUST Joseph and his grandfather in the room.

"Are you okay?"

"Tired," Eric said.

"What made you keep the guns?"

"You."

"Me?"

"Yeah. As you got older, I wanted out. But it was clear I was in too deep for all of that. I was an asset for them. I'd made a choice. It was the choice of a desperate and, honestly, depressed man. I was in a dark place after your nan passed away. After she was gone. No job. A daughter and grandson to provide for. I thought I needed their money. And, I was good at it. Never got caught, did I?'"

Eric grinned. So did Joseph.

"No, Grandad, you didn't."

"But as you grew up, I couldn't take the guilt. I'd look at you, all the good in the world in your smile, how happy you made your mum. It was tough for her, don't get me wrong, but we made it work, the three of us. And I just knew I couldn't take it. I couldn't have you one day finding out that your grandad was a criminal. Which I am. Make no mistake about it."

The words made Joseph flinch.

"I was stuck though. I couldn't admit what I'd done. Maguire would've killed me. So, I decided I'd try and do some good one day. I stopped getting rid of everything and I started keeping records. He can't kill me now. Cancer's already done that. Hopefully what I've provided will help you build a case."

"Why have you kept the money in the loft a secret?"

Eric signalled for Joseph to help prop him up in the bed.

When comfortable, he said, "You're a copper. I'm proud of that. But you will have to walk amongst your colleagues and hear the snide comments about all of this. There'll be press coverage: Grandad of police officer worked for city's biggest criminals. The fact you've brought this to your bosses might make your career. Or it might make it harder. That's my fault, not yours. Your whole life, I've tried to do the right thing to give you a chance. My idea of what that was got lost somewhere. I woke up one day and it was just gone. That money in my loft is my way of saying sorry. The choice is yours what you want to do with it. You want to tell your bosses about it, you do that. But if you want to use it to give you, Ellie and your mum a better life, that's up to you too."

Joseph watched his grandfather's eyes close. He looked at the old man he loved more than anyone in the world, the man who had taught him everything he thought he knew about life, and started to cry.

LAUREN ARRIVED AND sat next to her son, silently watching her dad's chest rise and fall. She held his frail hand and waited for the change in him that she knew was inevitable now.

"I need to tell you something about Grandad," Joseph said.

"What?"

Eric's breathing became raspy, shorter.

Joseph took his grandfather's free hand and held it tight. 'It can wait,' he said.

Eric Phillips took his final breath.

Here. Then gone.

MINDY HORMANN

by

Nathan Pettigrew

SOLDIERS BLOCKING THE way out from Southdown West were both armed with submachine guns and grenade vests. A mere intimidation tactic.

"License," the white one said.

Mindy couldn't stand her DMV pic.

"Mindy Hormann of 115 Algiers," the soldier said, as if he didn't know by now. "Where are you off to this evening?"

"I'm off to see the Wizard of Oz," she said.

"You need to take this serious, ma'am. Unless you're going out for official business, we're asking you to turn around."

"It's my brother's birthday," Mindy said. "And he lives next door in Summerfield."

"You're not supposed to see family, right now," the soldier said.

"I said it's his birthday. Jesus. Are you listening?"

"I understand," he said. "But I'm asking you to turn around."

"Can I have my license back?"

Mindy nearly ran over his boot when driving past, but he didn't shoot or give chase. Soldiers weren't ordered to go that far just yet, and the two guarding Southdown West had to make sure no one else got out.

ARRIVING AT HER brother's house, Mindy let herself inside and Kevin greeted her with the good news of crawfish season not being cancelled this year.

"Thank God," she said, hanging her new Coach purse and Saints jacket on his hall tree.

"Drove past the soldiers again, eh?" Kevin said.

"Morons," Mindy said. "You know I'm all for safety, but not allowing us to see family?"

"At least they're letting us get together for crawdads," Kevin said.

Their father used to say a smart society allowed citizens to unwind and taste the illusion of freedom. Carnival season had served that purpose for Terrebonne Parish before Mardi Gras was cancelled yet again, but come April, Mindy could visit family on Fridays without a hassle.

Her brother's house was a modern one story near the wide ditch dividing Summerfield from the older brick homes in Southdown West and had become the gathering place for birthdays, anniversaries, and Saints games—an arrangement that Mom and Dad were glad to accept until the soldiers showed up.

Mindy fixed herself a drink while Kevin found sports. His bar in the living room was a bonus, a flatscreen wall-mounted with satellite channels and surround sound, a grill on the back patio firing the smell of barbecue into the air.

"Well, sorry Mom and Dad aren't coming," Mindy said.

"They're old, sis, and scared."

"Those soldiers are a joke," she said. "They've never seen combat like you or Cousin Manny. God rest his soul."

"How's Grandma?" Kevin asked, still flipping through sports.

"The same."

"And Tim?"

Mindy sipped her drink. "You care?"

"'Long as he doesn't go too far," Kevin said, settling on The Rich Eisen Show.

"I watch Rich Eisen on YouTube," Mindy said.

"Of course, you do," Kevin said. He grabbed his beer from the coffee table. "Come on. I should check on the steaks."

Mindy smiled when seeing he'd remembered to leave the ashtray out, but cursed while trying to light a Marlboro beneath the patio fan.

"Really, Kevin? During a cold front?"

"What's that?" he asked, tending to the grill.

"I'm turning the fan off," she said.

"Look on the bright side," he said as she lit up. "We don't have to cut these fuckers into four."

"I get it, Kevin, but weren't they always lecturing us about protecting our freedoms?"

"I said it's fine, Mindy. Ready to eat?"

Kevin's ribeyes were the first and only to ever melt on her tongue. Before her brother had learned the trick in Afghanistan, Mindy saw the pitch of a steak melting in one's mouth for a marketing scheme.

"Yeah, I'm in shock about crawfish season," Kevin said.

"Stop," Mindy said. "Bad juju."

"You're right," he said. "I'm more concerned about my job."

A popular salesman for local drilling, Kevin was used to taking customers down Bayou Dularge to fish and losing graciously at golf, but the government had said no more, deeming such activities as unsafe.

"My base salary won't float me for much longer," he said.

"Try not to stress," Mindy said. "My YouTube's blowing up."

"Yeah, but I hate to—"

"Come on, Kevin. The bright side. Your bald ass ain't forty just yet."

"One more year," he said. "With you not too far in the rearview."

"Don't remind me," Mindy said. She set her knife and fork on her plate. "Well, supper was to die for."

"Damn, girl. Already?"

"You eat too slow, like Dad."

"Glad you enjoyed it," Kevin said. "'Cause those were the last of 'em."

"Can you believe this new shit where Geautreaux's is only allowing us to buy a pound of ground beef?" Mindy asked, grabbing her jacket. "What about families with children?"

Kevin sipped his beer while she reached into her purse.

"Here. Got you something."

"Don't tell me," he said, taking the phone. "I mean—thanks, Mindy. Mine still works."

"It's cracked to shit," Mindy said.

"And the new monthly?" he asked.

"All taken care of, Kevin. Happy Birthday."

She gave her brother the biggest hug and flipped off the soldiers when speeding past them.

HER HOUSE WAS the second to last on the left before the dead end, both homes isolated from others on Algiers Drive by half a mile of uncut grass. People had long given up on building—not that anyone could afford to build right now.

The couch was unoccupied. Tim had put Grandma to bed and wandered out back.

Mindy left her jacket on a chair and was looking in the fridge when the light came on.

"Hey, you," she said. "Sitting out in the dark again?"

Tim slapped her. "Drove past the soldiers, again?"

"Jesus," Mindy said. "It's his fucking birthday."

He slapped her a second time. "I was worried about you."

"Will you calm the fuck down, Tim? You drank the whole bottle?"

"Outside," he said.

Turning the patio light on, Mindy saw enough bourbon for maybe three glasses.

She sat to enjoy a Marlboro, waiting for Tim.

"Fuck, Mindy. I'm sorry. The drive to Lafayette's wearing on me is all."

"At least you still have a job," she said.

"Yell, but the soldiers and their checkpoints are turning my two-hour commute into four," Tim said, and Mindy couldn't help smiling.

She used to have two cameras inside, but now had four.

Using her phone, Mindy turned her equipment on.

"But with all these assholes not working? My job's secure," Tim said, "and I stole us some paper towels."

"We needed toilet paper, Tim. And water."

"Nothing's ever good enough," he said, reaching for the bottle.

"I just can't believe they don't have the most basic shit, by now," Mindy said. "An Amazon warehouse?"

"What do you want me to say, Mindy? We still have two rolls."

"Two rolls of sandpaper, Tim. That shit's making our butt holes bleed. What if Grandma bleeds?"

Mindy caught their neighbor LaVar watching them through his kitchen window.

"Come on," she said, stubbing her cigarette out. "It's cold."

"Seriously?" Tim asked. "You prefer the humidity?"

Inside was like most nights. Tim went nuclear over mainstream media and how so many folks were willing to give up their freedoms and wandered out for a smoke break. He slapped Mindy a third time, but she was able to reel him to the couch where he finally passed out.

Returning to the patio, she uploaded tonight's episode of Tim Gets Drunk on her YouTube channel.

Sitting back, Mindy refreshed and smiled when seeing the views.

"MORNING," LAVAR said, always checking mail at the same time.

He had on his Trinity Baptist tee, but his body was chiseled, and his Caribbean green eyes never failed to smile.

"Morning," Mindy said, smiling back.

"Anything good?" he asked.

"Just junk," Mindy said.

"Things are good at home?" he asked.

"Fine. Why?" she asked, still smiling.

"No, it's just—y'all were loud again last night."

"Well, your yard still looks like shit," Mindy said.

"Can you believe the HOA sent me a letter?" LaVar asked. "So, I'm like sorry about the dead grass but I'm focused on finding food. You know? Lord Jesus will provide, I'm sure, but not a lot of construction going on in Terrebonne these days."

"Have a good one," Mindy said.

"Wait," LaVar said, standing on her driveway. "Look, I hate to ask, but is there anyone I can call?"

"About what, LaVar? You've called the cops twice on us and nothing came of it. Now, please. Keep your distance and mind your business."

"God bless you," he said.

Yeah, Mindy thought. *Fuck you, pal.*

SHE WENT STRAIGHT to the couch, shaking Tim awake.

"Jesus," he said.

"Yeah," Mindy said. "Jesus wants to call someone again."

"He won't," Tim said, rolling over. "You're worried about Clement threatening to arrest me next time?"

"That's right, genius. Now, get up. Brush your teeth while I take care of Grandma."

"The guy wants you, Mindy. He's ain't doing shit."

"Get your ass up," she said.

Mindy found Grandma sitting up against her backboard and smiling at thin air.

"Morning, Grandma."

"Good morning, Mindy. I thought you might be an angel."

"Let's get you to the bathroom."

Tim had his sneakers on by the time she'd helped Grandma to the couch, still in the clothes he'd slept in.

"You're all wrinkled," Mindy said.

"I'm good," Tim said.

"Whatever."

Mindy found a cooking show, cranked the volume, and left the remote on Grandma's lap.

"We'll be right back, Grandma. Don't go into the kitchen and try not to use the bathroom."

"So many rules these days," Grandma said, and Mindy kissed her forehead.

TOO HUNGOVER TO drive, Tim took shotgun in his new pickup and played air drums to Stevie Wonder's "Superstition" until seeing customers in the Geautreaux's parking lot.

"Shit makes no sense," he said. "Masks have never worked, and now Terrebonne wants to fine us three large?"

"It's for our safety," Mindy said, waiting for a blue Accord to back out. "Nothing wrong with protecting our neighbors."

"Our neighbors?" Tim said. "They're the ones we need to worry about."

"The only neighbor we need to worry about is on your dumb ass," Mindy said.

A young couple pulling a cart from the corral had stolen his attention.

"Fuck it," Tim said. He reached into the glove box for his Saints do-rag and turned the rearview his way before tying the black and gold fleur-de-lis around his face.

"Badass," he said. "I look like a bank robber."

"You look like a moron," Mindy said. "Water and toilet paper before you run off to the meat."

Soldiers in Geautreaux's forced customers waiting for automated checkout to stand apart by eight feet in two aisle-long lines behind traffic cones. Even families.

"Did you bring the Visa or just the debit card?" Tim asked in produce.

"Why?" Mindy asked.

"No, it's just—they're only letting us buy a pound of that shit meat, right?"

Mindy nodded, waiting for potatoes.

"I say we split up with two carts and buy a pound each," Tim said. "Then we do it again. Should be enough for spaghetti and hamburgers, right?"

"If I can find pasta," she said, giving him the debit card. "Water and toilet paper first."

She continued waiting for an older couple putting their hands all over the potatoes to move on before grabbing two—the most each customer could buy.

"Don't be mad," Tim said when finding her. "I did look for water and toilet paper."

"It's fine," Mindy said. "They had pasta. No sauce, though."

Tim's scam proved successful but had taken close to three hours to pull off, the human herd lined up for checkout looking far more like cattle than the cellophane packs of browning beef.

THE COUCH BENEATH Grandma's bum was soaking wet.

"Christ," Mindy said. "I knew we were gone too long. Grab the Resolve, Tim."

She helped Grandma to the bathroom in the hall, and the couch was spotless by the time they returned.

Watching Tim bring in groceries, Mindy fixed him a drink.

"Seriously?" he asked. "You get so mad, and want me to do it again?"

He wasn't wrong, but with mounting debt and Kevin seeking support, Mindy needed a new episode of Tim Gets Drunk to upload.

SHE RANG HER brother's doorbell and checked her views.

"Sorry," Kevin said. "Could've sworn I left it unlocked."

Mindy headed for the bar dropping her phone in her purse.

"Is everything okay?" Kevin asked, finding sports. "'Cause I watched last night, and—"

"Did you let the episode play in full?" Mindy asked, pouring her drink.

"Of course," he said. "Anything for family."

"Thanks, Kevin."

"It's getting intense, Mindy."

"And bringing more views," she said. "Mind if I bring the bourbon home?"

"I don't know," Kevin said. "Think I might need something stronger than beer tonight."

"Oh, yeah?" Mindy asked.

"I was finally let go today," he said.

Mindy set her glass down. "Jesus, Kevin. I'm so sorry."

"I feel bad," he said, finding Rich Eisen. "But it looks like I'll need more help than expected."

"Told you not to stress," Mindy said.

"Shit, then," Kevin said. "Take the bottle, but fix me one first and join me outside."

He clinked her glass when she sat with him.

"Yeah, Tim's out of his gourd when it comes to safety," Kevin said. "But he's right about neighbors."

"I spoke to LaVar," Mindy said. "He won't hurt us."

"You don't know that, sis. Your neighbors could be killers."

"That's the soldier talking," she said, watching her brother sip his drink. "We're not in the Middle East, Kevin."

"No, we're not," he said.

Mindy lit up and took a quick drag. "Look, I explained Tim's parole. Okay? I just thank God for Chief Clement. The man's a saint."

"LaVar wants to hurt Tim," Kevin said. "And so do I, but I'm your brother."

"Well, good," Mindy said. "'Cause Mom and Dad can't save us. Tim goes back to Ashland and then what? They'll stick Grandma in one of those awful death camps."

"Come on," Kevin said. "Bad juju."

"Touché," Mindy said, smiling. "Well, I'm glad you're in better spirits. I'll pray for you on Sunday."

"Shit's as useless as our government," he said.

"A government you fought for," she said.

"No, Mindy. I fought for family. Those fuckers fly our planes into our buildings in broad daylight? I mean—what's next? A bomb dropped on one of our houses?"

"Okay, so that's what you're thinking?" Mindy asked. "Will they even take you back?"

"Reenlisting? No," Kevin said. "Seems like I'm needed at home, right now."

PASTOR COLETTI WAS the only "man of God" in Terrebonne who refused to close his church.

"How do you close God's house?" he yelled from his pulpit. "Separation of church and state no longer exists, and they can arrest me every week, but I'll still be here for God. Can I get an Amen?"

The tiny auditorium of Trinity Baptist down Bayou Blue had reached full capacity despite city guidelines.

In a pew across the aisle, LaVar was sitting with his mother, and Mindy could feel his eyes locked on her tight green dress, the back of her neck, and her new extensions.

"Don't give in to fear," Coletti yelled. "Can I get an Amen?"

"Can we get him to shut the fuck up?" Tim whispered, and Mindy couldn't help laughing.

She punched his knee. "Stay focused."

The collection baskets were coming.

"And don't forget to say a pray for Chief Clement," Coletti yelled. "God bless the man for waiting until after services to arrest me."

The ushers came and went, and Tim and Mindy were among the very few who stepped out.

"Well?" she asked in the truck.

"Almost two hundred," Tim said, counting the bills a second time.

She turned the ignition. "Want to go to lunch?"

"Sure. What's open?" he asked.

Mindy smiled. "I miss those days, too, Tim. We should get out more."

"To where?" he asked.

"Bayou Black, maybe?"

Bayou Black was all folks online were posting about. Gone were the junk food wrappers and beer cans. In place of the pollution were slow-moving gators that had emerged to disrupt the sill calm reflection of the green oaks and gray moss while giant turtles swam happily to the surface.

Tim shrugged her off.

"Oh, come on," Mindy said, "It's not like I'm asking you to spend time with my family."

"I mean—I would," he said. "But your mom hates me."

"You really are a moron, Tim. My entire family hates you."

THE COUCH BENEATH Grandma's bum was dry when Mindy helped her up.

"Okay, good. Let's get you to the bathroom."

"No worries, Grandma," Tim said. "We got you."

"Oh, hi, Kevin. When did you get here?"

"No," Mindy said. "That's Tim. He lives here, remember?"

"See why I shouldn't call her that?" Tim whispered in the hall.

"Now's not the time," Mindy said. She flipped the switch in the bathroom. "Ready, Grandma?"

She gave Tim the okay to leave, as he raised no objections to wearing a mask when it came to Grandma's number twos.

Returning, he held Grandma while Mindy wiped.

"Damn it," she said, showing him blood.

"Are you fucking serious?" Tim asked.

"Just hold her," she said.

"Is Tim your boyfriend?" Grandma asked.

"No, that's good," Tim whispered. "Means she's not in pain."

"But she's bleeding," Mindy said.

SHE KNOCKED HARD on LaVar's kitchen door.

"Hey, neighbor," he said, still in his Sunday best.

"Grandma's bleeding," Mindy said.

"What?" LaVar asked. "Did Tim hit her?"

"No, asshole. She was using the bathroom. Do you have any more of that good stuff?"

"The last roll I gave you is gone?" he asked.

"That was a month ago," Mindy said.

"Listen," LaVar said. "I would, but—"

"But what?" Mindy asked. "I said she's bleeding. Jesus. Are you listening?"

"No, of course, Mindy. Hold on."

She didn't mind waiting outside. LaVar wasn't married or a father or the owner of any pets, his home devoid of the simplest décor.

He almost tripped in his kitchen when hurrying back.

"It's Charmin," he said.

Mindy took the roll. "Stalk me again, and I'm the one calling the cops."

"Okay, but—"

"But what, LaVar?"

"I can't just do nothing while he slaps you around," LaVar said.

"God bless you," Mindy said.

BEING A DOUCHE, she rang her brother's doorbell twice.

"Sorry," he said.

"Save it," Mindy said. "That's the second time."

Kevin watched her sip at the bar instead of finding sports. "What happened?"

"Outside," she said.

He sat with her, waiting for Mindy to light up.

"Fucking LaVar wanted me to beg him for toilet paper," she said.

"So, there's more," Kevin said.

"I'm just not sure what else," Mindy said.

"Well, you know I'm more than capable of finding out, Sis. Next Sunday while he's in church?"

Mindy took a long sip.

"A condition," her brother said, and she damn near threw her drink in his face.

"For me, Kevin? Really?"

"I don't want Tim to know I'm going in there," he said.

"Are you a soldier or not?" Mindy asked. "'Cause I'm the one taking care of this family now and I'll determine Tim's involvement."

"Of course," Kevin said.

TIM HAD MADE it to the fourth quarter of Monday Night Football before slapping Mindy for the first time, and she slapped him just as hard.

"Jesus," he said.

"Yeah, Jesus," she said. "Be a man and fuck me, already."

Tim threw the bottle above the couch. "Like you fucked LaVar for that toilet paper?"

"Damn it, Tim. That was good bourbon."

"You're right," he said. "I should go over there."

Mindy stood in his way. "Are you stupid? Clement said he's arresting you next time."

"I don't give a fuck," Tim said.

"Fine," Mindy said. She took his hand and pulled her phone. Their conversation needed editing, but Mindy could end the night's episode at the point where she asked Tim for a fuck.

Outside, her eyes met LaVar's before she turned to Tim.

"Go on. Be a man"

He slapped her, and LaVar ran outside.

"Back off, Tim. I'm serious."

"Bitch," Tim said. "Call the cops."

LaVar could've crushed him with one fist, but tried to bring his phone to his ear before seeing his hand blown off from a sniper shot.

In shock, he fell to his knees, watching his wrist bleed out.

"Jesus," Tim said. "A soldier's coming."

"That's right," the soldier said, his suppressed subsonic .308 aimed at Tim's chest. "Now step away from my sister."

Tim obeyed, and Kevin fired another shot into LaVar's head.

You never had a chance, Mindy thought.

"Fuck," Tim said. "Oh, fuck."

"Shut up," Kevin said, aiming for Tim again.

"Yeah, man. No—no problem, Kevin."

"Mindy and I got this," her brother said. "Now, go inside and sleep it off. 'Cause you're getting up in a few hours."

"For what?" Tim asked.

"Dead Jesus has an attic full of water, toilet paper and meat," Kevin said. "Premium stuff, too, and enough to last until summer."

CHIEF CLEMENT KNOCKED on Mindy's front door as Terrebonne's horizon bled beneath the evening sky and stars.

"Hey, stranger. How's Sheila and the boys?"

"Dying to get out more," Clement said.

"Cabin fever's the worst," Mindy said. "So, to what do I owe the pleasure?"

"Have you seen LaVar?" he asked.

"Not since checking the mail the other day. Why?"

"The other day meaning which day?" he asked.

"Come to think of it," Mindy said. "I haven't seen LaVar all week."

"His mother hasn't heard from him, either," Clement said. "And the soldiers haven't picked him up for breaking curfew. But it's strange. His truck's home and his door's unlocked. Like he just upped and disappeared."

Mindy waved him inside, and Clement became distracted by the sight of Grandma on the couch.

"Ms. Hormann," he said, removing his hat.

"Oh, hi, Calvin. How's your mother?"

"She passed last spring," Clement said.

"I'm so sorry," Grandma said. "Mindy didn't tell me."

Mindy offered a cold can of Miller Lite—the police chief's favorite.

"I brought her to the wake," she said.

"I remember," Clement said, cracking his beer open.

"Well, he can't be gone with the wind," Mindy said. "Have you checked Bayou Black? It's all the rage these days. Maybe LaVar went on foot and fell ill somewhere. I get that's not the most optimistic thought, but—"

"No," Clement said. "That's good thinking."

"And how are the soldiers treating you?" she asked.

He took a long sip. "Pretty well, overall. I think. Where's Tim?"

"Out back," Mindy said. "Want me to get him?"

"Not if he's keeping his nose clean," Clement said.

"Well, you definitely put in the fear of God in him last time," she said. "But yes, he's behaving himself."

"Good," Clement said.

He downed the rest of his cold treat, leaving Mindy with the empty.

"Thanks for the beer," he said.

"Any time," she said. "Don't work too hard."

"With all the red tape these days?" Clement said. "I can barely work at all. Enjoy your evening, Ms. Hormann."

"Oh, hi, Calvin. How's your mother?"

Clement turned to Mindy. "You'll call if LaVar shows up?"

"Of course," Mindy said, smiling. "What are neighbors for?"

FRIENDLY FIRE

by

S.E.Moorhead

THE MOSQUE HAD become a place of war.

How could there be worship when there was no peace?

It was silent, the last adhan had been called eighteen months previously, before dwindling phosphorus reserves had finally broken down the fragile relationship between the United Kingdom and Morocco. The fields of Europe were barren without its fecundity. Morocco would only sell to the highest bidder.

How could there be friendship if there was no food?

Now soldiers stood where the imam had once called to prayer, the mosque a battlefield, the town a war zone. The squad, five men, two women, crept across the green and golden marble tiles, dusty and brown in the darkness. Glass gritted beneath government issued boots. Sergeant Travis held up a fist. The squad halted as one body, a khaki desert lizard, eyes swiveling.

Leila checked her 360° vision camera. Travis and her brother, Zak, were ahead with two other squaddies, twin brothers. Another one of the lads, Max, was bringing up the rear with Cassie. There was no one else. She was beginning to wonder if this mission to find a rebel cell had been a wild goose chase.

They stood in silence for a minute, cicadas emitting a continual high-pitched whine, a dog barking somewhere outside in the heat and the darkness. Leila tapped the side of her helmet and statistics flashed on the eyescreen inside her transparent visor. Heart rate steady, body temperature 37.2, external temperature 47 degrees. Her hydration bars were low. She heard the drip, drip of the taps in the ablution room nearby, as if her brain was automatically searching out a water source.

Travis dropped his fist and they began moving again. Leila knew he could be cruel. A hardened tough man, but his decisions had kept them alive.

Leila's mouth was dry. The skin beneath her helmet strap itched, a bite from some invisible foreign bloodsucker. Focusing beyond the tiny bright green lights of her eyescreen, she spotted Zak stumble and right himself. Immediately her helmet recorded a change in body chemistry, a peak of adrenaline followed by raised levels of dopamine and oxytocin. She swiped the display away, not needing digital information to tell her how she felt about her twin.

It wasn't unusual for siblings to be deployed together, in fact the army encouraged twins in particular. Stronger loyalty, fiercer defence. *Brother warrior* she called him, affectionately taking the piss. Leila and Zak had spent a lifetime protecting each other. When they'd signed up, they—it was never she/her but always they/them—she'd worried they might not pass the psychometrics and psychological tests. Would they pick up on the damage? Twins with a couldn't-cope-absent-mother, raised by their Muslim grandfather until they were ten years old, and then deposited in a care home after he died. She assumed they would be rich pickings for cannon fodder.

Until one of the scientists had asked a question that got her thinking.

Do you ever know what your brother is thinking without him saying?

What, like how he's feeling?

No, specifically, what he's actually thinking. Maybe words pop into your head and then he'll say them...

No, well, yes, sometimes, I guess.

When his eyes had lit up behind his nerdy glasses, she'd realised she was onto something, embroidered her answer. She'd told Zak to do the same.

They signed up the same day.

AN EXPLOSION NEARBY rocked the building. A chandelier of crystals, which had somehow survived—defiant in the face of the horror outside—tinkled violently above the soldiers.

A shudder like an aftershock vibrated through Leila's body. Zak glanced over a hunched shoulder, making eye contact. Nodded his head. She nodded back. He turned away again. The bite beneath her chin-strap throbbed now.

She undid the strap and scratched at it, blood on her fingernails. It would sting later. For now, her helmet automatically stimulated her pain response.

Leila looked up, her gaze following the curves of the arches and the deep azure dome, the thousands of gold stars, no doubt hand-painted as an act of devotion, glowed in the light of the military torches. They echoed the ones she had seen outside, crisp around a crescent moon in a much darker sky, as they had crept between the squat whitewashed buildings.

She recalled the care home's broken promise of mosque once a week. Now here they were, Friday night, but instead of searching for God, they were looking for the enemy. *Get in, find the cell, take them out, establish ownership of the mosque...* Travis' orders lodged in her mind like shrapnel and now crouching in the pitch black she was starting to wonder if the intelligence they'd been given was wrong. Maybe they could do with heatseeking visuals on the helmets. They had everything else; built-in navigation maps, long range broadband comms, smart foam preventing head-injuries, infra-red, thermal imaging, night-vision, geotagging, facial recognition—friend or foe?— birds-eye views from headquarters and even views relayed from other soldiers. Her and Zak. Two orphan kids trialling the latest in military technology, the thought still gave her a buzz. Was the army really working on telepathy, using them both as guinea pigs? Zak had laughed when she'd suggested it was something to do with mind-control. Could the helmet already read their minds? She wasn't smart enough to figure out how them being twins could help, but if it was to protect the squad from the enemy, give them victory, then she was in.

A noise, muffled in the blanket of darkness. The squad froze, blood rushed in her ears. Travis' head turned a few degrees to the right. A closed door nearby, the madrassa, Leila assumed by the sign on the door—*The seeking of knowledge is obligatory for every muslim.* An almost indiscernible nod and they followed him as gently as a bomb-disposal unit at a landmine site. As they had drilled so often, two of the squad flanked either side of the door, Zak and Cassie hanging back so all angles were covered. Travis gave another nod, one of the other soldiers, his twin brother near by—kicked the door in, and Leila and Max burst into the room.

Four boys, maybe aged thirteen or fourteen years old, sat smoking around a rough wooden table on which a dog-eared deck of playing cards was dealt. The only source of light was a few stumps of candles. One ancient rifle leaned against a wall. Two of the boys stood and raised their arms in startled surrender. One of them dropped to the floor and placed his hands on his head. Leila recognized his words as those of prayer. The fourth boy jumped up, the cigarette falling from his lips, snatched at the nearest rifle, his face a picture of terror and determination.

Leila directed her target, a beam of green, towards the centre of the boy's chest, waiting for the order to shoot, the words *enemy, other, threat* like a mantra in her mind. She studied him, the same skinny coltish frame as Zak had once, the same dark eyes and hair—a strange disconnect in her brain as though she knew she should somehow feel more for this boy. He was of her tribe, her's and Zak's, not like the fair-skinned Travis, not like the rest of the squad. And yet she felt nothing. As though something had gone from her. Had been taken.

Another green spot of light danced with her own over the dirty white cotton of the boy's garment, his shoulders trembling, chest heaving with fear, but he held his weapon resolutely.

Her trigger finger itched like the insect bite at her throat.

'Now what do we have here?' Travis' voice low. Menacing. Leila had seen him like this before, merciless, but he got the job done, didn't he? Protecting the squad at all costs. The praying boy suddenly jumped up and grabbed a stool, launching it at the adults. It hit Leila, knocking her down, her loosened helmet crashed to the floor and spun like a tin can. Disorientation overwhelmed her until her brain rebooted. She surveyed the scene again and instead of seeing the enemy, she now saw shabby, malnourished, fearful kids. A bunch of boys playing cards, playing at soldiers, their one weapon as dusty as the Moroccan roofs outside. The boy in front stared at Leila as she scrambled to get up. He dropped his rifle clattering to the ground and put his hands in the air screaming, 'La la la salam! La tutliquu alnaar! *Don't shoot!*' The other boys whimpering in chorus with his words.

Travis gave Leila a look of disgust and turned to Zak. 'Kill them all,' he commanded.

Zak aimed his rifle.

The boy's eyes widened.

Travis turned to leave.

Leila felt Zak's heartbeat as her own as his finger squeezed down on the trigger.

'No!' she shouted and flung herself at her brother.

There was a split second of silence, the eye of the storm, a moment of stillness, the sound of the gunshot muted, even the projectile seemed reluctant to leave its barrel. The bullet exploded into a crumbling wall with a puff of powdered plaster. Nearby hung a wooden board painted with the words *It is not the eyes that are blind but the hearts*. Zak shoved her angrily to the ground, the worst betrayal.

Moments later, a cacophony, her hands a poor substitute for the ear protection her helmet usually provided, the smell of hot metal and blood, and a tangle of dead children on the madrassa floor, their learning at an end.

"JESUS FUCKING CHRIST, Leila! You nearly cost us our lives out there!" Travis roared in her face. "Kill the enemy or they kill your squad, your brothers. Where's your fucking loyalty?"

The others stood nearby, their backs to her. Zak hung his head.

"Sarge, they were kids...we could have..."

"You're supposed to be a fucking super-soldier! You can deal with a few kids. You follow *my* orders!"

"They were just children..."

His face flushed at her insubordination, he stepped in closer to her and spoke very quietly but with great force. "Weaponized children! Killing civilians sometimes is necessary. It's collateral damage, that's what it is, kids or not. If someone gets in the way of us doing our job, then you kill them. It's as simple as that. Message received?"

"Yes, Sarge. Kill them. Collateral damage."

Leila glanced towards Zak, but he wouldn't look at her.

"There is no morality here, soldier!" Travis yelled in her face. "There are no emotions, no decisions for you to make! Just do your fucking job!" More quietly. "And keep your fucking helmet on in future."

"Yes, Sarge."

She put it on as he moved away from her, hiding her shame. Glad the stats on her eyescreen couldn't register despair.

LATER, THE OTHERS sat together in a huddle eating on the other side of the mosque. Zak looked to Travis and he nodded. Zak brought over two mess tins and handed one to her. It looked like chicken stew. They placed their helmets together on the floor and ate for a few minutes in silence, ignoring the looks from the others. Finally, Zak said, "Why did you try to save that boy?"

What could she say? He'd reminded her of Zak when he was young? She hadn't wanted her twin to live with the consequences of killing a child? She'd had a moment of madness wondering what the fuck they were doing out here? But she said nothing.

"We've killed before in the line of duty." His eyes mirrored her own. "Didn't bother you then."

"That boy wasn't duty. That was murder."

Travis laughed a little too loudly at something one of the other set of twins had said and glanced over. His smile disappeared, morphing to one of disappointment or distaste. Leila felt blood rush to her face.

"Just keep your helmet on in future, when we're working. It'll keep you out of trouble."

"What's that supposed to mean?"

His eyes flashed over to where the others were sitting, huddled together, excluding. Then looked back and said quietly, "Look inside behind the ear protectors."

She turned the helmet around on the floor so she could see into it. There was a nub of metal on either side that she hadn't noticed. She didn't need to know the ins and outs. She just had to wear it.

She looked at him and shrugged.

"Affects the TPJ," he said biting at his lips to catch a stray bean. "With magnetic pulses."

"What are you talking about?"

"I read up about it, temporoparietal junction in the brain. Stops your moral judgment from interfering with the mission."

"Interfering? You're fucking joking, right?"

"Jesus, Leila, they've injected us with all sorts, pumped us full of God knows what, practically made us into machines, and you're worried about a couple of magnets? Get a fucking grip." His spoon scraped against his mess tin and the noise grated on her.

"Why tell me then?"

He shrugged. "Just thought you should know."

"I don't want to turn into an emotionless monster like him." She nodded towards Travis.

"It's to protect us, Lei, so we can *control* our emotions, do the job. It's only while we wear the helmets. It keeps us alive. Look what happened when you lost your helmet. That could have been fucking disastrous."

She sighed. Her mess tin dropped from her hands to the tiles. "What if there are side effects?"

"There are no side effects," Zak said, licking his lips and dropping his spoon into the tin with a clatter.

"I think those dead kids are side effects. What did he call them—collateral damage?" The words burned her lips. "They're making us into killers."

"We *are* killers!"

"I mean they're making us into more effective killers—sociopaths. Unfeeling, indiscriminate killers."

Zak put down his mess tin and grabbed her hand. Squeezed, hard. Hissed, "Lei, this is not the time or place. If you have doubts, if you're going to rock the boat, you're gonna get someone killed. We, *I*, don't need this now."

"Why didn't you tell me sooner? About the magnets?"

He shrugged again. "Figured it was easier just to get on with it. We're not paid to think, Leila."

Not paid to feel either, it would seem.

"What Travis says is true. We're super-soldiers, designed to kill. Whatever these helmets do for us, make us, give us—faster responses, more resilient to pain, better informed, more efficient—it's all for the good, to make us the best at what we do. Now just leave it alone."

"He'll punish me for this."

"What? Shoot you at dawn for not following orders?" He laughed but his eyes remained cold.

"He's done it before. He's a fucking monster, Zak."

"We all are, Leila," he said, sounding tired. "We all are."

THE SQUAD WERE trying to get a few hours kip before Beta Squad relieved the post in the morning. Leila lay awake, knowing in her heart Travis *would* watch her burn. Punishment for not following orders. Probably a kangaroo court martial. Military prison.

Max and Cassie were outside, on watch. Zak was flat out. The other twins were deep in sleep. A *clear conscience is a soft pillow* their grandfather used to say.

Travis approached her silently, still wearing his helmet. His way of letting her know this was official.

He ordered her down to the washrooms, the same sort of place her grandfather had done his ablutions in preparation before prayer.

Maybe this too would be a purification.

But it was worse than that.

"This is what we do when someone breaks the trust in our squad, soldier. When someone doesn't toe the line, follow orders." He frowned. "I always said they shouldn't have women in the forces." He took a deep breath, swelled his chest and sighed. "I loathe the weakness you showed today. But I'm going to toughen you up so that you shut that emotional bullshit down."

He took her helmet from her and balanced it on one of the taps above the drains. "Not much of a punishment if you're getting pain relief, is it?" he grinned.

LATER, WHEN SHE returned to the main prayer room and lay down on the hard tiles, Leila wondered who the real enemy was. She remembered what her grandfather had taught her that the greater jihad—the struggle inside oneself—was the hardest struggle of all. There was no such thing as telepathy. Leila knew that now. If there had been, Zak would have come running into that wet room, and killed Travis.

She pulled her helmet on, the pain relief almost instant and substantial— and stared up to the gilded stars above blurring through the lens of her tears.

THE SQUAD AWOKE at first light, the ghost of the call to prayer ringing in Leila's ears after three hours of a roulette wheel of emotions and thoughts in the darkness. Body aching. She wanted to put her helmet back on to take the pain away, but she needed to think clearly. Anger raged within her.

There was no way she could speak of what had happened. She was already a pariah. Could never win against Travis. She had heard once of another woman who had claimed the same thing had happened to her, and Leila had shaken her head in disgust with the rest of them, even when the woman had taken her own life after being accused of being a liar, and disloyal—a trouble-maker.

If Leila told anyone she would lose her place in the army, her living, her vocation. She might never see Zak again. Where would she live? How would she exist alone, a unit of one?

Max took a piss near the mihrab. She thought of her grandfather, an image of him in his white taqiyah as it reached the ground as he bent to pray and her heart ached. The boys' corpses had already been removed. A new squad would soon be bringing in proper kit on trucks. Camp beds, trestle tables, computers, stoves. Soon the mosque would be a hustling, bustling operations centre, a point in gained territory for their side. Then her squad would be back on their way to camp and her chance would be lost.

She frowned over at the ablution room as Travis came out of its doors after his morning wash, short grey hair damp and dark. Looking no different to the day before.

Her hand reached out automatically for her helmet, then her rifle.

The bastard, the bastard, the bastard.

As if he'd read her mind, Zak turned quickly towards her.

There's no such thing as telepathy.

Her heart beat rhythmic explosions like mortar fire in her chest. Tears streaming from her eyes, nose running. She hid her face with her helmets visor.

Suddenly the whole world calmed, her pain, her distress dissipating and then simply gone.

Travis joined the rest of the squad, making a joke. They all laughed.

Leila growled.

Her twin moved towards her, concerned, but stopped when she took a firing stance and aimed at Travis. Her green light dancing on his spine.

The others saw her before he did. They stopped laughing. Travis turned around slowly.

Zak raised his hands, trying to placate her. "Lei, what are you doing?" His words steady, but she could hear the fear in them.

"I'm going to kill the bastard."

"Lei, no, don't…"

At that moment, the helmet did its job. She didn't feel anything. No pain, no emotion. Blissfully free of her humanity, she embraced the efficient killer that she was, that the army had made her into.

Travis' face a picture of outrage.

Zak yelled something.

She pulled the trigger.

The green line between her and Travis, the trajectory of her hatred, was suddenly broken as Zak, instinctively protecting one of his squad, jumped in front of Travis.

Leila felt nothing as his chest opened in a wet rosette, just relief when he hit the ground and her target was clear.

"Collateral damage," she said, as Zak looked up at her, his eyes horrified, imploring, the light in them darkening.

Leila fired twice at Travis and she didn't feel a thing, not even when she saw his lifeless face turned towards the painted stars.

Death will find you even if you hide in fortresses built up strong and high...

She lowered her weapon, the only movement in the mosque, the squad stunned by her action, Travis dead, her twin lying nearby, his arms splayed out as if embracing the next world, an angel flying up to Jannah.

Leila's rifle fell to the tiles beneath, her hands reached up to remove her helmet, to face the worst horror of all.

GOD OWES NOBODY ETERNITY

by

M.Sean Coleman

GOD OWES NOBODY eternity. There was no better message. After all, he'd said it often enough. His aide-memoir of the abhorrent and unnatural thing his bloody-minded son-in-law had done. If he could have chosen a different business partner, he'd have done it in a heartbeat, but the boy was a genius and, although he hated him, what they'd created together was something incredible. But Dan had broken the fundamental rule—he'd changed time, destroyed lives, played God—and he'd lied about it.

Well, God owes nobody eternity. So, stick that in your pipe and smoke it.

HE TOOK A deep, calming breath. It all came down to this. Live or die. This exact moment would change everything. Shame he wouldn't live to see it. But then, that *was* the whole point. There was no other way. He steadied himself. Deep breath in. Count to three.

One.

Two.

Three.

The hum of the condenser provided a solid backdrop of white noise, a light buzz which filled the silence, pumping life through the machine. Their machine. Dan's baby. Not for the first time, that familiar flicker of fear licked at his throat. What if it didn't work? What if all of this ended up being for nothing? What if he simply died, and his life's work died with him? No. It *would* work. Dan had already proved it. Now it was up to him to put things right. Time unwinds.

It all came down to this.

He checked the clock. Checked the settings. Checked the wires which bound him, life and soul—thank God he believed in such things—to the system they had created.

Tick. Tick. Tick. Thunk.

The minute hand clicked on one place. 6.57.

"Play," he said quietly. And into the silence came the first bars of Gabriel Fauré's *Cantique de Jean Racine*. Slow, gentle, melodious, but played at a volume appropriate for the spectacle which would unfold here in the next three minutes.

He lifted the gun from the desk. A small pistol. Solid and cold. Who would have thought the greatest breakthrough in quantum physics could be brought about by such a blunt instrument? He turned it over in his hand, feeling the heft of it, weighing it on his palm, fingers caressing the trigger. So real. So simple. So fundamental. No margin for error. He noticed the slight tremor in his hand. He was right to be nervous.

He let the growing fervour of the choral piece flow through him, steadying him. So familiar. His power song. The one that lifted and carried him through everything, no matter what happened.

Tick. 6.58.

He turned to the metal disk on the floor. The spot where he would take his own life. A titanium platform, gleaming silver, with a low, pulsing blue light surrounding it. Silly, really. No need for the light at all. It had been Dan's nod to the 1970s Sci-Fi shows that had enthralled his childhood brain. As the music rose—the tenors taking centre stage, underpinned by the bass voices he'd always aspired to but never achieved—he stepped into the circle, and imagined the buzz of electricity coursing through the wires filling his veins with energy.

Tick. 6.59.

A final check everything was running exactly right. The console gleamed. Glowing figures flashed. Now the buzz was real, the sound of energy rising to an inevitable crescendo. It all came down to this.

He raised the gun to his head, its cold metal kissing the warm skin on his temple. His pulse thumping against the tip of the barrel.

Thump. Thump. Thump.

The countdown before him measured in mere seconds now. This was it.

Faure's haunting choral reached its final note, and the silence rushed back into the room. The buzz of the machine. His breath. His pulse. The inexorable ticking of the clock. Deep breath.

Three. Two. One.

Click. Bang. Thud.

He was dead before he hit the floor.

/

CLICK.

Silence.

A breath, slowly exhaled, as though to test the waters.

He took the gun from his temple and bellowed a euphoric roar. It had worked. He had lived. And yet, looking at the glowing lines on the monitor—like strings on a harp— he knew that in another, parallel universe, he had died. Another gateway had been built. His very own gateway. He'd bloody done it! How do you like that, Dr Dan Goddard? I told you I'd put things right.

He laid the gun back on the desk and turned to stare straight down the lens of the camera.

"And there you have it," he said. "My own gateway moment. Now for the real work to begin. Not so hard, after all, is it, Dan? Sorry son, you're just plumb out of time."

He reached across and stopped the recording, allowing himself just a moment of satisfaction. He had done it. But now it really <u>was</u> time for the real work to begin.

"GOD OWES NOBODY eternity," had been the old man's dying words. A bitter retort, aimed directly at the son-in-law he'd grown to hate, reported to me now by my ex-wife—his daughter—over a crackling and distorted international phoneline. Her voice was staccatoed by the same abrupt, snorting sobs that had been the soundtrack to our inevitable divorce. By the time I finally left her, I'd lost count of the number of times *'It will kill my father if you leave me!'* had been her full stop in an argument. Words that kept me at her side far too long.

Ultimately, it hadn't been me leaving her that had seen him off. Neither had it been the discovery of his precious daughter's seemingly limitless capacity for infidelity, despite the vows she had made in front of the Lord— his Lord. I must admit, petty as it was, I took great delight sharing every detail with him. The bitter discovery *had*, in fact, nearly seen him off—the stress had caused his first heart attack. That, and a lifetime of poor diet and hard liquor, obviously.

"But that was *all* he said," she sobbed. "No 'I love you'. Not a shred of comfort for me. Just some cryptic message for you. And he hates you. What does it even mean, Dan?"

Not that I was going to tell her, but I knew exactly what it meant. And I knew exactly what he'd done. It was no cryptic message. It was clear as fucking day. He was taking my daughter from me, as punishment for what I'd done, and there was nothing I could do to stop him. Well, almost nothing. I checked my watch. 4 p.m. 1 a.m. in Australia. Surely there wouldn't be enough time left to fix this. Fuck!

God, fuck him! He'd timed it perfectly—I'd only gone away for a week. But he knew that the distance between Australia and the UK meant I would inevitably lose time on the return trip, anyway.

"When, *exactly*, did he do it? And were you with him when he died?" I asked, my voice colder than it should have been.

"What the hell, Dan? No, I wasn't with him. He shot himself in the fucking head! If I'd been with him, I'd have fucking stopped him! Fuck's sake. Tell me what he meant. And why was it so important that I tell you at midnight? Dan? .... Dan?"

My name still sounded bitter in her throat. She knew I hated her using my name as punctuation in every damned sentence. I ignored it for now. Shit. My heart paused.

"Tell me how he did it, exactly?"

"Jesus Dan, what is wrong with you? Whatever happened to 'I'm so sorry for your loss?' I know you two had fallen out, but..."

I don't have time for this.

"It's important, Bel. Just tell me what happened and I'll explain what he meant."

"He shot himself. In the head. Point fucking blank. Is that what you want to know? He was hooked up to that stupid machine. Your machine. He called me earlier in the day and told me to tell you 'God owes nobody eternity'. He made me repeat it back to him. I asked him what he meant, and he just said to promise to tell you. He said I had to call you at exactly midnight. Local time."

"What time?"

"Midnight. I just said. I know it's gone one now, but it's been a…"

Jesus, this woman did not shut up.

"No. What time did he die?"

"What? Why is th…"

"It's important." It was all I could do not to scream at her.

"Somewhere around seven last night. Local time, obviously. What's that got to do with anything?"

It has everything to do with everything. Ripples flow quicker through time than water. Those words he'd made her repeat to me said he'd finally done the one thing I thought he'd never do. He'd killed himself to spite me. He'd come after my daughter, my only child, my Lily. And he'd done it in a way I could do little about—little, but not nothing. He'd played me like a fiddle—waiting until I was on the other side of the world, with Lily in tow, to visit my own parents. Boy, had I underestimated him.

"Dan? Tell me what he meant." She sobbed another strangled, snipping sob.

I had no time for her crocodile tears. I had no time for her guilt. There was just no time.

"I'm coming back."

"We don't need you…"

She did, but in a way she'd hopefully never understand. I needed to save our daughter, again.

"Lily does. I'm bringing her back."

It was enough to halt her protests.

"What have you done, you bitter old bastard?" I muttered as I hung up. But I knew exactly what he'd done, and I had a matter of hours remaining to stop the effects of his actions. It may even be too late already. He'd vowed once he would take my daughter from me, and now he'd set that plan in motion.

I SHOULD PROBABLY explain a few things.

A year ago, I was absorbed in my work, adrift from my wife—who had stopped loving me many years ago anyway—and distant from my teenage daughter. My father-in-law, Michael, was growing frustrated with my lack of progress, and was threatening to pull the funding he had so generously provided for the past five years. I couldn't let him do that. I was on the cusp of the greatest discovery in Quantum Physics. I was obsessed. Nothing, and no-one else mattered. Only HARP—the simple name I'd given the most complex of systems.

The Many Worlds theory was just that—a theory to be explored and proved. The idea that there are many, interconnected versions of our own lives, each playing out simultaneously, differing only because of decisions made, and actions taken—sometimes our own, sometimes those of others who directly affect us. What I'd created in HARP was something from science fiction, brought to life by my genius, and my father-in-law's deep pockets.

When I realised that I could actually find a way to observe multiple versions of the universe at the same time, and even bend time to choose our path through those universes, I'd immediately though of the old Star Trek adage *Live long and Prosper*. A silly geeky reference, but there was more truth in it than I had acknowledged at the time. You see, I had created a system which could ensure long life, unparalleled wealth and eternal happiness, by harnessing the tenuous lines of time and space, and knitting them together to create a meandering path of pure joy.

The problem is, most people are too boring. I soon discovered that the multiple, infinitely expanding versions of an average person's life bob along quite peaceably, close enough to affect each other, sometimes even bending and weaving across each other, but with very few significant differences between each version. People just don't take the kind of deliberate risks required to cause a significant enough of a split in time. Simply stepping out into the street and getting hit by a bus is not even enough—that's an accident. It would create ripples, of course, but because it isn't the consequence of deliberate choice, it wouldn't create the clear split I needed.

To create the kind of schism HARP needs to link and cross universal pathways, there had to be a moment of significant black-and-white change. Live or die. Nothing in between. And more than that, the moment needed to be deliberate, and simultaneously observed in all versions of the universe. A schism of that magnitude would temporarily bring all versions of the universe back together in a single, simple A/B split. And for that, suicide was the cleanest answer. Which was where Michael and I had started falling out.

What you have to understand, is that Michael Kinsella is a devoutly religious man for whom suicide is an act of absolute betrayal to God. He had been fully supportive of my research because I'd pitched it cleverly, avoiding any hint that I wanted to manipulate fate and destiny. This was about science and the future. Absolutely nothing to do with me wanting a better life. Michael firmly, resolutely believes that everything that happens—good, bad or ugly—is God's will. It is this ridiculous notion that led to an almighty argument, in which I finally explained exactly what I had built and what I needed to do to achieve the success we craved. Namely, shoot myself in the head. Well, he exploded. Accused me of playing God. Of abandoning my family for some ridiculous notion that would likely never work anyway.

The thing is, it did work. But it wasn't my suicide that provided the gateway moment I needed. It was my beautiful daughter's. Exactly one year ago, she took her own life. And in that moment, I finally proved the Many Worlds theory. The problem was, in order to prove it, I'd lost everything.

So I created a world where I got it all back.

The panic bubbling in my gut now told me that there was every chance I would lose it all again.

This time, forever.

WITH TWO HOURS to wait until we can leave for our flight back to Melbourne, I've sent Lily upstairs to get ready, and I've locked myself in my office. That wily, deceitful bastard. I should never have shown him it worked. Like I said, I underestimated him. It's highly unlikely I'll be able to find him in time, but I have to try, for Lily. I've already noticed she's glitching. It's barely perceptible, but she's becoming more vacant and forgetful. She's not meant to be in this universe. She deliberately took herself from it, and selfishly, I put her back in it.

I'm staring at the 3D graphical representation of my life—or the multiple versions of my possible lives—on the screens in front of me. There, in as straightforward a display as I was able to render it, are a series of bending, rippling lines representing the various versions of the universe on which my own life has a direct influence. Like the strings on a harp, the multiple universes run parallel to each other, and like the waveforms created when a string is plucked, the many interconnections between those multiple, parallel universes bend, cross, ripple and intersect with each other on the screen. It's a beautiful representation of a complex and mind-bending thing, but I need to see it like this, simply to keep track of the consequences of every action and reaction. I have been manipulating my timeline for a year now, ever since I switched Lily back on to it. It is a twisted, glowing trail of my deceit.

The lines dance on the screens in front of me, hypnotising me with their rippling vibrations. This is my life, my influence, my universe. Here, I am in charge of my own destiny—puppet master. God. Or I was, until Michael Kinsella created a gateway moment of his own, and started pulling the strings himself. I stare at the screens again, willing the truth to change. But the dancing lines taunt me. My patches are already unravelling. The graft I made to make sure Lily stayed in my life is already fraying. She will soon be gone completely if I don't find him in time.

I tap a few buttons on the keyboard, my fingers beating an angry, frustrated rhythm. The screens change, rolling back through the last twelve hours of time. There it is, as clear as day. The moment my father-in-law changed everything. Seething, I turn the rotating scrub dial to roll the timeline back and forth, like a video editor finding the right insert point. There is no doubt. Lily's line is there, entwined with my own line, like the vines of an ancient rainforest, and tied, too, to her neurotic mother, and her controlling grandfather. I roll back a year, and zoom in on the incision point where I put her back in my timeline. It had been so close to becoming permanent, but it was already beginning to fray.

Just after Lily had taken her own life, through my fog of grief and guilt, I realised that I could get her back. Carefully, delicately, like a botanist creating new hybrid plants, I spliced the version of Lily's timeline where she survived onto the cut nub of the one in which she had recently departed. I felt God-like. She would live again. And I would never have to feel the pain of losing her. Or the guilt of not having been there for her, and not realising what she was feeling. It was a good analogy—the hybrid plant. When a cut shoot was spliced to another plant's root stock, it needed to be bound on, and it needed time and care to knit properly, for life to flow from one part to the other, and for the shoot to flourish and grow into a new plant, significantly different—stronger and better—than the original.

This is what I had developed with HARP. While the gateway moment is significant enough to bring all the multiple parallel universes back to just two lines, even temporarily, the echoes from the other lost universes still bounce across those new lines, reverberating, and throwing up memories, reminders, feelings of déjà-vu and a conviction that one has been somewhere, seen something, felt something like this before. It takes time for those echoes to fade. It takes time for the ripples of the universes to settle again and become one, single, observed life.

Some people will feel the echoes for longer, convinced they can still hear voices of the deceased, sure that they have seen their faces on the street. They are not the false memories we write them off to be, they are simply stronger echoes of other universes, just beyond our sight. Or, at least, they had been beyond sight until I created HARP.

The problem is, Michael realised what I had done. And he was sickened. It had been him that had found Lily after she'd killed herself, and the memory of what she had done was etched strongly in his mind. More than a vivid dream. When he saw her alive again, he knew exactly what I'd done. I had used my daughter's suicide to complete my life's work. And I had used the system to ensure she was still with us. It went against everything he believed, and everything he stood for. Lily had taken her life—a sin in his eyes.

He tried to tell the rest of the family what I'd done, but of course, for them, it had all just been a bad dream. As far as their memories were concerned, she hadn't gone anywhere. She'd tried to kill herself, and it hadn't worked. The family gathered around her, and her grandfather's strange ramblings about me bending time saw him medicated by doctors to help him through the trauma of nearly losing his grand-daughter. Of course, the echoes of the shock of learning of her death still played on her mother's mind, but over time, as the splice I had made strengthened, those, too, faded.

Not so for Michael Kinsella. He had written it down, to remind himself every day of what I'd done. *"God owes nobody eternity."* That's what he'd said to me on the day he'd realised. And he'd promised that he would undo my work one day, and return everything to its rightful time and place. Even if that meant losing his grand-daughter. After all, what she'd done was unforgivable to him, and he would never forget that, either. The fractures her actions, and then mine, had caused meant that the whole family fell apart. Michael banned me from the laboratory, hoping to cut me off from my system while he figured out how to put right my wrongs. Of course, I had a duplicate system in my own home, and a satellite version of it here in London. He even tried pulling the plug on it, to see if that would reset the balance. But it doesn't work like that.

I, meanwhile, took the opportunity to get to know my daughter—to build a life and a relationship together that we had never really shared before. She became my shadow. But I could never tell her what I had done, and my action haunts every single moment of my life. I, too, have become neurotic and paranoid about keeping her alive. But it turns out, now, with good reason. My action was irrevocable. The timeline I had spliced the living Lily from had long since withered and died. This is the only version of her life in which she is still alive. And it doesn't matter how many times I patched it over, the inalienable truth is that, in every version of my life, apart from this one, my Lily is dead. And now, Michael has used my own system against me, and is somewhere, deep in my past, unpicking every event that brought us to the point where I had a daughter to lose in the first place.

"GLAD OUR NAME'S Evans," Lily smirked under her breath, having heard the tall man in the check-in queue in front of us have to repeat his name—Highcock—in an even louder voice.

The check-in clerk stifled a smirk as he tried to find the booking reference, and then presented the man's boarding passes and passport back to him.

"You're all ready to fly, Mr Highcock," he said, smiling. A slight, childish over-emphasis on the second half of the man's surname.

The clerk was still smirking when he greeted us, looked Lily up and down, almost earning himself a dressing down, and took our passports. Realising that her father had clocked his appraisal of her, he got busy with our check-in.

"Good news, you've been upgraded to business," he said, handing us back our passes. That really was good news. I had booked the only available seats on the next flight back to Melbourne out of London Heathrow, and hadn't been looking forward to sitting upright next to a fidgety teenager for the best part of twenty-four hours. Lily squealed her delight, looked to the ceiling and mouthed; "Thanks Gramps."

I had nothing to thank that old scrote for. He had properly stitched me up. I knew I should have moved everything out with me when I'd gone. Even though he'd paid for it all, HARP was my baby. It should never have left it with him. I held Lily's hand tight as we made our way through the airport, and made her sit beside me in the lounge, refusing to let her out of my sight. I needed to feel her presence. I needed to make sure she was still with me. He didn't have her yet. But I urgently needed to get back to the machine he used, and find where—and how far back— he had gone.

GATE 12, BOARDING NOW. The board flashed its message in bright green. It was time.

"Hiya! You alright?" Lily chirped to the tall man, Highcock, in front of us in the queue at the gate. I'd already given him the side-eye as we'd waited for boarding to start—I didn't like the way he'd looked at her. And now, somehow, he'd managed to place himself directly in front of us in the queue. When he'd turned back, pretending to look at his fellow passengers, his gaze had landed on Lily and, to my surprise, she'd suddenly perked up, as though she knew him. The man looked from her, to me—glaring, and back to her. He returned a muted, confused hello, and cocked his head, narrowing his eyes as though trying to figure out where he knew her from. He looked at me again, frowned, and turned back to hand his boarding pass to the gate steward.

"Who's that?" I asked.

Lily shrugged, frowning.

"Not sure," she said. "I thought I knew him for a minute there, but I don't know where from." She shrugged again, then whispered, "Oh God, what if he's off the telly or something, and I've just made a tit of myself?"

"If he is, I'm sure he gets it all the time," I reassured her. "Don't worry about it."

But I was worried about it. I recognised him now. From a different place and a different time. He'd looked at me, half-feeling the same echo, and half-feeling my paternal animosity. He had every right to. Matthew Highcock was the man Belinda was due to marry until she'd met me. The man who'd accused me of stealing his life. Even though we'd never met face to face, I'd seen enough pictures of him to recognise him. In fact, Michael still kept a picture of Belinda and Matthew on a skiing trip together on his desk.

"GO ON. NOW everyone's sat down, you'll be fine," I said to Lily. "Do you want me to come with you?"

"No, I'll be okay." She gave my hand another squeeze, stood up, eased out of her seat into the aisle and tottered away. I watched her make her way down the narrow aisle towards the toilets at the back of the cabin. She pushed the door cautiously, even though the overhead light indicated it was vacant. She stepped in, closed the door, and only when the light switched to occupied did I turn back to my in-flight movie.

Lily had always been a nervous flyer. She'd always been nervous of a lot of things. As she'd got older, she'd increasingly learned to hide her fears and anxieties behind a steely detachment which could sometimes come across as aloof. It was a trick she'd been forced to learn thanks to having a mother who would exploit those fears and anxieties to score points against me. Don't get me wrong, I've been no angel. I wished, countless times that I could start over. I've even wished that we never has a child together. But that was the problem, right there. From the moment I'd first held Lily in my arms, I knew there was no going back. Which was why I was rushing back now, to stop Lily's grandfather from taking her from me once and for all.

I settled back in my chair, adjusted my headset and took a sip of wine. The film wasn't holding my attention, and my eyes wandered to Lily's seat, facing mine and already covered in her clutter. Her own glass sat empty on the tray table, and one of the two small coke cans was on its side with a twisted napkin wedged into the opening like the fuse of a cartoon bomb. Her college branded hoodie was scrunched up into the arm rest. I leaned forward, picked it up and folded it, inhaling the scent of her. I placed the hoodie back on her seat, smiling at the thought of how she would roll her eyes at my habitual fussing.

I looked back over my shoulder again. The lavatory light still glowed red. Occupied. She was taking her time. She'd no doubt be sitting in there, having splashed some cold water on her face, muttering to herself repeatedly to pull herself together. Her father's child. She'd started feeling queasy just after take-off. I'd put it down to nerves. And being upset at what her grandfather had done. And anxiety about going home, knowing that yet again her feelings would have to be subjugated so that her mother could radiate in her own grief.

The plane bucked in the air. Turbulence. Lily wouldn't like that. It would probably hurry her back to her seat. I leaned over to glance out of the window. Nothing below but a flat sheet of grey cloud. A flash of lightning bounced off the blank canvas, lighting up a line of distant cloud from within. The plane bumped and kicked again. And again. A real drop—big enough to spill drinks—sent a collective shriek up from a number of passengers. A dull ping signified the seatbelts light had been switched on.

"Ladies and Gentlemen. This is your captain speaking." His voice was deliberately calm and reassuring. "As I'm sure you've noticed, we've hit a spot of turbulence. Please return to your seats and fasten your belts." The last word caught in his mouth as another bump struck. The cabin was filled with the sound of buckles clicking shut. I hesitated in putting mine on, looking back over my shoulder to the toilets. Where was Lily?

I could see the stewardess in the galley at the back of the plane checking the latches on the serving hatches. And then I saw it. The lavatory light was green, and the sign read: vacant. My heart skipped. My stomach lurched. Lily.

I glanced at the seatbelt light. At the stewardess in the galley. And I made my decision. Up out of my seat and heading for the back of the plane, ignoring the tuts from my fellow passengers, convincing myself that she's just getting a bottle of water from the staff at the back of the plane.

I reached the toilet, only to have my way blocked at the last minute by the same stewardess.

"I'll have to ask you to return to your seat, please sir. The seatbelt lights are on."

"I'm looking for my daughter," I said, hearing the choke of panic in my voice. Surely not here. Not up here at thirty-thousand feet. Not so soon. "She was in the toilet."

"There's no one in there now, sir," she says, hands out, palms spread, ushering me back without touching. "Now please go back to your seat, I'm sure she's there already."

"She's not," I said, pushing forwards. She took a step back, unsure of my intentions, and I slammed the door to the toilet open. There was no one inside.

"Sir," the stewardess warned.

I rounded on her. "I will go to my seat when I'm bloody ready. Right now, I want to find my daughter, and the last time I saw her she was right here. If she'd come out, I would have seen her."

"There is no one here, sir. I am going to have to insist that you go back to your seat right now."

I pushed past her. She was right. There was no one in the galley. There was no sign of her anywhere. Lily was gone.

/

UP IN THE first class cabin, Lily Highcock returned to her seat beside her father, and sat down. She shuddered.

"You okay?" he asked.

"Yeah, I just had a really strange feeling. Like deja-vu, but not quite."

She shook her head, frowning, and shuddered again.

"Someone must be walking over my grave."

A DRINK IN PEACE

by

Ken Teutsch

WAYNE RATTLED THE chain, finding it surprisingly difficult to express complete innocence and utter sincerity with his hands cuffed and tethered to a table. "Like I told you," he said, voice cracking, "One minute I was in the bar with this old guy, and the next…" He tried to shrug and was brought up short again. "I don't know what else to tell you."

The bigger of the two cops thrust out his lower lip and tapped a fingernail as thick as a poker chip against the table top. "Yeah?" he said amiably. After a moment he leaned wearily back in his chair and half-turned his head toward his partner, whose own chair was tilted on two legs and leaning against the wall. "You hear that, Ray? He doesn't know what else to tell us."

"I heard," said the other cop, who had not looked up from his phone since they entered the room. 'Ray' was the smaller of the two, but that didn't mean he was small. He was dressed almost identically to Bigger Cop: brown jacket, khakis, and cheap, black shoes. He even had a similar haircut, as though the two used the same barber, who used the same bowl. "But," he went on reasonably, "he needs to tell us something else."

"That's kinda what I thought, too," said Bigger Cop. His head rolled around to aim his bloodshot eyes once more in Wayne's direction. "Tell us something else."

Not for the first time that night, Wayne felt as though he might throw up. He closed his eyes to the glare of the horrible fluorescent lights and the horrible, muck-spattered walls. This made his head spin and his nausea worsen, so he opened them again. Bigger Cop watched with a mix of impassive boredom and deep malevolence, like some demonic Galapagos turtle.

"Okay," he sighed. "One thing at a time." He paused to let out a seemingly painful burp, and grimaced. "How'd you get into the vault," he finally continued, "without setting off the alarm?"

"He did set off the alarm," said Ray.

"Yeah," said Bigger Cop, "But that was after he was already in there!"

"Oh," muttered Ray. "Yeah."

"So, the question is, how did he get in there?"

Ray shrugged. "Ask him." He still hadn't looked up from his phone.

"I just asked him. You want to maybe pay a little attention? So? What? You hid in there somehow before they closed it?"

Wayne moaned. "I'm telling you, I was just *there*! Poof!"

Ray giggled. "Poof!" he said, shaking his head.

Wayne tried again to gesture, again only rattling his chain. "You tell *me* how I got in there! I wish somebody would!"

"You must not watch much TV," said Bigger Cop. "If you did, you'd know that's not how this works. We don't tell you things. You tell us things."

"Oughta watch more TV," said Ray, nodding at his phone.

Wayne laid his forehead on the cool surface of the table. How could he make them believe him? He didn't even believe himself. His head throbbed; he could swear the pulsing vein in his forehead was actually lifting his face off the table. He had told one white lie: he'd said he'd had a "couple of beers" at the bar; in fact, he'd had a lot of beers. In between, he'd had shots of something called Firewater or Firewhiskey or some damn thing. He'd come with a girl he met while drinking in *another* bar, but at some point, she had ditched him. He was already half-loopy before he struck up a conversation with the old guy in the ratty jacket. Then this nightmare started.

"I must have blacked out," Wayne whimpered. "The old guy in the bar. Talk to the old guy in the bar!"

Bigger Cop shook his head. "Why would we want to talk to a guy in a bar? We're talking to the guy who tried to rob the bank."

Wayne sat up. "I didn't try to rob the bank!"

Ray chuckled. "Maybe he was making a deposit."

"Well," said Bigger Cop grimly, "I guess somebody had to make that joke."

"What bar was it you were in?" said Ray. For the first time he looked up from his phone. His eyes were watery, but less red than his partner's.

"Who the hell cares about that?" Bigger Cop rumbled.

"Me. I'm curious."

Bigger Cop didn't look happy about the digression. He glared at Wayne. "Well?"

"The Boiled Owl," said Wayne.

"The Boiled Owl?" both cops repeated in two-part disharmony.

"On 4th Street. Near the stadium."

"Geez," said Bigger Cop, "You're the shittiest liar I ever met. There's no 'Boiled Owl' on 4th Street. Or anywhere else."

"Sure there is," Wayne said.

Bigger Cop sat forward and pointed a sausage-like finger. "You think I don't know the downtown bars?" he said menacingly.

"Hey," said Ray.

"That's where I was."

"Hey!" Ray said, louder.

"You think I'd forget a stupid-ass name like the *Boiled* fucking *Owl?*" A challenge to his comprehensive bar knowledge had finally gotten Bigger Cop to sit up straight in his chair.

"Hey!" Ray shouted, "Shut up a minute!"

"What?" Bigger Cop looked ready to reach for the rubber hose. "Lying little…"

"I looked it up," said Ray, holding up his phone. "There *is* a Boiled Owl on 4th Street."

"*What?*" roared Bigger Cop.

Ray turned the phone toward his partner. "On 4th Street in *St. Louis!*" He started to laugh in ugly little snorts.

"Where else?" said Wayne.

Bigger Cop's voice was truly icy now. "I guess we kind of thought you meant Cincinnati."

Wayne looked from one of them to the other, his jaw hanging loosely. "What are you talking about?" His chain rattled once more, weakly. "What's Cincinnati got to do with it?"

Bigger Cop sprang to his feet, his chair tipping over and banging onto the floor. He leaned across the table. Wayne cowered as far back as his handcuffs would let him. "All right, you rotten little shit," the big man growled, "I've had just about enough. I'm gonna ask you just —"

He stopped talking. His tongue popped against the roof of his mouth. His eyes widened as his pupils shrank to pinpoints. The room went deathly still.

The rotten little shit was gone.

"Ray?" The big man's voice was suddenly that of a bewildered six-year-old. Ray, however, could conjure no voice at all. He leaned against the wall, mouth open, eyes wide, staring at the empty handcuffs. Neither of the men moved for a long moment, then they both jumped, stooped and nearly smacked their heads together looking under the table.

But there was nobody there.

WAYNE JUST SAID, "Hah?"

The big scary cop was gone. The snickering cop was gone. So were the buzzing fluorescents. He looked at his wrists. The handcuffs were gone. He was sitting in a chair at a table, but it was a formica-covered table—dingy, scuffed formica with cigarette burns around the edges. Instead of blank, green walls there was a refrigerator and a sink with dishes in it. To his right was a dim room with a ratty sofa with some posters hanging askew above it. Instead of a metal door with a peephole, there was a dirty, white, wooden door with a window with one pane replaced by cardboard.

"Hah?" Wayne said again.

"Hope you didn't have too rough a time."

A man sat across the table. He had a bald head with a wispy rim of graying hair. Soft, blue eyes, bloodshot, over round cheeks, also bloodshot. Grey, stubbly beard.

"You!" said Wayne. He raised both hands, forgetting they were no longer shackled together, and pointed. "It's you. From the bar."

The man nodded. "Yeah. You want some coffee?" He hoisted himself out of his chair and moved toward the counter. "Sure you do. Anyway, I do."

The man was no longer wearing the battered hat he had worn in the bar, but otherwise looked the same. A brown, tweedy jacket with scuffed patches on the elbows, a checkered shirt, corduroy pants and brown shoes that had clocked a lot of miles and never been shined. In the better light he didn't look quite as old, but he looked worn and very tired. He shuffled rather than walked. His shoulders sagged. Wayne watched as he poured coffee into two cups, and shied away when he wheeled and set one of the cups on the table.

"Take it easy. It's all over now." The old man nodded in a way presumably meant to be reassuring and sank into his chair with a slight groan. The smell of the coffee reached Wayne and he reached for the cup. "I'm Larry," said the old man.

"Wayne," said Wayne. It seemed like the thing to say.

"Look, Wayne," the stranger went on slowly. "I know this is freaking you out." He lifted his own coffee cup and planted both elbows on the table. "But everything's okay now."

Wayne sipped the coffee. The cup trembled in his hands. "You sure? Because I don't feel very okay." He set the cup down and took a deep breath. "Have I been dreaming? Tripping? Did somebody spike my booze? Did *you*?"

The old man seemed to consider a moment, then shook his head. "No. That won't fly. I could tell you that's what happened, but it won't fly. Cops have your stuff, right? Wallet and so forth?"

Wayne felt his pockets. "Yeah. My phone and... What are you saying? You saying it really happened?" He put both hands on the table to keep from sliding out of his chair. "How did I get there? How did I get *here*? How long have I been out?"

The old man—Larry—made the 'calm down' gesture, pumping the air with both hands. "You haven't been 'out,'" he said. He sighed and rubbed his eyes. "It's always been right now. It's the morning after the night before!" He leaned back in his chair and crossed his arms. He gazed at a point on the ceiling. "You'll be hearing from them," he said, and looked at Wayne once more, his expression peeved, verging on hostile. "Okay. Listen. As soon as you get home, call the police. Report that your wallet and phone and so forth were stolen." He pointed at Wayne. "And you by-God leave me out of it."

"Out of what, exactly?" Wayne said.

The old man ignored the question. "Tell them the stuff has been gone for a couple of days. You thought at first maybe you just lost it, left it somewhere. That's why you waited to call. They didn't fingerprint you, did they?"

"No," said Wayne.

"Okay then." The man picked up his coffee and plunked his elbows down once more. "Somebody stole your stuff, and that's who they picked up in Cincinnati."

Wayne's voice squeaked. "Why does everybody keep talking about Cincinnati?"

"You got plenty of witnesses to say you've been here in St. Louis. It's okay."

"Stop saying that!" cried Wayne. "I'm losing my mind. That's not okay!"

Larry's eyes flashed anger again, then he slumped. He looked almost as tired as Wayne felt. "Okay," he said resignedly, "I'm gonna explain it. You should try to accept it."

Wayne did not commit to that. He reached a still-trembling hand for the coffee cup. "I'm listening," he said.

"I was just having a drink or two, minding my own business, and you come over and start with your life story. All your troubles. Losing your job, rent due, child support, blah, blah, blah..." Wayne winced. *Child support?* He remembered a sob story to get the old guy to pay for the drinks, but he didn't remember going that far. "You... got on my nerves." Larry closed his eyes and began to rub his temples with two large, flat thumbs. He took a deep breath. "I have a temper. When I'm drinking, I..." He trailed off. Wayne waited.

Larry opened his eyes and squinted at Wayne. He stood and shuffled toward the sofa in the other room, stopped and seemed to study the larger of the posters on the wall. It was a theatrical poster. On it a bearded man in a tuxedo gestured flamboyantly. On one side of him stood an empty cabinet with an open door, on the other a cabinet with a scantily clad woman emerging from it. "Bottom line," said Larry, "I got this, oh, it sounds silly when you say it out loud. But I got this... power." He looked back over his shoulder.

"Uh huh," said Wayne.

Larry moved slowly back into the kitchenette. "I can send people places. I think them somewhere, and they go there. It's something I can do. And I can bring 'em back again. Usually." He glanced back at the poster. "And you should believe it, because I did it to you. You were such a pain in the ass, going on and on, bitching and bitching about money." He looked at Wayne from under bushy eyebrows. "So, I sent you to the bank." He gave a shrug.

Somewhere nearby a cat let out a loud meow. Larry glanced at the kitchen door.

"Uh huh," Wayne repeated.

"Thing is, I can only send people to places I've been myself. There's always *rules* for these things, you know? I couldn't send anybody to China or Mars or whatever." *Sure,* thought Wayne, *because* that *would be ridiculous.* "So, I sent you to *my* bank. But I'm drunk, see?" The old man looked away. "I sent you to the bank I used to go to when I lived in Cincinnati. The vault, right?"

"There was no money," Wayne said. Was it a memory? Or a dream? "Not laying around. Just lockboxes and stuff. I mean, once the lights came on. At first it was just dark." He felt tears start to well up. "I was really scared."

"And the alarm went off?"

Wayne nodded, too choked up by the memory of terror to speak.

"People shouldn't bug me," snapped the old man. "Not when I'm drinking."

The meow came again, longer and louder. There was a scrabbling outside the door. Larry glanced at it again, turned, opened a cabinet and pulled out a bowl. "Anyway, I got back here and sobered up a little. I started thinking. By the time I worked it out and reached out, you weren't there." The old man shook his head and wiped his mouth. "You weren't there," he repeated, his voice trembling like his hand. His eyes darted to Wayne and he seemed to pull himself together. "Then I figured the cops must have got you. No other way you could have got out." He set the bowl next to an electric can opener and pulled over a can from the back of the counter. "So, I thought where they might take you." He clamped the opener onto the can. The can opener whirred into life and the meowing became frantic. "Lucky they took you to the downtown headquarters. I been there. If they'd taken you to some sub-station or something, I'd never have found you." He paused again, then, "Anyway... No harm done." He whacked the can on the rim of the bowl, knocking cat food out into it.

Wayne thought that, to the contrary, harm had definitely been done, but he let that go. "So you're saying," he said, "that you... magically... sent me into a bank vault in Cincinnati?"

"Yeah, that's it. Magically."

The cat outside the door gave a loud "Meee—," and Larry held out his hands.

"—Oooow!" said a grubby Siamese in the old man's arms. The cat looked around and blinked once, spotted the bowl, scampered up his arm, over his shoulder and down onto the counter. It began scarfing down the food.

"So that's the situation," said Larry. He scratched between the cat's ears. "Where do you live?"

Wayne didn't answer. A cat had just popped into existence from thin air, and that always distracted him.

"Hey!" Larry said, snapping his fingers. "I asked you a question. Where do you live?"

"Uh..." Wayne couldn't take his eyes off the cat. "Apartments. Royal Oak Apartments."

"What's that close to?"

"Close to?"

"Come on, buddy! Focus!" Wayne looked at the old man. His face was yellow in the light from the kitchen fixture. "Is it close to anything? A park? Major highway?"

"Uh... It's not far from I-44 and Kingshighway."

"Yeah, I know that place," said Larry. "Bye."

The light went out and the chair beneath Wayne's butt was no longer there. A chill breeze bit into his face in the split second before he flopped onto his back on the cold, wet dirt. A roar filled his ears. He let out a shriek of terror and gripped the ground.

After several panic-stricken seconds, he realized that the roar was traffic zipping across the interstate overpass above him. He was lying next to a sidewalk. After a few more seconds of gripping the earth as if it might shift beneath him, he sat up to see the first red glimmer of dawn over the spikey, leafless trees on the east side of Kingshighway Boulevard.

THE MANAGER WAS none too pleased to be awakened at that time of the morning, his displeasure compounded by the fact that Wayne was two weeks overdue on his rent. But after a few choice words he let Wayne into his apartment. Wayne shut the door, fell onto his couch and went to sleep.

He awoke a few hours later, called the pawn shop where he worked and told them he was sick. He took a shower, scrambled and ate all the eggs in the refrigerator. By this point he had decided that the incidents of the night before had simply never happened. It had merely been an unusually drunk night out. He made a solemn vow to nevermore touch Firewhiskey or Firewater or whatever, and another even more solemn to never give the rest of the night another thought. Then came a knock on the door and the detective with the St. Louis Police Department.

"Yeah, I'm Wayne Rice. My wallet? My phone? Uh, yeah! You know, I was just gonna call you guys about that… No, I haven't been anywhere… Sure, lots of people can vouch for that. Cincinnati? Whoa, that's weird. When will I get my phone back?" As the cop walked away, Wayne was struck by an urge to say, "Tell Ray I said, 'Hello.'"

Then he sat down on his couch and did some serious thinking.

WAYNE HAD NOT been exaggerating much when he told Larry he was broke. He had about three bucks in that wallet in Cincinnati, about a hundred more in the bank, and a moderately decent-sized pile of change in an ashtray on the dresser in his bedroom. He would get paid in a couple of days, but practically all of that would have to go to the rent he already owed. He had a credit card, but couldn't even pay the interest on what was already on it.

On the plus side, though, he had just met a guy with magical powers.

He started thinking of all the places—casinos, check-cashing shops, payday loan joints, even bank vaults, during business hours—where large quantities of cash were left lying around in easily grabbable piles.

Wayne cleared a space on the kitchen counter and put his pawnshop laptop on it. A quick click confirmed that his neighbor hadn't changed his Wi-Fi password (12345678), and he was soon staring at the Google Doodle. Okay. What did he have? The name "Larry" and The Boiled Owl. Searches for "Larry" near that address turned up nothing. Similar searches for "Lawrence" and "Laurence" turned up similar nothings. Wayne was stumped already. Then he thought, "Trust in Google!" and typed in "Larry Lawrence magic disappear Cinncinnati." He clicked the button. Corrected the spelling of "Cincinnati," clicked the button again.

There were a lot of people named Larry Lawrence, and seemingly random mixtures of "magic" and "disappear." He clicked through page after page of nothing useful, then he spotted something. There was the boldface word **magic**, and on the other side of an ellipsis, the name Lawrence Marovich. Next to that, separated by another ellipsis, "Lorenzo." Lorenzo. *Lorenzo!* The poster over the old man's couch! Wayne closed his eyes and pictured it again.

"Lorenzo the Magnificent! Master of Time and Space!"

Wayne clicked the link and was taken to a website on which some magic nerd was trying to compile some kind of comprehensive magician encyclopedia. There were pages and pages of bios of every card flipper and rabbit puller who ever worked a birthday party. Among them was Lorenzo the Magnificent. No picture, but it had to be his guy. "Specialized in teleportation illusions. Worked with his wife. Retired after she passed away." The old man really was a magician. Only he *really was* a magician! At least now Wayne had a full name.

But the name did him no good. There were a surprising number of Larrys Marovich on the internet, but none was his. No search he could think of turned up an address or anything else about a Lawrence, Larry or even Lorenzo Marovich in St. Louis. Magic Larry was off the grid.

Wayne pondered. The internet had let him down. Back to the real world. He would stake out the Boiled Owl. In the meantime, he settled into making a formal list of places with money. Money easily grabbable, left lying around.

LARRY/LORENZO WAS not at The Boiled Owl that night. Or the night after that. Wayne walked the neighborhood, checking the other bars. No luck. He scanned the rundown buildings in the area, looked at names on mailboxes. He kept an eye peeled for Siamese cats.

Nothing.

After blowing off work for two more days he was, unsurprisingly, fired. But Wayne didn't want a job. By now his list of places with scoopable money had grown to two full pages and was all he could think of. In moments of doubt, he just reminded himself of the cat and the detective and Cincinnati and his wallet and phone. He did occasionally speculate on the old man's origin story, though. Encounter with aliens? Bitten by a radioactive travel agent? He hoped it wasn't an ironically doomed deal with the Devil. It didn't matter. What mattered was the money. From time to time he heard a little voice ask, "What if the old guy doesn't *want* to go into business?" That was something to worry about when the time came.

On the fifth night he started his usual systematic check of the bars along 4th Street. It was tedious and it was discouraging. By the time he came once more to the Boiled Owl, he was operating on autopilot. Look left. Look right. Check the booths in the back. He hit the men's room, then started back toward the street. Glancing left he saw a little booth at the end of the bar that he had missed on his way in, and a small, hunched figure leaning, elbows on the table, lifting a glass with brown liquid.

Lorenzo the Magnificent.

Wayne literally screeched to a halt, his sneakers slipping on the concrete floor. He hurried to the bar. "The guy there at the end," he said. "Give me a double of whatever he's drinking. And start a tab!" When the drink came, he carefully picked it up and strolled back to the booth. One more deep breath and he slid in opposite the old man.

"Hi, Larry!" he said.

Larry/Lorenzo looked at him over the rim of his glass with glazed eyes and no sign of recognition.

"It's me!" Wayne continued cheerily, "Wayne. Remember? The bank? Cincinnati?"

Larry slowly lowered his glass. "What do you want?" he said.

"Nothing. I just saw you over here and thought I'd buy you a drink. I kind of left you holding the check last time. Not exactly my fault, but still…" He grinned and slid the glass across the table. "On me," he said.

Larry eyed the glass warily. Wayne waited, then shrugged. "Hey, if you don't want it…" He reached for the glass.

Larry's hand fell on it first. "Didn't say I don't want it," he said. His voice was thick and slurred; the drink in front of him obviously wasn't his first. With a practiced move he tossed back the remainder of that one, clunked the empty glass down and drew the new glass toward him.

Wayne smiled. "So, how's it going?" he said. "How's the wiz biz?"

"The *what*?" said Larry. He took a hefty sip from the new glass and shuddered.

"The whole, you know…" Wayne made a showy gesture. "Ala-kazaam!" This drew a cold stare. He was overdoing it. He shrugged and leaned back in the seat. "You know what I mean."

Larry took another sip. "All right. You bought me a drink. Now we're even."

"Even?" Wayne leaned forward, his expression serious now. "How do you figure? You know what your little magic trick did for me? The cops have my stuff and won't give it back. I don't have my license, can't get around. I lost my job!"

"Thought you said you didn't have a job."

Wayne ignored that. "But look. No hard feelings. Neither of us is exactly the height of prosperity, are we? And I've been thinking about that. About how this, you know, mojo of yours could be made to pay off. Pay off *big*. All you need is a partner."

Larry looked at Wayne with hooded eyes. "A partner?" He lifted the glass again.

"Yeah." Wayne grinned. "Like in the old days, Lorenzo. You know. A beautiful, young assistant." He flashed his best salesman smile, and saw instantly that somehow he had just stepped in it.

The old man stiffened and dropped the glass. It bounced, splashing onto the table, but didn't tip over. He sat straight up, his eyes wide with anger, and he slammed both hands down onto the table top.

"Mind if I join you?"

The voice seemed to come from nowhere and was followed by the grating screech of a heavy chair dragged across the floor. Wayne turned to see a large man in a suit coat taking a seat at the end of their table. He blinked once and the man's face clicked into place in his mind. It was Ray, the not-biggest but still-pretty-damn-big cop from Cincinnati. The big man smiled a very unpleasant smile. "Yeah. Yeah, you know me, don't you, asshole?" he said.

The cop did not look good. There were bags under his eyes, and his skin had a peculiar grayish tinge. His eyes were redder now than his partner's had been, and that was very red indeed. He seemed to be wearing the same clothes he had worn that night, too. Wayne tried to pull himself together.

"I... uh... I don't, uh, I don't think..."

Ray laughed, the same snorting bark Wayne had heard before. But the laugh contained no mirth. "Poker face," he said. He glanced at Larry, who was now frozen, eyes darting back and forth between Ray and Wayne. Ray's brow furrowed for a moment, but his attention switched back to Wayne. He plopped a wrinkled paper bag onto the table.

"You are Wayne Rice?" he said.

"I uh... I don't..."

"Yes, you're Wayne Rice, you piece of shit!" Ray hissed. "I been following you for two days. I got your property." He reached into the bag, pulled out a wallet, flung it at Wayne's face. Wayne recoiled and managed to catch it, but not without banging his head against the back of the booth. Next Ray pulled out a cell phone. This he threw sidearm into the back wall, sending glass shards spraying into the air. "Oh yeah, your keys." He dangled a key ring for a moment, threw it across the room. Somewhere a startled woman's voice yelled, "Hey!" He balled up the paper bag and tossed it onto the table.

"I want to know how you did it."

Wayne swallowed with difficulty. "Did…"

"If you say, 'Did what?' I'm gonna put your head through that fucking wall."

Wayne looked at Larry, who was sitting perfectly still, eyes narrowed, jaw tight, hands on the table. Ray the cop looked at Larry, too. "Do I know you? You look familiar."

"I don't know either one of you," said Larry. "I was having a quiet drink. All I want," his teeth ground together, "is a quiet drink."

"This the old man?" said Ray to Wayne. "The mysterious old man in the Boiled Owl on 4th Street? In St. Louis?" Wayne said nothing. Ray pulled his chair up closer to the table. "Remember Marty, my partner?" he said.

Wayne almost said, "I never got the name," but stopped at the last second.

"He's in the hospital," Ray went on. He tapped his chest. "Infarction, infraction, whatever they call it. From the stress." He shook his finger at Wayne. "You got us into all kinds of trouble. Because you went 'poof.'" He looked at Larry, who remained completely still. "Son of a bitch went 'poof!' But nobody believed he went 'poof.'" He turned back to Wayne, leaning on the table. "Remember how you said you went 'poof' and then I laughed at you?" Ray sounded jovial now. "That's on the tape, me laughing at you. And then you went 'poof' on the tape!" He spread his arms as though to say, *Can you believe it?* "And guess what? hey say we must have fucked with the tape. Because, you know, people don't just go 'poof!'" He shook his head, laughed. "They said we must have done something with you, and edited the tape. Because, you know, *where did he go?*" Ray looked all around in mock amazement, looked under the table, picked up the crumpled bag and looked under that, tossed it over his shoulder. He took a deep breath to get his laughter under control.

"So, they put us on administrative leave. Grilled the *shit* out of us. What did we do with you? Where did we put you? Only now it wasn't even you! Because you're in St. Louis and never were there in the first place. And finally poor old Marty—he was always wound too tight—he stroked out. Or whatever. In the hospital, anyway." He touched his face. "Tubes up his nose. Couldn't talk to me. May not make it." He shrugged. The laughter was gone from his voice now. "So, I drove over, and here we are. You are not under arrest and are not under any obligation to answer my questions." He gestured at the bar around him. "I'm outta my jurisdiction! And it's been established to everybody's satisfaction that you were never in Cincinnati at all, anyway. Nevertheless—" He held up a finger. He slowly smiled a smile decidedly less pleasant than his earlier very unpleasant smile. *"Nevertheless!* You need to understand that if you do not tell me how you did it, you are not going to walk out of this bar alive."

With that, Ray the not-biggest-but-definitely-big-enough cop leaned back in his chair and looked expectantly at Wayne.

Larry upended his glass and emptied it. He blew out a breath and wiped his mouth on his sleeve. "This is between you two," he said. He moved to slide out of the booth.

"What?" Wayne yelped. "Where do you think you're going? This is all your fault!" He pointed at the old man. "He did it! Don't take it out on me!"

Ray moved a large leg across the opening of the booth, trapping the old man in his seat. "What's he talking about?"

"Get out of my way," Larry growled.

"It's this guy!" Wayne said frantically. "He sent me to the bank! He brought me back. He's a magician or something."

"A what?"

"It's true! You were there. You saw me disappear! He did it."

Ray now took a long look at Larry, who was looking down at the table top, the muscles in his jaw visibly working. "Magician?" He leaned over, took a harder look at Larry's face. "I do know you! You're what's-his-name. Marovich! Sure. I remember you!"

Larry's eyes slowly met Ray's.

"Sure. A few years back. It wasn't my case, but I remember you now! The missing wife. One night this guy's neighbors hear a big fight. After the yelling stops, nobody ever sees the wife again. But we could never quite pin it on you, could we? Because no body. We never found the body. Magician. Yeah. He sure as shit made the little woman disappear."

Larry slowly raised his head. "Bastards," he hissed. His face had gone bright red. "Why can't you leave me alone? All I wanted... All I ever wanted," His voice rose to a coarse bellow, booming through the room.

"…was to have a *drink in peace!*" He slammed his fist down onto the table, and Ray the cop was gone.

A woman screamed. There was a crash of breaking glass. Larry wheeled around to face Wayne, his eyes wide and mad. Spit flew as he shouted. "We had a fight, okay? I was drunk, and she would never lay off me when I drank! I got mad! I sent her away, but I was drunk! And when I woke up…" He put a hand over his eyes. "I couldn't remember where I sent her. I couldn't find her!" He slumped forward, head in hands. "Until it was too late."

Thoughts of partnerships and piles of money had left Wayne's mind. What he wanted now was out. He began clambering out of the booth, but Larry suddenly lunged forward and grabbed him by the arm. He hissed whiskey breath into Wayne's face.

"You couldn't leave me alone, could you?" Wayne tried to pull away, but the old man's grip was like iron. "You couldn't just let me drink in peace!" Then Larry smiled at him, the most unpleasant smile of all.

"We used to go rock climbing," he said, "When we were younger. The two of us. Ropes and pitons. Out in the desert." The smile widened, the grip on Wayne's arm tightened. "The desert. Dry, see? Get it? Dry. That was the joke. That was the joke." The old man stopped smiling.

Wayne toppled into nothingness.

Darkness. A hard surface. Whipped by a cold wind, on all fours on what felt like solid rock. He looked up: no ceiling. A splash of stars and a bright moon. As his eyes adjusted, he saw he was on a rocky ledge, maybe six feet wide. A sheer wall rose to the right. To the left a drop to rocks, scrub, and sand faint in the moonlight, far below. Far, *far* below. The sand and scrub stretched away into nighttime nothingness. No lights or signs of life anywhere.

He heard panting, and farther down the ledge a shadow moved inside a deeper shadow. "Who's that?" came a voice. "Who's there?" The voice was weak and thin now, no longer gruff or threatening.

"It's me. Wayne." He started to crawl along the ledge. His hand landed on something hard and thin. There were things scattered about the surface. Hard objects and bits of tattered cloth. He saw something round, a lighter shade than the stone.

The voice came again from the shadow. "What happened? Where are we?"

Wayne leaned back against the rock wall. "Well, Ray," he said, "I'm not exactly sure. About either of those questions. But on the bright side..." He held up the skull in the fading moonlight. "I think we just solved your cold case."

Somewhere down on the desert floor a coyote yelped. Ray the cop yelped back.

GOOD NEIGHBORS

by

Bev Vincent

KANE ARRIVED IN the suburban neighborhood shortly after one o'clock in the morning, just in time to rendezvous with the U-Haul driver he'd hired to make it look like he was moving in. Arriving at such a late hour was bound to attract attention, set tongues wagging. He wanted people to notice.

After he and the driver carried several loads of empty boxes into the house, Kane set up temporary quarters in the already furnished living room. He moved the widescreen TV closer to the sofa and pushed an easy chair next to the window where he could monitor the residential street out front without being seen.

He perched a suitcase full of clothes on an end table, stocked the fridge with provisions from a cooler, put his shaving kit next to the bathroom sink and verified the WiFi password. After setting lights on timers in a few rooms upstairs to make the house seem more lived-in, he made himself comfortable on the sofa and watched two episodes of a Netflix series about a Flemish cop who talked with his deceased wife.

Tomorrow, he would begin in earnest.

Over a breakfast of Cheerios and toast, Kane reviewed the files containing everything Hector, the agency's computer specialist, had dug up on the neighbors. The house to his right was occupied by a minister from a non-denominational church and his wife. Their adult children no longer lived with them. A recently divorced probation officer and her three teenaged children lived on the other side. Her husband, a sketchy character according to the file, had moved out four months ago, so it wasn't likely he was involved in whatever had happened here. The Pratts, originally from Iowa, had been in the house across the street for the past twenty-five years, next door to another long-time resident, a former Houston police officer three years a widower.

The cop concerned him. Kane had a long history with HPD. If anyone might think his presence in the neighborhood was unusual, it would be Peter Lucas. Hector's file on him was an inch thick. He had racked up a few complaints for excessive violence, not that unusual after nearly three decades on the job, but there weren't any other red flags on his record. He'd retired with a full pension four years ago.

Kane rinsed his dishes and put them in the sink. His first task was a thorough search of the house. He went room by room, opening closets, looking in drawers, poking under beds and couches. He examined the carpets to see if any seemed like they'd been replaced recently. He opened bottles in the medicine cabinets and sifted through bags of rice and flour in the pantry. He looked in the toilet tanks and even melted the ice cubes in the freezer to see if anything was hidden in them. The garbage cans had all been emptied, depriving him of a normally reliable source of information.

He reviewed every document in a filing cabinet next to the computer. He couldn't log onto the computer itself, but he turned it on and inserted a WiFi-enabled flash drive that would let Hector attempt to gain remote access.

After scouring the house, he opened a sliding door in the dining room and stepped out onto the back deck. The backyard looked like a jungle. The trees and other foliage had been allowed to run wild, and the grass was knee deep. Kane knew enough about indigenous poisonous snakes to put on sturdy boots before venturing off the deck. He found a rolling garbage can beside the air conditioning unit, but it was empty. The rear fence was obscured by an impenetrable wall of bamboo, some of the shoots at least eight feet tall. Nothing seemed like it had been disturbed recently. No signs of a shallow grave, at least.

He went back inside and sat in the chair next to the front window, a pair of binoculars at his feet. The street, Chicory Lane, wove an irregular, winding course between two major intersecting thoroughfares. Three cul-de-sacs branched off from it, one on this side of the street and two on the opposite side. Kane spent the next three days familiarizing himself with the neighbors' activities and allowing them to get used to seeing him around. They were bound to notice that he didn't leave for work in the morning like many of them did. If asked, he would tell them he worked from home. People had a natural mistrust of strangers, but there were enough For Sale signs on the street to indicate a regular turnover among its residents.

He shopped for groceries at a nearby supermarket and ate breakfasts and lunches in the living room, either watching television or peering out the front window. There was a Mexican restaurant, an assortment of fast-food options, a sushi bar and a pizza place with an outdoor patio all within a few blocks. He made a habit of walking to one of them at around the same time each afternoon.

The suburb prided itself on its hundreds of miles of hiking and biking paths, and many of his neighbors took full advantage of them, especially now that it was autumn. He soon identified a group of regulars. There was an older man he nicknamed Ralph, who lived four doors up on the opposite side of the street. He could be counted on to arrive at the cluster mailbox across the street just as the USPS van was pulling away, as if getting the mail was the highlight of his day. Maybe it was, Kane thought.

There was the Walking Lady, about sixty and as skinny as a rail, who passed his house at eight thirty, noon and again at four o'clock each day. A short, squat woman of about fifty went out twice daily, led by a pack of four small, yappy mutts that made Kane think of the Iditarod sled dog race. He dubbed her the Energizer Bunny because of the exaggerated way she swung her free arm. Neon John wore glow-in-the-dark shirts while walking a dog that required a muzzle. In hindsight, Kane realized he should have brought a dog with him. It would have given him an excuse to be outside at any and all hours.

He checked the mail each afternoon. People seemed more inclined to engage with each other at the mailbox. A few barely spoke or merely grunted a greeting, but most would at least pass the time of day with him.

His longest conversation by far was with a pretty young woman with a wild mop of hair who reminded him of the cavewoman from an insurance commercial. She was jogging behind a double-occupancy stroller with twin girls who looked to be about eighteen months old. She paused to welcome him to the neighborhood, continuing to jog in place, breathing heavily and sipping from a water bottle as she asked where he came from and what he did for a living. She shared details about herself and some of the neighbors, although nothing she said was particularly helpful. She ran one hand over the front of her thin, sweat-soaked T-shirt, as if daring him to look. He had the feeling she was flirting with him, but then the twins started crying, putting an end to their conversation. She glanced over her shoulder at him as she continued down the street.

He watched until she was out of sight, admiring the view and thinking of *Desperate Housewives*, a TV program a former girlfriend liked to watch. That show had probably tainted his view of suburbia. None of the people he'd encountered so far seemed like murderers, but you could never tell. He'd met many affable killers over the years.

On the fourth morning, he decided it was time to take more direct action. He had to find out what his neighbors knew. His first target was the minister next door. He'd be easy to approach because he often paced in his driveway while holding loud conversations on his cell phone. Kane couldn't hear what he was talking about, but he always knew when the man was outdoors. He lingered near the garage until he heard the minister wrap up a call, then strode past as if he was heading out for a walk. On the way by, he caught the man's eye and nodded.

"Howdy, neighbor," the minister said.

Kane returned the greeting with a wave and what he hoped was an inviting smile.

"We didn't even know the house was for sale," the man said. He extended a hand. "Clifford Kingston, but you can call me Cliff."

"It was a private transaction," Kane said. "A friend of a friend of the previous owner."

"Carl," Kingston said with a shake of his head. "Strange thing, that."

"What?"

"You don't know?"

Kane shook his head. "All I know is that the house was available, fully furnished."

"The guy who used to live here, Carl Eads, disappeared. Gone. Vanished. No one has any idea where he went."

Kane looked back at the house, feigning puzzlement. "I found it odd that there were so many personal belongings in the house. Sort of like renting an AirBnB. It's bigger than I need, but the price was right. Disappeared, huh?"

The minister gave Kane the lowdown, all of which he already knew. Eads had lived on Chicory Lane for three years. He had an advanced degree in computer science and worked for a company on Technology Drive, two miles away. He was unmarried, lived alone, and was an avid cyclist, clocking fifteen to twenty miles a day on his high-tech Peugeot bicycle after work, and going on longer rides on weekends.

"Wore those tight Lycra shorts," Kingston said. "Looked ridiculous if you ask me."

"How did you find out he was missing?" Kane asked.

"The community newspaper was still in the driveway a few days after it was delivered. It'd rained a couple of times, so it was a soggy mess, even though it comes wrapped in plastic. I thought he was away on vacation, so I threw it in the trash. Then a couple of his coworkers showed up, asking if anyone had seen him. He'd missed work two days in a row and wasn't answering his phone or emails. Didn't come to the door when they knocked, either. They peeked through the front and back windows but couldn't see anything."

"Huh," Kane said.

"A squad car showed up an hour or so later. It was a welfare check, they said, which Pete says allows them to enter the residence." Kingston nodded in the direction of the house across the street where the retired cop lived. "They didn't find anything suspicious. The back door was unlocked. No signs of violence. His car was still in the garage, his keys were on a hook in the kitchen and his cell phone was beside the bathroom sink. Only thing unaccounted for was his wallet."

"Maybe he went for a bike ride and got hit," Kane said. "Lying dead in a ditch."

Kingston shook his head. "Bike's hanging from a hook in the garage. Guess you haven't had a chance to go in there yet."

"Not yet," Kane said. He'd parked his car in the driveway so people would notice his presence.

In addition to what Kingston told him, Kane knew there hadn't been any credit card activity since Eads got home from work that Friday afternoon. The police canvas hadn't turned up anyone who could remember seeing him during the weekend, and his last phone call had been to his parents in Amarillo on Saturday morning. It had been a routine call, they'd told Kane. Nothing to indicate why he might suddenly go missing.

"The cops poked about a bit, but there wasn't a crime, so that was pretty much that. Carl's brother showed up the next week. He stayed for a while, cleaned up a few things, but no one has been back since." Cliff looked at the property. "Lawn needs to be mowed," he said.

"I'll get to that soon, I promise," Kane said.

The minister's cell phone chirped. He looked at the display and held up a finger.

"I'll let you go," Kane said. He hadn't learned anything new, but Kingston didn't seem a likely suspect. He continued down the street. It was a cool October morning, so he went farther than he'd planned. He could get used to this walking thing.

That afternoon, he synchronized his trip to the mailbox with the time the couple across the street walked their dogs. They owned two big Labrador retrievers, one pitch black, the other off-white. Shortly after they arrived home from work each day, the Pratts changed into casual clothes and took them out.

Kane wasn't fond of big dogs that strained at their leashes the way these two did, but he had a job to do. After confirming the Pratts were about to leave by peering into their kitchen window with his binoculars, he ambled across the street. He pretended to be preoccupied with his phone and didn't notice them until he was directly in their path. Then he looked up, muttered an apology, and shuffled awkwardly out of their way. The wife gave him an appraising glance, but the husband and both dogs ignored him.

He went through the pretense of checking his mailbox. There was a flyer from a Chinese restaurant with a discount coupon, nothing more.

"You're not going to get much out of those two," a man's voice called out.

Kane glanced down the street. The dog-walking duo were already two hundred yards away. He looked across the lawn at the house next door. A grizzled old man was sitting on a folding chair in the driveway, a can of beer in the holder on the arm and a cooler on the ground beside him. The retired cop, Peter Lucas, presumably. The man leaned over, picked up another can of beer from the cooler and held it out.

Kane folded the flier, tucked it in his pocket and sauntered to the driveway.

"I call this 'driveway happy hour,'" Lucas said. "Well, to be honest, my wife came up with that name. Back then we drank wine, but I prefer beer these days, now that she's gone."

"Sorry for your loss." Kane accepted the can of beer and popped the top.

"It's been a while." Lucas indicated the open garage behind him. "Grab a chair."

Kane found a second folding chair in the corner, wiped off the cobwebs and set it up next to the cop. The beer was cold and went down easy. He eased himself into the seat and was about to introduce himself when Lucas spoke first.

"Yeah, those two—I don't think they've said more than a hundred words to me the whole time I've lived next to them." He scratched his chin. "That's about four a year, on average, although they came in bursts of a dozen or so at a time on a few different occasions. Mostly when they wanted me to do something for them, like pitch in on replacing the fence between our houses."

"Quiet folk," Kane said.

"From the Midwest. Don't talk to anyone. Never came around to the southern way of being hospitable." He twisted in his chair to look at Kane. "I knew your father, by the way."

"Huh?" Kane said. "I don't—"

"Quiet, now, son. Don't think you can put one over on me. I know why you're here."

Kane remained silent.

"Your pa was HPD for a good many years, but then there was a spot of trouble and he retired. Set up a private agency. Had a couple of sons, one of them a cop, too. That'd be you, I'm guessing." He didn't give Kane a chance to respond. "Quit the force to join your old man's agency, but he died not long after."

Kane took a sip of beer. He hadn't expected anyone would recognize him. Not up here in Houston's northernmost suburb.

"Good man, your pa. Got a raw deal, if you ask me. I worked with him a few times. He was proud of his sons, let me tell you. I saw your picture in the paper a couple of times, when you brought in fugitives or found missing people. Knew it was you right away. Was watching from right in there." He pointed to a street-facing window behind a grove of bushes and trees. "Like to keep an eye on things," he said. "Especially when someone goes missing."

Kane finally nodded. "Benjamin Kane," he said, extending his hand.

"Peter Lucas," the cop said, squeezing hard enough to make Kane wince. "Pete. But you probably knew that already. You're looking for that young Eads fellow, right?"

"His family hired us to investigate. They weren't getting much satisfaction from the police. They filed a missing persons report, but nothing came of it. They want me to look around, talk to people, see what I can come up with. Quietly, in case it turns out there's an innocent explanation for his disappearance. They don't want me disturbing the neighbors too much."

"Considerate of them. Except maybe one of the neighbors needs to be disturbed. You decided to go undercover and get to know everyone. Not a bad plan, if you have the time."

"The ones close by, at least. People he'd be most likely to have a run-in with."

"Including me, huh?" Lucas grinned, then scrunched up his mouth. "It's a quiet street, mostly. Had a little drama a while back when the Internet Crimes Against Children task force searched the house around the corner. They'd caught the husband watching child pornography on his laptop computer in a coffee shop earlier in the day. I'd say he was a little senile. I was sitting out here, like I am now, when about fifteen cars pulled up all at once. Even had Homeland Security involved in that one."

"Is he still around?"

"Nope. In prison. Not a great place for someone like him, you know? I feel bad for the wife. Not to mention his kids, even though they're all grown up."

Kane nodded.

"Then there was *her* husband," Lucas said, indicating the house where the parole officer lived. "Had a problem with prescription pharmaceuticals. Kept this big old boa constrictor as a pet. It got loose once. Almost gave Cliff over there a heart attack when he found it in his hedge one morning. But he's been gone a while. Lives up in Huntsville now, I hear."

He paused for a sip of beer. "Eads was a nice enough fellow. Not unfriendly, but not outgoing, either. Worked with computers. That sort. Can't say I ever recall him having visitors. Not of the overnight variety, anyway. Rode that bike of his all over. Can't imagine sitting on a tiny seat like that for as long as he did. Makes my ass ache just thinking about it."

"My brother does century rides," Kane said. "Hundred miles at a time. He says the most important thing about a bicycle is how you adjust your ball bearing."

It took Lucas a few seconds to get it, but then he cackled and slapped his leg. "Ball bearing. Oh, that's good. I like that." He plucked two more cans of beer from his cooler and handed one to Kane.

Kane drained his first can and opened the second. Driveway happy hour, indeed. "He got along with everyone on the street?" he asked.

"Far as I know." Lucas opened his beer, took a long swig and wiped his mouth with the back of his hand. "Now that I think about it, though, there was one funny incident a while back."

"Oh?"

"One afternoon, maybe a week before he disappeared, I see a woman coming around the corner over there." He pointed to the cul-de-sac up the street a few houses. "The sort of woman you'd notice under any circumstances. Pretty little thing, wearing a cut-off shirt and skimpy shorts. I see her going by from time to time and I always sit up and pay attention. If I was thirty, forty years younger, she'd be just my type." He shrugged. "Who am I kidding? A woman like that will always be my type." He grinned and took another swig of beer. "Anyhow, the strange thing was that she had a bunch of reeds in her hand. Bamboo shoots, you know?"

Kane nodded. Eads's backyard was full of it.

"She marched down the street clutching them like she was going to battle. They had to be at least five feet long, almost as tall as she was. I admit I was more interested in watching her than anything else, but I also saw someone else hanging back at the corner. Her husband, I figured, keeping an eye on the situation but not brave enough to take part in whatever was fixing to happen."

"Which was?"

"She went up to the front door of the place you're staying and pounded on it with her fist. Eads opened up. I couldn't hear what she was saying, but boy oh boy, she gave him what for. Shaking that bamboo like she wanted to hit him over the head with it. All the while her husband is pacing back and forth over there like he's trying to decide whether he needs to intervene. Eads just stood there and nodded and maybe he got in a few words, but that was it. Once she'd said her piece, she turned and headed back home. Still carrying the bamboo, mind you. She walked right past her husband and he had to trot to catch up with her. Funniest dang thing I ever saw. Better than TV, that's what I would have told Sadie if she'd been here."

"That is strange."

"I was curious, so I did a little research." Lucas shrugged. "I have plenty of free time these days. Seems there are two kinds of bamboo. There's what they call clumping bamboo, which stays pretty much where you plant it, and then there's running bamboo, which spreads like the dickens. It forms these long, underground runners that can pop up ten, fifteen feet away."

Kane thought of the wall of bamboo behind the house across the street. "Into a neighbor's yard, for example."

"That'd be my guess. And she was none too pleased about it."

"Huh," Kane said. When he and his brother and Hector had been researching Eads's neighbors, they hadn't considered the residents on the other side of his back fence. Kane had no idea who was in the house behind him back in Houston. They never crossed paths. It was like they lived in different worlds.

"Something to consider," Lucas said.

Indeed it was. However, Kane didn't want to visit these back-fence neighbors until he knew more about them, and not with the smell of booze on his breath. He thanked Lucas for the beer and the conversation.

"Come on by any afternoon. It's always happy hour here."

"I just might do that," Kane said. As he stood, he remembered the flier from the Chinese restaurant in his pocket and a sudden craving overtook him. He set off toward the nearby strip center, coupon in hand.

By the time he got back to Chicory Lane, it was getting dark. The neighborhood looked like a different place. Less inviting. Somewhere bad things could happen. He had an uneasy feeling about this case. People vanished voluntarily from time to time, but they rarely left everything behind. Still, Eads was a computer guy. If anyone knew how to cover his tracks, it would be someone like him.

The next morning, Kane teleconferenced with Hector at their office in Houston. He'd finally gained access to Eads's computer. "Nothing out of the ordinary," the analyst told him. "His taste in porn was pretty mainstream."

"Mainstream porn. Is that a thing?"

"Sure," Hector said. "At least that's what Nate says."

Nate was Kane's younger brother, his partner in Kane Investigations. "Did you look into the family across the back fence?"

"Tamara and Earl Cochran. He's thirty-two, she's thirty. He's a FedEx driver. She doesn't work outside the home. Two young kids, girls. No criminal records. Lived in the house for two years. Their credit's a train wreck. All their cards are maxed out and they've missed a few mortgage payments."

Financial stress could make people do crazy things, Kane knew. He decided to drop in on the Cochrans at five-thirty. Hector didn't know the husband's work schedule, but Kane figured that was the best time to catch them both home at the same time.

He spent the afternoon drinking coffee and watching the final episodes of the Flemish crime series on Netflix. Later, as he set off down the street, he waved at Lucas, who was sitting in his driveway with another cooler of beer.

Edgewood Court doglegged to the left, ending in a turnaround loop. The third house from Chicory Lane on the left belonged to the Cochrans. Kane had used Google Earth the previous evening to confirm that their backyard shared a section of fence with Eads. There was a car in the driveway, a beat-up eight-year-old Honda, so there was a good chance someone was home.

He had considered a variety of strategies, but decided it was time for the direct approach. He rang the doorbell and waited. Eventually a timid-looking man pulled the door open a few inches. He had a quizzical look on his face.

"Yes?"

Kane held up his ID. "Benjamin Kane. I'm a private investigator looking into the disappearance of Carl Eads. He lives over there." Kane nodded in the direction of the man's backyard. "I was wondering—"

Cochran's face lost all color and he stumbled back a few steps. Kane thought he was going to pass out. "Oh God, oh god, oh god," he said.

Kane was familiar with that reaction. He stepped inside and closed the door behind him.

"Earl? Who was it?"

Cochran opened his mouth to speak, but no words came out. A few seconds later, a young woman appeared. Kane recognized her—the friendly woman with the wild hair. It did not escape his attention that she was holding a large carving knife in one hand.

"It was an accident," Cochran said.

"Honey? Why is he here? What accident are you talking about?"

"The guy... the one who planted the bamboo that spread into the backyard. The one you got so mad at."

"You shut up about that, Earl," she said, but Cochran was on a roll.

"He came by to apologize. We took him out back to show him the mess he'd made. Things got out of hand. Tammy didn't mean to hit him." He lowered his head. "At least not that hard, I guess."

"Where is he?" Kane asked.

Tammy glared at her husband, but the damage was done.

Cochran tossed a thumb over his shoulder. "In the flower bed."

Kane pulled out his cell phone to dial 911. He kept an eye on the femme fatale clutching the deadly weapon in her right hand. He detected indecision in her eyes and had a brief vision where he joined Carl Eads in the backyard. Pushing up daisies, he thought. Then the fire in her eyes went out and she put the knife on a table by the front door.

Kane told the emergency dispatcher what was needed and where. When Cochran went to console his wife, Kane grabbed the carving knife in case she had a change of heart.

Soon, the quiet neighborhood was a hub of activity as cruisers, unmarked vehicles, Child Protective Services and forensics vans descended on the cul-de-sac. Kane told his story to the lead detective and said they could find him at the house around the corner that evening, but he'd be heading back to Houston in the morning.

Many of the residents of Edgewood Court and Chicory Lane were standing at the ends of their driveways when he returned to his temporary lodgings. On the way, he spent a few minutes bringing Lucas up to speed. He'd provided the vital clue, after all, and no doubt the detectives would want to speak with him before long, too.

The next morning, as Kane packed up his belongings in preparation for abandoning suburbia for the comparative safety of Houston, he thought about Robert Frost's poem in which a man argued that his apple trees would never cross a stone wall to eat the cones under his neighbor's pine trees. He wondered what Frost would have made of invasive bamboo plants that could extend runners under a wall.

Sometimes it took more than a good fence to make good neighbors.

MUST LOVE DOGS — OR YOU'RE GONE

by

M. H. Callway

ON A FRIGID January sunrise, my ex, Rudy, did a nosedive off the Leaside Bridge. Gone just like that. When I heard the news, I downed a mickey of rye though I was, as they say, sorry, not sorry.

I mean, Rudy and I did have some fun times during our five-year marriage, at least until he dumped me for Maxine, his stock broker "friend". And blew my investments on his failed Bitcoin trades.

My real grief was for our dog, Flea.

You see, Rudy was out walking Flea when a hit-and-run driver launched him 200 feet down into the Don Valley. So weird. And Rudy willingly doing Flea's stoop-and-scoop? Even weirder. Not that it mattered.

Why, oh why had I agreed to joint custody of our dog?

And where was Flea? The police wouldn't talk to me. I scoured the internet news and came up dry.

Flea had to be as dead as Rudy.

I cried myself to sleep.

NEXT MORNING, A heavy pounding on my front door hauled me off the sofa. Bleary-eyed and dying of thirst, I peered through the spy hole. A heavy-set, fifty-ish stranger with a shaved head and no eyebrows leered back at me. Was he a cop? No, not wearing that pricey black cashmere overcoat he wasn't.

"Open the door, Frieda. We make nice conversation."

He knew my name. Not good.

"Come on." Bang-bang-bang. "I know you are in there."

"Go away!" I shouted through the door.

"Okay, fine, no problem." He reached inside his coat, pulled out a huge Luger and aimed it at my lock.

"Stop! Wait!"

Hands shaking, I unbolted the door, ran and dived behind the sofa as he burst his way inside.

"Your condo is crap," he said looking around.

Fair comment, I guess. "What do you want?" I asked, muffled behind the couch.

"Get up."

Heart pounding, I pulled myself off the floor.

"Over there." He gestured toward my fake granite countertop with his gun. "Now sit."

I plunked myself down on the bar stool. "Who—who are you?"

"My name is Viktor Volkov." He smiled like a king cobra. "Rudy did not tell you about me?"

I shook my head.

"Never mind. We will have little chat." He said easing his bulk into my solitary armchair and running his free hand over the torn upholstery. "You do not look after your things."

Well, Flea did have a bad habit of eating anything—including furniture. Besides I'd let things go after Rudy took off, even myself.

"Is this about money?" No, duh! What else could it be?

"Your late husband, Rudy, owes me one million dollars. For bad Bitcoin trade."

"What!"

"American dollars. Not crap Canadian currency."

"But-but Rudy dumped me six months ago."

He shrugged one massive shoulder. "Too bad. Now Rudy's debt is your debt."

"I'm *broke*. He stole all my money!"

"Then you must sell your crap condo."

"He mortgaged it behind my back. Here, I'll show you." I scrabbled through the detritus on the counter, found my bank's latest threatening letter and shoved it at him.

He read it through. "Your bank did not get good deal. No way they will get one million for this place. So, we still have problem. You have good job. Rudy said you are accountant with big firm."

"They fired me last week. Rudy forged my signature on a bogus invoice. I don't know how he did it."

Viktor cracked a smile. "Yes, Rudy was creative guy, but sadly, as trader in Bitcoin not so smart." He picked up his gun. "Sorry, Frieda, your time is gone. This is business. This is matter of family honour."

"Wait! Stop! What happened to Flea?"

"Flea, what is this 'Flea'?"

"My dog. I named him after the bass player in the Red Hot Chili Peppers. Rudy was walking Flea when you, um… Please tell me Flea isn't dead."

"So, you are dog lover." He thought for a long minute. "Okay, fine, maybe we can work this out. Get dressed. Today, Frieda, is your lucky day."

THAT'S HOW I ended up working at Doggie's Day Spa to pay off Rudy's debt. For Marisa, Viktor's twenty-five-year-old, erm, niece. With those big brown Animé eyes and that figure? Sure, whatever. I knew better than to pry.

Marisa hugged Viktor, disappeared into the back of her crystal and marble boutique and returned with a chilled bottle of Stolichnaya Vodka. She filled three shot glasses decorated with happy Schnauzer faces.

"*Nostrovia!*" she cried, raising her glass.

She and Viktor downed their shots, banged down their glasses and beamed. I downed mine, breathed fire and coughed like a drowning victim. But when I surfaced, my hangover was gone.

"Now you be good girl." Viktor squeezed my shoulder and left.

"You love dogs, yes?" Marisa asked. "Good, we work together. I show you everything."

She handed me a pink tunic adorned with an inanely smiling poodle. For the rest of the day, I shampooed, brushed and trimmed doggy fur and clipped doggy nails. I learned how to restrain the biters and dodge the bladder-voiders —often the hard way.

It was exhausting, muscle-burning work, and being up close and personal with dogs made me tear up. All I could think about was Flea.

Late that afternoon, a muscular young man named John Makar dropped by to deliver Marisa's favorite treat, a cinnamon latte. Turned out, he owned the café next door.

"Looks like you could use a latte, too," John said to me. "Drop by, I'll make you one on the house."

I could have fallen in love with him right there if I hadn't felt so miserable.

"Frieda, what is wrong?" Marisa asked after he left. "You look so sad!"

I'm a sucker for kindness, so I spilled my guts about Flea and Rudy. Hardly a secret since Rudy's accident was all over the news. But I kept quiet about his Bitcoin debt—I wasn't stupid.

"So sorry for that," Marisa said. "Maybe Flea run away after accident. Look, I do dog rescue. I know all animal shelters in Toronto. Tonight, I will call my friends."

"Thanks," I sniffed.

But next morning, Marisa gave me the bad news: no sign of Flea.

"Never mind, I cheer you up," she said. "Come in the back. I fix your hair."

"With *dog* products?"

"Better than stuff for humans. Cheaper, too. Here, I cover your grey with fresh blonde colour. Same as product I use on toy poodles. I make you look younger, maybe fifty years old."

Thanks, I'd just turned forty-five. "No way!"

"Please, I do for free."

Free? Check and mate. Afterwards, I had to admit, I did look better.

"Now I have favour to ask," Marisa said. "This afternoon, I have date with John. You will be alone, but you can handle it. Think of owners as bigger dogs."

Marisa took off after lunch. Between grooming the dogs and placating their owners, I spent the afternoon in chaotic stress. Those dog owners— *woof!* In their eyes, I was lower than a lazy slave. Worse they hated tipping. The beavers on their nickels didn't just scream, they bellowed out Wagnerian operas. By closing time, I was ready to use Viktor's Luger.

And for the icing on my crap cake, I ran straight into Viktor himself. Right outside the shop after I locked up. He was walking a champagne-colored toy poodle.

Must love dogs…

"Where is Marisa?" he asked—and he meant business.

I thought fast. "You just missed her. We ran out of Canine Cuddle shampoo."

Viktor smoothed his bald head. "Okay, you tell Marisa that my stockbroker friend is bringing Jo-Jo here to the spa. Tomorrow, two o'clock. Whatever my friend wants, you give. Even Canine Cuddle shampoo."

He flashed his snaky grin. "Your hair, it looks like Jo-Jo's. Cute." He squeezed my shoulder. "Now you be good girl, Frieda."

With that he led Jo-Jo away, leaving me to shiver in the icy wind blowing down Bloor Street.

After another sleepless night missing Flea, I decided to kick-start my morning with that promised cinnamon latte in the café next to Doggie's Day Spa. Sadly, the hot John Makar wasn't there to serve me.

That's because he and Marisa were locked in a heavy embrace in the spa's back room. I had a front row centre view through the window in the reception area. Dazzled by young lust, they'd forgotten to pull the blind.

I slammed the front door and made a lot of noise.

"Oh, hi there," John said, straightening his T-shirt over a stellar torso. "Um, hi."

He grinned on his way out the door, but Marisa looked like she was facing a zombie attack. "Please, Frieda, say nothing to Uncle Viktor."

"You mean Viktor really is your uncle?"

"Of course. He is my mother's brother. What you think?"

"I think you and John are both adults. Do what you want."

"Please, Frieda, please! John is Turkish, I am Russian. Viktor is old school. He will not understand."

"Don't worry, I won't tell," I said. "I've got enough problems with Viktor."

"Of course, you have problem," Marisa said, adjusting her spa uniform. "That is why he gave you job here, is it not?"

"Look, Viktor showed up here last night."

A blaze of fear crossed her face. "What did he want?"

"He said his stockbroker *friend* is bringing her toy poodle, Jo-Jo, here to the spa at two o'clock. And we better be extra nice to her."

"Holy crap, Liliana Reynolds! She is Viktor's private money advisor." Marisa collapsed on the reception area sofa. "We must cancel our customers. We have no choice."

"Because you front for Viktor's business."

"Of course! You think I can afford rent on Bloor Street? I launder money for Viktor like everyone in my family."

"So, we're both trapped."

"This is true." Marisa tied back her mane of dark hair and stood up. "Come, Frieda, we have much to do."

She switched the spa's neon window sign from "open" to "closed". While I rebooked the day's clients, she ordered delivery of French pastries and champagne. From the back cupboard, she produced fancy china and crystal. By two o'clock sharp, the coffee table in reception was set, the goodies laid out and the champagne cooling on ice.

We, too, were primped and waiting. But the feast was strictly for Liliana. We would have to go hungry.

Marisa fetched the vodka and the Schnauzer glasses. "For courage before Liliana," she said, pouring out two shots. I almost beat Marisa downing mine.

Now what?

Marisa peered out the front window and swore. "Here she is! Quick, hide the vodka."

Message received. I stashed the vodka in the mini-fridge out back and hurried to rejoin Marisa by the front window.

Together we watched the hulking black Cadillac Escalade parked in the space outside the spa.

A woman in a hooded down coat leaped out of the driver's seat. Teetering on stiletto-heeled boots, she went round to the rear passenger door and yanked it open. First, she dragged out an oversized Versace purse and then, after considerable tussling, a Husky dog by its collar.

My heart gave a leap. Those black and white markings—no, it couldn't be.

"That's Flea! That's my dog!" I cried.

"What are you saying?" Marisa said.

Flea plunked himself down on the icy sidewalk and refused to budge. The woman hauled on his collar. Her hood fell back. I stifled a scream: I'd recognize that dyed scarlet hair and those surgically enhanced cheekbones anywhere.

"And that's not Liliana Reynolds!" I said.

"What you mean? Here I am seeing Liliana with my own eyes."

"That's Maxine! Rudy's girlfriend!"

"What!" Marisa thought for a moment. "Quick, hide in the back." She grabbed a spare leash from the counter and dashed out of the store in a blast of cold air.

I fled into the spa, shut the connecting door and jerked the blind down over the spectator window.

And not a microsecond too soon.

Noise burst through the reception area: the shrill voice of the ersatz Liliana, Marisa's alto urging calm and Flea's anxious yelps as they dragged him inside.

"I will give him a treat to calm him down," I heard Marisa say.

"Don't you dare feed him!" Liliana snapped. "Where's my champagne?"

I peeked round the edge of the blind. Marisa slipped Flea a treat, while Liliana flounced around, swearing. Flea sighed and lay down, resting his pointed nose on his crossed front paws.

"Aren't you listening? My champagne, right now!" Liliana said.

Flea winced at the sound of her voice. While Marisa popped the cork of the champagne bottle, he eyeballed the platter of French pastries on the coffee table. Quick as lightening, his tongue flicked out and disappeared the nearest éclair.

Oh, no! Chocolate made him sick.

Marisa poured champagne into the single tulip glass on the coffee table. Liliana dumped her stuff on the sofa and snatched up her drink. She downed half of it.

"Where is Jo-Jo?" Marisa asked.

"With Viktor. I'm delivering this dog to Cleveland tonight. To a nice Russian family. Go fetch your rescue van."

"Are you kidding? I cannot drive all night to Cleveland and back for one dog. I have business to run."

"That's your problem." Liliana held out her glass for more champagne.

"Border guards will ask questions. Always I bring rescue dogs *from* United States *into* Canada. Not other way round."

"Stop stressing. I've got the necessary paperwork for him."

"No, I have a date."

"Break it." Liliana's eyes narrowed—as much as her facelift would allow. "Or do I tell Viktor about your sexy Turkish boyfriend?"

"How you know about John?" Marisa clutched the champagne bottle in a death grip.

"I'm very observant." Liliana's eyes fell on the platter of pastries. "Why are there only seven pastries? I always order *eight*. And what's that dog doing?"

Flea had sensed me. He scratched and whined at the connecting door to the spa.

"Who's out back?"

Liliana strode toward the door, but I beat her to it and flung it open. Watching her pale under her salon tan felt better than sex.

Flea yelped for joy. He leaped into my arms and tumbled us down onto the coffee table. Pastries, china and glass flew everywhere. I clung to my lost dog while he licked me frantically—and gobbled down the ruin of pastries squished all over my uniform.

"Y-you!" Liliana sputtered through the chaos. "What the hell are you doing here?"

"Viktor hired me."

"*Viktor?*"

I extricated myself from Flea. "Looks like we're both working for him, Liliana. Or should I say *Maxine*."

"What's with the frizzy blond hair?"

"What's with your tenth facelift?"

"Nice, Liliana." Marisa folded her arms. "Very nice. You were cheating on Uncle Viktor with Frieda's ex, Rudy."

"Frieda's a pathological liar!"

"Dogs do not lie." Marisa picked up the champagne bottle from the floor. "You are Frieda's dog, right, Flea?"

Flea wagged his tail and swiped a glob of icing from his nose.

"Now *I* have juicy story to tell Viktor," Marisa said.

"OK, OK." Liliana scraped Chantilly cream off her leather pants. "So, I had a little fling with Rudy. No biggie."

"It was a lot more than that." I grabbed the champagne bottle from Marisa and took a swig.

"Viktor doesn't have to know. Anyway, Rudy's dead," Liliana said.

"I see you're really broken up about it," I said.

"No more than your crocodile tears. Look, Marisa, I won't say anything about your Turkish barista babe if you don't tell Viktor about Rudy. Deal?"

Marisa thought it over. "Okay,, but on one condition. You give Flea back to Frieda now."

"NO! Flea goes to Cleveland."

"You're not taking my dog anywhere!" I said, ready to fight to the death.

Liliana lunged for Flea's collar. I swung the champagne bottle at her and missed. Its contents sprayed out, giving us an unholy baptism.

"You bitch!" Liliana shrieked. "You wrecked my Versace bag!"

"Too bad it wasn't your head!"

Flea erupted in a frenzy of barking.

"Shut up, shut up, all of you!" Marisa clapped her hands over her ears. "Fine, Flea goes to Cleveland, but Frieda comes, too. To look after Flea."

"No way!" Liliana and I shouted together.

"Do it or I call Viktor now! And Frieda, you cannot cross American border smelling like a drunk. Go in the back and change. Take Flea with you."

Liliana shuffled through her handbag, hauled out a box of doggie-doo bags and threw it at me. "If he goes, put it in there."

"Do it yourself!" I said.

Marisa sighed. "Please, Frieda. Do as Liliana says. I cannot drive 12 hours with you two fighting."

I grabbed the box and took Flea with me into the back.

MARISA STORED HER dog rescue van in the parking lot under the grooming salon. While she and Liliana moved the Escalade down into its spot and brought up the van, I changed into a clean uniform.

Behind me, Flea uttered a fluid cough. Uh-oh! I knew that gurgling sound. The next instant, he barfed copiously over the floor tiles.

"Flea, *ohmigod!*"

Mixed in with the hideous remains of half-digested chocolate pastries lurked shining bits of glass. The champagne goblet! He'd eaten it!

"Don't die, Flea. Please don't die!" I fell on my knees beside him.

But Flea, relieved of his stomach contents, panted happily. Nothing like a dog who'd eaten glass. Maybe I was seeing things. I grabbed a handy rag and wiped up the mess to make sure.

My heart sank. He'd eaten glass all right, but why was it in little cubes like pieces of a shattered windshield? I plucked out a bit and held it to the light.

A flame of brilliance shot through it. Not glass: a cut gemstone.

A diamond!

I filled a bucket with soap and water and ever alert to the sounds of Marisa and Liliana's return, performed the icky task of straining, rinsing and collecting. I ended up gazing at a glittering handful of diamonds.

"You poor thing," I said to Flea. "No wonder Liliana wanted your Number Twos."

I clutched the fortune in my fist. Here was my way out!

The spa's front door whooshed open. Marisa and Liliana were back. Now what?

The vodka! I tore open the door to the mini-fridge, unscrewed the top of the bottle with my free hand and poured the diamonds into the alcohol. Transparent gemstones in a transparent liquid, the best hiding place I could think of for now.

I seized a bottle of air freshener and sprayed madly as Liliana rushed into the spa with Marisa close behind her.

"Why is the floor wet?" Liliana coughed and waved.

"From cleaning up your eight pastries," I said.

Luckily, she bought it.

THE FOUR OF us trooped outside to the neon pink dog rescue van. Marisa threw open the back door, emblazoned with the spa's goofy poodle logo, and revealed a large dog cage.

Flea refused to climb into it. Even I couldn't persuade him.

"Okay, we all ride up front," Marisa said over Liliana's protests.

She took the wheel and Liliana, naturally, claimed the roomy passenger seat. That meant I had to squeeze onto the narrow back seat behind them with Flea stretched out on the floor under my feet. My next few hours promised to be cramped torture.

Liliana dropped her oversized Versace bag on the van's floor with a loud thump.

"What have you got in there, free weights?" I asked.

"None of your business."

"Shut up, please!" Marisa tossed her electronic key into the van's cup holder. "Weather report calls for big snow tonight. Buffalo border crossing is closed. We have to take Rainbow Bridge in Niagara Falls."

Not that our route mattered. I didn't have my passport with me and couldn't get into the USA without one. If I didn't get Flea away from Liliana before the border, I'd lose him forever.

Time to get creative.

The snow began falling thick and fast. Our endless stops and starts through Toronto's rush hour traffic bought me time to think and slowly the plaques of idiocy peeled from my brain. I sat up: I'd been a complete idiot.

Hadn't Marisa practically begged me to escape from the spa with Flea? She'd left us alone together when she and Liliana went to fetch the van. Mind you, in my defence, I'd been busy salvaging millions of dollars in diamonds—diamonds Liliana planned to ferry across the American border *inside* Flea.

Because—no, duh! - Rudy had dropped him off at her condo *before* Viktor knocked him off the Leaside Bridge. Because he and Liliana were in on the scam together!

I pounded my knee with my fist, jostling the bench. That explained why Rudy had fought me for joint custody of our dog. Flea would eat anything: he was the perfect smuggler. As long as he didn't eat or drink...

So where did Rudy and Liliana get the money for those diamonds? From Rudy's Bitcoin trades? Are you kidding? Obviously, they'd stolen it from their brokerage clients.

Clients like me—and Viktor.

Viktor had been onto Rudy and Rudy had paid the price. Viktor would be onto to Liliana soon. No wonder she was desperate to leave Canada tonight.

I had to get Marisa alone. Tell her what I'd figured out, but the blinding blizzard made pulling off Highway 403 impossible. It took three gruelling hours until we finally turned south toward Niagara Falls.

The misty lights of a shopping centre beckoned in the distance. Marisa signalled right and headed for the exit ramp. Here was my chance!

"What are you doing?" Liliana demanded. "I'm hours late. We must go, go, go!"

"I cannot drive through this snow any longer without food," Marisa said.

"And I haven't eaten since breakfast," I put in.

"No one cares about you, Frieda." Liliana rummaged through her purse and extracted a plastic bottle of water and a chocolate bar. "Here, Marisa, eat this."

Marisa wrinkled her nose in disgust. "That is not decent food."

"Fine." Liliana unwrapped the chocolate and took a bite herself. Flea lifted his head and sniffed the air. Oh-oh.

"Flea's hungry," I said. "Thirsty, too."

"I said, he gets no food!"

"For Flea to be thirsty is cruel." Marisa reached for the water bottle but Liliana snatched it away.

"That's my vitamin water!"

"Now you make me miss exit." Looking grim, Marisa kept driving.

Every time, she made to pull off the highway, Liliana squawked. All the way to Niagara Falls.

Its snow-clogged streets lay deserted. Even the signs of the tourist traps on Clifton Hill had gone dark.

Marisa pulled up at the traffic light at the bottom of Clifton Hill. The iron underbelly of the Rainbow Bridge, the gateway to America, reared over our heads.

"*Bliatz!*" Marisa swore. She veered the van right, away from the bridge.

"What the hell are you doing?" Liliana sat up. "You're going the wrong way. Turn around!"

"I am the driver. I decide." Marisa drove down the Niagara Parkway toward the frozen blur of Horseshoe Falls. Lit up, they looked like an Arctic fairyland, but the spectacle was lost on me.

Think! I had to think!

We were passing Table Rock at the edge of the Falls, when I spotted a familiar yellow sign. "There's a Tim Hortons Doughnut Store," I cried.

Marisa skidded across the parkway into Table Rock's empty parking lot. But luck was against me: the inside of the coffee shop looked dark.

"It's closed, obviously," Liliana said. "Now can we leave?"

"Shut up!" Marisa switched off the engine, flung open the driver's door and climbed out into the cold. Through the windshield, I watched her pull out her phone, probably to check for a Tim Hortons that *was* open.

Finally, my chance. "Let me out, Liliana. Flea needs to go."

Liliana smirked, crossed her arms and refused to budge.

"Move your scrawny butt!"

"Time to switch drivers." Quick as a snake, she snatched the van key from the cup holder, tossed it into her purse and punched the passenger door, locking the three of us in the van.

Marisa heard her. She threw herself against the passenger door grappling with it. Liliana tried to wriggle into the driver's seat.

I launched myself up and over the front seats crash-landing on Liliana's stick-insect legs. She kicked me in the face. The pain! I screamed.

Flea reared up, barking. He toppled over the driver's seat. Thumped down on Liliana's chest. With a flash of white fangs, he chomped down on her shoulder.

Liliana howled like a rabid coyote. I fumbled with the door lock. The passenger door flew open tumbling me out onto hard ice.

The perpetual mist off the Falls had turned Table Rock's parking lot into a skating rink. I lay there stunned, staring at Marisa's Kodiak boots.

The boots leaped over me. I saw Marisa dive into the van through the open passenger door. She was trying to get a grip on Liliana's kicking legs, but Liliana fought like a tigress.

"Frieda, help!" Marisa shouted.

I staggered up. Slipping and sliding, grabbed onto Liliana's foot. Her Louboutin boot slipped off in my hand. I tossed it away. Latching onto her bony ankle.

"Pull! Pull!" Marisa yelled.

"I'm trying," I screamed back.

We hauled and heaved: Liliana's claw-like fingers clung to the steering wheel.

"Harder!"

Three humans and Flea avalanched out of the van.

Liliana thudded onto her hands and knees. Marisa sprawled on her back like a snow angel. I ended up, clinging to the open door.

Flea bounded up and ran over to me.

Where was that damn key? I grabbed Liliana's bag off the floor of the van—and slipped onto my butt. US cash, the chocolate bar, the vitamin water and a .22-calibre gun spun out over the ice.

Liliana caught the gun. She teetered to her feet and pointed it at us.

"Stay back or I'll shoot!" she said. "I'm taking that dog."

"NO!" I cried.

"And you, Marisa, pick up my damn stuff."

Even in the dim light, Marisa's expression scared me. But she grabbed Liliana's bag from where it had fallen the ground.

Flea leaped on the chocolate bar. Down it went. His jaws closed on the plastic bottle.

"My vitamin water!" Liliana aimed her gun.

I threw myself over Flea. And Marisa swung Mr. Versace like a baseball bat.

Home run!

Two seconds later, she had the gun pressed to Liliana's forehead. For the first time I saw the family resemblance between her and Viktor.

"Don't, Marisa, please," Liliana pleaded.

Marisa's finger tightened on the trigger.

"Stop!" I said. "She's not worth it."

"Okay, we throw her over the Falls for a swim."

"No! Lock her in the dog cage. Then decide."

A long moment passed. Marisa's shoulders relaxed. "You heard Frieda. Get in the damn cage."

She herded her around the van. I threw open the back door. Liliana seemed pathetically grateful to climb into the cage.

"Can we discuss this?" she asked, after I locked her in.

"No, you try to steal my wheels. Worse to shoot Flea." Marisa slammed the back door shut.

I pried Liliana's vitamin water bottle out of Flea's mouth. His teeth had punctured the plastic. Water was dribbling out, freezing where it landed. I stashed the bottle in the van's cup holder and gathered up the rest of Liliana's paraphernalia. Even her lost boot.

But we couldn't find the key.

"It's got to be here," I said. "She dropped it in her purse. I saw her."

Marisa turned on her cell phone's flashlight. Shivering and drenched, we kept searching.

Nothing.

"We'll freeze if we don't stop," I said through chattering teeth.

Marisa nodded, too numb to speak. We retreated with Flea into the shelter of the van, Marisa behind the wheel and me in the passenger seat. Flea stretched out on the back seat behind us.

"We are stuck," Marisa whispered.

"What? No spare key?" I whispered back.

Marisa shook her head.

"I can hear you two perfectly well," Liliana said.

"Oh, no!" Marisa pointed through the windshield. "Police! This is disaster!"

A police car was crawling down the parkway toward Table Rock.

Liliana banged the sides of the cage. "Help, police, help!"

My heart was thumping. A van parked in a deserted parking lot with a screaming, caged human inside. Not suspicious, no, not at all.

I thought fast. "Your key's electronic. If it's close enough to the van, the engine might still start."

Marisa jammed down the start button. The engine fired! Warm air flowed out through the vents in the dashboard.

The cop car signaled and turned into the parking lot.

"Go, go!" I said.

Marisa dropped the gun in my lap and gunned the motor.

Bad idea.

We skidded. And slid backwards toward the railing and the swirling black water of Niagara River.

Marisa steered madly. The van spun like a carousel. Round and round.

Silence: we'd stopped moving.

We'd stalled.

Liliana renewed her frantic banging. "Help! They're going to kill me and my dog."

Desperate, I punched the start button. The engine fired again!

"What did you do?" Marisa said.

"I don't know!"

Marisa slammed the gear into second. I felt our tires grip the icy ground. We inched away from certain death into the centre of the parking lot.

The cops pulled level with my window.

I twisted my face into a smile and waved to them like the Queen in a motorcade. Only this queen had a gun in her lap. Heart pounding, I held my breath until they waved back.

"Get us out of here!" I whispered. "And take it slow."

Marisa nodded. She eased the van back onto the parkway and heading back toward town well below the speed limit. "How my van started? This is miracle!"

"No, Liliana shut up. That's the real miracle," I said.

"I'm thirsty," Liliana whined from the cage. "Can I have my vitamin water?"

I picked up the bottle from the coffee holder. Under the passing street lights, something sparkled.

Hello, diamonds at the bottom! Translucent gems in a translucent liquid, just like the diamonds hiding in the vodka back at Doggie's Day.

"Look!" I held the bottle so Marisa could see. "Diamonds!"

"*Bozhe moy!* If those belong to Viktor, we are in bad trouble."

"Well, Liliana, *do* the diamonds belong to Viktor?" I asked.

Only silence from the dog cage.

"There's your answer," I said. "Remember how she ordered me to save Flea's poop?" Marisa nodded.

"She and Rudy stuffed a crap-ton of diamonds into Flea. He threw them up back at the spa." Quickly I filled her in on what I'd figured out about Liliana's and Rudy's fraud.

Liliana let out a wail. "I'll cut you in, Marisa."

Marisa scowled. "Forget it. Diamonds are mine now."

To my surprise, she drove up onto the Rainbow Bridge and stopped. Through the snow, I could just make out a black oblong at the far end of the bridge: the border crossing.

OK, Liliana," Marisa said. "Here is the deal. If you wish to live, walk over Rainbow Bridge to America. And never come back."

"How will I get to Cleveland?"

"Take Uber. Not my problem."

Marisa covered Liliana with the gun, while I released her from the cage and handed over her stuff. I watched her stumble down the bridge's slippery sidewalk, her Versace purse in one hand, her boot in the other while Marisa made yet another phone call. I prayed she'd found an open cafe. I desperately needed a coffee—or preferably something stronger.

"WHAT DO WE tell Viktor?" I asked as Marisa drove away from Rainbow Bridge. "She stole from him. Look what he did to Rudy."

"Viktor did not do anything to Rudy."

"He killed him! He knocked him off Leaside Bridge."

"*Think*, Frieda." Marisa threw me a look. "Liliana killed Rudy. She wanted the diamonds for herself."

That made horrible sense. I saw poor Rudy strolling over the bridge, dreaming of his future together with Liliana in an extradition-free paradise, when bam! She drives her honking big Escalade into him and whacks him into oblivion.

"We just let a murderer go free!"

"No, trust me, we have not." Marisa's smile chilled me. "My brother is border guard at Canadian customs. He will keep Liliana waiting until Uncle Viktor's men arrive. Then they will take her for nice swim in Niagara River."

BACK AT DOGGIES Day, I spread out the diamonds from the vitamin water and the vodka bottle while Flea took a well-deserved nap.

"Wow, millions." Marisa couldn't stop staring. "This is much more than Viktor's money."

"Right! There's the money belonging to all of Rudy and Liliana's clients. Including me."

"Viktor will take everything. You and I know this."

"So, what do we do?"

She thought for a moment. "We negotiate big finder's fee. What Rudy stole from you and enough for me to buy my freedom from the family business. Free to be with John. This way we get Viktor's respect."

"Won't he just laugh at us?"

"Relax, Frieda. Viktor *likes* you. He says you remind him of Jo-Jo."

Great, wonderful.

"And he will make millions out of this. Too bad for other investors," she went on.

"I guess that'll teach them to invest in risky Bitcoin," I said.

We spent the rest of the night cleaning up the spa.

"One thing I still do not understand," Marisa said as we finished up. "How my van started second time? What did you do?"

"Your answer's sitting right there." I pointed to Flea. "When I dropped Liliana's purse, Flea went for her chocolate bar. But your key and the chocolate bar look about the same and he swallowed your key. Because he was in the van with us, your key was, too."

"A new key is expensive!"

"Let nature run its course. Your key should appear in a day or two—and maybe more of Liliana's diamonds."

She smiled. "Bigger finder's fee for us."

Soon Viktor's black cashmere overcoat darkened the front door of the spa. He strolled in with Liliana's poodle, Jo-Jo, on a leash.

Flea and Jo-Jo sniffed each other, while Marisa fetched the vodka and the Schnauzer glasses.

"We are drinking early," Viktor said. "Have you been good girl, Frieda?"

"Oh, yes, very good," I said.

Marisa poured out three shots. "First, we drink, then we talk. And you, Uncle Viktor, will listen."

Viktor raised his non-existent eyebrows, but lifted his glass with us.

"And when you down your shot, be careful," I said. "There's a prize at the bottom."

LOST LADY

by

Jacqueline Seewald

PRIVATE DETECTIVE, NINA Harris, studied the attractive blonde dressed in a designer suit sitting opposite her. Sharon Lester exuded charm. Nina placed the woman in her early thirties. She oozed wealth and class.

"How can I help you?" Nina asked.

"Attorney John McDermitt is a friend of my husband and myself. I asked him to recommend a detective and he gave me your information."

Nina nodded. "We've done some investigative work for him from time to time. Do I understand you're interested in engaging the services of our agency?"

Sharon Lester nodded. "However, Ms. Harris, before we go any further, can I have your assurance that everything I tell you will remain in confidence whether or not I hire you?"

"Mrs. Lester, we are always discreet." Nina gave the potential client a reassuring smile.

"Who or what would you like us to investigate?"

Sharon Lester licked dry lips. "It's complicated. You see my husband has a daughter and she seems to have disappeared—well that might be the wrong word. Let's just say she's gone."

Nina leaned forward in her chair placing her elbows on her desk as she reached for a notepad and pen. "Name and age of the daughter please."

"Caroline, age eighteen. I'm not certain of her last name."

Nina's brow rose questioningly. "Isn't it Lester?"

Sharon shook her head. "My husband, Alex, had a situation with his first wife, Michelle."

Mrs. Lester squirmed in her chair.

"What sort of situation?"

Mrs. Lester cleared her throat. "He caught his wife cheating on him. It turned out she was pregnant. They had a contentious divorce. She left New York." The tension in her voice was brittle.

"Did Mr. Lester ever take a paternity test?"

Sharon Lester's eyes cast downward. "Not that I know of."

"What brought on this sudden interest in Caroline?"

"Michelle came to our house after the funeral of Kevin's father. She brought Caroline with her. Kevin was furious at the intrusion. They argued in Kevin's study. I was not invited to join them, but their voices were so loud, I couldn't help overhearing them. Sadly, Caroline was standing there right next to me. She heard some terrible things."

"Such as?"

Mrs. Lester looked away. "Michelle said she'd only come to drop off Caroline who was now graduated from her school. Michelle said she was about travel to Asia with her current boyfriend. Caroline would have been an inconvenience. It was time for Kevin to take responsibility for his daughter."

"And how did he respond?"

Mrs. Lester shook her head. "He blew up. Said she wasn't his daughter and for Michelle to get out and take Caroline with her."

"And I take it she did."

"Yes, but not before saying some ugly things to Kevin."

"How did Caroline react?"

"As you would imagine. She started to sob. I truly felt for the girl. None of it was her fault. I gather she'd led a sheltered life, educated at a private school up in the Boston area. I placed my arms around her in a gesture of comfort. We bonded in that moment."

"Mrs. Lester, are you a second wife?"

Sharon crossed her arms. "Actually, I'm Kevin's third wife. His second marriage also ended in divorce. But please don't think badly of Kevin. He's really a good man. I was his executive assistant in the company for several years before we became involved romantically. He was unhappy with his second wife before he turned to me."

Nina was getting a picture of Kevin Lester and it wasn't a pretty one. Likely, Sharon was not as innocent as she would like to appear either.

"Since your husband has denied Caroline, why do you want to contact her?"

"I feel sympathetic. Her mother seemed like a self-centered individual. Kevin's ex appeared to have no real maternal feelings for her daughter. It troubled me. I had divorced parents. I just want to contact Caroline and make certain that she's all right."

"Did the mother mention where she intended to leave the girl since your husband wouldn't let her stay at your house?"

Sharon was thoughtful for a few moments. "Michelle mentioned a name, a cousin. Kevin said something derogatory about him."

"Would you have his name? That would be a good starting point."

"No, I don't remember. He was no one Kevin had ever talked about."

"How long ago did this incident at your house occur?"

"It was several weeks ago. We've heard nothing since then."

"Mrs. Lester, finding Caroline might not be so easy. But if you give me a retainer fee, I'll start working on it."

"I'll write you a check right now. I do want to help the girl. Please start searching for her as soon as possible."

AFTER SHARON LESTER left the office, Nina placed the generous check in the top drawer of her desk. Mrs. Lester wouldn't be happy, but Nina realized it was necessary for her to have a talk with Kevin Lester. That was the logical starting point. She decided to discuss the matter with her husband before proceeding. He always offered intelligent advice.

Nina fixed coffee for both herself and Bob. Then she knocked at his office door. Bob called out to enter. It sounded as if she'd interrupted an intense telephone conversation. But he looked relieved to see her enter the office carrying the tray holding coffee and two cups. He waved her in and promptly ended the phone call.

"I thought you might need some refreshment," she said.

"Sometimes I think you have E.S.P. Just what I need, some caffeine to stimulate the mush in my brain."

The Sweethearts Detective Agency, founded by Bob and Nina Harris, two N.Y.P.D. detectives who opted for early retirement from the force, was strictly a small-time gumshoe operation. They'd met on the job, been attracted to each other from the first, and were married a year after their first date. When Bob, a tall, husky former marine, met Nina, a feisty, blue-eyed redhead, he started to think it was time to consider marriage.

It was Nina who initially suggested the name for the P.I. firm. At first Bob had groaned, but the truth was it drew a lot of female clients. Ironically, these women were generally checking up on husbands they suspected of cheating.

After a short coffee break, Nina told Bob about the new client.

"I'm hoping you'll talk with the client's husband. I have a feeling he'll be more cooperative with another man than a woman."

Bob arched a brow. "That sounds a little sexist to me. I don't think any man alive could resist your interrogation techniques."

"I get the feeling this one could," Nina responded with a wry smile.

"You haven't even met the man yet. You could be jumping to conclusions."

"Somehow, I doubt it."

She and Bob researched Kevin Lester on the internet.

"This guy's a big spot," Bob said. "I'm impressed his wife contacted you. Interesting, did you notice the photos of him with his various wives? All of them are attractive blondes. Appears he goes for a certain type."

Nina managed to talk Bob into phoning Kevin Lester at his office. Unfortunately, he couldn't make an appointment to see Lester.

"Sorry, I couldn't get by the front line."

"That's all right. Obviously, Lester seems to be well-insulated from the public."

"Yeah, fifty million bucks, give or take a few, does that for a guy."

"I'll skip the office and make a house call," Nina said.

"And you think they'll just let you in?"

"Not a problem," Nine said. "I'm calling on Mrs. Lester first." Nina tossed Bob a kiss and returned to her own office.

She used the cell phone number Sharon Lester had written down for her and was pleased when Sharon picked up promptly. Nina explained she needed to see Sharon regarding some follow-up questions.

"I want to come over to your home so we can talk."

"I don't know. My husband will be home soon."

"That's fine."

There was a pause. "The thing is, I haven't told him that I'm trying to find Caroline."

"Don't you think he ought to know?"

"I'm not so sure of that."

"Mrs. Lester—"

"Please, just call me Sharon.'

"All right, Sharon. Your husband may be the only one who can help us."

Nina took a cab to the Lester residence, a penthouse in the fashionable East Eighties of Manhattan. According to the internet search, he also owned a large house in the Hamptons as well as an estate in Florida used during the winter months. Lester's company was apparently doing very well, but then most of the wealth had been inherited from the senior Lester.

There was a private elevator to the penthouse with red velvet upholstery and gold mirroring. A maid answered the door. Nina was led through a high ceiling foyer and into a massive living room. The glass curtain walls, and barrel-vaulted ceiling provided a spectacular view of the Manhattan skyline. The furnishings all appeared to be custom-made. Nina noted the rooftop garden and the pool with hot tub. She thought of her own simple apartment and sighed.

Sharon Lester joined her. She was now dressed in casual attire—a blue jumpsuit which matched her eyes and golden hair pulled back in a ponytail. Sharon offered her a drink but Nina refused. Years of never touching alcohol on duty stayed with her. She might no longer be a policewoman, but still the training and discipline were ingrained as part of her.

"My husband is changing out of his office clothes. He'll join us shortly," Sharon explained in a small, nervous voice. "What are you planning to say to him?"

"The truth—that a client has hired me to find a person that may have gone missing. I won't be mentioning your name."

Sharon breathed a sigh of relief. At that moment, Kevin Lester strode into the room. He was a tall man. Nina, at five-foot-ten was not short herself, but Lester was well over six feet, probably as tall as Bob. He immediately demanded to know why she was there.

Nina gave her explanation. "I'm a detective looking for your ex-wife's cousin. It appears Michelle left the country recently. So, I can't contact her. I believe you may have information regarding him."

"Gerald Davis? I don't know where he is. He lives somewhere in the city. I'm not surprised a detective is looking for him. He's a slippery character, has a bad reputation. Michelle told me she was going to leave her daughter with him. I didn't believe her. She said it just to aggravate me."

Seeing that Lester would be of no further help, Nina thanked him and left the residence. At least she now had a name. It was good she and Bob still had friends at their former precinct. Nina took the subway this time and rode downtown.

Sam Manger was a police captain who got things done. A former Marine like her husband, he took his job seriously. Luckily, he was on duty and made the time to talk with Nina. She explained the case to him.

"I can get Gerald Davis's info for you," he said.

"Thanks, I appreciate it."

"Say hello to Bob for me."

Nina promised she would. N.Y.P.D. proved to be efficient. Sam had a file and mugshots ready with surprising speed. Nina followed up the next morning.

Davis lived in an old apartment building on the lower East Side, far away from the Lesters's glitz and glamorous penthouse. Graffiti decorated the crumbling brick exterior. The outside railings rusted.

Nina found Davis's apartment on the third-floor walkup. She rang the doorbell but there was no answer. She waited and tried again. Starting to feel impatient, she gently tried the door. It creaked open. Nina walked cautiously inside and called out Davis's name. A few steps inside and she discovered why there had been no answer.

A man lay on the floor drenched in blood from a chest wound. Nina bent down and felt for a pulse. Nothing. She removed her cell phone from her handbag and called 911.

"I WASN'T EXPECTING to see you again so soon." Captain Manger turned out to be one of the policemen responding to her call.

Nina was aware that he was a homicide cop, but she didn't expect that he'd be in on the call. He was a captain after all and it wasn't even his precinct. By that time, she'd already given her information to the two uniform policemen. Now she was repeating it again. It occurred to her that it would have been smarter to just wipe her prints from the door and have left the building.

The building super, Juan Gonzales, came upstairs to find out what was going on. While the plainclothes detectives were busy with CSI, Nina had a chance to ask him some questions.

"Who lived in this apartment with Mr. Davis?"

Gonzales raised bushy brows over bright dark eyes. "He had a girlfriend. The last few weeks, a teenager lived here too."

"Do you know their names?"

Gonzales scratched his stubbly beard. "The woman paid half of the rent. I have her name and phone number downstairs. The young girl, I have no idea. But Lisa, she comes in to clean here. Lisa might know more. She does some of the apartments in the building, mostly when people come and go. The landlord, he rents month to month."

"How long had Davis and his friend lived here?"

"Not so long. Maybe six months. He owed his part of the rent for the last three. The landlord was getting ready to kick them out. You want to know more, talk to Lisa. She's nosy and snoops around when she cleans."

Nina asked where the woman could be found, and Gonzales was cooperative. While the police were searching the apartment, Nina slipped out. She located Lisa, the cleaning lady, where the super indicated she would be, up on the fourth floor cleaning an empty apartment reeking of marijuana.

The woman looked tired and appeared glad to shut off the vacuum cleaner she was using when Nina called out to her, and especially glad when Nina removed fifty dollars from her wallet and placed the cash in front of the woman.

"Please tell me whatever you know about Gerald Davis and the woman living with him."

Lisa nodded her agreement. Nina handed her a twenty-dollar bill as incentive to start speaking.

"Mr. Davis, he had bad friends. They come around and make a mess in the apartment. His lady friend, she would get angry at him, and they would argue, have big fights. She pays me to clean up sometimes. I know she worked, but she wasn't respectable."

"What about the young girl that stayed with them? When did she arrive?"

"A few weeks ago. She was unhappy here. She wanted to leave."

"Did she leave?"

Lisa shrugged. "I don't know. Maybe." She eyed the money Nina held out.

Nina handed her the rest of it, certain there wasn't any further information to be gained.

She went back upstairs and waited for Sam Manger.

"Where were you?" he said, turning to her.

"Upstairs talking to the cleaning lady. I didn't find out much though."

"We got hold of the landlord. He was about to evict Davis. He had some useful info. The girlfriend's name is Tiffany Archer. She's a hooker by trade and Davis pimped her. He also called himself a professional gambler, except he wasn't very good at it. He owed some very unsavory people big bucks. We'll be looking for Tiffany and your girl Caroline. I'll let you know when we come up with something."

Nina thanked him and left. Looking over at the super, she was certain he knew more than he'd shared with either her or the police. She decided to return and see him again offering a financial incentive.

As to who killed Gerald Davis, obviously he was a shady character who made enemies. Loan sharks could get very nasty if they weren't paid. Then there was the girlfriend who Lisa said fought with him. And what about Caroline? Where had she gone? What did she know?

The following afternoon, Nina was on the phone with Sam Manger. He had more information to impart.

"Gerald Davis took a bullet in the heart. Death was quick."

"Did you find the murder weapon?"

"No, the apartment was clean. Not even a spent bullet casing. Have to wait for the M.E.'s report for further details. We'll get more once we pick up Tiffany Archer."

NINA PUT THE case on the back burner for the time being. She had other clients to contend with and the Lester case had turned into a serious police matter. She and Bob were more comfortable with divorce cases, getting the goods on cheating husbands or wives. However, her latest concerned a podiatrist who was being sued by a patient who claimed her feet had been crippled by his treatments. The podiatrist had foolishly allowed his insurance to lapse.

Nina sat opposite the woman's Brooklyn home and waited. Several hours later, she was rewarded by the sight of said patient walking gingerly down her driveway to pick up the mail in her box at the curb. Nina captured it all with her phone camera.

"Gotcha!" she whispered, content no jury was going to award that faker the huge damages she was seeking.

Nina returned to the agency satisfied with herself for a job well-done. She had intended to tell Bob about it, but the phone was ringing in her office, and she rushed to answer it. It turned out to be Sam Manger.

"We got Tiffany. I'm inviting you to sit in and listen to the interrogation."

"I'll be right there," she said.

Since this wasn't Manger's precinct, he joined Nina behind the one-way mirror glass. Tiffany Archer appeared to be in her middle to late thirties. She wore heavy make-up, a short skirt with a tight cropped top and had shoulder length hair of garish green.

The questioning started slow and basic at first. The female detective in charge was an African American homicide detective. Like Nina, she wore her hair cut short and dressed conservatively.

Manger observed Nina studying the policewoman. He leaned over and whispered. "St. Croix is good. Wait and see."

"Ms. Archer, did you shoot Gerald Davis?"

Tiffany nearly jumped out of her chair, a startled expression on her pale face. "Hell, no! Why would I?"

"Because you were overheard arguing with him," St. Croix said.

"Look, we did argue about money. Gerry owed people. He also hadn't paid rent for the last three months even though I contributed my share. He had this gambling problem. Naturally, I got angry."

"How angry?" St. Croix's eyes were intense.

Tiffany squirmed. "I'd forgiven him. Gerry said he got several thousand dollars from his cousin for letting her daughter stay with us for a while. He planned to get her a few gigs. Said the people he owed would accept the girl in trade. Otherwise, we'd have to skip town, maybe head to Vegas."

"Davis planned to pimp his cousin's daughter?"

"Well, yeah, I guess." Tiffany worried her lower lip.

"Did the girl happen to hear this?"

"She was in the spare bedroom at the time. She might have overheard us. We were kind of loud."

Nina sat up straight. Likely Caroline did overhear their conversation and was naturally petrified.

"What happened after that? Did the cousin confront Davis?"

"No, but she wasn't in the room in the morning. Her clothes and suitcase were gone. Gerry and I figured she must have cut out during the night while we were sleeping. He was upset. We ended up arguing again. I slammed the door. Got out of there."

"When you left, Davis was alive?"

"Absolutely," Tiffany said.

"Was that the last time you saw him alive?"

She gave a quick nod.

"Do you know who killed him?"

Tiffany looked down. "I don't know, but it wasn't me."

"What about those people who he owed money? We need names."

She shook her head hard from side to side. Scared now. "I've told you everything I know."

"We need more."

"Those people, they're dangerous. They could kill me."

"We could offer witness protection in exchange for testimony."

Tiffany shook her head more vehemently. "I don't know their names."

Nina was certain she was lying. Could tell that Detective St. Croix was of a similar opinion. But this wasn't her case or her problem. Nina reminded herself that she still had to find Caroline for Mrs. Lester. That was what she had been paid to do. The girl remained missing. New York was a big, dangerous city. A young girl like Caroline without much in the way of street smarts could really be in trouble. The whole case was starting to feel more than just a job. Nina was worried about the girl.

SEVERAL DAYS LATER, Nina finally caught a break. The call came from Sam Manger. Not a surprise.

"I thought this would interest you. A woman came into the local precinct claiming a young girl had fallen in front of her shop and hit her head on the concrete. She called her son who worked with her and the two of them helped the kid—bleeding from where she hit her head and barely conscious, into the shop. The girl's description sounds like the one you gave us: blond teenager, slim, about eighteen. Anyway, the woman, Frances Dennis, claims the girl can't seem to remember much of anything. Dennis's shop is in the

East Village. This happened about a week ago. Corresponds with your girl's disappearance. Want the address?"

"Does it snow in the mountains? Of course, I want the address, and thanks."

As it turned out, Mrs. Dennis's shop sold antiques. It was small but interesting. Frances Dennis was fiftyish and plump. Her son looked to be about twenty-five or so and well-muscled.

Nina sat down with Frances Dennis while her son tended the shop.

"I got some of the story already. But where is the girl? Is she here?"

Frances nodded. "Upstairs, in the apartment over our shop."

"She's suffering from memory loss? Amnesia?"

"I guess so. I took her to our family doctor. He said she had a mild concussion, that her memory should start coming back soon. It's been over a week. I thought it was best to check with the police and see if anyone filed a missing person's report on her."

"Good thinking. She didn't have any I.D. with her?"

"There was a suitcase, but some fellow came along and grabbed that and her purse before we got to her. It happened fast."

"Nothing coming back to her as of yet?"

"She says not. If her family is reaching out, that would be great. I'll get her for you."

Nina waited impatiently glancing at the various antiques on display to try and distract herself.

Finally, Frances returned followed by the blond teenager. Nina identified herself and asked the girl to join her.

"Let's step outside," she said. "I think we need to talk privately."

The girl followed her silently.

"There's a coffee shop on the corner. My treat," Nina said.

It was an off-hour and Nina was relieved to see there were few customers. The girl appeared anxious, still not speaking at all. Once they were seated and had their orders in hand, Nina began.

"Are you Caroline Lester?"

The young girl remained silent, twirling the spoon in her coffee. Nina studied her. It seemed as if the girl had something to hide.

"You do remember who you are, don't you, Caroline." Nina was careful to make her words a flat statement rather than an accusation or a question. She recognized this was a delicate situation.

Again, no response. Nina poured a sachet of sugar into her own coffee, tried once more, "At least tell me your name."

"All right, yes, I'm Caroline." For the first time their eyes met.

"Why didn't you tell Mrs. Dennis?"

"Because they'd send me back to Gerald." Caroline burst into tears.

"What if you could go somewhere else?"

"Where? No one wants me. My mother dumped me on Gerald, gave him some money to take care of me. But I heard him tell Tiffany that he was going to prostitute me like he did her."

"So, you ran away?"

"Yes, that night while they were asleep. I packed my bag and ran for it. The trouble was, I hardly had any money. I wandered around, mostly lost because I don't know the city. I didn't have any idea where to go. I wanted to return to my school, but I don't suppose I belong there anymore either." Caroline took a long sip of her coffee and swallowed hard. "Mama got regular alimony payments, except she was forgetful about paying my tuition. The two sisters who ran the school tried to get in touch with Mama, but she traveled around a lot. Things were all right though for a while, because the sisters liked me, and I was helpful. I'd been a good student. I helped teach the younger girls. I made myself useful. You might say I earned my tuition and board. It was all fine until Mama finally decided to send a check. The sisters wrote back that it wasn't necessary since I was working at the school, and I'd finished high school graduation requirements. They wanted to know if Mama was going to send me to college. Mama got upset and came for me. But then she didn't know what to do with me since she planned on going away. She wants to marry the guy she's with now. A wealthy guy just like Mr. Lester."

Nina saw how lost and forlorn the girl was and felt sorry for her. "So, you wanted to stay with Mrs. Dennis?"

"Yes, she's been so nice, and so is her son. They've been generous, buying stuff for me, clothes to wear. I didn't really fake losing my memory, not exactly. My head hurt bad at first. I was confused, really thirsty, hungry. I'm not even certain if I fell or someone pushed me down."

"The man who stole your purse and suitcase?"

Caroline nodded. "I think so."

"You realize you have to tell Mrs. Dennis and her son the truth. You can't just stay here indefinitely. The current Mrs. Lester hired me to find you. I want to take you to see her."

"Mr. Lester can't stand the sight of me." Caroline's lower lip trembled.

"He may be ill-tempered, but he's had time to calm down."

"What about Gerald?" Nina saw the fearful expression come over Caroline's face.

"He's dead. Someone murdered him."

Caroline's eyes opened wide. The look of surprise appeared genuine.

"Let's talk with Mrs. Dennis and then go over and speak with the Lesters, okay?"

SHARON LESTER HUGGED Caroline fiercely and blinked away tears.

"I'm so grateful you were able to find her, Ms. Harris. You're a miracle worker."

"Hardly that," Nina said. "I had help from the N.Y.P.D. When I phoned earlier, you said your husband would be here as well?"

"That's right. He's in his study. Always working even when he's home. I'll get him."

"I'm scared," Caroline said to Nina. "I shouldn't be here."

"You absolutely should be here," Nina said, giving the girl a gentle pat on the shoulder.

Kevin Lester strode into the room, glanced at Caroline and then frowned at Nina. "Why is she here?"

"You're legally considered to be Caroline's father. Don't you think it's time you took a paternity test and found out for certain."

"I don't consider it necessary," Lester said. His expression that of a pit bull ready to bite.

Nina didn't plan to back down. She suddenly wondered if Lester had anything to do with Gerald Davis's death. Davis could have tried to hit him up for money. According to Tiffany Archer, he was desperate for money.

"You've heard about the murder of Gerald Davis I presume?"

Kevin and Sharon Lester exchanged long looks.

"We read about it," Sharon said in a guarded voice.

"Did he try to extort money from you?"

"What if he did?" Kevin Lester responded angrily. "I wouldn't give that vulture a single red cent. Michelle has taken alimony from me for years. I'm sick and tired of that family."

"So, you went to his apartment and shot him?"

"What? No, I did not. Don't be so utterly ridiculous." Lester's face had turned as red as a rare roast. "I'm going to ask you to leave and take that girl with you."

"Absolutely not," Sharon said. "I've never stood up to you, Kevin. You can be a bully, but I'm drawing the line about this. You get that paternity test. Let's find out if your DNA is a match. If you don't, I'll leave you. Caroline deserves better, and so do I."

Mrs. Lester went to Caroline and placed her arms protectively around the girl.

"Very well," Lester said, backing down.

NINA KNOCKED ON the door to her husband's office.

"Bob, are you busy?"

"Not, now. Come in, sweetheart."

"I brought coffee and donuts," she said.

Bob greeted her with a big smile. "What's the occasion? You usually say I shouldn't have donuts because it's bad for my cholesterol."

"Well, it is, but I'm celebrating. I received a very generous check from Sharon Lester today. She included a note."

"What did it say?" Bob asked, as he grabbed a chocolate cream donut and took a big bite out of it.

"Sharon said the DNA test proved her husband *is* Caroline's father. She's his only child. He's now accepted her and will be paying her college tuition."

"Good news," Bob said through a mouthful of donut. "And while we're on the subject of good news, Sam Manger called while you were out of the office. He said they got Gerald Davis's killer. They leaned on Tiffany Archer to get the name of the loan shark Davis owed bigtime. Turns out his enforcer got over-zealous. Tiffany is going into witness protection. She'll be called on to give testimony at the trial."

"Like Shakespeare said: All's well that ends well." Nina said smacking her husband's hand when he tried to grab the last donut, snatching it up herself and taking a bite. Bob saluted her with his coffee cup and winked. And then the telephone rang.

ALL GONE

by

Gordon J. Brown

"OKAY, YOU TAKE first shift with the shovel," the professor says.

He focuses his torch beam in front of the cutting blade. I plunge the spade into the grass.

"Clear the turf first and then we'll dig out the earth," he orders.

I make a second cut. He bends down to lever up the sod and I slice the section free before he throws it to one side.

"See, Kevin," he says. "Piece of piss."

"Piece of piss, professor. Really? It's two in the morning. It's raining like an open tap. We're in a cemetery, digging up a grave. A piece of piss *isn't* the way I'd frame what we're doing."

IT WAS MY dog that found the headstone. We often walk through the old Cathcart Cemetery, Jonty and I. Him sprinting ahead to sniff at some random, but dog interesting, bush or stone. Me trailing behind, head in the clouds, feet of lead. Jonty is a mongrel's mongrel. A product of a thousand generations of indiscriminate canine sex. If there's a scale that runs pedigree to mutt, Jonty is the benchmark for the non-pedigree end. And that's why my dog and I get on so well. Him a combination of scraggy coat, twisted ears and a tail that points three ways at once. Me a scraggy coat, twisted ears and hair that points a *million* ways at once.

"Get out of there, Jonty." I shout, knowing it'll have no effect on his actions, but you need to pretend you're in control; don't you?

Jonty has a predilection for poo that bounds on the incredulous. He's inexorably drawn to the substance and, around here, late-night revellers

357

provide plenty of samples of the human variety for him to sniff. If I don't get him out quick he's apt to roll in the stuff. I jog over and try to snatch at his collar, but he's buried deep in a bush.

"Jonty, if you come out stinking of shit, I'll throw you in the river on the way home, I bloody promise."

In response he pushes further in. There's a gravestone between him and I. It's the resting place of a George Blake and his wife, Mary; both cold and below ground since 1882. There are older graves than George and his spouse's around here, but not many. I step over the grave, apologising to Mr and Mrs Blake for the intrusion, and pull away at the bushes to reach Jonty. Thick and unyielding, the undergrowth makes me wonder who in the heck forced their way through it to vent their bowels. You'd need an industrial chain saw to get to where Jonty is snuffling around.

"Just get your skinny backside out here," I snarl.

A lady, out walking a five-star labradoodle, *hrrmphs* at me and I turn, giving her a crooked smile. With a shrug of my shoulders I utter, "Dogs."

She walks on, nose in the air.

"Look, you pain in the tonsils, just get out of there," I growl, turning back to the bush.

With no response, I opt to move around to the far side where the foliage is a little thinner. In the late evening light I can just see the outline of Jonty. I stick my head into the bush and begin to wriggle my way towards him. Twigs and branches scratch at my hand and I've almost reached him when, with a bark, he backs off and escapes.

"I swear..." I shout, without finishing the sentence.

I try to reverse out, but my twenty plus year old C&A duffle coat snags on some thorns. I pull at the material, but the coat is stuck fast. I hear Jonty run off.

"Stay, Jonty. Stay," I shout.

My words will have the same effect as trying to stop a runaway double-decker bus with a stick of candy floss.

I shuffle back into the thicket to try to loosen the tension between the thorns and my jacket. I trip, tumble forward; my forehead planting hard on stone. Flopping to the ground, head deep in the bush, I fumble around and push my face out of the earth; the rotting smell of damp leaves filling my nose. As I reach up for support, my hand touches the stone I've just headbutted. Struggling backwards, my eyes are presented with a well-hidden gravestone. Thick with moss and dirt, it's small—less than two feet high; maybe eighteen inches wide. As I use it to lever myself up, barbs, spikes and spurs grab at my clothes and skin. It's as if I'm being pinned down by the undergrowth. Cursing Jonty, my eyes, level with the middle of the stone, catch a single word etched into the surface.

"GONE"

Above it there are some scratches, maybe letters, but the light is too poor to be sure. I twist and turn, hearing a few rips from the ancient wool of my coat as I begin to break free. A last branch holds me, snagged in my hood. A hand pinning me in place, my face a few inches from the ancient carved stone. For a moment I'm scared that I'm not getting free. That the branch is hell bent on holding me here. I throw myself back and, with a snap, the limb breaks. I roll across the bare earth.

Jonty runs up, licking my face.

At least his tongue doesn't smell of crap.

That night, as I collapse into goggle-box mode, Jonty at my feet, Glencairn Glass in my hand, well-filled with a decent malt—my mind wanders back to the gravestone.

"GONE"

Makes perfect sense when you think about it. It's hard to think of a better word to describe those that are laying in their last resting place. I assume there will be a more illuminating inscription on the far side of the stone; names, dates, epitaph and the like.

I try to tune into the telly but something about the gravestone haunts me. A simple thought that worries itself into a repeating cycle. *Who is gone? Who is gone?* The stone was lost to the vegetation. Impossible to see from any point around it.

Hidden.

Lost.

"GONE"

Who is gone?

Two days later the question will not be shifted. There are hundreds of graves in the cemetery and none have ever held any more than a passing interest for me. Sometimes a name catches my attention. Dates that talk to a long life. Words causing pause with their beauty. None of these, though, hold me for more than a moment. Except this grave. The branch that snagged me, the hand of the dead holding me close to the stone's cold bosom, planting a virus. A nasty little bug that has wormed its way into the core of my skull. Interrupting the workings of my brain.

Who is gone?

By day four I give in and return to the cemetery, Jonty in tow, a pair of secateurs in my pocket.

It's late afternoon, the cemetery is at its quietest, people reluctant to be caught in here once the sun dies. I climb to the spot where the gravestone lies and work my way back around to the rear. Finding the break in the bush where I'd crawled from, I get to work with the secateurs. Jonty is no longer interested in whatever it was he had smelt here. He digs at some leaf litter a few yards away as I start to cut the undergrowth around the gravestone.

It takes a few minutes to carve out a hole big enough to allow me to better examine the stone. The single word sits square in the middle and I can now see that the scratches above it are three letters, scored into the rock as capitals.

A L L

Beneath them a crude arrow, also scratched into the surface, points down.

I lean over to examine the far side of the stone, flipping on my phone's torchlight. The stone on the other face is dressed, but lacks any inscriptions. I root around at the base in case the earth is hiding some words, my stomach resting on the top of the gravestone. Nothing. I pull back and shine the light on the single word. Run off a few photos and move back, standing up. *Who would bury someone with a single word? And who scored the letters above it? And the arrow? What's with the arrow?*

I stand, a chilled wind zipping through the trees around me. Jonty nuzzles at my legs, breaking the spell. I look down and he's all but invisible. I shake my head. Around me is darkness. How long have I been standing here? I check my phone. Somehow, I've lost nearly an hour. I use the torch light to navigate out of the cemetery as quickly as I can.

Who is gone?

The next day I decide a little bit of detective work is the order of the day.

My first port of call is the local council, but it seems records on the dead's last resting place are thin on the ground. Certainly no one by the name of Gone is recorded in the registry of deaths—so I'm informed after a few phone calls. The free websites allowing me to search cemeteries, graveyards and crematoriums yield nothing useful. The ones wanting money to gain access go unsearched. My part time job at the local Sainsbury's doesn't allow me the luxury of unwarranted subscriptions.

I should just let it go, but I can't and, after another fruitless wander through the world-wide-web, I turn to my go-to font of knowledge, the Couper Institute Library. Less than a mile from the cemetery, its glass domed ceiling and ancient wood panelling have been a place of respite and escapism for me since my first days of Primary School.

After my Friday morning shift at the supermarket, I enter the library to enquire about books on local history. Specifically, about Cathcart Cemetery. I'm told there's a local *friends of* society I could contact. I'd stumbled on their website yesterday and have earmarked them for an email if the library proves a busted flush.

I know a little about the cemetery already. For instance, it was opened in 1878 on a greenfield site to the south of Glasgow to replace the older cemetery a few miles further north. The site was designed by William R. McKelvie of Dundee. A man whose expertise in such areas was "unequalled in Scotland". The librarian asks what my interest is in the cemetery, and I tell her about the grave marked GONE. She smiles, asks if I can wait a minute, then vanishes into the back office to reappear, a few minutes later, pamphlet in hand. She passes it to me.

"This might help." she says, still smiling.

It's title, in dark ink, is intriguing.

Alicia Gone, Serial Killer?

The pamphlet is authored by a Professor James Taylor.

I take it through to the reading room where a set of chairs and tables are laid out for the public to use. Some are weighed down with computers; allowing access to the internet for the digitally challenged. There is a lone occupant, an elderly man, sitting at the table nearest the entrance, reading a copy of the Daily Record. He looks up and nods at me as I enter.

I drop into a seat and place the pamphlet in front of me. Above the title is the photograph of a woman. An old black and white portrait from the days when full evening dress was the garb of choice for such sittings. She's sitting next to a large potted plant and behind her is a screen of scenes from China. The woman is slightly side on to the camera, her legs totally hidden by a voluminous skirt that rises up to a pinch at a miniscule waist. A blouse with overblown sleeves and a ruffled neck are topped off with a face that is more scowl than smile. She could be pretty but her face is set hard, almost in a grimace, warping her features. She has a tight bun of hair to the back of her head and is resting both hands on her lap.

Opening the pamphlet to the first page provides me with a brief biography on the professor. He's from Glasgow University and a chemist; although he has a private interest in forensics and crime. The pamphlet is dated some twenty years back. On the second page is a simple paragraph.

If you are reading this, let me assume that you have stumbled upon the gravestone in Cathcart Cemetery with the word GONE inscribed upon it. If you want to know more— read on.

And I do.

An hour later I spin back through the pages and re-read parts. The opening section is almost a mirror to my own blossoming obsession with the grave. The big difference being I've only spent a few days trying to crack the small mystery, whereas the professor spent some two years. The pamphlet, forty-five pages in length, is academic in nature and lean on anything but facts. Professor Taylor doesn't do waffle.

Alicia Gone was born in 1878 to John and Victoria Gone. An only child, she was brought up in the coastal town of Dunoon in a home overlooking the firth of Clyde. Professor Taylor was unable to find much about Alicia's childhood other than she left home at eighteen to take up a job as a junior secretary with a shipping firm based in the centre of Glasgow. It was there, two years later, she met Allan Wardthrope, a clerk in a rival shipping firm. Allan was the son of the company's owner. His father, a wealthy Glaswegian, had insisted his offspring learned the business from the bottom up, hence the son's role as a clerk. Alicia and Allan married on Saturday the 4th of June, 1898, at Govan Old Parish Church.

In 1905 Allan vanished, never to be seen again. At this point in the pamphlet the professor has inserted a series of pages taken from the notebook of a Detective Constable McAdam. The professor points out it was only a year earlier that the Glasgow police had appointed their first Chief Inspector of Detectives and the first Detective Constables—all based at Turnbull Street, near Glasgow's historic centre. When the professor had contacted the police museum, by then located in the same building DC McAdam used to work in, they had kindly unearthed McAdam's police notebooks for him. The professor has lifted what he considers are the key pages from the notes.

August 19th, in the year of our Lord, 1905.

'I interviewed Mrs Alicia Wardthrope (née Gone) at her home on Aikenhead Road the day after she reported her husband (Allan Wardthrope) missing. She is a lady of severe manner and given to few words. Her demeanour did not, in my opinion, sit well with that of a lady whose husband had left suddenly, and with no warning. She explained that she had been taking tea with her friends at the Willow Tea Rooms the previous Saturday and had returned home to discover her husband, who had told her he was going to spend the afternoon reading in the garden, to be gone. She pointed out that a small suitcase he used for business trips was missing, as was a quantity of clothes and toiletries. She also said that a safe, that lay in the drawing room, had been emptied. When I asked her as to why it had taken near on a full week to report her husband missing she informed me that he regularly left for business trips at short notice. It seemed odd to me that a Saturday would be a day for an unplanned business trip. In addition, Mr Wardthrope had not left a note as to his whereabouts. Mrs Wardthrope did not seem unduly worried that her husband had not returned in the intervening days between him leaving and her reporting it. I asked if she had contacted Mr Wardthrope's place of work or his father. She said she had not; pointing out that her husband pointedly forbade her from any contact with his place of employment or his father, without his express permission. I was allowed to search the home of Mr and Mrs Wardthrope and I also examined the safe. Everything seemed in order, maybe a little too so. The smell of cleaning products and lack of dust suggested that the home had been recently cleaned, and done so thoroughly. I concluded by asking what had been in the safe. Mrs Wardthrope shook her head and told me she had no idea. I left with a promise to investigate further. I reported the incident to the Chief Inspector who, in no uncertain terms, informed me that wandering husbands were to be low down on my priority list.'

There was more on the disappearance of Allan in the pamphlet. Allan's father, the owner of Wardthrope Shipping, had employed a private firm called Makepeace and Simon to undertake enquiries when it was clear that the police were drawing a blank. The only matter of note they discovered was a one-way rail ticket to London that had been purchased in the name of Wardthrope for the Saturday afternoon of Allan's disappearance. This purchase had been ordered over the telephone some days earlier and the ticket collected by a gentleman roughly fitting Allan's description fifteen minutes before the train departed. But, when the Detective had shown a photo of Allan to the ticket attendant, the attendant could not confirm if it was or wasn't Allan who had collected the ticket. Further investigations in London proved fruitless.

Another extract from McAdam's notes concludes Allan's story. It reads,

August 29th, in the year of our Lord, 1905

'Having investigated further into the disappearance of Mr Wardthrope, against my superior's wishes, I now understand that, although Mrs Wardthrope indicated she was unaware of the contents of the safe, I have ascertained that there had been substantial gifts of money from father to son over the years. When confronted with this information, Mrs Wardthrope claimed she had been left in poverty by her husband's disappearance. 'If there had been money left by Allan, Constable, you would not find me here eating bread and drinking water. New York is where I would go. And since I'm here, not there, there is no money.'

The professor noted that Alicia, under the Presumption of Life Limitation (Scotland) Act, 1881, would've been required to wait seven years to have Allan declared legally dead—but she never did. Instead, she made the inside pages of a local newspaper by asking a Mr Lionel Morlock to move in with her two years after Allan had vanished. Lionel was a recent widower whose wife was the heiress to a large estate in Stewarton. By recently widowed, we're talking very recent. Lionel buried his wife on the Monday and shacked up with Alicia on the Tuesday.

Given the title of the pamphlet it was of little surprise to me that Lionel also vanished. Another note from DC McAdam summarises the circumstances:

December 5th, in the year of our Lord, 1907

'I interviewed Mrs Wardthrope in an interview room at Turnbull Street on the Thursday morning. Having visited her home, the day before, I was not comfortable with the answers she had provided. Mrs Wardthrope was a little put out at the request to come to the station and arrived with her lawyer, Mr Alistair Tore. Mr Tore is more than a little well known to myself and the other Detective Constables I work with. The circumstances of Mr Morlock's disappearance have uncanny similarities to those of Mr Wardthrope's. Mrs Wardthrope was taking tea at the Willow Tea Rooms and returned to discover Mr Morlock was missing. On this occasion, Mrs Wardthrope waited three

days to report the disappearance. She pointed out that he was a man who liked fishing and was of a mind to take to the sport at short notice. It is true that no fishing tackle or clothing could be found on the premises and Mrs Wardthrope assured me that the spare room was usually full of such material. Two questions raise themselves in my mind time and time again. The first question is simple. Was it not highly unlikely to lose a second partner in such a manner? This question was dismissed by Mrs Wardthrope in an almost casual manner. 'Maybe it was me?' she had said. I had jumped on this phrase, but she insisted she did not mean she had killed them, rather that she was the cause of them leaving. Both men having grown tired of her. The second question related to a missing sum of money. It is important to note that the Stewarton house, that Mr Morlock had inherited from his late wife, was sold barely a month before Mr Morlock vanished. It fetched some Two Thousand Eight Hundred Pounds Stirling, of which Mrs Wardthrope claims she saw none. She, once more, told me that if she had been left any money she would surely be in New York.

Dig as he might DC McAdam could find no evidence of foul play, although the professor noted it was clear the Detective Constable was convinced of Alicia's involvement in both disappearances.

Mrs Wardthrope's final 'victim' was a Mr Gerald Stuart, a prominent business leader in the Glasgow community and man of considerable means. It was rumoured that Geoffrey could count himself amongst the ten richest people in the city. A man of many relationships, Gerald moved Alicia into his mansion in the village of Eaglesham, some ten miles south of the city, in the late summer of 1910.

Gerald lasted until 1911, when he too vanished. DC McAdam undertook the investigation and, by all accounts, this was a far more in-depth enquiry as Gerald had taken to the wind in the same manner as his two predecessors.

September 27th, in the year of our Lord, 1911

Once more I find myself in the interview room at Turnbull Street with Mrs Wardthrope and her lawyer. On this occasion the Chief Inspector joined me. We have the same circumstances to deal with as the last two disappearances. Mrs Wardthrope taking tea, Mr Stuart absent on her return and some confusion over monies. On this occasion Mrs Wardthrope informed us of Mr Stuart's regular trips to a cottage in the Highlands. Again, her partner had given no indication he was leaving and once more a travel bag was missing. I searched the home, a massive sprawling building, from top to bottom and stumbled upon a trapdoor in the pantry, under which was a locked strong box. Mrs Wardthrope claimed to have no knowledge of the box but a maid, Miss Mandy Caldwell, told me that she had seen Mr Stuart place 'a lot of money' in the box on numerous occasions. With some effort I forced the lock and found the box to be empty.

After two hours of questioning we had little to hold Mrs Wardthrope on. When she left, the Chief Inspector made it abundantly clear to me that he believed in her guilt and that if I couldn't find the evidence required to convict her, then I would be relieved. It did not help that Mrs Wardthrope's last words, as she left the interview room, were to inform us that had Mr Stuart left her any money she would now be in New York sipping champagne.

McAdam visited the Highland cottage to find it empty and unused for some time. The last page of the pamphlet contains—as all good mysteries should—a twist, in that it has a copy of Alicia's death certificate, dated 3rd of March 1912. The cause of death is noted as Cerebral Haemorrhage. Alicia was buried in Cathcart Cemetery on Monday the 4th March 1912. The author describes the burial as 'a quiet ceremony attended by a few close friends and one Detective Constable McAdam'.

The professor mentions the single word on the gravestone but makes no guess as to why such a brief inscription was placed on the stone. By all accounts Alicia was buried under her married name which is why I could find no record of her death.

I push the pamphlet away and, far from being satisfied I've got to the bottom of the whole thing, I'm left frustrated. I stare at her photo. *Did you do it, Alicia? Did you kill those men? And why the single word on your grave? And what about those initials and the arrow?*

For the next few days the story of Alicia Wardthrope whirls in my head. A full load on spin. I can finger no reason why this has grabbed me in such a way. *Why does it matter what happened over a hundred years ago?* And yet it does. Not least, because if Alicia died suddenly, who had commissioned the grave stone? Of course, Alicia might have commissioned her own stone, but wouldn't someone else have at least added dates before it was set in the ground?

It takes me a week before deciding to contact Professor Taylor; unsure if he is still a professor, still at Glasgow University or still alive—the internet informs me he is all three. I call the main switchboard from my mobile, while standing in the loading bay outside my work. I'm put through to the professor. He agrees to meet me at the Tinderbox Café on Byres Road that Saturday afternoon.

Having borrowed the pamphlet from the library, I re-read it on the bus as I travel to meet the professor.

"Hi," I say, as I sit down across from him in the cafe. "My name's Kevin."

He was easy to spot, *"A BOF wearing a white jacket."* He had said on the phone. *"A BOF?"* *'Yes'* he'd replied. *"Bald old and fat."*

"Hi Kevin, coffee?"

"Black Americano," I say. He rises, crosses to the café bar and orders up my drink.

Once he is back, my coffee in hand, he asks me, "So what can I do for you?"

His manner is easy, his speech soft, his eyes watery.

"This," I say placing the pamphlet on the table.

He sits down, "So you said on the phone. But what about it? Do you want to know if I think she was guilty?"

"No, it's not that, but, since you ask, do you?"

He sips at his coffee, coating his upper lip in froth. He doesn't wipe it away.

"I can't say for certain but, if you add it all up, she *had* to have something to do with it." He pauses before speaking again, "But if it wasn't that you wanted to know, what was it?"

"The stone," I say.

"The gravestone?"

"Yes."

"And why it has that single word on it?"

"Yes."

"Well, for a start it's her maiden name but, more than that, I think Alicia was a bit of a player, Kevin. A real little devil. My one thought was that she arranged that inscription."

"Why?"

"Because she was Alicia. I wrote a pamphlet, but I could have written a novel. There were all sorts of rumours about affairs, lies and all sorts in her life. She seemed fully centred on herself, with no regard to others. And, despite her protestations about having no money, she lived a good life, even when she had no partner. I'd guess she was cocking a snook at McAdam with that epitaph. Telling him that she was gone and that was that."

"And the other markings on the stone?"

"What other markings?"

"Scratched in above the word GONE. There are three capital letters, A L and L and there's an arrow below them."

I pull out my phone and show him the letters and the arrow.

He smiles as he studies the photo "That is new. Those weren't there when I last looked."

"What do they stand for?"

"That's easy. Alicia Lidia Longannet. That was her full name. A L L are her initials."

"And the arrow?"

"Not a clue."

"But who would have scratched them into the stone."

"No idea. Maybe someone else has been looking into her story. I get the odd call on it, but you are the first person that has asked to see me."

I sit back and we drink our coffee in silence.

"Although," he says, a few moments later. "A L and L. Now that is a little odd."

"What is?"

"It's certainly Alicia's initials but it's also the initials of the first names of her husband and partners who vanished."

"No, it's not," I say. "There was Allan, Lionel and Gerald. That's A L G."

"True, but something I didn't put in the pamphlet was that for some reason Alicia called Gerald by his middle name, Les. McAdam said she used it a lot when talking about him. Allan, Lionel and Les. A L and L."

"And the arrow?"

The professor smiles again. "Oh my."

"WHY ARE WE doing this," I say, as I dig into the earth.

"You want to solve the riddle of Alicia and if she killed those men. Don't you?"

"But professor, digging up a grave?"

It had been the constant texts from him that had finally worn me down. That and my dumb obsession. You'd think agreeing to dig up a century old body would be the matter of a deranged mind. And that's probably true. I was surprisingly easy to persuade. A tarpaulin to hide the light of our torches. The stone buried deep in the cemetery, where few would venture this late at night. The pouring rain to keep even the nutters out of the way. The professor's insistence that it would take no time at all. And me, with a head that wouldn't let Alicia lie.

"Just dig, and be quick," he says.

It isn't quick. Once the bushes and turf are gone the earth is hard packed, but we spell each other on the shovel. Me expecting, every second, the voice of a policeman to pipe up and ask what we are doing.

The clunk is almost comical when it happens. Spade on wood? So clichéd. The professor digs some more and then starts scraping loose earth away, standing to one side of the coffin lid as it reveals itself.

"She was buried in solid oak, if I remember correctly," he says. "But I'm still surprised it's lasted so well. Kevin, give me a hand to clear off the dirt from the lid."

I jump into the hole and we scrape away but, as we do so, the loose earth slides back into place, the rain turning it to mud. I take the spade from the professor saying, "This will take too long. The mud is beating us."

I raise the shovel high and bring it down hard on the lid. It cracks; a rift along the length of the lid appearing. I repeat and the crack widens. Stuffing the shovel's snout into the split, I stand on the handle, push down, and a large chuck of coffin lid flies up. We both freeze.

The professor moves first, shining his torch down into the coffin.

"Is she there?" I say.

He bends over. "No."

"No?"

I lean in to have a look.

Four black boxes are buried in loose earth within the coffin, all in a neat row. Each box is about a foot square. The earth inside the coffin is dry. There is no body. No bones. Just earth and the boxes.

"What's in them?" I ask.

The professor reaches down and pulls the first box out. It's made of dark wood. There's a catch on the top, holding a lid in place. It's rusty but, when the professor pushes at it, it breaks free. He cradles the box in one arm and lifts the lid. I jump back, as does he.

"That's a skull," I say.

The professor regains composure and shines the torch's beam into the box. A yellow tinged skull nestles in some cloth inside.

"Look," he says in a quiet tone.

Carved in the forehead of the skull is a single letter, A.

"Allan?" I suggest.

He puts the box down, doing his best to shield it from the rainwater pouring into the grave. He picks up the second box and springs the lock. Another skull. This one has an L on it.

"Lionel or Gerald," he says.

"And the next box, if you don't mind, sir," I say, thinking this would be a hell of game show.

A third skull lies within the next box, the letter L scored into the bone.

"Well that explains the initials and the arrow," the professor says. "Clearly someone else figured Alicia buried the men in here. The arrow was just their way of saying 'This way lies A L and L'."

"She buried *part* of the men," I correct him.

"She did that, but whoever thought they were in here wasn't prepared to dig up the coffin to confirm it."

"I wonder why?" I say.

The professor smiles.

We look down at the last box.

"Alicia?" I suggest.

"Could be."

The professor pulls the box out. This time the lock holds firm.

"Hang onto this," he says, handing me the box.

He pulls a pen knife from his pocket and jams one of the blades into the space between the lock and the wood. He levers it and the lock snaps. He pockets the knife before opening the lid.

There's no skull.

But it's not empty. The professor reaches in and removes a pouch about the size of a normal letter.

"Looks like it is made of leather," he says.

"Where's Alicia?" I ask.

"Not here, that's for sure."

"But there's a death certificate."

"And there was a funeral, but not hers. Knowing Alicia, she set it all up."

"How?"

"I suspect that a little money to a corrupt doctor for his help with the certificate, a little cash to a bent undertaker and a few pounds of soil in the coffin to weigh it down, would all add up to one fake death."

He opens the pouch and, keeping his head over it to prevent it from getting wet, he extracts a piece of paper. From this angle I can't read it but he can.

He studies it and places the paper back in the wallet, laughing.

"What?" I say. "What is it?"

He recovers after a moment. 'Put the box down and look for yourself, but make sure you keep the paper dry.'

He hands me the paper. I focus my torch light on it. As I do so the professor reminds me, "Remember Alicia kept saying if she had the money that she would be in New York?"

I nod, open the piece of folded paper and read it.

It is a yellowing receipt, and reads:

Received the Sum of Forty-Two Pounds and Seven Shillings for a First-Class Ticket, One-Way Only. Sailing Date; Wednesday 10th April, 1912.

"Well," the professor says, laughing again. "Maybe Alicia made it to America or, maybe she didn't."

I look at the paper and can't help but join him, laughing. As with Alicia's gravestone, the receipt signs off with three initials and a single word.

RMS Titanic.

ABDUCTOR, ABDUCTEE

by

Mike McHone

IT WAS JUST before midnight when Molly Fetterly slipped into bed, closed her eyes, and, of course, heard the ring of her cellphone. "Shit." That was the worst thing about being on-call. Sometimes people actually called.

She reached over, turned on the light, and grabbed her cell off the nightstand. Jim's number lit up the touchscreen. "Hell—" She yawned. "Hello."

"You asleep?" Detective Jim Biggins asked.

"At this hour? God, no. Don't be ridiculous."

"I could use your help down here at the Gas and Go station on West First."

"Put the hose in the tank, swipe your debit card, and fill it up. Are we good?"

"Quit goofing around and get down here, would you?"

"All right, relax. I'll be there in…" Another yawn. "Be there in twenty."

THIRTY MINUTES LATER, a patrol officer lifted the yellow caution tape to the gas station entrance and Molly pulled her Impala into the parking lot. Jim stood beside a white BMW parked at a gas pump, arms folded, a scowl on his face. Molly pulled up behind the Beamer and got out. Jim was polite enough to wait a whole three seconds before he gave her shit. "I thought you said twenty."

"I got caught by a train, for Christ's sake." She slammed her door and walked over. "I left as soon as I could. I didn't even have time to brush my teeth."

"I know. I'm downwind."

"Shut up. Why am I here?"

"There's been an abduction."

"Serious?"

"As a heart attack. About forty-five minutes ago, the owner of the gas station reported the driver of the Beamer got out of the car, and not but a couple two, three seconds later, a tan colored F-150 pickup tore across the lot. He said a tall guy with long, blond hair and a ballcap jumped out, grabbed the woman and sped off."

Molly nodded at the BMW. "Did you run the plates?"

"I didn't have to. The station owner recognized the woman. It's his niece. Jasmine Collins, maiden name Jasmine Antar."

"Antar? As in—"

"Sam Antar's daughter."

An atom bomb would've made less of an impact. "Son of a bitch."

"Like Smokey said, 'I second that emotion.'"

And as if it were on cue, Sam Antar, President of the Midport City Council and CEO of Southeastern Michigan Bank and Trust, stormed out of the gas station. Captain Janet McKart followed behind the man and had to jog to keep up with him. Antar told the captain he wanted every available police officer in a hundred-mile radius dispatched to find his daughter. The man was usually high-strung anyway, but that night he was understandably manic, his arms gesturing wildly. "Everyone, and I mean *everyone* needs to look into this, understand?" Antar said.

"Yes, sir," McKart told him. "We're on it."

"What the hell's Janet doing here?" Molly whispered to Jim.

"She told me Sam called her directly," he answered. "Wanted someone of authority over the department on the scene when he got here. And since the chief is on vacation..."

"When isn't the chief on vacation?"

"Exactly."

"I kinda wish I would've brushed my teeth now."

"Yeah, me too."

"Again, shut up."

Captain McKart and Mr. Antar approached the BMW. "I can assure you, sir, Detectives Fetterly and Biggins are the best we've got," she said. "They'll find your daughter." The Junoesque blonde turned to them, her eyes like hazel-colored rapiers. "Right?"

With zero hesitation, Molly and Jim issued a series of yep's, and you betcha's.

"The best, eh?" Sam Antar said to Molly.

"Uh, yes, sir."

"Tell me, then, what clues have you gathered?"

Molly stammered. "Well... I..."

"Anything? Anything at all?"

"Uh..."

Antar turned to Janet. "The best?" He went back inside the station. Before she followed him, Janet made sure her glare sliced Molly in half.

CHRISTIAN ANTAR, SAM'S younger brother, owned and operated the Gas and Go on the east-side of the city. He had purchased the business only a week prior and ran the station by himself that night after an employee had called in sick. At approximately 11:40 pm, he made a cash drop in the office safe when he noticed the BMW pulling into the lot on the surveillance monitors on his desk. A young woman emerged from the car who looked remarkably like his niece, and when he looked closer at the monitor, he realized that's exactly who it was. He wondered why Jasmine was out at such an hour, but the inquisitiveness morphed into panic because, not three seconds later, a pickup sped into the lot, a man jumped out, grabbed her by the waist and threw her into the cab.

"By the time I got outside," Christian said, his voice breaking. "The truck was already half-way down the road."

"Did you happen to get the license plate?" Jim asked.

"No," he said. "I couldn't see it. It was much too dark. So, I ran inside and called the police and my brother." The five of them, Molly, Jim, both Mr. Antars, and Janet, were crammed into the small office. The younger Antar took a deep breath and sat on the worn leather chair next to the desk. "I'm sorry, Sam. I'm so very sorry. I promise you, I tried to get to her in time! But I just... I just couldn't! It all happened so fast!" His brother knelt beside him and hugged him around the neck. "It's not your fault, Chris."

After a few moments, Christian composed himself. "If I would've known this was such a bad area, I would have never purchased this place to begin with!"

In truth, it wasn't a bad neighborhood in the slightest. As far as Molly could remember, she'd never received a call to come out and investigate anything in the area. There were never any reports of break-ins, robberies, or assaults, and all in all, that area of Midport was considered the quietest in all the city.

McKart's cellphone rang. She dug it out of her back pocket and answered. "Hello...Yes... Okay... Great... All right, stay put. Thank you." She hung up. "I sent a patrolman over to your daughter and son-in-law's house," she told Sam. "He tried the doorbell, pounded on the doors. No one answered."

Molly asked him, "Do you have a key to your daughter's place?"

"I do."

JIM STAYED BEHIND at the station to collect anything he could from the car, while Molly and Sam headed over to the house on the other side of town. They searched through the entirety of the five-thousand square foot home. There was no sign of a disturbance, a burglary, and, disturbingly, no sign of Marcus Collins. His Jaguar was in the garage, the clothes and other items in his closet and dresser seemed untouched, and nothing else in the house was out of place as far as Sam could tell. The man, like Jasmine, was simply gone.

"I'm going to try him again," Sam told Molly, punching his son-in-law's number into his iPhone.

Molly walked from the living room into the kitchen out of earshot from Sam and called Jim.

"Hello?" he said.

"Find anything?"

"I got Onstar to unlock the car but the only thing inside was the owner's manual and a pine tree air freshener. No purse, no cell, nothing else. How about you?"

"About the same. The husband's gone. No sign of him anywhere."

"Antar put a call into the Navy SEALs or the Army Rangers yet?"

"Not yet." She looked down the hallway and saw him leaving a voicemail for his son-in-law. His words were urgent, his gestures animated. "But he's getting worried. This isn't good, Jim."

"I know. McKart's getting frazzled too. She's hanging around here, asking me every five seconds if I've made any headway. Woman's sticking to my ass like three-day-old underwear."

"Thank you for the visual."

AFTER SHE WENT home to clean up and catch a quick nap, Molly was back in the office by six that morning. No leads had come in. She had requested a copy of the surveillance footage from Christian Antar, and dropped by the gas station to pick it up on her way to work. He had saved it on a thumb drive, and Molly, Jim, forensic scientist Ginny Proctor, and Sgt. Dave Gerlock gathered in Molly's office to review the footage on her desktop. After they ran through the video three times, they compared insights.

"Thoughts?" Molly asked them.

"Obviously the guy followed her," Ginny, a stout woman in her early fifties offered. "The way he pulled in right behind her and didn't hesitate?"

"Exactly," Gerlock said. "It's not like he spotted her in passing and all of the sudden he decided he wanted to kidnap her."

"So," Molly said, "he's been keeping tabs on her, stalking her?"

"Could be," Ginny answered.

"But what was she doing out at that hour on a Tuesday?" Jim asked.

"Maybe she's a night owl," Molly said. "She doesn't have a job as far as the million or so selfies of her lying out near her pool in a bikini on a daily basis would suggest. She also isn't involved in any sort of charity work or social activities as far as I can tell. She might just be the type of person who stays up all night doing Christ-knows-what and sleeps till noon."

"If she weren't missing, I'd probably envy her," Ginny stated.

"What about the husband?" Molly said. "Same kidnapper?"

"Or someone associated with the kidnapper," Gerlock added.

"Dave, you've been here a lot longer than most of us," Molly said. "And you're way older than dirt. Ever see something like this in Midport before?"

A frown formed on Gerlock's otherwise stone like face. "First, thank you for those words. Second, fuck you for those words. And third, no, never. We've had our usual missing persons, but nothing like this."

"Why though?" Ginny posed. "I mean, why these two? Why take them? Out of the twenty-thousand people in the city, why them? If it were a ransom job, surely someone would've been contacted with demands by now."

"Maybe they're involved in some shady stuff," Jim suggested. "Gambling. Drugs. Just because you come from money doesn't mean you know how to keep it in your pocket."

"Could be true. Have we heard from Toledo PD, or the Michigan state cops?" Molly asked.

"They're calling us with updates every hour on the hour, but they haven't seen or heard anything," Jim told her.

Janet poked her head into Molly's office. "Hey, I think you guys might want to take a look at the brand-new shit-storm that's in our forecast for today."

The five of them walked into the bullpen joining the fifteen or so officers and employees on staff that day, just as Sgt. Barb Bunkleman turned up the volume on the television mounted on the far wall. On screen, Sam Antar stood at a small podium adorned with microphones which bore the logos from the FOX, CBS, NBC, and ABC affiliates out of Midport, and neighboring Detroit and Toledo. He was joined by his wife, his brother, and a few members of the Midport City Council. At the bottom of the screen read a graphic, in a large, yellow font: ANTAR TO OFFER REWARD FOR DAUGHTER'S WHEREABOUTS.

"Oh no," Molly muttered.

"I will repeat," Antar's voice blared from the TV speaker, "I am prepared to offer ten-thousand dollars to any person who can tell me where my my daughter and my son-in-law are."

"Oh, God no."

"And to the kidnapper, if you are listening, I will tell you this: If you return them unharmed by this afternoon, I will urge the police and county prosecutor to go easy on you. If you do not... I will double my cash offer to anyone who can provide information as to where you are... Twenty-thousand dollars to anyone who leads me directly to you."

"Oh, sweet Jesus, God in Heaven, no."

"Twenty-thousand for your whereabouts. Or your head." He looked directly into the camera. "You are out of options. You are out of time. Be smart and think it through." Sam thanked the media for their time, took no questions, and walked out of shot.

The cops looked at one another and braced for impact. Jim broke the silence. "And cue the nonsense in five, four, three…"

The phones rang like all the church bells on Christmas morning and the voices of the station rose in a chorus of chaos as they answered the calls.

"No, sir… No… No, the missing woman is not the weather girl from Channel 2."

"You saw her where…? Dallas…? When was this…? Back in the seventies…?"

"No… No this isn't the number for information… Yes, ma'am, I'm sure."

By three o'clock that afternoon the police department fielded over two-hundred calls, none of them useful.

Molly sat at her desk, head cradled in her hands, certain the first waves of a migraine had started to crash down on her. She reviewed the security camera footage again, looked through all of the social media accounts for both Jasmine and Marcus at least three times each, checked in with Midport patrol officers and the admin officials from surrounding police departments and ran into dead end after dead end. She felt like she ran a marathon on a treadmill or took a nice afternoon dip in an inviting pool of quicksand.

"Hey," Jim called from the doorway.

"Yeah?"

"You might want to—"

"Do not say, 'Take a look at this.' Please? Anytime someone says, 'You might want to take a look at this,' it's never a good thing. On *Star Trek* it means Scotty's having trouble in the engine room or Bones is losing a patient."

"What are you, a twelve-year-old boy? Jasmine and Marcus Collins are out in the bullpen."

Amazingly, the headache seemed to disappear.

Molly darted from her office. And there they stood, both of them attractive and dressed in expensive clothes, exchanging words with McKart, flanked by almost every cop in the building. Patrolman Salvatore Parker had planted himself next to Marcus Collins, arms folded, looking irritated as usual. Parker was only on the force for two months at that point, and out of the academy for four months total, but he quickly adopted the attitude and demeanor of a cop three times his age and experience. Nothing impressed him, nothing shocked him, and nothing caught him off guard. At the ripe, old age of twenty-five, Sal Parker was a grumpy curmudgeon.

Molly asked the crowd what was going on.

"That's what I'd like to know," Marcus Collins said. "We get pulled over and this gentleman," he gestured toward Parker, and made sure to gloss the word "gentleman" over with a healthy coat of sarcasm, "says everyone is looking for us!"

"I am so upset right now my brain could literally explode!" Jasmine blurted.

"Literally?" Molly asked.

"Yes, literally!"

Sam Antar burst into the room. "My princess!" He pushed his way through the throng and grabbed his daughter in a bearhug that could've shattered the tiny girl's bones.

"Dad, what the fuck is going on?" his princess so eloquently inquired.

IN EVERY POLICE station throughout the world, from London to Los Angeles, Toronto to Tokyo, Paris, France to Paris, Kentucky and all points in between, there are a handful of stories that get passed down through the years that include retellings of impossible heroics, grizzly crime scenes, feats of strength, astounding detective work and deduction, and, yes, lurid tales about sex. The story of the "abduction" of Jasmine and Marcus Collins would become one of these stories, passed from one generation of Midport cop to the next, and much to the chagrin and embarrassment of Sam Antar it would forever fit snugly into the latter category.

While Sal Parker was out doing his routine patrol on the southside of the city, he spotted the tan F-150 the APB mentioned earlier that morning parked at a Tim Horton's donut and coffee shop just off the I-75 exit ramp near mile marker 10. He waited for the tall, blond guy to emerge, but instead witnessed Marcus and Jasmine Collins bound out of the place, hand in hand, leaning on each other, both of them replete with smiles and giggles. Parker leapt from his cruiser and informed them they had to accompany him to the station immediately. The couple protested and threw out their family names. Jasmine asked the young patrolman, "Do you know who my dad is, you idiot?" After he threatened them with arrest, they went quietly.

When pressed by Molly for details as to what exactly happened, with ninety percent of the Midport Police staff and her father present, Jasmine Collins stated the abduction was "a game" she and her husband played on a regular basis.

"What do you mean 'game?'" Molly said.

"Oh, my God, why do I have to talk about this?"

"We were worried sick!" Sam told his daughter. "You had me looking under every rock and stone, you brought your poor uncle to tears! We need to know!"

"Okay! Fine! God! Shit!" She took a breath. "Marcus and I…" Jasmine stopped, fidgeted with the spaghetti straps of her top, and began again. "Marcus and I like to role play."

"I assume you don't mean *Dungeons and Dragons*?" Molly asked.

"What?"

"*D&D*?"

Jasmine narrowed her eyes. "What are you saying to me?"

"Elves? Barbarians? Twenty-sided dice?"

Jim placed a hand on his partner's shoulder. "Just stop, Fetterly." He turned to Jasmine. "Please continue, Mrs. Collins."

The hands left the straps and folded themselves together in front of her. "We bought an old truck from this old junkyard down in Toledo. Marcus dressed up like someone else, put a hat and a wig on, and pretended to kidnap me. And then we, like, you know, went to a hotel near the state line, okay?"

The hotels and motels along the Michigan-Ohio border were the kind of establishments that would charge patrons by the hour instead of the day. They were not the kind of places one would go to expect a continental breakfast, a workout room, or around the clock room service. There were more mirrors on the ceilings than on the walls, and the films available to rent had more X's in the ratings than old-timey jugs of moonshine. Even the crackheads and junkies couldn't give the places more than a two-star review on Yelp.

Sam Antar looked on the verge of vomiting. "God, take me now."

"Well, I'm sorry!" his daughter shouted. "I obviously didn't want this out in the open, *Dad*, but apparently, I have to talk about it in a room full of people!"

"And just for the record, what we do behind closed doors is no one's business," Marcus added.

"You weren't behind closed doors," Molly answered. "You were at a damn gas station owned by your wife's uncle."

"Well..." Marcus folded his arms and nodded. "Okay, yeah, I can see your point. But Jasmine's right! We shouldn't have to stand here and tell all of you the ins and outs of our sex life. Even though, take it from me, it definitely makes the sex way more amazing."

"Enough!" Sam shouted and slammed his hand on a desk. "I've changed my cash offer. Ten-thousand dollars to any one of you that kills my son-in-law! I am prepared to fill out the check this very instant!"

THAT AFTERNOON, THINGS began to slowly return to normal. For Molly, Jim, and the rest of the police department at least. Sam Antar and his family, not so much. He rescinded his cash offer, of course, and Shock Jocks, talk show hosts, bloggers, vloggers, and gossip columnists for every newspaper throughout North America had a field day over the news of the exploits of his daughter and son-in-law. The "game" Jasmine and Marcus Collins played was the foremost thing trending on Twitter and Facebook the remainder of the day.

As the workday drew to a close, Jim entered Molly's office while she finished paperwork on the case that, frankly, wasn't a case at all. "Hey."

She looked up at him. "Hey yourself."

"I got you a present," he told her, and laid a long jewelry box on her desk.

She narrowed her eyes. "What the hell is this?"

"Open it," he said.

She did.

And emerged with a gorgeous new toothbrush.

"You know how to use one of those?" he asked.

"I hate you."

"I have a two-year-old niece that's just learning herself, so she can probably give you some pointers if you need them."

"You're an asshole."

Jim laughed and disappeared into the hallway. Molly grinned and tossed the toothbrush into her desk.

A few minutes later, her desk phone rang. "Midport Police Department, this is Detective Fetterly… No, ma'am. No… No, I'm sorry, this isn't the number for information… Yes, ma'am, I'm quite sure…"

MYSTERY LIGHTS

by

Scott Von Doviak

IT WAS FRIDAY night at the Lost Horse Saloon and Lyle Albright was itching for a fight. Someone had stolen his Ford Ranger while he was in the Dollar General picking up a bag of charcoal and a Snickers. Lyle was pissed because he'd just paid Hector Garces five hundred bucks to replace the water pump and the timing belt, and also because his wife of twenty-seven years had been in the truck at the time.

"It's kidnapping is what it is," said Lyle, signaling for another round. "But there ain't no ransom note, so what can I do except sit here and have another beer?"

"Now, Lyle," said Gus, the bartender, as he popped the cap on a cold bottle of Bud Light and set it in front of his customer of many years. "Isn't the more likely explanation that Yvonne simply drove somewhere in the truck herself?"

"Well, if I were an ignorant man, maybe I would jump to that conclusion. But that Ford Ranger is a manual transmission, and Yvonne never did learn to drive stick.

THE DOLLAR GENERAL was three blocks down and across Marfa's main drag, San Antonio Street. After discovering his truck missing, Lyle had tried to call his wife. He got her voicemail, which wasn't too surprising as cell reception in town was patchy at the best of times. A couple miles out of town, it vanished completely. He went back into the store and asked if they had security cameras on the front lot. They laughed at him, and he vowed never to return—an empty threat, since there were few other shopping options in Marfa.

He decided to head across the street and have a beer. It was a cool October evening, and the sky was turning purple as he trudged through the sandburs along the side of the road, collecting spiny stickers on the cuffs of his dungarees. When he arrived at the Lost Horse, he took a seat at the bar and set the bag of charcoal on the stool next to him. He'd already eaten the Snickers.

There were fewer than a dozen patrons in the saloon when Lyle arrived, but it would fill steadily as the evening progressed. The Lost Horse attracted a cross-section of what Gus liked to call 'the three true outcomes of Marfa'. You had the blue-collar crowd, mostly ranch hands and oil workers. Then there were those drawn by Marfa's growing reputation as an arts colony— an outpost attracting painters, sculptors, and a few freaks who fled Austin because they weren't keeping it weird enough anymore. The third category was the tourists who came to gawk at the collision of these two disparate worlds and overpay to spend the night in a hipster tepee.

Gus served them all with a smile. With his black Stetson, droopy mustache, and patch over his right eye, he looked like he was perpetually auditioning to play Sam Elliott's brother gone wrong in the kind of Western they didn't make anymore. He'd lost the eye in a rodeo accident, or when his tractor hit a rock that ricocheted at his face, no one was quite sure. A few locals speculated it was all show for the tourists, but never aloud in the Lost Horse, where Gus kept his shotgun on the wall behind him under a brass nameplate reading OL' SMOKEY.

"Why don't you call the sheriff's office and report it stolen?" he asked Lyle. "Hell, you don't even have to call them. There's always one sitting off the side of the road right past that dollar store, waiting to nail anyone who doesn't slow down on their way into town."

"I tried. They said I couldn't report it stolen if my wife was still in it, being as how the truck is in both our names. And I can't report Yvonne as a missing person for forty-eight hours. So, it's a Catch-22. They say they'll keep an eye out for it. I guess if someone drives it back into town at five miles an hour over the speed limit, they'll find it for me."

"How are you going to get home?"

"Hell, I'll worry about that when I need to worry about it."

Lyle owned a cattle ranch six miles out of town heading toward Fort Davis. It had been in the family for four generations, but now it looked ready to dry up and blow away whenever Lyle did. Ranching was in the Albright bloodline, or so his father had always told him back when Lyle planned on becoming the next Stevie Ray Vaughan. He'd put a band together in high school and they thought they were pretty hot shit, but gigging around West Texas was not a lifestyle suited to those short of patience and temper. When the van broke down on the way to Alpine in the summer after Lyle's senior year, he hitched a ride into town and joined the Army.

He returned after four years and married Yvonne, his high school sweetheart. His father had died in the meantime and his mother begged him to stay and help run the ranch. He was still doing it, more or less. Mostly less, truth be told. Yvonne ran the business side of things—inventory, payroll, invoices, and anything else that could be done with a computer and a phone. That ostensibly left Lyle in charge of operations, a set of duties that resembled work a little too much for his liking. His top hand Francisco Sandoval and his crew did all the care and feeding of his livestock and handled maintenance around the ranch while Lyle occasionally oversaw the work from the saddle of his horse or the seat of his ATV.

"The real question," said Lyle, picking the burrs off his pant leg and dropping them on the floor. "Is how am I getting to Terlingua tomorrow?"

Lyle had won the Terlingua International Chili Championship three out of the past four years. Often described as the Super Bowl of chili cook-offs, the Terlingua event served as the annual culmination of chili season in Texas. From modest origins, it had grown into a four-day festival complete with A-list musical acts, ancillary cooking competitions, and no shortage of drunken rowdiness. It all culminated in Saturday's showdown, pitting the best of the best against each other before a distinguished panel of judges who would taste-test each entry in search of that magic combination of meat, sauce, and spices (no beans, never beans): the perfect bowl of red.

"That's your primary concern?" said Gus.

"Well, I intend to defend my crown. Yvonne, wherever she is, would expect nothing less."

Gus doubted it, because he knew what Yvonne knew: Lyle's chili recipe was not his own. Lyle loved to lord it over the Weber on his spacious back porch, grilling up steaks and sausage, but that was the extent of his culinary expertise. Francisco, on the other hand, was a wizard with chili, adapting recipes that had been handed down from his *abuela* and concocting his own powders and sauces. He'd won the Terlingua competition once and would easily contend for the title every year, but somehow Lyle always had important errands for him to run or tasks that couldn't wait on the day of the cook-off. On those same Saturday mornings, Lyle would gather up all the leftover spices from Francisco's recent batches along with the freshest ground beef on hand and head down to Terlingua.

"Francisco," said Lyle, as if reading Gus's mind. "I bet he did this."

"Did what? Stole your truck with your wife in it? Come off it, Lyle."

"No, think about it. He's always been jealous of my championship trophies. I've got three to his one. He thinks he can distract me, keep me from going down there tomorrow and claiming what's rightfully mine. I oughtta fire his ass. Should have done it long ago."

"Well, it's Friday night after seven. He should be in here any minute if you want to have a reasonable discussion about it like two adults. Anyways, you're welcome to ride down with me tomorrow. I'm entering my famous Adios Pantalones in the margarita contest."

"Hell, I don't even need to fire him," said Lyle, oblivious to anything Gus had said. "All I gotta do is call ICE on his ass."

"Now, Lyle. You know I ain't gonna put up with that kind of talk in here." Gus wasn't exactly a bleeding-heart liberal, but he had no patience for reactionary immigration rhetoric. He'd grown up on the border and lived near it all his life, crossing it countless times over the years. If you walked into the Lost Horse shooting your mouth off about building the wall, Gus would personally escort you out to the parking lot and drop you on your ass. The CBP officers of Marfa Station knew better than to frequent the Lost Horse; they did their drinking at the local hotels instead.

The front door swung open, and Lyle's head snapped around like he'd been sucker-punched. It wasn't Francisco walking in the door, however, but a couple in late middle age; the man in a blue windbreaker and bad combover, the woman with a red sweater and a face full of regret. She took a seat at a table as the man stepped up to the bar next to Lyle.

"How you doin' this evening?" Gus greeted him.

"Could be worse, I guess. We came a long way to see these Marfa lights of yours. The wife thinks it was a big waste of time."

"Sorry to hear that, but hey, they led you here, so it's all good. What can I get you?"

"She'll have a gin and tonic and I'll take a margarita. The internet says you make a good one here."

"For once, the internet isn't lying." Gus got to work.

"I saw something out there for sure, but you know, I think it's just headlights. Maybe there's swamp gas or something, makes them bob and weave a little. As far as tourist traps go, I preferred the Cadillac Ranch."

"I'm sworn to secrecy myself," said Gus, setting the drinks on the bar. "Otherwise, the aliens might never return my family."

The man chuckled politely. "What do I owe you?"

"Eleven-fifty."

The man set fifteen dollars on the bar and told Gus to keep the change. As he joined his wife at the table, Lyle fixed Gus with a hard stare. "You making fun of me?"

"How's that, Lyle?"

"Your family abducted by aliens? Right after my wife disappears under mysterious circumstances?"

"Now, come on, Lyle. That's my standard line to the tourists. You've heard me say it a hundred times. I kindly doubt Yvonne was abducted by aliens."

Rufus, Gus's black Labrador, scurried in through the patio entrance and made a circuit of the bar, pursued by a couple of other dogs from the neighborhood. They chased one another back outside and returned a minute later, now with two more members of the canine entourage. This was a nightly ritual at the Lost Horse. The tourists got a kick out of it, but Lyle didn't even notice anymore.

In the corner by the neon Lone Star sign, a husky man in a checked Western shirt and faded Levis leaned on a stool and tuned a battered acoustic guitar, shuffling his boots in the sawdust.

"Oh, here we go," said Lyle. "Clyde the crooner treating us to another round of sad cowboy songs. Am I the only one here who's sick of 'Streets of Laredo?'"

"Don't you have somewhere to be, Lyle?" said Gus. "You're not making great progress on the case of your missing truck—or your missing wife—sitting here sucking down Bud Lights."

"What do you want me to do, hire a private detective? I don't think Magnum has an office in town."

"You could try calling her again. You could call around to her friends, ask if anyone's seen her. Unless she walks in the door, you ain't gonna find her here."

Before Lyle could answer, the front door squeaked open again. This time it *was* Francisco Sandoval, along with a couple of the other hands from Lyle's ranch, Raymond and Slim Jim.

"There he is," said Lyle, lurching to his feet.

"Hey, boss," said Francisco. He started racking balls on the pool table while Raymond approached the bar and Slim Jim chatted up a redhead in paint-spattered coveralls.

"Where's my Ranger?" said Lyle.

"Your truck? Ain't seen it since you drove it off the ranch this afternoon," said Francisco, rolling a pool cue on the table to ensure it was a straight-shooter. "You misplace it, boss?"

"Don't you smart me, Cisco. You plan this with Yvonne?"

"Boss, I got no idea what you're talking about. But this right here? This is *my* time. I am off the clock. So, I'll deal with your bullshit tomorrow morning when you all of a sudden need me to make a run to Fort Davis and pick up that special feed for Buster, or whatever other excuse you come up with to keep me from going down to Terlingua to cook my chili."

Lyle's face turned the color of the twilight Texas sky. "Now you listen to me, you little—"

"Fellas, fellas," said Gus, using his hands to call a timeout. "Clyde's about ready to get started. Ain't you, Clyde?"

Clyde looked up from his guitar, clearly lost. "Uh… sure, Gus. Whenever you want."

"Why don't you hold off just one minute," said Lyle, taking a couple of steps toward the pool table. "My integrity is being challenged by an underling, and I'm not going to stand for it. You got something to say to me, Cisco, why don't you just come right out and say it?"

By now Lyle had the attention of everyone in the bar, especially the couple who'd been disappointed by the Marfa lights. They were getting all the local color they could ask for now. Even Rufus and his friends took a break from their shenanigans, as if they could sense the abrupt change in the room's emotional temperature.

"Boss," said Francisco, softening his tone. "I don't know where your truck is. All I want to do is shoot some pool with my boys and drink a couple cold ones. But if you want me to help you look for it—"

"This is about the cook-off," said Lyle. "You're accusing me of coming up with excuses to keep you from entering, as if you could beat me."

"You're cut off, Lyle," said Gus. "You can leave now."

"Leave how? Leave in what?"

"Not my problem. You know the saying. You don't have to go home but you can't stay here."

Lyle wasn't ready to leave quite yet. He took another step toward the pool table. "You're fired, Cisco."

The woman in the red sweater gasped and her husband patted her hand.

"Say that again," said Francisco.

"I think you heard me. You're done. Slim Jim! You're top hand now."

"Kiss my ass," said Slim Jim.

"You're drunk, boss," said Francisco. "So, I'm gonna pretend we didn't even see each other tonight, and I suggest you do the same."

"Raymond," said Lyle. "You're top hand now."

"I don't think so," Raymond replied.

"Fine," said Lyle. "You're all fired. I'll have you all replaced by Monday morning, you can believe that. Won't be any problem at all."

"You got one more chance to take it back," said Francisco.

"I wouldn't take it back if you begged me on your hands and knees. You better brush up on your *español,* boy, because your days on this side of the border are over."

Francisco slammed his pool cue onto the edge of the table. It snapped in half, sending one splintered end spiraling until Rufus caught it in mid-air. "My family has been in Texas since before it had a name, you racist *hijo de puta.* And you know it. I tell you one thing, *pendejo.* You've won your last chili cook-off. I'm gonna go down there tomorrow and I'm going to kick your..."

Everyone knew how the sentence would end, but nobody could hear it over the sound of Lyle's forty-five. He squeezed off three shots, only one of which hit Francisco. The burst of red on his chest blossomed like a boutonniere and spattered across the pool table, leaving the felt streaked in Christmas colors.

Gus had his shotgun off the wall and trained on Lyle's neck. The woman in the red sweater cradled her husband's head in her lap. Her hands were slick with the blood that continued to gush from his temple.

The front door was open. Standing in the doorway was Yvonne Albright, her mouth hanging open in a way that would have struck Gus as comical under happier circumstances.

"Yvonne?" said Lyle.

"Drop your gun, Lyle," said Gus, tightening his finger on the trigger of Ol' Smokey.

"But I didn't mean—"

"Drop it right now."

Lyle dropped it.

"Is someone calling 911?" Gus asked. Clyde held up his phone, indicating he was on the case.

"Yvonne," said Lyle. "Where were you? I came out of the dollar store and you were gone."

Yvonne took in the scene before her as if she'd paid for a romantic comedy and accidentally walked into the theater showing a horror movie. "What have you done, Lyle?"

"I... the truck was gone. You were gone. I came out of the store. I came out the front door and..."

"Lyle. You parked in *back* of the Dollar General. Don't you remember? We came down Russell Street because you had to stop at Harry's and take a look at that guitar he's selling. Even though you already have a dozen guitars and never play one of them. I swear, Lyle, you'd forget your head..." She realized she was rambling, and that life as she knew it would never be the same. "So we came up behind the store, you pulled into the back lot, and I said I'd wait in the truck."

"I... wait a minute. You say..." Lyle looked like he was trying to do trigonometry in his head.

"I waited twenty minutes in that truck before I went inside looking for you. They said you asked about cameras in the front? Oh, Lyle. What have you done?"

Slim Jim had his flannel shirt wrapped around Francisco's chest to stanch the flow of blood. Francisco was still awake and muttering to himself. Slim Jim squeezed his hand.

"Ambulance is on the way," said Clyde. "Sheriff, too."

There was only one ambulance in Marfa. If it was otherwise occupied, you were shit out of luck. Francisco still had a chance, although the closest emergency room was thirty minutes away in Alpine. The sheriff's deputies were much closer.

"I want to wait for them outside," said Lyle. He turned to Yvonne. "Let's wait for them outside."

Yvonne looked at Gus, with whom she'd been having an affair for nearly twenty years. Gus nodded. Yvonne took Lyle by the arm and led him outside. Gus turned to Clyde.

"Play something for Cisco," he said. "Play one of his favorites."

Clyde played "Red River Valley."

LYLE LOOKED UP at the stars. He didn't know when he'd get another chance. He tried to think of something poetic to say about them, something more profound than that at night they were big and bright, deep in the heart of Texas, but his brain didn't work that way. The best he could do was something about diamonds spread across black velvet, but he thought he'd probably heard that in a song—maybe something Clyde always played.

"I'm going away for a very long time," he finally said.

"You're going to need a lawyer, Lyle," said Yvonne. "Not Danny Wagner. A real criminal lawyer."

"You think he's gonna live? Cisco?"

"I don't know, Lyle. I hope so. But the other one, the fella in the blue windbreaker. He's already gone."

"Friendly fire?"

"I don't think that's gonna work. But like I said. You need a lawyer."

Lyle took a few steps into the parking lot. Gravel and bottle caps crunched under his boots. The dogs were sitting outside the porch, all in a row. Waiting for something. Lyle turned back to Yvonne.

"You think I should apologize to that woman? The tourist? She and her husband were here to see the Marfa Lights."

"I don't think that's a good idea, Lyle."

"You know something? I lived here all my life and I never did see those lights. Never was in any big hurry to do it. You think the sheriff will stop and let me take a look?"

Yvonne put her hand on his shoulder and squeezed. There was no love behind it, but she couldn't help feeling a little sorry for him despite everything.

"I don't know, Lyle. I guess it can't hurt to ask."

She heard the sirens before he did.

RED DOG

CONTRIBUTORS BIOGRAPHIES

Richard Chizmar is a New York Times, USA Today, Wall Street Journal, Washington Post, Amazon, and Publishers Weekly bestselling author.

He is the co-author (with Stephen King) of the bestselling novella, Gwendy's Button Box and the founder/publisher of Cemetery Dance magazine and the Cemetery Dance Publications book imprint. He has edited more than 35 anthologies and his short fiction has appeared in dozens of publications, including multiple editions of Ellery Queen's Mystery Magazine and The Year's 25 Finest Crime and Mystery Stories. He has won two World Fantasy awards, four International Horror Guild awards, and the HWA's Board of Trustee's award.

His latest book, The Girl on the Porch, was released in hardcover by Subterranean Press, and Widow's Point, a chilling novella about a haunted lighthouse written with his son, Billy Chizmar, was recently adapted into a feature film.

Chizmar's work has been translated into more than fifteen languages throughout the world, and he has appeared at numerous conferences as a writing instructor, guest speaker, panelist, and guest of honor.

Trevor Wood has lived in Newcastle for 30 years and considers himself an adopted Geordie, though he still can't speak the language. He's a successful playwright who has also worked as a journalist and spin-doctor for the City Council. Prior to that he served in the Royal Navy for 16 years. Trevor holds an MA in Creative Writing (Crime Fiction) from UEA.

His first novel The Man on the Street, which is set in his home city and features a homeless protagonist won the Crime Writers' Association's John Creasey New Blood Dagger for best debut and the Crimefest Specsavers Debut Novel of the Year. It was also shortlisted for the Theakston's Old Peculier Crime Novel of the Year and has been optioned for television by World Productions, the makers of Line of Duty. It was followed by the highly-acclaimed sequel, One Way Street and the final book in the trilogy, Dead End Street was released in January.

Trevor is one of the founder members of the Northern Crime Syndicate and is a volunteer chef at the People's Kitchen in Newcastle, a charity that provides hot meals for around 200 hundred people every day.

Judith O'Reilly is the author of three thrillers featuring action hero Michael North (Sleep When You're Dead, Curse the Day and Killing State.) She is also the author of two memoirs including the UK/German bestseller Wife in the North which was a Radio 4 Book of the Week. She is a former journalist with the Sunday Times/ITN/BBC.

Awais Khan is the award-winning author of NO HONOUR (Orenda, 2021) and IN THE COMPANY OF STRANGERS (Hera, 2022; Simon & Schuster India 2019). He studied creative writing at Faber Academy in London and is the Founder of The Writing Institute. He has delivered talks at Oxford University, Durham University and American University of Dubai to name a few and his work has appeared in several anthologies. His short story THE VICTIM has been longlisted for the Short Story Dagger 2022. He is on the judging panel for the Gwyl Crime Cymru Novel Prize and the Cheshire Novel Prize. He is represented by Annette Crossland.

Charles Ardai is the founder and editor of Hard Case Crime as well as an award-winning author. His five novels include the Shamus Award-winning SONGS OF INNOCENCE, which the Washington Post called "an instant classic." In addition to the Shamus, Ardai has received the Edgar Allan Poe and Ellery Queen Awards. He was a writer and producer for six years on the TV series HAVEN, inspired by Stephen King's first Hard Case Crime novel, THE COLORADO KID. King has called him "a true renaissance man" and "a master of the short story." Ardai lives in New York.

M.E. Proctor is a European transplant. Born in Brussels, she now lives in Livingston, Texas, with her husband, James Lee Proctor, also a writer. As a former freelance journalist, she's more interested in the answers than the questions. Something she shares with Declan Shaw, her PI protagonist; the first book in that series will come out from TouchPoint Press in January 2023. Her short stories have been published in Bristol Noir, Mystery Tribune, Pulp Modern Flash, Beat to a Pulp, The Bookends Review, and Shotgun Honey among others. On Twitter @MEProctor3.

Ted Flanagan is a paramedic and former Recon Marine who lives and writes outside of Worcester, Mass., in the US. HIs novel EVERY HIDDEN THING was released in October by Crooked Lane, and his short fiction has appeared in several journals, to include Shotgun Honey and Mystery Tribune. He can be found at tedflanagan.com

Mark SaFranko's many novels and story collections have garnered rave reviews and a cult following, mainly in Europe. Putain D'Olivia (Hating Olivia) was recently nominated for the Prix Littéraire Rive Gauche à Paris and published in Italy in 2020. In 2018 he was named the first Author in International Residence at the University of Lorraine in Nancy, France. His latest novel, Amerigone, will be published in Germany in 2022 by Pulpmaster, and Tout Sauf Hollywood (Nowhere Near Hollywood) was just published in France. His stories have appeared in many magazines and journals, including Ellery Queen's Mystery Magazine and were cited in Best American Mystery Stories. His paintings have been exhibited in Europe, and he is also a musician.

Gabriel Hart lives in Morongo Valley in California's High Desert. He's the author of neo-pulp collection Fallout From Our Asphalt Hell and his second poetry volume Hymns From the Whipping Post, both out now from Close to the Bone. Other work can be found in Shotgun Honey, Rock and Hard Place magazine, Bristol Noir, Punk Noir, Expat Press, and Misery Tourism. He's a regular contributor at Lit Reactor, Los Angeles Review of Books, and The Last Estate. He is the lead singer/song and dance man of Jail Weddings and plays sax in the Lynchian jazz group The Former.

Megan Taylor is the author of four dark novels, 'How We Were Lost' (Flame Books, 2007), 'The Dawning' (Weathervane Press, 2010), 'The Lives of Ghosts' (Weathervane Press, 2012) and 'We Wait' (Eyrie Press, 2019).

In 2014, she had her first short story collection published, 'The Woman Under the Ground', and since then, further short stories have appeared in a variety of journals and anthologies, including the Dark Lane anthologies, 'The Invisible Collection' (Nightjar Press) and Neon.

Megan lives in Nottingham, where she's been running Creative Writing courses for many years. For more information, please visit www.megantaylor.info

Stephen J. Golds was born in North London, U.K, but has lived in Japan for most of his adult life. He writes loosely in the noir/crime genres, though is heavily influenced by transgressive fiction and dirty realism. His three novels are a trilogy of connected but stand alone novels that deal in themes of mental illness, trauma, betrayal and twisted love.

He enjoys spending time with his daughters, reading books, traveling the world, boxing and listening to old Soul LPs. His books are Say Goodbye When I'm Gone, I'll Pray When I'm Dying, Always the Dead, Poems for Ghosts in Empty Tenement Windows I Thought I Saw Once and the story and poetry collection Love Like Bleeding Out With an Empty Gun in Your Hand.

Noelle Holten is an award-winning blogger at www.crimebookjunkie.co.uk. She is the PR & Social Media Manager for Bookouture, a leading digital publisher in the UK, and worked as a Senior Probation Officer for eighteen years, covering a variety of risk cases as well as working in a multi agency setting. She has three Hons BA's - Philosophy, Sociology (Crime & Deviance) and Community Justice - and a Masters in Criminology. Noelle's hobbies include reading, attending as many book festivals as she can afford and sharing the booklove via her blog.

Dead Inside - her debut novel with One More Chapter/Harper Collins UK is an international kindle bestseller and the start of a series featuring DC Maggie Jamieson.

John Bowie was born in Northumberland, Northern England and studied in Manchester in the '90s. He has published poetry, novels and short stories. He now lives in Bristol, U.K.

John is the founder and editor-in-chief of Bristol Noir.

B F Jones is French and lives in the UK. She writes poetry and flash fiction. She has two flash fiction collections: Artifice (Alien Buddha) and Something Happened at 2 a.m. (Anxiety Press) and two poetry collections: The Only Sounds Left and Five Years (Alien Buddha)

Nils Gilbertson is a crime and mystery writer, UC Berkeley graduate, and practicing attorney. A San Francisco Bay Area native, Nils currently lives in Texas with his wife and German Shorthaired Pointer. His short stories have appeared in Mystery Magazine, Mickey Finn: 21st Century Noir Vol. 2, Rock and a Hard Place Magazine, Pulp Modern, and others. You can find him on Twitter @NilsGilbertson and reach him at nilspgilbertson@gmail.com.

Sebastian Vice is the Founder of Outcast Press, a small publishing house devoted to transgressive fiction and dirty realism. His short fiction and poetry has been published in Punk Noir Magazine, Close To The Bone, A Thin Slice of Anxiety, Outcast Press, Terror House Magazine, Bristol Noir, and Misery Tourism. He contributed a chapter to Red Sun Magazine's forthcoming book The Hell Bound Kids (May 1st, 2022) and writes a regular column called "Notes of A Degenerate Dreamer" over at A Thin Slice of Anxiety. His flash piece "One Last Good Day" was nominated for Best of The Net 2021. His debut poetry book Homo Mortalis: Meditations on Memento Mori was released April 4th, 2022 through Anxiety Press.

Sharon Bairden manages a small, local independent advocacy service just outside of Glasgow. By day she has a passion for human rights; by night she has a passion for all things criminal.

Sharon lives on the outskirts of Glasgow, has two grown up children, a grandson, a Golden Labrador and a cat. She spends most of her spare time doing all things bookish.

She confesses to have a bit of a book obsession and can usually be found hanging around Crime Writing Festivals across the Uk. She also blogs about her love of books over at Chapterinmylife.

Sharon is the author of standalone psychological thrillers, *Sins of the Father* and *You Need Me*, published by Red Dog Press.

Ailsa Cawley has been writing stories, poems and verses since she was a child. It's not always what is considered poetry by some, as she isn't a lover of sweet, schmaltzy rhymes.

She is currently editing her first novel. A psychological thriller with a paranormal element. She also hopes to bring out a poetry collection one day.

She lives on the Isle of Skye. While some of her stories and poetry are written from personal experience, others are written from her slightly dark and twisted imagination. And she may never admit how much of each is at play in each piece of work.

Chris McDonald grew up in Northern Ireland before settling in Manchester via Lancaster and London. He is the author A Wash of Black, the first in the DI Erika Piper series, as well as the forthcoming second - Whispers In The Dark. He has also recently dabbled in writing cosy crimes, as a remedy for the darkness. The first in the Stonebridge Mysteries will be released in early 2021. He is a full-time teacher, husband, father to two beautiful girls and a regular voice on The Blood Brothers Podcast. He is a fan of 5-a-side football, heavy metal and dogs.

Steven Kedie is a writer and co-founder of the music website www.eightalbums.co.uk, who lives in Manchester with his wife and two sons. He spends far too much time running, writing, and talking about albums. All of which get in the way of his football watching habit.

Steven is the author of two novels. Suburb tells the story of Tom Fray, a young man at a crossroads in his life – not a kid anymore, not quite an adult yet – who returns home from university to find no-one has changed but him. When he starts an affair with a married neighbour, his simple plan to escape home and travel becomes a lot more complicated.

Running and Jumping is the story of British Olympian Adam Lowe and his rivalry with American athlete Chris Madison. Set between Beijing 2008 and Rio 2016, the novel deals with the question: What if you had your greatest ever day and still didn't win?

Details of Steven's writing can be found at www.stevenkedie.com

Nathan Pettigrew was born and raised an hour south of New Orleans and lives in the Tampa area with his loving wife. His story "Yemma" was recently awarded 2nd Place in the 22nd Annual Writer's Digest Short Short Story Competition, while other stories have appeared in Deep South Magazine, Penumbra Online, The "Year" Anthology from Crack the Spine, Cowboy Jamboree, Stoneboat, and the Nasty: Fetish Fights Back anthology from Anna Yeatts of Flash Fiction Online, which was spotlighted in a 2017 Rolling Stone article. His genre stories have appeared in Thuglit, the Tripper anthology from Devil's Lettuce Press, the Savage Minds & Raging Bulls anthology from Bristol Noir, the Mardi Gras Mysteries and Mardi Gras Murder anthologies from Mystery and Horror, LLC, and at Punk Noir.

Born in Liverpool, **S.E. Moorhead** has told stories since childhood and uses writing as bubblegum for her over-active brain—to keep it out of trouble. Fascinated by meaning, motivation and mystery, she studied Theology at university.

Over the last twenty-five years, apart from teaching in secondary school, S.E. Moorhead has attained a black belt in kickboxing, worked as a chaplain, established a Justice and Peace youth group, and written articles for newspapers and magazines about her work in education and religion.

She still lives in her beloved hometown with her husband Seán, two sons and her black lab, Seamus.

Born in the UK and raised in South Africa, **M. Sean Coleman** developed a love for reading and writing novels in his early teens, thanks to two incredibly passionate English teachers who infected him with their love of words and stories. Over the intervening years, he has written film and television drama, cross-platform series, an interactive children's storybook and even a graphic novel series.

He finally found his niche as a (thriller) writer when he was asked to write a novel as part of the cross-platform project, Netwars. His first book, The Code, was published six months later, with the sequel, Down Time, hot on its heels. There was no going back. Since then, The Cuckoo Wood, A Hollow Sky and On Stony Ground have all been published

He is obsessed with crime, mystery and thriller stories, especially those with a fresh or surprising angle.

Sean lives with his girlfriend and family (including the Red Dogs) on the edge of the Peak District, where they often head out on epic walks.

He is also the founder and Publishing Director of Red Dog Press.

Ken Teutsch is a writer, performer and filmmaker whose stories have appeared in such diverse publications as Mystery Magazine, Andromeda Spaceways Magazine, Cowboy Jamboree, and Halfway Down the Stairs, as well as in the anthologies Shadow People, Old Weird South, From the Yonder, First Came Fear, and Strangely Funny. His comic/crime novella S-10 to Valhalla is available from Shotgun Honey Books. In addition to writing, Ken can be seen performing music and stand-up comedy in the guise of his creation, perennially failed country music "star", Rudy Terwilliger.

Bev Vincent is the author of several non-fiction books, including The Road to the Dark Tower and Stephen King: A Complete Exploration of His Work, Life and Influences. He co-edited the anthology Flight or Fright with Stephen King and has published over 120 stories, with appearances in Ellery Queen's, Alfred Hitchcock's and Black Cat Mystery Magazines. His work has been published in 20 languages and nominated for the Stoker (twice), Edgar, Ignotus and ITW Thriller Awards. Recent works include "The Ogilvy Affair" and "The Dead of Winter," the latter in Dissonant Harmonies with Brian Keene. To learn more, visit bevvincent.com

M. H. Callway's short crime fiction has appeared in many anthologies and publications and has won or been short-listed for several awards, including the Bony Pete, the Crime Writers of Canada Award of Excellence and the Derringer. Her novel, Windigo Fire, was shortlisted for the Debut Dagger under a different title and after publication for the Crime Writers of Canada Best First Novel award.

In 2013, Madeleine co-founded the Mesdames of Mayhem, a collective of leading Canadian crime writers whose work is showcased in five anthologies. The Mesdames are the subject of a CBC documentary by director Cat Mills (GEM and YouTube).

Websites: www.mhcallway.com ; www.mesdamesofmayhem.com

Jaqueline Seewald: Twenty of my books of fiction have been published. My short stories, poems, essays, reviews and articles have appeared in various publications such as: The Writer, The L.A. Times, Ad Astra, Pedestal, Surreal, Library Journal, Reader's Digest, After Dark, Gumshoe Review, Over My Dead Body!, Sherlock Holmes Mystery Magazine, Mystery Weekly, And Publishers Weekly. A story was published in the last issue of Hypnos. Another story is in a recent issue of Currents: Short Edition. The newly published issue #29 of Sherlock Holmes Mystery Magazine features one of my stories. I've also won multiple awards for fiction, poetry and plays.

Gordon Brown has ten crime and thriller books published to date, along with a novella and a number of short stories.

His new book, 'Any Day Now' is published by Red Dog Press and under his expat alias, Morgan Cry, 'Six Wounds', the latest in his Spanish crime series, is also out now.

Gordon helped found Bloody Scotland, Scotland's International Crime Writing Festival (see www.bloodyscotland.com), is a DJ on local radio (www.pulseonair.co.uk) and runs a strategic planning consultancy. He lives in Scotland and is married with two children.

In a former life Gordon delivered pizzas in Toronto, sold non-alcoholic beer in the Middle East, launched a creativity training business, floated a high tech company on the London Stock Exchange, compered the main stage at a two-day music festival and was once booed by 49,000 people while on the pitch at a major football Cup Final.

Mike McHone's work has appeared in Ellery Queen Mystery Magazine, Mystery Weekly Magazine, Punk Noir, Mystery Tribune, Guilty, Playboy, Sherlock Holmes Mystery Magazine, the AV Club, and is forthcoming in Alfred Hitchcock's Mystery Magazine. His short story "A Drive-by on Chalmers Road?" made the esteemed Ellery Queen Readers Poll for best short stories for 2020 and he was a recipient that same year for the Mystery Writers of America's Hugh Holton Award. Visit him online at www.mikemchone.com

Scott Von Doviak is a Derringer Award-nominated writer living in Austin, Texas. He is the author of Charlesgate Confidential (Hard Case Crime), which was named one of the top 10 crime novels of 2018 by Tom Nolan of The Wall Street Journal. His short crime fiction has appeared in Mystery Tribune, Shotgun Honey, and Tough, among others. He is a former film critic for the Fort Worth Star-Telegram and has written three nonfiction books on film and television, including Hick Flicks: The Rise and Fall of Redneck Cinema.